MILLAIS SCHOOL
ART DEPARTMENT

AFRICAN ART

AFRICAN

Ezio Bassani

ART

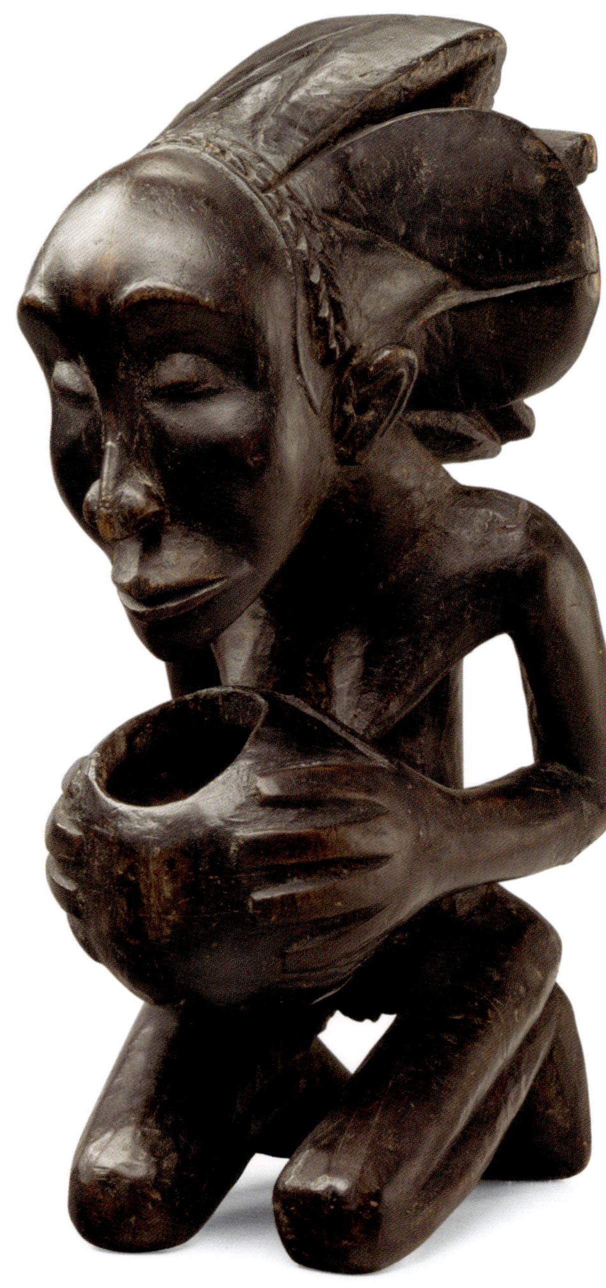

SKIRA

Cover
Hemba artist
Democratic Republic of the Congo
(Luika region)
Ancestral figure
Private collection
Photo Hughes Dubois, Bruxelles
(no. 222)

Page 3
"Master of Kateba"
(formerly "Master of Buli")
Luba-Hemba, Democratic Republic of the Congo
Kneeling female bowl-bearer
Musée Royal de l'Afrique Centrale, Tervuren
(no. 161)

Design
Marcello Francone

Editorial Coordination
Emma Cavazzini

Editing
Timothy Stroud

Layout
Serena Parini

Translations
Paul Metcalfe for *Scriptum*, Rome

Iconographical Research
Paola Lamanna

Marco Zanella, Certosa di Pavia, for the map

The publisher is at the disposal of the entitled parties as regards all unidentified iconographic sources

First published in Italy in 2012 by
Skira Editore S.p.A.
Palazzo Casati Stampa
via Torino 61
20123 Milano
Italy
www.skira.net

Printed and bound in Italy. First edition

ISBN 978-88-572-0869-5

Distributed in USA, Canada, Central & South America by Rizzoli International Publications, Inc., 300 Park Avenue South, New York, NY 10010, USA.
Distributed elsewhere in the world by Thames and Hudson Ltd., 181A High Holborn, London WC1V 7QX, United Kingdom.

Acknowledgments

This book could never have been produced without the help of the museum directors and personnel whoin generously provideding information on the works from their collections, which are discussed and illustrated here. The same holds for the private collectors involved, some of whom have preferred to remain anonymous. As the names in both cases would be far too many to list, I thank them all collectively, as well as the authors of the photographs that illustrate the various chapters, and those colleagues and friends who helped assisted me with information and clarification on specific problems as they emerged over the years, first of all, Jean-Louis Paudrat.
I also wish to express my personal gratitude to Massimo Vitta Zelman and Stefano Piantini for their belief in this project and their determination to make it a reality, to the personnel of the Skira publishing house, especially Emma Cavazzini, Marcello Francone, Paola Lamanna and their co-workers, and to the translators, all of whom managed to overcome the many difficulties involved.
A final word of thanks to my family for their support all through this work and especially to Chiara for her patient help with that infernal device the computer, and the countless problems it caused me.

Note

No dates are given for works believed to have been produced in the late 19th century and the first half of the 20th

Contents

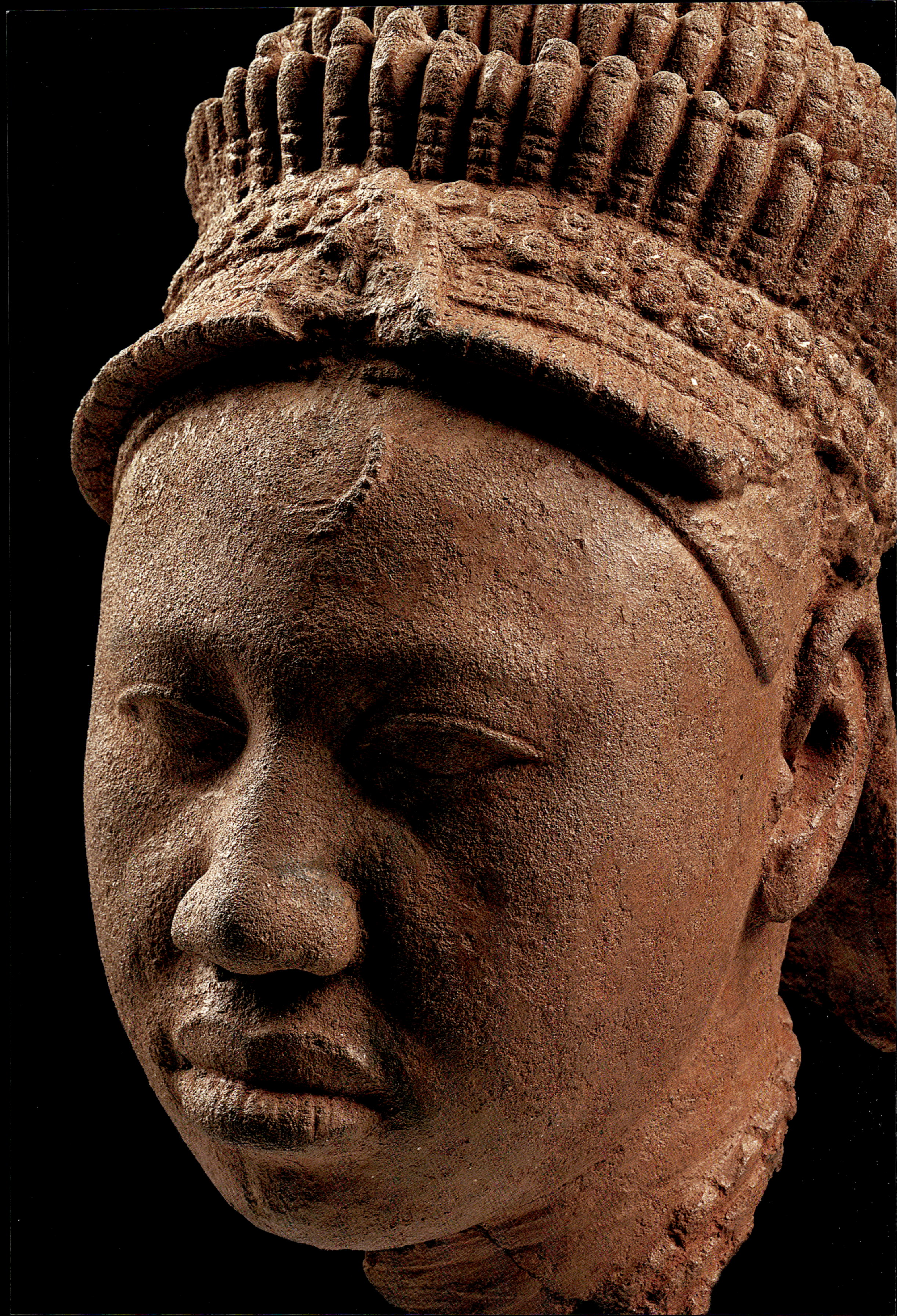

Introduction*

Overall examination of the traditional figurative arts of Sub-Saharan Africa today is an undertaking that would give pause even to someone who has seen or handled a vast number of works, over a period of many decades. The aims of this book are to present traditional African sculpture at the highest possible level and provide a concise and straightforward exposition of the author's knowledge of the different historical, formal, symbolic and functional characteristics that distinguish it, while bearing the difficulties of the task clearly in mind. As William Fagg wrote nearly half century ago (1963, p. 40), "Art in its purest form is concerned with the communication of the ineffable, which is beyond words."

The adjective "traditional" defines works created explicitly not for the art market, but in response to the religious, political and also aesthetic needs of African societies of the past. It is used here in the absence of any more appropriate term, but with full awareness of its vagueness and ambiguity as well as the contaminations that it hides.

Groups of artefacts – figures, masks and utensils – are shown and discussed in order to exemplify some of the key problems addressed and results obtained in the study of the arts of Sub-Saharan Africa today. The questions comprise dating and historicity, relations with the first European clients, the attribution of works to their authors, the artistic value of many artefacts, diversification in the form of works performing the same function, and the variety of formal solutions invented by the artists in response to the constraints of their commissions. It should be understood that the examples are necessarily chosen so as to exclude works regarded as atypical.

While sculptures in wood and (less frequently) ivory are the best-known examples of traditional African art at present, works using other techniques and materials do exist. These include the increasingly numerous pieces of metal and terracotta sculpture brought to light by the excavations that have intensified over the last few decades and are now altering our idea of the continent's artistic panorama, while revealing unsuspected cultures of the past alongside the classical and well-known ones of Ife and Benin.

The boundless universe of African sculpture is the result of a complex and diversified evolutionary process, a variegated mosaic that emerged from a history rich in stylistic cross-fertilization due to contacts, migrations, wars and alliances. This universe has been described in thousands of books and articles and shown in thousands of larger and smaller exhibitions, but always with a predominant focus on the (often uncertain) use and meaning of the items displayed or illustrated. The artefacts in question were in fact considered primarily in ethnographic terms and confined to museums of ethnography until half a century ago. The still largely unsolved problems limiting our knowledge of artistic creation (as understood by Westerners) in that part of the continent south of the Sahara were seldom taken into consideration. Egypt and the northern regions of Africa have had a different history and therefore a different form of art, albeit with points of contact over the centuries, since ancient times, as in the case of Nubia.

Artist of Ife
Nigeria (from Ita Yemoo), 12th–15th c.
Head of a queen
(no. 29a)

It would appear advisable at this point to provide some brief general clarification as regards the nature of the works presented here, with the forewarning that the questions and uncertainties often outnumber the definite answers.

The African artists of the past expressed themselves primarily through sculpture and, as Michelangelo also noted, this medium does not lend itself to landscape. They focused almost exclusively on the human figure, which they used to represent important personages in the community, both real and symbolic, as well as entities facilitating contact with the supernatural realm. Isolated in a metaphysical space that it makes its own, the figure is motionless, expressing no emotions and making no gestures. At most, these are suggested by means of slight irregularities that disrupt the symmetrical and frontal quality of the work to transform it into a living organism.

The few exceptions to this state of isolation include mother and child works and the rare groups that adorn some emblems of religion or office and various furnishings.

Identity is suggested by external attributes – tattoos and scarification, particular deformities, hairstyle, weapons and tools – and is not individual but rather categorical (e.g. personal or group ancestors, images of spirits and magical statues). It must be pointed out here that our information as to the true nature of the subjects represented is often insufficient or incorrect and terms such as "ancestor figure" and "power figure" are unquestionably vague and sometimes mistaken, as revealed by the precise investigations of some scholars.

Animals are not usually represented, though rare ceremonial seats, Kongo magical statues, Dogon and Senufo equestrian figures and above all zoomorphic masks provide the best-known exceptions. The inclusion of sculpture in architectural complexes is also infrequent. Exceptions here include the reliefs in the royal palaces of ancient Dahomey and the pillars in the palaces of Cameroonian monarchs and the Yoruba in Nigeria, as well as the doorways of the granaries and sanctuaries of the Dogon, the Senufo and (though rarely) the Baule. The comparatively limited number of subjects depicted is in any case one of the characteristics of religious art all over the world.

The works are generally of modest size, ranging from a few centimetres to just over one metre, and neither monumental nor rhetorical in intent. At the same time, however, the proportional balance of these "humble treasures", as Dominique de Menil poetically described them, prevails over their limited size to endow them with monumentality.

It should also be remembered that the African artists created their works without making any preparatory drawings, sketches or models. The works are carved or moulded directly on the basis of mentally visualized images.

It must be pointed out that sculpture is not the only form of art practised in Sub-Saharan Africa. Architecture is another, albeit naturally in the forms appropriate to the climate of the continent and the political and economic systems of the various populations. The environmental conditions that have led to forms of nomadic pastoral life in many regions have also fostered other forms of expression such as ornamentation of the body and costume, which are not taken into consideration here.

The appreciation of African art in the West has seen a change during the last few decades. The transformation of the criteria relating to the exhibition and hence selection of works adopted by some of the museums in question – including a number of newly created ones – constitutes the first step in this direction. In a nutshell, these institutions have been turned from ethnographic museums into museums of art (albeit with no change in name), in which the works are no longer relegated to the status of documentation, but bear witness to human creativity.

Though carried out with no fanfares, this operation has produced results that can be appreciated by all visitors as regards the elimination of simple accumulations of objects in the museums involved and a decrease in the number of items on exhibit. This development reflects the criteria of formal excellence adopted in the selection of works to be displayed and the use of adequate and innovative methods to show them to their best advantage.

The selection criteria evidently attach different values to ethnographic materials and artworks, the latter being an end in themselves, since they are an autonomous manifestation of the artists' creativity within the culture of their society. The United States provides some great examples of the second approach, such as the Metropolitan Museum of Art in New York (whose collections were transferred from the Museum of Primitive Art in accordance with the wishes of its founder Nelson Rockefeller, in 1976), the Detroit Institute of Art and the Museum of African Art in Washington, D.C.

As regards the choices guiding cultural policy, Sylvia Williams, the first director of the latter institution, summed up the new approach and the difference in function with respect to the Smithsonian Institution's existing and nearby ethnographic museum in the pithy statement that her museum would exhibit "only the best". In other words, the items would not be regarded as interchangeable, like so many implements, and each one exhibited would be chosen for its value in formal terms.

As regards Europe, the new arrangement of the Museum Rietberg in Zurich, where just over a hundred African works of art are exhibited with the greatest visibility, constitutes a good example of the new trend.

In my view, the conflict between art and ethnography has instead not been resolved in the most recent and largest museum of its kind, built by Jean Nouvel in Paris, namely the Musée du Quai Branly, the heir to the glorious Musée de l'Homme and Musée national des Arts d'Afrique et d'Océanie, whose collections it incorporates. The items exhibited in the permanent section are too numerous and cannot be appreciated in their exemplary uniqueness as works of art. The extraordinary "tower of music", into which thousands of musical instruments of different origins are crammed like a gigantic "accumulation" by Arman, takes this approach to the extreme. It should be noted, however, that the new museum does organize excellent exhibitions of non-European art and offers facilities for the study of the cultures where it originated – including libraries of both printed and video material – that have no equal in the world today.

Hopes were raised by the decision to adopt the opposite approach in creating the Pavillon des Sessions in the Louvre, where a few dozen sculptures (forty-three of which are African) establish the universal value of the non-European arts by virtue of their sheer quality, making no claim to present an exhaustive survey of the field. The selection of items for display and the use of resources, technologies and inventions ensuring the most effective, appropriate and appealing revelation of the intrinsic beauty of the works, namely their formal perfection, have endowed them with the power to communicate with visitors not involved culturally or religiously in the rationale of their creation.

As John Pemberton III noted acutely in his examination of a Yoruba mask a quarter of a century ago (Fagg, Pemberton 1982, p. 192), "When ritual art is removed from its cultural as well as its religious context, it necessarily becomes an object of art, the significance of which is shaped by its new cultural milieu. Rarely can the object continue to convey with the same force the world and the experience of those who created it and used it. [...] Thus, when an object continues to convey, even to the eye of a stranger, an insight of the world of its origin, we must wonder at its power and ponder the artistic skill of its maker."

Jacqueline Delange, head of the Département d'Afrique Noire of the Musée de l'Homme, one of the temples of ethnographic studies, had in any case made this observation some twenty years earlier in the catalogue of an exhibition of the museum's masterpieces (Delange 1965, p. 45): "If an ethnological museum exhibits the finest of its works of art and exhibits them essentially as such, this means that the time has come when these, like the masterpieces of the historical civilizations, can be admired for what they are, above and beyond their purely scientific interest, namely perfect expressions of the aesthetic values of the culture that generates them."[1]

Every real encounter begins in fact with wonder and admiration, the first steps towards understanding or at least a willingness to understand. For that matter, it is unquestionably and inevitably true that if the African works held by the museums and private collections of the West returned to their countries of origin, they would no longer be looked at, enjoyed and interpreted as they were by those for whom they were initially created. In any case, this holds also for the works of the West's artistic heritage.

This is not to say that the African works of art, the ones we most appreciate, were created solely for reasons of aesthetic enjoyment, but on the contrary that formal perfection and correspondence to function are mutually complementary requisites in the birth of what we call masterpieces. This is indeed true of religious art as a whole and of the art celebrating institutions and individual members of society in every era and every part of the world. The Sistine Chapel, the friezes of the Parthenon and certain Mayan terracotta works are good examples of this, as are the cave paintings of Lascaux, whose possibly propitiatory purpose remains unknown.

What we often know about African works of art, which are unquestionably decontextualized when exhibited in museums but no more so than an image of the Madonna created for an altar, is their "Western life", the names of their collectors and owners. We are instead nearly always totally in the dark as regards the circumstances of their creation, the formal innovations introduced by their creator, and indeed the very existence of a creator as distinct from a mere instrument.

In actual fact, even though denied the condition of absolute freedom enjoyed by their present-day Western counterparts, African artists are the conscious creators of works that are inherently valid, expressive in their own right, and capable of generating emotion and understanding. Even though the subject matter of every work of art, including the African, is imposed by the group for which it is created, it owes its form to the genius of the person who made it, whose powers of expression are not limited by the client. The latter expresses a prior judgment of value on the work by choosing a specific artist, who has his or her own personality and way of working.

Everything that provides insight into the process of African artistic creation is unquestionably useful, be it iconography or ethnography, because the artists' activities were determined by the social, political and economic reality in which they operated. It should be borne in mind, however, that most of the elements involved in investigations of this kind (the meaning, purpose and chronology of the works, their place of creation, which often differs from the place of discovery, and the figurative tradition from which deductions can be drawn) are uncertain, often contradictory and indeed even non-existent, above all due to the absence of writing in the past amongst the peoples living south of the Sahara.

The lack of this tool, upon which the success of studies into the arts of the European past rests, does not mean the absence of memory, which was handed down in oral rather than written form. Unfortunately, the priests, officials and storytellers (*griots*) acting as the depositaries of memory and knowledge are disappearing – or have already disappeared – through death or have been marginalized by the new forms of communication. Moreover, the data supplied orally by native informants are then written down by the people gathering them, with the inevitable risk of the latter fitting them into the interpretive frameworks of their own culture.

The criteria used to assess the formal value of a work of art vary in relation to the culture within which they are formulated. Many scholars, and ethnologists above all, claim that traditional African societies had no category corresponding to the Western "work of art" and that the parameters used by Westerners to define such works are ethnocentric – which they certainly are – and hence vitiated by cultural colonialism. Unfortunately, the African contribution to our knowledge of these criteria is modest as yet, not least because of the dramatic political and economic conditions in the continent and the fact that many of the works of traditional art left Africa long ago.

The aid of African scholars is nevertheless indispensable, since investigations carried out within one's own society, facilitated by knowledge of the language and by direct access to any surviving oral tradition, is crucial in seeking to clarify the meaning attributed to works of art, the value attached to form, and the concept of beauty in the respective cultures, which are – it should be remembered – highly diversified. Suffice it to recall the fundamental contribution to the understanding of Yoruba art made by the Nigerian scholars Ekpo Eyo, Wande Abimbola and Rowland Abiodun, to name just a few.

I believe that formal perfection (not to be confused with attractiveness, which is a matter of taste) is an intrinsic quality of every work of art and the result of conscious choices on the part of its creator, whether African or Western. It therefore always exists – regardless of the ability or inability of the viewer and even the author, African or Western, to articulate it verbally – because form and the organization of form are the language of the figurative art of all times.

Many Western scholars have attempted to take what are assumed to be African aesthetic categories as their terms of reference. This seems unrealistic because African thinking has been inevitably influenced by Western colonization, also in cultural terms, during the last few centuries and above all in the last few decades, with the advance of globalization. For this reason, use of the terminology and the criteria developed by Western culture appears unavoidable here, not because they are infallible, but because the author has no better tools at his disposal, at least for the time being.

These socially and historically determined categories are by no means immutable and possess no universal value. They are indeed highly changeable, like every other construct of culture, which must as such be constantly revised, tested and measured against the categories of others in a dialectical relationship that brings enrichment through confirmation or modification. For this reason, the previously unrecognized value of artworks, both African and non-African, becomes evident at a certain point with the transformation of society and the acquisition of new interpretive keys.

The African continent has undergone radical and irreversible changes in the fields of social and political organization, economy and religion during the last century and above all the last fifty years. The ancient rituals have fallen into disuse or have gradually given way to new religions rituals (Christianity and Islam). The increasingly well-established market economy and the political and social organization of the newly created sovereign states founded on Western models in the post-war period (without taking into account the ethnical and cultural identities of their populations) have gradually destroyed the usefulness of the type of artistic creation that responded to the spiritual, religious and political needs of the African world of the past, already dramatically transformed by European colonial occupation. In step with the process of globalization, new forms of expression are inevitably being established with the creation of works aimed at the art market, first national and then international, which have increasingly tenuous links with those of the past. These older forms do survive in some cases, above all in rural areas.

It should be recalled, however, that also in the field of art, and above all African art, there is a period of transition between past and future during which codified forms and innovations coexist and overlap so that it is difficult to draw any clear dividing lines.

The art summarily described as "traditional" was the expression of societies differing greatly in terms of numbers (from a few thousand to millions), forms of government (from acephalous structures to absolute monarchies) and economic systems. African art did, however, possess a common ground in religion, or rather in the religions hastily and incorrectly lumped together under the label of "animism" (an oversimplification incapable of doing justice to the complexity of the African spiritual and religious world), meaning a view of the universe in all of its component parts – things, animals and people, both living and dead – as animated by forces of good and evil that interact with human life and determine its meaning. These forces and the numerous divinities making up the

Boyo artist
Democratic Republic of the Congo
Royal effigy
(no. 253)

pantheon of the various peoples had to be won over and placated with suitable instruments, ceremonies and forms of worship, which involved, in many cases, the creation of artworks.

These differ in quality, of course, no more and no less than the symbols and instruments of Western religion, whose function and effectiveness are not determined by their greater or lesser degree of formal perfection, which may even be non-existent, but by the faith of the believer. This does not rule out the possibility of formal perfection being appreciated by Africans, even though theories about beauty like those developed in the West over the millennia have not been articulated in such abundance. Or perhaps they have but we know nothing about them and it is now too late to remedy our ignorance.

In this volume the creativity of artists from some cultures is given more space than others, but solely on the basis of the representativeness of the selected works in relation to the themes treated. Some of the works that belong to categories discussed in specific chapters are also referred to in other chapters to support the theories put forward therein.

Information of an ethnographic nature has been obtained from the writings of the experts who have studied the different topics, whose names appear in the bibliography.

The sculptures were selected in accordance with the space available and, inevitably, the vision, knowledge and personal experience of the author of the text. Consequently, the panorama is necessarily partial and fragmentary and I would not presume to suggest that it constitutes an ideal "museum" (many works could be substituted by others of the same quality that are equally representative).

Above all, I have no desire to usurp the Africans' powers of judgement, to speak for them in a way that smacks of ethnocentrism, or, even less, to assume an attitude of cultural superiority, being well aware that my approach to African art is that of a European.

My one desire is to pass on the information that I possess and have gleaned from my colleagues and teachers (William Fagg, Albert Maesen and Father François Bontinck, some of the most eminent scholars to have studied the various specific issues) and, above all, to share with readers the emotions and enjoyment I have experienced through these works.

* The author has addressed the various subjects developed in this work over a number of decades in papers, books, lectures and conferences. These are revised, rearranged and presented here so as to give an organic picture of the current state of knowledge as regards the arts of the past in Africa south of the Sahara and the countless associated problems, which Western but also and above all African scholars are called upon to help solve.

[1] "*Si un musée d'ethnologie expose les plus belles de ses œuvres d'art et les expose essentiellement comme telles, c'est que le temps est venu où elles peuvent, semblables en cela aux chefs-d'œuvre des civilisations historiques, être admirées pour ce qu'elles sont par-delà de leur intérêt directement scientifique: les expressions parfaites des valeurs esthétiques propres à la culture dont elles sont issues.*"

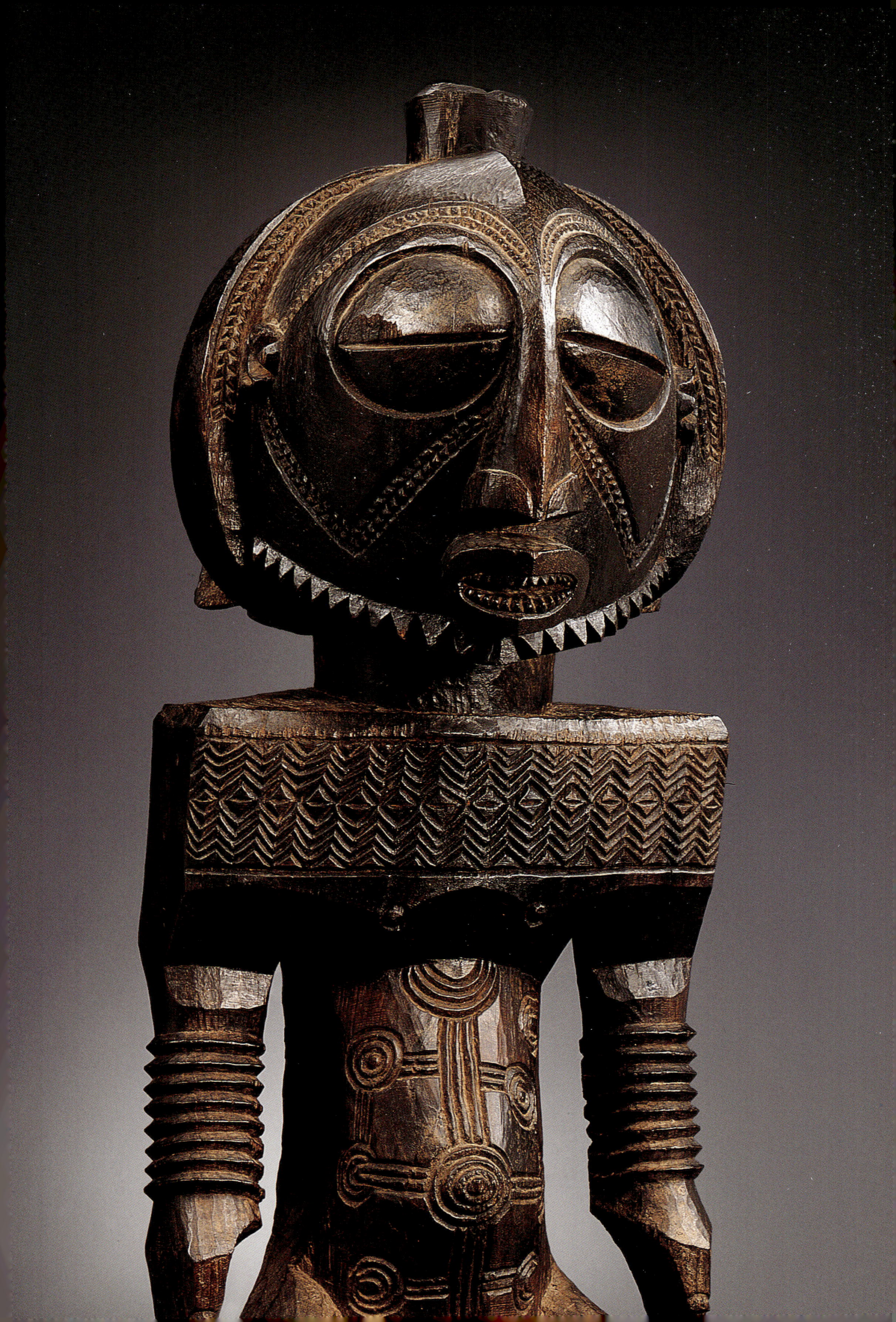

Ethnic groups and cultures whose works are described in this book

1 Akan (Ghana)
2 Baga (Guinea)
3 Bamana (Mali)
4 Bamileke (Cameroon)
5 Bamum (Cameroon)
6 Bangwa (Cameroon)
7 Lower Niger – Region (Nigeria)
8 Baule (Ivory Coast)
9 Bidjogo (Guinea Bissau)
10 Boa (Democratic Republic of the Congo)
11 Boyo (Nigeria)
12 Bura (Niger)
13 Chamba (Nigeria)
14 Chokwe (Angola, Democratic Republic of the Congo)
15 Dan (Ivory Coast)
16 Djenne (Mali)
17 Dogon (Djennenke, Niongom, Tellem) – (Mali)
18 Edo (Benin, Nigeria)
19 Ejagham (Nigeria)
20 Fang (Gabon)
21 Fon (Republic of Benin)
22 Grebo (Liberia)
23 Guro (Ivory Coast)
24 Hemba (Democratic Republic of the Congo)
25 Ibibio (Nigeria)
26 Ife (Nigeria)
27 Igbo (Nigeria)
28 Igbo-Ukwu (Nigeria)
29 Jaba (Nigeria)
30 Konde (Mozambico)
31 Kongo, formerly Congo (Angola, Republic of the Congo, Democratic Republic of the Congo)
32 Kota (Gabon)
33 Kpelle (Guinea)
34 Kuba (Democratic Republic of the Congo)
35 Kwele (Republic of the Congo)
36 Lobi (Burkina Faso)
37 Luba (Democratic Republic of the Congo)
38 Luluwa (Democratic Republic of the Congo)
39 Mahongwe (Gabon)
40 Mambila (Nigeria)
41 Mangbetu (Democratic Republic of the Congo)
42 Mbembe (Nigeria)
43 Mboye (Nigeria)
44 Ndengese (Democratic Republic of the Congo)
45 Ngbaka (Democratic Republic of the Congo)
46 Nok (Nigeria)
47 Nyamwezi (Tanzania)
48 Ovimbundu (Angola)
49 Owo (Nigeria)
50 Punu (Gabon)
51 Sakalawa (Madagascar)
52 Sapi (Sierra Leone)
53 Senufo (Ivory Coast, Mali)
54 Shona (Mozambico, Zimbabwe)
55 Sokoto (Nigeria)
56 Songye (Democratic Republic of the Congo)
57 Suku (Democratic Republic of the Congo)
58 Teke (Gabon, Republic of the Congo)
59 Tikar (Cameroon)
60 Yangere (Republic of South Africa)
61 Yoruba (Nigeria)
62 Zande (Democratic Republic of the Congo)
63 Zulu Zulu (Democratic Republic of the Congo)

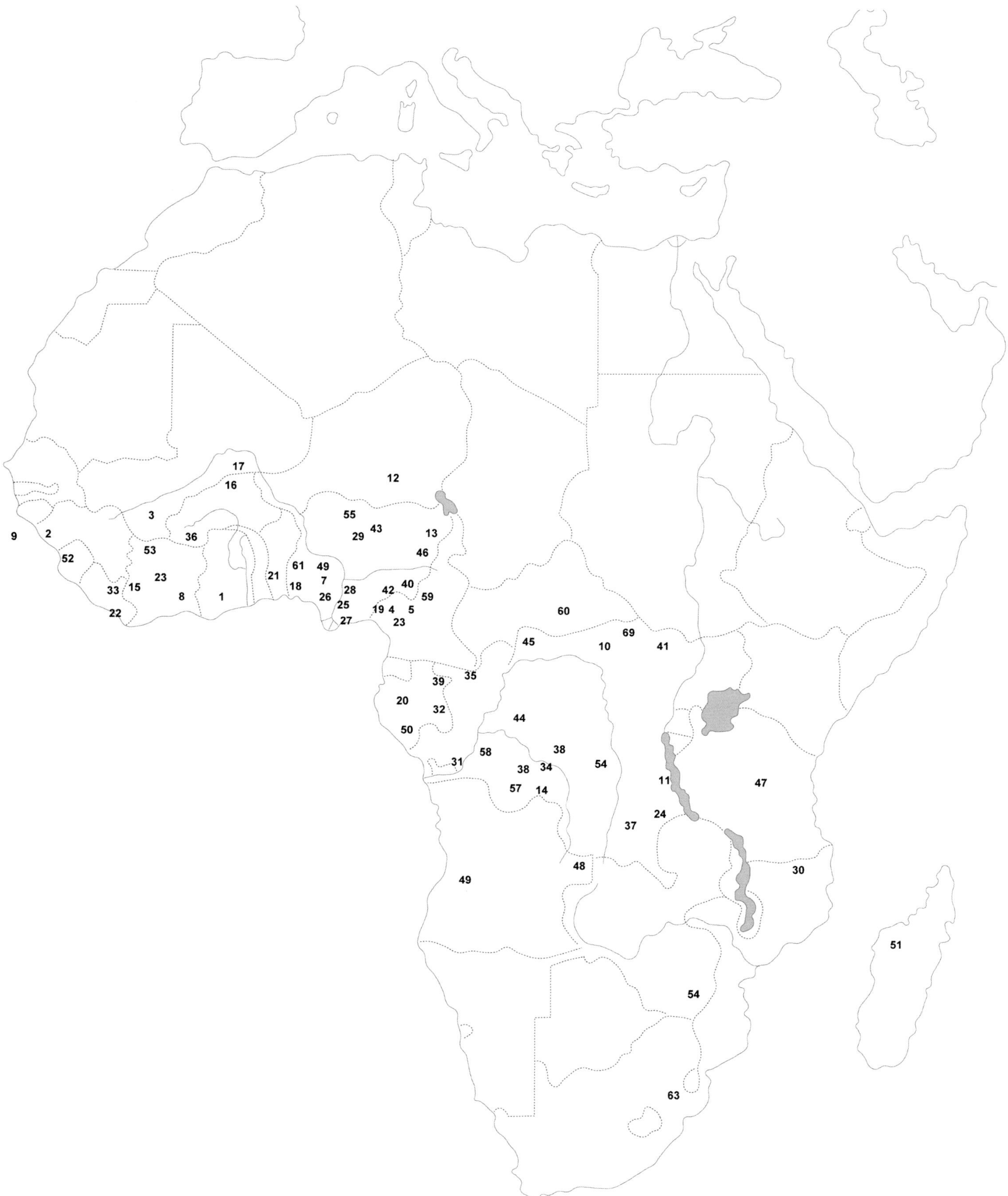

17
16
12
3
55
43
29
13
9
2
36
53
52
46
61
49
7
23
21
18
15
33
8
1
28
26
42
40
59
25
19
4
5
22
27
23
60
69
45
10
41
35
39
20
32
44
50
38
58
31
38
34
54
11
47
57
14
24
37
48
30
49
51
54
63

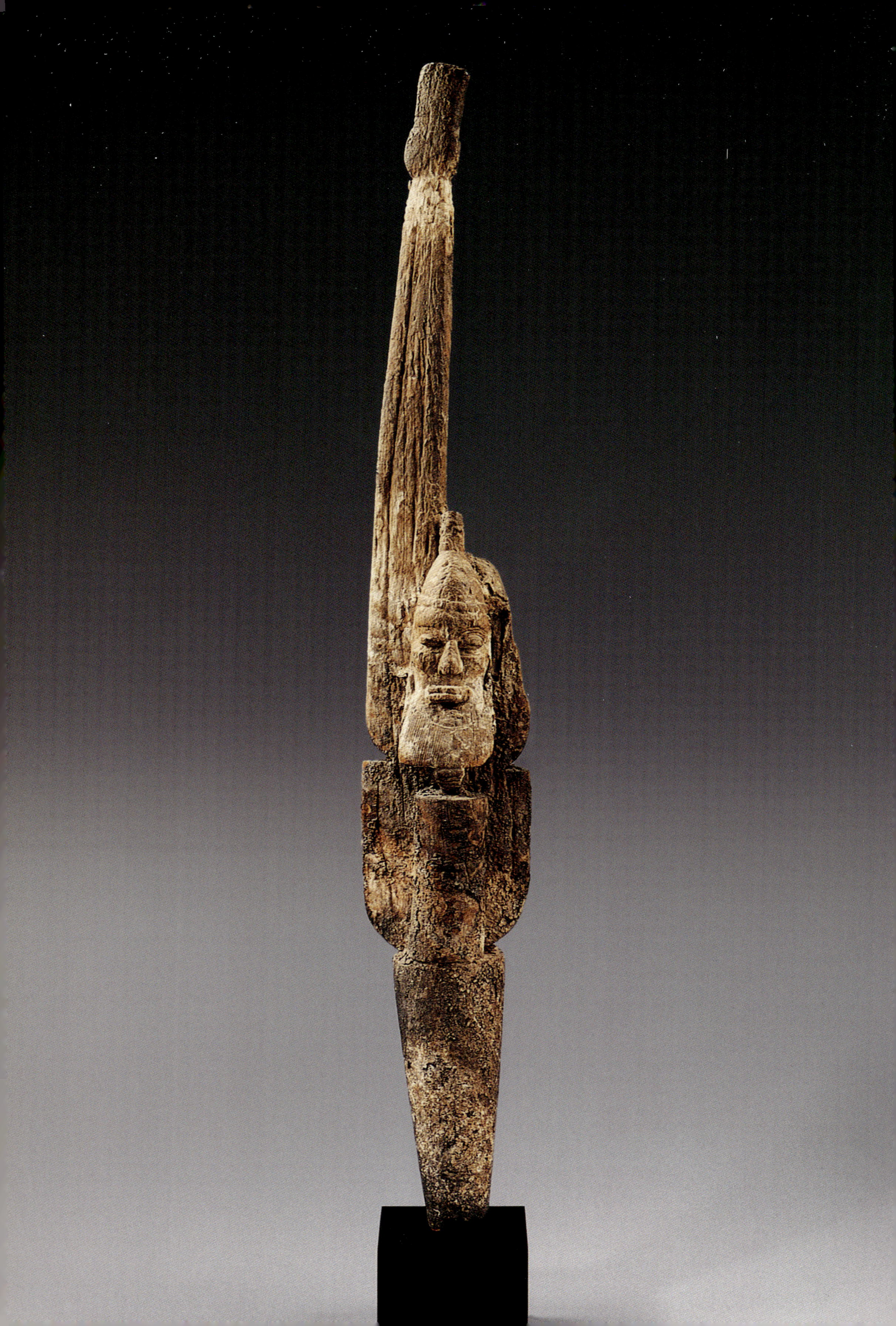

Dating and Historicity

The historicity of the African arts was ignored until a few decades ago. Dating the works and above all ascertaining their antiquity are tasks that Western scholars did not address until quite recently, about midway through the last century. An age of no more than a hundred years was in fact usually attributed to wooden works of art – which account for most of the hundreds of thousands of African items held by the public and private collections in the West – on the grounds of the perishable nature of the material in a humid environment unfavourable to preservation, the voracity of xylophagous insects, and the inherently replaceable nature of the artefacts involved. While these conditions certainly do exist, above all in equatorial Africa, they have not prevented works crafted in wood many centuries ago from arriving in the West.

The works in terracotta, bronze and ivory of two cultures of ancient Nigeria, namely the Ife (or Ile-Ife) and the Benin, were not swallowed up in this sort of timeless limbo. The former were brought to light by the German scholar Leo Frobenius a century ago and the latter at the end of the 19th century by the arrival in Europe of about two thousand items, the spoils of a British punitive expedition that destroyed the city, as we shall see later. The great art of the Egypt of the pharaohs and the countries north of the Sahara is not taken into consideration here for the reasons outlined in the general introduction.

For the many other artworks of Sub-Saharan Africa, whose forms were assumed to have been handed down since "time immemorial", no effort was made to document and quantify the time spans actually involved, almost as though such matters were of no importance. It was not until 1941 that the Belgian scholar Frans Olbrecht far-sightedly called attention to the urgent need to date the works, despite the inadequate means of investigation then available and the existence of "incalculable difficulties".[1]

Olbrecht's views found confirmation in the evidence obtained from archaeological excavations and the use of new methods of dating, which refuted the spurious assumption that Sub-Saharan Africa had no past civilization. It does have an artistic history, just like the West, and one that even stretches back for thousands of years in the case of the cave paintings and sculptures of southern Sudan.

The lack of written evidence certainly makes it more difficult to pinpoint the stages of this history. While countless events had already transformed African societies before the arrival of Europeans, the impact of colonization from the mid-19th century caused change on such a scale that it is legitimate to divide the creation of the artworks into two separate historical eras, albeit with the awareness that it is practically impossible to identify those created in one or the other on the basis of formal analysis alone.

It should be added that not all the countries of Sub-Saharan Africa have revealed the treasures of their artistic past. This does not mean that such riches do not exist, but probably that they have yet to be identified or even looked for in some cases.

1. Pre-Dogon artist (Djennenke)
Mali, 10th c.
Figure with raised arms
(the left broken and lost)
Wood and pigments, 103 cm
Musée Dapper, Paris

Establishing the exact age of an African work of art in the absence of documentary evidence is impossible at present. Even the dating of finds through examination of the layers from which they are unearthed – the stratigraphic method normally used by archaeologists all over the world – is unfortunately often impossible, because most of the works that arrive on the market are the result of illegal excavations that permanently destroy any information that might have been used for the purposes of scientific, albeit approximate, dating.

Despite all these adverse circumstances, the panorama of the ancient African arts began to develop depth and consistency year after year with the discovery of new methods of investigation, and the synchronous vision established in the past has been shown to lack foundation. The corpus of works of ascertained antiquity is increasing gradually as new items appear for examination, albeit emerging more through the pressure of the market than of scholarly study.

The process of determining the period in which a work was created often suggests comparisons with others with similar material and formal characteristics and provenance, which thus come to constitute more or less homogeneous sets that can legitimately be assigned a common dating. Unfortunately, in the absence of supporting evidence obtained by means of other disciplines, the characteristics listed are sufficient neither to confirm the dating nor above all to establish temporal sequences, since the pace of formal transformations is much slower in Africa than in the West, even though similar situations have arisen in Europe, in the case of icons of the Orthodox Church for example. Apparently similar and coeval works, like some Dogon figures, can be assigned dates centuries apart on the basis of carbon 14 testing.

A further problem is that the person who commissioned the work (a crucial element for the dating of a great deal of European art of the past) is nearly always unknown and the oral tradition, another pillar for the dating of African works, offers no certainty because many societies do not measure the passing of time on the basis of revolutions of the earth around the sun, but by reference to mythic events, the dates of which are sometimes manipulated for reasons of power.

In conclusion, we can neither establish nor expect the exact dates, based on precise documentary evidence, to which the study of Western art has accustomed us, and new chronological acquisitions emerge like islands or archipelagos in the ocean of timelessness. The amount of terra firma is, however, increasing with the development of studies.

The individual works and groups reproduced in this chapter – a total of about seventy dated to between the first millennium BC and the end of the 18th century AD – provide an albeit schematic picture of the richness of the African artistic heritage of centuries past. Though insufficient for the purpose of tracing a history of the African arts in all their development, they do afford a glimpse of stretches of the mainstream and suggest its depth.

Mali

The regions through which the immensely long River Niger runs on its way from Mali to Nigeria occupy a predominant place in the study of the past art of Black Africa because they appear to have provided the greatest number of ancient works. Created in wood, terracotta, bronze and ivory within different figurative cultures, with links already identified or perhaps to be discovered, and characterized by different stylistic devices, these works give a fascinating picture of the African sculpture of past centuries.

The route from north to south is illustrated here through a selection of emblematic works.

The chronological sequence, functions and assumed meaning of the artworks created in the region of the Bandiagara Escarpment (or Cliff of Bandiagara) in Mali, with the plateau above and the Seno plain below, are among those most extensively studied in the field of wooden African sculpture as a whole. While uncertainties have yet to be dispelled, science is beginning to provide some approximate yet reliable data, at least, on the unexpectedly ancient periods in which the works were created, and to put forward hypotheses as to the particular ethnic groups of their authors, even though this operation often presents insurmountable difficulties due to the lack of documentary evidence.

Until a few decades ago, the sculpture of the Bandiagara region was attributed indiscriminately to the Dogon, a people who became famous in the early 1930s through the studies and publications of Marcel Griaule and his colleagues.

The Dogon did not, however, find an empty land on their arrival in the region in the 13th–14th century. The Tellem, an ethnic group whose existence remained in doubt for decades until the mists of legend were dispersed by more recent studies, inhabited the escarpment and the adjacent areas, and would continue to do so with some autonomy for a few centuries before being assimilated by the newcomers.[2]

Moreover, the area above the Seno plain, between Pignari and Douenza, was inhabited some centuries before and concurrently with the Tellem by other peoples, whom Jean-Louis Paudrat[3] (1994) cautiously refers to as pre-Dogon. Vincent Bouloré (2000[a]) uses the same term also for the author of the celebrated snake-shaped figure in the Louvre regarded for decades as one of the masterpieces of Dogon art (no. 8 in this volume), which is identified by Hélène Leloup as Niongom or Nongom.

The works illustrated here in approximately chronological order are intended to provide some idea of the formal richness of the ancient art of this region.

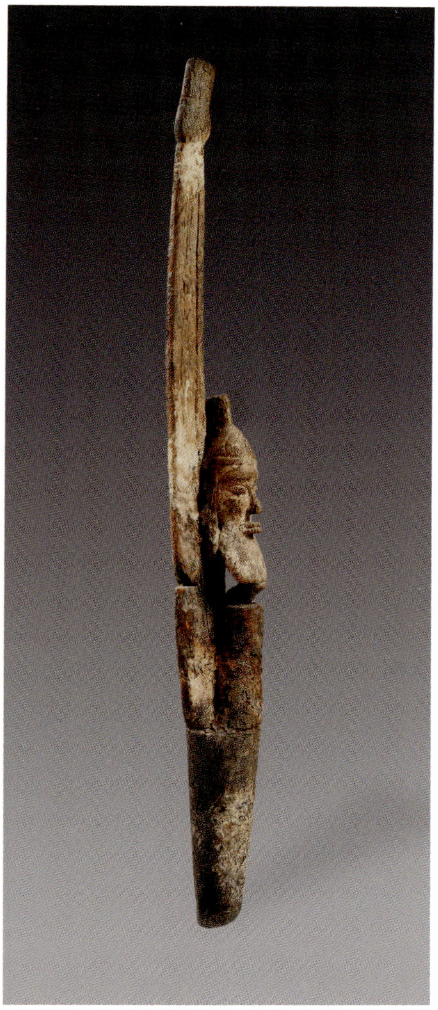

1. Pre-Dogon artist (Djennenke)
Mali, 10th c.
Figure with raised arms
(the left broken and lost)
Wood and pigments, 103 cm
Musée Dapper, Paris

Pre-Dogon

The unfortunately incomplete figure with raised arms (no. 1) now in the Musée Dapper, Paris, is attributed to the 10th century, the earliest date assigned to any work of art from this region and wholly unexpected for a wooden African sculpture. The pose, which we shall see repeated in numerous figures, has given rise to many different interpretations, the most frequent being an appeal to the divinity to send the rain essential to the agriculture upon which the life of the population largely depended. While this is the most plausible view, given the arid conditions characterizing the region, it could also and more simply represent an indeterminate appeal to the higher powers that govern human life. The focus of the figure is the head and the very long right arm (the left having been lost) raised above the body, which is suggested rather than actually represented by an assemblage of three solids, whose abstract quality serves, by contrast, to highlight the realism of the splendid head, endowed with all the nobility of a medieval king or saint.

The imposing sculpture now in the Musée du Quai Branly (no. 2), regarded by Hélène Leloup as a symbolic image of the mythic union of the two sexes, represents an anatomically composite figure with the beard and topknot of a man and the breasts of a woman. The two small forms, one male and one female, carved in high relief on either side of the navel on the flat belly seem to emphasize the dual essence of the figure, while the abundance of jewellery – bracelets and necklaces – suggests high rank. The most striking features of the sculpture are the large breasts, pendulous and distended, which allude metaphorically to fertility.

This unusual work is an assemblage of apparently disparate elements: a large, rectangular and almost flat panel, a series of cylinders for the raised arms and the proportionally minute head on a long neck, and two large cones for the breasts. These parts, embellished with sophisticated decoration and deftly arranged, are combined, however, to create a figure of extraordinary power and sublime spirituality at the same time.

A private collection holds the eroded remains of a similar figure of the same size dated to the 11th–12th century.[4]

Hermaphrodite figures are more frequent in Dogon and pre-Dogon sculpture than in any other African culture, and the works in which this subject appears are thought to illustrate creation myths.

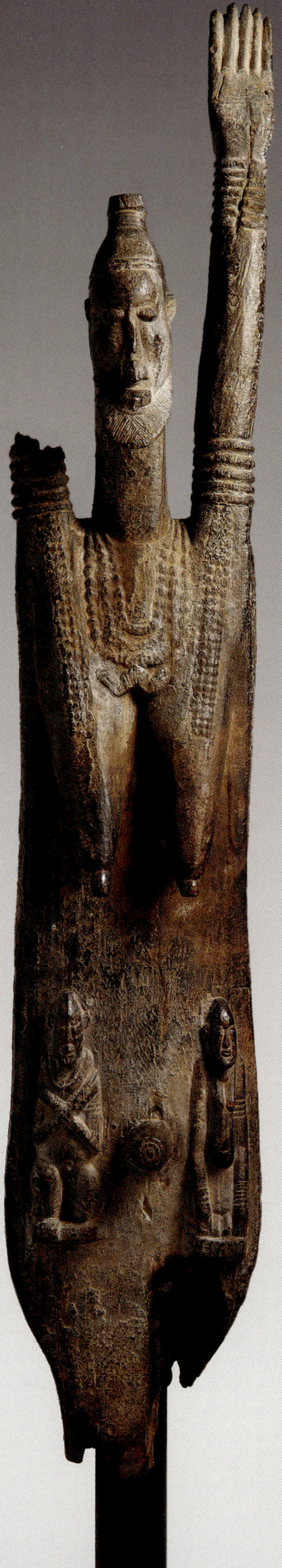

2. **Pre-Dogon artist (Djennenke)**
Mali, 10th c.
Figure with raised arms
(the right broken and lost)
Wood, 191 cm
Musée du Quai Branly, Paris

3. Pre-Dogon artist (Djennenke)
Mali, 12th c.
Maternity figure
Wood with sacrificial patina, 69 cm
Private collection

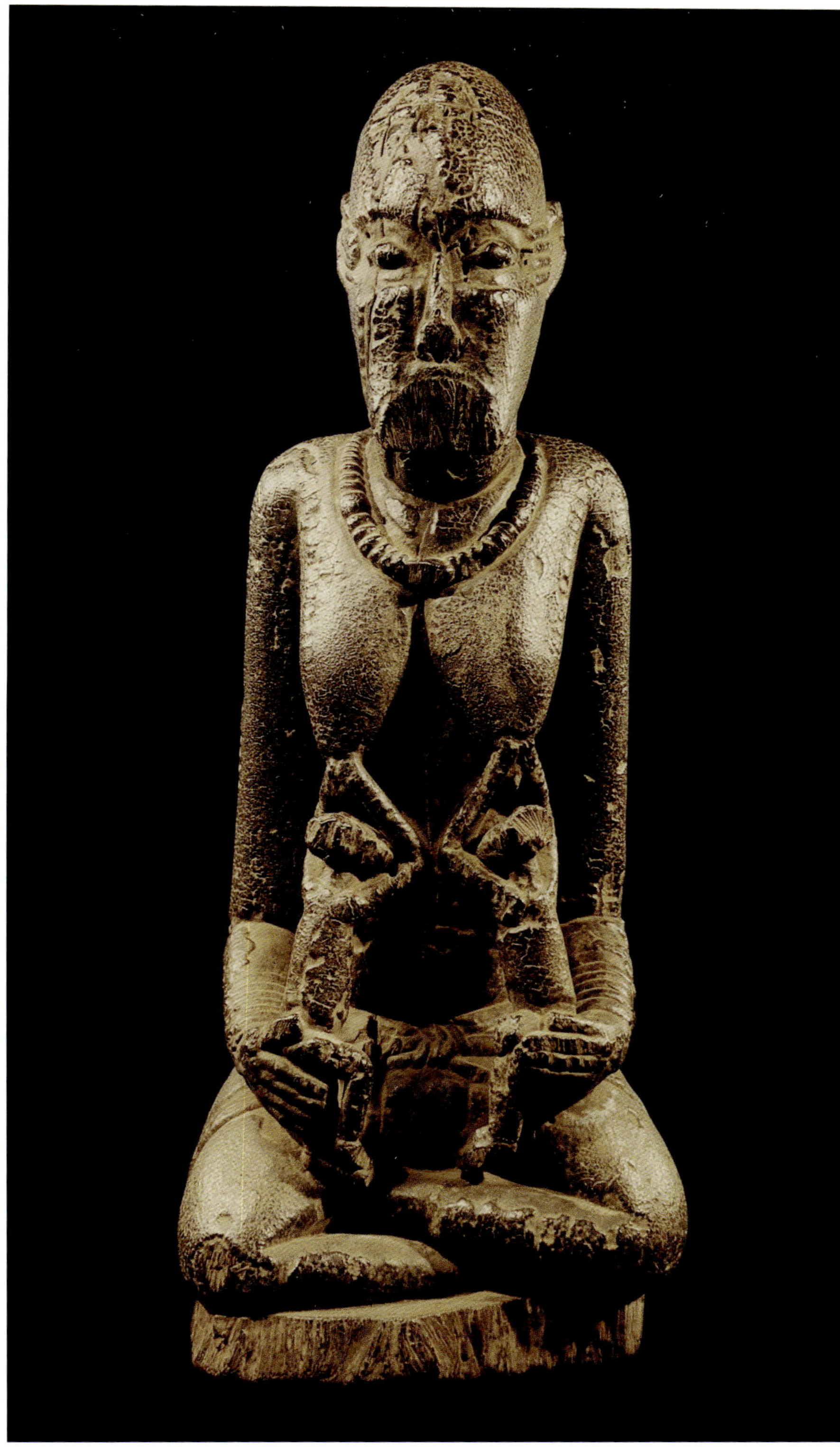

Female fertility was evidently extremely important in the life of all the African peoples, due to the high infant mortality rate, and propitiatory maternity figures are therefore frequent.

The theme is, however, addressed fairly rarely in the art of the pre-Dogon population. Moreover, as far as I know, this piece (no. 3) is the one of the few specimens to feature two children.

Even though this splendid image of a mother and twins is no more than 70 cm in height, the first adjective that comes to mind in order to describe it is "monumental". The long torso and large oval head of the woman rise from the plinth of the crossed legs, made still more powerful by the slenderness of the two children seated in the crook of her bent arms. Volumes of equal size echo one another in studied balance. The generous breasts and thighs of the woman, the thin arms and legs of the children, the elongated heads in an unnatural position, and the complex interplay of elements in relief (fingers,

4. "Master of the Red Maternity", pre-Dogon (Tintam)
Mali, 14th c.
Maternity figure
Wood and pigments, 75 cm
Musée du Louvre, Pavillon des Sessions, Paris (on deposit from the Musée du Quai Branly)

5. Pre-Dogon artist (Djennenke)
Mali, 14th–15th c.
Equestrian figure
Wood, 54.3 cm
Private collection

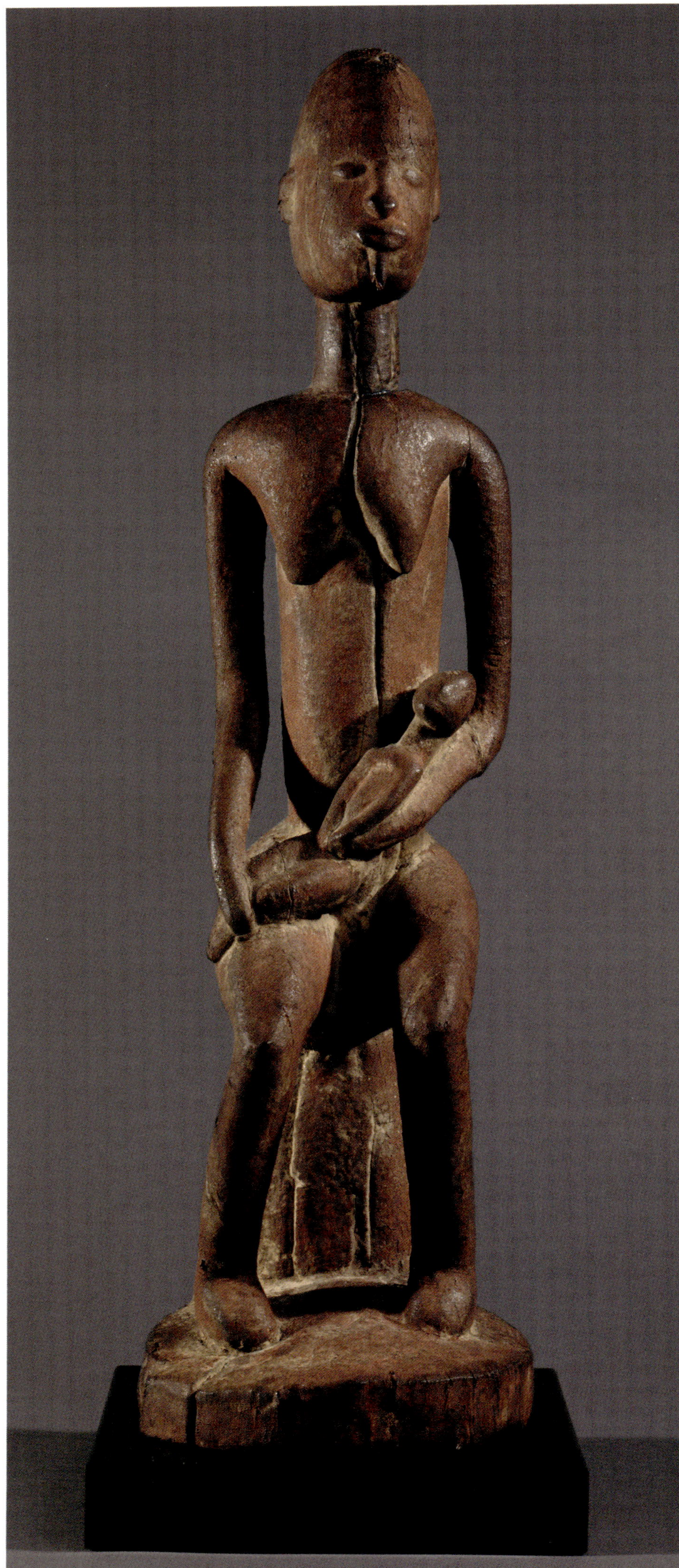

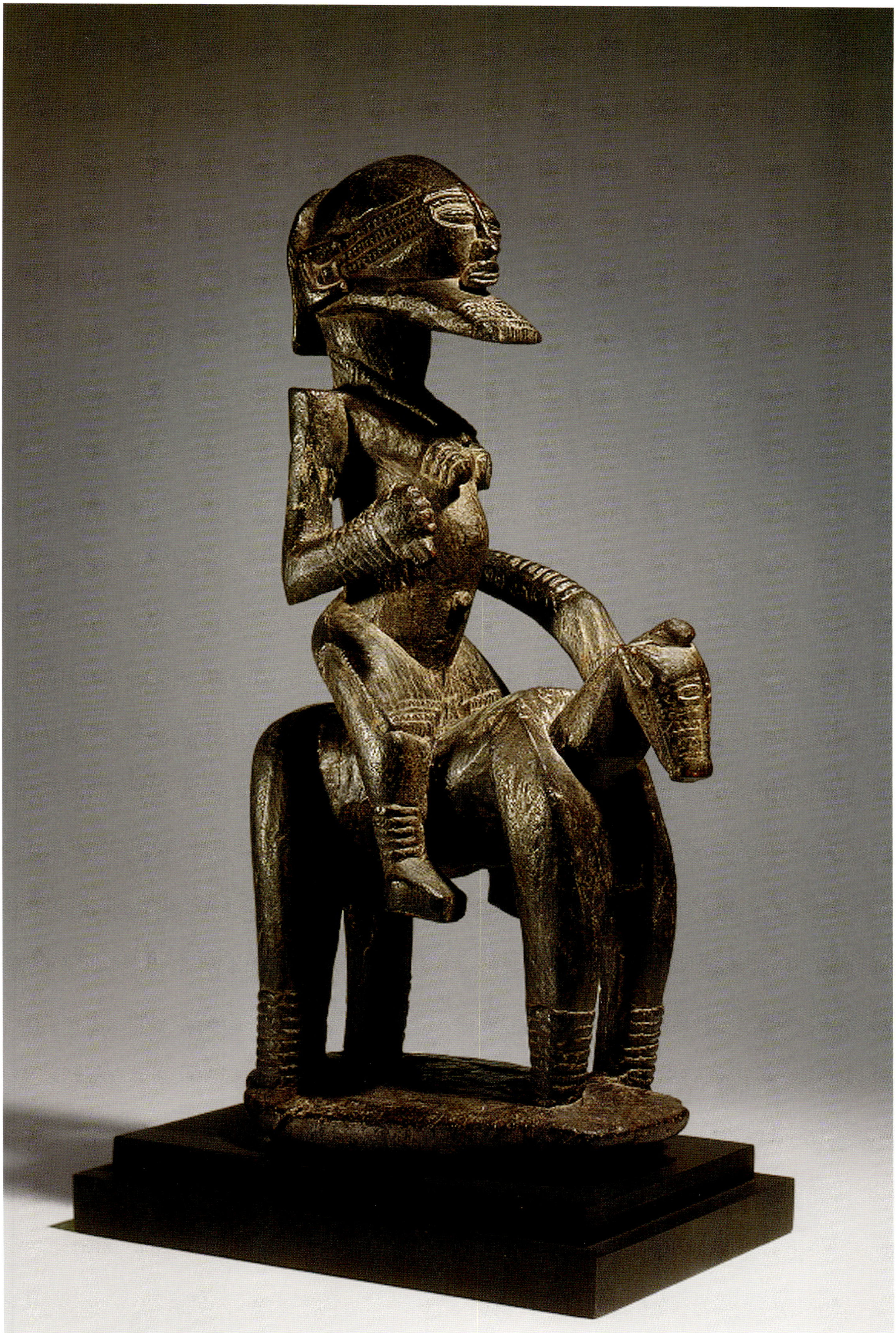

6. Tellem artist
Mali, 11th–16th c.
Figure with raised arms
Wood with sacrificial patina, 43 cm
Musée Dapper, Paris

bracelets, necklace and scarification marks) together create a skilfully fashioned structure imbued with energy and vitality.

According to Hélène Leloup, the maternity figures of the Djennenke represent the female ancestor of a lineage, a symbol not found among the other inhabitants of the plateau, which suggests that this people had a matriarchal system at some point in the past.

The maternity figure now in the Louvre (no. 4), one of the great masterpieces of Mali art, is a work of uncertain origin. According to the results of carbon 14 dating,[5] it was produced in the 14th century, and therefore prior to the arrival of the Dogon in the Bandiagara region.

Despite the hieratic pose, the absence of any eye contact or gesture of tenderness between the two figures, and the evident employment of pure volumes in the creation of the work (ovals for the heads and cylinders for the necks, torsos, arms and legs), the work conveys a moving sense of humanity through minimal elements such as the delicate features of the woman's face, the large hand holding the tiny child, and the knees turned slightly inward in a typically feminine pose. The thick red patina of mineral origin imprisons but does not obliterate this human quality.

The horseman is a recurrent image in the art of the pre-Dogon and Dogon peoples. An example now in an American private collection (no. 5), dated to the 14th–15th century, illustrates this theme in all its iconographic richness. The scarification at the temples, the heavy necklace, the bracelets, the arm dagger, the trousers with a side split and embroidery, and the absence of a saddle are elements shared with the clay sculptures brought to light in the Djenne-Jeno region, as will be seen below. Our information about the significance of the equestrian images and their function is unfortunately inconclusive.

Though actually modest in size, the work has a monumental character that derives from the erect pose of the figure enthroned on his mount, which evidently performs the subordinate function of a pedestal. This is suggested by the simplified forms, immobility and very small head of the animal compared to the complexity of the rider's body, enlivened by a parallel arrangement of slanting volumes and the ornaments and scarification marks in relief. The qualities listed above are exemplified and encapsulated in the whole formed by the chin, beard, ears and scarified temples of the proudly raised regal head.

Tellem

As mentioned above, the Bandiagara Escarpment was inhabited approximately between the 11th and 16th centuries by the Tellem, a people whose origin is still uncertain. The Dogon, who found them on the plain below when they arrived and assimilated them over the centuries, called them simply "the men before". Their culture and their very existence were controversial subjects until just a few decades ago, and their works of art were confused with those of the Dogon, who incorporated them to some extent into their own rituals.

In 1954 Pierre Langlois devoted a chapter of his slender volume *Art soudanais – Tribus Dogon* to the "Tellems", with twelve figures to illustrate their artistic creations. Five years later the Hanover Gallery, London, exhibited 43 sculptures, no fewer than 30 of which were attributed to the Tellem,[6] who were still vaguely described by Michel Leiris[7] in the preface of the catalogue as the predecessors mentioned in the Dogon traditions.

The later studies carried out in situ, above all by Dutch teams and in particular by Rogier Bedaux on his numerous expeditions, led to the discovery of valuable material that confirmed the existence of this mysterious people, who used to bury their dead in the caves halfway up the escarpment, where they also kept their stocks of provisions. The items found there include terracotta jars, iron and bronze ornamental objects, wooden furnishings for domestic and ceremonial use, and well-preserved fabrics. Unfortunately, there were only two examples of sculpture and, as Bedaux himself pointed out, these were discovered in a somewhat unconvincing context.

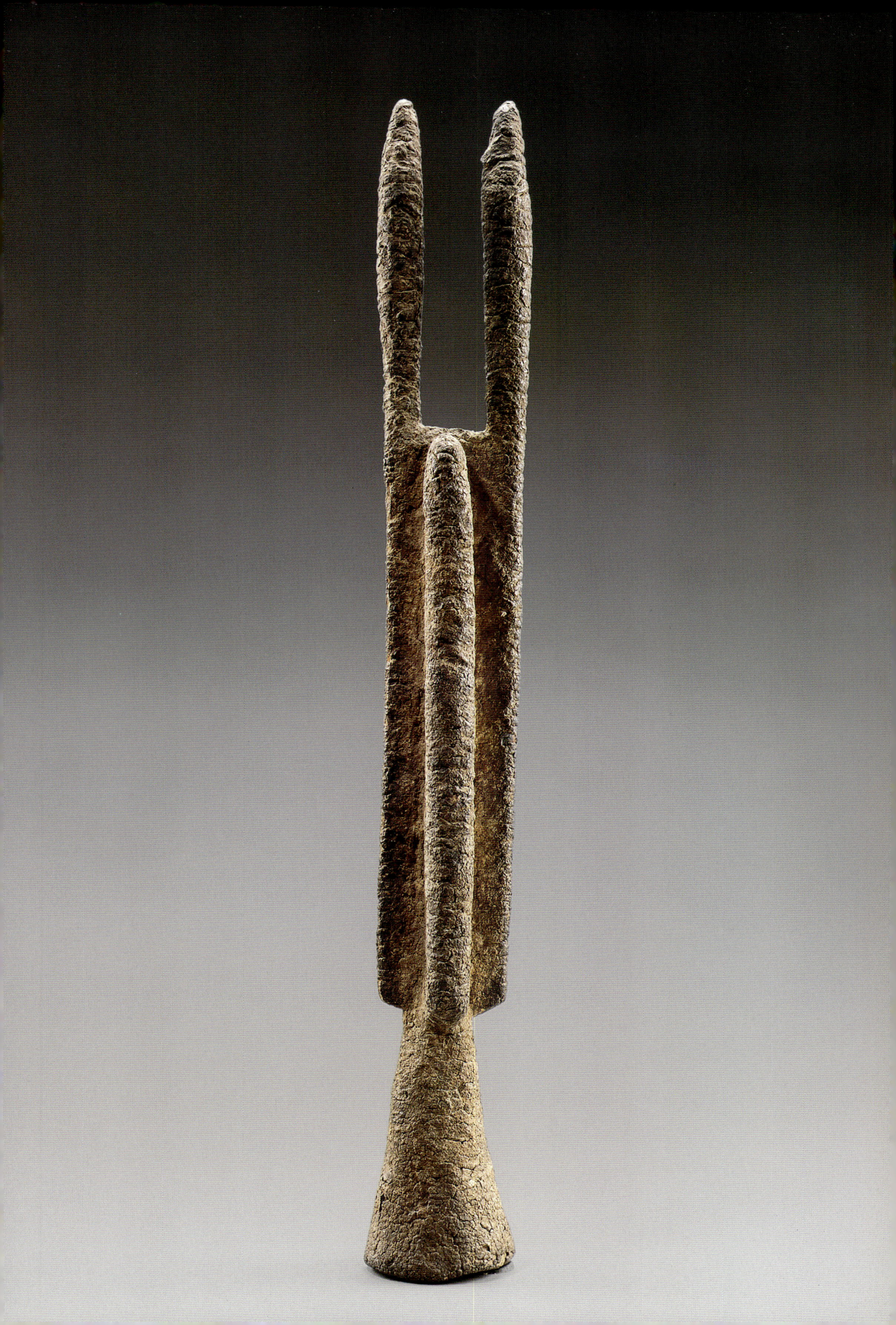

7. Tellem artist
Mali, 11th–16th c. (?)
Figure with raised arms
Wood with sacrificial patina, 68 cm
Private collection

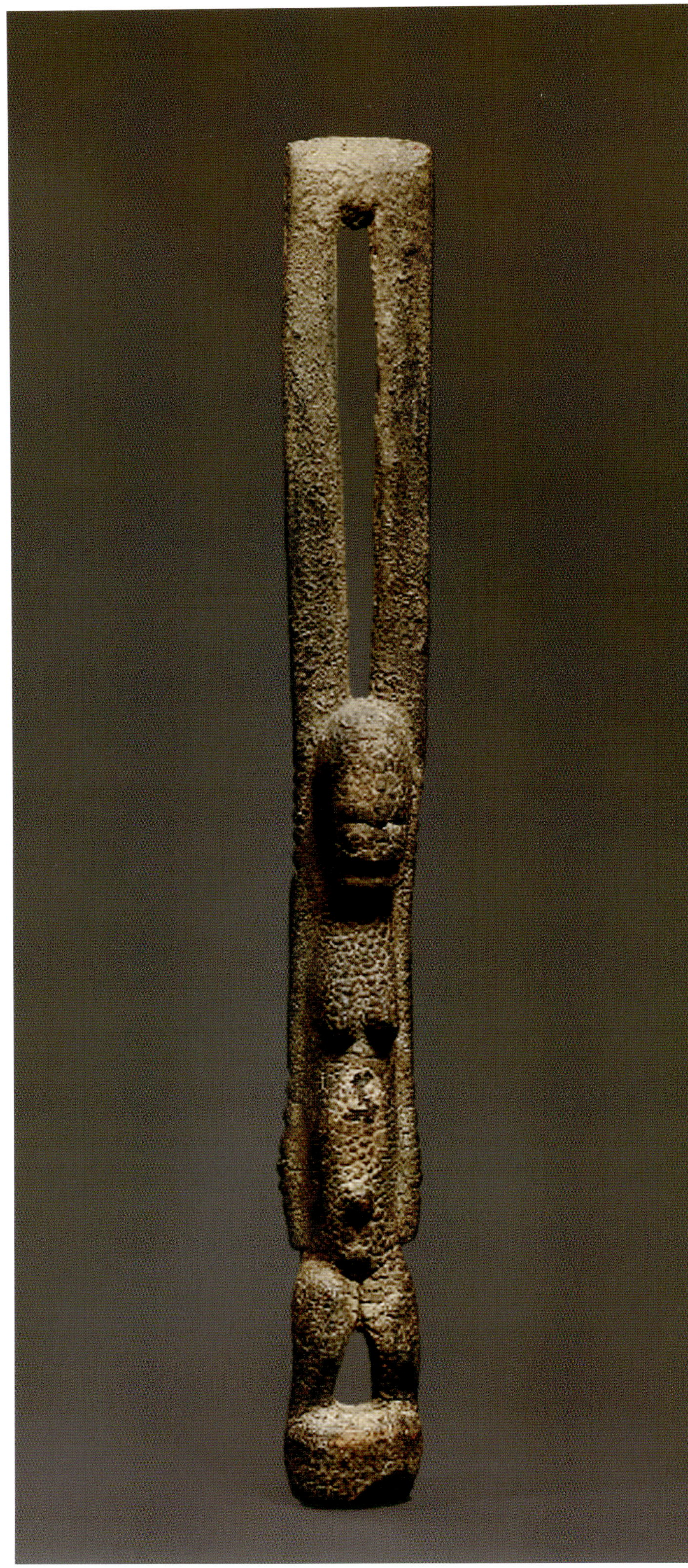

Numerous evocative, sober, wooden sculptures, found in the region of Bandiagara primarily in the 1960s, are today attributed to the Tellem on the basis of their formal characteristics, and scientific confirmation of their antiquity is being increasingly provided by laboratory tests.

Most of the works by Tellem artists are isolated human figures that are more abstract than any other form of sculpture in the region. Their petrified patina of blood and millet endows them with a distinctive stone-like appearance.

The first work illustrated here (no. 6) is a significant example of the Tellem artists' above-mentioned capacity for abstraction. The set of simplified and almost cylindrical elements of suitable length making up the figure suggests an ascetically stark idea of mankind.

In the next figure (no. 7), the large head with its features that are barely hinted at and the torso soberly animated by anatomical details in relief (in the complete absence of scarification, clothing and jewellery) emerge like a work of high relief from a flat surface that continues its impetuous upward motion in the unarticulated arms whose joined hands are merely suggested. The extraordinary tension running through and almost lifting the figure seems to be discharged into the very long panels tilted slightly forward.[8]

Dogon

Fleeing from Islam, the Dogon arrived at the end of a long migration, presumably between the 13th and 14th century, in the region of Bandiagara, which was or had been already inhabited by other peoples (as mentioned at the beginning of this chapter). Their culture then established its hegemony with a mythology and a religion from which the artists drew inspiration to create works of an unmistakable character despite their stylistic diversity.

A population of less than 300,000, little known in the Western world and still referred to at the time also as the Habé or Habbé (meaning "pagans" in the Peul language), the Dogon made their entrance on the academic scene in 1907 with the publication of *Le Plateau central nigérien*, a monumental report on the mission carried out in 1904–05 by Lieutenant Louis Desplagnes of the French colonial army.[9] As regards the art of this people, however, no significant works were brought back either by the Desplagnes mission or by the celebrated German explorer Leo Frobenius from his journey through the region during 1907–09.

It was not until the 1930s that the Dogon impinged themselves forcibly on Western consciousness through the reports of various missions organized by Parisian scientific institutions in order to gather both ethnographic information and material for the Musée d'Ethnographie du Trocadéro and then for the Musée de l'Homme, which later replaced it.

Led by Marcel Griaule and manned by Michel Leiris, Germaine Dieterlein, Solange de Ganay, Déborah Lifszyc and Denise Paulme, these missions brought thousands of items back to France. The first campaign alone, the famous Dakar-Djibouti Mission of 1931–32, saw a haul of some 3,500 pieces consisting primarily of artefacts with few works of art, which were in any case not the object of a systematic search.

The *Instructions sommaires pour les collecteurs d'objets ethnographiques* given to the French team just a few days before their departure made this explicit statement: "A collection of ethnographic items is neither a collection of curiosities nor a collection of artworks. Objects are nothing but evidence and must be considered for the information they supply on a given civilization rather than for their aesthetic value."[10]

It is not merely by chance that the legendary studies of the great French ethnologist Marcel Griaule make no reference to the formal qualities of the sculptures created by Dogon artists within and at the service of the immensely spiritual world evoked above all in *Dieu d'eau. Entretiens avec Ogotemmêli*. Published in 1948, this fascinating fresco of the Dogon world of myth and religion was written on the basis of information obtained in the space of a decade

8. "Master of Yaye",
Pre-Dogon artist (Niongom)
Mali, Cliff of Bandiagara,
16th–early 17th c.
Human figure
Wood, 132 cm
Musée du Louvre, Pavillon des Sessions, Paris (on deposit from the Musée du Quai Branly)

from an old, blind hunter named Ogotemmêli, the (perhaps) unwitting poet and mythographer of his people.[11]

The attitude of French ethnography was shared at the time by practically the whole of the international scientific world. The function and meaning of the comparatively few Dogon works of art to be found in Western museums in the past and of those collected by Griaule and his followers as from 1931 were painstakingly examined, albeit with contradictory results, whereas the dates or rather periods of their creation and their artistic quality did not generally receive due consideration. It should also be remembered that the studies carried out after the mid-20th century demonstrated that the statuary discovered on the escarpment did not constitute a single homogeneous group and that not all the works were attributable to the Dogon. In many cases, they were created by the peoples that inhabited the region over the centuries, as mentioned above. The later arrivals then made use of them and incorporated them into their own culture, while remaining aware of their true paternity. Before the tools for dating made available to researchers during the last fifty years came into existence, it was commonly held that the African wooden sculptures were at most a century old, because of the climatic conditions and the destructive action of xylophagous insects. The research of the last few decades has refuted this unfounded belief.

Before introducing the group of works that experts have definitively attributed to the Dogon, it is worth pausing to consider the snake-shaped figure found by Denise Paulme and Déborah Lifszyc in the village of Yaye (no. 8), which is a further example of how difficult it is to assign a sculpture to a specific period in the history of the arts of the Bandiagara region. In actual fact, from the time of its acquisition in 1935 until a few years ago, the work, now attributed by Hélène Leloup to an artist of the Niongom culture, was regarded as a noteworthy example of Dogon art even though the two French scholars wrote explicitly to Georges Henri Rivière, assistant director of the Musée d'Ethnographie du Trocadéro, that they had discovered "a statue 1.3 metres tall in a previously unknown style that was unquestionably earlier than the arrival of the Dogon".[12]

The dating (16th–17th century), if it is confirmed, indicates, however, that the sculpture was created when the Dogon had already been settled in the region for a few hundred years and would therefore be evidence of a period of coexistence with the previous inhabitants.

While its meaning was unknown to them, Denise Paulme and Déborah Lifszyc had no doubt that the work was a masterpiece. The letter to Rivière continues as follows: "[...] the very long, curved body with the arms flat against the hermaphrodite body. The head arouses a deep emotion that makes this piece a masterpiece in the true sense of the word."[13]

Paulme had written a month earlier to André Schaeffner of feeling a lump in her throat and being on the verge of tears as the work emerged from the earth in which it was buried up to the shoulders, and that she did not dare to touch it.[14]

The emotion felt by the two scholars is quite understandable, such is the spiritual power that emanates from the sinuous form, curving gently in and out from the feet up to the small breasts and on to the finely proportioned head with its strongly defined features. The very long arms pressed against the body and the genitals follow the line of the log from which the work was carved and thus confirm the deliberate choice made by its sculptor, who also took advantage of the vertical grain of the wood.

A small and severely damaged sculpture of a horseman, possibly by the same hand, was brought back from Griaule's third mission in 1935.[15]

Full discovery and appreciation of the greatness of Dogon sculpture did not come, however, until the 1960s, when the triumph of Islam and consequent abandonment of the traditional religion, of which the artworks were both ritual objects and evidence, led to sales and thefts that emptied the sanctuaries previously hidden from outsiders. Great masterpieces were thus brought

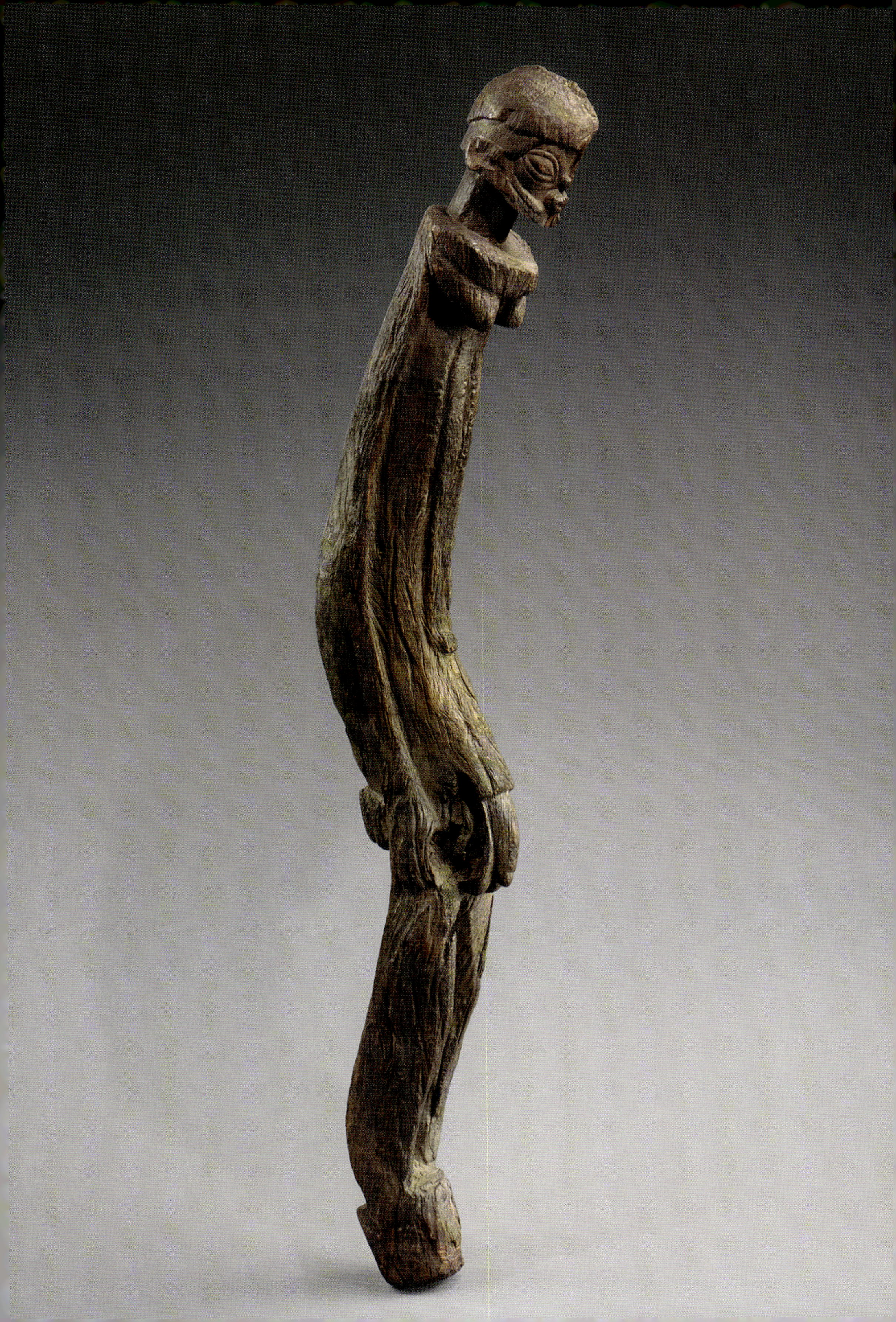

9. Dogon artist
Mali, 16th c.
Figure with raised arms
(the right broken)
Wood, 210 cm
The Metropolitan
Museum of Art,
New York

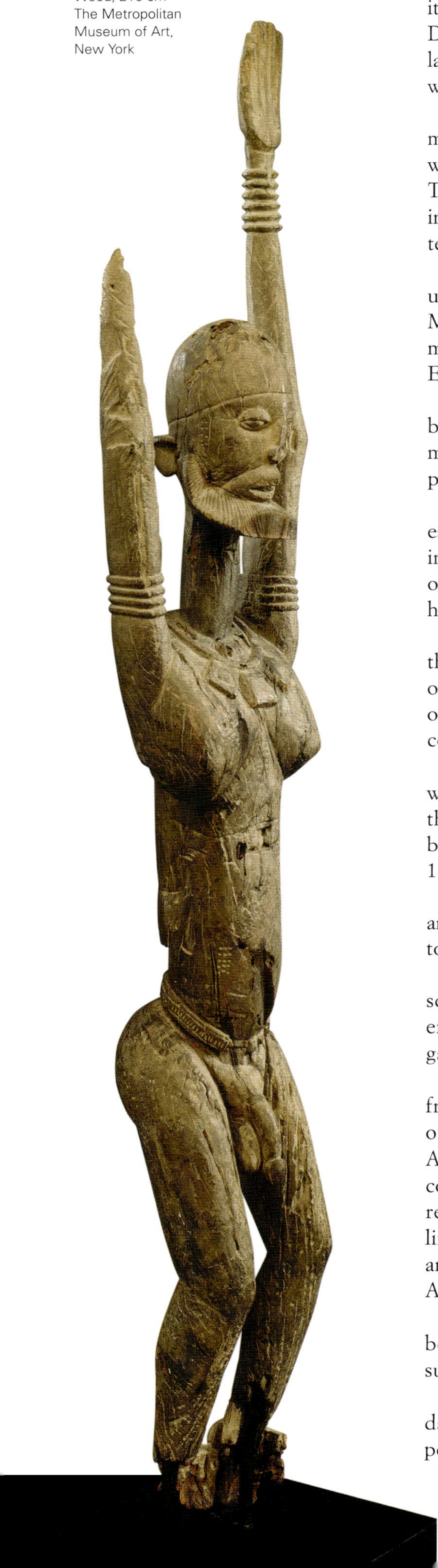

to Paris by Muslim dealers and from there they were distributed all over the world.

The regal figure from the village of Tintam (no. 9) now in the Metropolitan Museum, New York, is one of these and indeed one of the most moving Dogon works by virtue not only of its exceptional size, which makes it the largest known piece of Mali sculpture, but also of its austere gravity combined with monumental nobility.

The simple, unadorned structure consisting of soft elongated volumes marked only by the traces of a necklace and bodily scarification is endowed with rhythm by the complementary protrusions of the breasts and buttocks. The thrust of the long cylindrical arms emphasizes a vertical quality that is not inert, but animated by an inner life that the noble head expresses through austere reserve.

While figures with similar characteristics can be found in various museums and private collections, none of these has the nobility of the one in the Metropolitan Museum. Something similar can, however, be found in certain maternity figures, such as the piece formerly in the renowned collection of the English sculptor Sir Jacob Epstein and then owned by Carlo Monzino.[16]

In African art, as in the art of Europe and every other part of the world, be it "civilized" or "primitive", the depiction of the same subject does not mean sameness in terms of formal rendering. This is demonstrated by a comparison of the three maternity figures illustrated here.

Great composure and a complete absence of pathos usually distinguishes the figures of the mother and the child that sits in her lap. In the piece held in the Musée Dapper in Paris,[17] both gaze straight ahead, apparently unaware of each other apart from the tenuous link suggested by the way the woman's hands rest delicately on her son's body.

The frozen detachment of the two figures, however, melts in the moving third sculpture, which Hélène Leloup has attributed to the northern-centre of the Bandiagara Plateau (no. 10). The tender act of feeding the child, whose open mouth shows its hunger, subtly suggests a close relationship and uncommon affective involvement.

The complementary rapport between the full volumes of the two bodies within an evident spiral movement – note the parallel and enveloping lines of the mother's forearm and the child's legs – conveys a warm sense of mutual belonging that makes this work quite exceptional. It has been dated to the 18th century,[18] though it is probably earlier.

The (now broken) chameleon carved on the top of the woman's head is an ambivalent symbol because of its ability to change colour and, also according to Hélène Leloup,[19] the most ancient animal in the Dogon pantheon.

The meaning of the horseman in the Dogon culture is not clear. Some scholars think that the equestrian figures are images of *hogon* (religious leaders) linked in some way to the myth of the creation of the world. Others regard them more simply as portraits of important personages.

The piece illustrated here (no. 11), assigned to the 16th–18th century and from the N'duleri region like the two figures that follow it, is one of the most outstanding works of this type. Although it is modest in size (yet large by African standards), it has an extraordinarily monumental quality and bears comparison with the great equestrian statues of the European Renaissance as regards the harmony of its simple volumes, arranged in a moving, formally limpid composition, the calibrated proportional relationship between rider and mount, the expressive power of the noble head, and the perfection of the Apollonian body.

While the unusually curved arm dagger and quiver are elements also to be found in the terracotta sculptures of Djenne, the presence of the saddle suggests a different origin.

A sculpture in a private collection, devoid of attributes of status and not dated scientifically, resembles this work in some formal and volumetric aspects.[20]

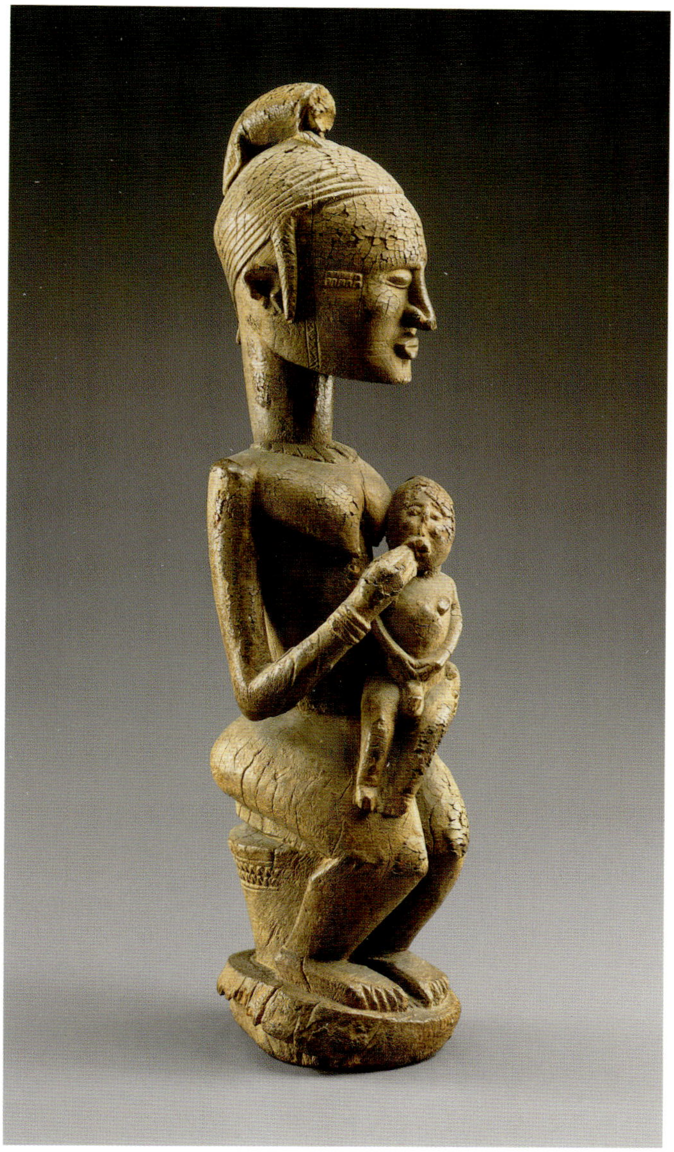

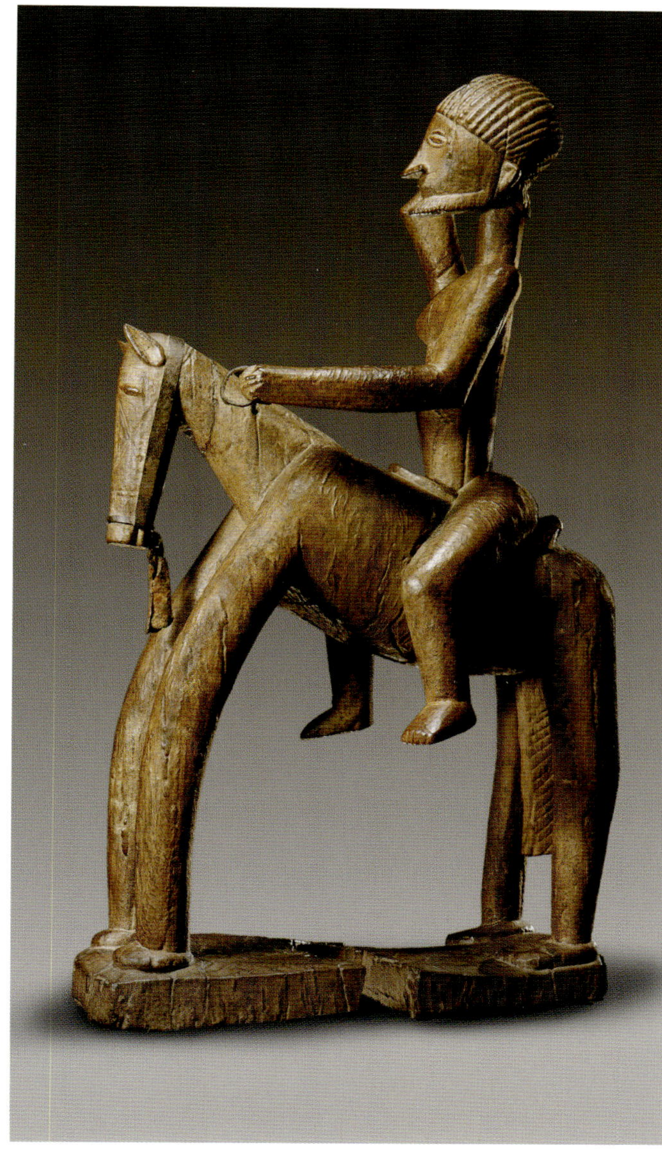

10. Dogon artist
Mali, 16th–18th c. (?)
Maternity figure
Wood and pigments, 68 cm
Private collection

11. Dogon artist
Mali (N'duleri region), 16th–18th c.
Equestrian figure
Wood, 91.5 cm
Private collection

The husking or pounding of millet in a mortar is a subject seldom depicted in Dogon art, at least not in recent times, even though this cereal is one of the basic foodstuffs for the Sahel peoples and also, together with blood, one of the components of the sacrificial patinas covering many antique sculptures.

The stark linearity and limited corporeal substance of this slender figure, also from the region of N'duleri (no. 12), probably the most poetic of all those illustrating this theme, are echoed in the calculated verticality of the mortar and above all of the pestle, which is a very long, cylindrical stick, like the slender arms of the woman.

The meaning of the image has yet to be precisely ascertained. Citing Denise Paulme, Kate Ezra[21] has suggested that similar works might be the sculptural equivalent of an oration celebrating the work of Dogon women.

This arbitrary overview of Dogon sculpture ends with the rare subject of a couple of figures playing the xylophone-like instrument known as the *balafon* (no. 13).

Carved in the 15th–16th century, this is the work of a great artist who has created a complex structure that is perfect from every point of view in its masterly combination of cylindrical and polyhedral, squared and rounded volumes.

The instrument and the seats act as a solid base for the musicians' bodies and, by contrast, set off their lithe, clear-cut elegance. The heads of the two almost identical figures seem to express concentration and involvement in the task they are performing.

12. Dogon artist
Mali (N'duleri region), 16th–17th c.
Woman pounding millet
Wood, iron and pigments, 101 cm
Private collection

13. Dogon artist
Mali (N'duleri region), 15th–16th c.
Couple playing the balafon
Wood with sacrificial patina, iron, 44 cm
Private collection

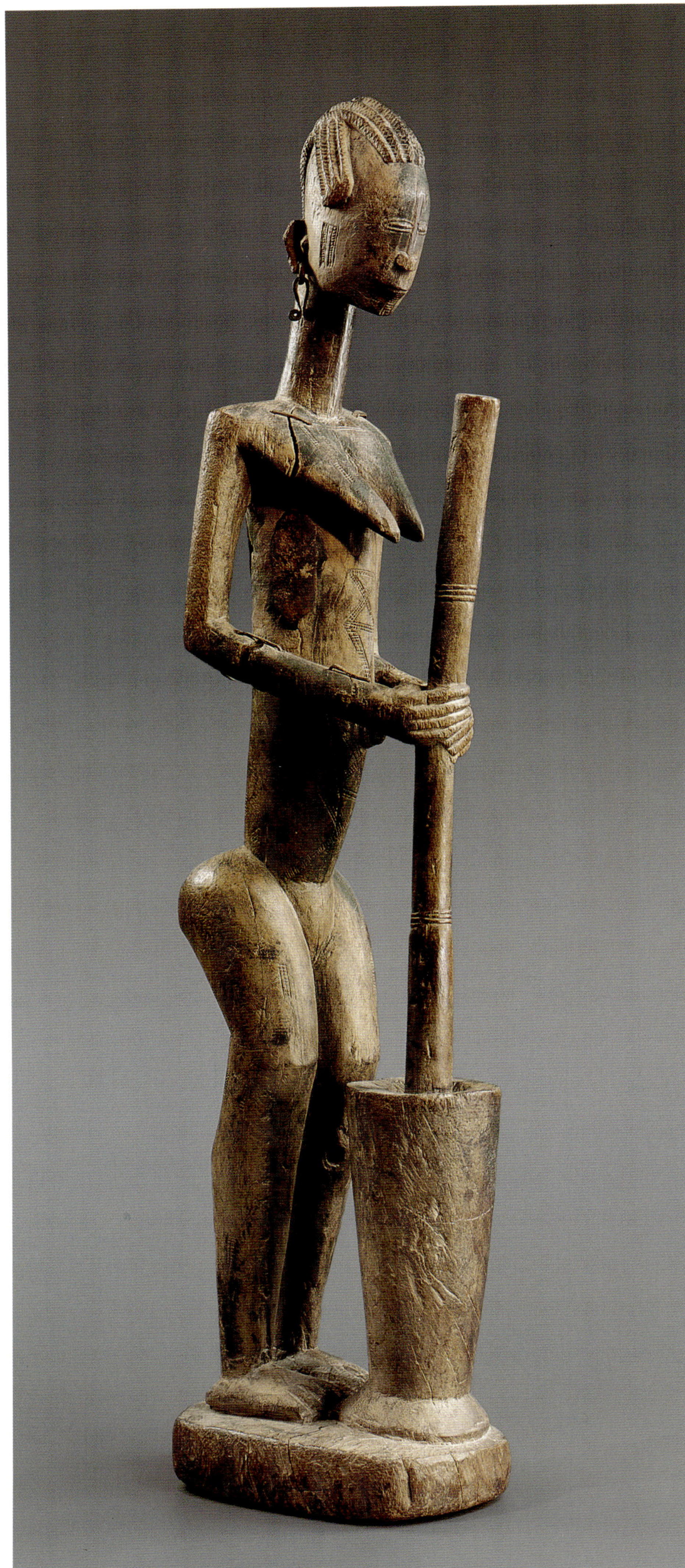

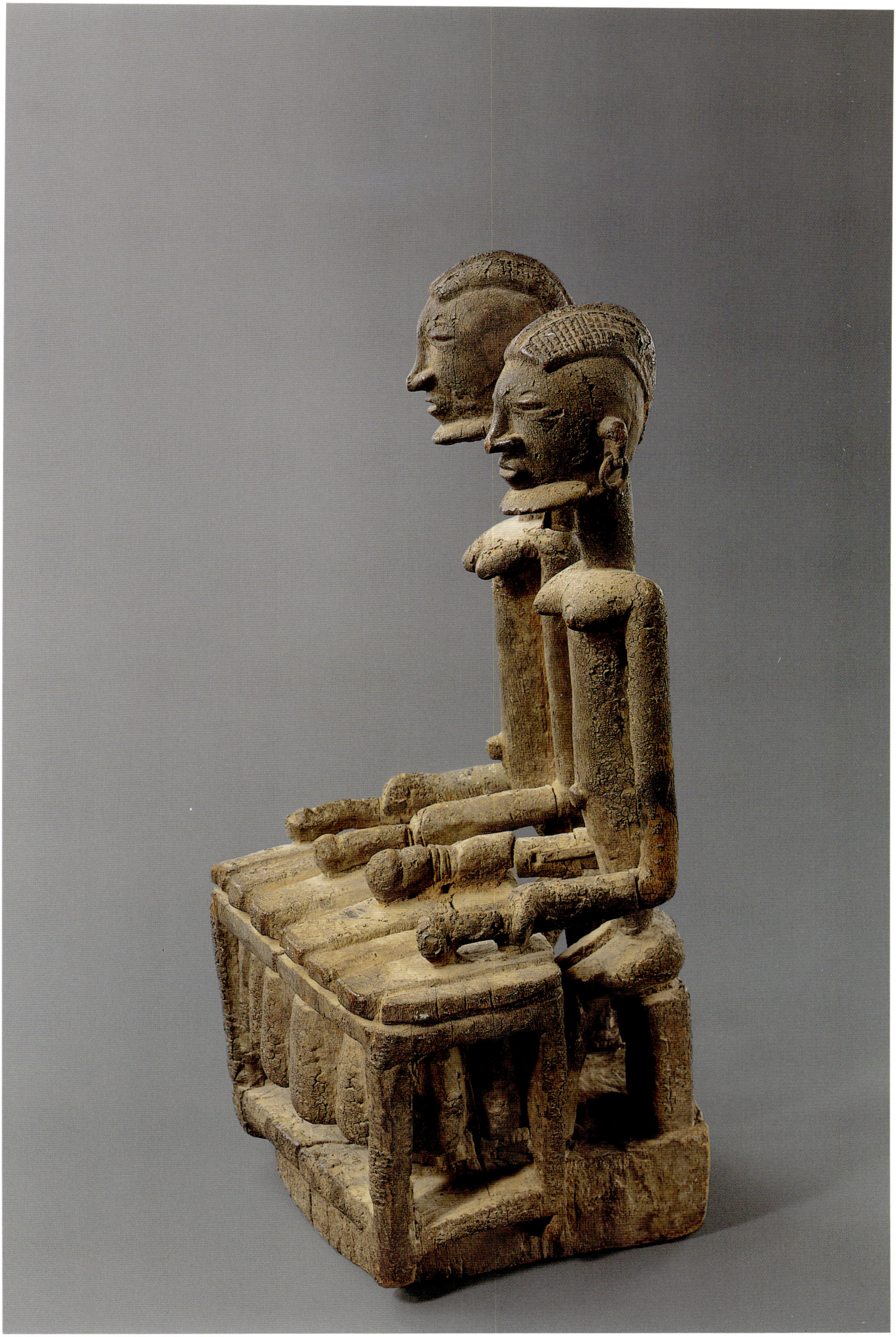

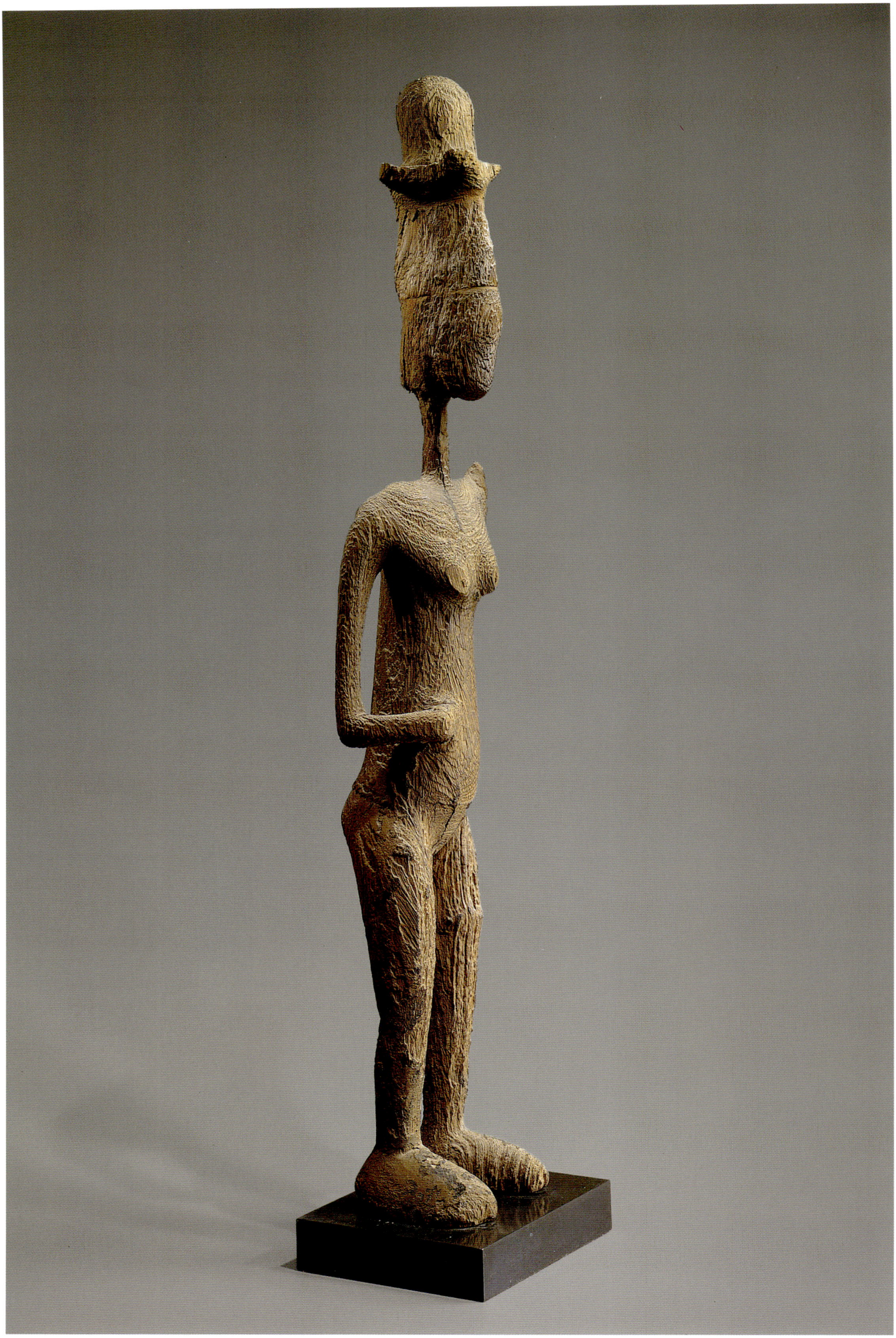

14. Bamana artist
Mali (Banan region), 12th–16th c.
Female figure
Wood, 116 cm
Private collection

According to information gleaned in 1993 and reported by Jean-Louis Paudrat,[22] the work represents a man and his sister playing an instrument used only during the funeral rites of priests.

Bamana

The artworks of the Bandiagara region are not, however, the only ones to date back over hundreds of years. A series of sculptures by the Bamana,[23] the most numerous ethnic group in Mali, make it possible to broaden our knowledge of the country's art during the past centuries.

In the mid-20th century, the conversion of most of the population to Islam led to the abandonment of some sanctuaries of the ancient traditional religion and the destruction or sale of ritual objects, including large wooden figures. When they appeared on the market, some of these were purchased by illustrious institutions like the Museum of Primitive Art, New York, (subsequently incorporated into the Metropolitan Museum of Art) and by private collectors, though no mention was made of their age.

It was not until 1986 that Kate Ezra reported in *A Human Ideal in African Art: Bamana Figurative Sculpture* (the catalogue of the show she curated at the Metropolitan) the results of the carbon 14 testing carried out on some of the sculptures exhibited, which gave a surprising series of dates between the 13th and 17th centuries.[24]

Fourteen years later, in the catalogue of the exhibition held in their gallery in Paris,[25] Hélène and Philippe Leloup published two figures dated respectively 1419–1526 and 12th–16th century,[26] together with a third figure and an unusual animal from the same sanctuary, neither of which was dated.

It should be noted that three of the ancient sculptures in the 1986 Ezra catalogue (nos. 25, 27, 34) apparently belong to a different stylistic and temporal universe from the two figures in the Metropolitan Museum and the four in the Leloup Collection. Above all, they are not homogeneously eroded like the others. Differences in provenance and date must therefore be assumed, unless the more complete items were kept in a different environment that was conducive to their preservation.

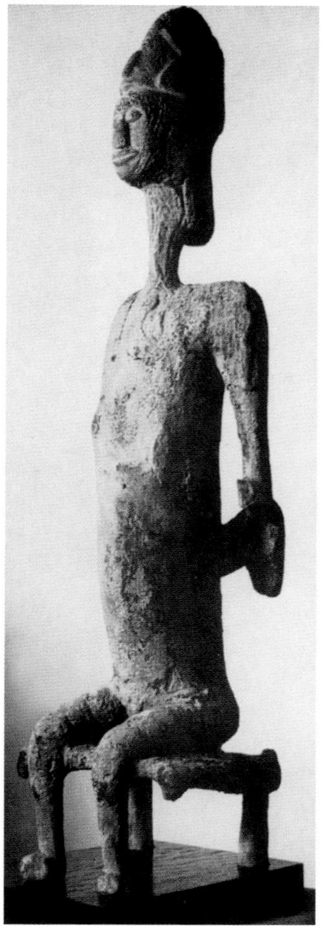

15. Bamana artist
Mali, 12th–16th c.
Seated figure
Wood, 98 cm
The Metropolitan Museum of Art, New York

To make matters even more complicated, a test executed in 2003 assigns a probable age of 200±45 years to a figure similar to these eroded works,[27] which calls into question the assumption that the works in the group were created in the same period. The problem is evidently anything but resolved and will entail both a re-examination of the Metropolitan sculptures and an analysis of the other works in the homogeneous group, which are not scientifically dated but all from the same sanctuary in Mali.

The specific significance and use of the figures are thought to have been connected with the rituals of the male and female Jo initiatory societies and the Gwan cult, both intended to foster fertility. Their religious purpose and original meaning are, however, subject to verification, which is anything but easy in the case of an oral culture, especially if the earlier dates are confirmed. The persistence of purpose and significance, with minimal variations, is customary and proven, however, for the images of religions and societies that possess a written language, which provides certain – or in any event less uncertain – information on cultural phenomena even of the remote past, albeit with some divergence of interpretation. There is thus no reason why the same should not also hold for the artworks of African cultures, which developed different mechanisms for the transmission of knowledge.

The ruthless passage of time has dried out these noble figures carved in compact wood and eliminated the perishable part to reveal their innermost spiritual essence and tender, attenuated beauty, which some loss of limbs has not diminished. The moving, austere, monk-like bodies are created through soft lines that flow from the legs to the shoulders in an elegant continuum, interrupted by the Gothic slenderness of the necks that set off the mass of the noble heads. The deft composition makes up for the erasure of facial features and adds a further touch of ascetic immateriality to the images.

16. Artist of the Djenne culture
Mali, 13th c.
Androgynous figure
(head and right leg missing)
Terracotta, 27 cm
Musée National du Mali, Bamako

According to the authors of the Leloup catalogue of 2000, the missing left arm of the first sculpture (no. 14), now in an Italian collection, probably supported a small cushion on which a mortar rested.[28]

The body of the second figure (no. 15), seated on a low chair, retains a regal presence despite mutilation. The author skilfully made the lower part of the body smaller and gradually expanded the very long torso crowned by a noble head. The hat, which looks pointed when seen from the front, contrasts with and enhances the imposing body, so that the whole acquires an aura of spiritual majesty accentuated by the white patina.

The Djenne culture

A great art of terracotta and bronze also flourished alongside the great art of wood carving on the banks of the Niger. The numerous clay works found in the region of ancient Djenne and now held by many museums and private collections constitute a prime example of this. They were mostly unearthed during illegal excavations and hence there is no information that would make it possible to place them within a cultural context and thus shed light on their nature. These items were subjected to thermoluminescence testing and have been dated to between the 12th and 15th centuries, which makes them coeval with some pre-Dogon and Dogon works in wood.

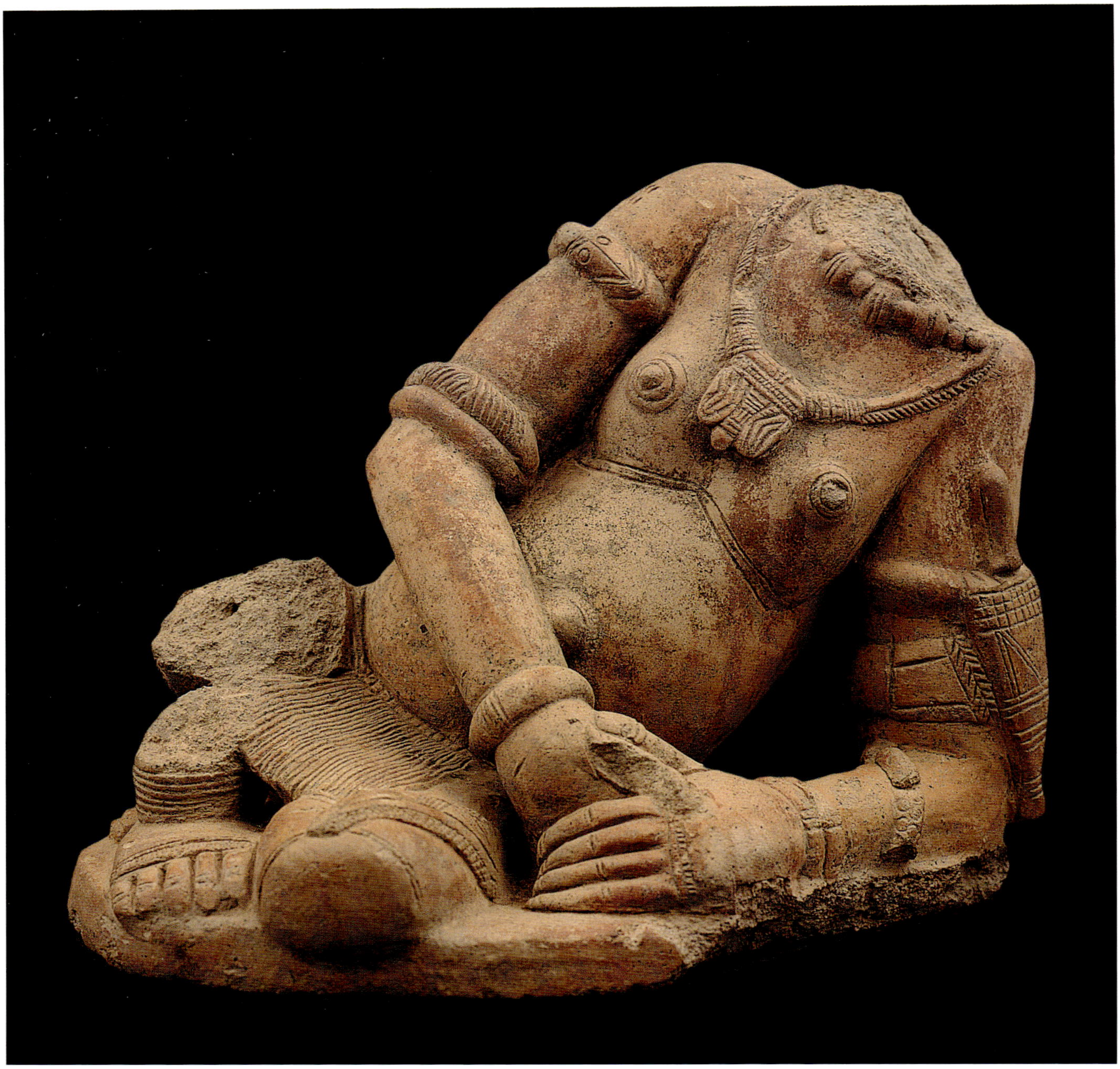

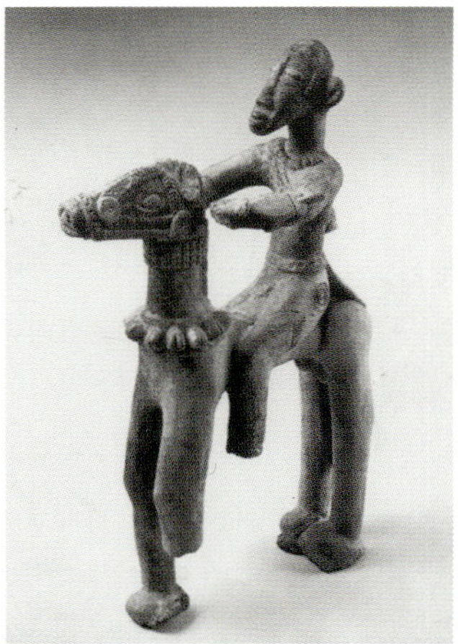

17. Artist of the Djenne culture
Mali, 13th–15th c.
Equestrian figure (found in pieces and reassembled)
Terracotta, 47 cm
Private collection

The headless figure from the Bamako Museum (no. 16) is one of the few found in an excavation carried out scientifically, by Roderick and Susan McIntosh in 1981. Though incomplete, it is evidently the work of a very gifted artist.

Arranged in a soft diagonal whose ends are unfortunately the missing head and the left knee, the full forms of the body are emphasized by the right angle of the rigidly bent left arm. The rich ornaments and the arm dagger indicate a personage of high rank.

A comparison of the headless figure, the sculpture shown here[29] (no. 17), and the pre-Dogon horseman (no. 5) is illuminating as regards the relationship between the two cultures, even though the works differ in volumetric terms. While all the figures wear trousers with a V-shaped split at the side that has a decorated edge and bear arm daggers, a wooden figure on foot, now in the New Orleans Museum of Art, has the same number of bracelets as the wooden equestrian figure. It should also be noted that the hair is worn in a topknot, as in the monumental figure now in the Musée du Quai Branly, Paris (no. 2).

Niger, the Bura necropolis

The finds unearthed between 1980 and 1985 in the necropolis of Bura-Asinda-Sikka in the Niger Republic – which were a few hundred large, terracotta

18. Artist of the Bura-Asinda-Sikka culture
Niger, 3rd–11th c.
Equestrian figure (lower part of rider's body and most of the mount missing)
Terracotta, 52 cm
Institut de Recherches en Sciences Humaines, Niamey

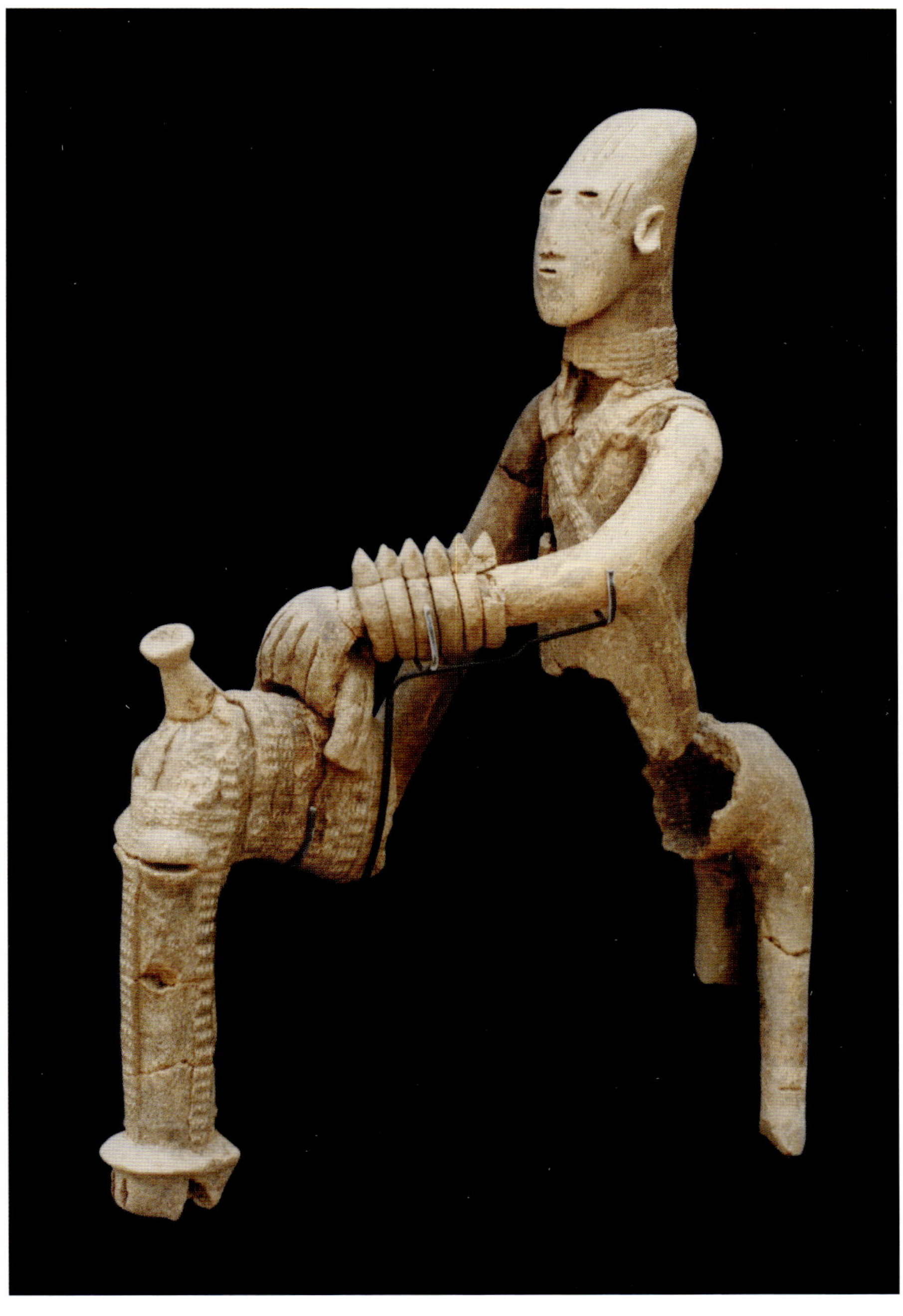

19. **Artist of the Nok culture** (from Rafin Kura)
Nigeria, 5th c. BC
Head
Terracotta, 33.8 cm
The National Commission for Museums and Monuments, Nigeria

burial urns surmounted by images of standing and mounted human figures, dating from between the 3rd and 13th centuries – add an important chapter to our knowledge of the civilizations of ancient Africa.

The rare statue shown here (no. 18) is an incredible work in volumetric terms and rich in precious decorative elements. Articulated and dynamic when seen from the side, the sculpture is endowed with an extraordinary vertical quality when viewed frontally, which the sculptor felicitously suggests through the abnormal elongation of the animal's head. This is underscored by the elegant bands of the harness that seem to be echoed in the scarification on the rider's temples and forehead.

The impressive bracelets, the necklaces, the crossed bands (one probably holding a knife) and the horse's rich harness are indicative of the importance of the personage buried.

Before going on to Nigeria, it should be remembered that a vast number of ancient terracotta works have been found in other countries south of the Sahara. Small animals and human heads attributed to the Sao and dated 1200±200 years and 500±75 years (in 1979) were unearthed south of Lake Chad. Many hundreds of crudely fashioned figures, human heads and animals dating from the period 1200–1800 AD were found in the excavations of Koma-Bulsa in the north of Ghana.

Nigeria

The sculpture from the African region corresponding to present-day Nigeria, however, is unique in that it spans nearly three millennia, though it is marked by different ethnic forms of expression. The art of Benin is unique in that the European scientific world was aware of its existence as early as the beginning of the 17th century, and then came into direct contact with it at the end of the 19th century through the arrival in London of some thousands of works, the spoils of the British expedition that destroyed the city in 1897.[30]

These works aroused wonder and incredulity in the Western world by virtue of their quality and realism. Put on sale by the Admiralty and by members of the expedition, they were bought immediately by some important museums and dealers. Other sculptures remained in the possession of the families of members of the expedition and then came onto the market over the years. The art of Benin, though the most famous, is also, however, the most recent of the Nigerian ancient figurative cultures.

Nok

An accidental find made in 1928 during work in a tin mine near the village of Nok (in the Jos area of what is now the Plateau State) and the discovery of a group of terracotta sculptures as a result of the scientific excavations begun in 1943 by Bernard Fagg (an archaeologist with the British colonial service in Nigeria) revealed the existence of an artistic culture that had developed over a period of approximately a millennium, from 500 BC to 500 AD.[31] Finds have multiplied during the last few decades and spread over a vast area as a result of excavations that are mostly illegal,[32] and the countless works and fragments brought to light confirm the thematic variety of Nok art, as well as the artists' ability not only to create, but also to fire large works without them shattering.

The heads and figures are made immediately recognizable by a series of stylistic elements that can be summarized as follows: pure volumes (spheres, cones and cylinders) for heads and limbs; large triangular eyeballs that together with the upper eyelids and eyebrows form an unmistakable pattern; perforated eyes, mouth, nostrils and ears; a sophisticated interplay of solids and voids; variety in the positions of the figures.

The vast size of the area in which the sculptures have come to light[33] and the diversity of certain stylistic characteristics found in some of them have raised doubts as to the homogeneity of the Nok culture, and suggest the existence of independent traditions that will require new investigations to clarify

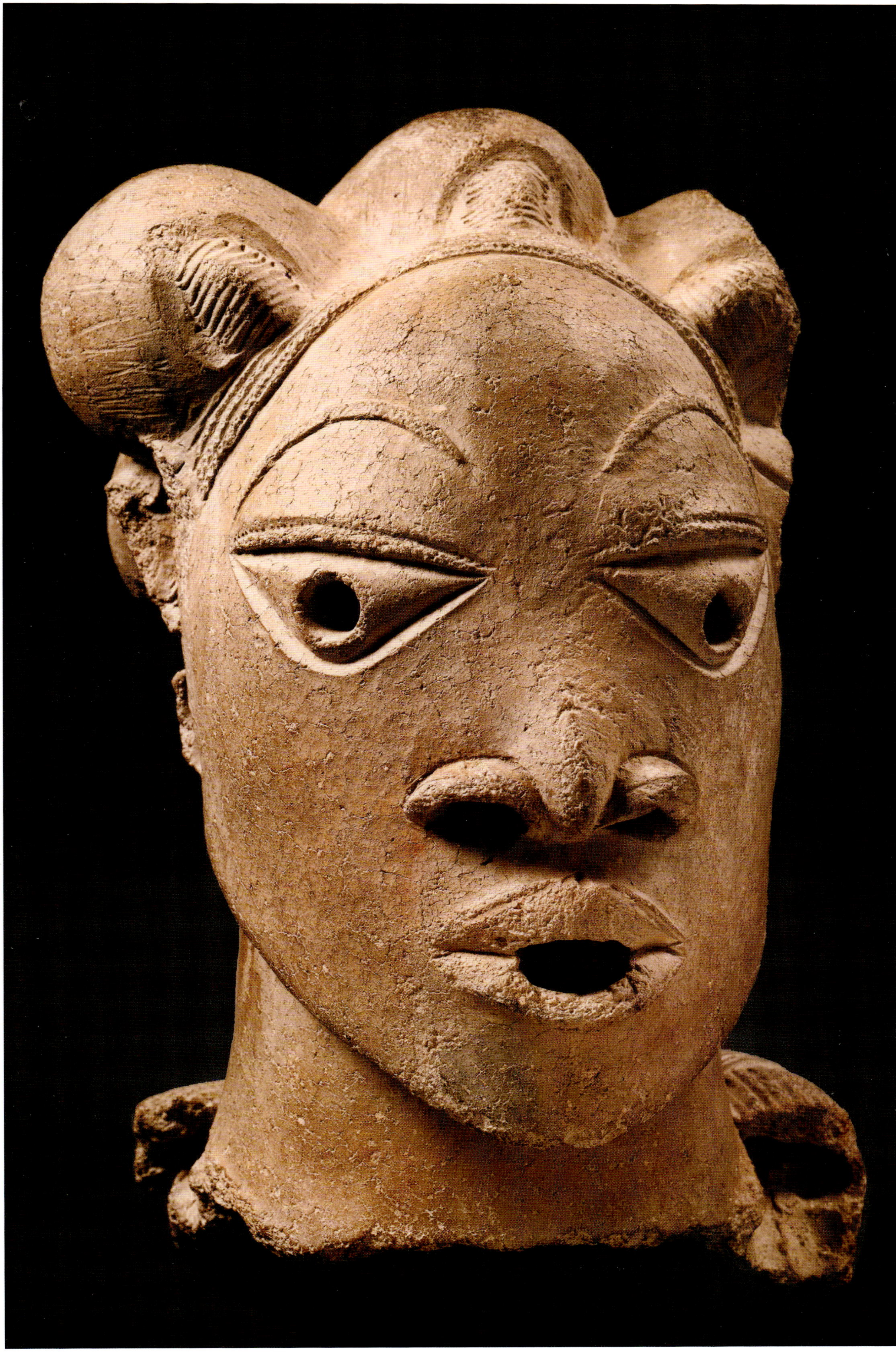

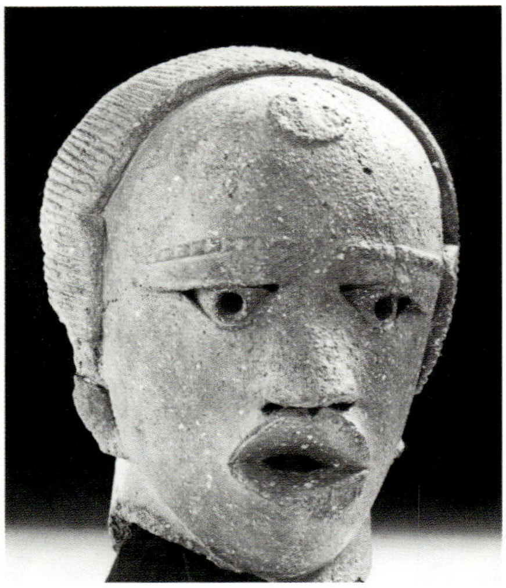

20. Artist of the Nok culture
(from Tsauni Camp, Jemaa)
Nigeria, 5th c. BC
Head
Terracotta, 25 cm
The National Commission for Museums and Monuments, Nigeria

the differences and provide some indications about the as yet unknown purpose of the works. Bernard de Grunne (1998, p. 21) suggests that the figures may be images of important personages worshipped in special holy places.

The large head from the National Commission for Museums and Monuments of Nigeria (no. 19) is a paradigmatic example of the sculpture discovered in Nok and of its artist's sophisticated sense of form. It must have belonged to a lost figure that was probably over a metre in height. The strong features of the face are imprinted on the surface of the almost cylindrical volume without diminishing its perfection in any way. The three narrow crowns encircling the broad brow subtly separate the smooth surface of the face from the controlled animation of the hemispherical locks of hair, fully in keeping with the monumental quality of the head.

The spherical module is illustrated by the second sculpture (no. 20), again a head that belonged to a larger figure, now lost. The dating assigned on the basis of thermoluminescence testing is placeable at 510±230 BC.

Except for the triangular eyeballs with large perforated pupils, the facial features correspond less closely to the canons of Nok sculpture. The arrangement of the hair in narrow parallel bands emphasizes the roundness of the skull like a helmet and contributes in its simplicity to the mysteriously imperious aura that seems to be sealed by the circular relief on the forehead.

The figure now in the Louvre (no. 21), which is in the style of Katsina Ala, a locality some 200 miles south of Nok, is evidence of how widespread the culture, whose name comes from the area where the first discoveries were made, had become. This name is retained because the works are the result of the same process of production and share some iconographic elements, despite the distances that separate them and their different dates. These similarities suggest a shared culture and a constant exchange also at a material level (through trade

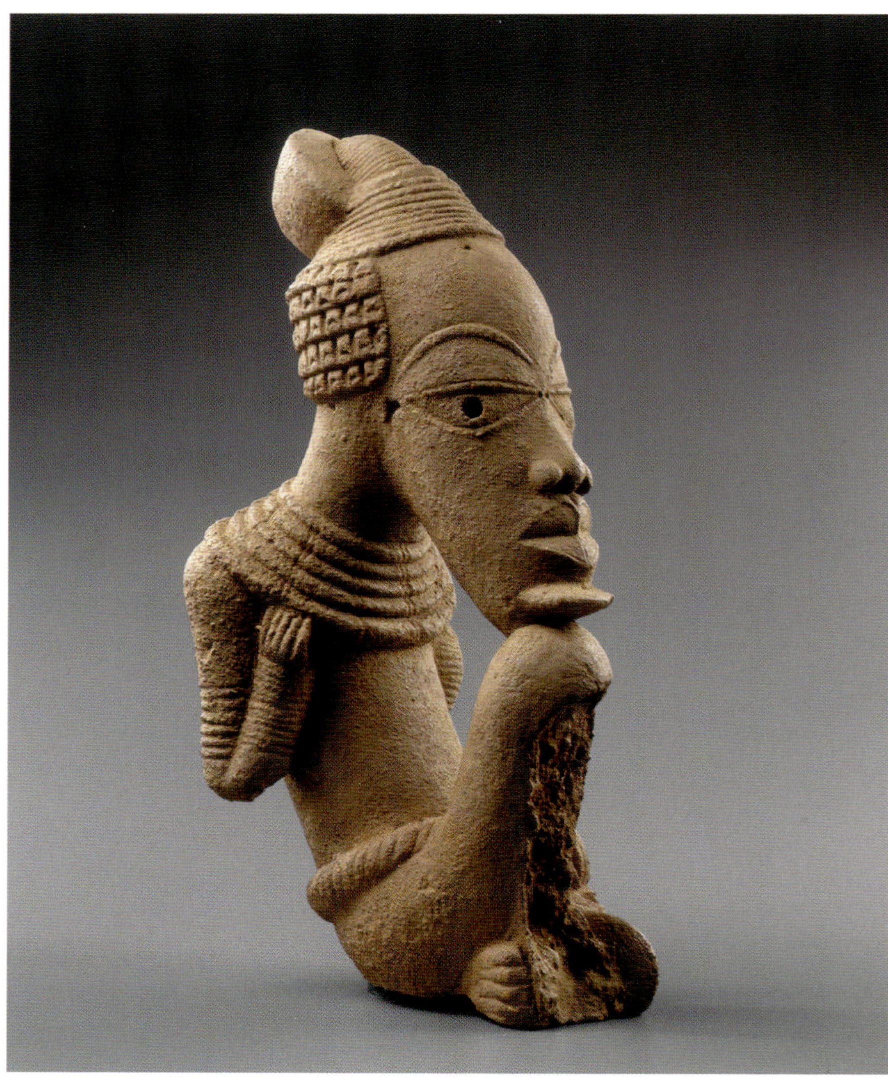

21. Artist of the Nok culture
(Katsina Ala style)
Nigeria, 500 BC–500 AD
Seated figure (lower part damaged)
Terracotta, 38 cm
Musée du Louvre, Pavillon des Sessions, Paris (on deposit from the Musée du Quai Branly)

22. Artist of the Sokoto culture
Nigeria, 500 BC–100 AD
Male head
Terracotta, 33 cm
Musée du Louvre, Pavillon des Sessions, Paris (on deposit from the Musée du Quai Branly)

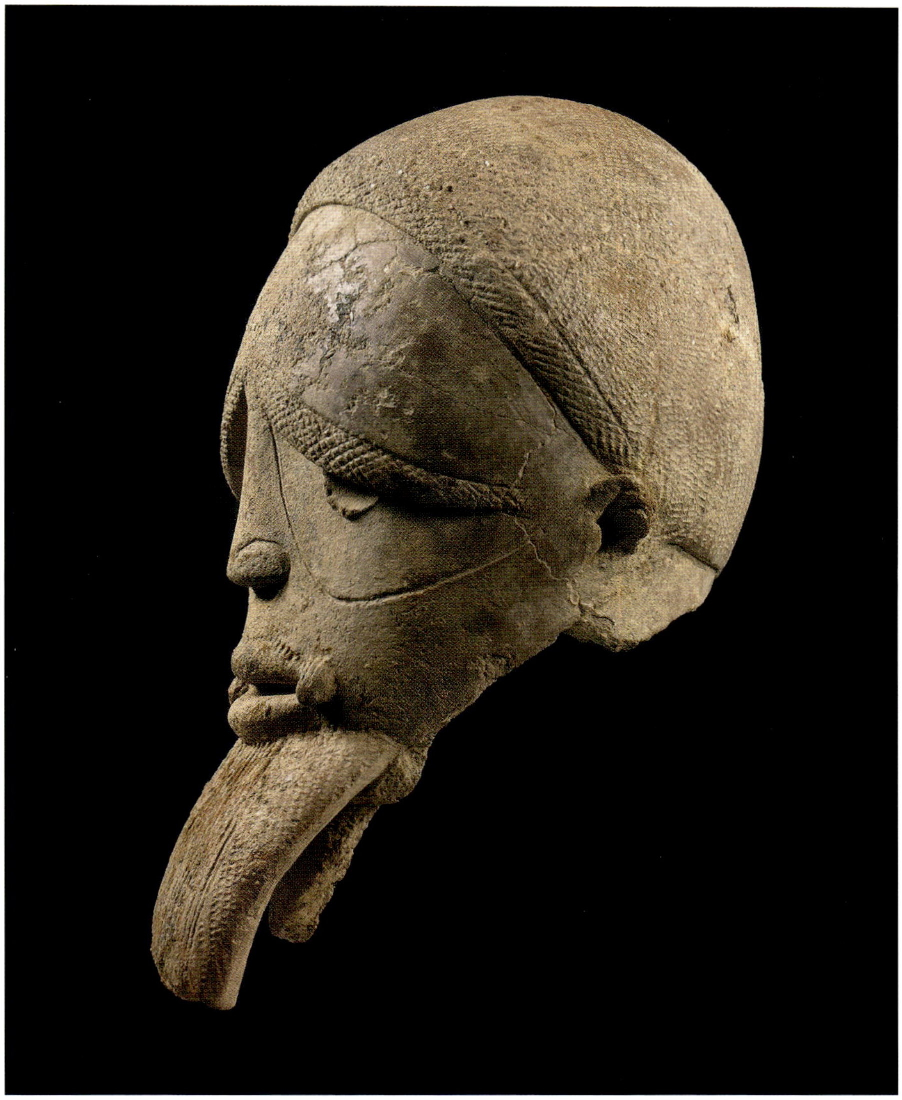

or by other means) between the inhabitants of the various regions in which the works were found.

The volume of the enormous conical head accounting for half of the entire seated figure is integrated into the overall structure of the work, which is a deft assemblage of cylindrical elements firmly marked by the transversal relief elements of the belt, bracelets and necklaces, as well as the superb hair. The space between the backward-tilted torso, the upper part of the right leg and the elongated chin resting on the knee is skilfully integrated into the overall structure of the work, so that it acquires lightness without losing its monumental quality.

An echo of the Nok culture can also be perceived in the terracotta works discovered in the Sokoto region on the northern border of Nigeria. The large male head (no. 22) also in the Louvre (beside the seated figure) bears exemplary witness to this artistic phenomenon. Like the heads discovered in Nok, it almost certainly belonged to a large figure. Claire Boullier, the author of the description accompanying the image of the work in the Louvre catalogue, draws attention in this connection to a similar work that may be by the same hand.[34]

The general appearance of the head is similar to typical Nok works (a similarity suggested by the use of the same material), but it is distinguished by the wholly original arrangement of the elements of the face, first of all the very long, arched and slanting eyebrows, which almost conceal the round holes of the pupils and form a harmonious pattern with the unusually narrow nose, the light semicircular reliefs of the eyes and the slightly open mouth with curious small moustaches at the corners. Separated from the broad forehead by a raised band similar in shape and decoration to the eyebrows, the hair (or close-fitting headgear?) adapts naturally to the spherical volume of the head and its

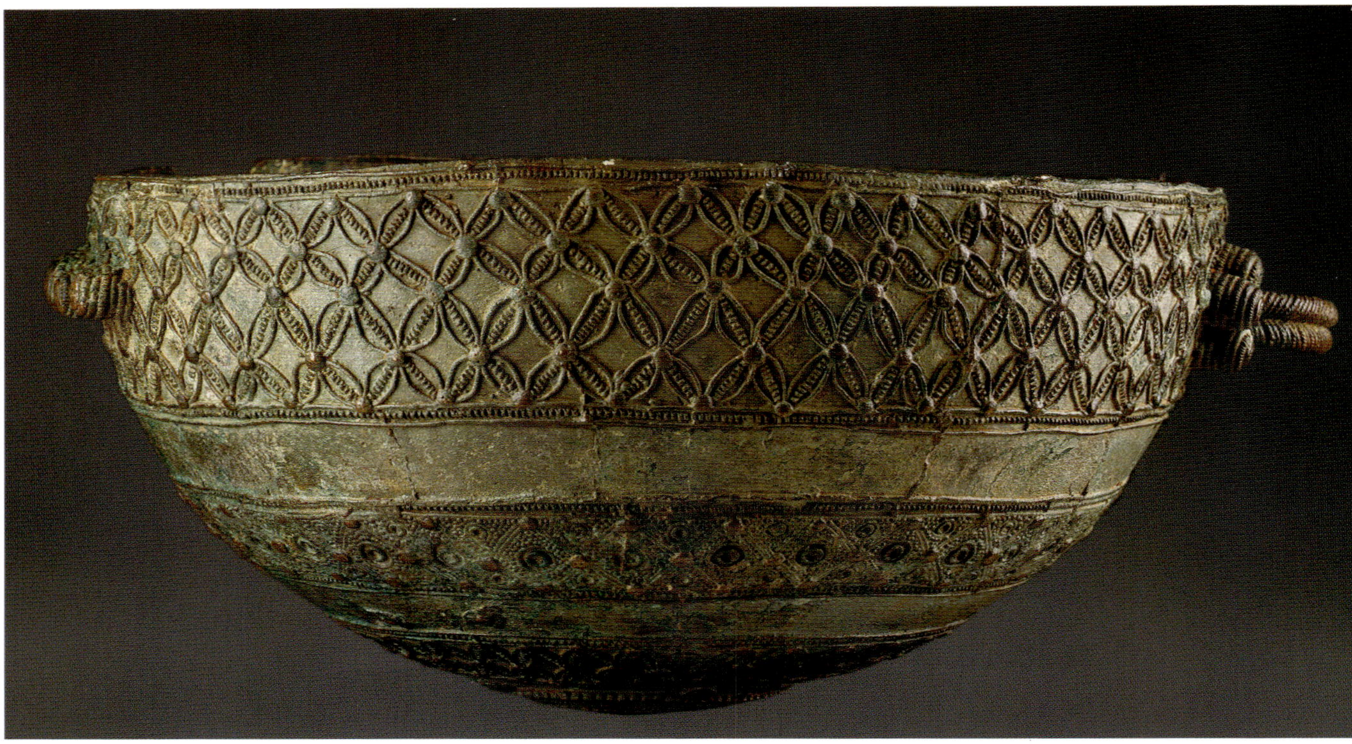

23a–b. Artist of the Igbo-Ukwu culture (from Igbo Isaiah)
Nigeria, 10th–9th c. BC
Ceremonial bowl
Bronze with a high percentage of lead, diam. 26.4 cm
The National Commission for Museums and Monuments, Nigeria

simplicity contributes to the balance of the composition. The long, tapering beard that starts immediately beneath the lower lip accentuates the impression of concentrated thought conveyed by the monumental head.

Igbo-Ukwu

The most ancient bronze works of art found south of the Sahara owe their name to the village of Igbo-Ukwu in the state of Anambra, where the first items were discovered quite by chance, in 1938, in what was thought to be a buried deposit of ritual objects by Isaiah Anozie, who was unaware of their true nature and distributed them among his friends.

On realizing the importance of the finds some time later, officials of the British colonial administration saw to it that they were collected and handed over to the National Commission for Museums and Monuments of Nigeria. It was not until 1959–60 and 1964 that systematic investigations were carried out by the archaeologist Thurstan Shaw, which led to the discovery of two more sites, one a burial chamber and the other a storeroom for disused ritual objects. The three sites were given the names of the owners of the land on which the discoveries were made: Igbo Isaiah for the first deposit of ritual objects, Igbo Jonah for the second and Igbo Richard for the burial chamber.

Surprisingly enough, the human figure is represented on only two or three of the finds brought to light.

An examination of some of the bronzes revealed that four of them dated from the 10th–9th century. The artists of Igbo-Ukwu were therefore the first inhabitants of Sub-Saharan Africa, in an era prior to any contact with Arabs and Europeans, to create works in an alloy of copper by means of the lost wax process, and display an extraordinary mastery of this technique despite the rudimentary means at their disposal.

Unfortunately, nothing precise is known about the Igbo-Ukwu culture (just like the Nok) or its religion and social organization. The artists of what must have been a prosperous society with a mature and refined culture used bronze because they were aware of the difficulties presented by copper in the pure state and possessed the ability to create complex works by means of repeated casting. This technique, which must have taken a long time to develop, combined with an inventiveness that was both unbridled and controlled, produced splendid works, whose perfect surfaces are covered with equally perfect decoration that one is tempted to describe, in many cases, as frenzied.

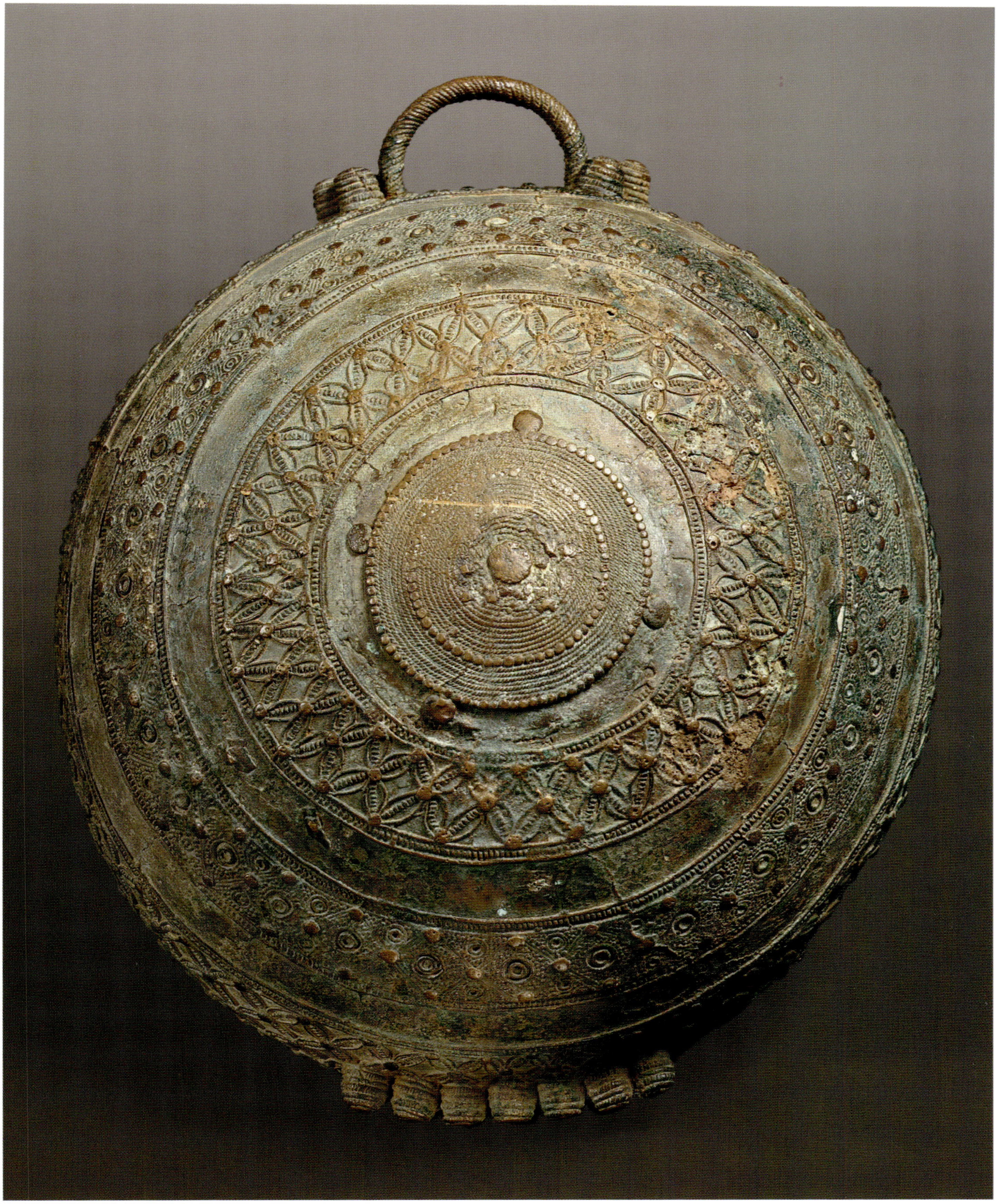

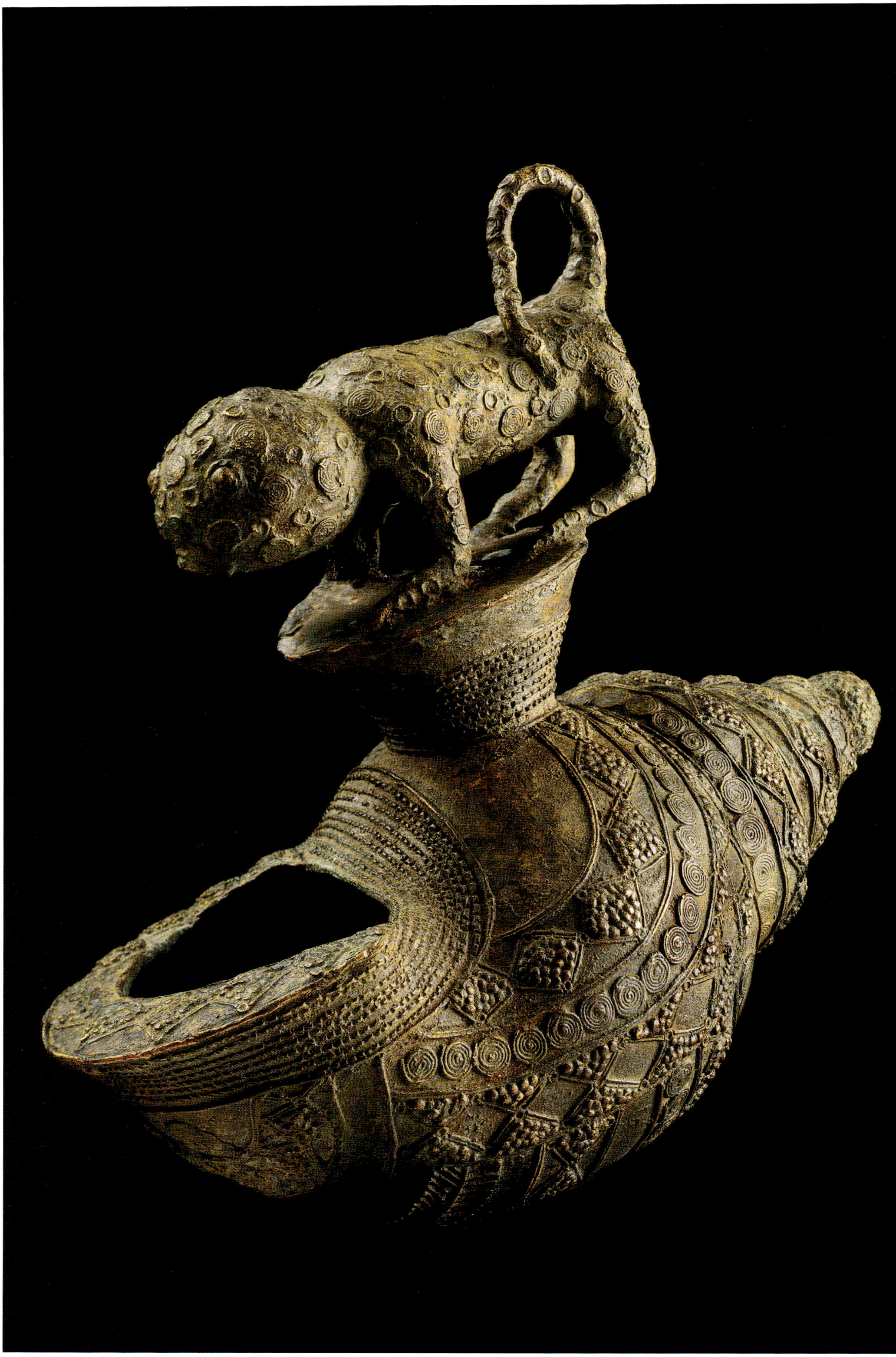

24. Artist of the Igbo-Ukwu culture (presumably from Igbo Isaiah)
Nigeria, 10th–9th c. BC
Ceremonial vessel shaped like a giant shell
Bronze with a high percentage of lead, l. 20.6 cm
The National Commission for Museums and Monuments, Nigeria

25. Artist of the Igbo-Ukwu culture (presumably from Igbo Isaiah)
Nigeria, 10th–9th c. BC
Cylindrical ornament for a staff
Bronze with a high percentage of lead and glass beads, h. 14.5 cm
The National Commission for Museums and Monuments, Nigeria

26. Artist of the Igbo-Ukwu culture (from Igbo Isaiah)
Nigeria, 10th–9th c. BC
Vase
Bronze with a high percentage of lead, h. 32.3 cm
The National Commission for Museums and Monuments, Nigeria

The extremely stark and simple shape of the bowl (no. 23), probably based on a vessel fashioned from a gourd with the addition of handles, is an initial example of the above-mentioned combination, which is seen here in its most understated form.

There is a marked change of expressive register in the vessel (no. 24), since the surface of the giant shell is completely covered with spirals (which also alternate with small circles to simulate the spots of the leopard surmounting it), lozenges and parallel lines of minute reliefs that embellish it. The leopard is a recurrent symbol of authority in many African cultures.

A prime example of this riot of decoration is provided by the cylindrical ornament (no. 25), whose surface is decorated with birds of sumptuous plumage, orderly arrays of tiny granules and small rings attached to strings of multicoloured glass beads. Ekpo Eyo regards this as the main ornamental element of a ceremonial staff or emblem of authority.

Further proof of the technical expertise of Igbo-Ukwu casting is provided by the globular vessel (no. 26) in a wide-mesh net resting on a support with a perforated pattern of elegant plant motifs. Frank Willett lists the stages of its production as follows: casting the body of the vessel and the upper part of the base; casting the lower part of the base and the cord net, without the lower rings, which is placed around the vessel and adapted to its shape; welding the upper edge of the vessel and the lower edge of the support and the lower rings of the net. As he notes in conclusion, "One can only suppose that the smiths of Igbo-Ukwu enjoyed demonstrating their virtuosity".[35]

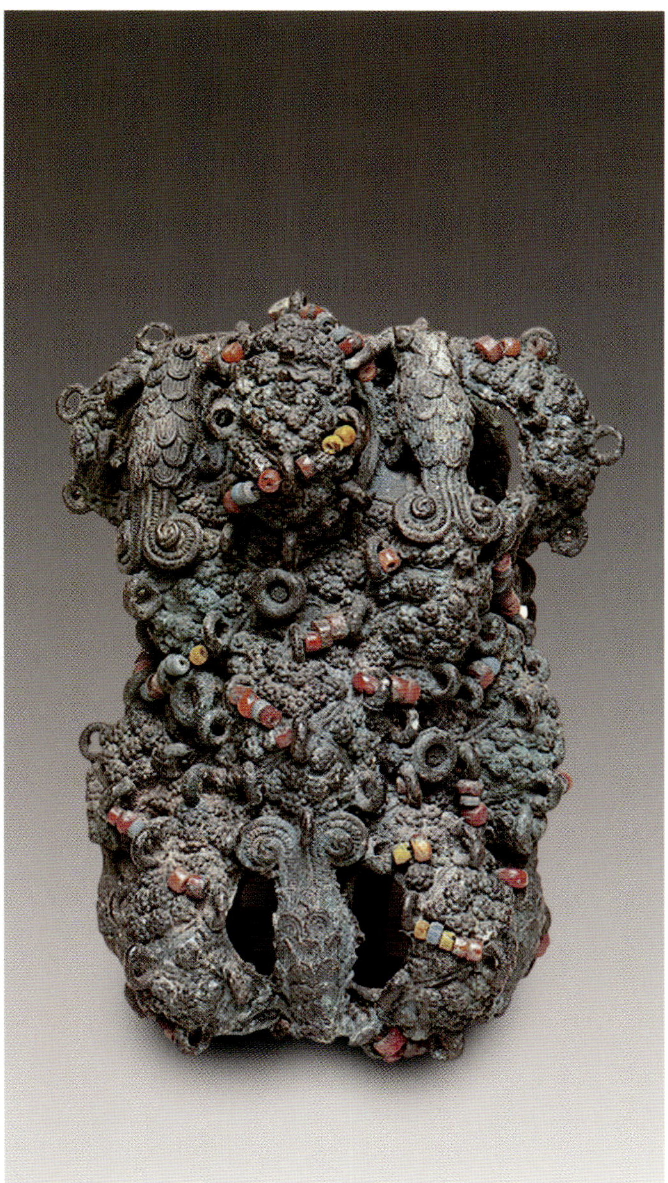

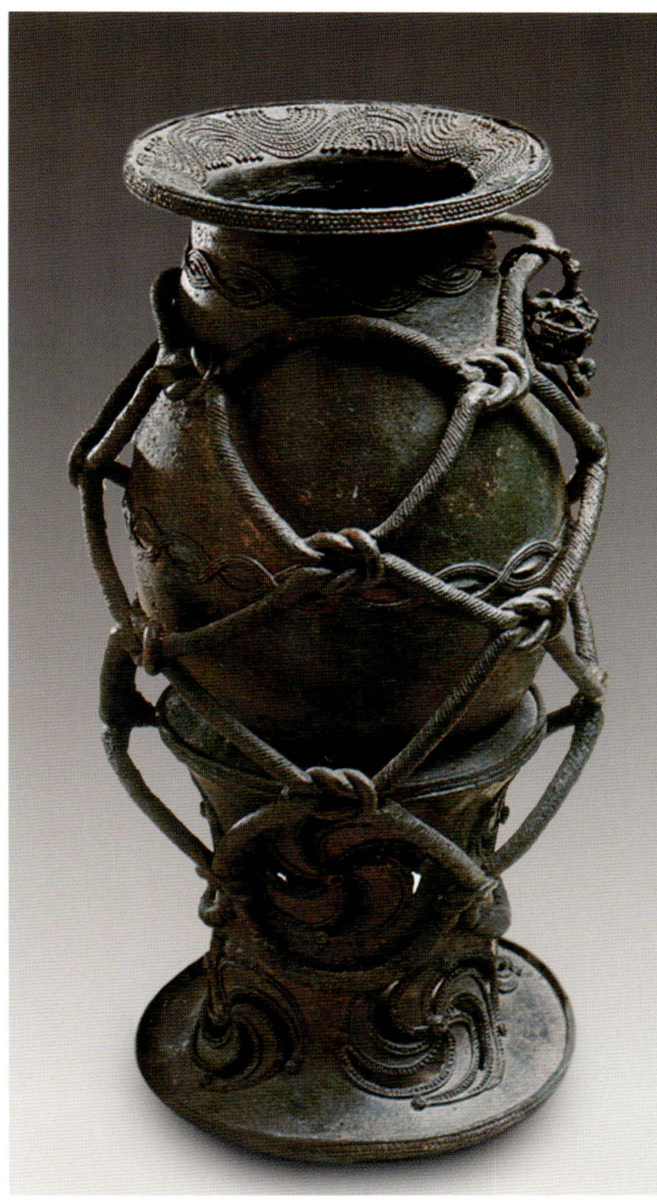

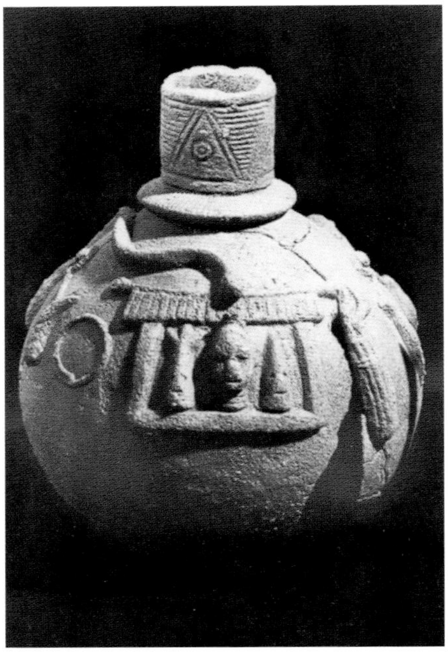

27. Ife, Nigeria
Terracotta vessel with three heads of different shapes

28. Artist of Ife
Nigeria (from the palace of the Ooni, Ife) 12th–15th c.
Head thought to represent the usurper Lajuwa
Terracotta, 31.7 cm
The National Commission for Museums and Monuments, Nigeria

Ife

Produced between the 12th and 15th centuries, Ife sculpture is the ancient African art form that has most impressed Westerners. Such is its perfection also in terms of the canons of the classical European tradition that the German scholar Leo Frobenius even suggested that there must be artists from the Mediterranean in the region when he discovered some works of this culture, then unknown in Europe, in 1904. In fact, he described the art of Ife as "reminiscent of Ancient Greece; and a proof that, once upon a time, a race far superior in strain to the negro had settled here."[36]

Ife has been the holy city of the Yoruba for centuries and is ruled by the Ooni, a priest king whose moral and religious authority is still recognized by that people even at great distances. The information handed down by the oral tradition is borne out by the results of archaeological investigations and above all works of art that bear witness to the society's very high degree of civilization and its readiness to open up to the outside world. In fact, metal was obtained from North Africa, while the glass and stone beads found on many sculptures were almost certainly produced locally.

Interest in the antiquities of Ife was fairly limited in the years that followed Frobenius's discovery. Even when eleven bronze heads were found by chance in 1938 and six more shortly afterwards, the West remained unconvinced that the works were of local origin, having forgotten about the figures and plaques that had arrived in Europe from Benin forty years earlier.

The investigations continued over the following years and led to new discoveries that generated fresh interest. As a result, Ife sculpture is today unhesitatingly recognized as belonging to the highest levels of the artistic heritage of mankind as a whole and has been the object of countless studies, both general and focused on particular aspects or items. Many questions, however, are still awaiting an answer.

The monumental catalogue compiled by Frank Willett, the greatest expert on the Ife culture and formerly an archaeologist with the Nigerian Department of Antiquities and curator of the Museum of Ife Antiquities, sums up the present state of knowledge on the culture of the ancient holy city and its art, which is concisely described as realistic in style, classical in form, perfectly crafted, and the product of advanced technical skill.[37]

This description applies perfectly to the terracotta and bronze sculptures, in which realism and idealization are blended to sublime effect.

It should be remembered, however, that the works from Ife also include a small number of conical and cylindrical heads of an abstract character, which Willett regards as connected with different forms of worship, as well as deformed or monstrous figures (no. 27).

The "overhanging of the corners of the lower lid by the upper; the incised line parallel to the edge of the upper lid; the raised edge of the lips; the impressed corners of the mouth"[38] are all distinctive morphological characteristics making it possible to identify Ife figures.

A slight deviation from the vertical axis in the representation of the lips brings the faces to life.

In the opinion of scholars, borne out by the results of scientific tests, the works were created between the 12th and the 15th centuries, as stated above. The "classical" nature of Ife art was therefore achieved independently by the artists of that African society prior to any contact with Europeans. The same tests also suggest that the terracotta works preceded and anticipated the formal perfection of the bronzes.

The splendid head (no. 28) from the Ooni's palace, dated to the 12th–15th century and thought to represent Lajuwa, usurper of the Ooni's throne,[39] or the court servant of the Ooni,[40] is one of the most important examples of the terracotta art of Ife.

Every element of the spiritual face is perfect and integrated into the overall design of the work, from the slightly parted lips and the dainty, shell-like ears to the hair, wavy in front but straight at the back, and the narrow hori-

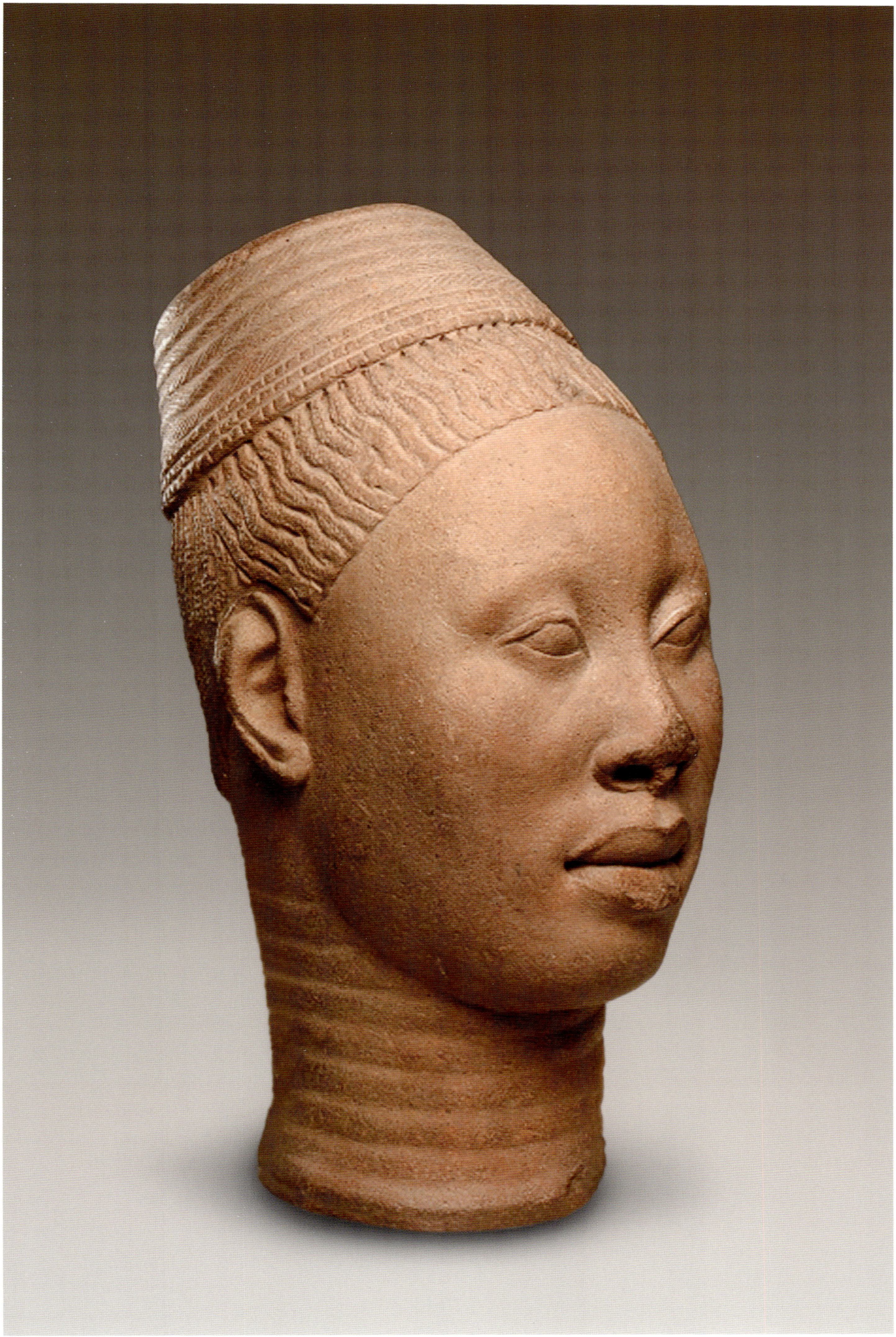

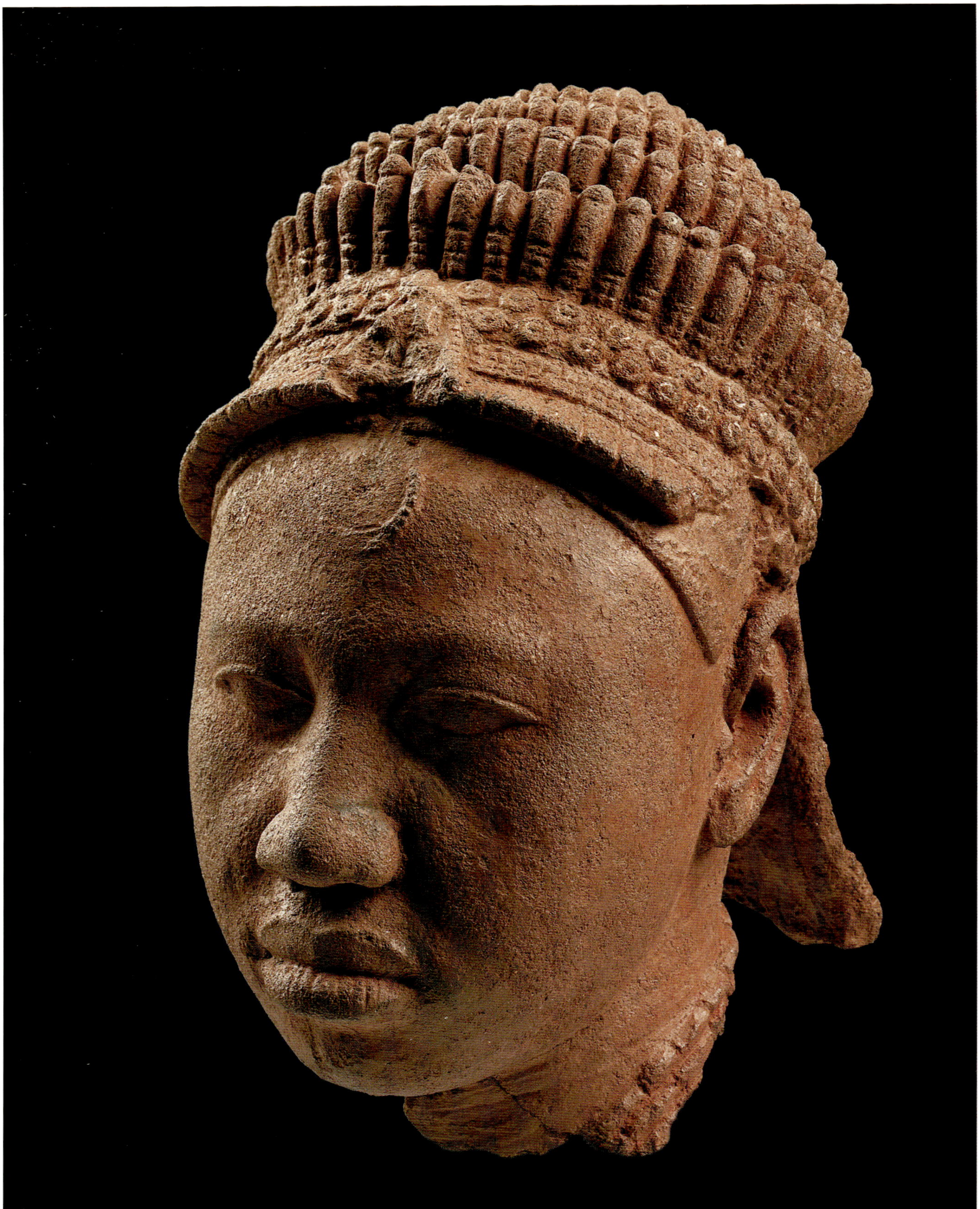

29a–b. Artist of Ife
Nigeria (from Ita Yemoo), 12th–15th c.
Head of a queen
Terracotta, 23 cm
The National Commission for
Museums and Monuments, Nigeria

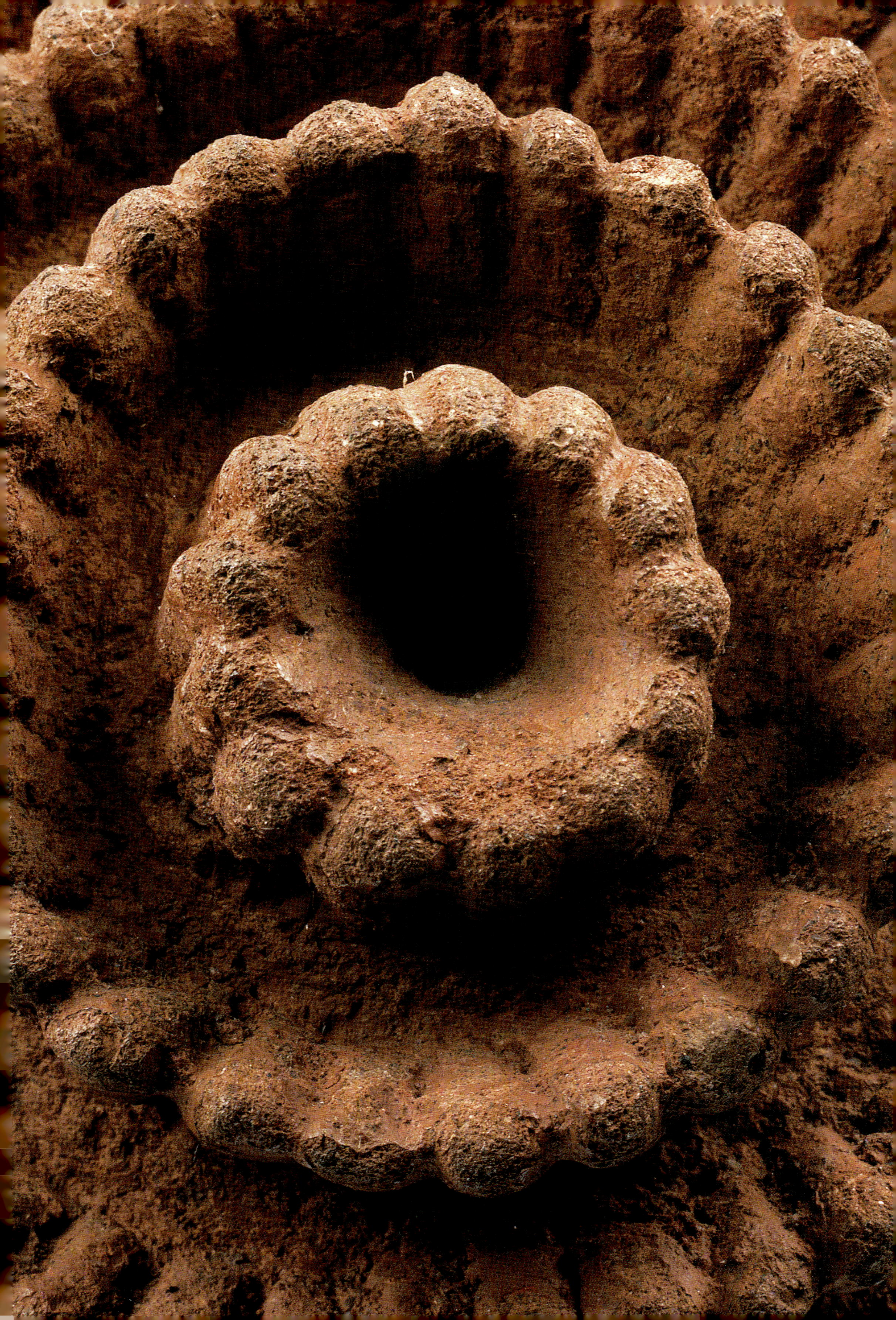

zontal bands of the hat echoing the ringed neck of the figure portrayed, whose serene nobility is almost otherworldly.

The head (no. 29) unearthed during the Ita Yemoo excavations and dated to the 12th–15th century probably belonged to a full-length figure that must have measured over 70 cm in height, given the standard African ratio of the size of the head to the body. The rudimentary conditions in which the works were fired make this no negligible achievement. It should be mentioned, however, that terracotta works of this size have not been discovered in Ife. The lofty pride characterizing the previous image is attenuated in this portrait of a queen with slightly swollen features by a sort of human awareness combined with incomparable majesty. The five-tier crown of beads that adorns her attests to the high rank of the personage portrayed.

Despite its small size and the fact that it is little more than a fragment, the enchanting head (no. 30) unearthed during agricultural work in 1953 is one of the most fascinating Ife artworks by virtue of the vibrancy of the delightful face and the exquisite sensitivity of the moulding that is confident and precise. It is not by chance that William Fagg described it as "possibly the most beautiful human representation yet discovered at Ife".[41]

The "cat's whiskers" scarification (also visible on some other sculptures) introduces a touch of mystery that makes this small masterpiece still more captivating.

The bronze works were created by means of the lost wax process, a technique used by the great Italian Renaissance sculptor Benvenuto Cellini among others, which makes it possible to obtain only one copy of the work because

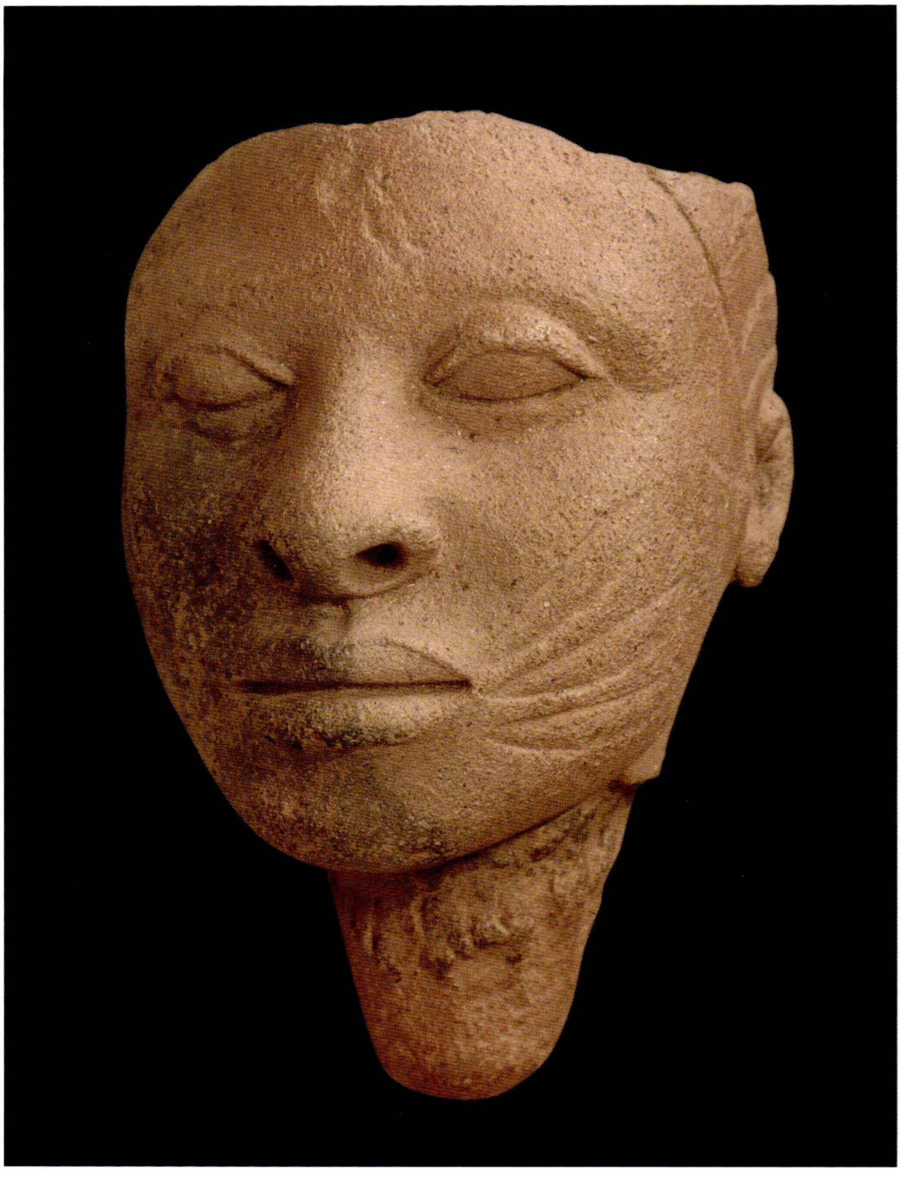

30. Artist of Ife
Nigeria (from Grove of Olokun Walode), 12th–15th c.
Head with "cat's whiskers" scarification marks
Terracotta, 13 cm
The National Commission for Museums and Monuments, Nigeria

31. Artist of Ife
Nigeria (from Wunmonije Compound), 14th–15th c.
Head of Ooni
Brass and gold, 29.5 cm
The National Commission for Museums and Monuments, Nigeria

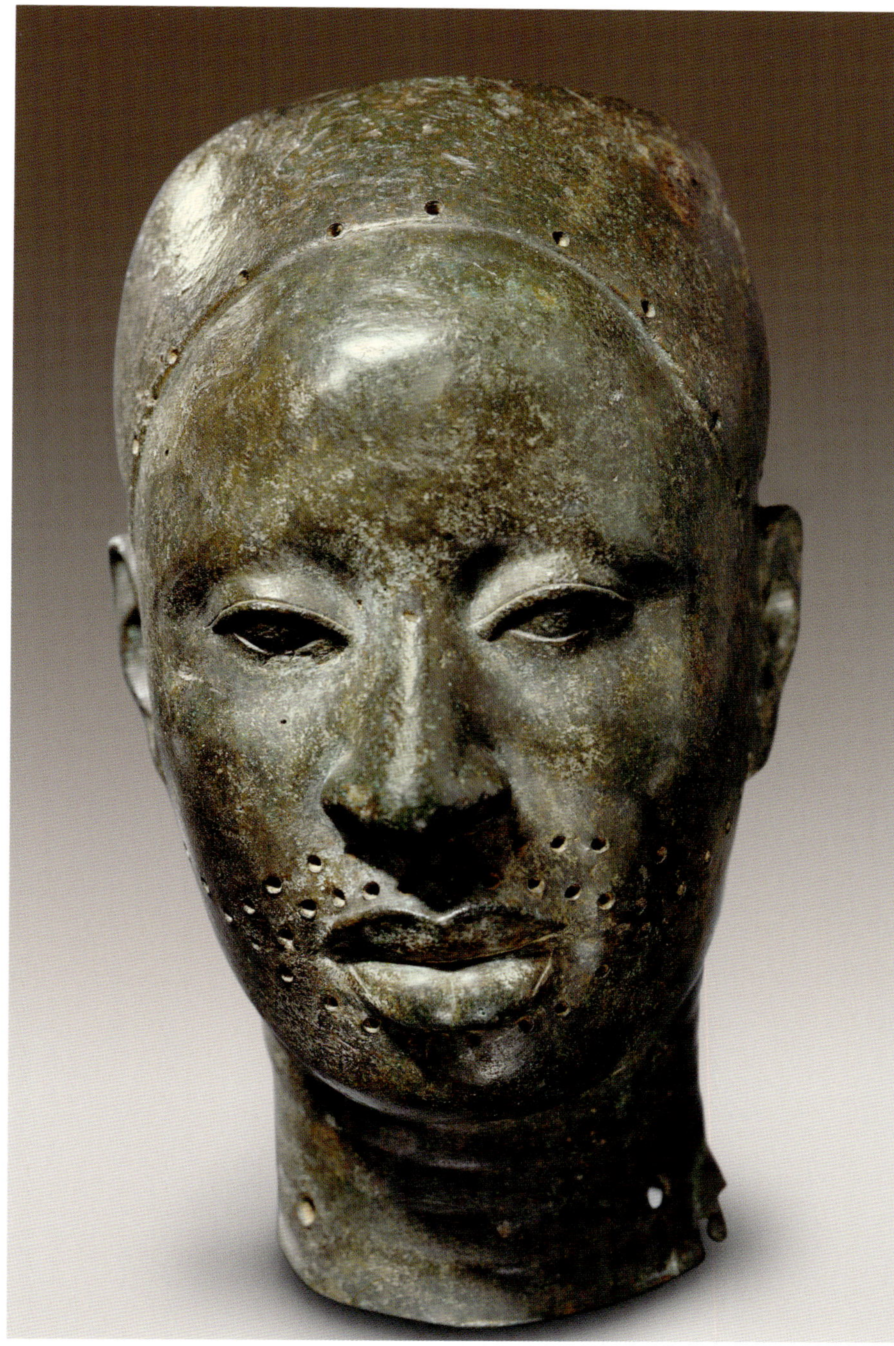

the mould is broken. Though described for the sake of brevity as bronze, the material is actually an alloy of copper and tin or lead, whereas brass is an alloy of copper and zinc. The traces of a greenish colour visible on parts of some faces indicate that a small percentage of gold was also used.

The cohesive style of a group of very beautiful heads induced Henry Drewal to hypothesize that "they were done, if not by a single artist, then by a group of artists over a relatively short period of time, perhaps by only in a single workshop."[42] Some display traces of colour.

The first head considered here (no. 31), discovered in the Wunmonije district in 1938, is probably an idealized portrait of an Ooni, both a monarch and a divinity, and is unquestionably one of the highest achievements of Ife bronze sculpture. An impression of spirituality is conveyed by the austere features of the perfect face tempered by a sense of aristocratic humanity.

The holes at the base of the ringed neck made it possible to attach the head to a wooden body that performed a function after the death of the priest-king in the ceremonies of what Willett describes as the second funeral, designed to establish the deceased in his role in the afterlife. The hole in the top of the head probably served to attach a crown, a symbol of power also found, for example, on some terracotta heads.

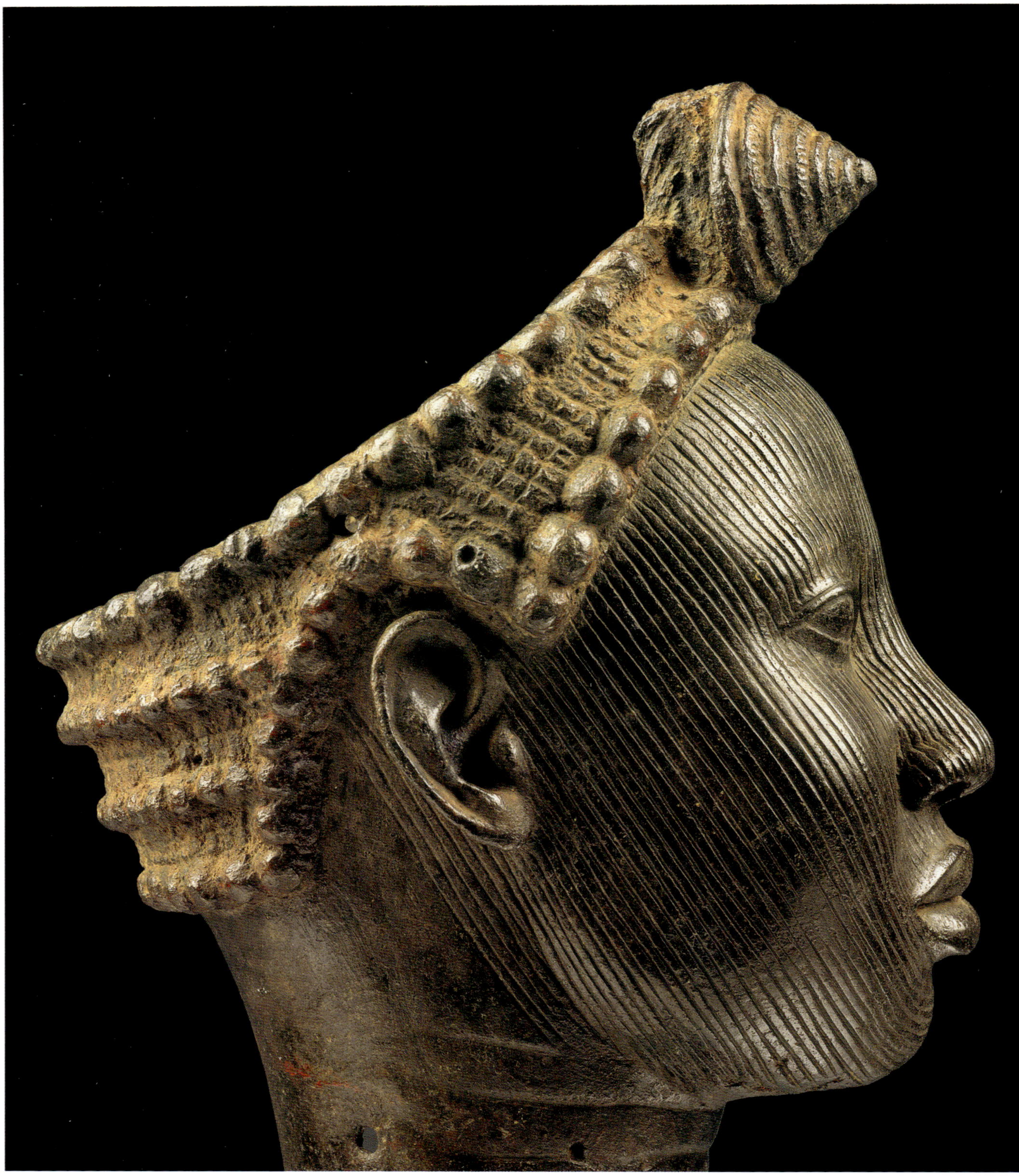

32a–b. Artist of Ife
Nigeria (from Wunmonije Compound), 12th–15th c.
Head of Ooni with crown
Brass, 24 cm
The National Commission for Museums and Monuments, Nigeria

Pages 56–57
33a–b. Artist of Ife
Nigeria, 15th–16th c.
Upper half of Ooni figure
Brass with a high percentage of lead, 37 cm
The National Commission for Museums and Monuments, Nigeria

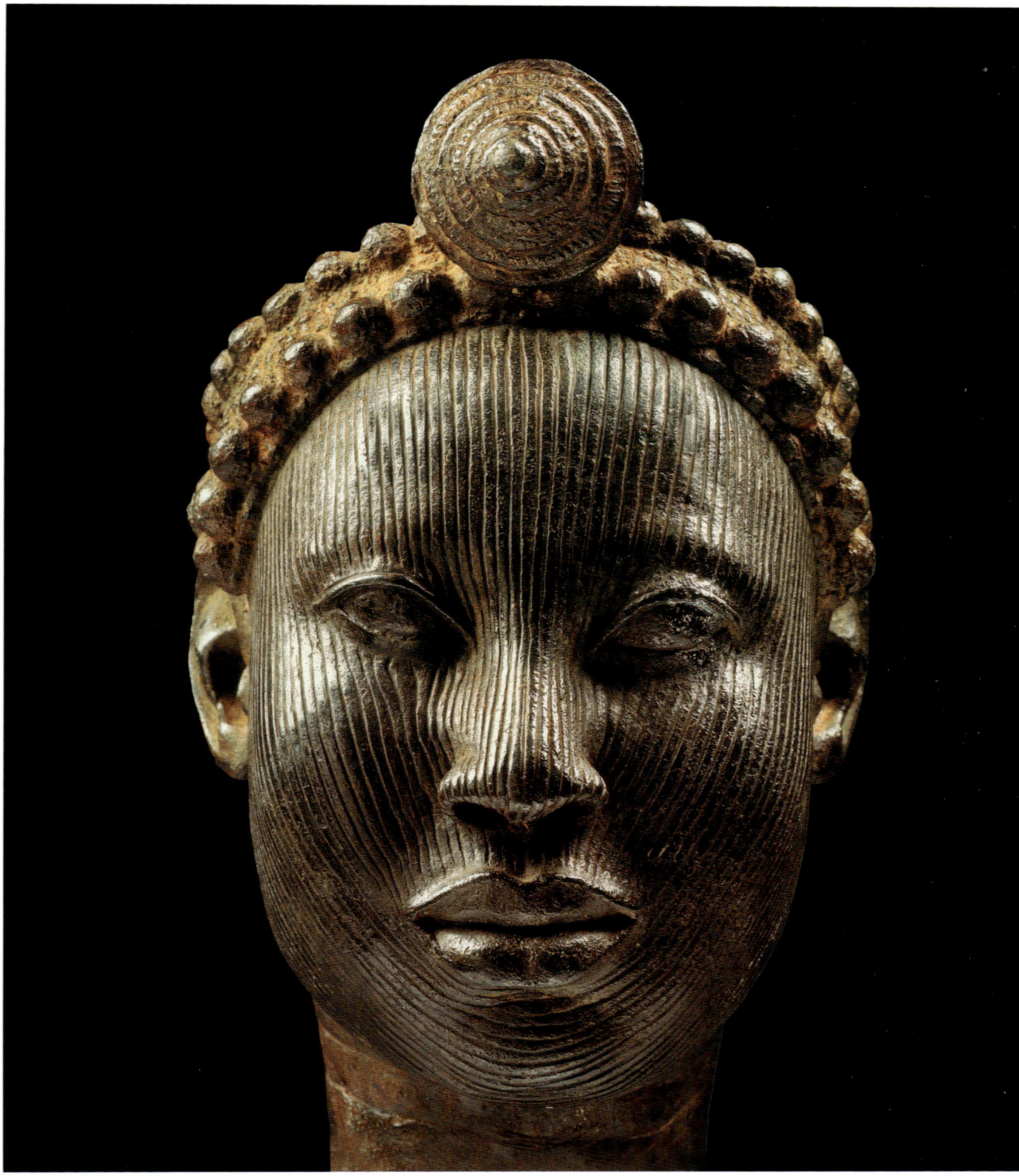

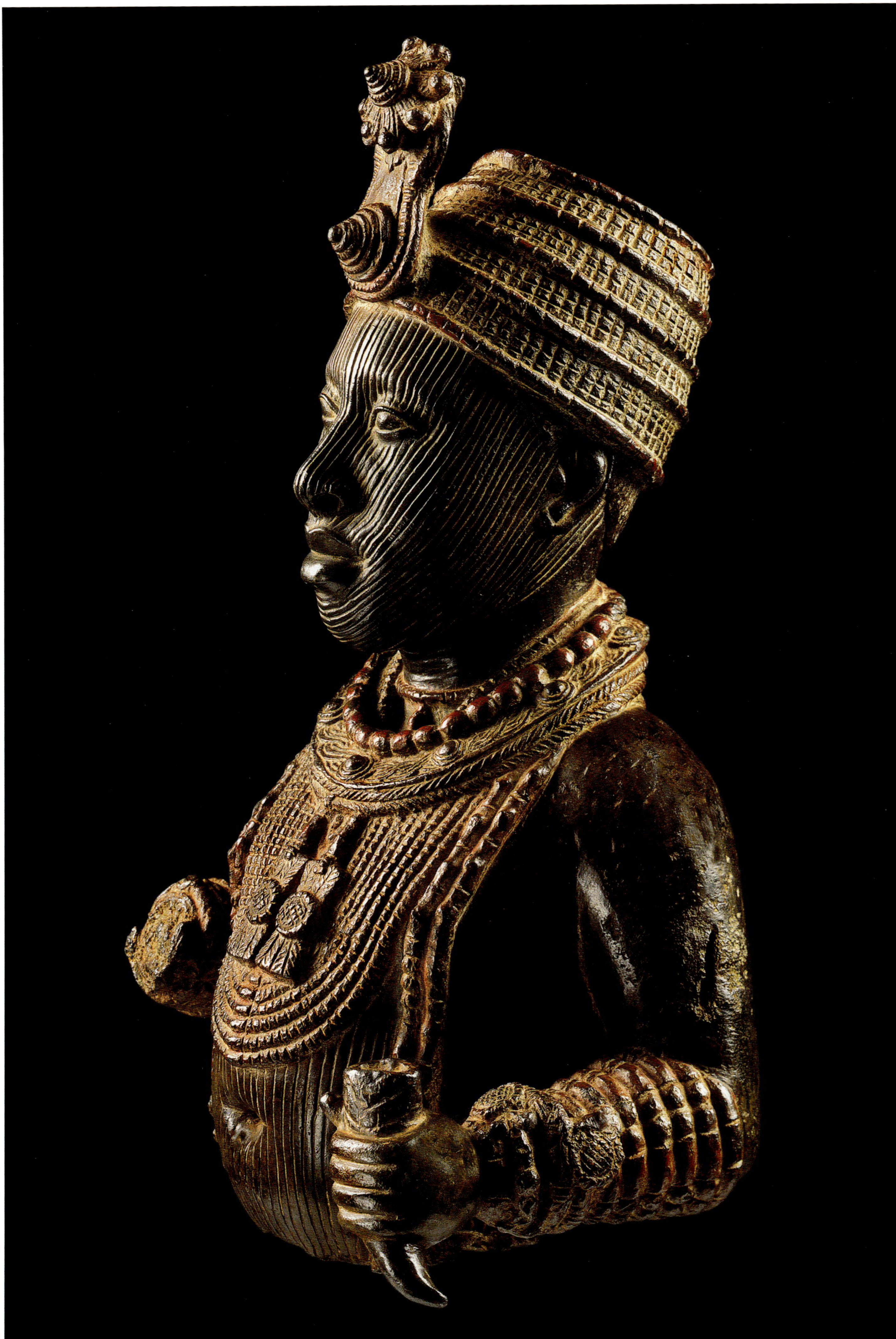

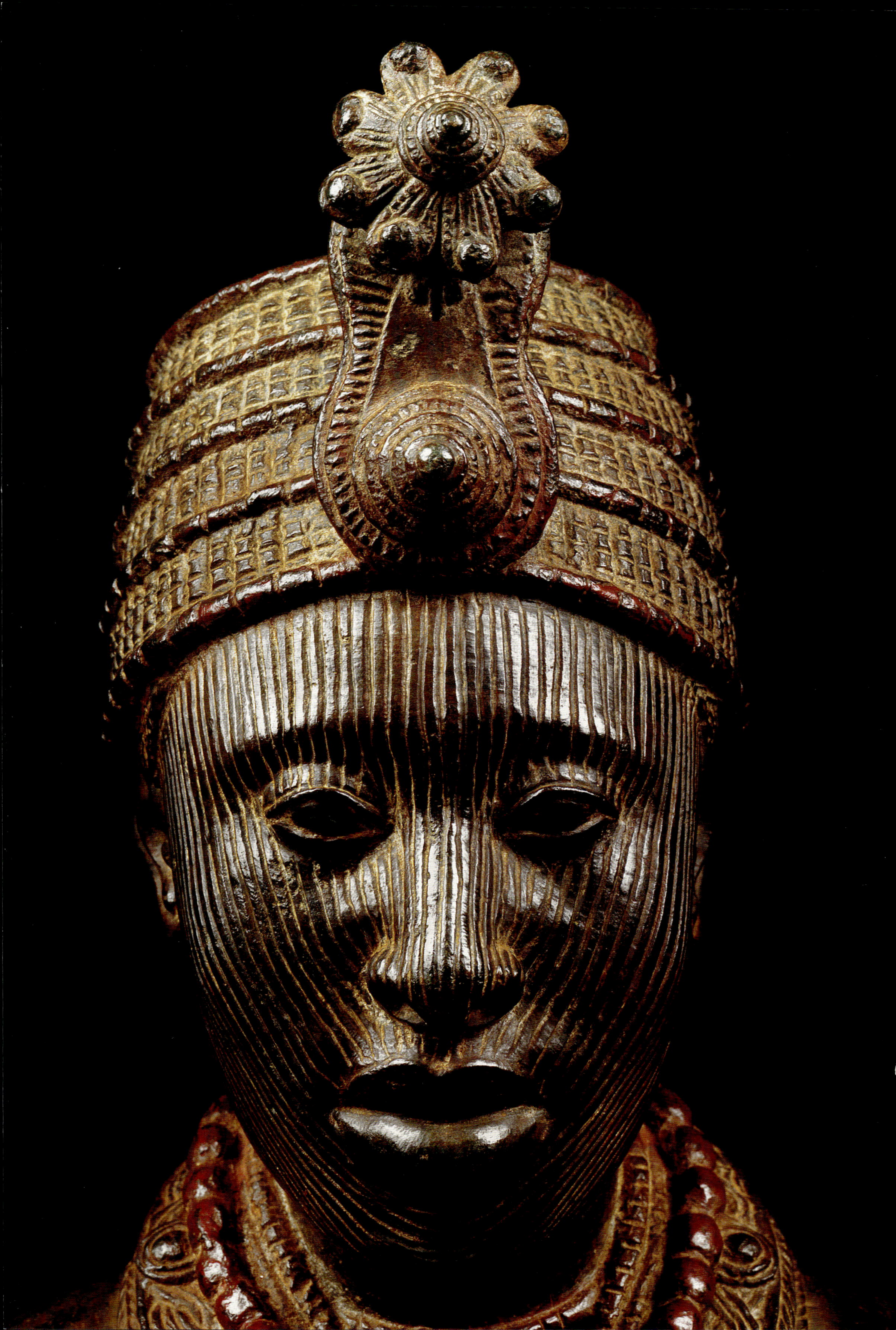

34. Artist of Ife
Nigeria (from the palace of the Ooni), 14th–15th c.
Mask thought to represent the Ooni Obalufon
Copper, 33 cm
The National Commission for Museums and Monuments, Nigeria

The function of the holes around the lips and on the cheeks is unclear. While they may have served to attach a veil of beads concealing the monarch's face, their absence in many sculptures increases the uncertainty and further research is needed to establish what they really were.

The face of the second head (no. 32), unearthed on the same site and slightly smaller than the first, is entirely covered with narrow parallel grooves (also present on other items) that probably represent scarification but have given rise to various hypotheses. While the extremely delicate features make the gender of the personage represented uncertain, the similarities between the crowns of two Ooni statues and the one visible on this head (albeit devoid of part of the frontal decoration) suggest that it is the image of a monarch.

The upper half of one (no. 33) of the two Ooni figures mentioned above, which were discovered together, is distinguished by its four-tier headgear and sumptuous decoration of necklaces of different shapes and lengths. The vertical and horizontal reliefs of the ornaments and the narrow incisions on the face, the abdomen and the smooth parts of the body are arranged in a complex interplay that is unusual in the sculpture from the Nigerian holy city.

The Ooni holds a horn for magical substances in his left hand and presumably held a sceptre in his right hand, which is broken and lost.

The Ife artists also cast some heads and figures in pure copper, an extremely difficult operation technologically speaking, because oxidation prevents the unmixed molten metal from flowing inside the mould. It therefore required considerable technical expertise, which the craftsmen, who were well aware of the difficulty, unquestionably possessed.

Mask no. 34, dated to the 14th–15th century, is the most perfectly successful casting in copper because it shows no sign of repair. It is traditionally held to represent Obalufon, the second king of Ife, who is said to have introduced the technique of casting. Apart from the technical skill involved, the mask (which was almost certainly worn, as indicated by the slits below the eyes) is above all an admirable creation from the artistic viewpoint by virtue of the impression of human serenity it conveys.

The most mysterious and important work of Ife art is, however, the seated figure (no. 35) that takes its name from the village of Tada on the River Niger, now inhabited by the Nupe, where it was found. The presence of the sculpture in a locality hundreds of miles away from the holy city of the Yoruba could be an indication of the ancient dominion of Ife over that territory.

The surface of the sculpture is worn because of the annual rubbing with sand to which it was subjected for ritual purposes by the local inhabitants. The work was moved to the National Commission for Museums and Monuments of Nigeria during the 1970s to ensure its preservation.

Frank Willett writes that the Tada figure is "undoubtedly artistically the finest Ife casting, but its conception appears to have taxed the available technology to its limits."[43]

The sculpture is distinguished by the head of natural proportions and the complex asymmetrical position of the body, which in no way impairs the harmony of the whole. The opulent nudity, enhanced by the elaborate motifs of the loincloth, and the features of the thoughtful face, which suggest inner serenity, bear the expressive hallmarks of the art of Ife.

Benin

As mentioned in the introductory note to the chapter on Nigerian works, the sculpture of Benin was the first of the ancient African forms of art to become known in the West, in somewhat dramatic circumstances, and remained synonymous with the ancient art of the continent for decades. It had been discussed, albeit in vague terms, by the Dutch scholar Olfert Dapper in a celebrated work printed in Amsterdam in 1668[44] (later translated into German, English and French) and by David van Nyandael in 1702. It was, however, the arrival in Europe of a few thousand artworks in bronze, terracotta and ivory, the spoils of the British punitive expedition that destroyed the capital of the

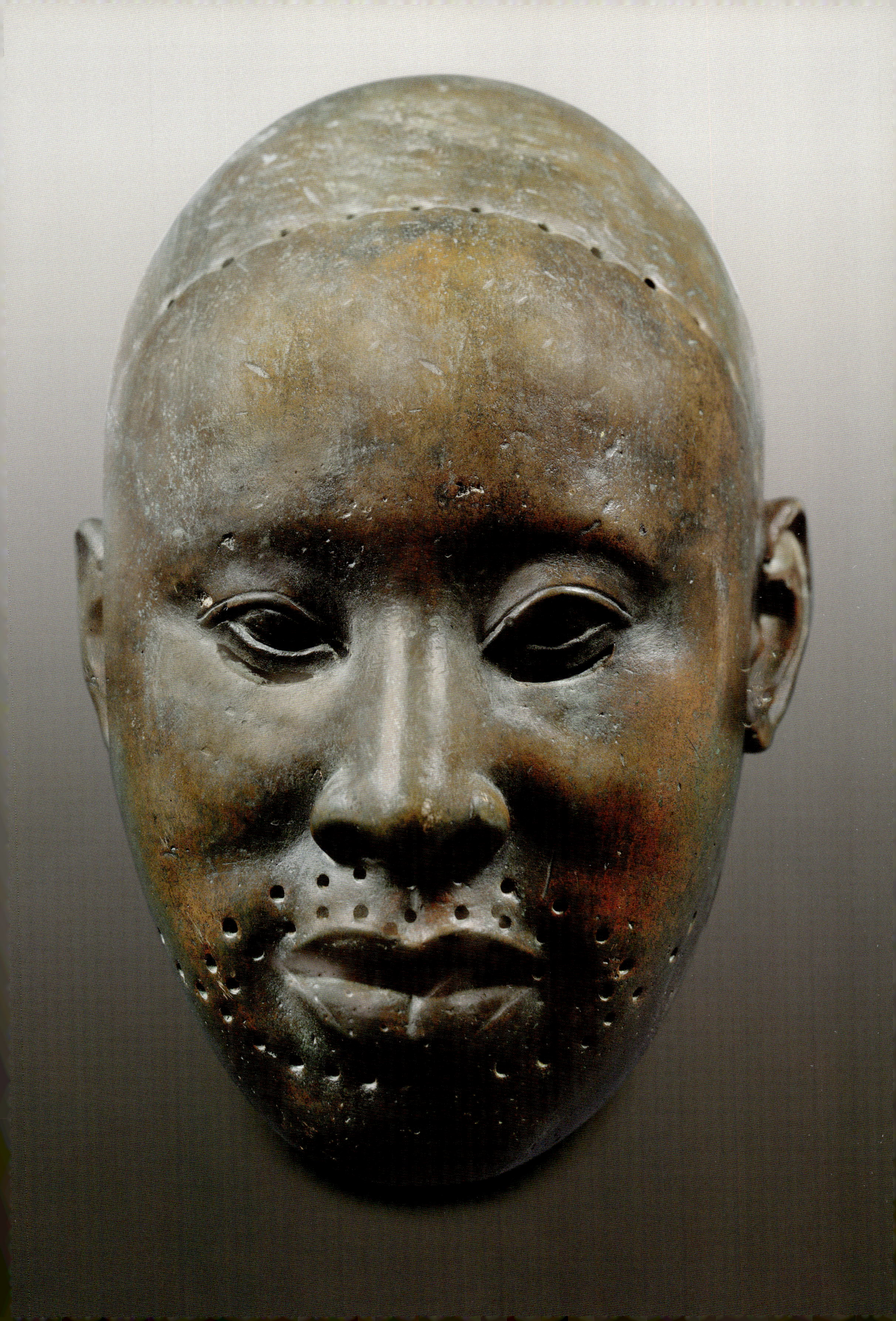

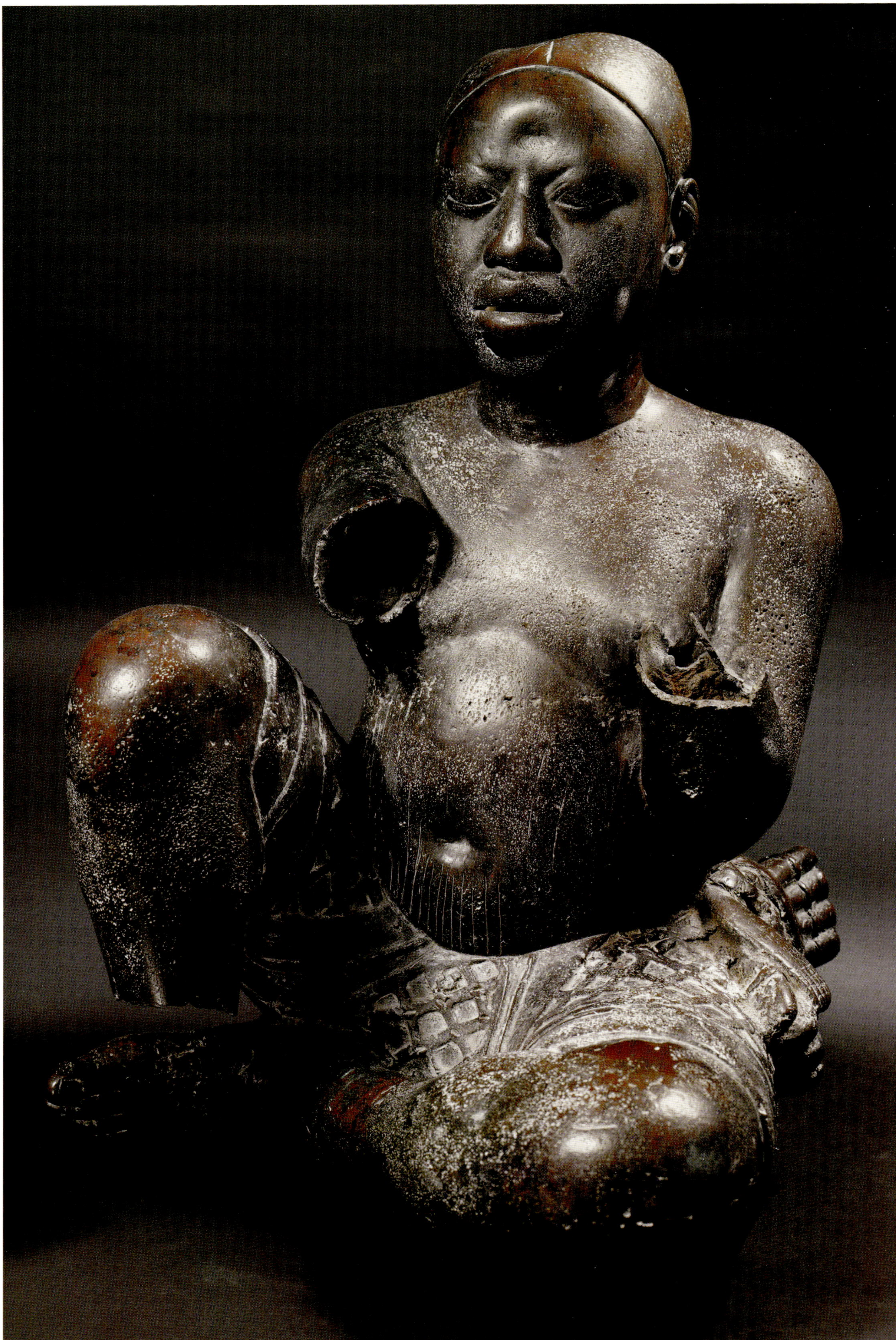

35. Artist of Ife
Nigeria (formerly in Tada), 14th–15th c.
Seated figure
Copper, 54 cm
The National Commission for Museums and Monuments, Nigeria

36. Members of the British punitive expedition with some of the spoils to be sent to Britain, 1897
Archives of the British Museum, London

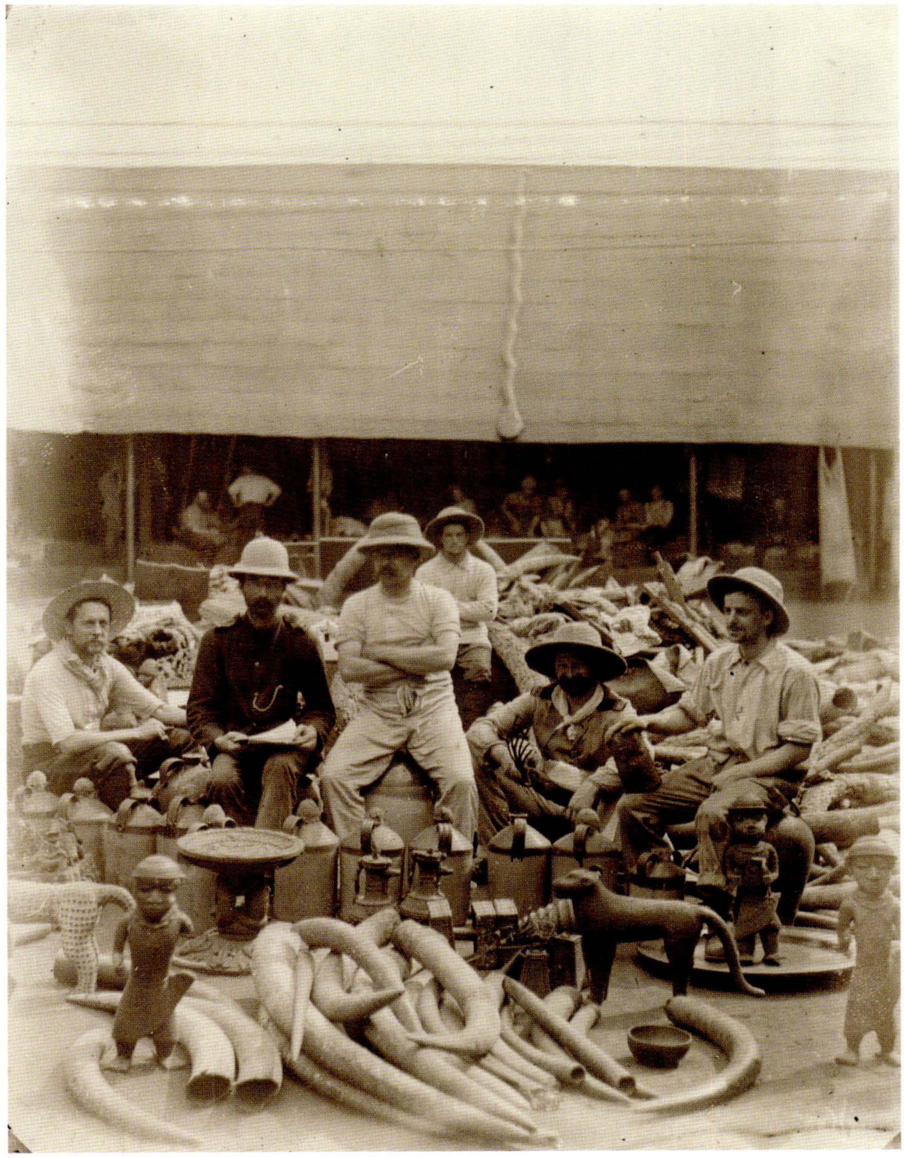

ancient kingdom in 1897[45] (no. 36), that brought it to the astonished attention of the West.[46] 'Benin Kings and Rituals: Court Art from Nigeria', the major exhibition organized by Barbara Plankensteiner that travelled to Vienna, Paris, Berlin and Chicago in succession a few years ago, is the most recent stage in this process of cultural acquisition, even though the interest of the curator and her team appears to have focused on the historical and ethnographic rather than the art-historical aspect of the works.

The Oba, absolute ruler of the kingdom of Benin (whose inhabitants fall within the Edo culture), was at the centre of a perfectly organized state machinery and exercised his power through a court of officials and dignitaries. A strong army was responsible for defending the state and extending its borders. Artists and craftsmen were organized into guilds (*Igun eromwon* for bronze and *Igbesamwan* for ivory) with their own statutes and particular districts, where they lived and produced the works required for religious purposes and to glorify the monarch and dignitaries.

Jacob U. Egharevba, the leading expert on the history of the Benin, has published a list of the thirty-eight sovereigns to have ruled from about 1,200 to the present (a reconstruction that has given rise to some disagreement). As the Nigerian historian Philip Aigbana Igbafe[47] points out, however, the birth of the state still remains shrouded in myth and uncertainty despite the numerous studies undertaken by Western and local scholars

The art of Benin was soon made known to the Western world through the works of Charles H. Read and Ormonde M. Dalton in 1899, Augustus Henry Lane Fox Pitt Rivers in 1900, and above all the monumental study by Fe-

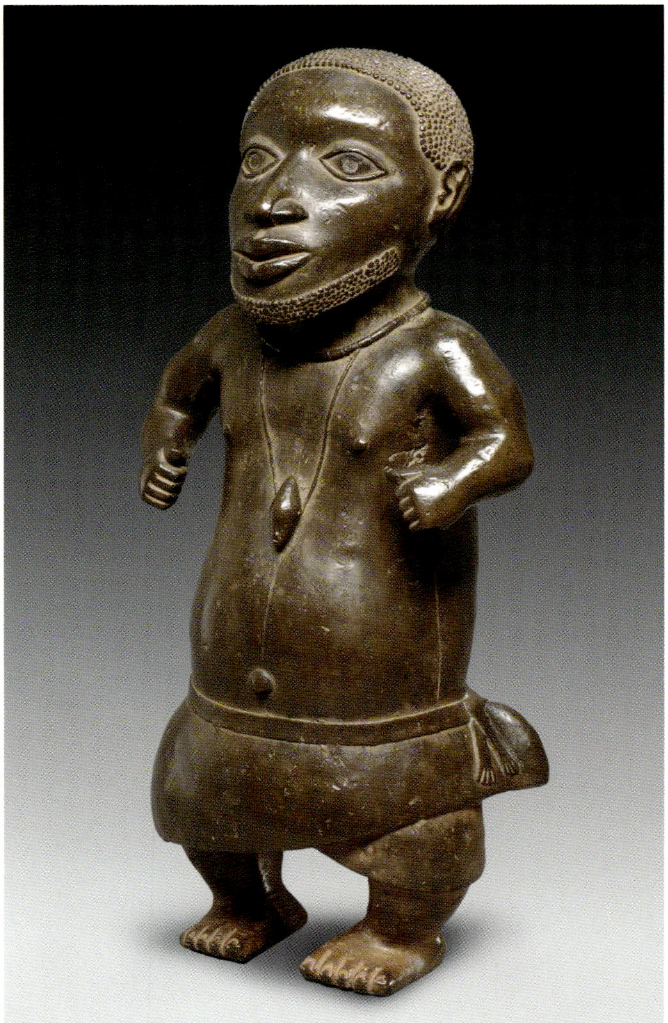

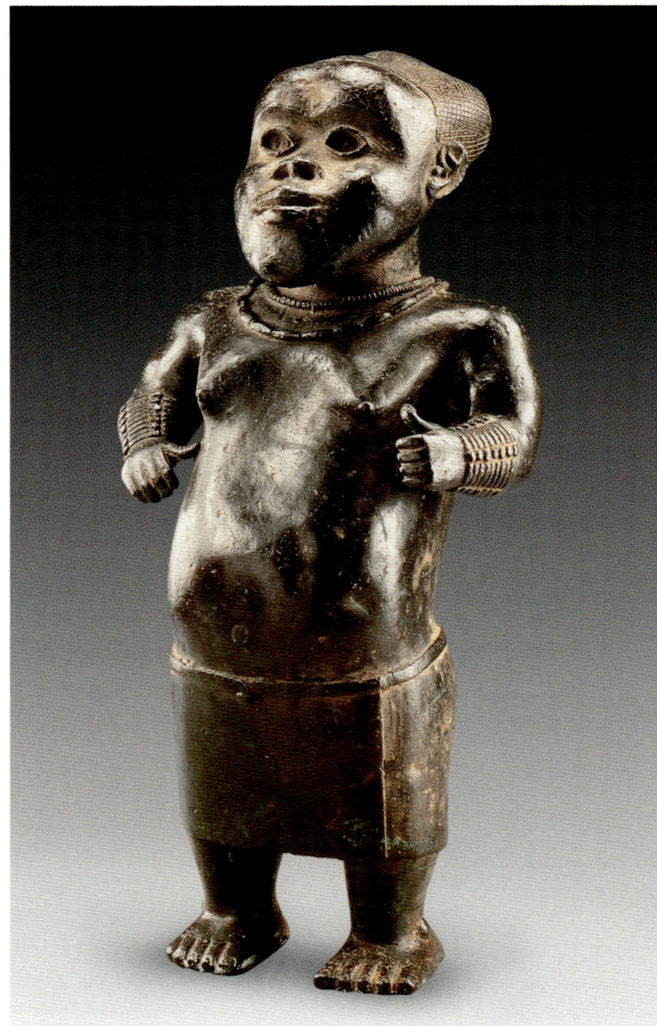

37. Edo artist
Benin, Nigeria, first half of 14th c. (?)
Court dwarf
Bronze, 60 cm
Museum für Völkerkunde, Vienna

38. Edo artist
Benin, Nigeria, 14th–15th c.
Court dwarf
Bronze, 59 cm
Museum für Völkerkunde, Vienna

lix von Luschan entitled *Die Altertümer von Benin*, published in 1919, not to mention the countless authors to have addressed the subject from various angles ever since.

The chronology put forward by William Fagg, which suggests a development from naturalism to increasingly rigid stylization, appears to have retained much of its validity.[48] Rigidity accompanied by summary execution becomes increasingly evident over the centuries, together with an overabundance of decoration that attests to the subordination of artistic creation to the celebratory requirements of the ruling class rather than free expression. Stylistic comparison of the Ife heads with those of the Benin first period provides important evidence for dating.

The two dwarves (nos. 37–38) now in the Museum für Völkerkunde, Vienna, which are almost certainly the work of different artists, are generally regarded as among the finest bronze figures from Benin and also probably the most ancient. On being subjected to thermoluminescence dating in 1985, one of these (no. 37) proved to be about 660 years old and was therefore produced in the first half of the 14th century. This very early date reopened the fascinating question of the relations between the art of Ife and Benin, which were very close according to the oral tradition. For William Fagg, "it is even conceivable that they are Ife works."[49]

As regards the deformity of the other figure (no. 38), Frank Willet has drawn attention to a series of fragmentary terracotta images unearthed at Ife that present very accentuated deformation of the head.

The calibrated blend of naturalism and distortion, the voluptuously rounded volumes reminiscent of the seated Tada figure, and the surfaces shot through with inner vitality all contribute to the extraordinary fascination of these sculptures, which were probably made for the altar of a monarch.

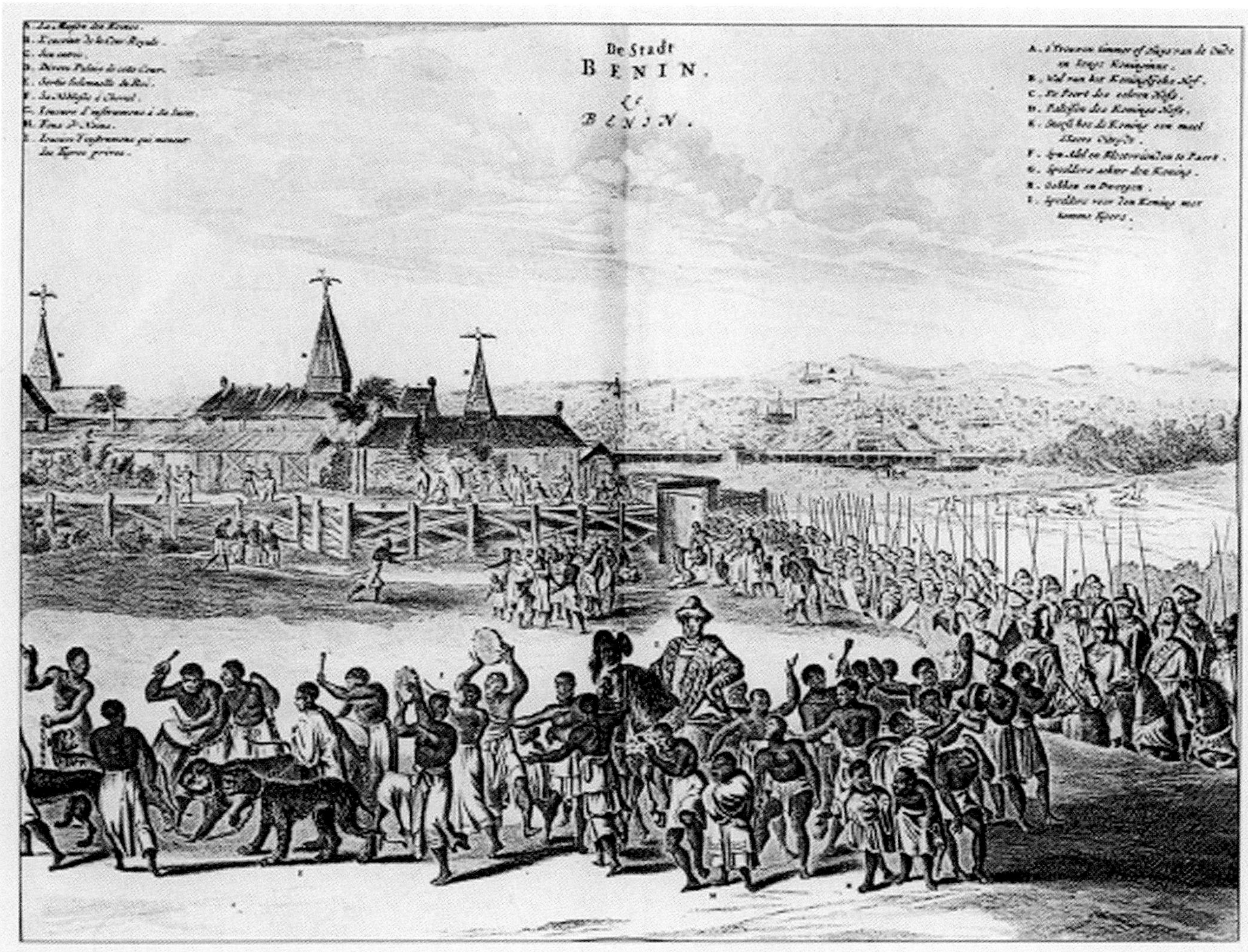

39. View of the city of Benin, in Dapper (1668)

Pages 64–65
40. Edo artist
Benin, Nigeria, mid-16th–17th c.
Pair of leopards
Bronze, l. 79 cm and 77 cm
The National Commission for Museums and Monuments, Nigeria

The presence of dwarves of uncertain status at the court of the Oba is mentioned by Olfert Dapper in connection with the monarch's annual procession outside the palace and shown in the illustration accompanying the description,[50] where leopards and horn players also appear (no. 39).

Leopards are the subjects of some of the most ancient and spectacular Benin artworks. The pair in the National Commission for Museums and Monuments,Nigeria (no. 40), which are the most perfect, capture the animal's combination of elegance and ferocity: on the one hand, its beautiful spotted coat, human eyes and leaf-shaped ears, and on the other, its menacing fangs.

Somewhat attenuated by the precious nature of the material and by wear, the same ferocity characterizes the splendid ivory head (no. 41) in the Museum für Völkerkunde, Vienna, which dates from the 17th century and probably belonged to a full-sized figure.

As the king of beasts, the leopard was a symbol of the Oba, the king of men.

The ancient works also include male and female human heads, which were placed on the altars of ancestors. The earliest of these have thin walls and are shaped with great sensitivity even though they appear more rigid and stylized than the pieces from Ife, above all in the rendering of details such as the ear. This tendency increased over the years until it virtually became a stereotype in the increasingly spectacular works of the 18th and 19th centuries (no. 42).

The nature of the ancient male heads, few specimens of which are known, is not clear. Some scholars see them as commemorative works and others as trophies of vanquished enemies.[51]

The head in the National Commission for Museums and Monuments of Nigeria (no. 43) dated to the 15th–16th century, is a good example of ancient artwork. The reliefs of the coral necklaces and neatly arranged coiffure har-

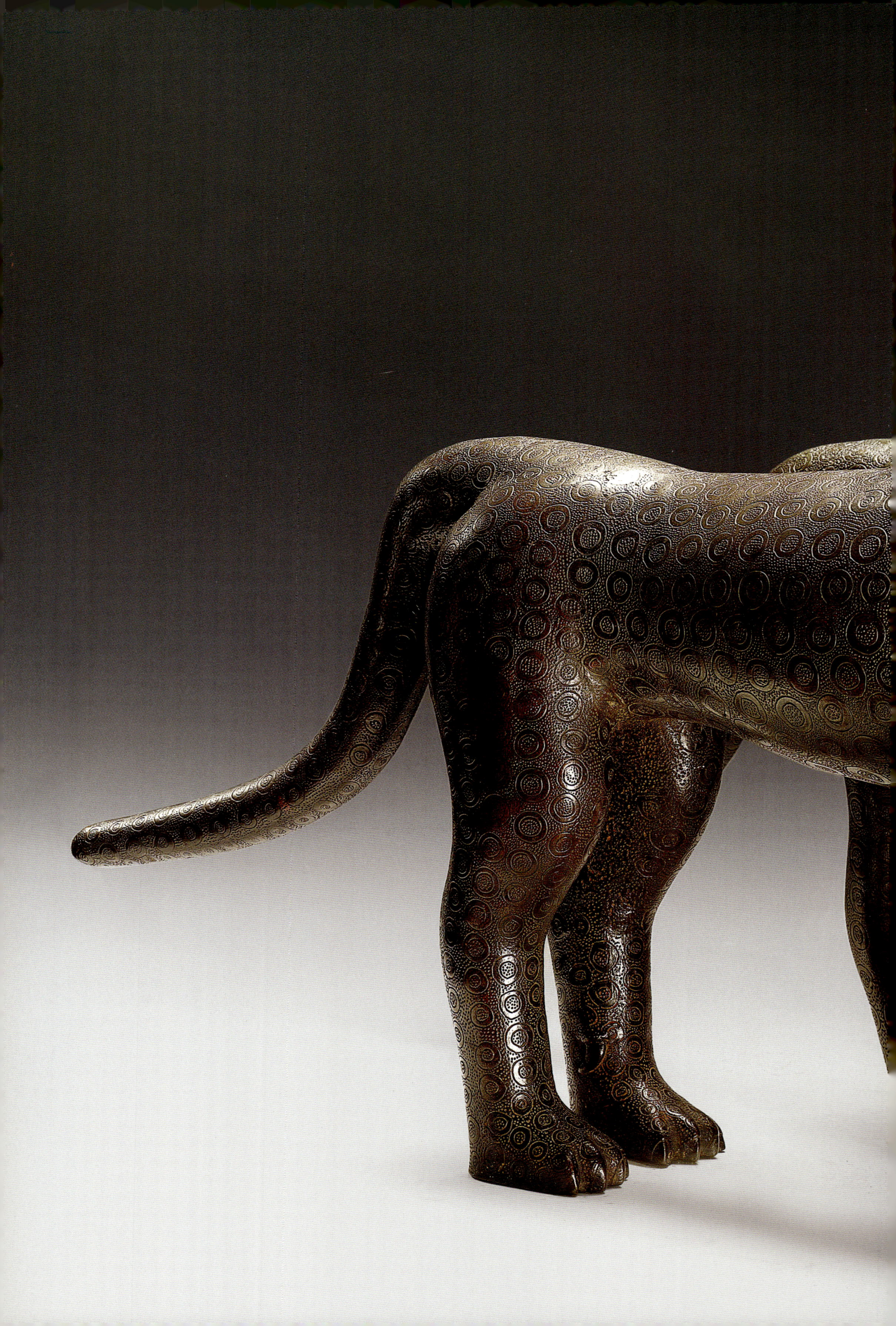

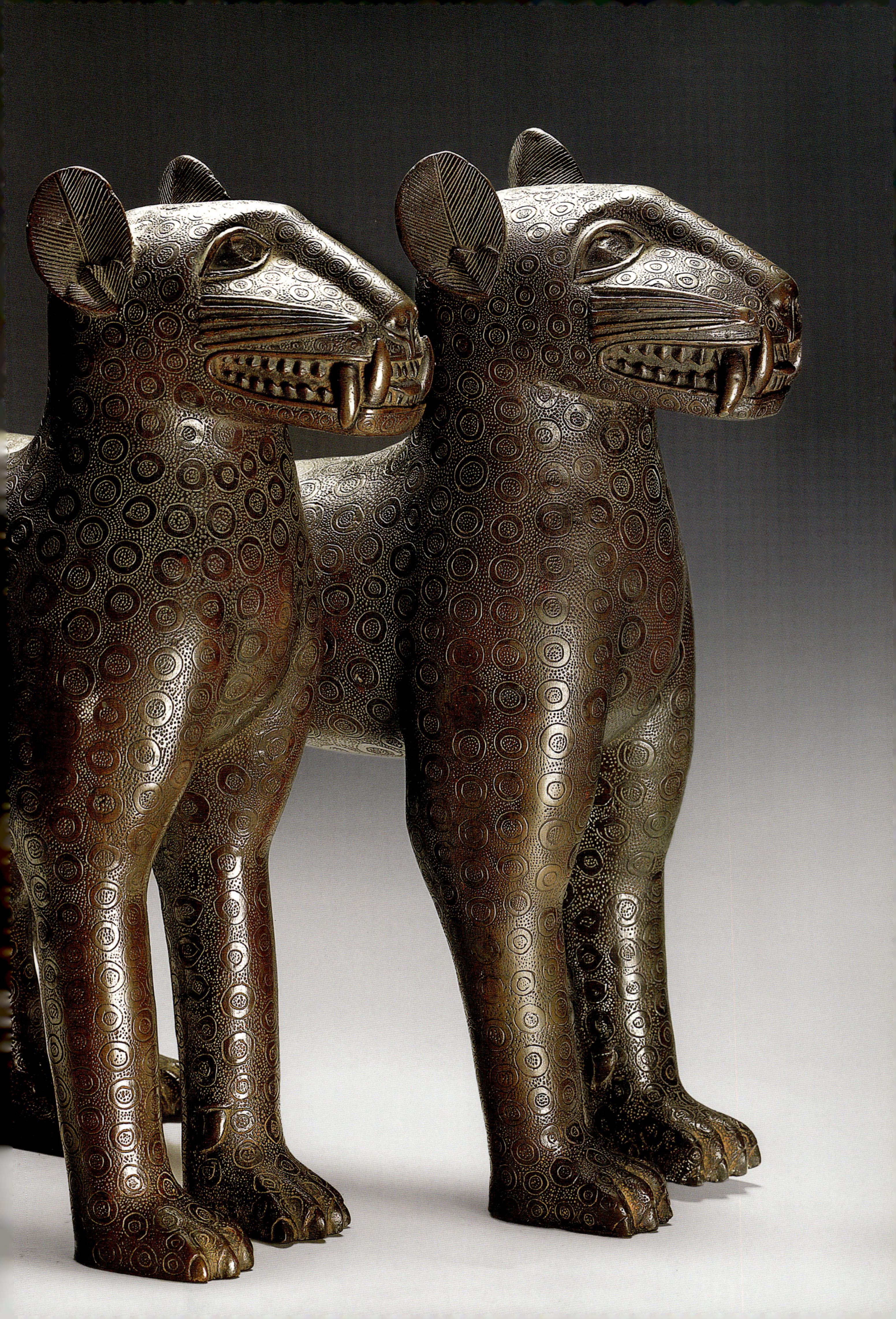

41. Edo artist
Benin, Nigeria, 17th c.
Head of leopard
Ivory, iron and copper, 18 cm
Museum für Völkerkunde, Vienna

42. Edo artist
Benin, Nigeria, 19th c.
Head of Oba
Bronze, 30 cm
Museum für Völkerkunde, Vienna

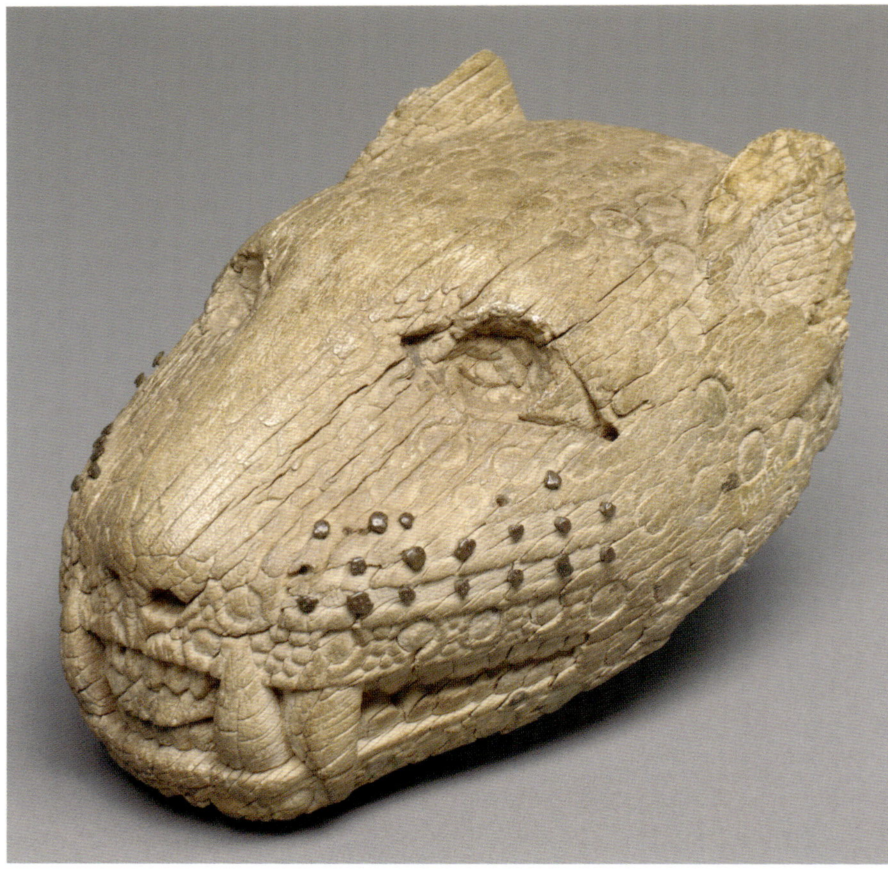

monize with the subtle rendering of the features of the regular face, illuminated by wide-open eyes and enlivened by the two scarification marks on the forehead, which once contained iron with a propitiatory function.

The rarer female heads are stylized portraits of *iyoba* or queen mothers, probably to be understood as "mothers of the kingdom", important counsellors of the monarch, rather than in the biological sense.

The sensitive naturalism of the features and the extraordinary conceptualization of form are combined in these heads with delicate workmanship to produce works of great sophistication.

The remarkable degree of formal invention (as exemplified in head no. 44) is evident above all in the side view. The slight prognathism naturally paves the way for the tapering and the change in direction of the horn-shaped hat. The integration of the symbol of power into the overall volume enhances the perfection of the work. Note how the decoration of the headgear – similar in shape to the *corno* worn by the Venetian doges – is visually linked by narrow vertical strands of coral beads to the band encircling the slender neck and the elegant motif of the very appropriate base, which prepares for the upward thrust of the composition it supports.

Five ivory masks of extremely sophisticated workmanship, probably worn by the Oba on special occasions, bear evident similarities to the bronze heads, with which – although designed to be viewed from the front – they share the mixture of naturalism and stylization as well as the same scarification marks on the forehead. The actual nature of the personage represented is not clear. Barbara Plankensteiner suggests that this sculpture may be a portrait of a queen mother.[52]

The two finest works (no. 45 shown here and the other in the Metropolitan Museum, New York) were found in the Oba's bedchamber by the members of the punitive expedition.[53] They are almost certainly by the same artist, a contemporary of the authors of the bronze heads described above.

Visually linked by the calibrated projection of the ears and the rings for attachment, the fretwork decoration beneath the chin and the crown of stylized, bearded Portuguese heads enclose the face in a perfect oval. The balance of the composition and the perfection of the features, rendered with great sub-

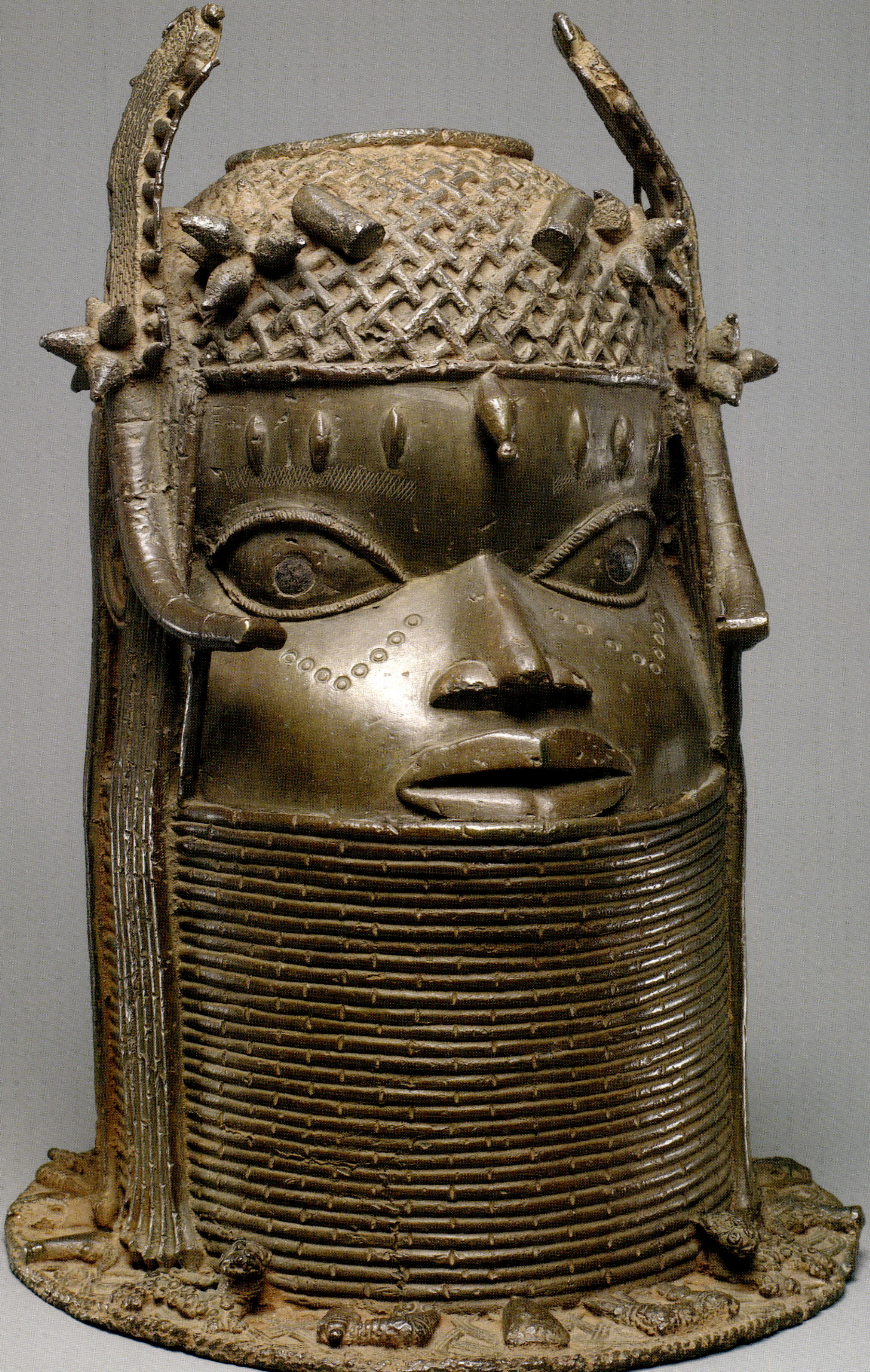

43. Edo artist
Benin, Nigeria, 15th–16th c.
Head of Oba
Bronze, 20.8 cm
The National Commission for Museums and Monuments, Nigeria

44. Edo artist
Benin, Nigeria, 15th–16th c.
Commemorative head of queen mother
Bronze, 51.5 cm
The National Commission for Museums and Monuments, Nigeria

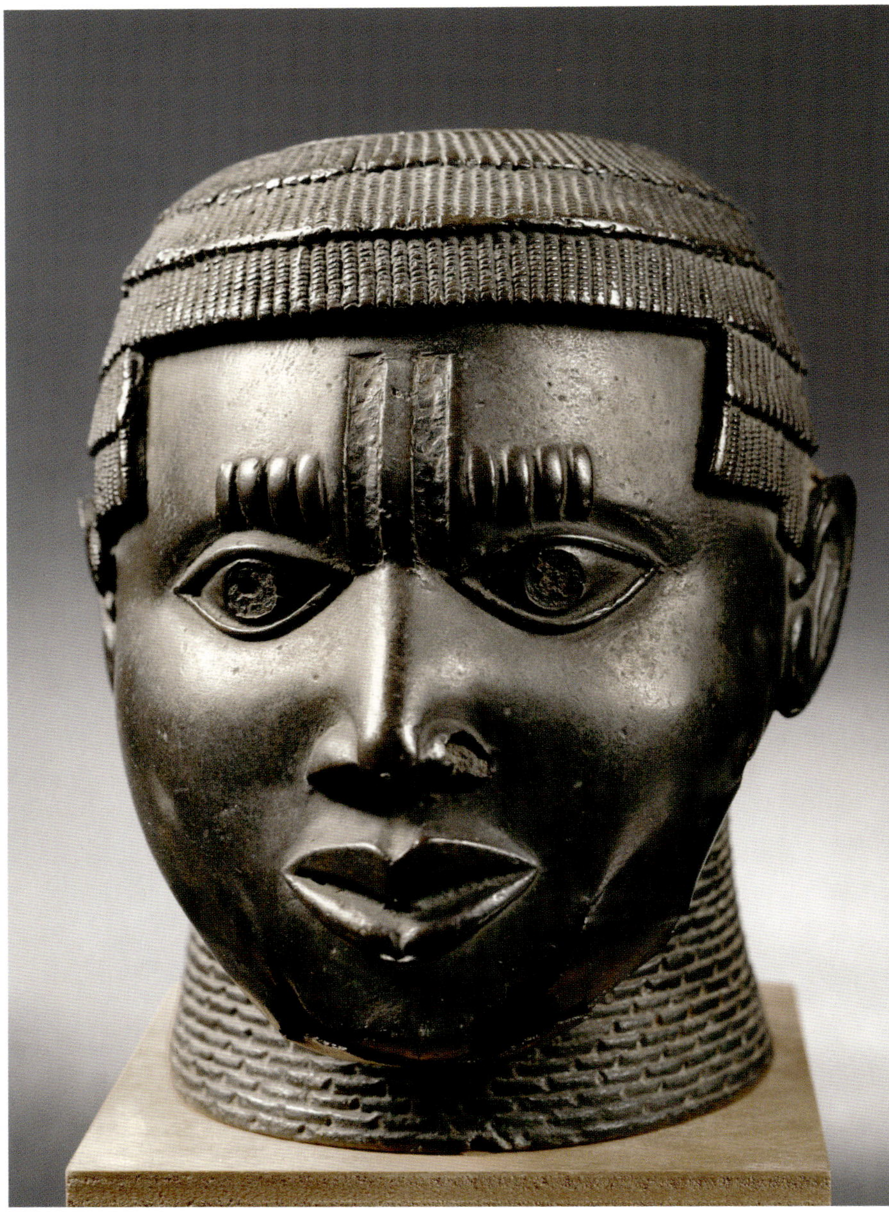

tlety and sensitivity, combine in this mask to make it a work of exceptional beauty.

Numerous figures in the round, including musicians, horsemen, messengers, royal attendants and warriors, date from the period of transition between the classical and intermediate styles, between the mid-16th century and the first quarter of the 17th.

The horn player (no. 46) now in the British Museum is a significant example of this group of works. Displaying a sophisticated combination of immobility and movement, realism and expressive distortion, the figure stands firmly on very large feet. The stocky legs support a slender torso apparently lacking in musculature, like the thin arms holding the long horn with a side mouthpiece. The oversized head, made still more monumental by the tall hat, restores the overall balance. The rigidity of the frontal pose is modified both by the musician's graceful gesture and by the slanting line of the lower part of his garment and its prolongation upwards, which is underscored by the rich decoration in low relief.

Olfert Dapper wrote in 1668 that the wooden pillars of the main portico of the royal palace in Benin were covered from top to bottom with copper plates on which the victories of the monarchs were engraved.[54] These plaques are the most emblematic creations of the middle period: an enormous artistic and cultural heritage of about 900 items – many of which are in museums in the Western world – that extols the exploits of the sovereigns, depicts the symbols of their power (images of animals) and portrays the personages of the

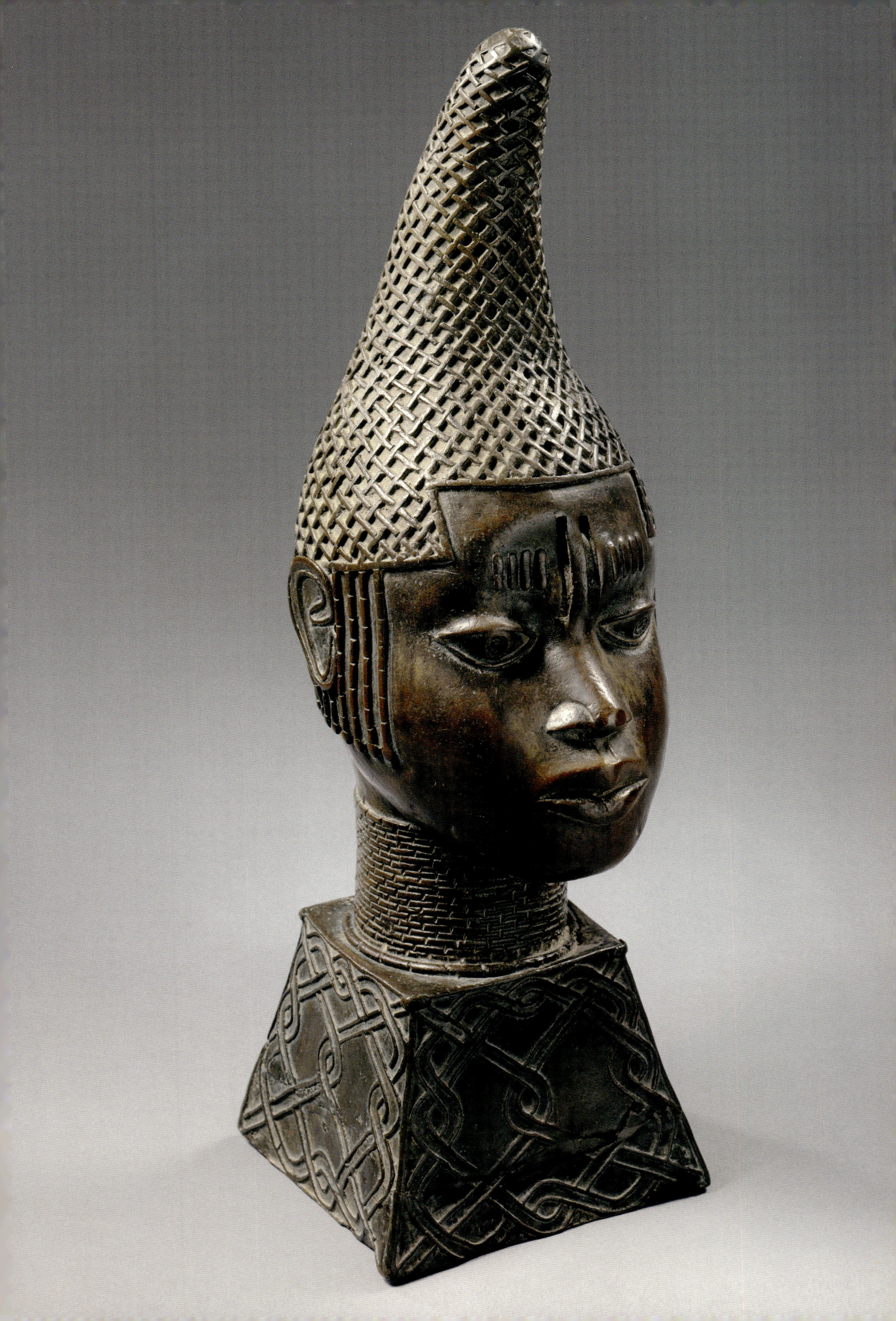

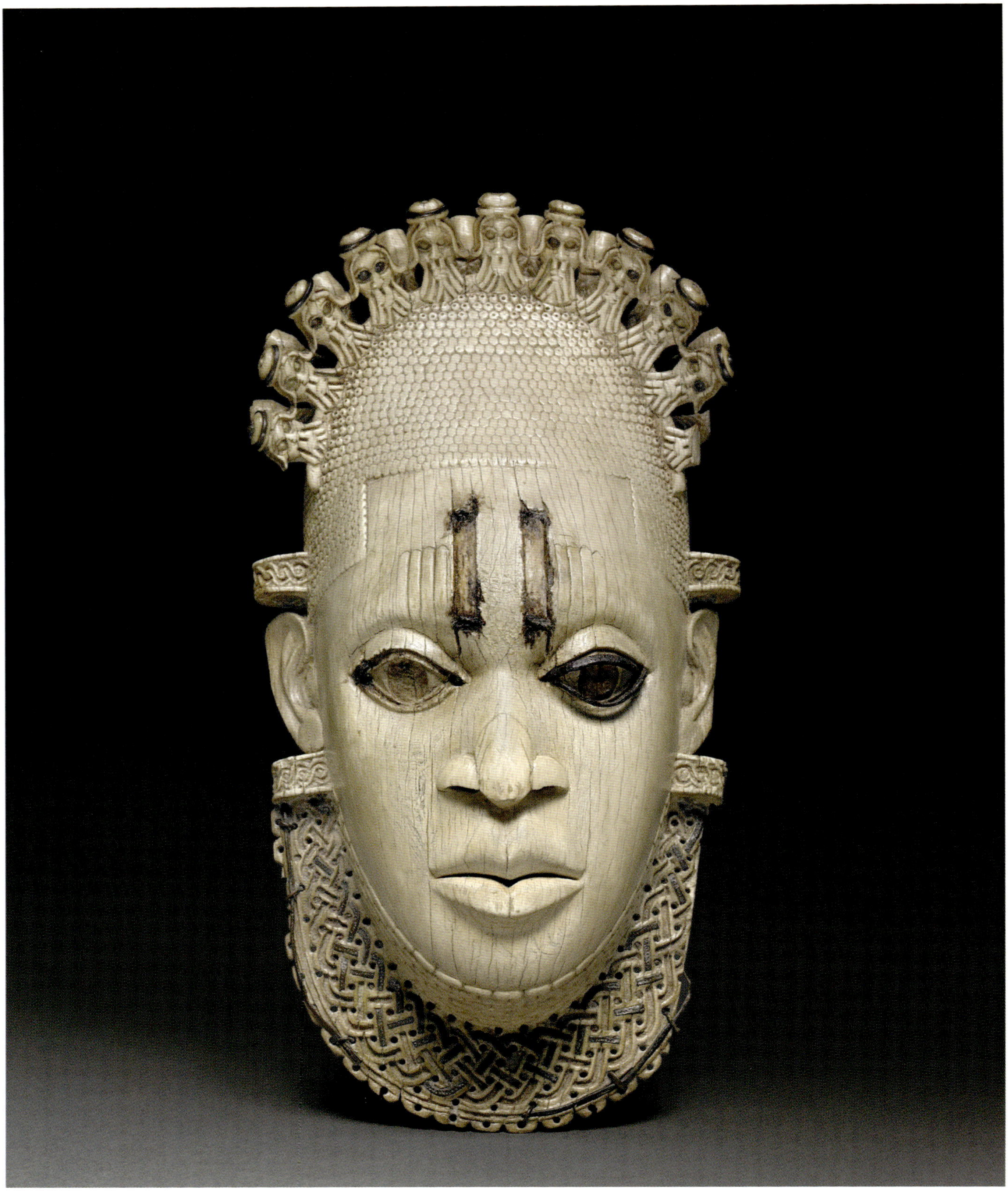

45. Edo artist
Benin, Nigeria, 15th–16th c.
Mask of queen mother
Ivory, iron and copper, 25 cm
The British Museum, Ethnography
Department, London

46. Edo artist
Benin, Nigeria, 16th–17th c.
Horn player
Bronze, 62 cm
The British Museum, Ethnography
Department, London

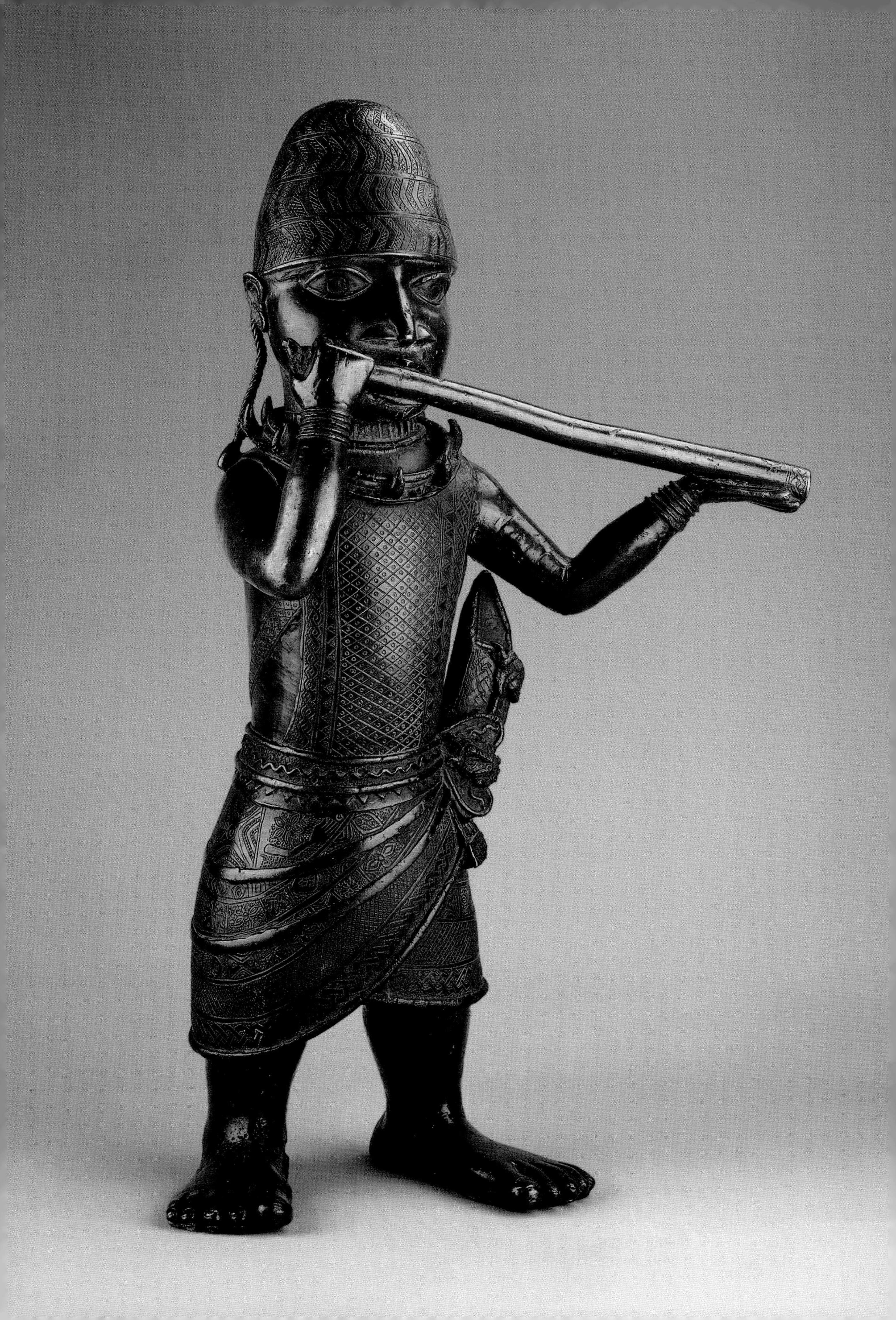

47. Members of the British punitive expedition with plaques piled up in a burnt building of the palace, 1897
Oxford University, Archives of the Pitt Rivers Museum, Oxford

48. Edo artist
Benin, Nigeria, 16th–17th c.
Plaque with Portuguese hunter
Bronze, 38 cm
Staatliche Museen zu Berlin, Ethnologisches Museum, Berlin

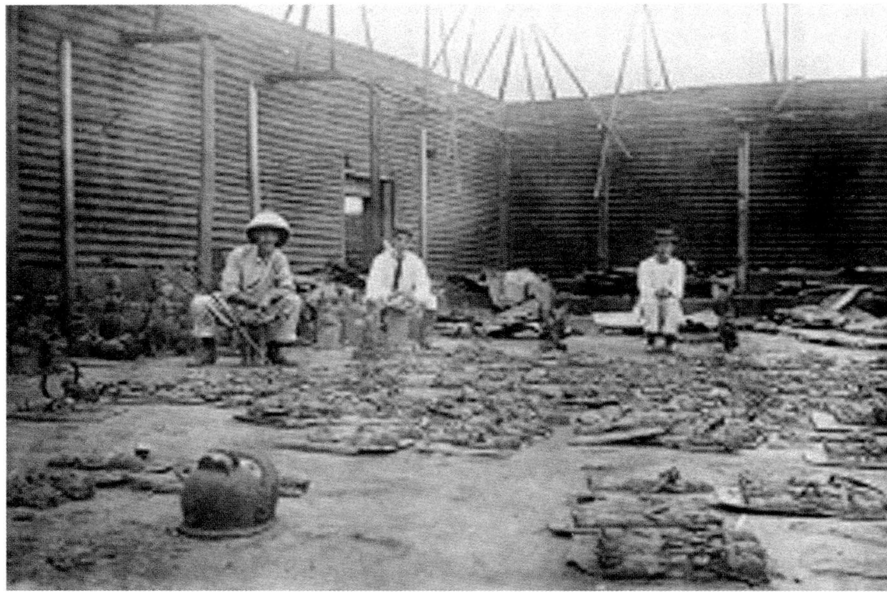

rigidly hierarchical court as well as the European visitors, who were presumably Portuguese. Their dress provides sufficiently convincing evidence that many of these works were produced in the 16th century.

The plaques were almost certainly removed a few years after Dapper's description, as David van Nyandael makes no mention of them in the account of his visit to Benin in 1702. The members of the punitive expedition found them piled up in a storeroom of the royal palace (no. 47). It has also been suggested that perhaps they were not all attached to the pillars, but rather constituted a kind of archive for display in appropriate groups on special occasions. The hypothesis has also been put forward that the square or rectangular format was borrowed from European illustrations, but there is no evidence of this. However, it is certain that the plaques are an indispensable source of information about life in Benin during past centuries, thanks to the situations illustrated, the dress of the figures and their position in the hierarchy.

While these works may appear at first sight to be the result of undifferentiated, standardized production, more careful examination reveals substantial differences in formal terms. For example, there is greater complexity in the handling of space than appears at first sight. This ranges from the rigidly frontal presentation of figures to the rendering of the third dimension by means of appropriate techniques, such as the accentuation of the relief of some elements, the positioning of figures along a diagonal or vertical axis, and the use of symbolism based on proportions. The three examples presented here give at least some indication of the inventiveness and mastery of the Edo sculptors – the name recently established for the inhabitants of the kingdom – in solving the problems posed by the depiction of the various subjects.

The figure of a Portuguese hunter (no. 48) now in the Ethnologisches Museum, Berlin, exemplifies the first and simplest approach, namely the frontal view. An idea of movement is nevertheless suggested by the diagonal of the man's arms and the reliefs of the bird and the crossbow, deftly balanced by the two stylized crocodile heads.

Lying diagonally like a rug, the flattened carcass on the plaque depicting the sacrifice of a bull (no. 49) is the compositional focus of a scene crowded with those who have performed the sacrifice, whose decreasing size and positioning create the impression of spatial depth.

Another plaque (no. 50) in the Vienna Museum provides a good example of the combined use of relief and the symbolism of proportions. In a crowded yet still airy composition, dressed in a splendid warrior's costume that was traditionally supposed to confer invulnerability, the figure of the sovereign Ozolua[55] emerges from the background, against which the two warriors accompanying him appear flattened. His arms holding the emblems of power stand out sharply from the plane of the king's body to suggest the depth of the space, in which two

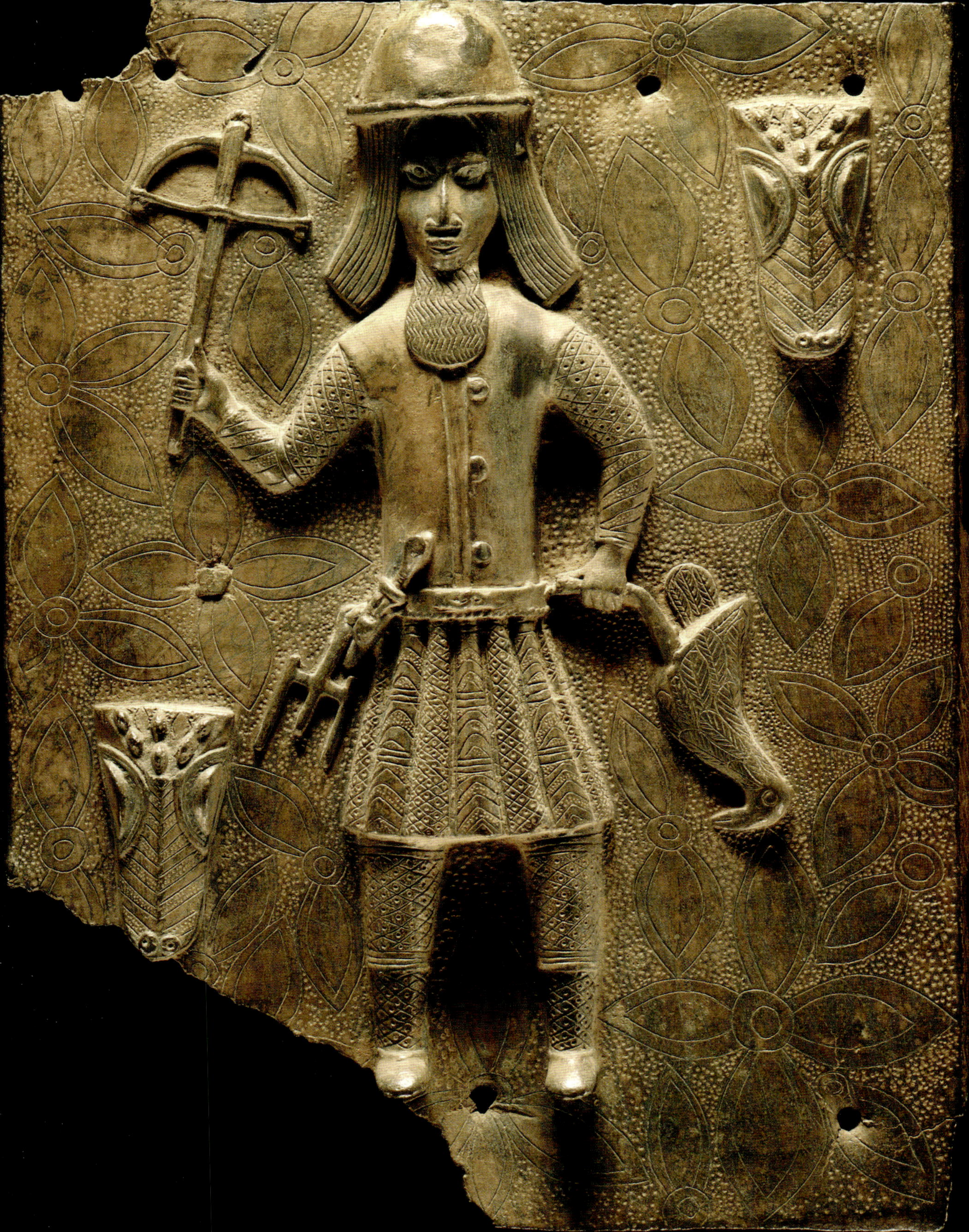

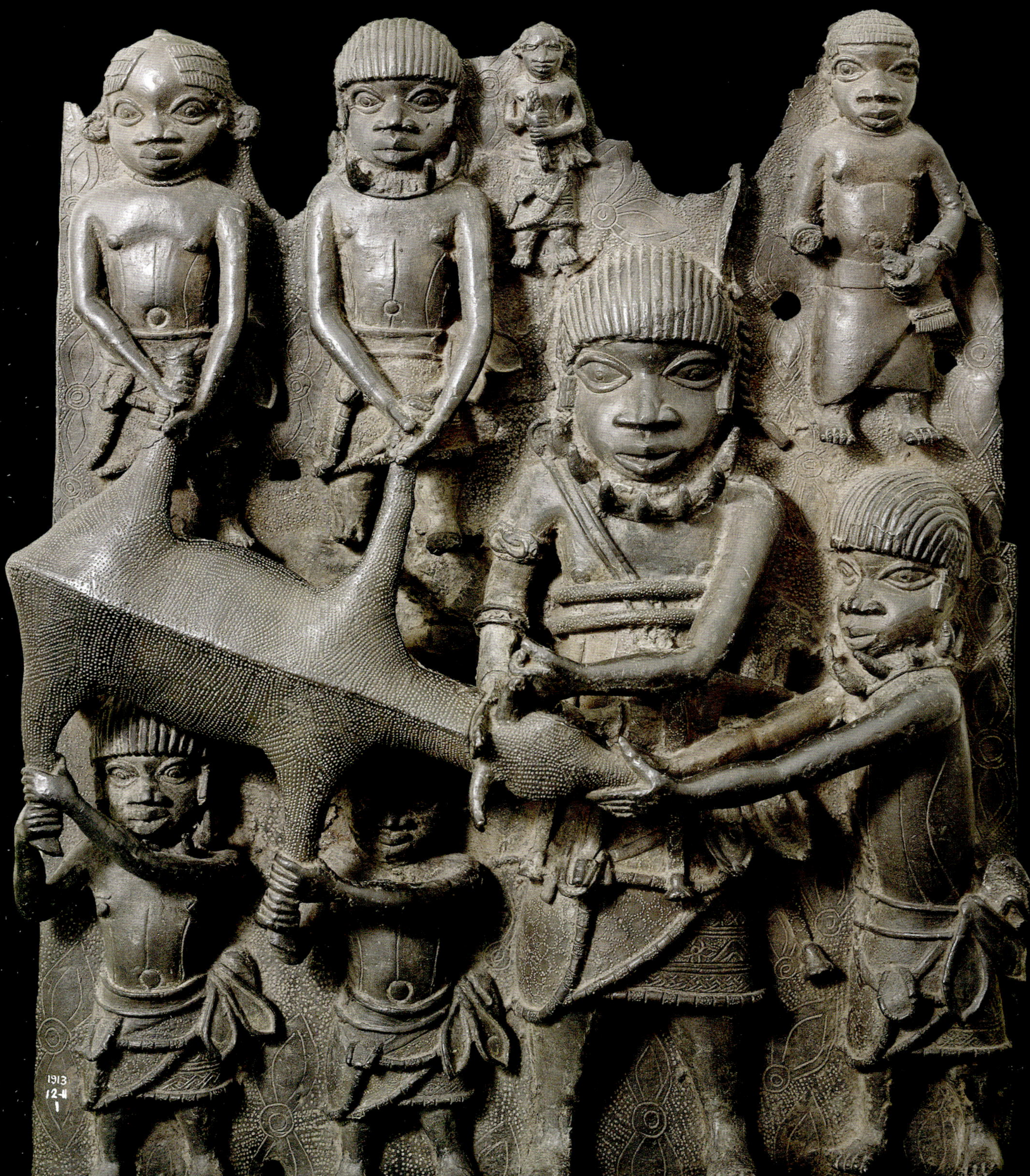
1913
12-11
1

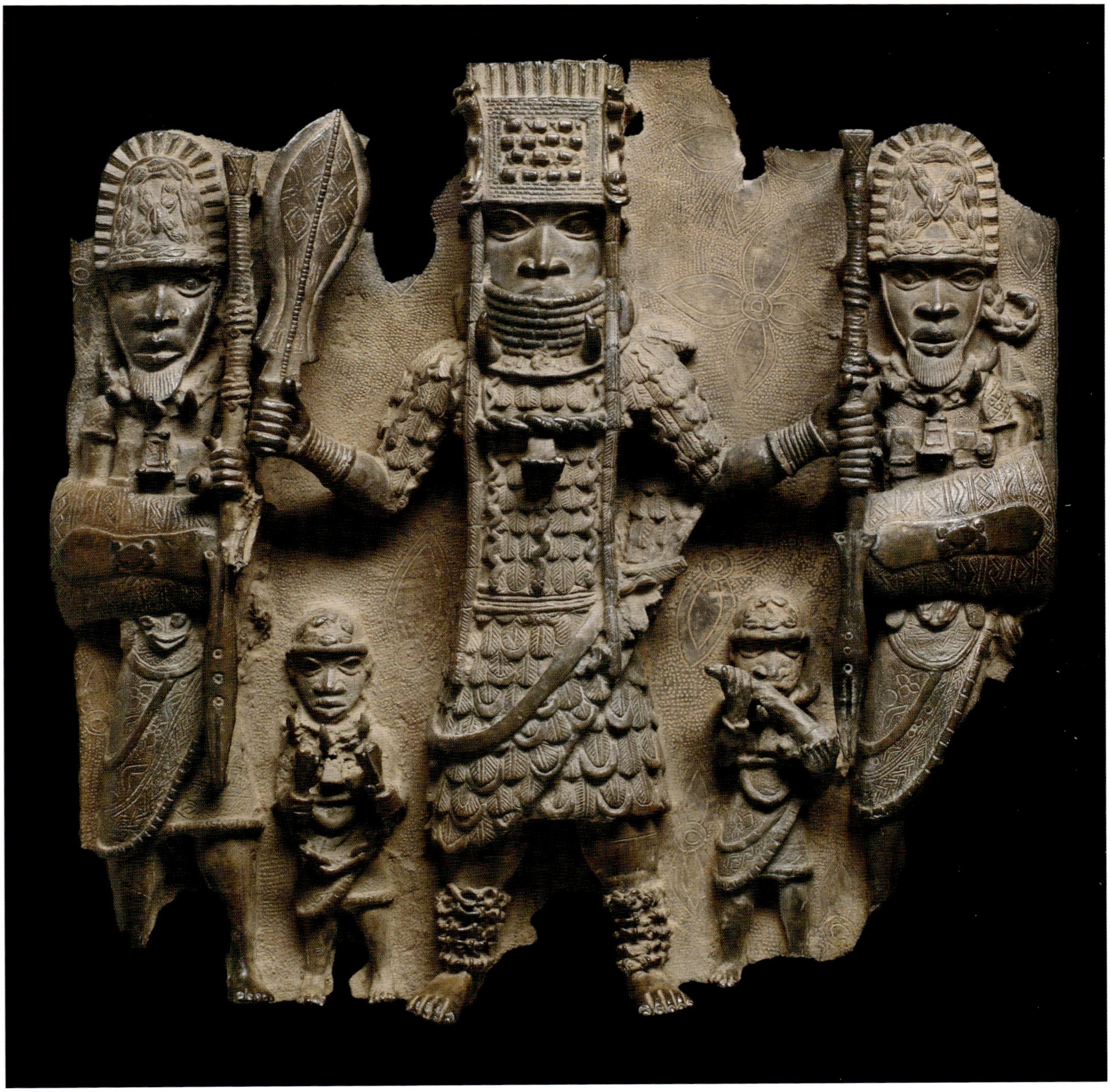

49. Edo artist
Benin, Nigeria, 16th–17th c.
Plaque with sacrifice of a bull
Bronze, 50.4 cm
The British Museum, Ethnography Department, London

50. Edo artist
Benin, Nigeria, 16th–17th c.
Plaque with the Oba Ozolua and four attendants
Bronze, 41.3 cm
Museum für Völkerkunde, Vienna

51. **Artist from Owo**
Nigeria (from Igbo 'Laja), ca. 15th c.
Head
Terracotta, 17.4 cm
The National Commission for Museums and Monuments, Nigeria

52. Artist from Owo
Nigeria (from Igbo 'Laja), ca. 15th c.
Head
Terracotta, 10.1 cm
The National Commission for Museums and Monuments, Nigeria

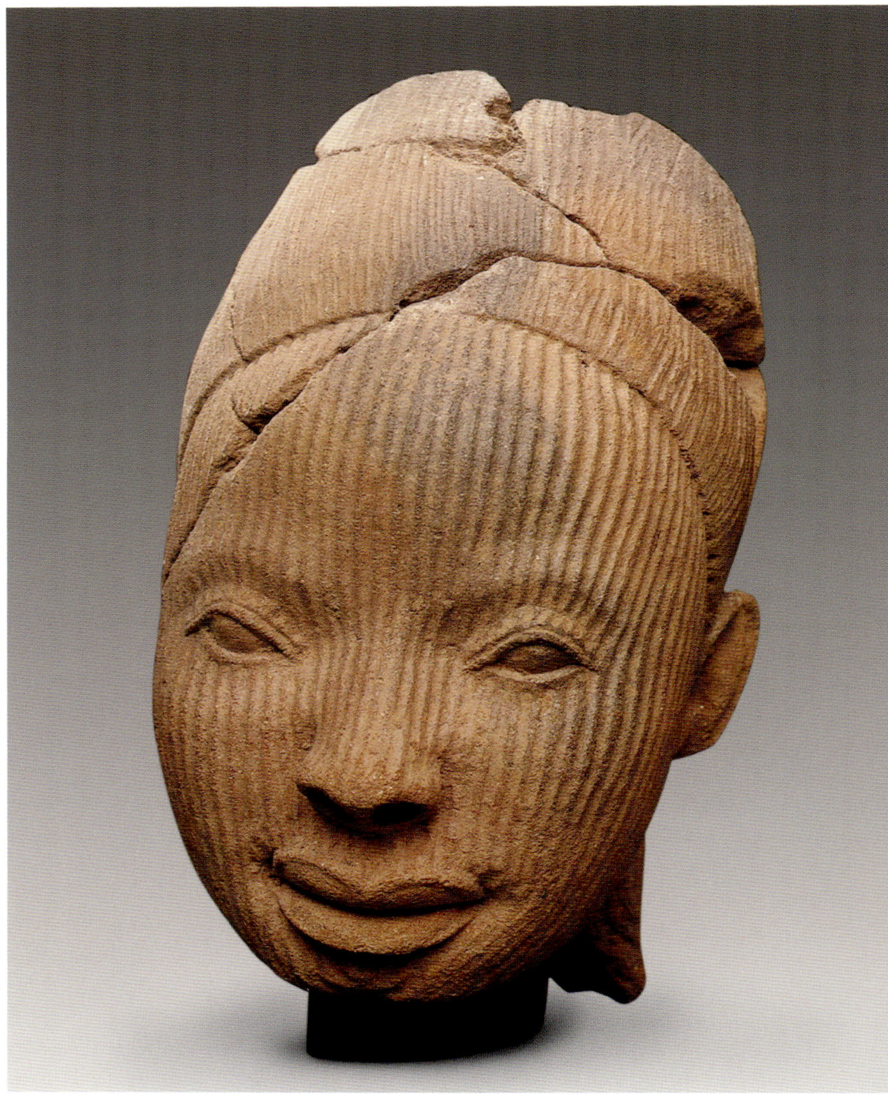

musicians on a smaller scale, in accordance with hierarchical order, one ringing a bell and the other playing a horn, occupy the middle ground.

Owo

Owo was a city state situated halfway between the kingdom of Benin, whose rival it was for a certain period, and Ife. Like the latter, it had a Yoruba population.

Many of the ivory works of uncertain age produced in the city (some in European collections probably date from the 17th century) were already known midway through the last century, but erroneously attributed to artists from Benin. The bronze and terracotta sculptures dating from the early 15th century, most of which are fragmentary, were instead only discovered in 1971 by Ekpo Eyo, who carried out the first scientific excavations in the region.

These works display the influence of Ife in their tendency towards naturalism and of Benin in terms of subject matter. Head no. 51 is a good example of the former by virtue of its classical serenity and a series of shared details such as the vertical scarification marks on the face – inexplicably extending also to the coiffure or hat (unless the author intended to represent a veil) – the shape of the lips, and the way the upper eyelids overlap the lower at the corners. It is, however, distinguished by the subtle sense of melancholy that seems to emanate from the beautiful face with its ineffable human quality.

Head no. 52 probably belonged to a full-length figure and perhaps to a small group that was dispersed and lost, as seems to be suggested by the way the left part of the fragment is barely sketched, since the sideburn and ear are lacking in detail. This head conveys a very different impression from the previous work, as the knitted brows seem to suggest anger.

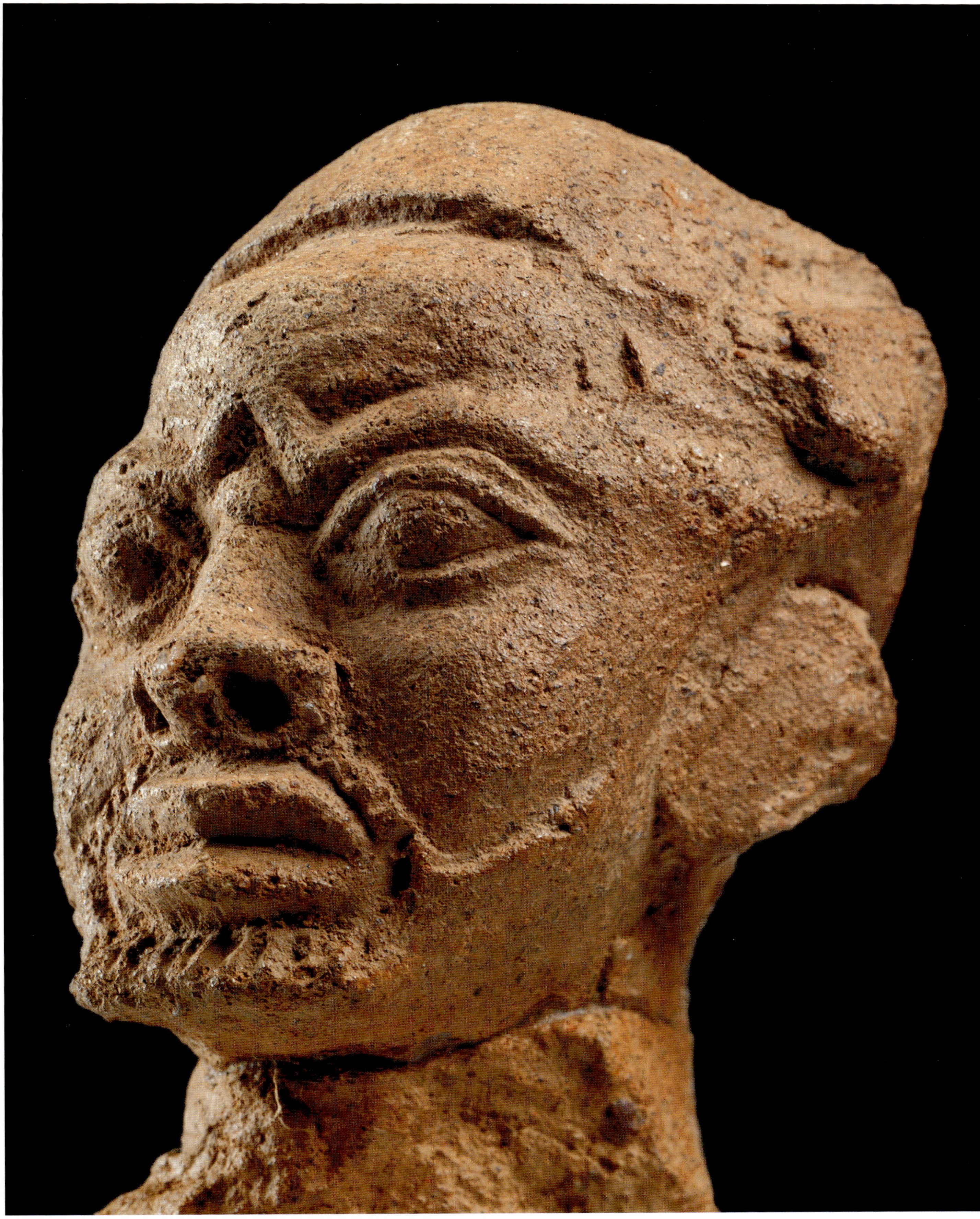

53. Artist from Owo
Nigeria, 15th–17th c.
Striker for Ifa oracle
Ivory, 44.5 cm
R. Miehler Collection, Munich

53a. Detail of lower section of the striker no. 53

54. Artist of the Lower Niger culture
Nigeria (formerly on the island of Jebba), late 14th–early 15th c.
Archer
Bronze with tin, 95 cm
The National Commission for Museums and Monuments, Nigeria

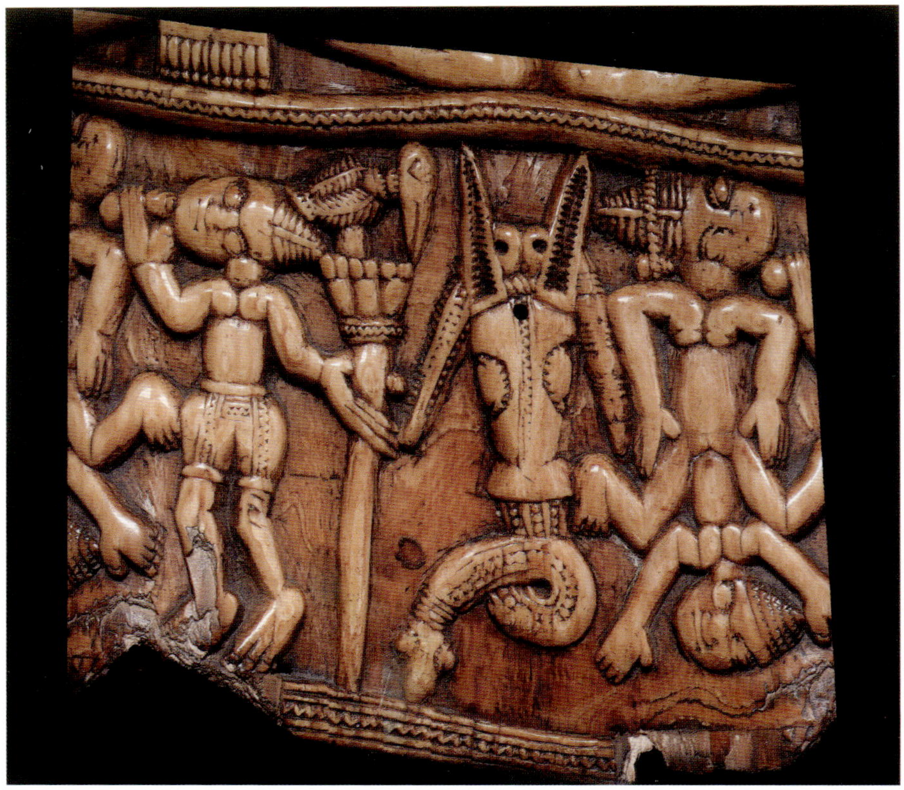

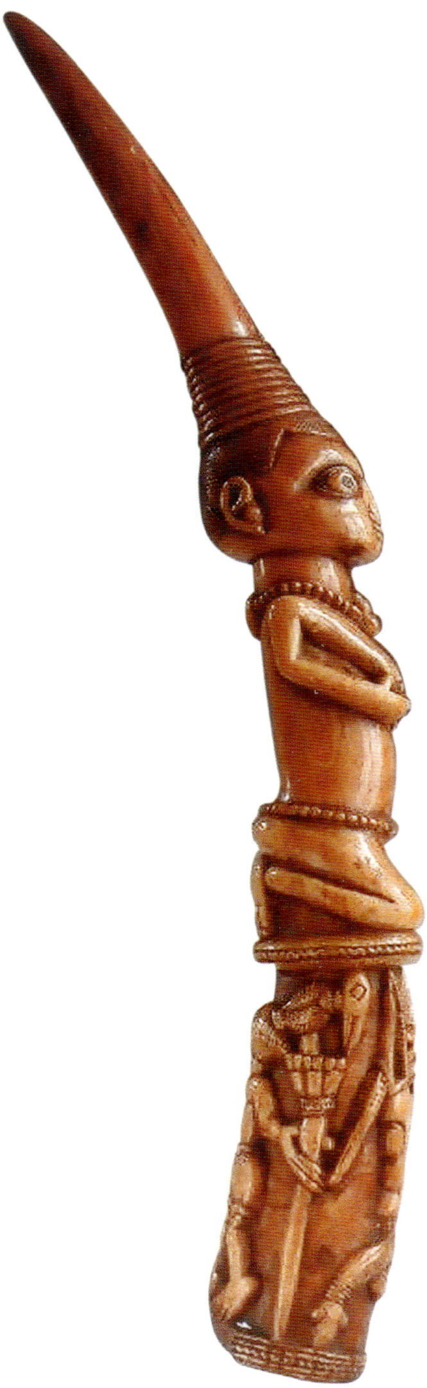

The very interesting ivory striker (no. 53) used in the Ifa oracle ceremony was recently subjected to carbon 14 testing and dated with a probability of 95.4% to the 15th–17th centuries.

The iconography of the instrument is extraordinary. While an elegant, nude, female figure with her hands on her breasts, a recurrent motif in Owo sculpture, is carved on the pointed upper section, the usually smooth lower section (no. 53a) is covered with complex and – to the best of my knowledge – unique decoration in a different and more intricate expressive register. Viewed as a whole, it shows a ram's head (of gigantic size with respect to the figures carved on either side of it) with a snake emerging from its mouth, flanked by a woman giving birth and a figure holding a staff apparently surmounted by a bird.

The ram's head is a motif found on Owo ivory bracelets in the 17th and 18th centuries or even earlier, while, aside from the subject matter, the human figures flanking it are curious, since their outsized heads look as though they have been detached from the body and set horizontally on the neck.

The birth scene is unusual and obscure in meaning, as the figure being born is the same size as the one giving birth. Given the absence of any other reason, to the best of my knowledge, this may be for the purely formal purpose of balancing the volumes of the upper figure. Also evident in this pursuit of internal order is the great rigour of the parallels established not only between the heads, but also between the legs bent at right angles of the upper figure and the arms of the lower one, and between these arms and the head of the snake and the very long feet of the figure on the left, who appears to be dancing.

The staff in the man's hand is most probably an iron rod used in divination ceremonies, which is larger than life size, probably to meet the requirements of the composition.

The long pointed beak suggests that the bird may be a woodpecker, a motif sometimes found on the staffs of the Osugbo association, whose members performed a judiciary function among the Yoruba.

The Lower Niger Culture

The expression "Lower Niger Bronze Industry", coined by William Fagg[56] in 1963 to describe a group of bronzes with characteristics differing from the works created within the other ancient Nigerian cultures examined above, is indicative of the vagueness of our knowledge in this connection.

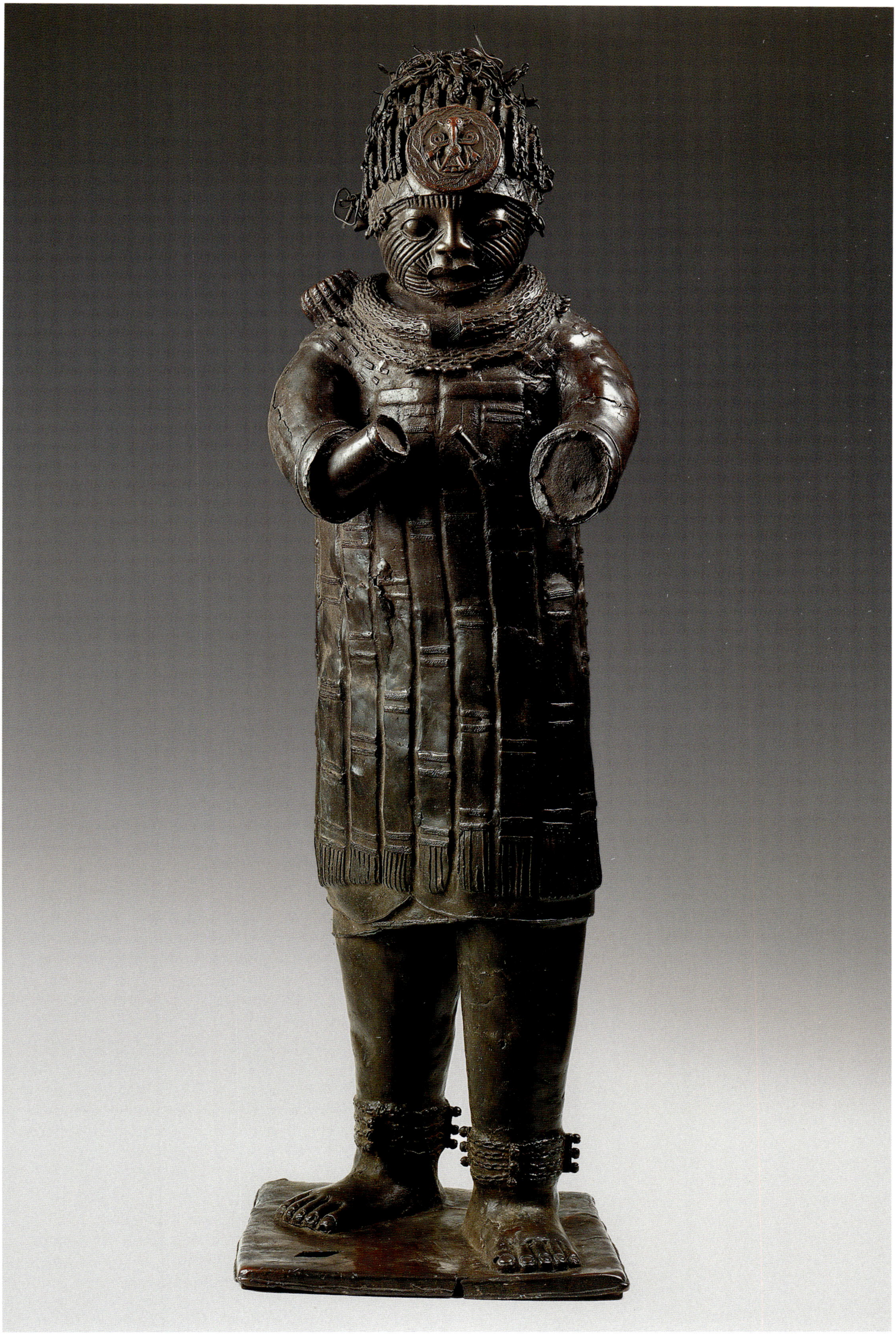

55. Artist of the Lower Niger culture
Nigeria, 15th c. (?)
Hunter with antelope
Bronze, 35.6 cm
The British Museum, Ethnography Department, London

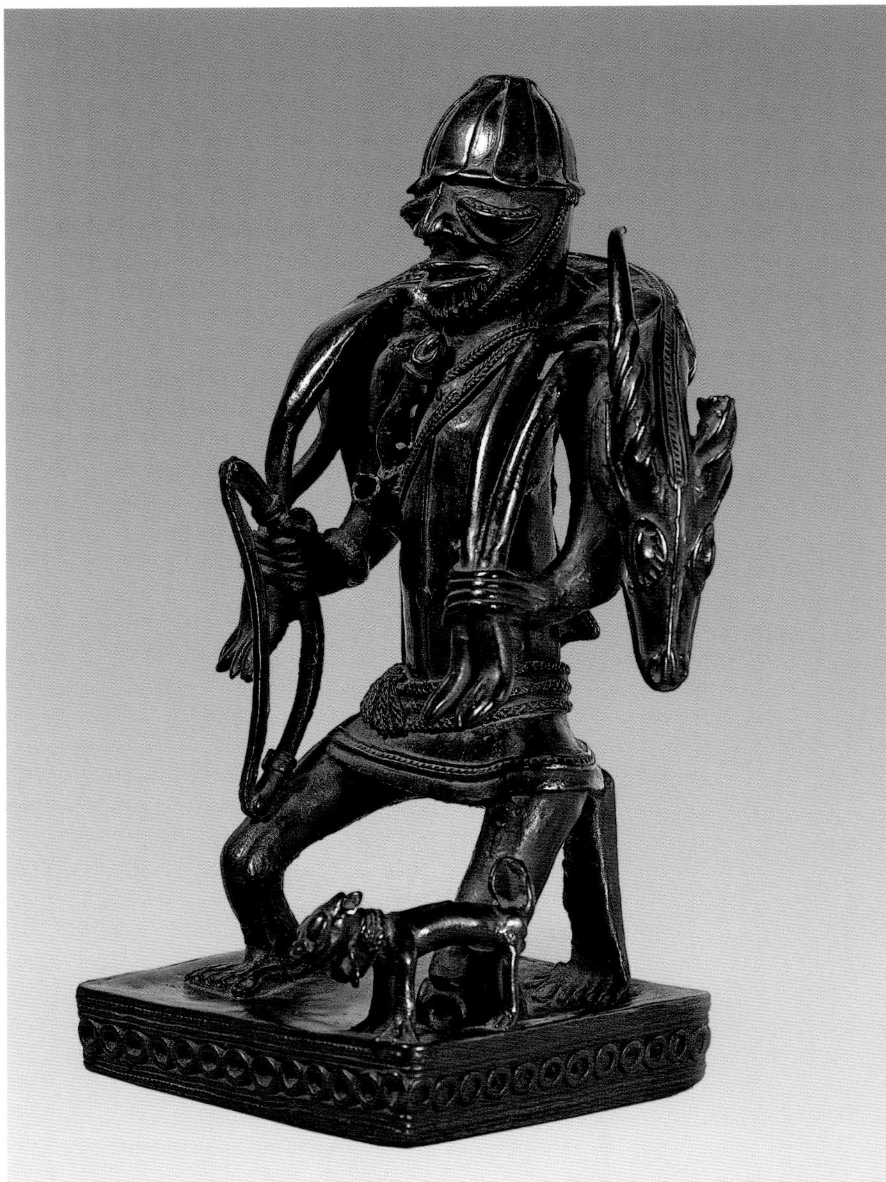

Nine of these figures (five men, one woman and three animals), all large, though differing from one another in style, were located in the village of Tada and on the island of Jebba in the Nupe region[57] until the 1970s, when they were moved to the National Commission for Museums and Monuments, Nigeria, to ensure their preservation. They were referred to collectively as the "Tsoede bronzes" after the legendary founder of the Nupe kingdom, who is supposed to have left them in the places where they were found during his escape from Idah. In actual fact, the sculptures belong to different cultures whose earlier history is unknown.

Unlike seated figure no. 35 identified by Fagg as an Ife work, the monumental figures of the archer (no. 54) and the warrior from the island of Jebba, probably produced in the late 14th or early 15th century, belong to a figurative culture that is diffiult to identify, but is in any event not Ife. Frank Willett[58] suggests the influence of Benin and Owo, but this is difficult to discern except in some details. The monstrous bird with snakes instead of wings that decorates the medallion on the archer's forehead, for example, also appears on an ivory gong from Benin.[59] The lively face of this figure, with its protruding eyes and diagonal scarification, contrasts with the immobility of the tubular body wrapped in thick fabric, whose subtle relief elements emphasize the figure's weighty immobility.

The extraordinary hunter (no. 55), one of the masterpieces of Nigerian art, was instead apparently found in Benin in 1897[60] but does not belong to that culture. The questions about its origin are still awaiting a satisfactory an-

56. Ejagham artist from the northeast, Bakor clan (village of Etinta)
Nigeria, pre-16th c.
Monolith
Stone, 174 cm
Musée du Louvre, Pavillon des Sessions, Paris

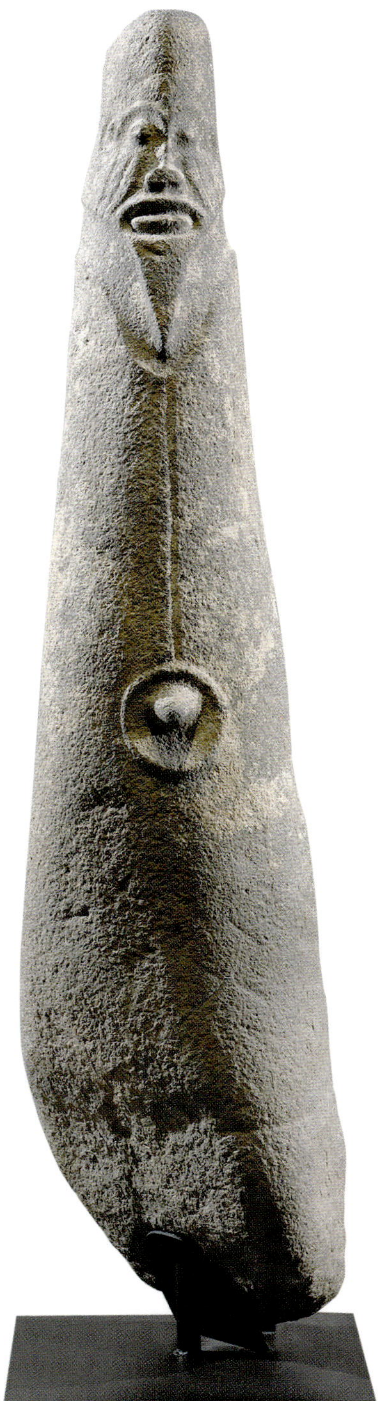

swer. It has therefore been included, temporarily I hope, in the sculptures provisionally grouped together by William Fagg as being from the Lower Niger Bronze Industry, and tentatively dated to the 15th century.

There can instead be no doubt as to the outstanding formal quality of what the eminent English scholar describes as a fundamental example of conceptual art. Using a completely free hand, the anonymous African sculptor has distorted the shape of the human body and the animal, but without destroying the harmony of the perfectly balanced composition, indeed enhancing it.

In addition to the works grouped together partly for reasons of convenience, but also because of the real or apparent links thought to exist between them, attention should be drawn to some other ancient works of sculpture identified in Nigeria, such as the Ejagham monoliths, the ornamental figures on the Mbembe drums, and the rare Mboye statues.

Ejagham Monoliths

The existence of over 300 basalt monoliths of between 90 and 180 cm in height, mostly in abandoned villages of the Cross River region on the border with Cameroon, was reported in 1968 by Philip Allison, a British official serving in Nigeria. Carbon 14 testing of items found, where the monoliths were partially buried, suggests that they were created prior to the 16th century, but their actual nature remains uncertain. While they could represent legendary figures such as warriors and hunters, they could also be emblems of secret societies.[61]

The monumental example now in the Louvre (no. 56) is distinguished by the extraordinary economy used in representing the human figure, a tendency towards concision that is not commonly found in the Ejagham sculptures of the Bakor clan. The head with its boldly sculpted, severe features is a continuation of the otherwise undifferentiated conical body, from which it is distinguished only by a carefully calibrated groove running all the way around it and causing it to stand out in all its mysterious power. A narrow incision runs from the lowest point of the groove beneath the pointed beard to the large and perfectly rounded navel, perhaps alluding to a complementary relationship between the two elements.

Mbembe

A few years before the eye-opening discovery of the monoliths, the arrival in Europe of a dozen wood sculptures brought to light another chapter of the ancient art of Nigeria,[62] namely the work of the Mbembe, a small ethnic group living on the border with Cameroon. According to the information available, ten of these formally similar human figures adorned the edges of large slit drums used to send messages that could be heard dozens of kilometres away. This ornamental function is deduced from the presence of fragments of the original drum in some cases and the fact that the figures are unusually carved against the grain of the wood, lengthwise to the instrument. The only two maternity figures in the group are carved in the normal way with the grain, and therefore constitute separate works.

The only complete drum in existence, purchased in 1908 and now in the Berlin Ethnologisches Museum,[63] is 330 cm long and thought by Kurt Krieger to be four or five centuries old. This is apparently confirmed by the results of carbon 14 dating.[64]

The figure of an executioner, now in the Horstmann collection in Zug,[65] the only sculpture in the recently discovered group to have been dated, was apparently carved in 1785±35 years. The dates of the Berlin drum and the executioner, and the similar appearance and degree of wear of all the other works in the group, bear witness to the constant creative skill of the Mbembe artists through the centuries. The additional process of natural erosion of the materials, unforeseen by their authors, gives these figures an undeniable attraction.

The figure (no. 57) now in the Pavillon des Sessions, Musée du Louvre, resembles other similar works in various private collections in its aura of solemn detachment and the hieratic gravity also found in certain figures from the Middle East and ancient Egypt. The proudly held head gazing intensely towards the horizon conveys a sense of eternity. At the same time, the vibrant grooves attenuate the rigour and endow the figure with a poignant touch of humanity.

A marked change in expressive register was necessitated by the dramatic subject of figure no. 58, a man with a severed head in his left hand. The wrestler's body, the aggressive profile of the shoulders, and the spherical head with brutish features set on the short neck, all reinforce the dramatic impression made by this disturbing work.

The concentric circles that spread out as though from an explosion shaking the lower part of the figure reveal the heart of the original tree trunk, a giant no less than two metres in diameter.

Hélène Kamer (1974) regards the statue as a portrait of Chief Appia carved seventeen years before his death in 1613.

The carving of the mother and child (no. 59) follows the grain of the wood, which is more appropriate for this domestic subject in that the grooves on the surface create a less dramatic effect. This does not mean that there is an idyllic rapport between the two figures as the mother seems to ignore the presence of the child, who has adult features, and she does not even touch him

57. Mbembe artist
Nigeria, 16th–18th c.
Seated figure
Wood, 64.5 cm
Musée du Louvre, Pavillon des Sessions, Paris

58. Mbembe artist
Nigeria, 16th–18th c.
Man holding a severed head
Wood, 89 cm
Private collection

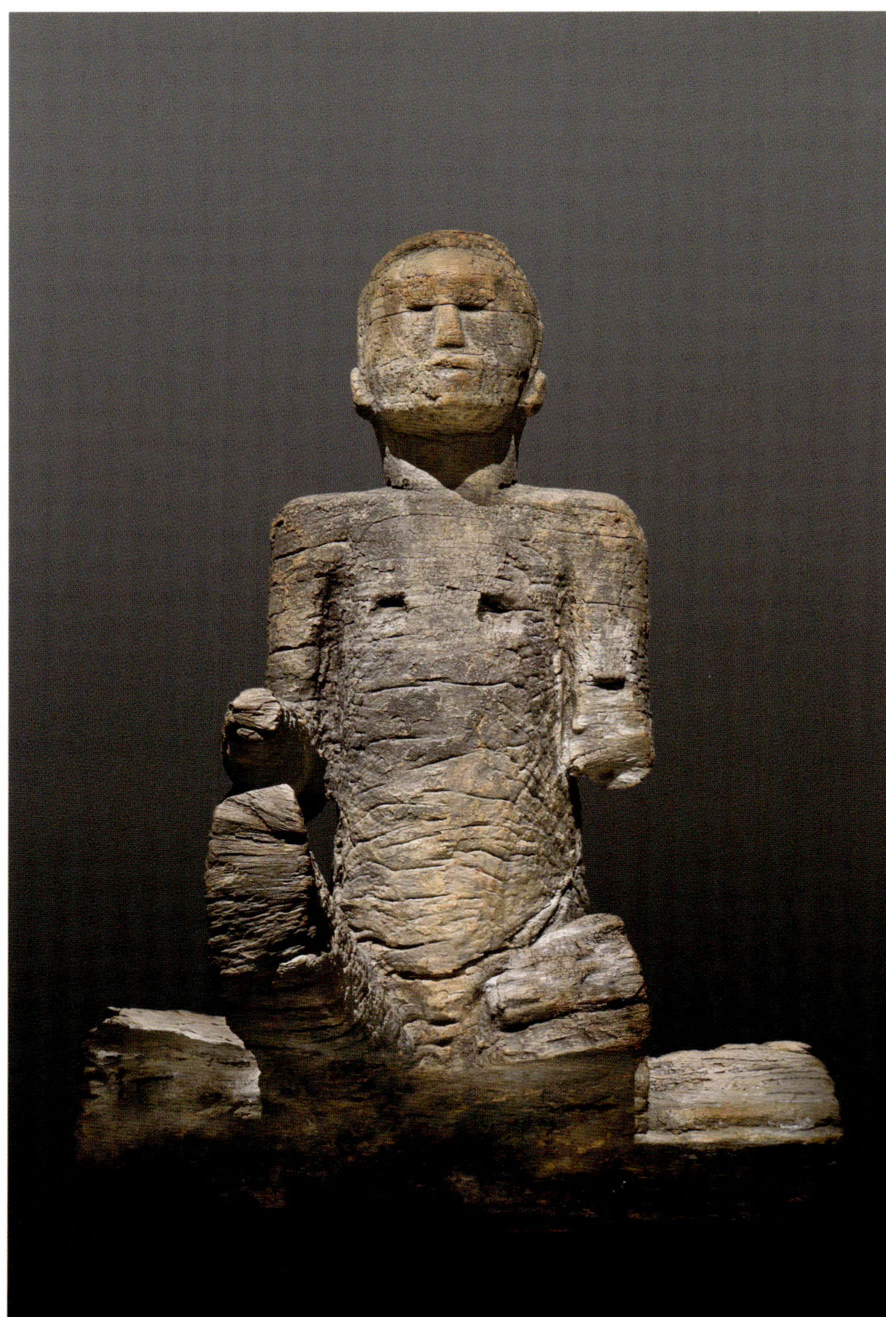

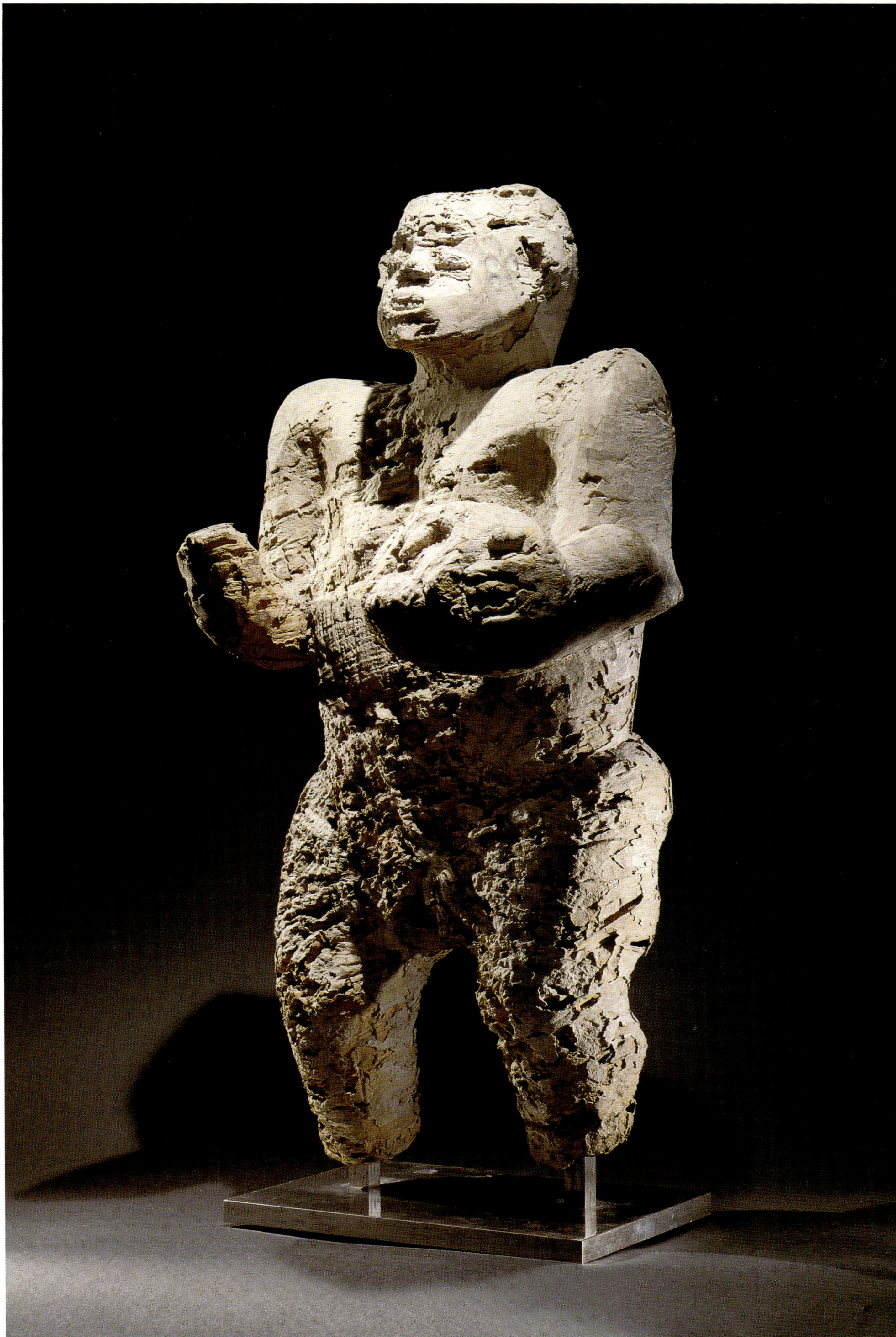

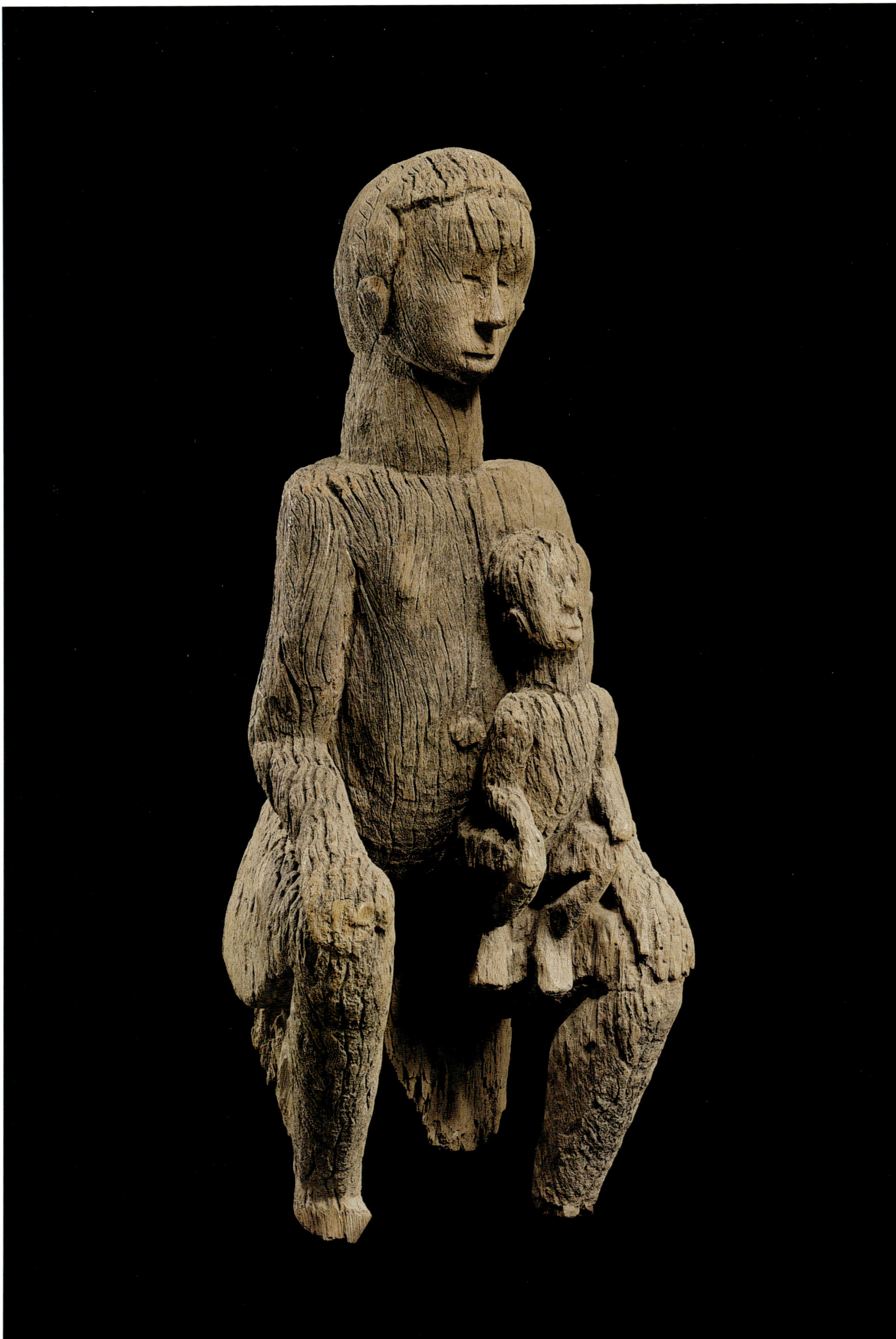

59. Mbembe artist
Nigeria, 16th–18th c.
Maternity figure
Wood, 94 cm
Private collection

with the enormous hands that rest on her knees. At the same time, the upward movement of the grooves that follow the fluid lines of the two bodies seems to generate a sense of elevation that transcends the material quality of the work, whose function and meaning are unfortunately unknown (as are those of another work on the same subject).

Mboye

Some rare large statues attributed to the Mboye, a small ethnic group in the north of Nigeria, made their appearance in the 1990s.

The presumably male figure (no. 60) dating from the 14th–15th century shown here is distinguished by the elegance of its elongated structure. The precise shaping of the body, avoiding both overemphasis and fragility, seems to have been neatly enhanced by erosion that has accentuated the flowing rhythm of its contours. The alignment of the arms with the trunk and, above all, the grooves following the grain of the wood accentuate the upward thrust.

The small oval head on the disproportionately long cylindrical neck is the focal point of the composition, whose constituent elements include the understated necklaces, the rendering of the hair and beard in attenuated relief, and the features of the serene face, which have survived the inexorable passing of centuries.

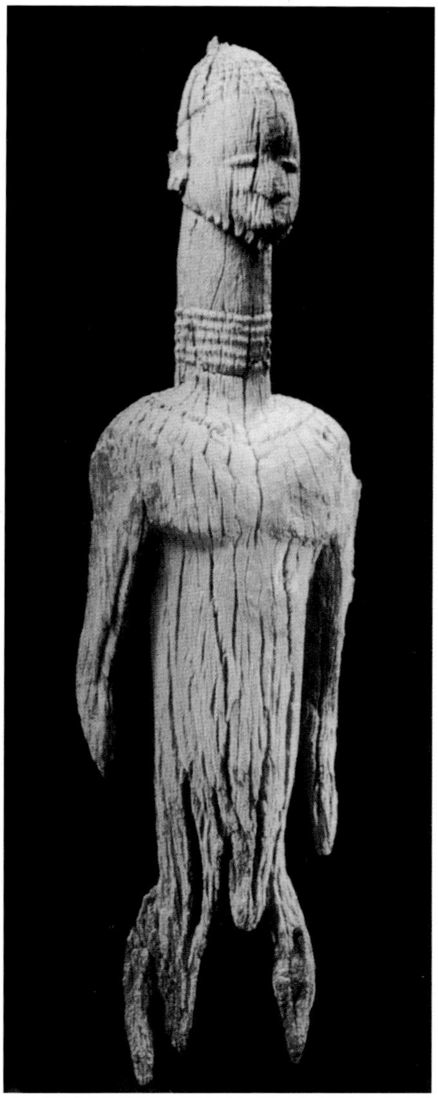

60. Mboye artist
Nigeria, 14th–15th c.
Human figure
Wood, 110 cm
Private collection

Investigation of the artistic creations of past centuries in the countries in the Niger Valley was prompted by historical, commercial and other factors, as we have seen in the cases examined above. This does not mean that great artists did not exist also in the other African countries, even if in smaller numbers than in Mali and Nigeria, but more probably that specific investigations have yet to be carried out. There is, however, increasing recognition of the importance of the problem of dating, and scientific testing and specialized studies are beginning to give some results, albeit often still isolated, also for works of art from countries other than the two mentioned above. Some examples are given below.

Sierra Leone and Liberia

Among other "curiosities", the collection of the renowned physician and scholar Eprit Calvet (1728–1810) from Avignon included a large horn (no. 61) described as a "musical instrument used in hunting in Germany, Switzerland and elsewhere around the 10th century" in the catalogue of the collection's major ancient works, probably compiled between 1796 and 1797.[66]

In actual fact, it is an extremely rare oliphant carved in Sierra Leone or Liberia, presumably in the 15th–16th century.

The pierced mouthpiece on the concave part of the horn and the absence of rings for a strap or cord provide confirmation that the piece is from Africa and intended for local use. The obvious similarities between the equestrian figure carved at the top of the instrument (no. 61a) and some steatite sculptures from the region (no. 62), known as *nomoli* and regarded by specialists as dating from the period prior to the arrival of Europeans at the end of the 15th century, provide evidence as to the place of origin and date of execution.

The valuable material, the subject of the unquestionably symbolic decoration (a man riding an unidentified animal) and the workmanship, which is less sophisticated but more expressive than that of the pieces produced for export (discussed in the next chapter), suggest that the horn was crafted for an important figure in the artist's community. This is borne out also by the absence of rings for a supporting cord.

Burkina Faso

The art of the Lobi was little known until the mid-20th century, after which a series of exhibitions and related studies began to reveal the presence of works of great quality and originality among the items of purely ethnographic interest. The question of their age was, however, not yet taken into consideration.

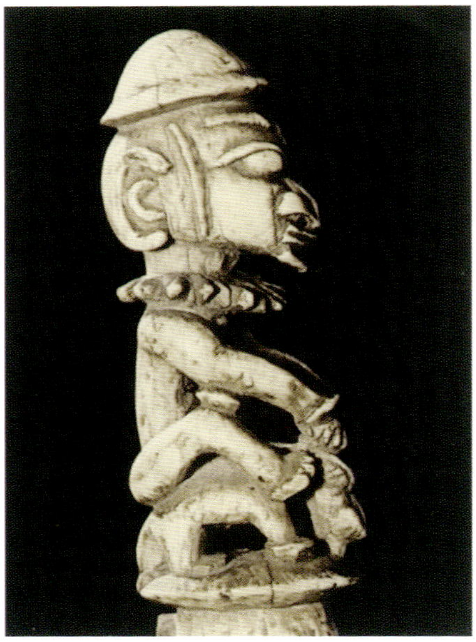

61. Sapi artist
Sierra Leone (?), 15th–16th c. (?)
Oliphant
Ivory, 79.2 cm
Musée Calvet, Avignon

61a. Detail of the oliphant no. 61

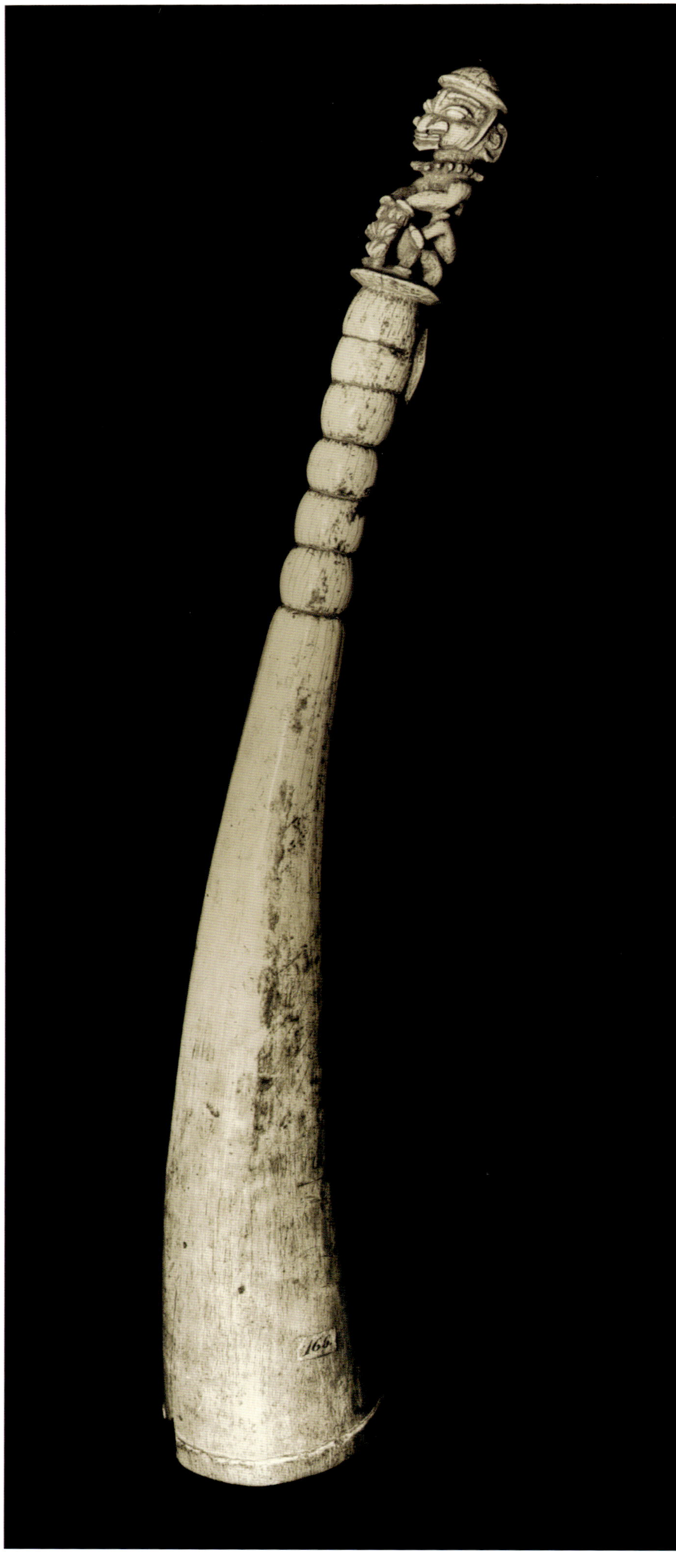

62. Sapi artist
Sierra Leone, 15th–16th c. (?)
Figure riding an elephant (*nomoli*)
Steatite, 22.5 cm
The British Museum, Ethnography Department, London

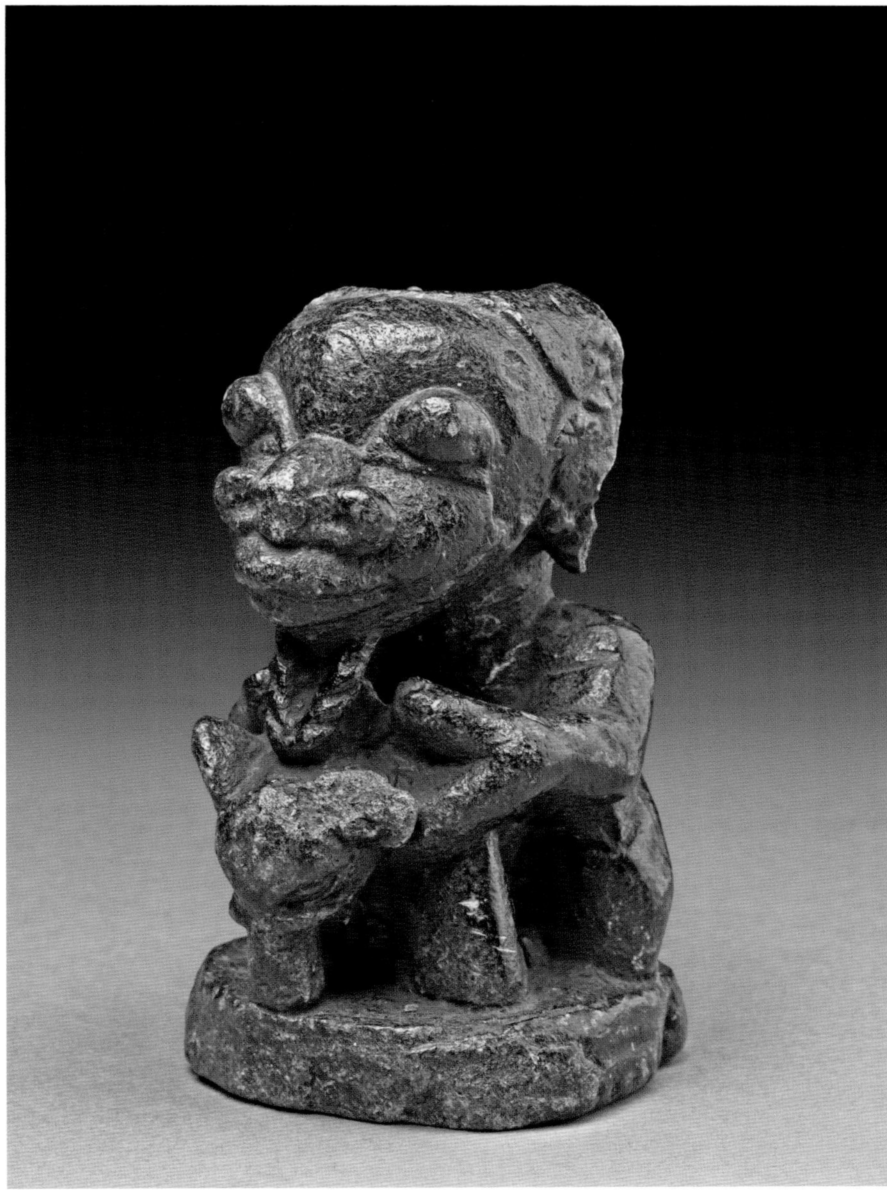

Figure no. 63, one of the first to be subjected to carbon 14 testing, has been dated to the 17th–19th centuries. The passing of time and limited erosion have dried out the slender figure, in which the original piece of wood is still perceptible, without detracting from its monumental quality. The result is an image of a young woman, tender, discreet and touching in her chaste solemnity.

Ghana

Unexpectedly early dates have also been assigned to many terracotta works created by Akan artists. Among the peoples of what is now Ghana, the ancestor cult involved the decoration of graves with commemorative sculptures, above all in the shape of a generally life-size human head. Attested as from the beginning of the 17th century by the Europeans who visited the country – Pieter De Marée (1602),[67] Willem Bosman (1705)[68] and John Barbot (1732)[69] – the practice died out in the mid-20th century.

In the work shown here (no. 64), assigned a date of 1607±40 years on the basis of thermoluminescence testing, the quite exceptional naturalism of the features is combined with precise rendering of the elaborate coiffure and the decorative elements, creating an elegant and composed whole.

Gabon

When Carl Einstein published the Fang figure no. 65 in his celebrated *Negerplastik*[70] in 1915, he was as unaware as everyone else of just how old the work was. The unexpectedly early date of 1745±40 years, assigned on the ba-

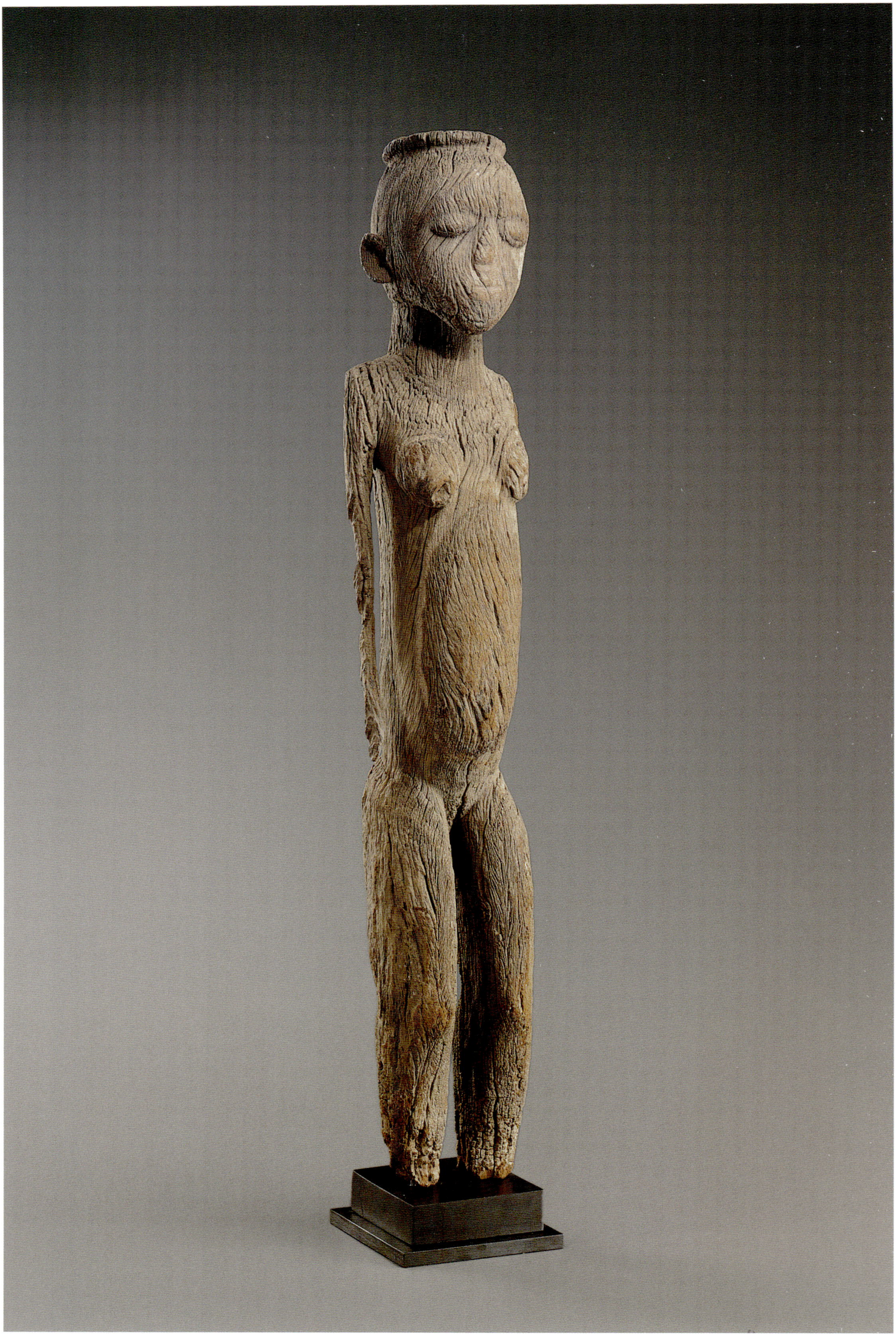

63. Lobi artist
Burkina Faso, 17th–19th c.
Female figure
Wood, 73 cm
Private collection

64. Akan artist
Ghana (Fomena-Adanse region), 17th c.
Human head
Terracotta, 27 cm
Musée Dapper, Paris

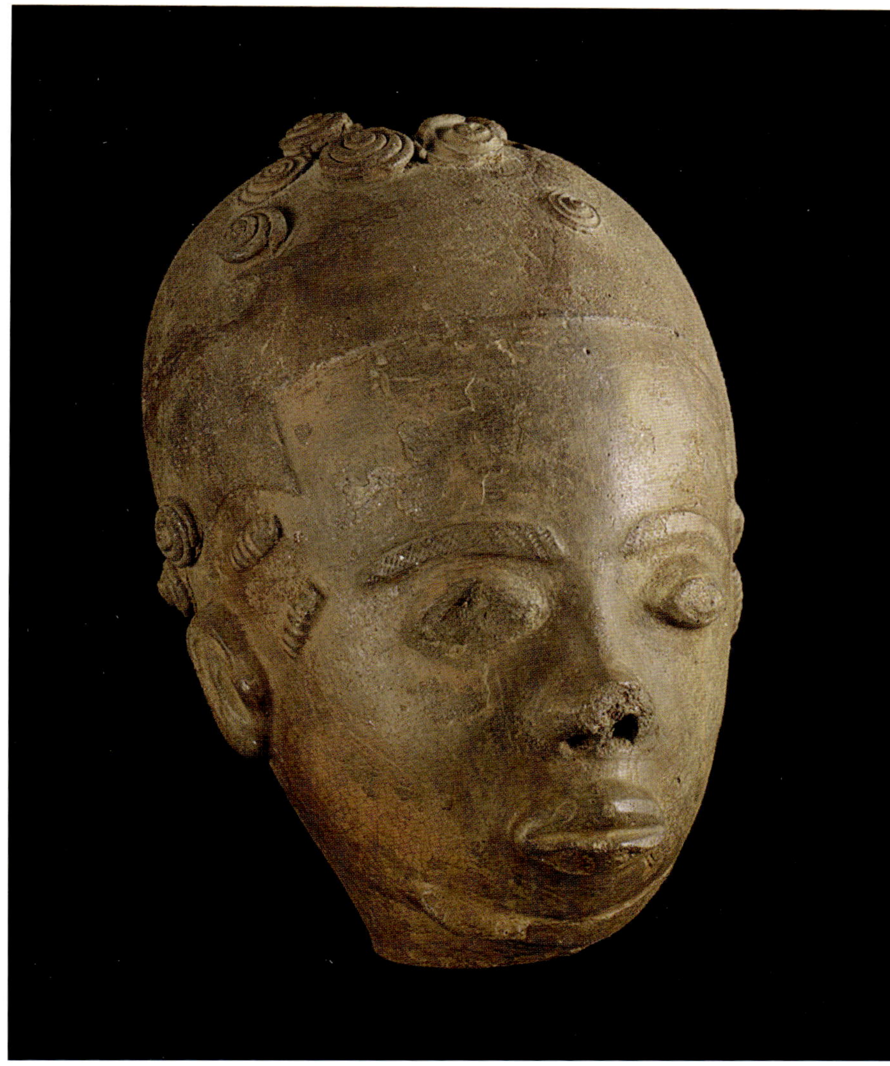

sis of carbon 14 testing a few years ago, sheds new light on the art of Gabon and calls for new studies on the many works held in museums and private collections, which are usually regarded as works from the 19th–20th century.

The inclusion of the piece in the book by the great pioneer of studies on African art constitutes unquestionable acknowledgment of its particular quality. The large trapezoid head, its severity accentuated by the whiteness of the eyes, is the apex of a symmetrical construction based on the central axis of the long, narrow torso. The view from behind reveals a harmonious assemblage of similar forms enlivened by minor asymmetries subtly exemplified by the central plait of hair that is slightly out of line with the spine. The side view, instead, reveals unexpected animation centred in the fingers, which are coiled around the remains of what may have been a musical instrument.

According to the information obtained *in situ*, the Fang people of Gabon and Cameroon used to place heads or simple figures like this one on the baskets used to contain the bones of important ancestors.

The ancient kingdoms of Congo and Angola

The ancient kingdom of Congo was one of the African territories with which both the Portuguese and the Vatican maintained close relations from the earliest explorations onwards. It is surprising that the collections in Portugal and other European countries should hold so few examples of the ancient art of this region, except for the valuable oliphants described below. It must be remembered, however, that the so-called "idols" and "fetishes" carved in wood were regarded by missionaries as products of the superstition of uncivilized peoples or, even worse, as demonic works to be destroyed in purifying bonfires.

A number of "idols" were brought to Rome in 1692 by the Capuchin missionary Andrea da Pavia, "wrested by brute force, and also at the risk of life,

65. Fang artist
Gabon or Cameroon, 17th c.
Reliquary figure
Wood, metal, pearls, teeth, 58 cm
Horstmann Collection, Zug

66. Congo artist
Democratic Republic of the Congo,
1470–1630
Human bust
Wood, 60 cm
Musée Dapper, Paris

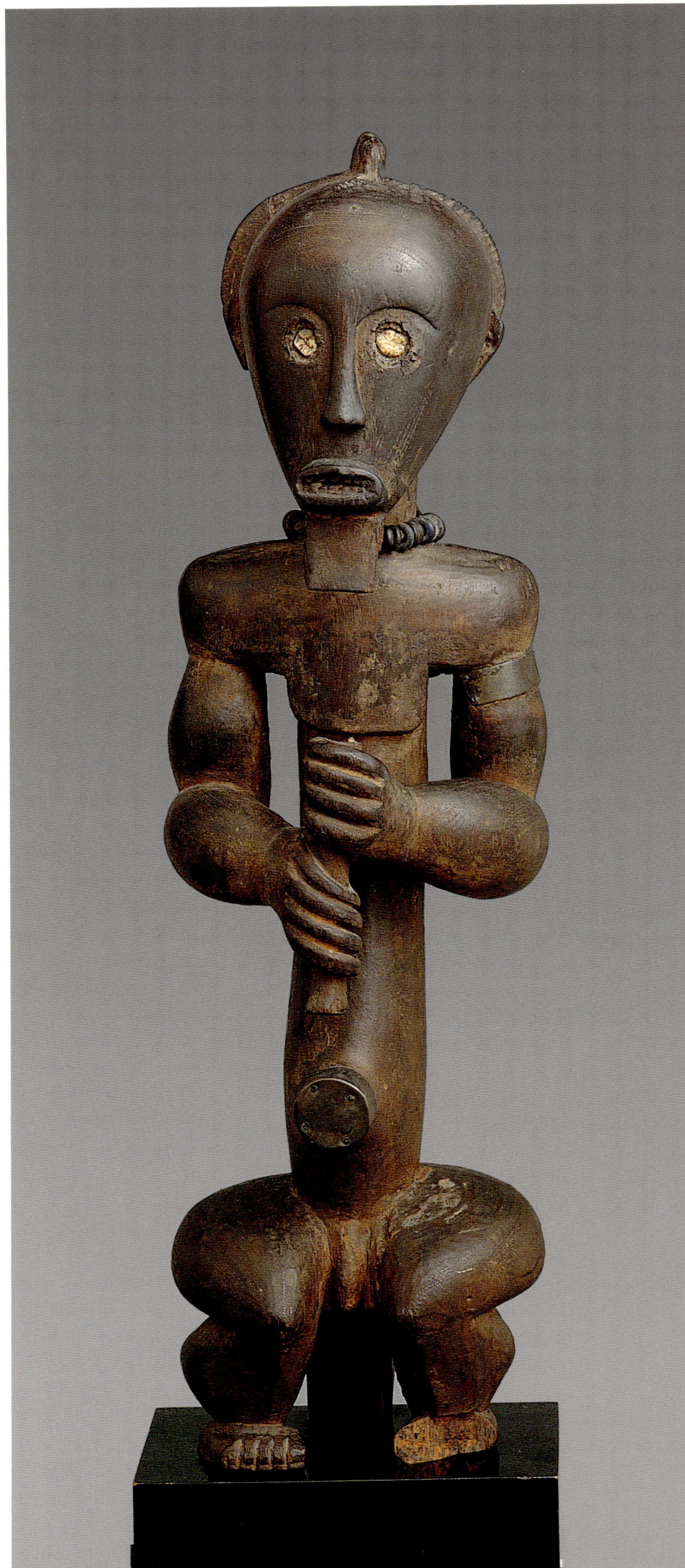

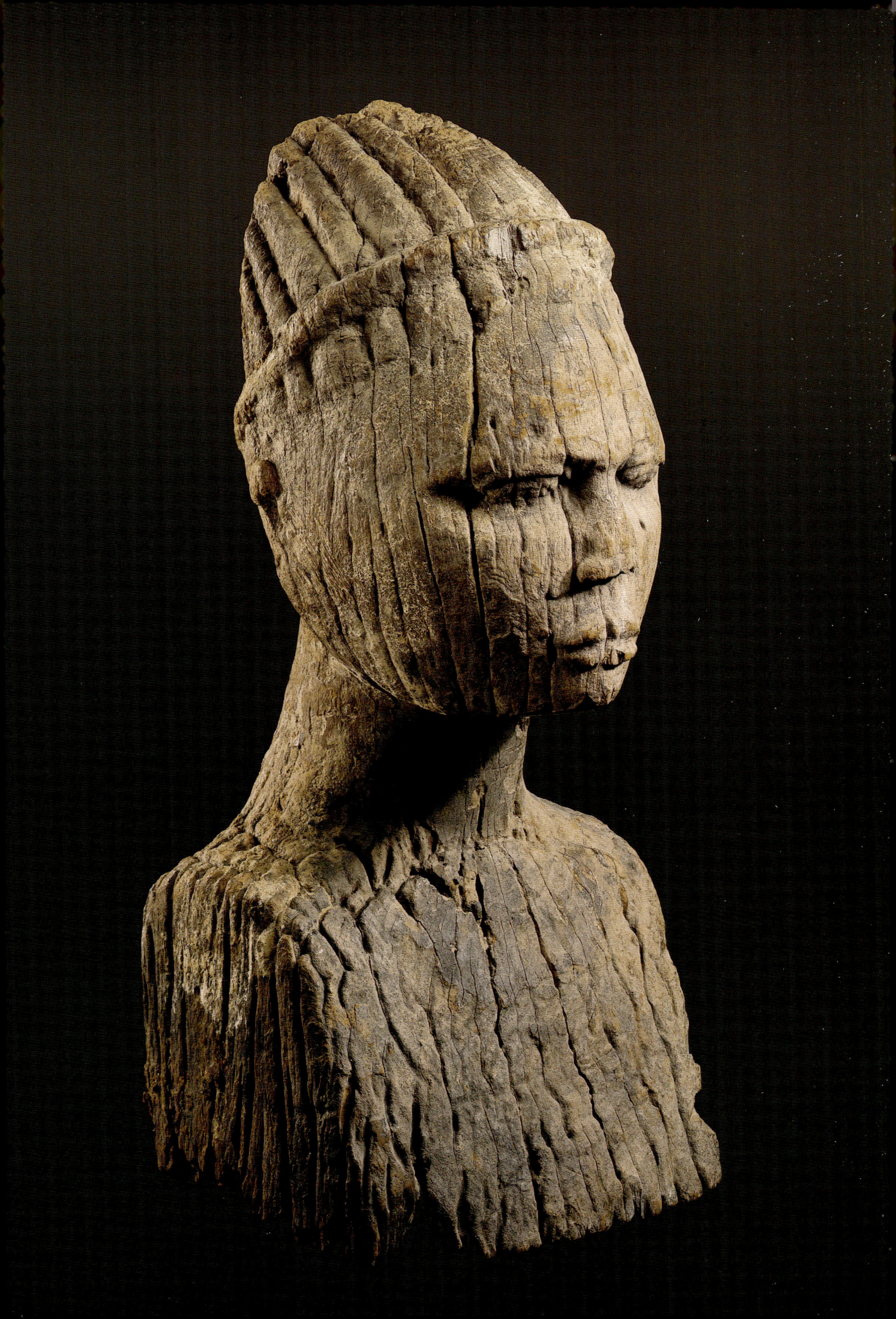

from the peoples of Sogno" (the Sogno or Soyo region in what is now Angola) as proof of the superstitious practices of the natives, as he wrote in his diary. Unfortunately, all trace has been lost of those valuable items, which were "confiscated" by the authorities in charge of missionary work.[71]

Other works spared from destruction by fire, the elements and termites have certainly remained in Africa or were imported to Europe in the 19th and 20th centuries without knowing their actual age.

The latter include a remarkable serene human bust (no. 66) now in the Musée Dapper, Paris, which can hardly be described as demonic[72] even though its function is unknown. According to the results of carbon 14 dating, it was carved between 1470 and 1630, and hence perhaps even before Diego Cao arrived in the kingdom of Manicongo in 1482.

An ineffable serenity is conveyed by the face of the figure, which has the solemnity of a herm enlivened by the cracks in the wood. The forms are simple and unadorned: a rectangular block for the base, a cylinder for the neck and a perfect oval for the head, animated by the carved relief of what may be a hat and the delicate features of the young man's face.

While we have no precise information as to the exact region in Angola that produced the two female statuettes (nos. 67–68) now in the Museo Nazionale Preistorico Etnografico "L. Pigorini" in Rome (inv. 4525 and 4526), it is known with almost absolute certainty that they arrived in Portugal between 1692 and 1697 with Francesco da Collevecchio, a Capuchin missionary in the ancient kingdom of Congo and Angola. He then delivered or donated them to Monsignor Giorgio Cornaro (1658–1722), Apostolic Nuncio to the Portuguese court at the time, who took them to Italy.[73]

Each of the statuettes is described in the inscription in Italian on the front of its base as an idol from "China", one supposedly named Mocorri (no. 4525) and the other Bamba Engo (no. 4526).

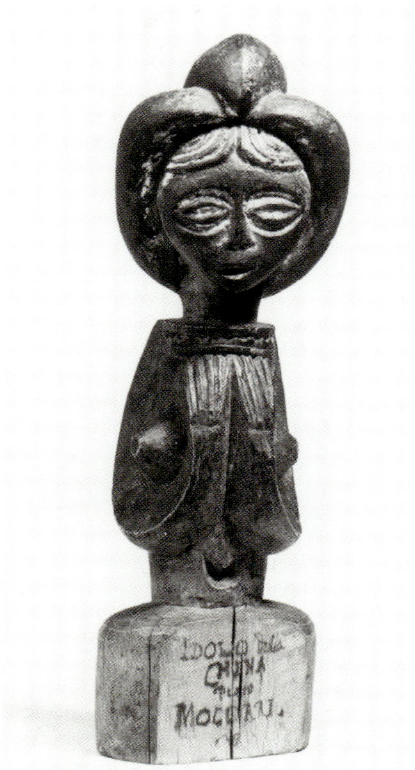

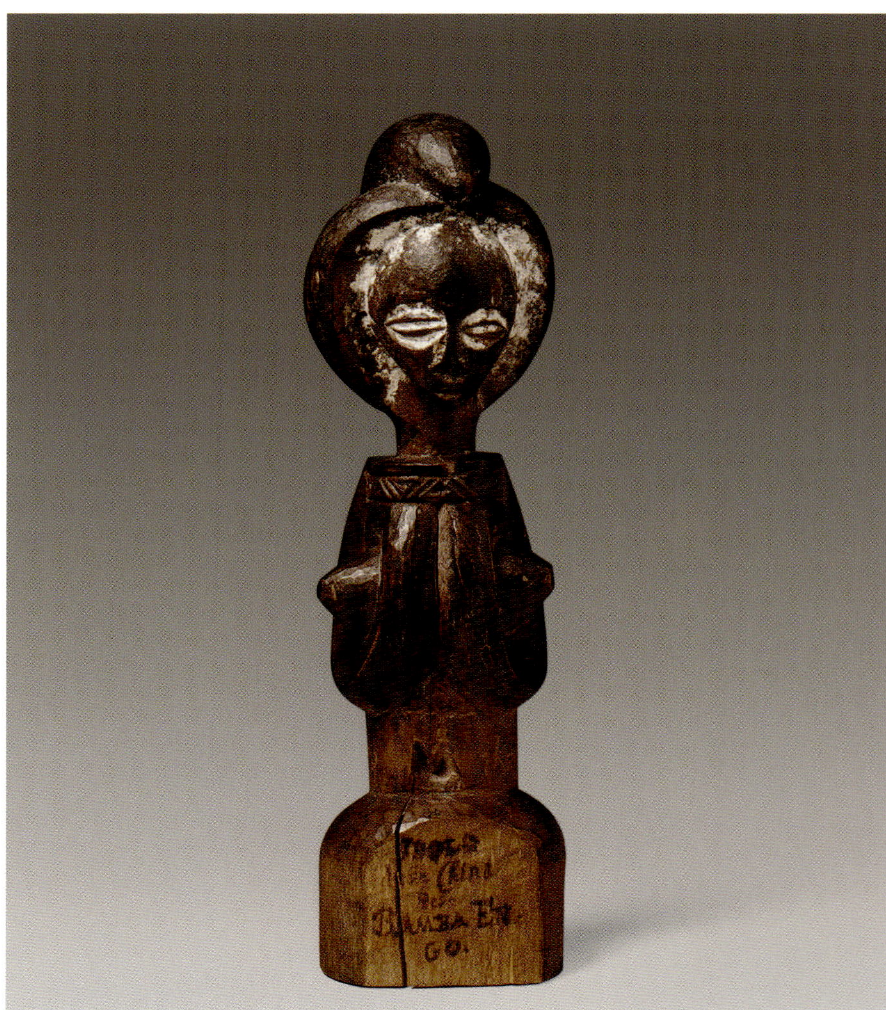

67. Congolese-Angolan artist
active before 1692
Female bust
Wood, 24.8 cm
Museo Nazionale Preistorico
Etnografico "L. Pigorini", Rome

68. Congolese-Angolan artist
active before 1692
Female bust
Wood, 22.2 cm
Museo Nazionale Preistorico
Etnografico "L. Pigorini", Rome

According to the study carried out by the late, lamented Professor François Bontinck with his customary thoroughness in 1979, "China" was simply the Italian spelling of "Kina", the name of a region in Angola that recurs in maps and treatises of the 17th and 18th centuries, while "Mocorri" and "Bamba Engo" were also the names of a region situated between the Kwilu and Kwango rivers. These two terms, which refer to both of the figures, were probably separated by the author of the inscriptions due to ignorance of their significance.

The iconography of the two works, in which I detect the coexistence of elements of Chokwe, Ovimbundu, Hungana and Suku sculpture, sheds no light on their origin. While the shape of the head, the three-part coiffure and the features bear similarities to the former, the bold approach adopted for the torso is closer to the latter.[74]

The two figures have also been examined repeatedly by Marie-Louise Bastin,[75] who was forced after a series of acute observations to admit defeat and acknowledge the impossibility of a definitive solution to the problem. In view of the migrations that took place over the centuries, this appears to be the only possible conclusion for now.

In their book on the art of the Punu people, Louis Perrois and Charlotte Grand-Dufay recently suggested that the larger of the two statues could be a "fairy" or genie, possibly a siren, and that Punu workmanship was identifiable in the head with its coiffure of large plaits.[76]

I find it hard to see the sculpture in question as a siren and regard the hypothesis authoritatively put forward by François Bontinck – namely that the works were obtained by the Capuchin missionary Francesco da Collevecchio[77] [s]in a region on the border between the ancient kingdom of Congo and Angola – as still the most plausible. This would rule out any attribution to the Punu.

There can instead be no doubt as to the creative skill of the artist who produced the two works, as unmistakably demonstrated by the balance between the imposing head and the torso when viewed from all sides and the perfect blending of stylistic elements to form a harmonious whole.

Madagascar

The age of the celebrated Sakalawa cenotaph from Madagascar (no. 69), purchased in 1901 by the ethnologist Guillaume Grandidier, was unknown until its transfer from the Musée de l'Homme to its present home in the Louvre, when carbon 14 testing revealed that it was carved in the 17th–18th century. This was quite unexpected, as the numerous specimens that have arrived in the West during the last few decades are normally regarded as dating from the 19th century if not later.

Consisting solely of the two figures and their base (with no supporting column) and previously in the renowned collections of the art dealer Joseph Brummer, the sculptor Jacob Epstein and Carlo Monzino, sculpture no. 70 is almost certainly the work of the same artist and was therefore carved in the same period. It is the only one of the sculptures in *Negerplastik* to appear in five illustrations. According to Susan Vogel, the two works may have originally stood in symmetrical positions on the same grave.

In both works, the figures of a man and a woman with a tall pot on her head, their bodies leaning slightly forward, emerge side by side from a trapezoid base into which their feet disappear. The frontal pose highlights their innocent nudity, like that of an ancestral Adam and Eve before the Fall.

The compact yet fluid volumes of their bodies, uninterrupted by the slender arms in low relief that are almost one with the torso, are like sturdy pillars supporting large spherical heads with severe features, gazing straight ahead. The deep sockets now visible due to the loss of the eyes they once held increase the sense of timelessness conveyed by the two extremely grave figures, whose only "decorative" element is the sober and orderly coiffure in relief. In the less static view from behind, the rounded buttocks contrast with the flat back.

The crocodile devouring a small animal carved on the column supporting the figures of the work in Paris (no. 69a) is an Indonesian motif attesting to the Afro-Indonesian origins of the island's population.

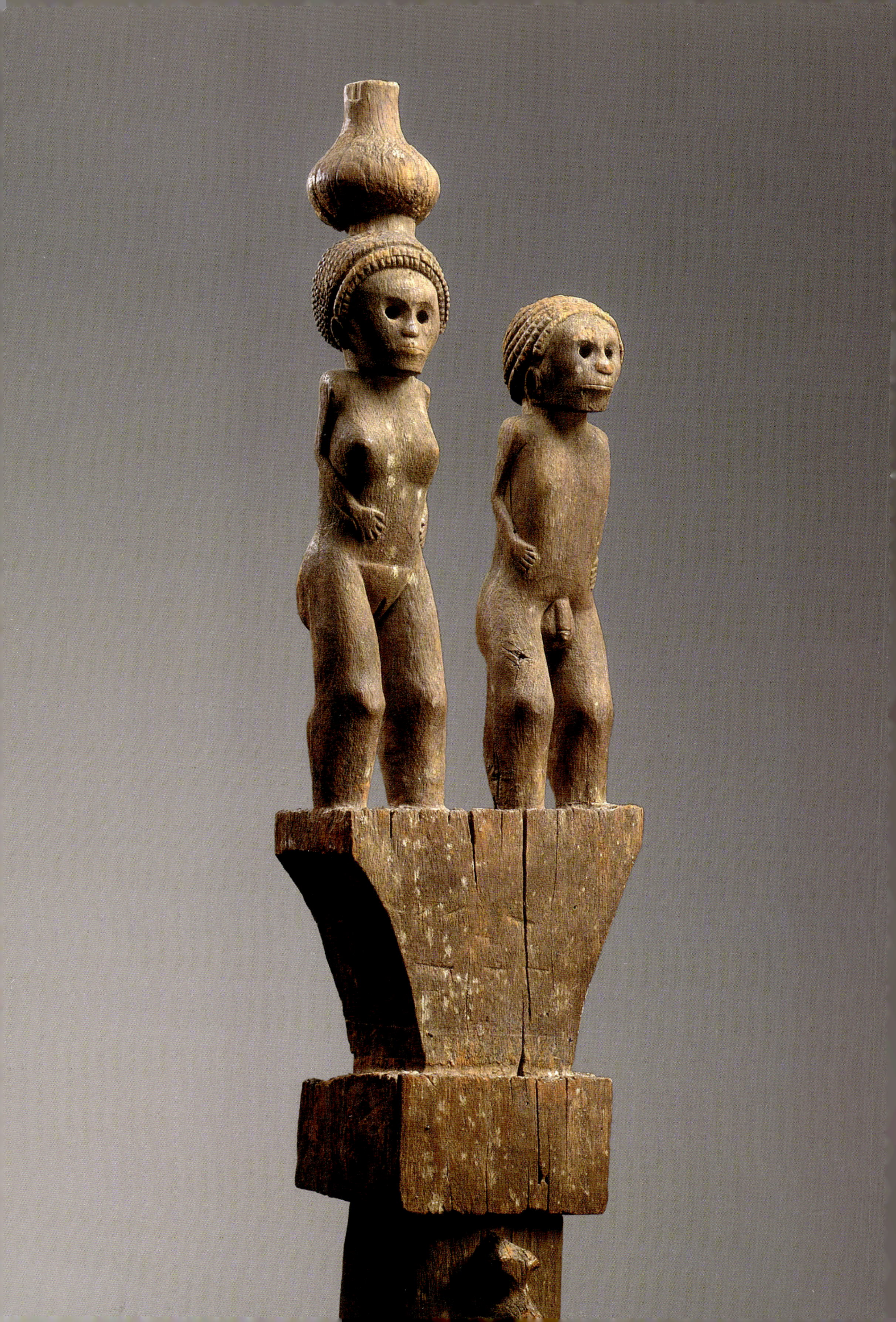

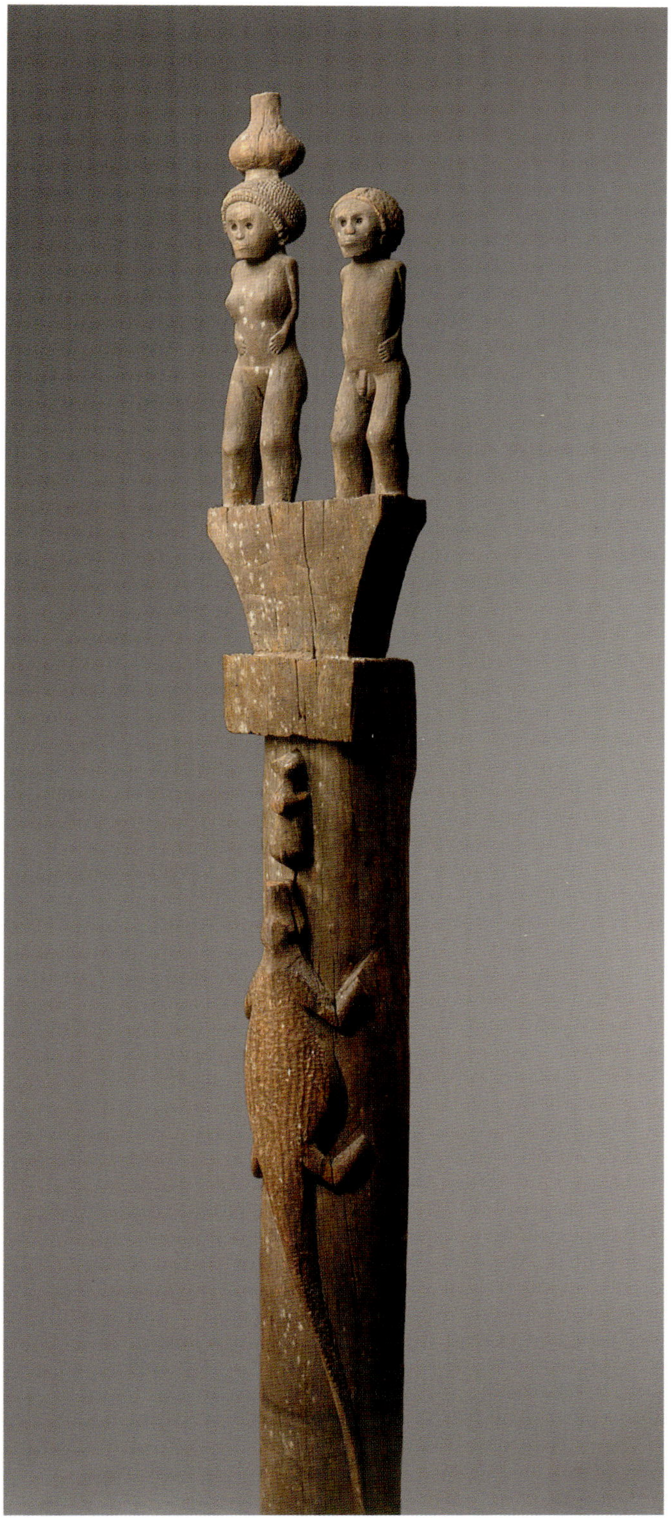

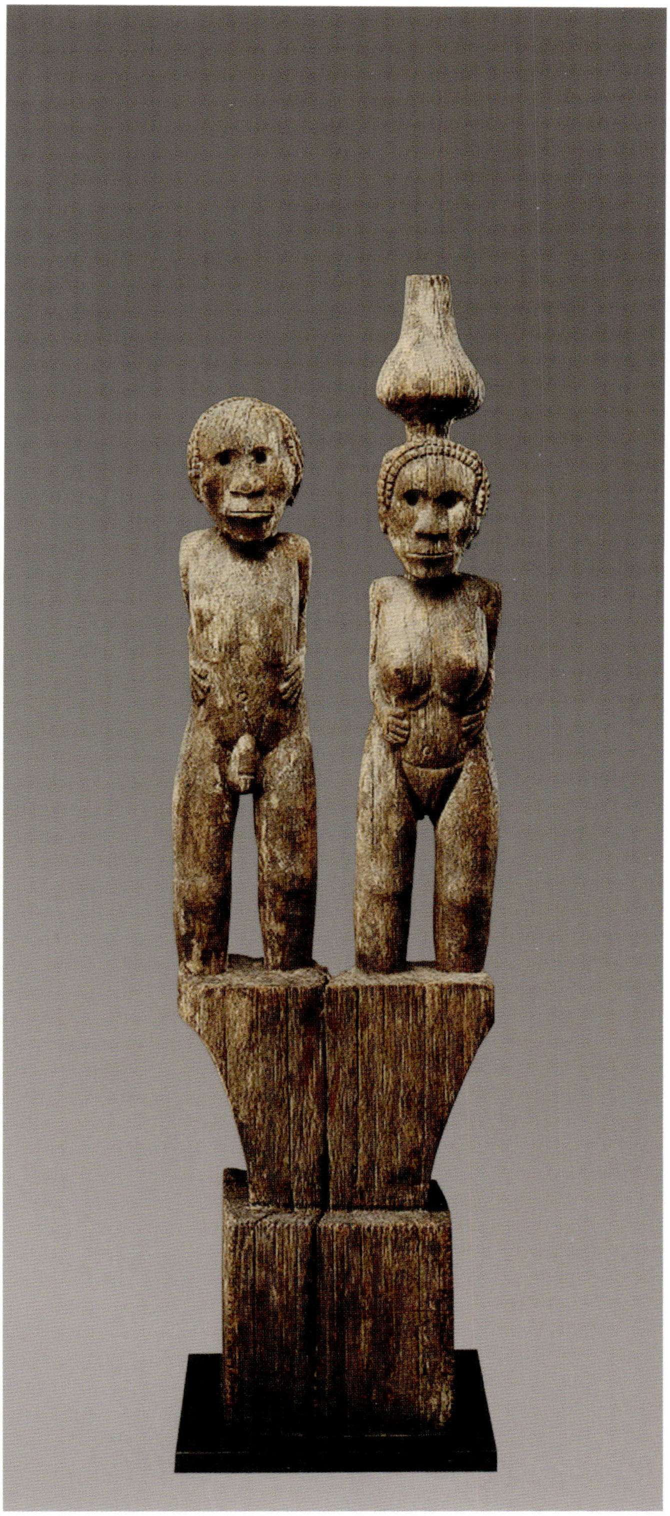

69–69a. Sakalawa artist
Madagascar, 17th–late 18th c.
Burial monument (detail of upper section and overall view)
Wood, 215 cm
Musée du Louvre, Pavillon des Sessions, Paris (on deposit from the Musée du Quai Branly)

70. Sakalawa artist
Madagascar, 17th–late 18th c.
Burial monument (upper section; supporting column lost)
Wood, 51 cm
Private collection (formerly in the Brummer, Epstein and Monzino collections)

[1] Olbrecht's study was published in Flemish in 1941 and in English, with a new title, in 1943. See the bibliography.
[2] The caves in the escarpment had been used by the Toloy, who inhabited the area before the Tellem, to house large storage containers for grain.
[3] *Dogon* 1994, p. 16.
[4] See Leloup 1994, no. 1; 2011, no. 1.
[5] Bouloré in *Sculptures* 2000, p. 93.
[6] Eight of these sculptures (nos. 3, 34–39 and 42) are not illustrated.
[7] Michel Leiris accompanied Griaule on the celebrated mission of 1931.
[8] In contrast, providing its attribution to the Tellem is confirmed, with its massive corporeity the sculpture exhibited in the Louvre (inv. 70,1999.7.1) would represent a comparatively important variant in the statuary of this people.
[9] The most valuable source is, however, his minutely detailed journal, full of drawings, now held by the Société des Africanistes in Paris.
[10] "*Une collection d'objets ethographiques n'est ni une collection de curiosités, ni un collection d'oeuvres d'art. L'objet n'est pas autre chose qu'un témoin, qui doit être envisagé en fonction des renseignements qu'il apporte sur une civilisation donnée, et non d'après sa valeur esthétique*" (*Instructions sommaires* 1931, p. 8).
[11] Griaule 1948. Translated into English as *Conversations with Ogotemmeli: An Introduction to Dogon Religious Ideas* (1965).
[12] "*nous avons une statue de 1 m 30, d'un style jusqu'alors inconnu et antérieure sans doute à la venue des Dogon*" (Rivière 1929 [ed. 1991, p. 589]).
[13] "*le corps très allongé et incurvé, les bras collés au corps, hermaphrodite; la tête dégage une émotion profonde qui fait de cette pièce un chef-d'œuvre, au sens véritable du mot*" (*ibid.*).
[14] "*j'avais la gorge serrée, envie de pleurer*" (N'Diaye 1995, p. 29).
[15] See Leloup 1994, no. 31. The author attributes the work to the Niongom culture.
[16] Vogel 1985, no. 1.
[17] *Dogon* 1994, p. 48.
[18] Leloup 2011, no. 40.
[19] *Ibid.*
[20] Leloup 1994, p. 16, n. 213.
[21] Ezra 1988, p. 43.
[22] "*un homme et sa sœur jouant d'un instrument* [...] *qui ne serait utilisé qu'au cours des rites funéraires des Hogons*" (Paudrat 1994, p. 80 and note 98).
[23] This correct name has now replaced the previous pejorative term *Bambara* used for non-Muslims.
[24] Ezra 1986, note 50. Works 31 and 32 are those shown in Goldwater (1960) as 98 and 99. Ezra's *Bamana: The Art of Existence in Mali* (2001, no. 125) also includes an illustration of a seated mother holding a tiny child from an American private collection. The date of 1432–1644 assigned to this piece is comparatively in line with the dating of the examples mentioned above.
[25] Leloup 2000: nos. 30 and 31, dated; nos. 32 and 36, undated.
[26] ETH Zurich, no. 21742 and ASA no. 11-24-36.
[27] ETH no. 26877.
[28] "*le bras gauche manquant devait soutenir un coussinet sur lequel était posé un mortier*" (Leloup 2000, n. 31).
[29] One of a group of four horsemen and one archer on foot with similar characteristics. See Grunne 1980, nos. 1.10–1.14.
[30] See note 46.
[31] From 500 BC to 200 AD according to Omotoso Eluyemi, the director of Nigerian museums (2003, p. 43; 2005, p. 43). The dates obtained by means of thermoluminescence testing must be treated with caution.
[32] Many of the works put on the market are fakes.
[33] "An area encompassing the middle valley of the Niger and the lower valley of the Benue", Ekpo 2005, p. 48.
[34] Boullier 2000, p. 123.
[35] F. Willett, in Eyo, Willett 1980, p. 30.
[36] Frobenius 1912–13, I, pp. 88–89. The work remains important despite the errors it contains. As noted by Stefan Eisenhofer (2003, pp. 46–48), it is also true that the idealized naturalism of Ife artwork is closer to the Western and Asian figurative traditions than the African.
[37] "The evidence that pointed to an African origin was scarcely considered." Willett 2003, also available on CD-ROM.
[38] *Ibid.*
[39] Eyo, Willett 1980, no. 49.
[40] Drewal, Schildkrout 2009, n. 39.
[41] Fagg 1963, no. 4.
[42] *Dinastía y Divinidad* 2009, p. 359.
[43] In the case of comparatively light works (up to 5–6 kg), successful casting was probably achieved by shaping the crucible to allow as little air as possible to enter during the transfer of the molten metal to the cast. The possible blow-holes or blisters found in some works were repaired by overcasting. The molten metal would have been poured from a number of crucibles to cast the large Tada figure. See Willett 2003, ch. 4, pp. 23–24. Drewal and Schildkrout (2009, p. 39) make the hypothesis that the work was made in several parts that have been joined together.
[44] Dapper never actually visited Africa and based his work on the accounts of various travellers (see *Olfert Dapper's* 1998, passim).
[45] The immediate cause of the destruction of the city and occupation of the region was the fact that the English acting consul-general James Phillips chose to proceed to Benin in order to persuade the Oba to respect the disputed terms of the commercial treaty signed with Britain in 1892 despite the latter's request not to approach. The ambush was set without the sovereign's knowledge and Phillips was killed together with his military escort. The crucial factor was economic, in that the British wanted no competition for trade with the region.
[46] The works of art were sold off by the Admiralty and the members of the expedition or their heirs at a later stage, and most of them were bought by major museums, above all in London, Berlin and Vienna.
[47] Igbafe, in *Benin* 2007, p. 41.
[48] Fagg 1963, pp. 30–39. Stefan Eisenhofen (2003, pp. 65–69) has cast doubt over the hypotheses put forward by prior historiography.
[49] Fagg 1963, p. 25.
[50] The fanciful illustration accompanying the description shows the royal procession, including the dwarves, leopards and horn players mentioned below, set against the background of a northern European city with towers surmounted by birds with outspread wings, to which the procession was added.
[51] The eight keloids on the forehead and marked "cat's whisker" scarification on the three heads would appear to support the latter hypothesis (see *Benin* 2007, no. 245).
[52] Plankensteiner, in *Benin* 2007, p. 144 (published in English and French).
[53] The two masks were allotted to Sir Ralph Moor, the civilian leader of the expedition, and later sold by his heirs. A third mask is in the collection of the

heirs of Sir Henry Lionel Gallwey, a member of the "Punitive Expedition", and the other two are respectively in the Linden Museum, Stuttgart, and the Seattle Art Museum.

[54] "*Elles sont soutenues par des piliers de bois enchassez dans du cuivre, où leur victoires sont gravées*" (taken from the French edition of the book, Dapper 1686, p. 308).

[55] Oba around the period 1481–1504 according to B. Blackmun. See *Benin* 2007, no. 320.

[56] Fagg 1963, p. 39.

[57] The female figure was stolen in the 1970s.

[58] Willett in Eyo, Willett 1980 and 1984, no. 94.

[59] Fagg 1963, no. 38a.

[60] Fagg 1963, no. 58.

[61] Eyo 1995, pp. 374–375; 2000, pp. 139–140. The existence of some specimens was first reported by Charles Partridge in 1905.

[62] See Kamer 1974.

[63] Ethnologisches Museum, Staatliche Museen zu Berlin, inv. IIIC 21947.

[64] Krieger 1969, II, no. 236. See also Nicklin, in *Africa* 1999, no. 63.

[65] Bassani 2007, no. 8.

[66] "*Instrument de musique pour la chasse, utilisé en Allemagne, en Suisse et ailleurs vers le Xe siècle*" (M.P. Foissy-Aufrère, personal communication).

[67] De Marees (1602) 1905, pp. 346–347.

[68] Bosman 1705 (reprinted in 1907), p. 252.

[69] Barbot 1732, p. 285 (see *Barbot on Guinea* 1992, p. 595).

[70] The first book systematically devoted to African art.

[71] Congregazione de Propaganda Fide (see Bassani 2000, pp. 160–161).

[72] Inv. 5250. Published in Lehuard 1989, vol. I, p. 244.

[73] An inscription on the rear of the base of figure no. 67 informs us: "*Portato da Portogallo dal Sig. Cardinal Cornaro Vescovo di Padova*" (Brought back from Portugal by Sig. Cardinal Cornaro, bishop of Padua). Lisbon was the port of departure and return for the missionaries sent to the African regions then under Portuguese influence. Giorgio Cornaro, appointed cardinal and bishop of Padua, formed close connections with that city's intellectual elite and appears to have given the two sculptures to Antonio Vallisneri or Vallisnieri, one of its members. They were then transferred in 1877 to the ethnographic museum in Rome (now the Museo Nazionale Preistorico Etnografico "L. Pigorini"), where they were inventoried as Chinese sculptures (an error not rectified until 1914) with the numbers 4525 and 4526. The word "China" in the inscriptions presumably gave rise to the confusion about their country of origin.

[74] Bassani 1978[a].

[75] Bastin 1994, p. 17.

[76] "*La plus grande de deux statue représenterait une 'fée', c'est-à-dire un génie, qui pourrait être une sirène (?) dont le visage est d'une facture punu parfaitement identifiable avec une coiffe à grosses tresses*" (Perrois, Grand-Dufay 2008, pp. 66–68).

[77] Bontinck 1979.

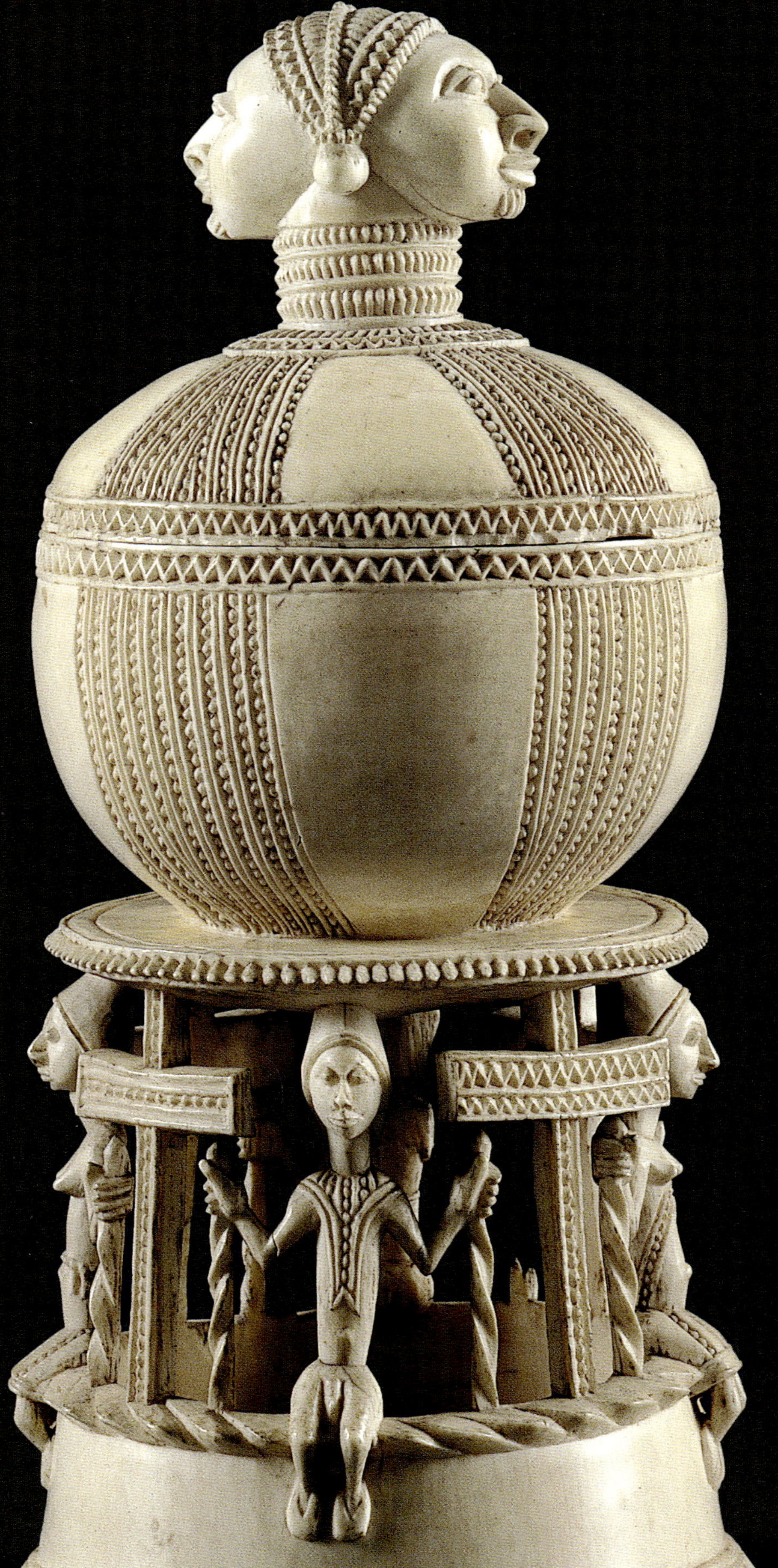

Commissioned Art: Afro-Portuguese Ivories

European attempts to gain overland access to the riches of Africa, especially the gold that gave rise to fabulous tales in the early centuries of the second millennium AD, did not meet with the hoped-for success, not least because the way was blocked by permanent Arab settlement in the Sub-Saharan regions.

Portuguese caravels started their voyages south in the mid-15th century, establishing stopping points on the coasts of present-day Sierra Leone, Nigeria and Congo, before pushing on to round the Cape of Good Hope in 1498, and thus open up the route to the East. The Portuguese sailors had products for trading, the primary objective of their travels, but they also brought examples of the material culture of the peoples they encountered and works of art back to Europe. Most of the items that have survived were produced specifically for export before the mid-16th century and commissioned by Europeans, as is evident from the subject matter of their decoration, the polished workmanship, and the addition of functional elements, such as rings for attaching straps to oliphants.

These Afro-Portuguese ivories, as they are known, are the result of interaction between the iconographic and stylistic elements of two different cultures and can therefore be described as hybrids. The term has no negative connotations, however, as the fact of being produced for Europe entailed no decline in quality. The Portuguese commissioned works in ivory from African artists both because of the abundance of that valuable material on the continent and because of the artists' recognized skills.

At the beginning of the 20th century, the German scholar Wilhelm Foy[1] suggested that the Afro-Portuguese ivories might have been made by African artists working in Portugal, primarily because of the absence of error in the reproduction of European motifs. This is refuted by the records of the treasurer of the Casa da Guiné for the period 1504–05,[2] which document the importation of ivory salt cellars and spoons as early as the beginning of the 16th century. The catalogue of the Museo dei Gesuiti in Rome, compiled by Fr Filippo Bonanni in 1709, also contains the unequivocal description of the instrument now in the Museo Nazionale Preistorico Etnografico "L. Pigorini" in Rome,[3] an ivory horn from Africa (*"Cornu eburneum ex Africa allatum cum figuris variis elegantissime sculptis"*). The identification is certain, because the item is shown in illustration 299 of the Bonanni catalogue.

About sixty salt cellars (including fragments, some of uncertain attribution), three pyxes, two dagger hilts, a dozen spoons, three forks and over forty oliphants, now in museums and private collections all over the world, evince the extraordinary skill of the Sapi sculptors of Sierra Leone, which was recognized by Europeans in no uncertain terms, during the first decade of the 16th century. "The men are very skilful and ingenious in Sierra Leone. They make works in ivory, whatever is asked, that are wonderful to see. Some make spoons, some salt cellars, and some hilts for daggers and any other kind of refined object",[4] as Valentim Fernandes wrote at the time.[5]

71. Sapi artist
Sierra Leone, 15th–16th c.
Salt cellar
Ivory, 24.5 cm
Museo Nazionale Preistorico Etnografico "L. Pigorini", Rome (formerly in the collection of Cardinal Fabio Chigi, deceased in 1693, and then in the Museo dei Gesuiti, Rome)

The similarities between the features of the figures carved on many ivories and those of the ancient, soft-stone *nomoli* found in Sierra Leone and Guinea – protruding globular eyes, arched nose and dilated nostrils (see no. 62) – suggest that both are the work of Sapi artists. As Fernandes wrote so admiringly, they adapted the considerable sculptural skills displayed in oliphant no. 61 to the requirements of their European clientele.

Sierra Leone was not the only part of Africa to produce carved works for Europe in the 16th century. Seventeen salt cellars and about sixty spoons from Benin, referred to collectively as Bini-Portuguese ivories (or Edo-Portuguese, to use the recently agreed-upon name for the inhabitants of the ancient kingdom), are now in European collections. Their name is suggested by the combination of decorative elements peculiar to the Bini or Edo culture[6] and typically Portuguese motifs, such as the dress and weapons of the figures carved on the salt cellars.[7]

The first and only reference in European literature to works produced for export in the ancient Nigerian kingdom is in the account of a voyage made by the English navigator James Welsh, who wrote as follows in 1588: "in Benin they make [...] spoons of Elephant teeth very curiously wrought with diverse proportions of fowls and beasts made upon them."[8]

This statement appears somewhat belated, since the Medici collections had already included five spoons since 1560. Nor can we rule out the possibility of Nigerian provenance for some of the ivory spoons and salt cellars (*colhares* and *saleyros*) recorded in the inventories of the Casa de Guiné for 1504–05 among the goods imported by Portugal.[9] The spoons, whose handles have carvings in the round of various combinations of animals and one instance of a European figure, are the most numerous of the Edo-Portuguese ivories to have survived. All the old princely collections contained one or more examples, even though they were described incompletely or incorrectly in the European documentation of the time.

The suggestion that the Edo-Portuguese ivories might also have been carved in Sierra Leone was recently put forward by Peter Mark in the catalogue of the exhibition 'Encompassing the Globe: Portugal and the World in the 16th and 17th Centuries' (Smithsonian Institution, Arthur M. Sackler Gallery, Washington, 24 June 2007–16 September 2007).[10] I would regard this as a somewhat rash claim and one refuted by the completely different form and decoration of both the spoons and the salt cellars. In particular, all the Edo-Portuguese salt cellars have two sections, one above the other,[11] and more compact bases with figures in European dress (larger than those carved on the items from Sierra Leone), which conceal the lower section completely.

As regards dating, the stylistic and thematic similarities between the various works in the classical style, both Sapi and Edo, are so marked as to rule out any possibility that they were produced over a period as long as two centuries. It is possible that production continued beyond the spans indicated by William Fagg and myself, but the works were not of such a high quality. Finally, it is curious that the ivories Peter Mark regards as possibly the work of artists from Sierra Leone should be indicated in the same Washington catalogue as Edo-Portuguese.

The above reference to quality recalls a problem raised by Susan Vogel in her introduction to the catalogue of the exhibition 'Africa and the Renaissance'. The scholar points out how difficult it would have been for African sculptors to acquire decorative elements of European origin, such as coats of arms and hunting scenes, solely on the basis of drawings and engravings, two-dimensional works of a kind to which they were certainly not accustomed. She therefore concludes that the unsuccessful works that were not purchased by clients must have been lost, together with all evidence of the intermediate stages in the acquisition of the new language, especially as no presumably rejected work documenting such a transition has ever been found in Africa. In actual fact, however, works with somewhat rough decoration that were apparently early attempts did arrive in Europe, and were especially to be found among the oliphants, whose degree of perfection ranges from masterpieces produced for European sovereigns to the clumsy results obtained during the learning stage.

The inclusion of oliphants of Congolese-Angolan origin in the category of Afro-Portuguese ivories is more problematic, as the only evidence that they may have been produced for export to Europe is provided by rings for attaching a cord or strap. The side mouthpiece is, however, an African feature and the refined geometric decoration derives from the figurative heritage of the Congo people.

The same considerations also hold for Nigerian oliphants and for a few from Sierra Leone and other unidentified regions. The side mouthpiece, decoration of European origin and polished workmanship all make it difficult to attribute these items to one category or the other.

Sapi-Portuguese ivories

The Portuguese used the term *saleyros* (salt cellars) for a group of items created by the ancient artists of Sierra Leone. These objects – which performed a more ornamental than practical function in the Renaissance, as exemplified by Benvenuto Cellini's celebrated work now in the Kunsthistorisches Museum, Vienna – were basically either cylindrical or conical in shape, with all the inevitable hybrids and variants. Moreover, they certainly offered clients greater freedom to express their preferences than spoons and oliphants, where shape is predetermined by function.

Clients' requests evidently played a limited part in the design of the items in the first group, because both the shape and the decoration (with the exception of the geometric patterns) were inspired by and reproduced elements from the local culture. The shape was probably suggested by a vessel (gourd?) on a stool. The fact that no antique stools decorated with figures are known in the region today does not mean that none existed at the time of the discoveries. Models for the almost exclusively African human figures, standing or seated, nude or wearing trousers or short skirts, were right before the sculptors' eyes.[12] The motifs are, however, repeated with inevitable variations from artist to artist, and from client to client, so that no two salt cellars are the same.

The geometric decoration, above all the rows of granules, is instead reminiscent of Manueline art, which flourished in Portugal from the late 15th to the mid-16th century and takes its name from Manuel I.

The elements decorating the lids of the surviving examples are, instead, all different with the exception of a group featuring a double human head, a subject also found, albeit infrequently, in stone sculptures.

The salt cellar (no. 71) now in the Museo Nazionale Preistorico Etnografico "L. Pigorini", Rome, is almost certainly the one described as "an ivory vessel with two heads on top of the carved lid" and listed as no. 745 in the inventory of Cardinal Chigi's possessions drawn up in 1706–07.[13] This is a significant example of the first type by virtue of the balanced relationship between the vessel and the light, airy, openwork base, the precise rendering of the figures, and the calibrated use of decoration consisting of zigzag lines and rows of granules, deftly combined with scarification marks and the crosses supporting the vessel. The scarification was a practice attested by John Sarke, who was in Sierra Leone in the mid-16th century.[14]

The salt cellar (no. 72) with a solid conical base now in the Musei Civici d'Arte Antica, Bologna, falls into the second category, the European model for which is thought to have reached African sculptors through engravings, particularly by German artists (no. 73).[15]

This work was almost certainly in the collection of Marquis Ferdinando Cospi (1609–1686) and is probably the "antique ivory goblet with lid and figured decoration" described in the inventory compiled by an anonymous author in 1680.[16]

The base of the salt cellar is carved in high relief with figures of men and women alternating with animals, perhaps dogs, confronting huge snakes that

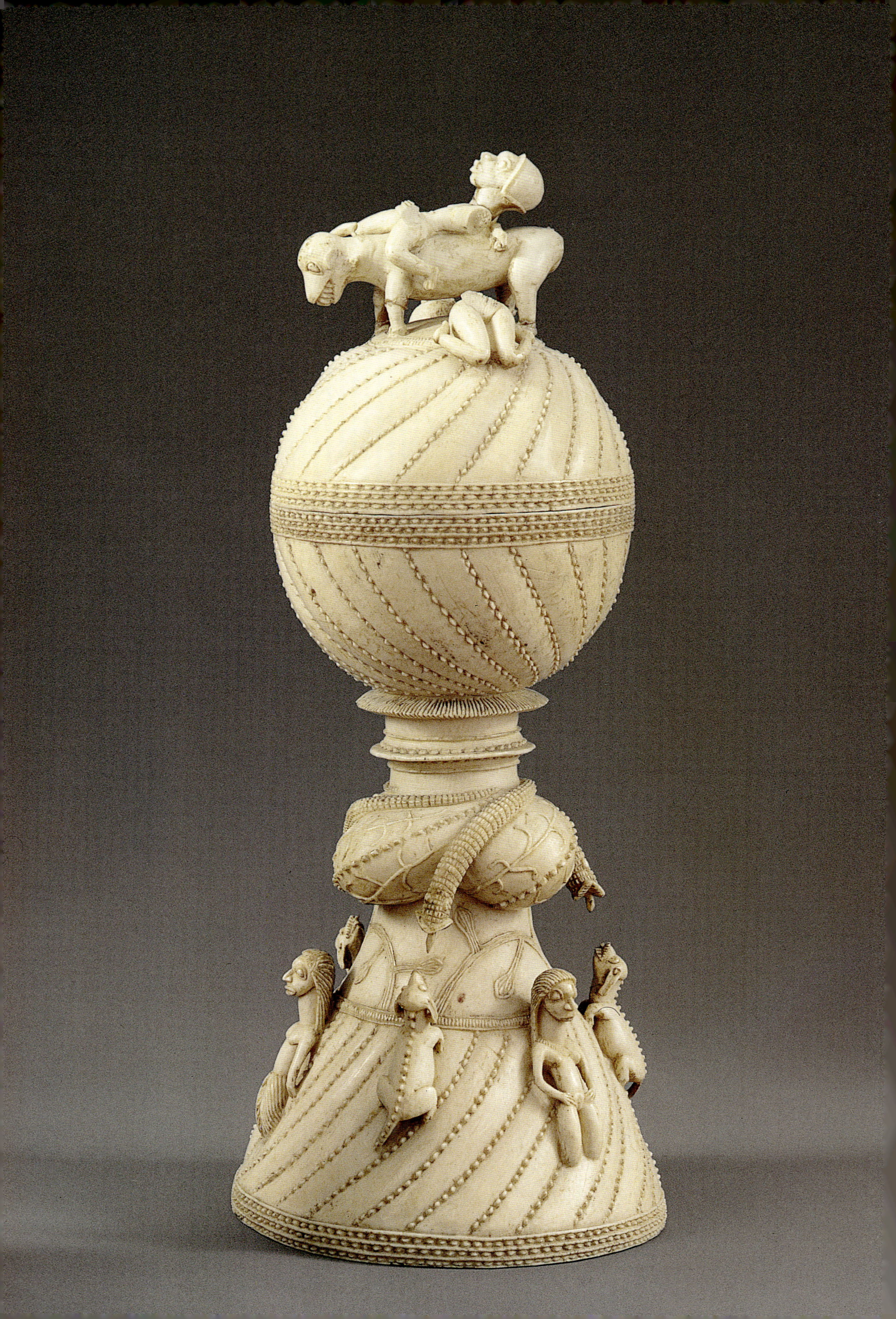

72. Sapi artist
Sierra Leone, 15th–16th c.
Salt cellar
Ivory, 24 cm
Musei Civici d'Arte Antica, Bologna
(formerly in the collection of Marquis
Ferdinando Cospi, Bologna)

72a. Detail of the salt cellar no. 72

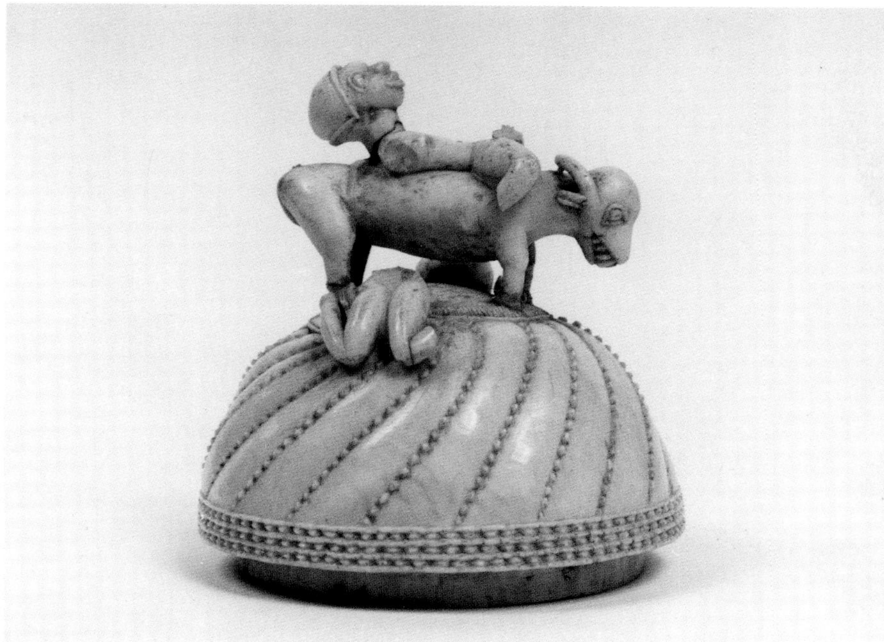

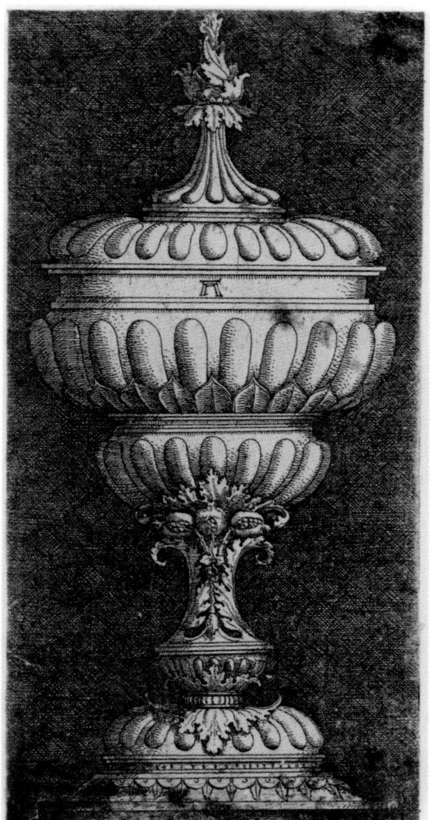

73. Albrecht Altdorfer
Vessel with lid, early decades
of the 16th c.
Etching

hang down from a sort of large cushion, in accordance with an iconographic model recurrent in ivories of this type. The sculpture in the round on the lid – a nude female figure stretched out on a goat, flanked by the surviving parts of two more female bodies – is instead a surprising depiction of a witch being carried to a sabbath by the devil (no. 72a). The arms are broken off at the shoulders, but a fragment attached to one thigh seems to indicate that the hands covered the genitals.

The subject was extraneous to African culture but highly topical in Europe, as attested by the trials for having sexual relations with the devil that led to the purification of "witches" by burning at the stake. In the light of this reading, the two female nudes with their hands framing their vaginas carved on the base also take on a specific significance in the general context.

The source both for the shape of the salt cellars and the witchcraft scenes is European. A comparison with engravings by Albrecht Dürer (1505–07) and Hans Baldung Grien (1510) (no. 74) and a drawing by Albrecht Altdorfer (1506?) leaves no room for doubt. The question of how the model was transmitted remains, of course, and the most likely answer seems to be through an engraving, even though this does not explain the blatant display of the sexual organs.

The smouldering eroticism of the subject in no way diminishes the elegant perfection of the work, which is created through subtle elements such as the finely proportioned volumes, the delicate plant motifs and the reversed spiral of the rows of granules imparting a musical rhythm to the bare surfaces.

The decoration of the salt cellar (no. 75) formerly in the collection of the Newcastle Society of Antiquarians and now in the British Museum[17] is completely different and equally exceptional in terms of subject matter. Apart from the snakes, the motifs are of European origin and connected with the Christian religion, with the exception of the European decorative elements of a geometric, floral and mythological (two sirens) nature. The coat of arms of the Portuguese royal family and the cross of the Order of Christ also in the decoration suggest that this salt cellar was intended for a member of the ruling house, perhaps even the king himself.

This piece may have been in the collection of George Allan (1736–1800),[18] which his son sold to the Newcastle Literary and Philosophical Society in 1822.[19] George Townshend Fox described the item in his *Synopsys* of 1827 as an "Antique pyx, in ivory, beautifully carved, 10 inches high, with a case" (pp. 183–185).

Dressed in splendid apparel decorated with rows of granules, the figure in the round standing on a dais on top of the lid, and holding a naked child

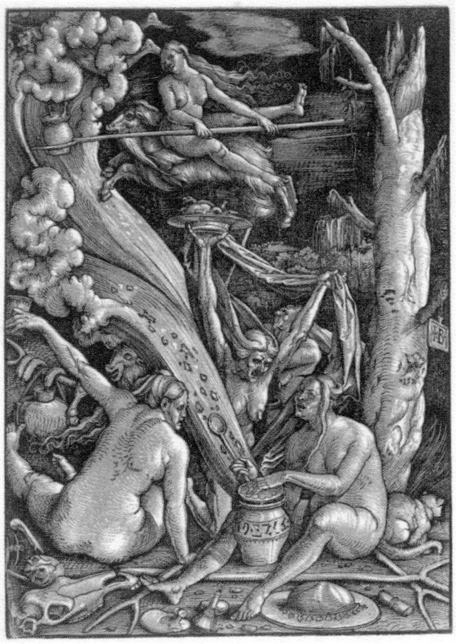

74. Hans Baldung Grien
Witches' Sabbath, 1510
Xilograph

wearing a cross around its neck, is most probably an image of the Virgin Mary with the Infant Jesus, curiously shown with adult features. Carved in high relief beneath the Virgin are three nude figures of youths holding hands. Their heads are covered by a veil and one of them holds a cross (no. 75a). They are almost certainly Shadrach, Meshach and Abednego, the three young Jews thrown into the fiery furnace by the king of Babylon for refusing to worship a golden statue. An angel sent by God spread a veil over their heads to protect them from the flames.

References to the Christian religion are also found on the base, where the image of a man kneeling between two lions, which seem to be patting him on the back, is readily identifiable as the prophet Daniel thrown into the lions' den by Nebuchadnezzar, king of Babylon (no. 75b). This motif was certainly in Portuguese religious iconography at the beginning of the 16th century, as attested by the bas-relief on the lower section of a splendid basalt window frame (no. 76) that once belonged to the Antiga Misericórdia do Funchal, built between 1507 and 1515, but which is now in the garden of the Museu Quinta das Cruzes, Madeira.

The subjects carved in the round and in relief would suggest connections with Christian liturgy and bear out Townshend's description of the item as a pyx, rather than a salt cellar, at the beginning of the 19th century.

The salt cellar (no. 77), which formerly belonged to the German imperial collection and is now in the Ethnologisches Museum, Berlin, corresponds to neither of the two main categories. It reveals the carver's surprising capacity for adaptation, not only by adopting an alien form but also by interpreting it with extraordinary sensitivity, in a figurative language fully in line with the client's expectations.

A kind of armillary sphere bearing a transversal band with the inscription *Espera in Deo*, the motto of Manuel I, king of Portugal from 1495 to 1521, is supported by an arched structure of entwined serpents resting on the backs of three lions, stretched out on an elegant circular platform of interwoven rope, with the coat of arms of the Portuguese royal family between their front paws.

The daring combination of the elegant design of the vessel and the platform base with the aggressively rendered snakes and lions results in a surprising, unusual and extraordinarily figurative work.

The cylindrical container with a lid (no. 78) from a private collection is unquestionably a pyx. The least damaged of three items that are identical in

75 Sapi artist
Sierra Leone, 15th–16th c.
Salt cellar
Ivory, 30.5 cm
The British Museum, Ethnography Department, London (formerly in the collection of the Society of Antiquarians of Newcastle upon Tyne)

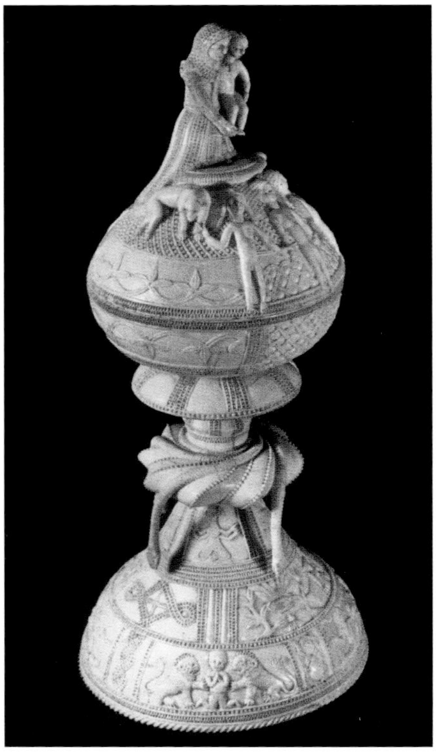

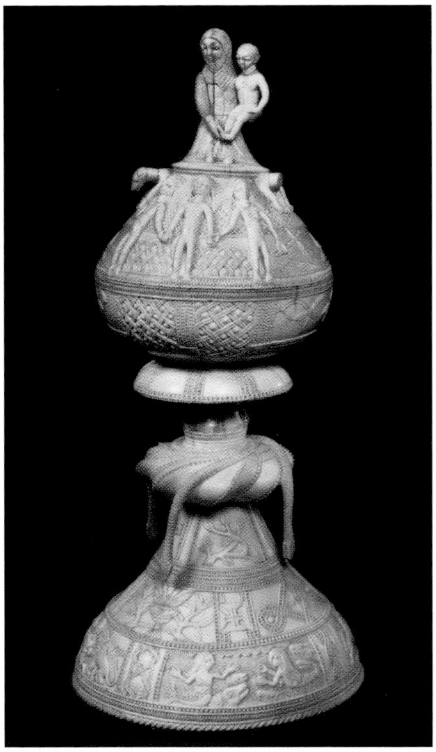

75a. The Virgin and three young Jews in the fiery furnace, detail of the lid of the salt cellar no. 75

75b. Daniel in the lions' den, detail of the salt cellar no. 75

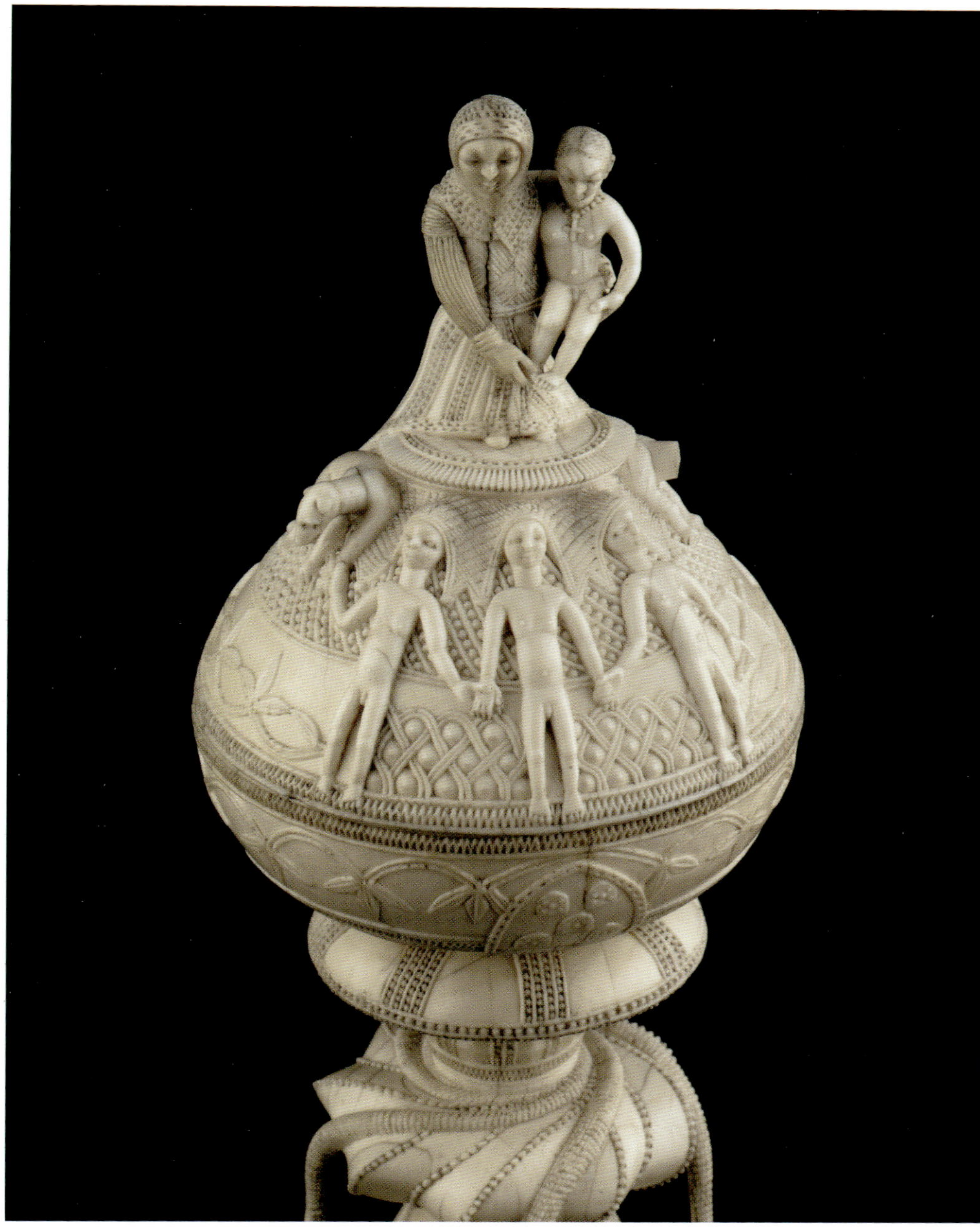

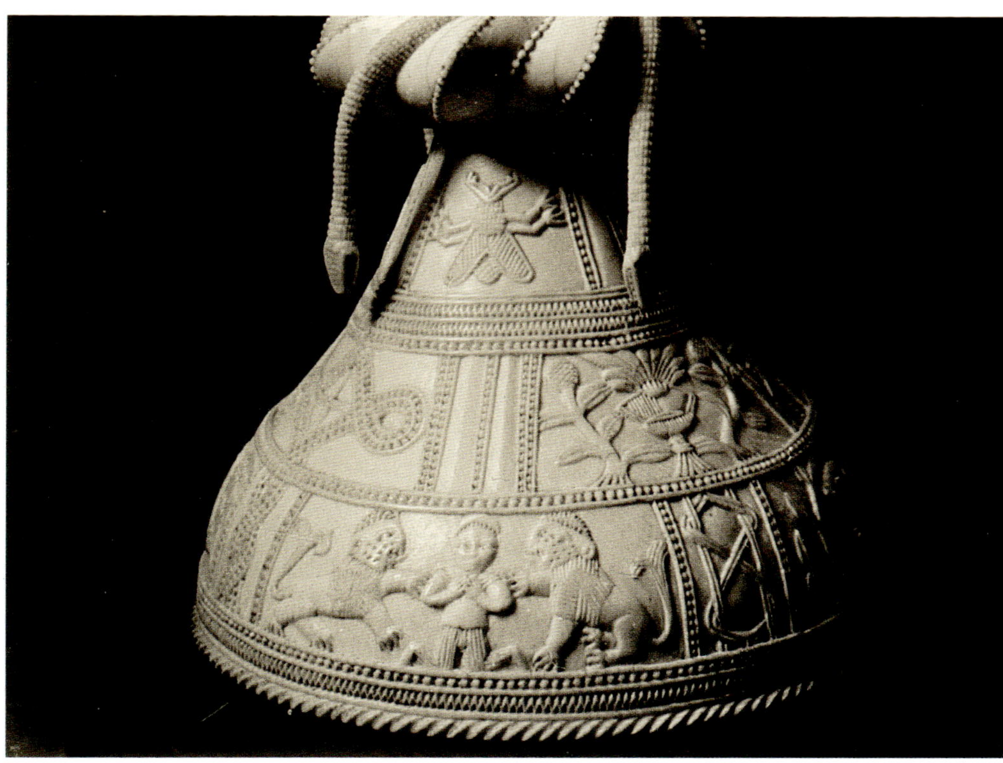

76. Basalt window of the Antiga Misericórdia do Funchal, now in the garden of the Museu Quinta das Cruzes, Madeira

77. Sapi artist
Sierra Leone, 15th–16th c.
Salt cellar
Ivory, 21 cm
Staatliche Museen zu Berlin, Ethnologisches Museum, Berlin (formerly in the imperial Kunstkammer)

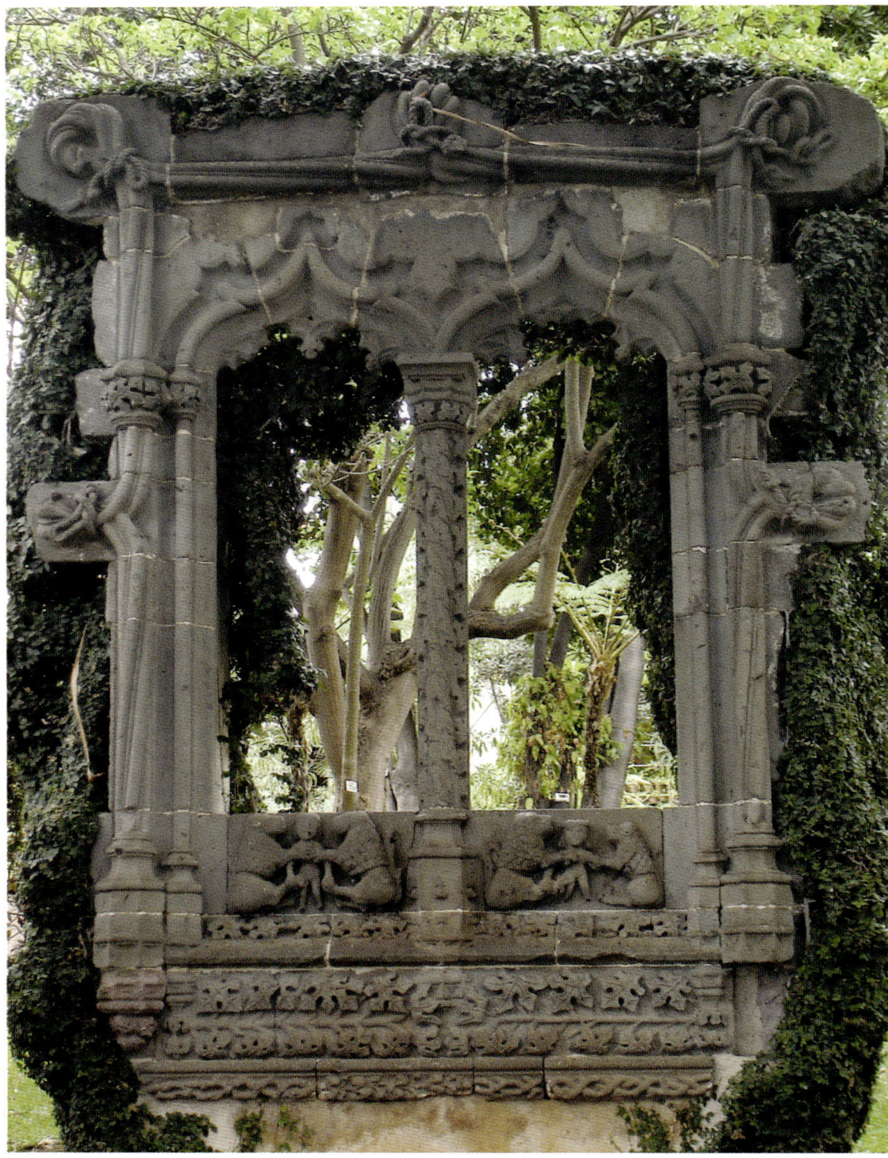

shape, quite possibly carved by the same Sapi artist and now in Western collections,[20] it resembles the work in gilded silver (no. 79) in the Museu Nacional de Arte Antiga, Lisbon, in form but is distinguished by its exuberant decoration. There is a group with the Madonna and Child and three other figures (fragmentary and unrecognizable) carved in the round on the lid, as well as a series of episodes from the life of the Virgin, in low relief, on the wall of the cylindrical vessel. This concentrated decoration leaves no breathing space and exemplifies what William Fagg would have described as *horror vacui*. Like the silver pyx, the vessel is supported by four small lions holding the coat of arms of the ruling house of Portugal between their paws.[21]

The images carved on the wall are copied with great precision from some devotional book that was probably on the trading ships that plied the coasts of Africa in the late 15th and early 16th centuries. The most likely sources are books of that period printed by Philippe Pigouchet and by Thielman Kerver in Paris, which were also used for the hunting scenes carved on oliphants, as we shall see below. A comparison of the Tree of Jesse on the pyx no. 78 and an illustration (no. 80) from a work printed by Pigouchet in 1498 bears out this hypothesis.[22]

While the garments of the figures are decorated with rows of granules, again borrowed from Manueline decoration, it remains unclear how the African sculptors were introduced to this and especially to the pyx form, which appears to have no counterpart in local works of art or artefacts.

The skill in miniaturization possessed by the Sapi sculptors of the past is evident in the few spoons and forks now in Western collections. While it is possible that many of these very small works perished due to their fragility, this

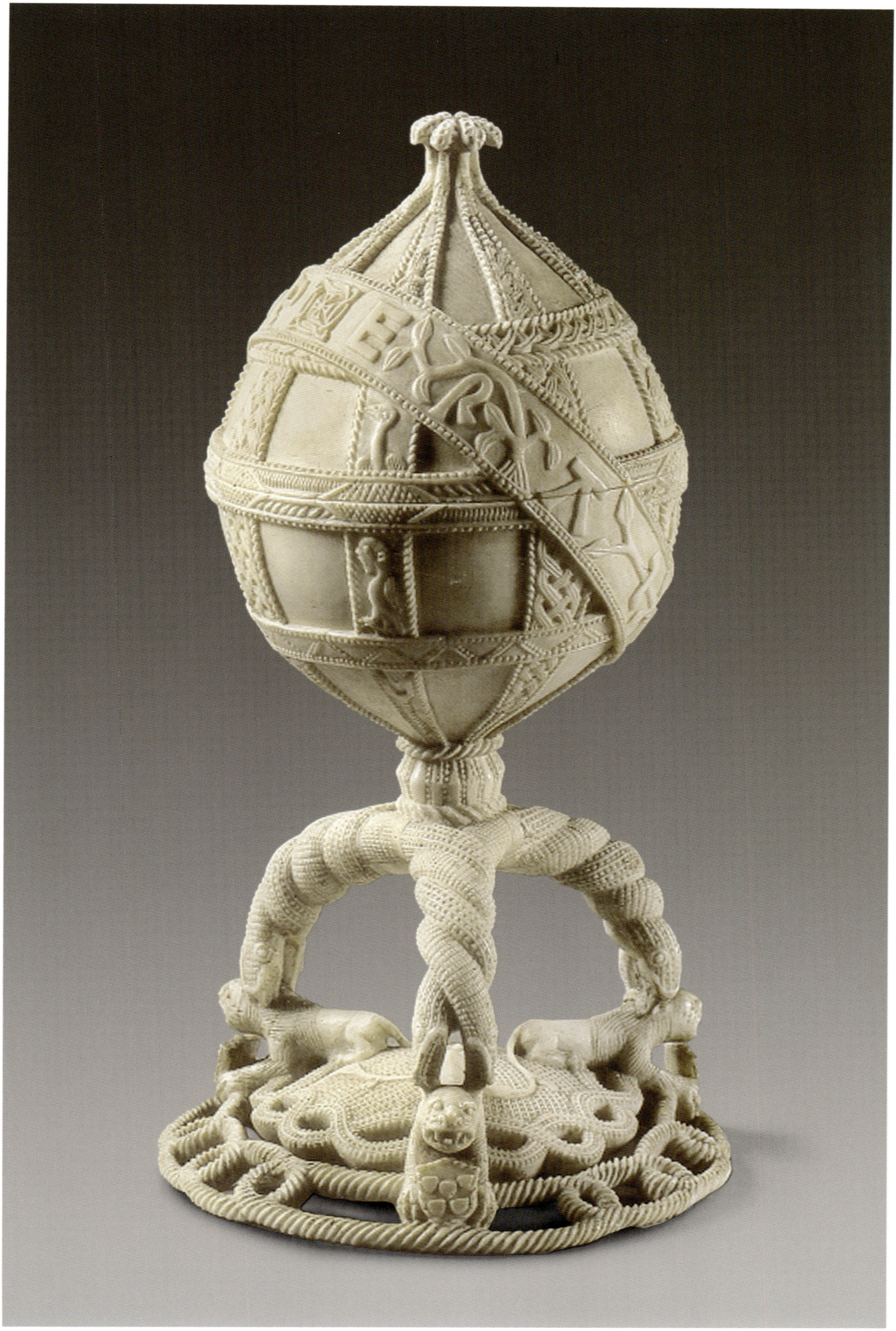

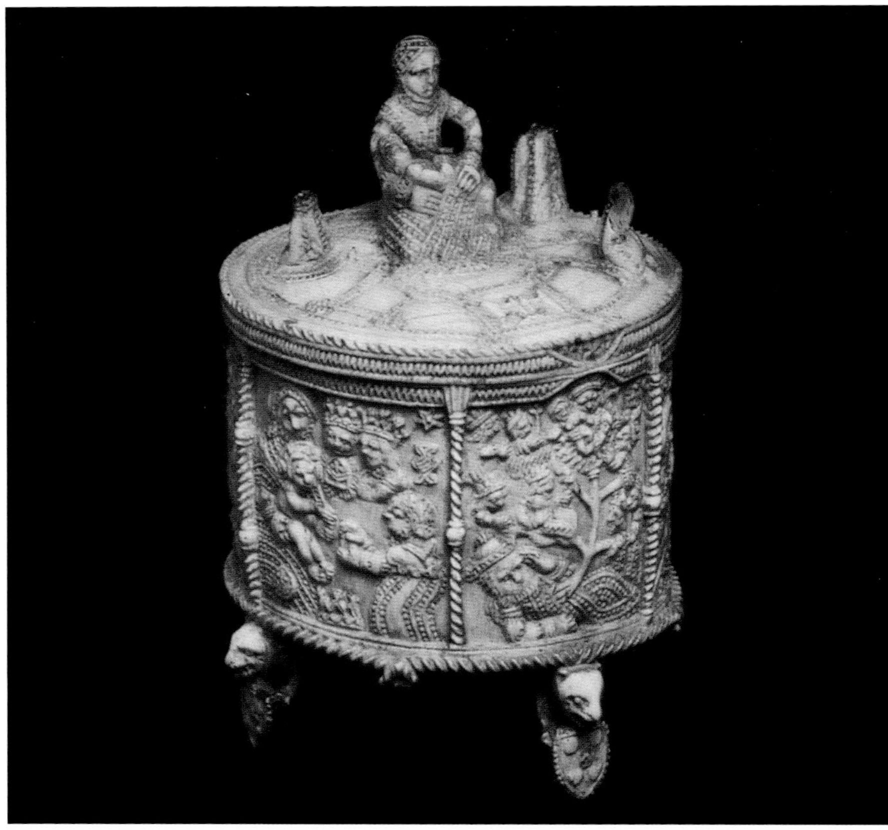

78. Sapi artist
Sierra Leone, 15th–16th c.
Pyx
Ivory, 23 cm
Private collection

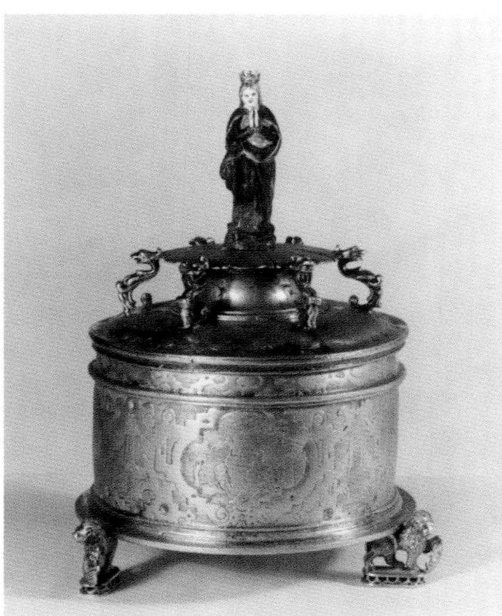

79. Portuguese artist
Pyx, 1537
Gilded silver, diam. 31 cm
Museu Nacional de Arte Antiga, Lisbon

does not square with the survival of a far greater number of Bini-Portuguese items. It therefore seems reasonable to assume that the former were simply produced on a smaller scale.

They correspond in shape to the European cutlery of the period with the addition of surrealistic invention or ascetic rigour in the decoration of the handles. A spoon now in Munich (no. 81) exemplifies the first type with its extraordinary flowing design, and a fork in Vienna (no. 82) the second with its minute replica of a Manueline column (no. 83).

Dagger hilts are also mentioned by Valentim Fernandes in the list of works "wonderful to see" produced by the sculptors of Sierra Leone. Despite the absence of a socket for attachment of the blade, an item of this nature in the British Museum (no. 84) could be one of the rare specimens to have survived. Incredible though it may seem for such fierceness to be suggested in so small a space, the ogre's head crowning the hilt measures no more than five centimetres. Though ennobled by subtle decoration, again of Manueline derivation, the blood-curdling image is fully in line with the lethal nature of the weapon for which the piece was designed. A crocodile is shown climbing up the back of the long neck in a combination of elements frequently found in the antique sculpture of Sierra Leone.

Surprisingly enough, unlike the works described above, oliphants do not figure among the Sapi pieces listed by Valentim Fernandes, unless of course the 16th-century scholar used the expression "*qualquer otra sotileza*" ("every other type of sophisticated work") precisely for the musical instruments not cited specifically in the list, even though these are the largest of the Sapi-Portuguese ivories and second only to the salt cellars in number.

The entry from the catalogue of the Jesuit collection in Rome regarding the above-mentioned item (no. 85), now in the Museo Nazionale Preistorico Etnografico "L. Pigorini", Rome,[23] dispels all doubt, however, as to the African origin of these works. At the same time, confirmation of the dating is provided by their close similarities to the illustrations in the small devotional books printed in the late 15th and early 16th century, which were almost certainly carried on board the few ships that then visited the coasts of Africa.

The oliphant now in the National Museum of Australia (no. 86) is one of the finest and most monumental of the group of forty identified items, by virtue both of its elegant shape and of the decoration in the round and in low relief. The position of the mouthpiece at the top rather than at the side and the rings on the concave part for attaching a cord or strap suggest that the instrument (and the others in its category) was produced for export.

The mouthpiece emerges from the fanged jaws of a beast of prey, whose fierce but elegant head recalls some coeval European gun barrels, just as the rings for the cord or strap, decorated with small heads of dragons or snakes, echo those used for hoisting cannons.

Two of the three figures carved in high relief on the convex side of the oliphant carry an animal on their shoulders. This derives from the Christian image of the Good Shepherd, but also from the classical myth of Orpheus, with an animal killed in the hunt in the place of the lamb, seen in low relief on the walls of the instrument.

The source for the images of the various stages of the hunt (no. 86a), a pastime of the aristocracy during the Renaissance, is unquestionably the miniature scenes decorating the margins of the devotional books printed by Philippe Pigouchet and Thielman Kerver, mentioned in connection with pyx no. 78. A comparison of the illustrations of hunting scenes (no. 87) leaves no room for doubt on this score. As the ritual of the hunt was extraneous to the African sculptor's personal experience, however, the illustrations were reprised as purely decorative elements.[24]

The same holds even more true for the inscription *Ave Maria* in Gothic lettering and for the coats of arms of Manuel I of Portugal, Isabella I of Castile and Ferdinand II of Aragon, complete with the latter's motto *Tanto monta*. Manuel I married two daughters of the Spanish sovereigns in succession, Isabella in 1497 and Maria in 1500, and it is possible that he commissioned an artist from Sierra Leone, obviously one of the best, to produce four oliphants with the coats of arms of the two ruling houses related by marriage, as gifts for his parents-in-law.[25]

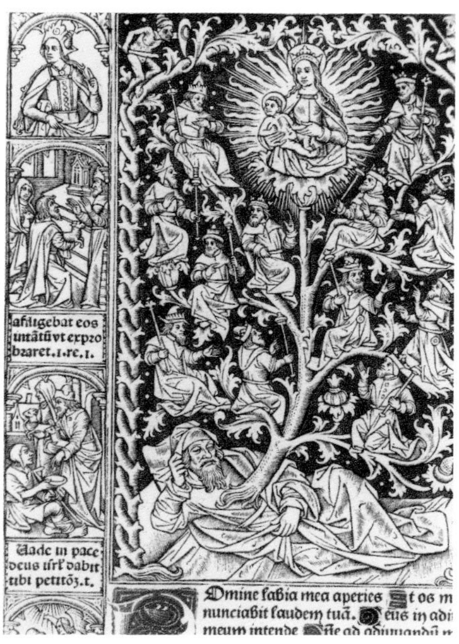

80. *Tree of Jesse*, illustration from the incunabulum *Horae Beatae Mariae Virginis* [...], by Philippe Pigouchet, Paris 1498

If this hypothesis is correct, the instrument must have been produced at the turn of the 16th century, an unusually precise date for an African work of art. Supporting evidence is provided by the fact that the Spanish coat of arms (no. 86b) includes a pomegranate tree, the symbol of the city of Granada, which was won back from the Arabs in 1492.

The oliphant (no. 88) now in the Armeria Reale, Turin, is another important example of ivory sculpture produced for export. The iconography of its decoration is even richer than that of the previous instrument. In addition to deer-hunting episodes, we see a horseman, an archer, hares, boar, an elephant, a heraldic lion, a unicorn and two gryphons with their necks entwined.

The convex side is decorated with two hunters in European dress in high relief and the concave has a proportionally huge snake devouring a hare, a crocodile and a menacing gryphon, strongly reminiscent of the attachments for hoisting cannons in the early 16th century. See in this connection the details of the Flemish (?) gun barrel of 1535 signed "Maistre Denis" (no. 89), now in the Tower of London, together with the previously-mentioned item.

The most interesting feature of the Turin oliphant is, however, the coat of arms of the Portuguese ruling house, which takes the usual form of a shield placed near the mouthpiece of the instrument, but hanging from a tree, flanked by two rampant unicorns (no. 88a). It also bears, with slight variations, the trademark of the printer Thielman Kerver, active in Paris at the end of the 15th century (no. 90). This provides not only evidence of the period in which the oliphants were produced, but also confirmation of the European sources of the decorative motifs embellishing them, which include the books printed by Kerver and Philippe Pigouchet.[26]

It is my view that the valuable instrument now in Turin, which was first recorded at the beginning of the 19th century, entered the rich collections of the dukes of Savoy in the early decades of the 16th century with the dowry of Duchess Beatrice d'Aviz (daughter of Manuel I of Portugal) on her marriage to Charles III of Savoy in 1521.

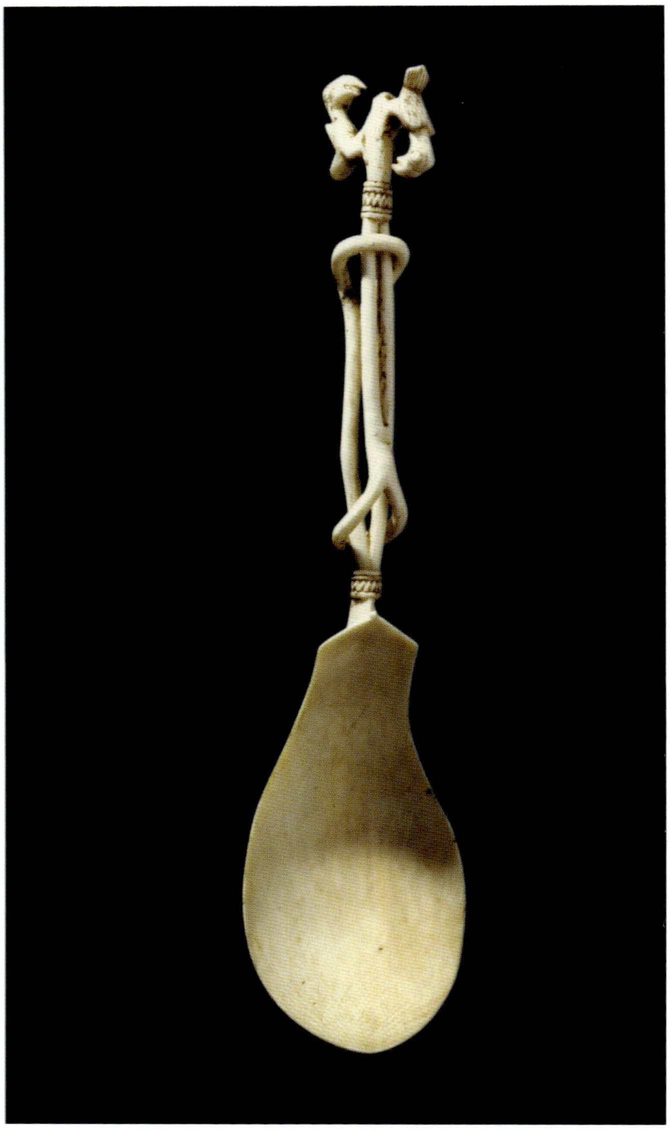

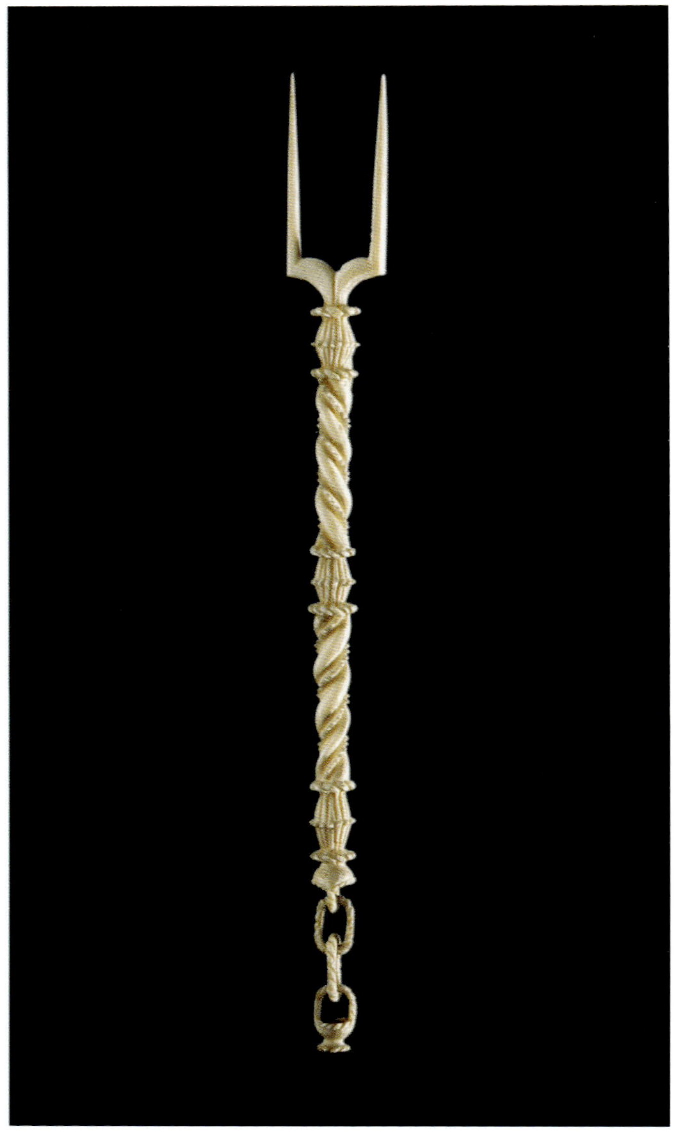

81. Sapi artist
Sierra Leone, 15th–16th c.
Spoon
Ivory, 24 cm
Staatliche Museum für Völkerkunde, Munich (formerly in the Kunstkammer der Residenz)

82. Sapi artist
Sierra Leone, 15th–16th c.
Fork
Ivory, 14.4 cm
Museum für Völkerkunde, Vienna

Edo-Portuguese ivories

The Edo-Portuguese salt cellars now in Western collections are less numerous than their Sapi-Portuguese counterparts and differ structurally from them by having two spherical sections instead of one. The lower section is encircled and almost concealed by figures, four on foot in the first type and two horsemen with other smaller figures in the second.

These items with two sections do not correspond to the European salt cellars of the 15th and 16th centuries or to Bini artefacts for local use. Their shape may have been suggested by the clients or adopted by the artists for compositional reasons connected with the addition of large figures to hide the function of the vessels.

The salt cellar now in the Musée du Quai Branly (no. 91) is one of the two intact examples of the first type: two static frontal figures alternate with two in three-quarter profile (no. 91a) to form a well-balanced composition. Attention is focused on the frontal figures, whose immobility is enhanced by contrast with the two flanking them, and takes on a regal aspect.

The dress and weapons are those of important members of the Portuguese court in the 15th century (no. 92), images of which probably reached the African sculptors through the illustrations in antique Portuguese books carried on ships. Many details of the apparel display elements derived once again from Manueline decoration, such as close-set rows of granules, and this is more difficult to explain.

One element appears, however, to contradict the hypothesis that all the decoration with European subject matter, including the group carved on the lid, derives from printed models. This point calls for at least some consideration. On the one hand, the simplified image of the ship is reminiscent of medieval vessels or in any event ships of a type no longer used for long ocean voyages at the time – see the seal of the Hanseatic city of Stralsund of 1301 (no. 93) – and the African sculptors must therefore have employed a model supplied by the client. On the other hand, the life-like representation of the sailors – one in a crow's nest that is disproportionately large with respect to the keel and the other climbing up the rigging – is in marked contrast to the somewhat static rendering of the imposing figures carved on the base. This suggests that the African artist was struck by a scene witnessed first-hand on a more modern ship and then incorporated it into his work, but in an expressive register more in keeping with the emotion actually experienced.

A salt cellar that is almost certainly the work of the same sculptor, but without the figure in the rigging, is now in the British Museum.

Similarities in structure and figuration can also be seen in the dozen (mostly incomplete) salt cellars of the type exemplified by the item (no. 94) formerly in the collection of Frans Olbrechts and now in the Antwerp Museum, characterized by the images of two evidently European horsemen with pronounced features and garments that again appear Portuguese.

The horses' harness (single rein, decorated bridle with no bit, collar adorned with crotal bells) corresponds to the harness seen on some Bini brass sculptures of African figures. The horse carved in the round on the lid has the same type of bridle and a cloth instead of a saddle in accordance with local custom.

The composition includes other European figures and, on the back, a curious winged nude that could be an angel but for its conspicuous male genitals.

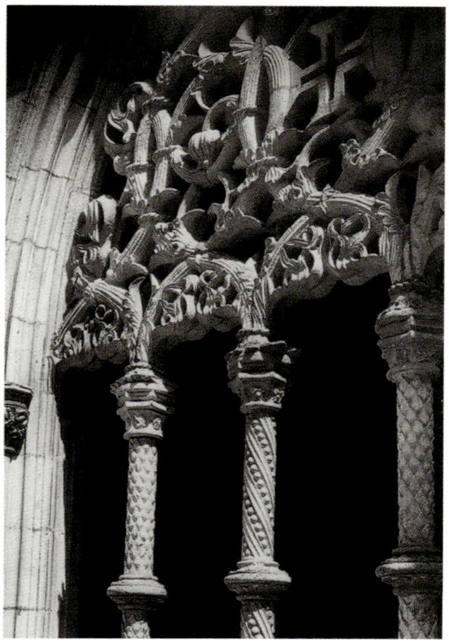

83. Cloister of the Batalha monastery, Portugal, Manueline architecture

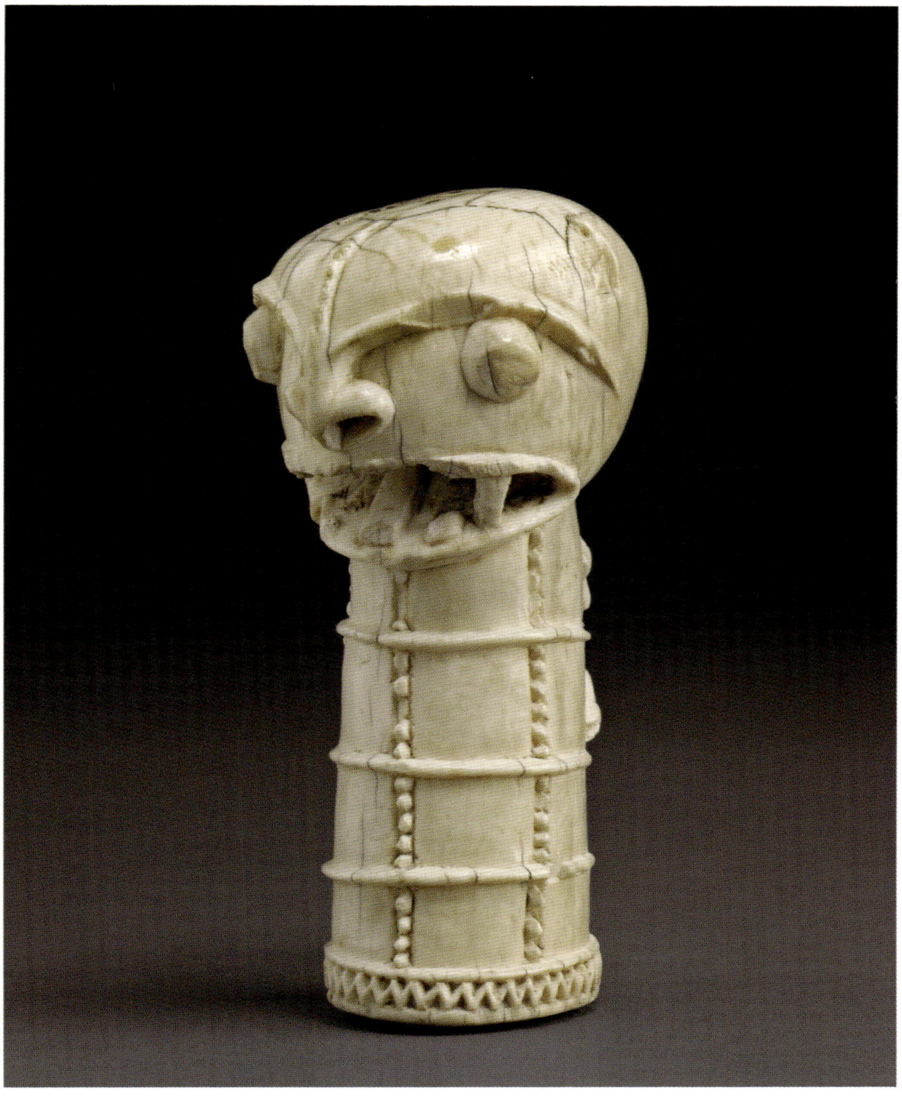

84. Sapi artist
Sierra Leone, 15th–16th c.
Dagger hilt (?)
Ivory, 11.4 cm
The British Museum, Ethnography Department, London (formerly in the Greville Chester Collection)

85. Plate no. 299 of the catalogue compiled by Fr Filippo Bonanni in 1709; illustration of the Sapi-Portuguese oliphant described on p. 235, now in the Museo Nazionale Preistorico Etnografico "L. Pigorini", Rome

86. Sapi artist
Sierra Leone, 15th–16th c.
Sapi-Portuguese oliphant
with hunting scenes
Ivory, 68.5 cm
National Museum of Australia, Canberra (in the George Ashby Collection [?] until 1802)

86a. Three deer hunting scenes, detail of the oliphant no. 86

86b. Coat of arms of the Spanish royal family, detail of the oliphant no. 86

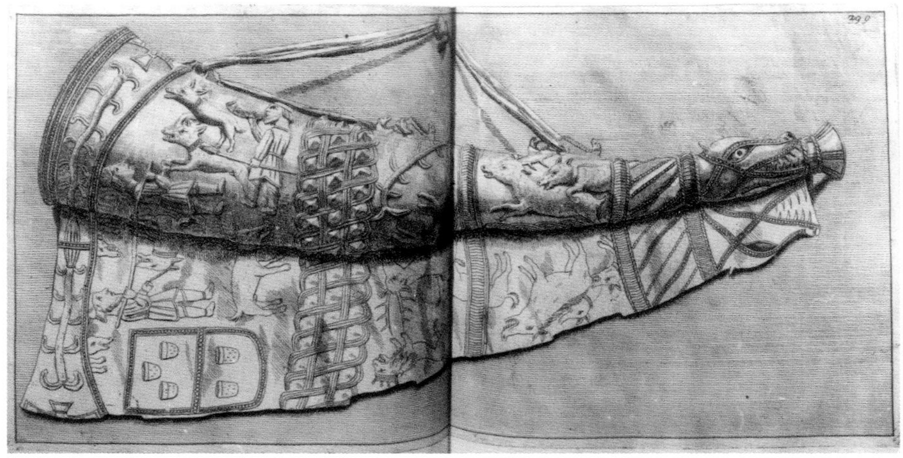

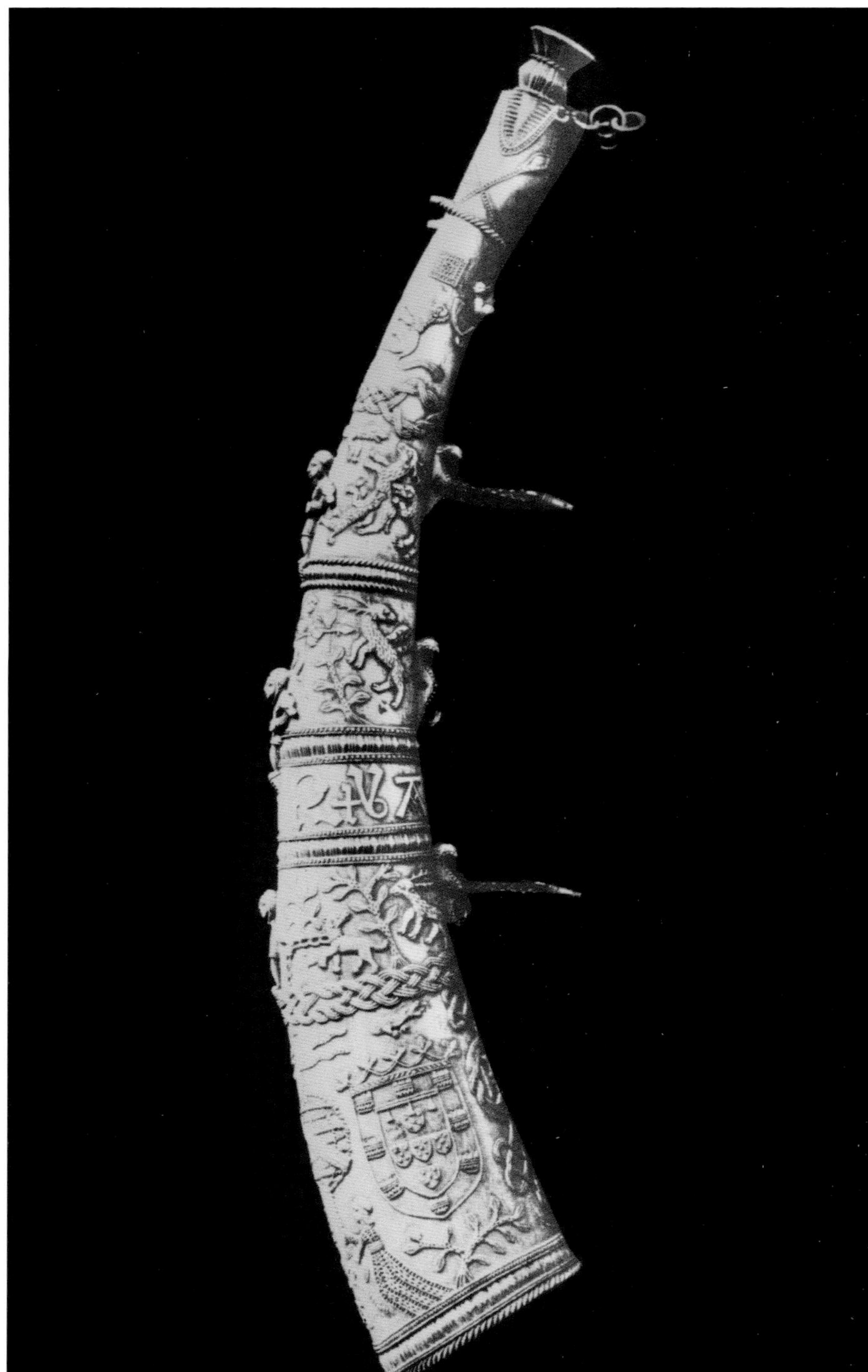

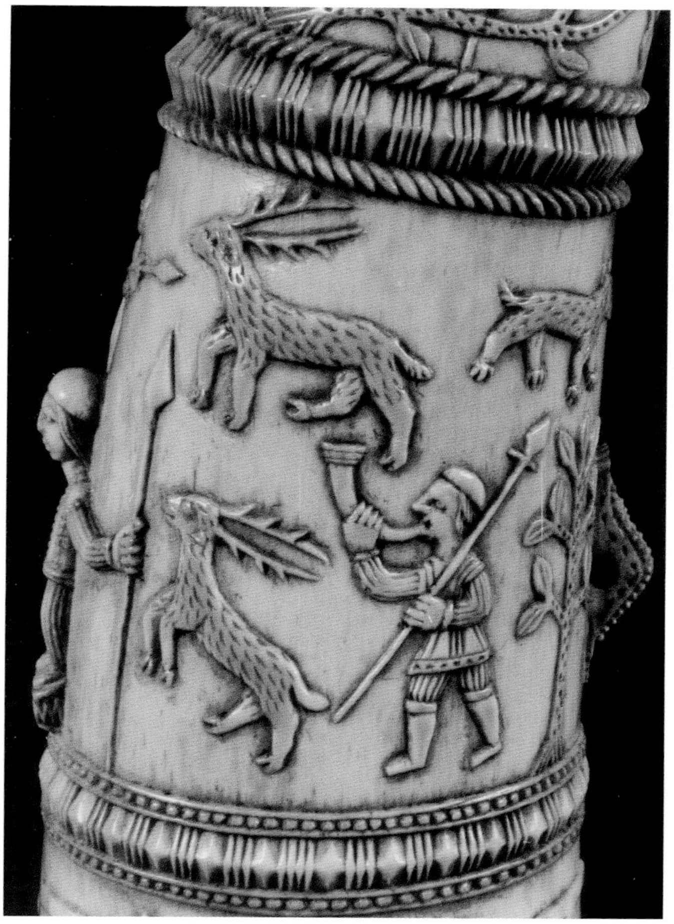

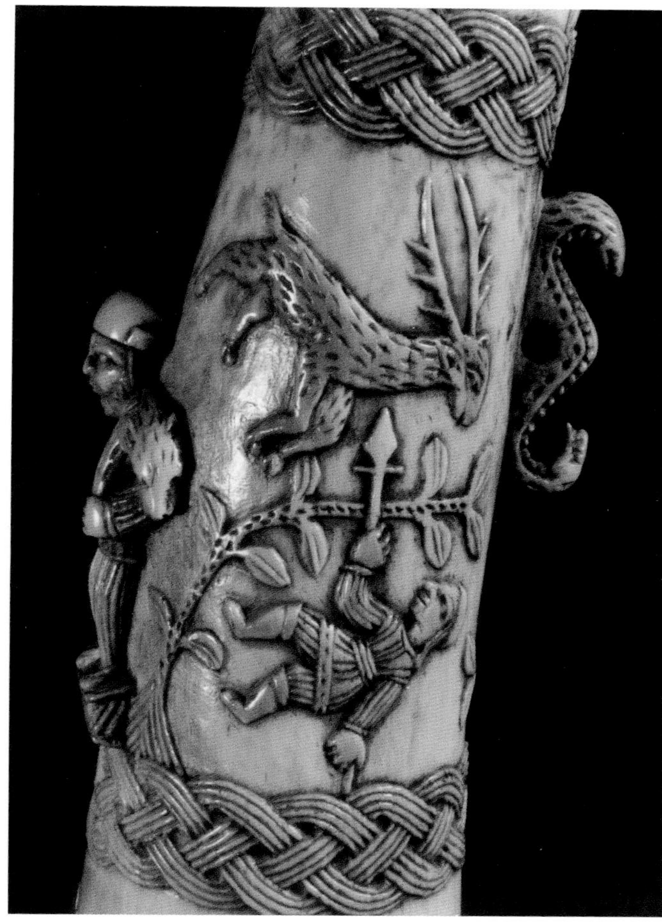

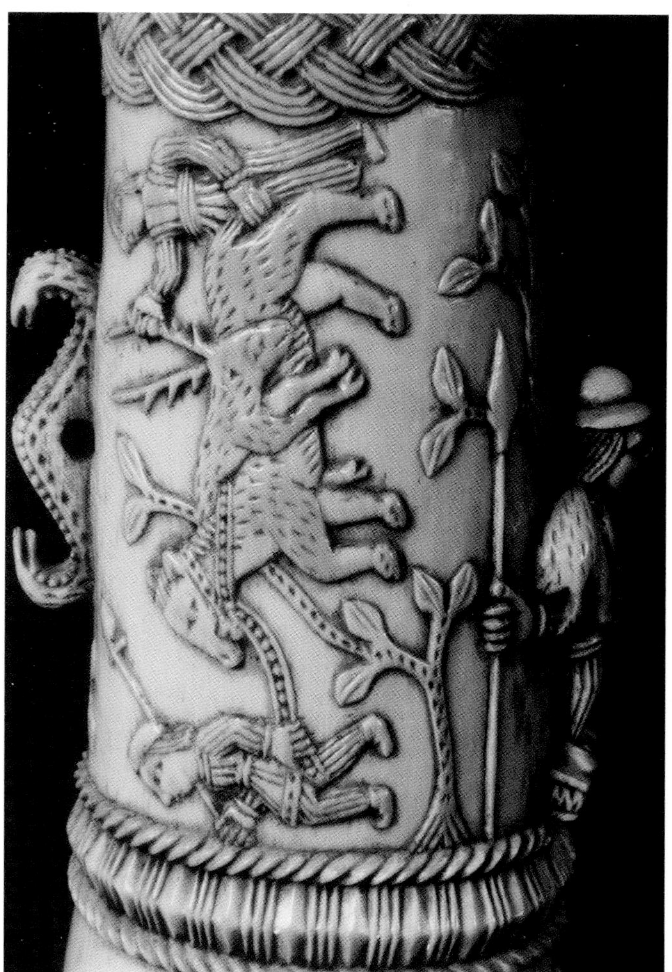

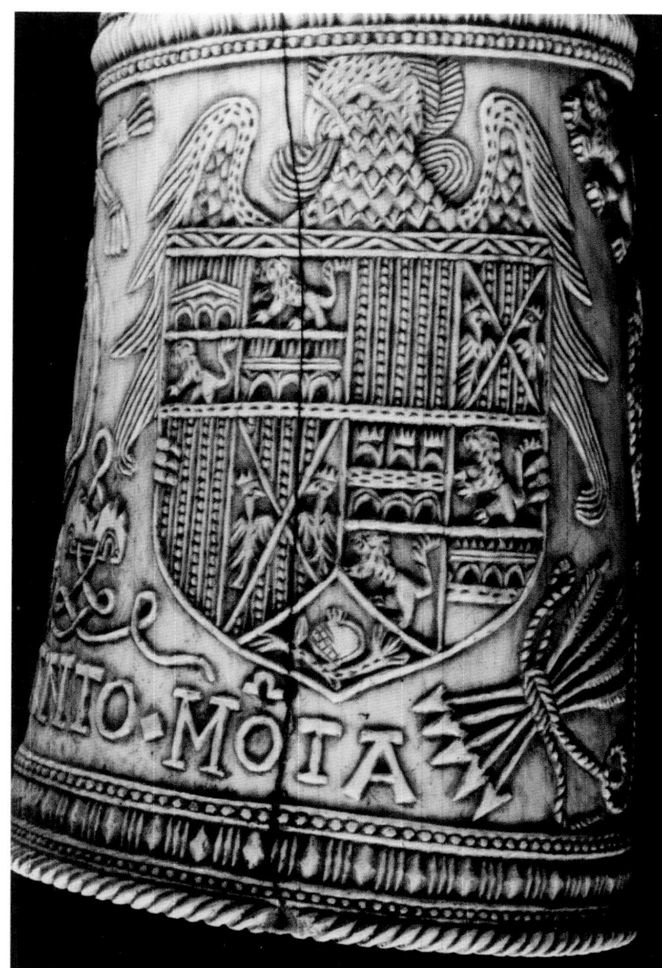

87. Page with deer hunting scenes from the incunabulum *Horae Beatae Mariae Virginis* [...], by Philippe Pigouchet, Paris 1498

88. Sapi artist
Sierra Leone, 15th–16th c.
Oliphant with hunting scenes
Ivory and gold, 63 cm
Armeria Reale, Turin (formerly in the collection of the dukes of Savoy)

88a. Coat of arms of Manuel I of Portugal, detail of the oliphant no. 88

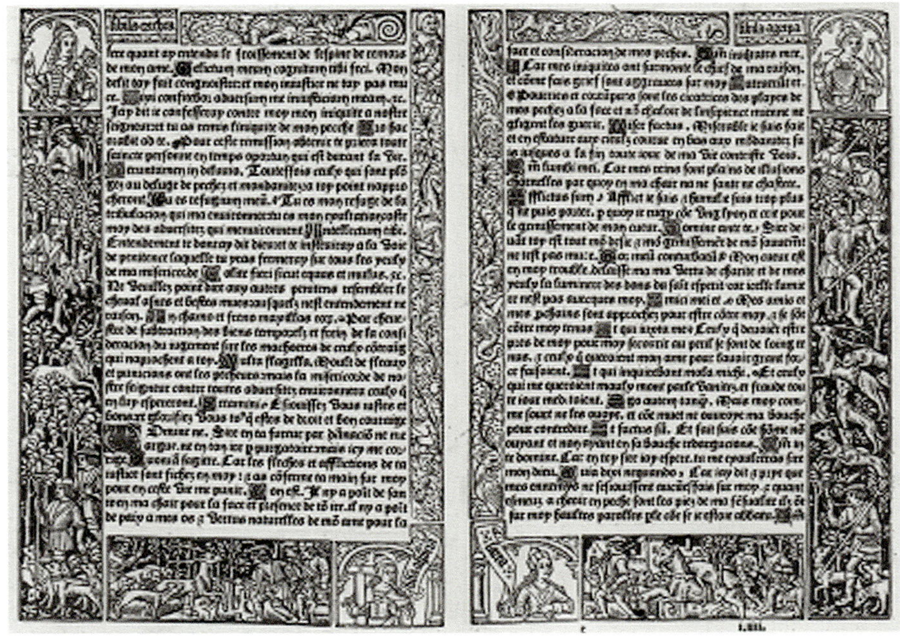

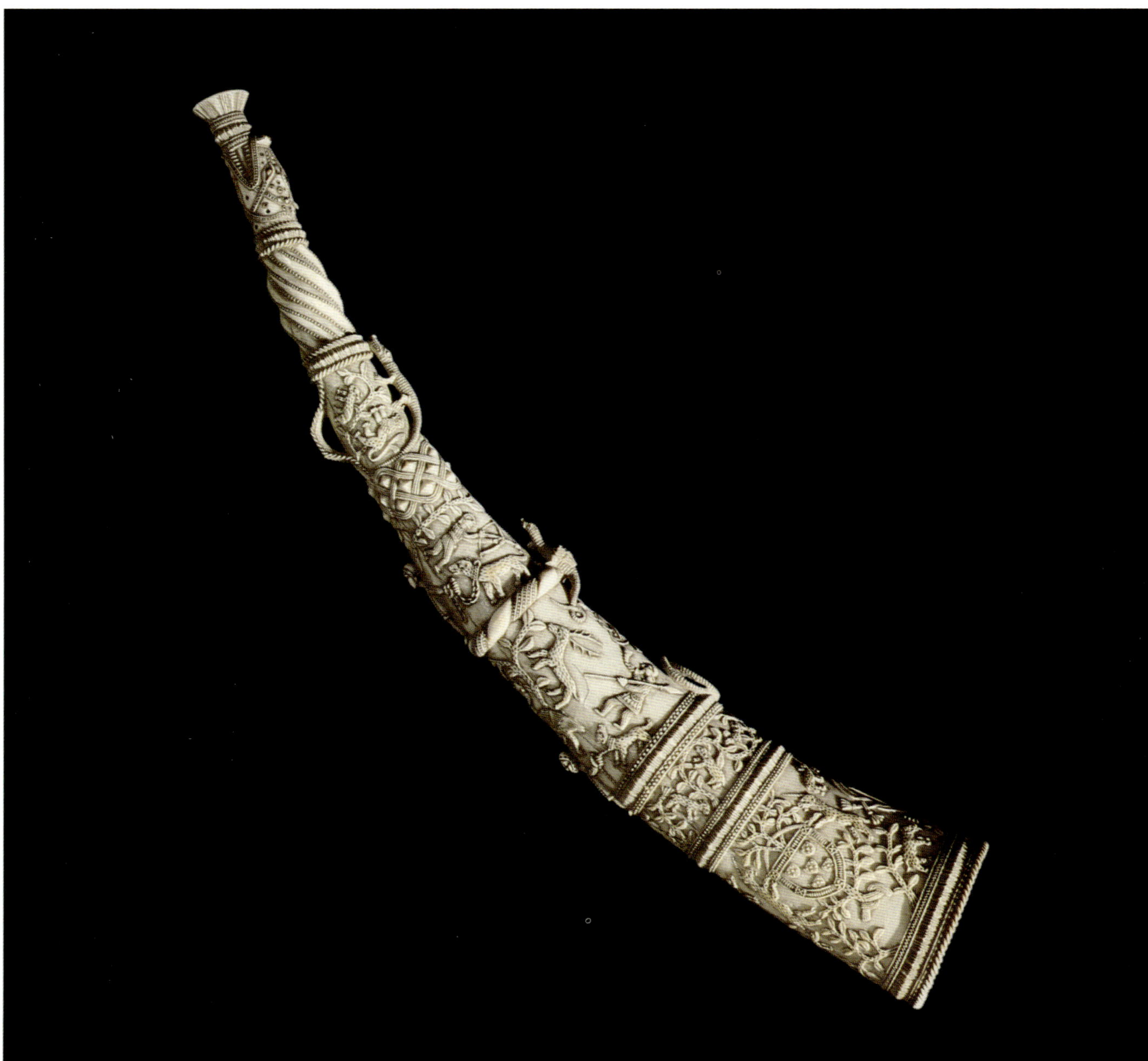

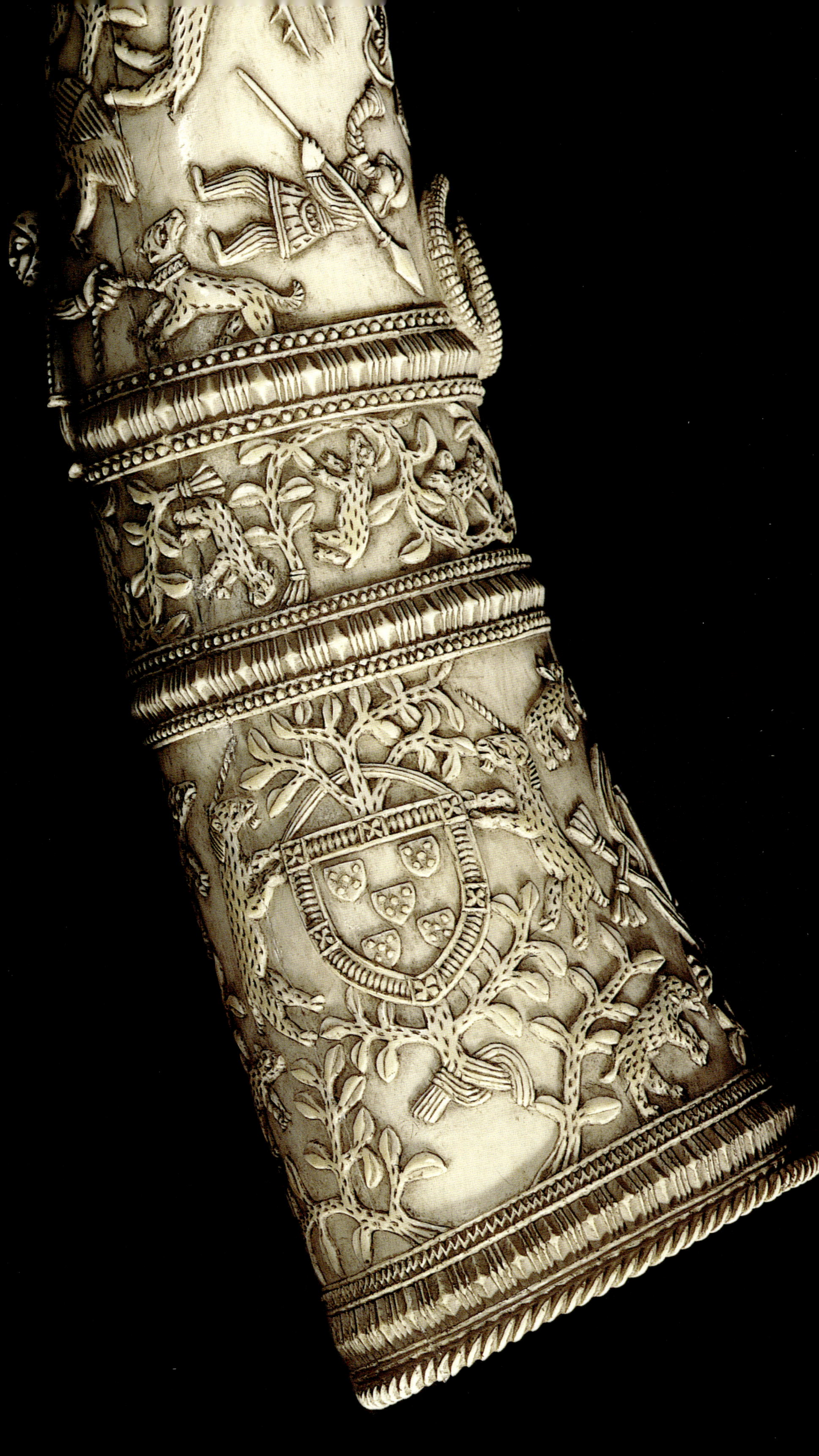

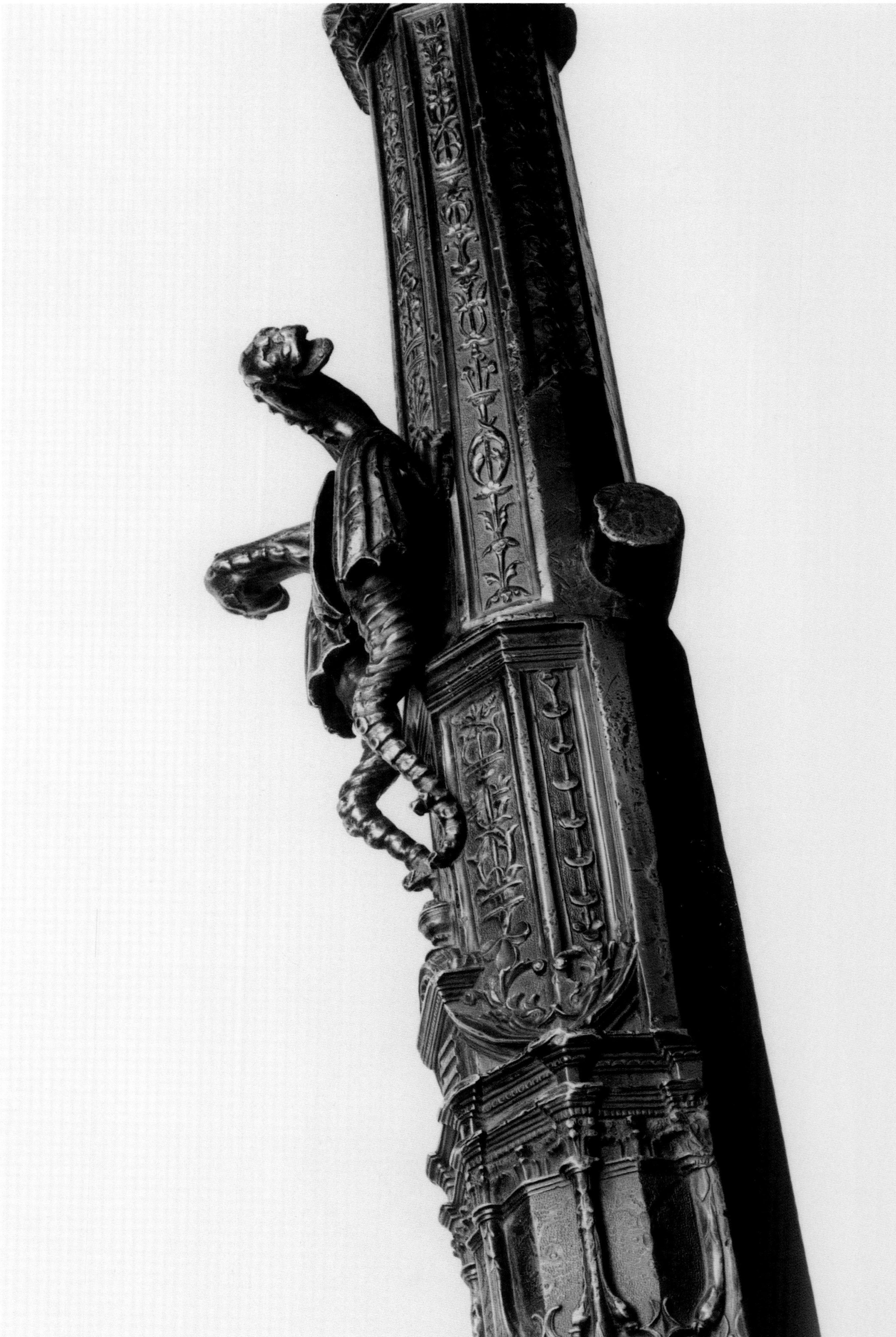

89. Detail of a Flemish (?) gun barrel signed "Maistre Denis", 1535
Tower of London, London

90. The trademark of printer Thielman Kerver, Paris, late 15th c.

Pages 118–119
91. Edo or Owo artist
Benin, Nigeria, 16th c.
Salt cellar
Ivory, 25.5 cm
Musée du Quai Branly, Paris

91a. Another view of the salt cellar no. 91

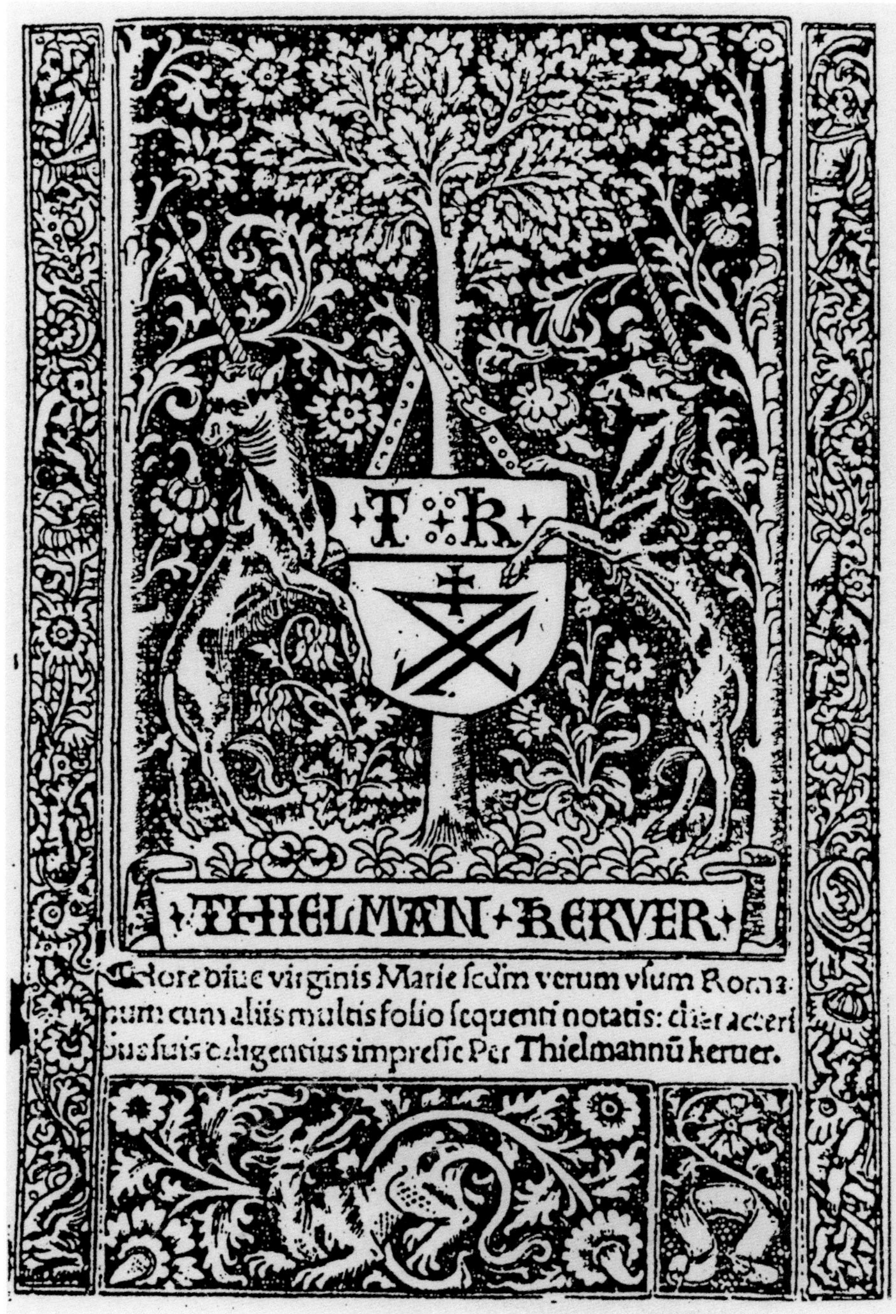

The central section of a salt cellar held in a private American collection that was recently made known to me by the owner (no. 95) compels re-examination of the rigorous classification of these salt cellars into one or the other of the two types defined at the start of this section. Two clearly European horsemen, seen in three-quarter profile, resemble the figures on foot in the item now in the Musée du Quai Branly (no. 91) down to the smallest detail. This demonstrates that one of the sculptors created salt cellars of both the first and second types, either because it pleased him to do so or to suit the wishes of his client.

The dense, bas-relief decoration on the visible areas is a combination of European images and Edo motifs, which confirms the hybrid nature of these artworks.

The spoons created by artists of ancient Nigeria were the African works most sought after by collectors during the Renaissance, especially in the North. The princes of Saxony purchased twelve in 1590 and three more in 1731, the Grand Duke of the Tyrol had six in his castle at Ambras, the dukes of Braunschweig three, and the aristocrat Christian Weickmann of Ulm five. Five spoons also appear, however, as early as 1560 in the inventories of the vast collections of the Medici grand dukes of Florence, where they are described as "mother-

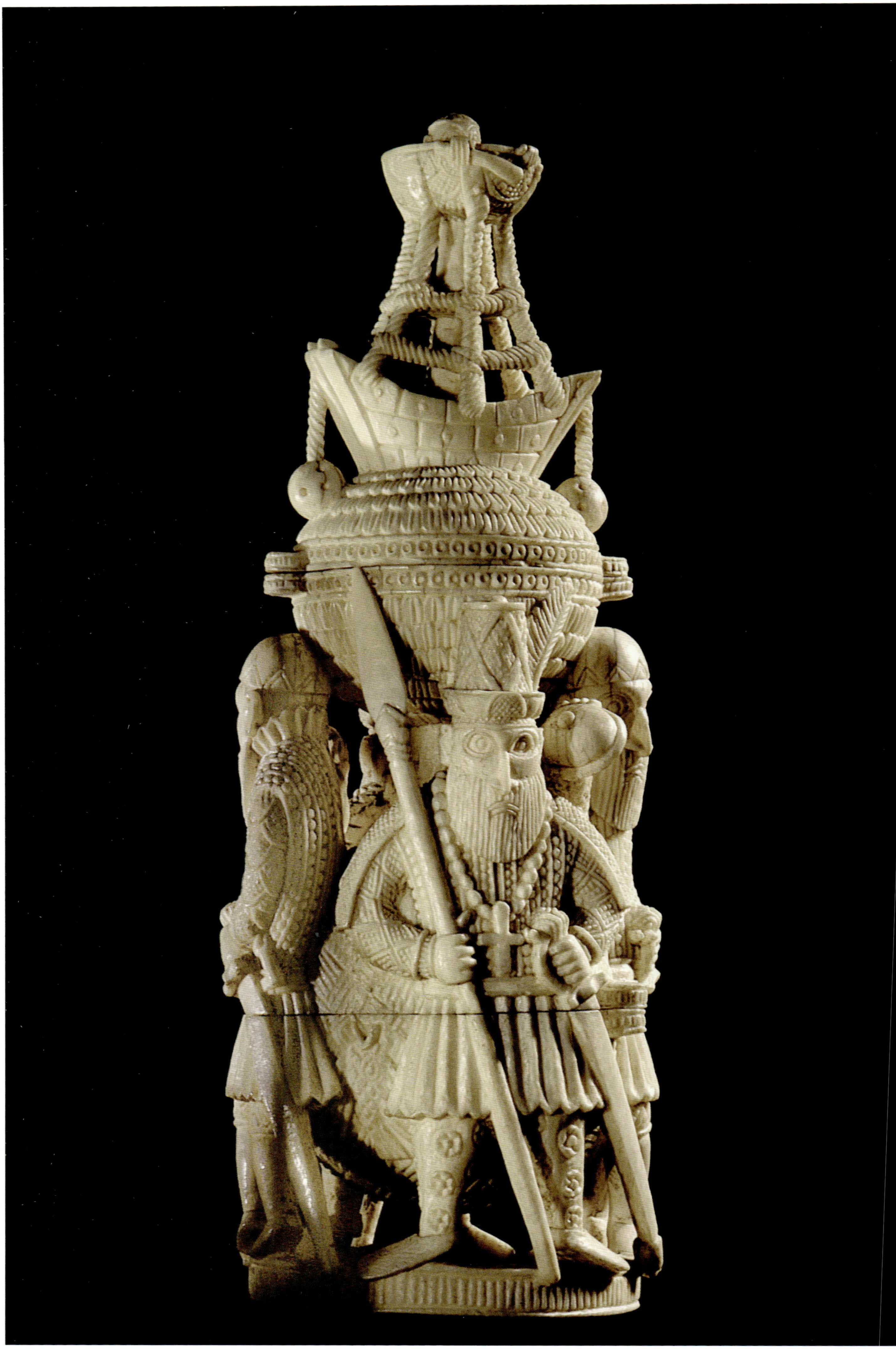

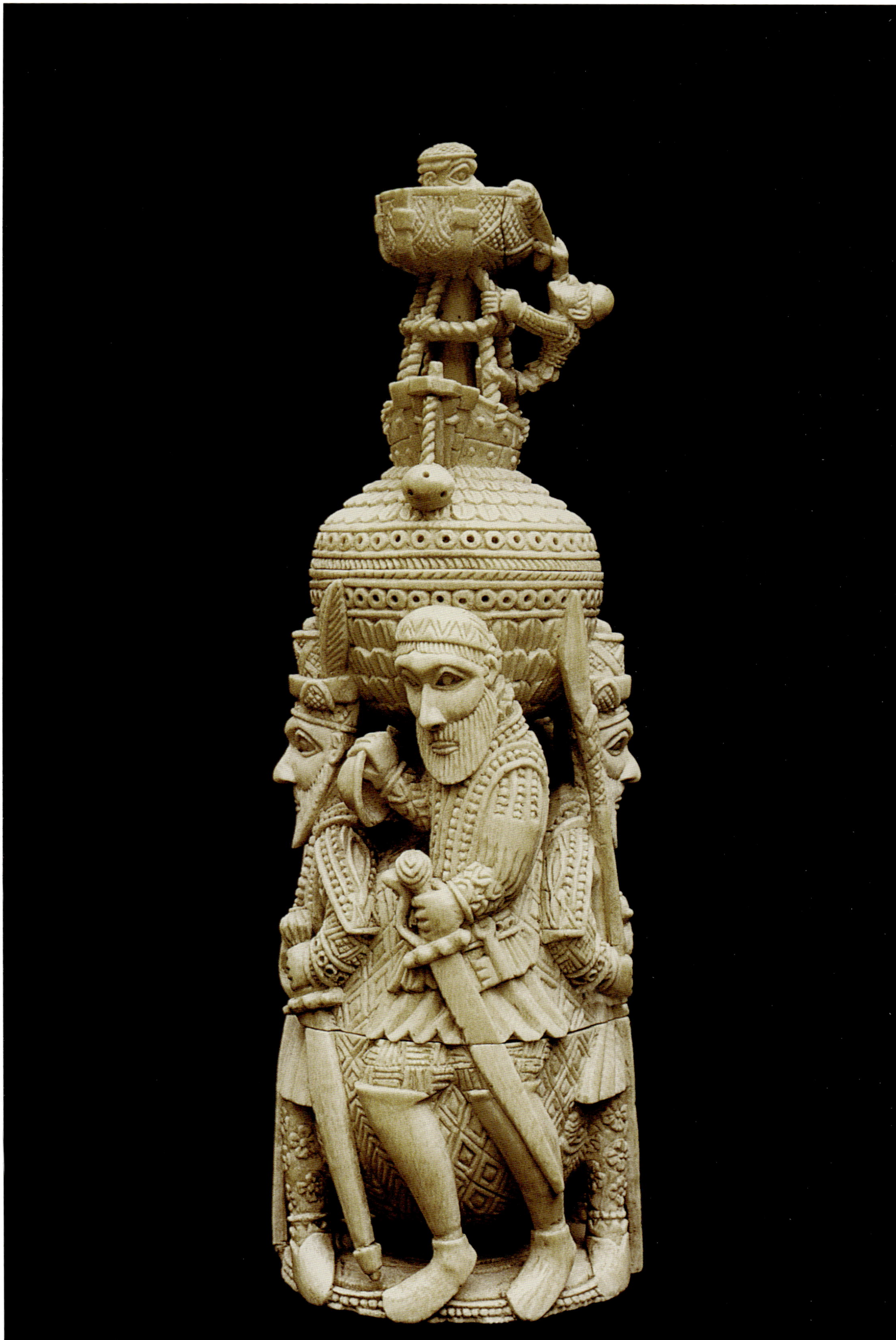

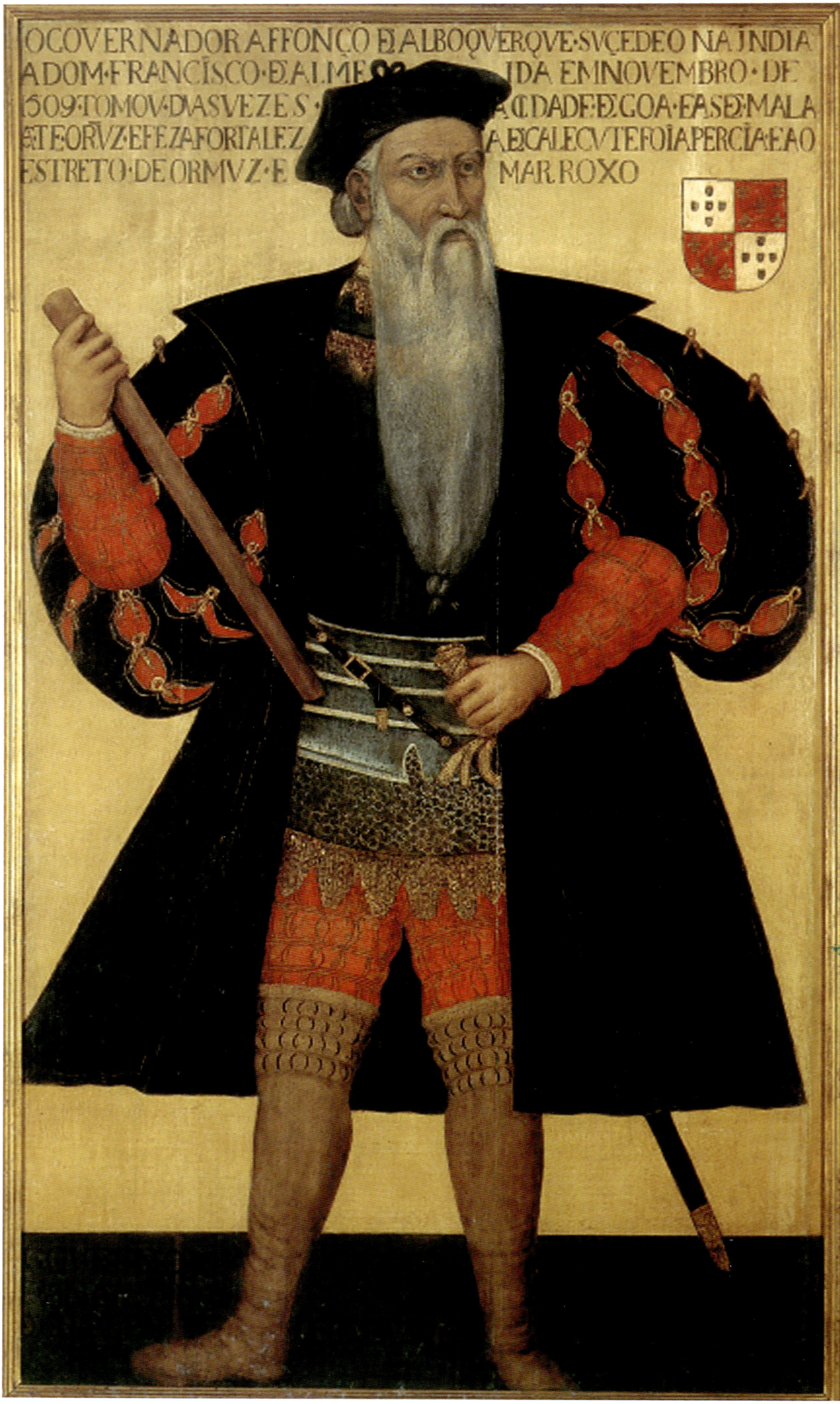
O GOVERNADOR AFFONÇO D ALBOQVERQVE·SVÇEDEO NA JNDIA
A DOM·FRANCISCO·D ALME IDA EM NOVEMBRO·DE
1509·TOMOV·DVAS VEZES A CIDADE DE GOA·E A SE DE MALA
TE ORMVZ E FEZ A FORTALEZA A DE CALECVTE FOI A PERCIA E AO
ESTRETO·DE ORMVZ·E MAR ROXO

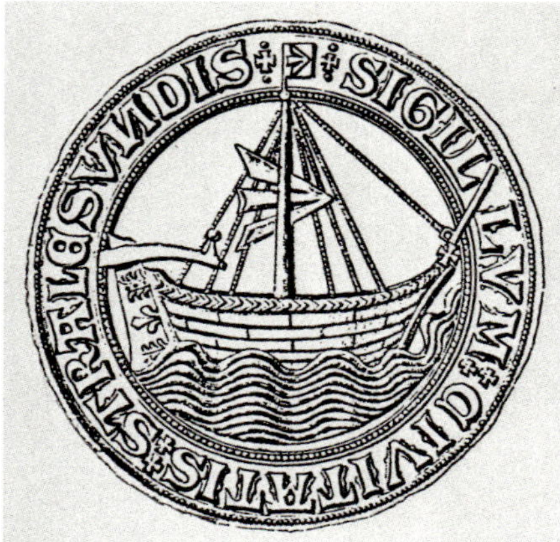

93. Seal of the Hanseatic city of Stralsund, 1301
Kulturhistorisches Museum des Hansestadt, Stralsund

Opposite
92. Indo-Portuguese art
16th c.
Portrait of Alfonso de Albuquerque, second governor of the Indies
Mixed media on wood, 102 x 108 cm
Museu Nacional de Arte Antiga, Lisbon

of-pearl" due to the translucent quality of the very thin concave part. This description was corrected in later records.[27]

These very small works of art were, however, erroneously attributed to Eastern artists. The spoons bought in Leipzig by Grand Duke Christian of Saxony were supposedly "made in Turkey", those at Ambras "of Turkish shape", and those in the collections of the Danish sovereign "East Indian" or even "Japanese".[28]

The first reference to their African provenance is found in the diary kept in 1588 by James Welsh, chief master of the British ship *Richard of Arundel*[29]

Unlike the Sapi-Portuguese spoons, the Bini items usually have an elongated bowl that curves in the shape of a very elegant leaf with marked ribbing on the convex part. The artist's imagination is given more or less free rein in the handle, a small space often crammed with quadrupeds, birds, crocodiles, snakes, fish and shells. A human figure also appears in one case, as we shall see.

The item from the Turin collection (no. 96) fully exemplifies the qualities of the spoons carved in the ancient kingdom of Nigeria. A fierce leopard sinks its fangs into an antelope at the join with the bowl and a sort of capital on its back supports a coiled snake, whose gaping jaws hold a support for an antelope eating a leaf. The sequence as a whole is a wonderfully balanced combination of the miniature and the monumental.

A combination of elements that are found separately on the sixty spoons existing in collections around the world is seen on a spoon in the ancient collections of the dukes of Braunschweig. Serpents, antelopes, monkeys and birds fill a space measuring fifteen or so centimetres.

The handle of the spoon now in the British Museum (no. 97) is the only one in the group that has a human figure, probably a European cabin boy, similar in dress both to the sailor in the rigging of the salt cellar now in Paris (no. 91) and to another figure, perhaps a merchant, holding a "manilla"[30] on a damaged salt cellar now in the Berlin Museum (no. 98).[31] These similarities make it reasonable to suggest that the ivories produced for Europe were carved in a locality close to a port on the Atlantic, where Portuguese ships usually anchored and Europeans could therefore be seen.

A further observation is prompted by the presence of small hollow cylinders in the decoration of the salt cellars (in particular the edges of the upper

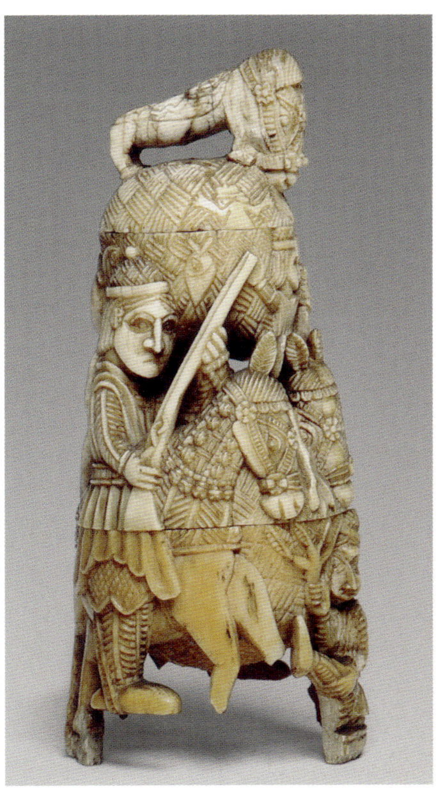

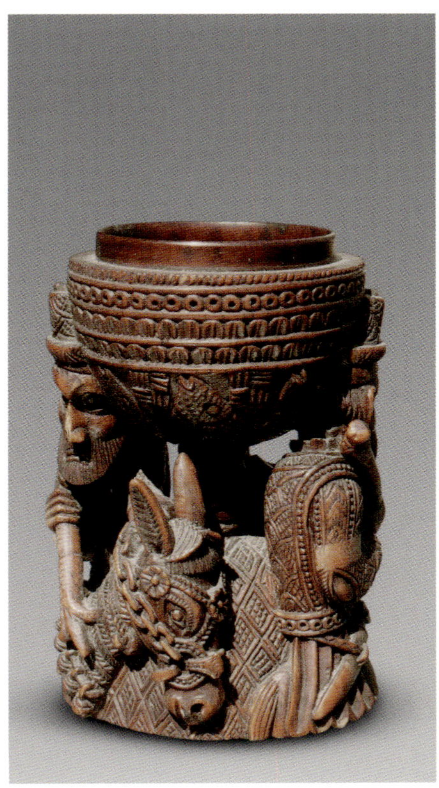

94. Edo or Owo artist
Benin, Nigeria, 16th c.
Salt cellar
Ivory, 19.2 cm
Ethnografisch Museum, Antwerp (formerly in the collection of Frans Olbrechts)

95. Edo or Owo artist
Benin, Nigeria, 16th c.
Central section of a salt cellar
Ivory, 11.5 cm
K. and D. Roth Collection, USA

Pages 122–123
96. Edo or Owo artist
Benin, Nigeria, 16th c.
Spoon
Ivory, 25.5 cm
Museo Civico di Palazzo Madama, Turin

97. Edo or Owo artist
Benin, Nigeria, 17th c.
Spoon
Ivory, 19.7 cm
The British Museum, Ethnography Department, London

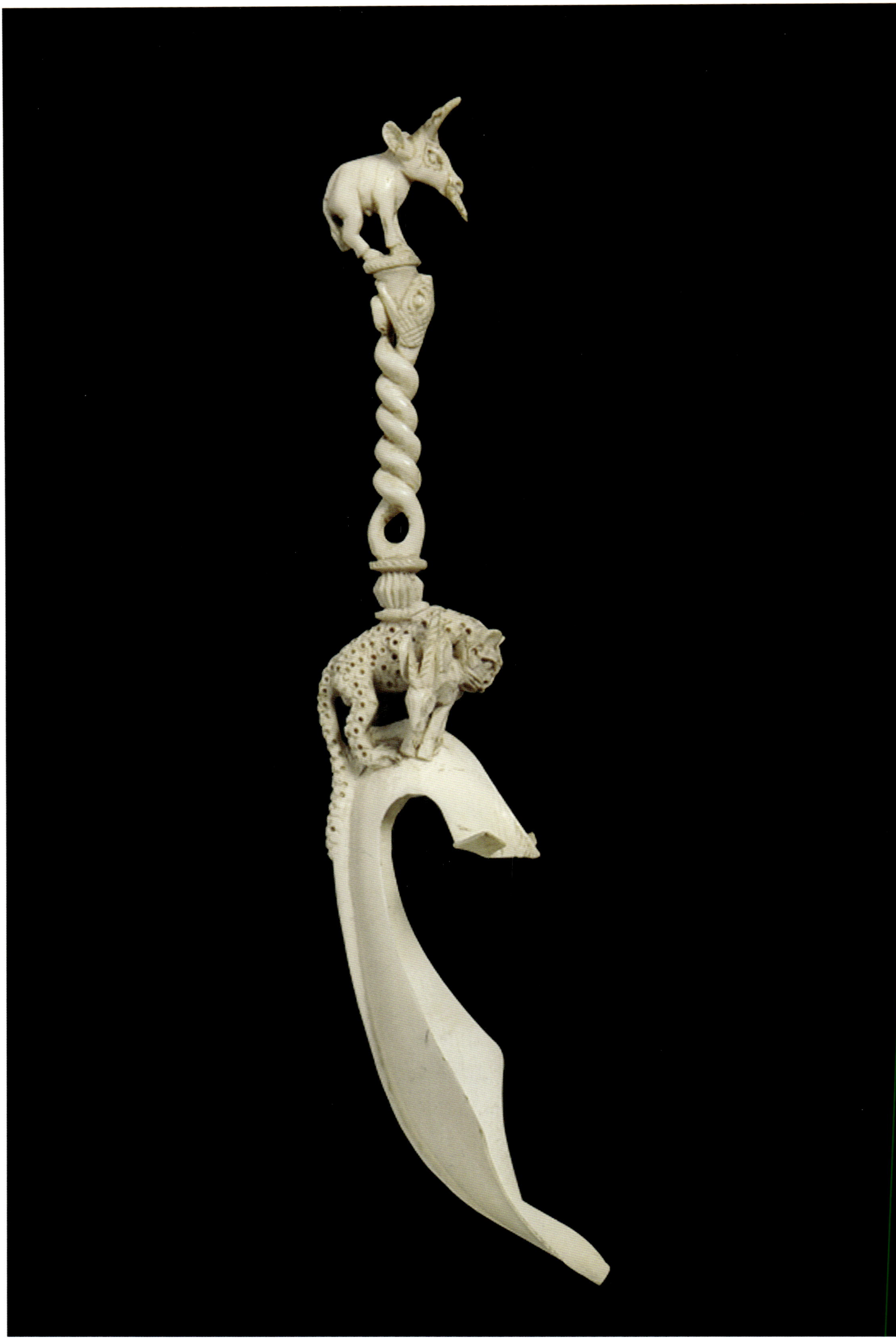

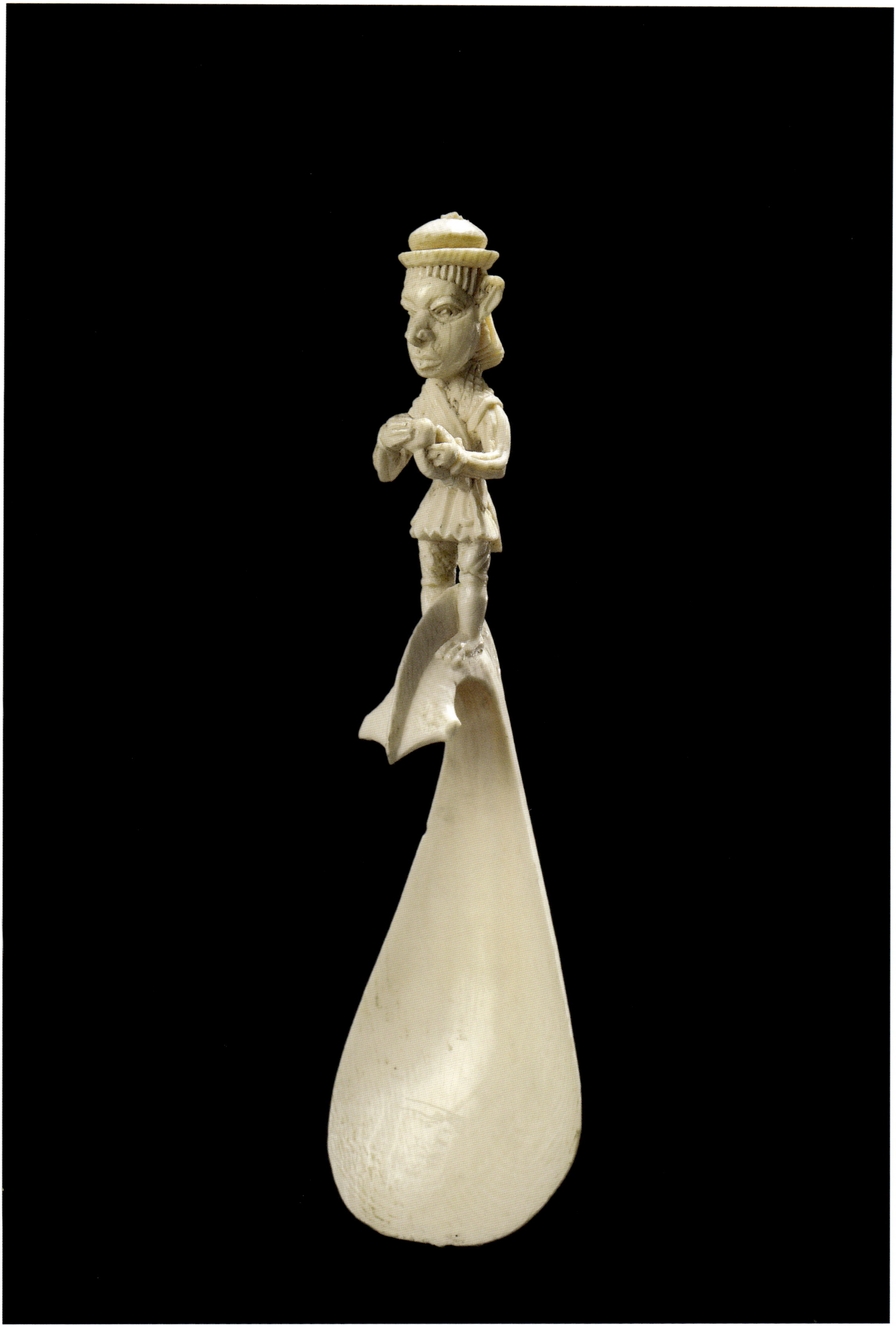

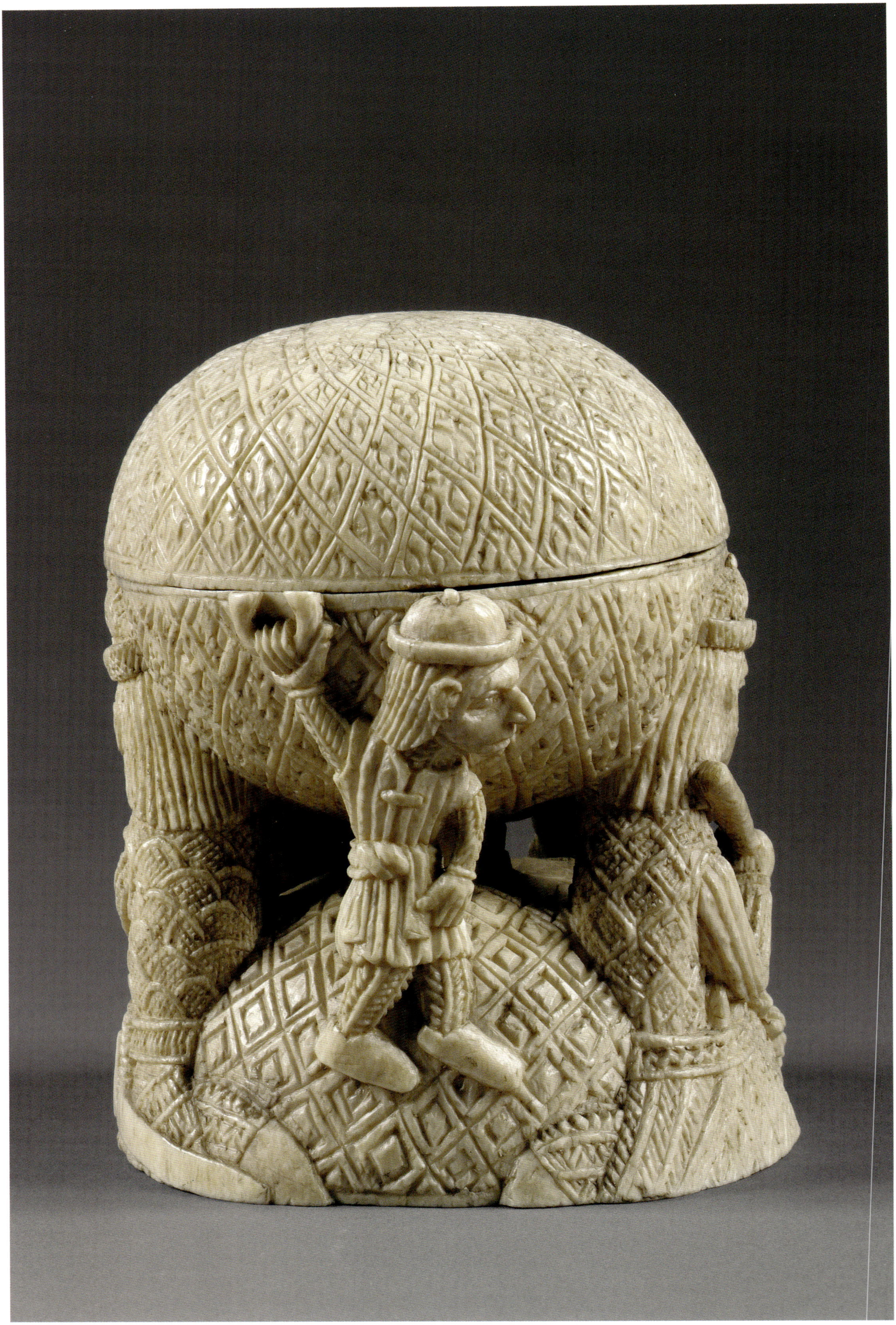

98. Edo or Owo artist
Benin, Nigeria, 16th c.
Salt cellar
Staatliche Museen zu Berlin, Ethnologisches Museum, Berlin (formerly in the imperial Kunstkammer [?])

99. Owo artist
Nigeria, 15th c.
Hand holding a small animal (fragment)
Terracotta, 16 cm
The National Commission for Museums and Monuments, Nigeria

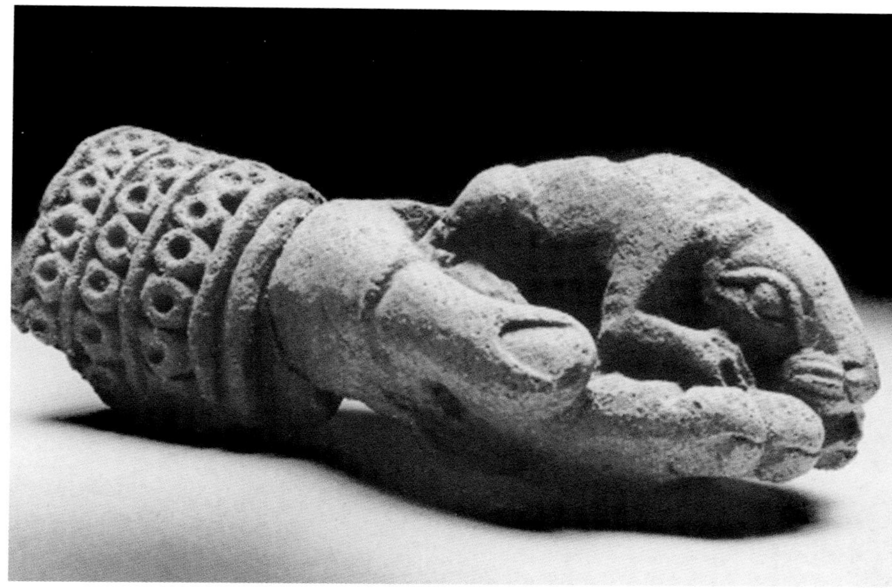

sections; see illustrations nos. 91–91a). These are absent in the Benin artworks produced for the home market but recurrent in Owo ivories, where they are the normal decoration for the bases of goblets with lids and many figures. They also appear in the 15th-century terracotta sculptures from the same culture (no. 99).

Images of antelopes eating leaves and monkeys eating fruit are to be found on Owo spoons and some goblets, but not in traditional Edo art. This appears to support the suggestion put forward by some scholars that the ivories produced for export were the work of artists from both ethnic groups, operating with royal permission in a single workshop. In this case, the term "Bini- or Edo-Portuguese ivories" would need to be corrected.

Hybrids

Some oliphants of different origin have formal and decorative elements characteristic of the works produced both for local use and for export.

One example is the splendid oliphant in an American private collection (no. 100), whose slightly raised, lozenge-shaped, side mouthpiece would suggest a work for the home market, whereas the presence of rings for attaching a strap, the decorative motifs and the polished workmanship are all characteristic of works produced for Europe.

The figures in high relief and the deer-hunting scenes so closely resemble those carved on some oliphants with the mouthpiece at the top in some of the items described below as to suggest that they are the work of the same hand. Other decorative elements are, instead, peculiar to this instrument, namely, the stars, the sun and the moon, and the coat of arms of the Portuguese royal family repeated on two sides, flanked in one case by two pelicans with horseshoes in their beaks and in the other by two harpies. A centaur archer looking backwards could have been taken, with the addition of the quiver, from an illustration in the book printed by Philippe Pigouchet (no. 101), mentioned in connection with the deer hunting scenes.

The most intriguing figure, however, is the galloping horseman brandishing a spear above his head (no. 100a), which is most unusual in European iconography. It is reminiscent of the decoration on a silver Iranian plate of the 7th–8th century (no. 102) in the double tuft at the end of the horse's tail, but this image is unlikely to have reached the African artist directly and how he found it remains a mystery.

Another "hybrid" is the rare oliphant now in the Rautenstrauch-Joest-Museum in Cologne (no. 103). The side mouthpiece set flush with the convex part of the tusk, the absence of rings for a cord or strap, and the geometric decoration all make it an African work and, to be more precise, an example of Benin art (see no. 104, an item for local use, now in the Museum für Völk-

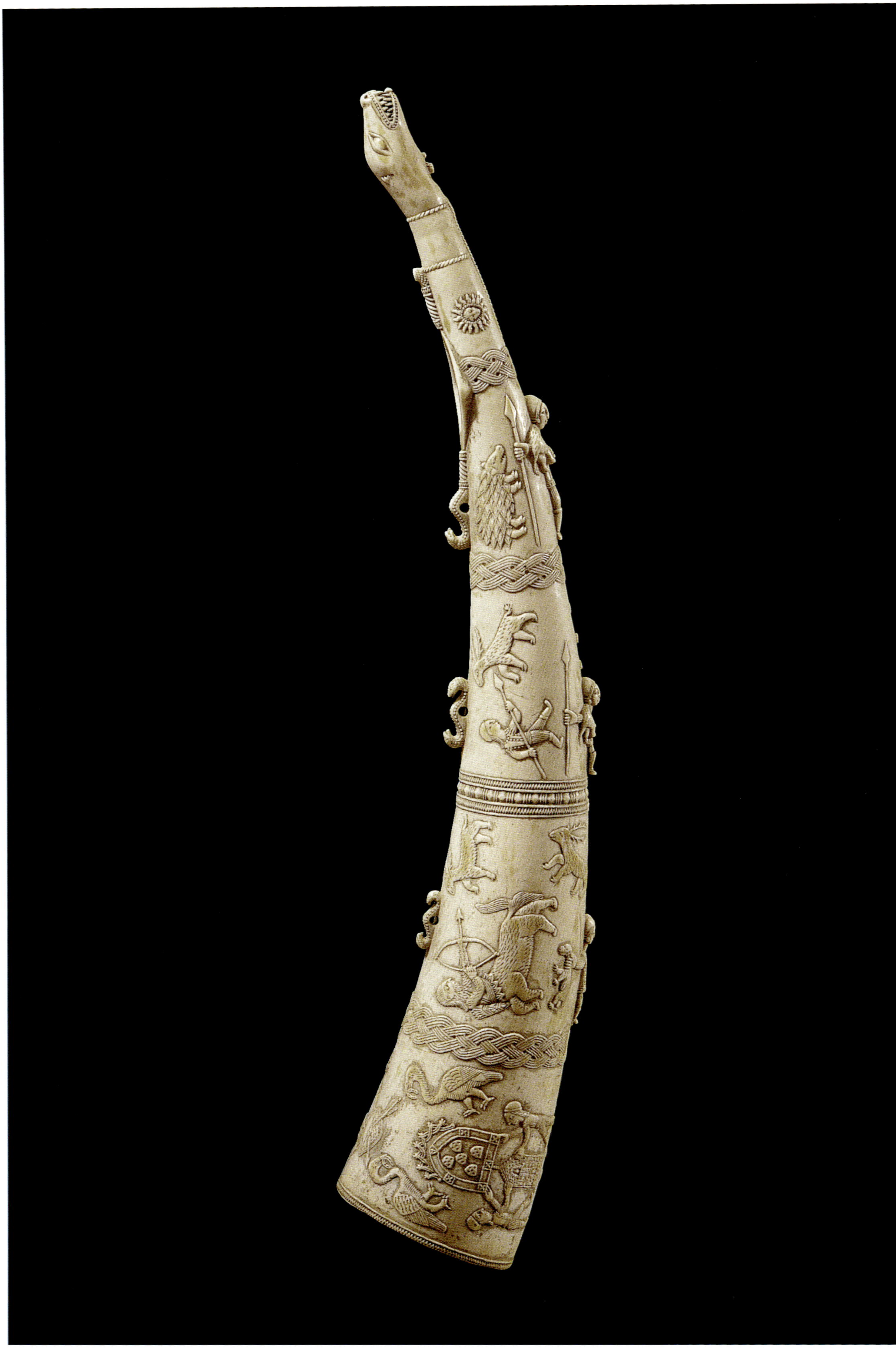

100. Sapi artist
Sierra Leone, 16th c.
Oliphant
Ivory, 54 cm
Private collection

100a. Detail of the oliphant no. 100

101. *Centaur*, detail of an illustration from the incunabulum *Horae Beatae Mariae Virginis* [...], by Philippe Pigouchet, Paris 1498

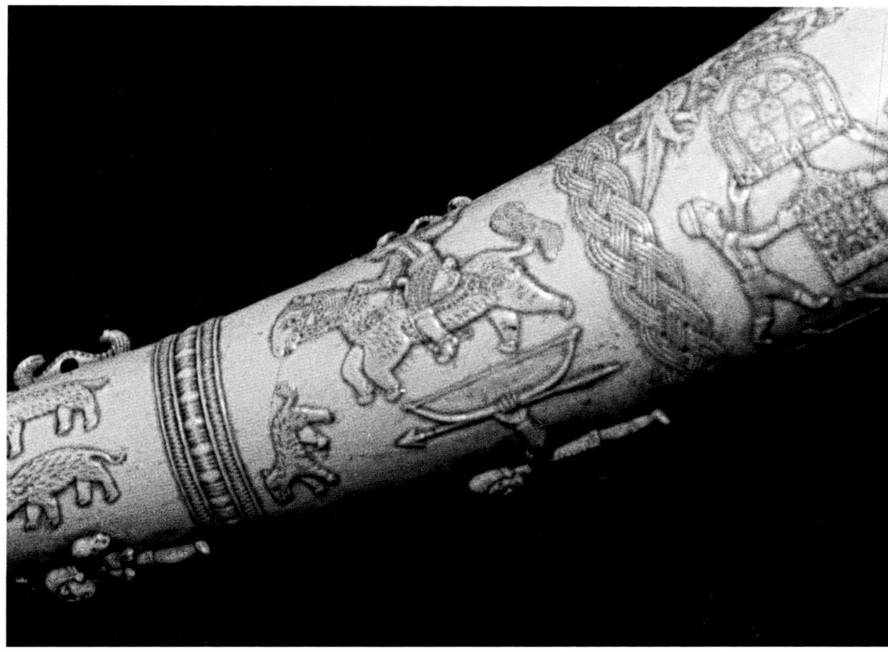

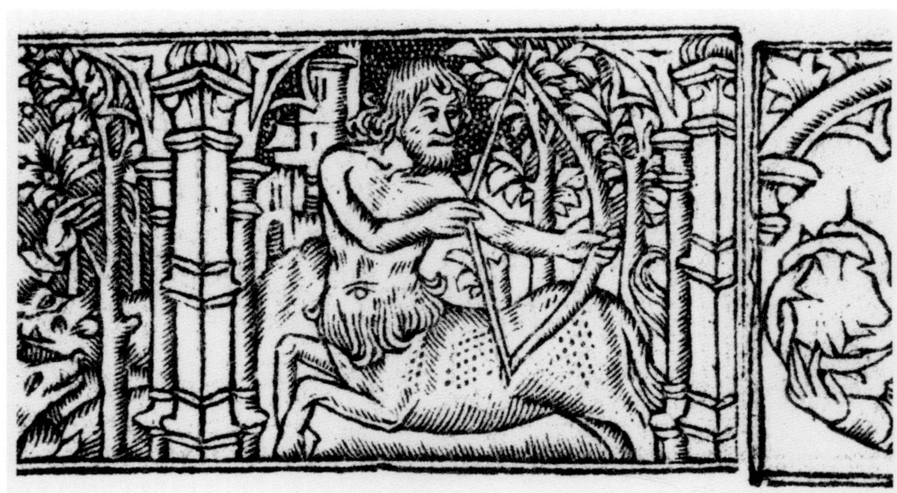

erkunde, Vienna). The coats of arms of the ruling house of Portugal at the time of the first contacts with Sub-Saharan Africa and the hunting scenes reminiscent of those visible on Sapi-Portuguese ivories, albeit less precisely rendered, are elements of European iconography. The animal head with menacing fangs at the top of the instrument resembles the one carved on the Sapi oliphant in the American collection (no. 100), which is purely decorative, the mouthpiece being on the side.

The characteristics summarized above make it possible to put forward two hypotheses. The first is that the instrument (the only complete one of three probably by the same hand) was produced for export to Europe and the sculptor introduced European images into the decoration whilst preserving the local morphological characteristics.

The second and more likely hypothesis, given the absence of rings for a strap, is that the oliphant was carved for an important personage or even the ruler of the African kingdom and the decontextualized European motifs performed a purely decorative function.

The two highly sophisticated instruments recorded in the inventories of the Florentine grand dukes in 1553 (nos. 105–106) are further examples of the hybridization mentioned above, even though the rings for the strap are the only elements that indicate that they were intended for Europe.

The motifs carved on the walls – which can also be seen on antique fabrics (nos. 107–108) and artefacts as well as recent sculptures and tattoos on human bodies (no. 109) – have been in the figurative heritage of the Congo[32] since time immemorial and certainly before any contact with Europeans, as is

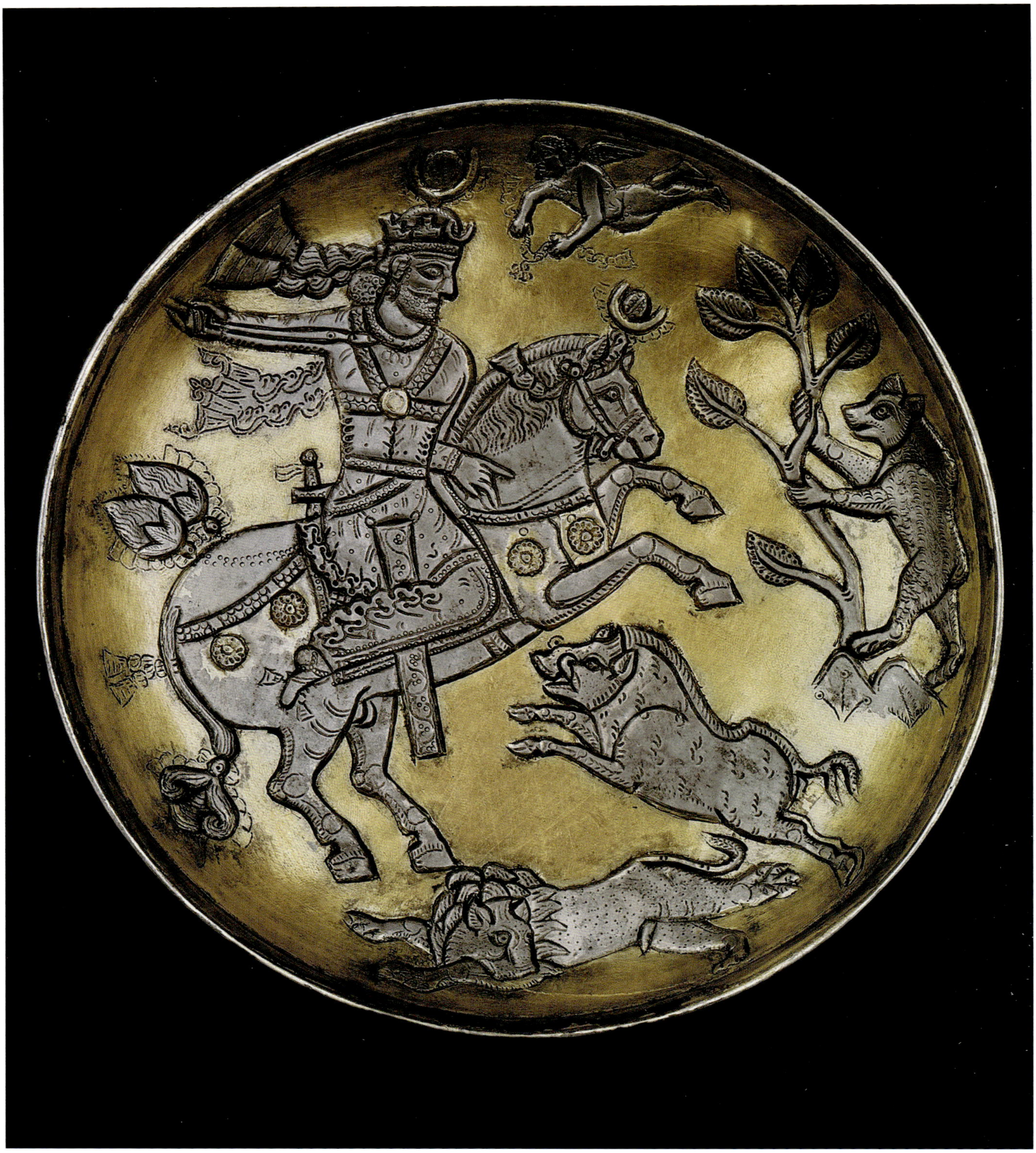

102. Iranian artist, 7th–8th c.
Plate with hunting scene
Gilded silver
Museum für Islamische Kunst, Berlin

103. Edo or Owo artist
Benin, Nigeria, 16th c.
Oliphant
Ivory, 57 cm
Rautenstrauch-Joest-Museum, Cologne

104. Edo artist
Benin, Nigeria, 17th c.
Oliphant
Ivory, 54.5 cm
Museum für Völkerkunde, Vienna

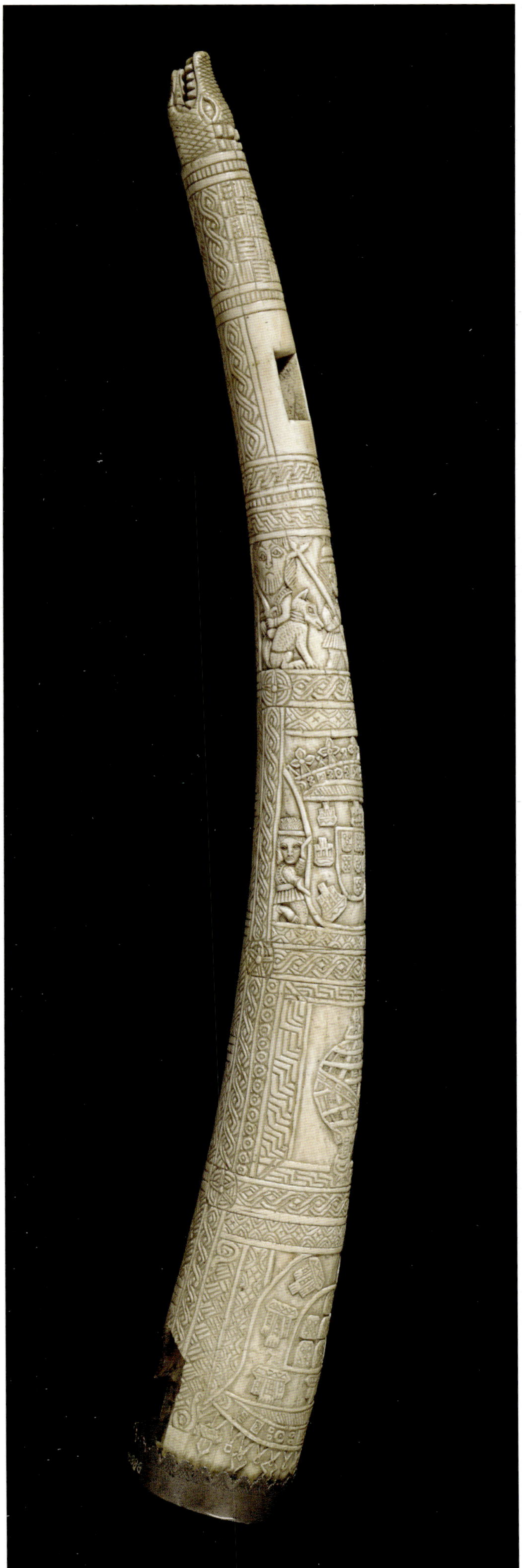

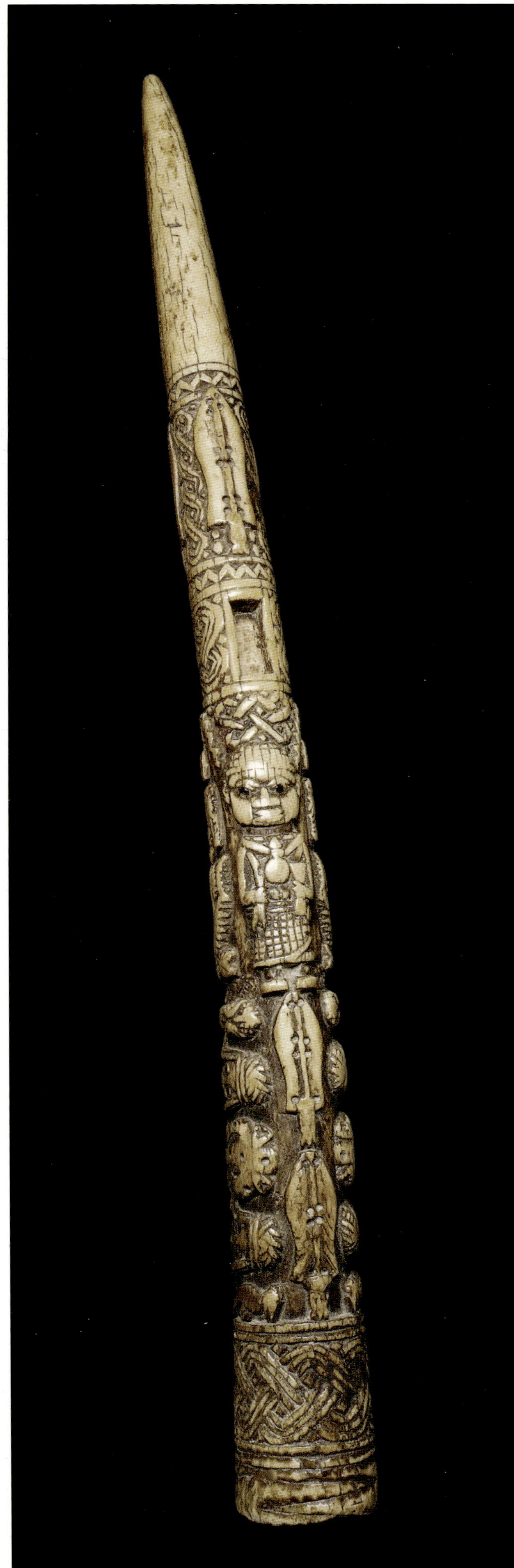

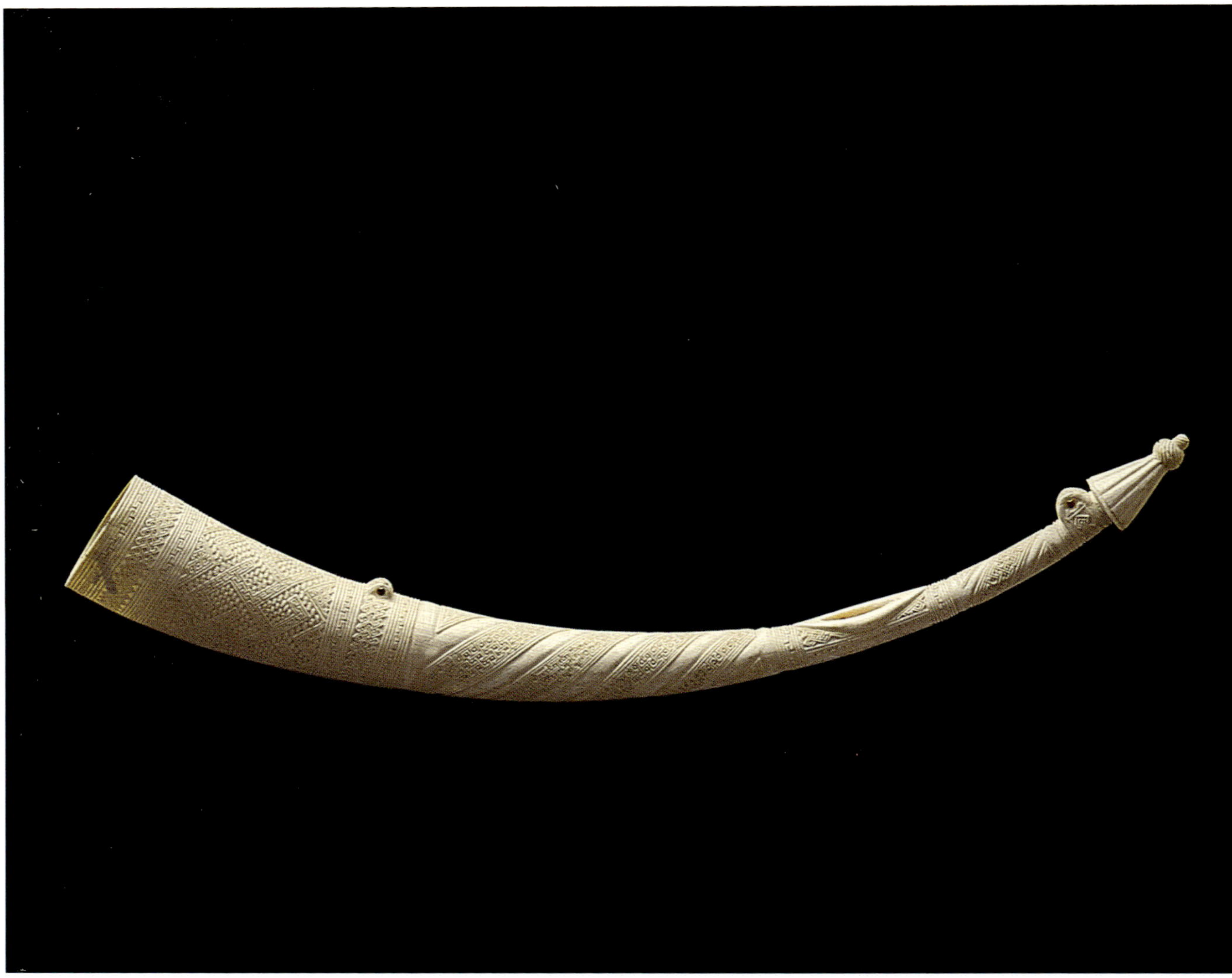

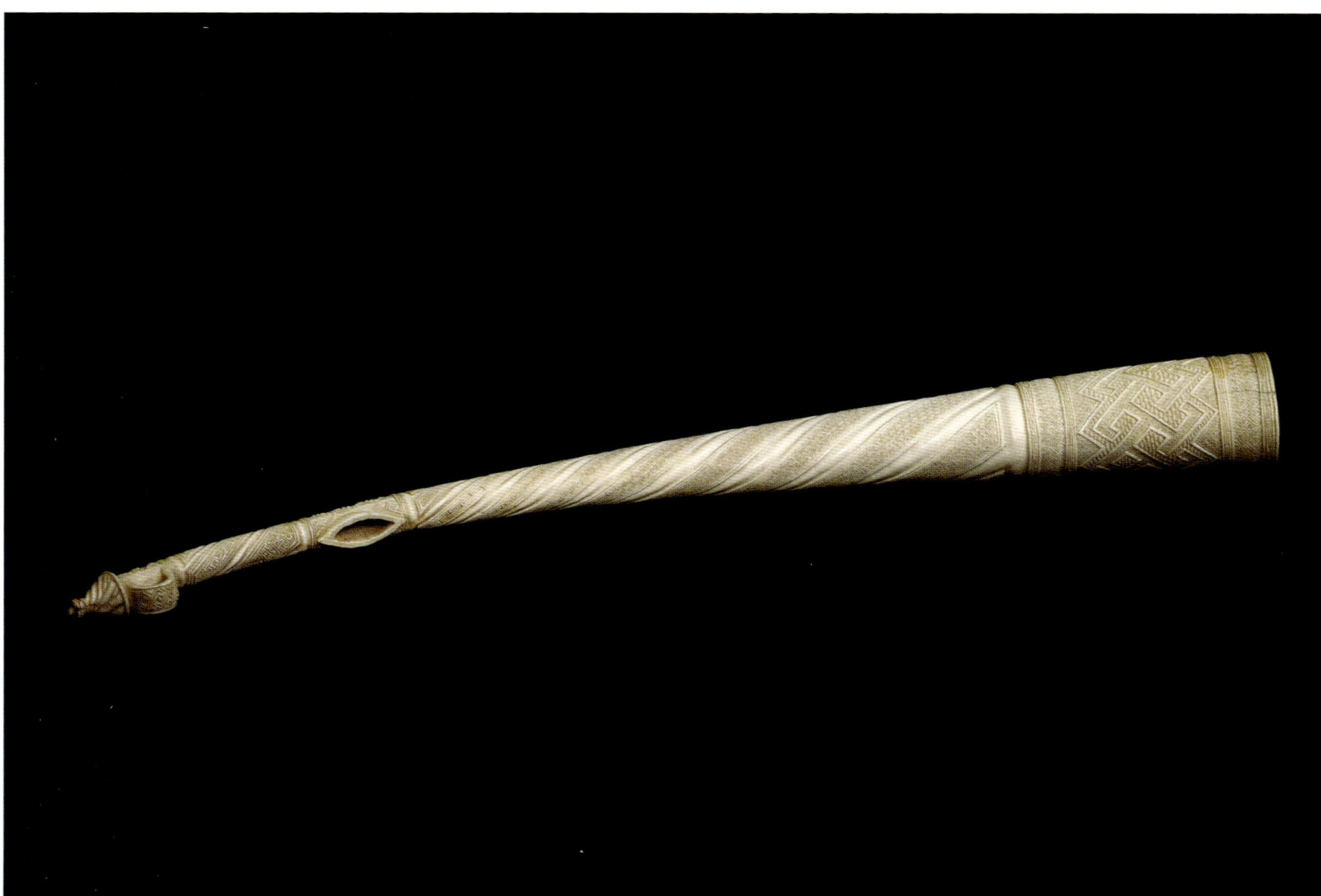

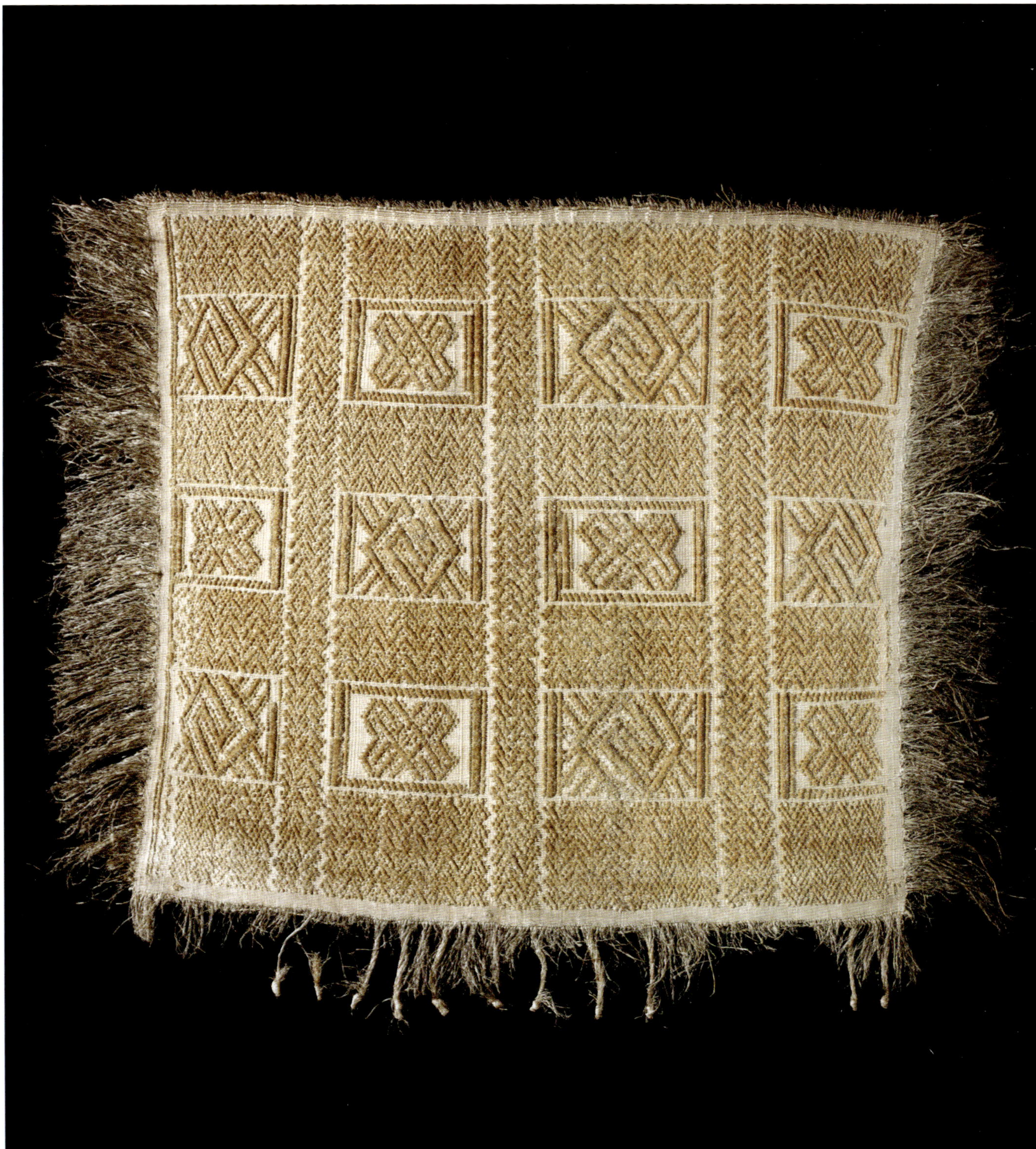

105. Congo artist
Ancient kingdom of Congo,
15th–16th c.
Oliphant
Ivory, 83 cm
Museo degli Argenti, Florence

106. Congo artist
Ancient kingdom of Congo, 16th c.
Oliphant
Ivory, 57.5 cm
Museo degli Argenti, Florence

107. Congo artist
Ancient kingdom of Congo,
16th–17th c.
Palm thread textile
Museo Nazionale Preistorico
Etnografico "L. Pigorini", Rome

le quei avesse parte da lei confessate, mi di propria bocca havendolo per più volte interroga
to sopra di ciò: Si pare bene, e conveniente quello facesti pigliarmi in Guerra, e

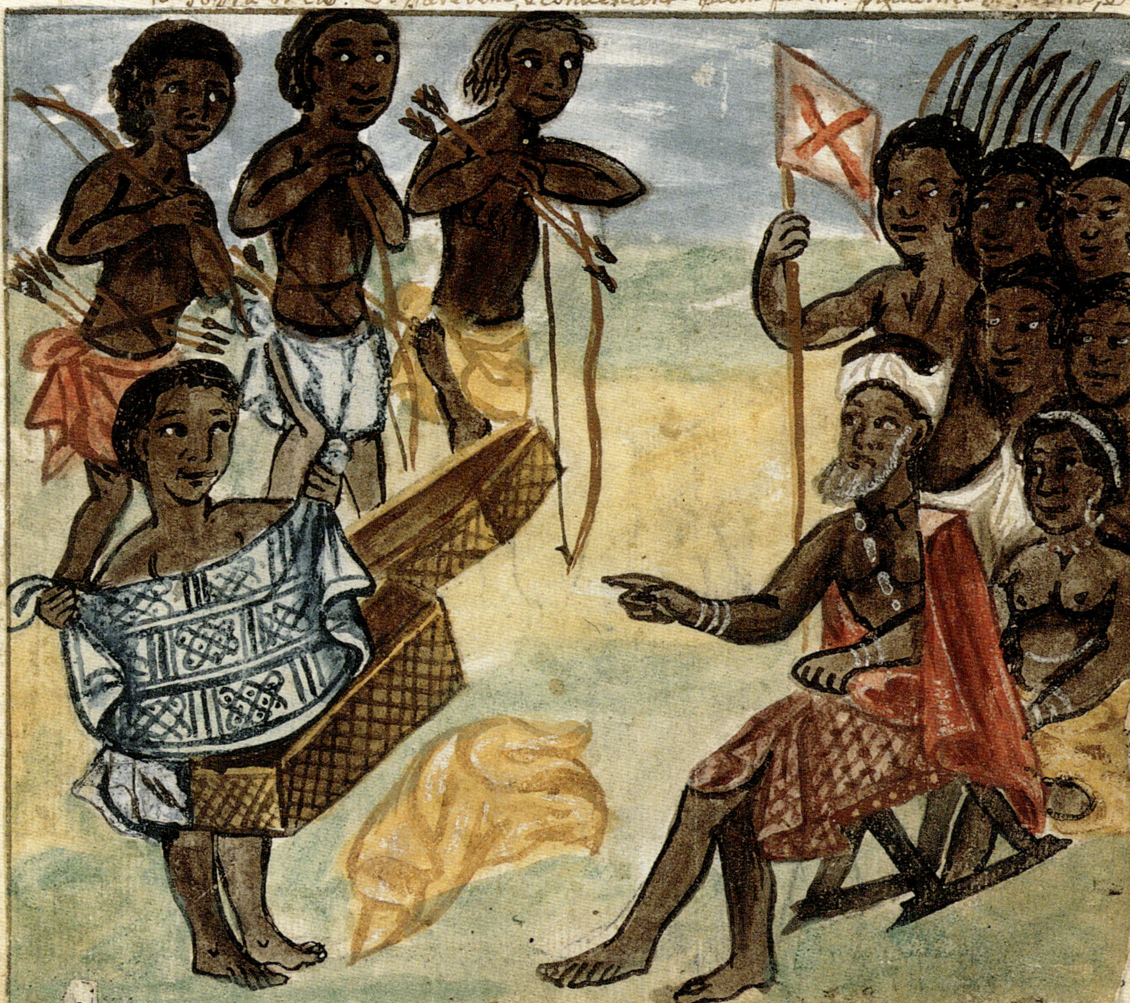

poi lasciarmi nel bosco. mandò senza dimora a [illegible] del [illegible]
facesti gettare, e portami alla Regina sua Sig.ra altrim.te facendo, non partirai
senza castigo, e questo per tre volte replicò sempre con maggior timore,

108. *Offer or sale of fabrics*, illustration from the manuscript of the Capuchin missionary Giovanni Antonio Cavazzi da Montecuccolo, produced in Congo-Angola before 1665

109. Kongo woman (Yombe group) with her back entirely covered in decorative scarification marks. Photograph taken before World War II by an ethnologist from the Tervuren Museum

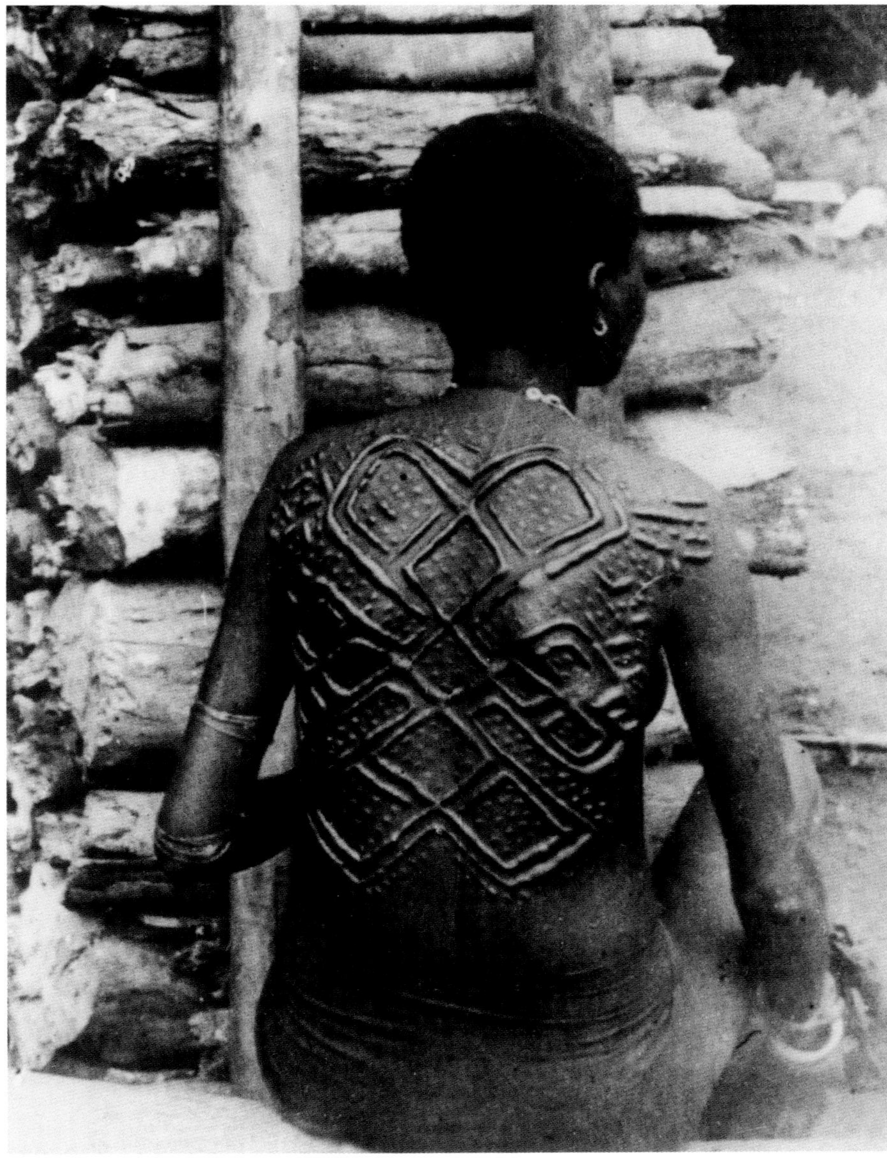

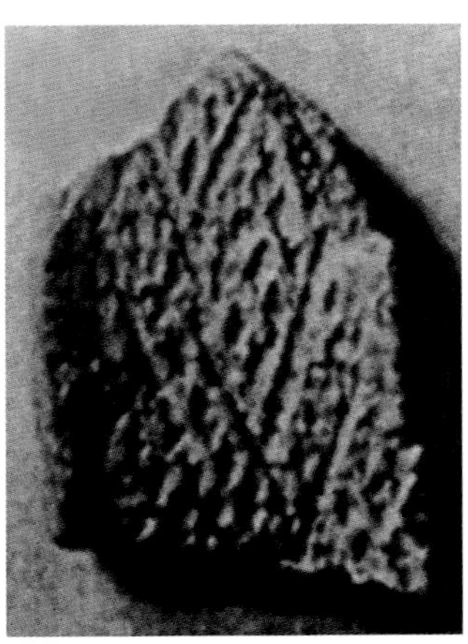

110. Terracotta fragment with printed decoration found by James Dembow during excavations on the coast of Loango together with other fragments dated to the 13th c.

evidenced by a terracotta fragment (no. 110) unearthed in 1990–91 on the coast of the pre-colonial kingdom of Loango (now part of the Republic of the Congo) and dated to the 13th century by James Dembow.[33]

Together with another four probably by the same hand,[34] the two instruments may have been a gift from the ruler of Congo to one of the Medici popes – probably Leo X,[35] who was repeatedly in contact with the converted African sovereign during his pontificate – or a gift from the king of Portugal, intent on securing Vatican support for his colonial policies.

The highly sophisticated carved decoration, dominated by a deft combination of lozenges, Greek frets and plaits, is skilfully distributed over a spiral-shaped space on the conical surface of the instruments. This intricate and crystalline geometric design reveals the hand of a virtuoso who has perfect mastery of his craft.

Works of uncertain ethnic provenance

A group of about ten oliphants (two of which are incomplete) with side mouthpieces, highly elegant in form and with minimal decoration (a crocodile head), raises more questions than the previous cases.

Only three of them have rings for a strap, two on the concave side and one on the convex. While unquestionably African, the crocodile head does not appear on any other artefact of this kind, which raises questions about their ethnic origin. What is certain, however, is the sculptural quality of their extraordinarily refined simplicity and their African provenance, even though the description accompanying the illustration (pl. XXX) of an instrument in

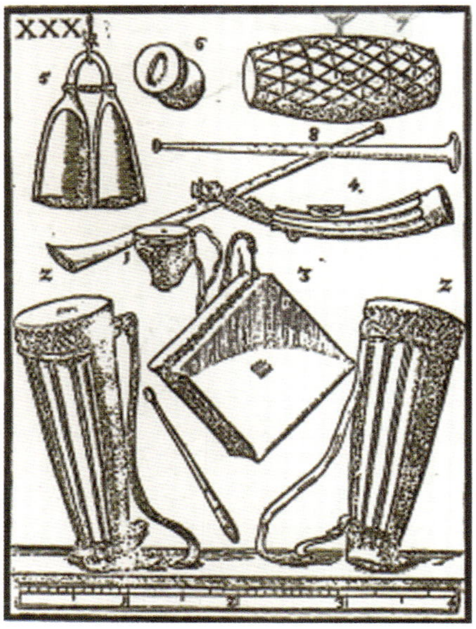

the *Theatrum Instrumentorum* by Michael Praetorius, published in 1619 – the earliest record of their existence – speaks of an "Indianische Horn von Helfenbein" or "Indian ivory horn" (no. 111). The date of this book constitutes, however, an indisputable *terminus ante quem* for the production of this kind of instrument.

The crocodile in the illustration reproduced by Praetorius has a human head in its jaws, a detail that appears in no other existing item, but is unquestionably authentic. The precision of the image is such that the illustrator must have drawn the instrument from life and may even, according to Pierre Sallée,[36] have used a camera obscura device for this purpose.

The oliphant (no. 112) formerly in the Kunstkammer of the dukes of Gottorp, Schleswig-Holstein[37] and now in the Nationalmuseet, Copenhagen, is almost identical to the one in the *Theatrum Instrumentorum*, including the ring on the convex side, and is therefore a good example of these works, which are so similar as to suggest that they were all produced by the same workshop within a very short space of time.

111. *Musical instruments*, pl. XXX of the treatise *Theatrum Instrumentorum* by Michael Praetorius, Wolfenbüttel, 1619. Oliphant no. 4 is described as an "Indianische horn"

112. Artist of uncertain ethnic origin, 16th c.
Oliphant
Ivory, 66 cm
Nationalmuseet, Copenhagen (formerly in the Kunstkammer of the dukes of Gottorp, Schleswig-Holstein, manuscript inventory of 1710)

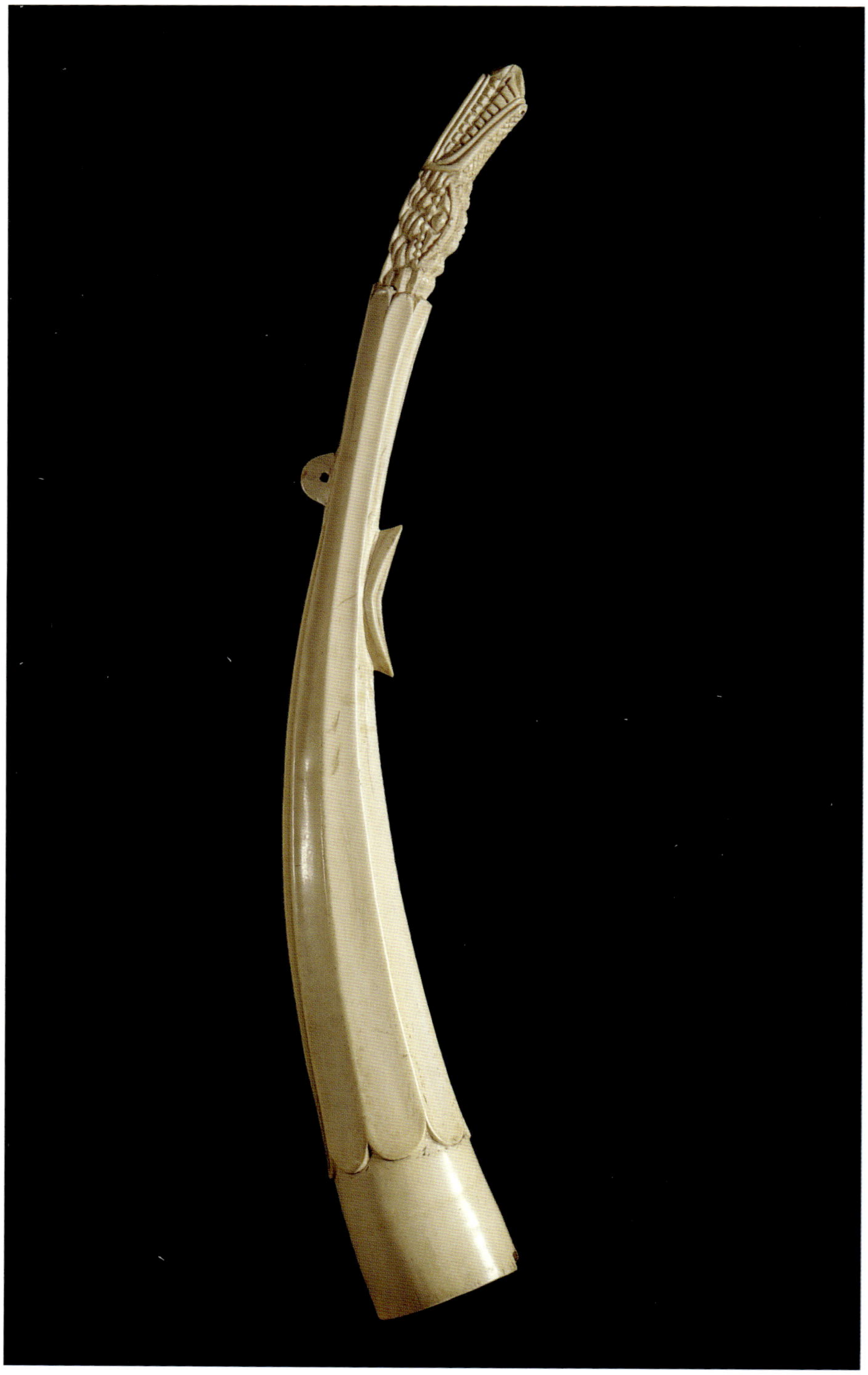

[1] Foy 1900–1, pp. 20–22.
[2] The entries are limited to the period September 1504–September 1505 because the previous and subsequent registers were lost in the 1755 earthquake that destroyed part of the city of Lisbon. The Casa da Guiné was a sort of customs house that recorded the arrival in Portugal of goods on which duty had to be paid.
[3] Inv. 108828.
[4] "*Em Serra Lyoa som os homês muyto sotijs e muy êgeniosos fazem obras de marffim muy marauilhosas de ver de todallas cousas que lhes manda fazer. s. hûus fazem colheyras outros saleyros outros punhos pera dagas et qualquer outra sotileza*" (Fernandes 1951, p. 96).
[5] A Moravian scholar resident in Portugal and author of a report drawn up between 1506 and 1508, Valentim Fernandes never set foot in Africa. His description of Sierra Leone, its inhabitants and their culture is based on the observations of Álvaro Velho, who spent many years in that country. See Hart 1995, p. 38.
[6] Elements common to the Yoruba culture are also found in the salt cellars as will be seen below.
[7] See Bassani, Fagg 1988.
[8] Welsh 1904, p. 452.
[9] Bassani 2000, pp. 180–81.
[10] Mark 2007, pp. 77–85.
[11] Only one of this type is to be found among the Sapi-Portuguese examples. See Bassani, Fagg 1988, no. 15.
[12] African figures wearing skirts and trousers were high-ranking personages. The European figures, which appear on only three items, are in 15th- or 16th-century dress. See Bassani, Fagg 1988, nos. 33, 34; Bassani 2008, nos. 44, 45; Bassani (forthcoming).
[13] "*Un vaso d'avorio con due teste in cima al coperchio intagliato*". *Inventario del Museo, che sta nel Giardino alle 4 Fontane*, Archivio di Stato, Rome, Notai A.C. 3248 – Francesco Franceschini, published by G. Incisa della Rocchetta, 1966, pp. 141–192.
[14] See Purchas 1625, p. 2. Note the similarity with those carved on the breast of a nomoli in the British Museum.
[15] See the prints by Hieronymus Hopfer (the great copyist of Dürer, active in Augsburg around 1520), Wenceslas of Olmutz, and Albrecht Altdorfer (1480–1538).
[16] "*Calice antico d'avorio con suo coperchio figurato*". *Inventario semplice* 1680.
[17] Recorded in 1981 with the inventory number 1981.AF35.1.
[18] The catalogue has been lost.
[19] This collection was to become the core of the present-day Hancock Museum collection. For a more complete European history of salt cellars, see Hart (forthcoming).
[20] The other two are now in the Museu Grão Vasco, Viseu, and the Walters Art Gallery, Baltimore.
[21] The silver pyx is decorated solely with an image of the Virgin in the round on the lid and four medallions with bas-relief portraits of the Evangelists and ornamental motifs on the wall.
[22] See also the essays by Jean-Michel Massing cited in the bibliography (Massing 2007[a] and 2007[b]).
[23] See the introductory note.
[24] The many sources for the decorations of the other oliphants include scenes of other animal hunts, on foot or horseback, as well as animals and monsters from the European bestiary (centaurs, dragons and harpies) copied from other devotional books or individual prints and drawings. The Indian elephant carved on the oliphant now in the Musée du Quai Branly (inv. 71.1933.6.1.D) is actually taken from a fresco by Raphael, a sketch of which by the Portuguese artist Francisco de Holanda was subsequently copied and sent to Africa as a model. See Bassani, Fagg 1988; Bassani 2000; Bassani 2008; Bassani (forthcoming).
[25] In addition to the specimen illustrated, there is one in the Museum of African Art, Washington, D.C., (formerly in the Tishman Collection) and another in the Museo de Pontevedra (Spain). Two pieces of a broken third instrument were turned into powder flasks. The fragment with the coats of arms and the inscription were once in the collection of Carlo Monzino. See Bassani 2000, nos. 768, 769, 770.
[26] The illustrations in the devotional books produced by the two printers are quite similar.
[27] Three of these spoons are now in Florence (Museo Nazionale di Antropologia ed Etnologia, inv. 216/1, 216/2, 216/3) and two in Rome (Museo Nazionale Preistorico Etnografico "L. Pigorini", inv. 6515/G, 6516/G).
[28] "*in Türkey sein gemacht worden*", "*auf den Turgischen furmb*", "*Ostindiske udskaren Skeer*" and "*Japonisk Skee*" (Bassani 2000, pp. 5, 12–13, 101).
[29] See note 8.
[30] Manillas were copper objects commonly used by Europeans in trade with Africa. The handle of a spoon in a private collection (Bassani 2000, no. 813) is the head of a crocodile biting an arm that holds a manilla.
[31] Ethnologisches Museum, Berlin, inv. IIIC4980, perhaps formerly in the imperial collection.
[32] A group of peoples now inhabiting regions of the present-day Republic of the Congo and Angola. In the recent literature they are named Kongo, which term will be used below for the recent works.
[33] Dembow 1991, p. 9.
[34] See Bassani 2000, nos. 280, 429, 483, 484, 513 and 576. There are also some examples of less polished workmanship with rings for a strap on the convex part of the tusk.
[35] Giovanni de' Medici, pope from 1513 to 1521.
[36] See Sallée 1985, p. 90.
[37] Recorded in the manuscript inventory of 1710 as no. VCI/7, one of a group of five "savages' horns made out of elephant tusks".

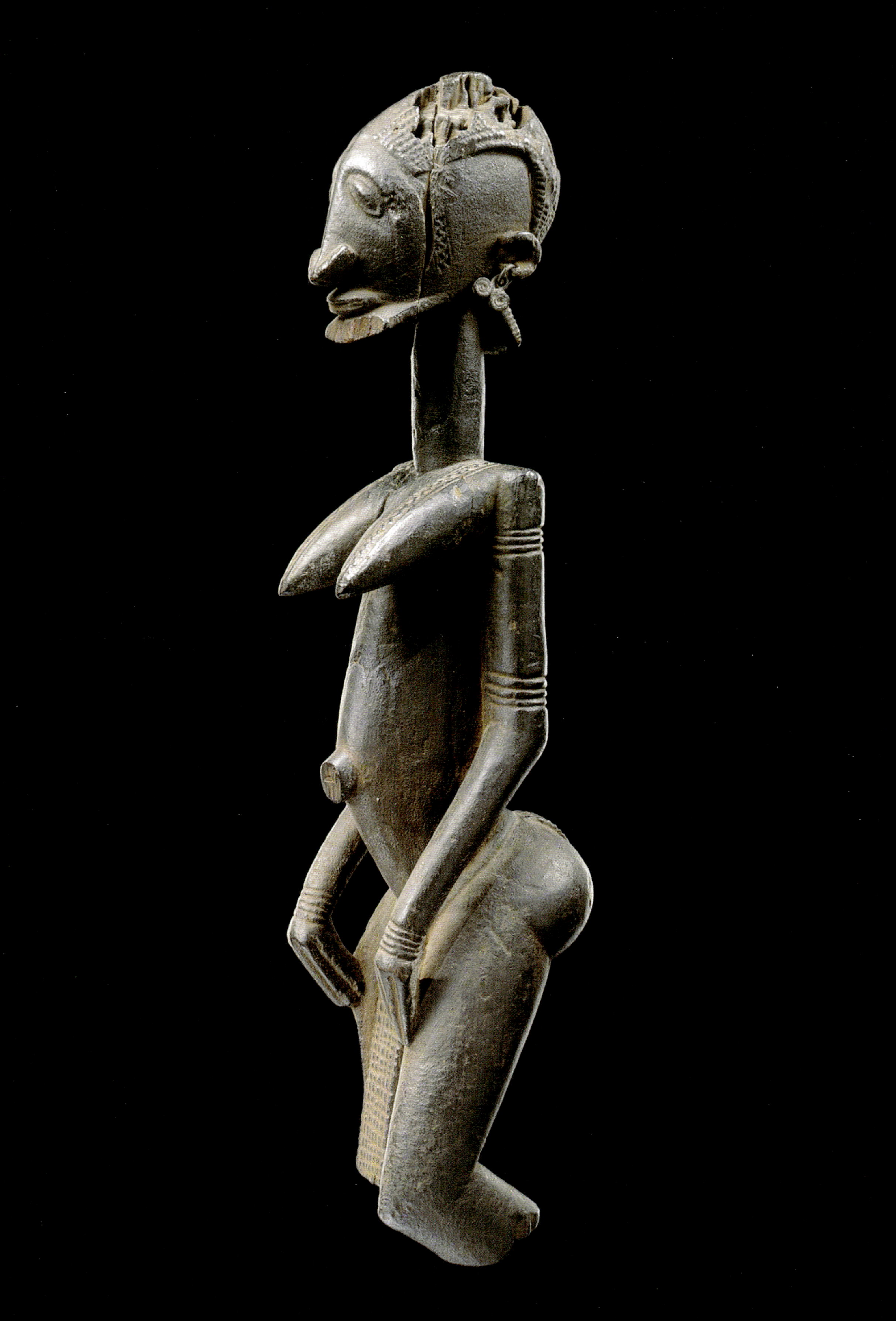

Attributions

The idea of an art scene where the leading actors are always off-stage may seem paradoxical, like something out of the theatre of the absurd, and it is certainly so for anyone working in the field. This was, however, the situation as regards African art until just a few decades ago.

The attempt to identify the authors of African artworks is a recent and very demanding development, made still more arduous by the absence of written documentation in Africa and by a lingering residue of intellectual racism in the West. African works were slighted for a long time by being described as "anonymous", an adjective that denied their individuality. A supposed widespread, impersonal, collective authorship, a hangover from colonialist ethnography in keeping with the image of a primitive Africa, was uncritically accepted. In reality, African artists of the past, usually professionals specifically trained through a long apprenticeship, not only responded to a need in their community, but also imbued their works with their own creative personality in the same way as the artists of the "civilized" West. In other words, they were the conscious authors of inherently valid works, expressive in their own right and fully capable of generating emotion and knowledge.

As William Fagg quite rightly points out, traditional norms were the framework within which African artists were required to work and create. The constraints imposed by the subject matter did not limit their freedom of expression, but regulated and channelled it, just as they did in Europe. To give just one example, being commissioned to sculpt a Madonna did not prevent Michelangelo from creating the masterpieces that we know so well.

Investigations in the field of attribution are, however, still in the early stages and the results are as yet modest compared to those obtained in the Western arts.

The attempt to establish authorship is made extraordinarily difficult both by the absence of a written language, and hence of documentation – a problem already noted in connection with dating – and by the fact that the works are dispersed today in hundreds of museums and private collections throughout the world, and are therefore only available for first-hand comparison when they are shown in exhibitions. A sculpture that may be the work of a specific artist is hard to attribute if it is isolated and can only be compared with photographs of others thought to be by the same hand; indeed, this situation is likely to lead to erroneous attribution on the basis of general similarities. Direct comparison, comparative analysis of wood, metal, earth and patina, and rigorous verification of all the information connected with the works, including where and how they were brought to light, are indispensable if reliable results are to be obtained. Consideration of how much has been and is being done in the study of the Western arts will give some idea of just how immense this task is.

A further difficulty lies in the fact that it is impossible – or rather that we are unable – to identify signs which enable us to see or at least glimpse the hand of a particular artist in apparently different works on different subjects.

113. "Master of the Slanted Eyes"
Dogon, Mali (N'duleri region), 17th–18th c. (?)
Female figure
Wood and metal, 59 cm
Musée du Louvre, Pavillon des Sessions, Paris

114. "Master of the Slanted Eyes"
Dogon, Mali (N'duleri region),
17th–18th c. (?)
Male figure
Wood and metal, 73.5 cm
Private collection

It is inconceivable that the authors of sublime, but apparently isolated works should not have created others and that none of them should have survived. The destruction of Africa's artistic heritage has been systematic in many cases, but certainly not selective. It is therefore more logical to assume a development in the artists' creative processes and hence changes in the canons of artistic expression, which are hard to identify in the absence of written documentation or direct comparison, as noted above.

This situation also means that the traditional African artists cannot be given their real names and we have to make do with pseudonyms, names used for the sake of convenience, which was in any case standard practice in the study of a great deal of European painting during the 19th century. Unfortunately, this temporary expedient will inevitably become the norm for African art, as it is impossible that documents revealing the names of the authors of the past will ever come to light, and the evidence gathered in situ is at best abgout artists from some comparatively recent time. As noted by a number of Western scholars who have addressed the problem, matters are made even more complicated by the fact that many African societies may have appreciated the best works, but attached no importance to their authorship, the name of the owner being often remembered but not that of the artist.[1]

Frans Olbrechts and William Fagg were the pioneers in the attempt to establish the authorship of African artworks. After examining and comparing the morphological characteristics of about ten Luba sculptures shown in Antwerp at the memorable exhibition 'Kongo Kunst' in 1937, the former concluded that they were the work of the same artist, or at least the same school or workshop, rather than examples of a regional sub-style.[2]

The stylistic individuality of a particular sculptor, referred to as the "Master of Buli" after the name of the village in the present-day Democratic Republic of the Congo, where two works in the group were found, was thus recognized for the first time in the history of African art. Further studies by scholars[3] in subsequent years led to the identification of about ten more works attributable to the master and a follower.

As regards the traditional canons in Africa, as early as 1951 William Fagg questioned "whether they are any more restrictive of genius than were the conventions of religious art in Renaissance Italy".[4] Thirty years later, he stated explicitly that "the work of art is the outcome of a dialectic between the informing tradition and the individual genius of the artist."[5]

These assertions echo the observation made with full artistic cognizance by the sculptor Jacob Epstein in 1931: "The finest works of art are the works of highly individualized artists, with an outlook and a technique of their own."[6]

The late 20th and early 21st century have seen a number of exhibitions, publications, conferences and other initiatives devoted to the problem of the authorship of African artworks, and Alisa LaGamma showed twenty-eight works by Nigerian artists active in the 19th and 20th centuries in the exhibition 'Master Hand: Individuality and Creativity among Yoruba Sculptors'[7] at the Metropolitan Museum of Art, New York, in 1997.

The first exhibition devoted to a traditional African sculptor was held in 1998, when Roslyn Walker presented forty-five works attributed to the Nigerian artist Olowe of Ise at the Museum of African Art in Washington, D.C.[8] In that year and the following one, two issues of *Authorship in African Arts* addressed the problem of authorship in African art. It was also in 1999 that Raoul Lehuard and Louis Perrois organized a colloquium on the subject entitled 'Ni anonyme ni impersonnel'. Finally, the works of no fewer than fifteen African masters active in different periods and countries, from Mali to South Africa, were presented in Brussels by Bernard de Grunne in the memorable exhibition 'Masterhands/Mains de Maîtres' in 2001.[9]

In addition to the exhibitions, authors such as Marie-Louise Bastin, Joseph Cornet, Eberhard Fischer, Hans Himmelheber, Lorenz Homberger, Hélène Leloup, François Neyt, Louis Perrois and Frank Willett have opened up previously unexplored fields of knowledge with studies devoted to the work of

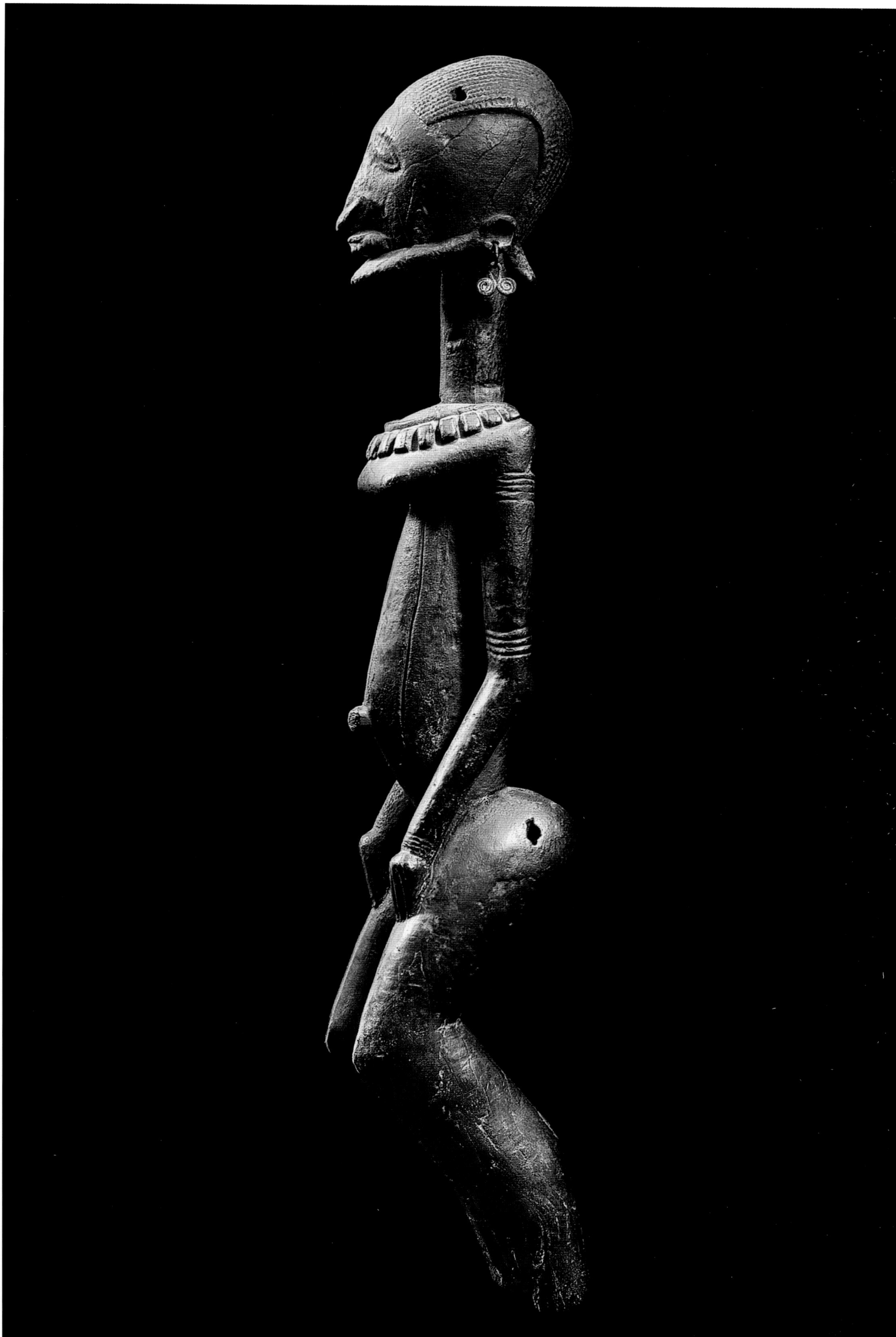

specific African artists or schools of sculpture. The process of attribution certainly poses enormous problems and the results are never definitive due to the countless replicas, copies and variants deriving from the masters' archetypes. Moreover, to quote Michel Laclotte, "it is imprudent to draw a distinction between an original and an excellent copy on the basis of a photograph". As pointed out above, it is only a first-hand comparison of the greatest possible number of homogeneous works that can give some indication of which might be attributable to the master, since creativity and individuality are inseparable. However, the unfortunate fact that this is seldom possible inevitably limits the sample presented here.

For reasons of space, this section will again provide only a sort of anthology, focusing on the work by artists from some ethnic groups who provide evident and significant examples, or, in any event, with whom I am most familiar. Due to the same constraints, fewer examples will be given of work by sculptors from some peoples, while others will receive little more than a mention.

After an initial group of ancient Dogon, Edo and Sapi-Portuguese sculptures, this section will follow the same course as the first chapter, starting with the Bamana, Senufo, Baule and Guro peoples and proceeding from north to south. It is hoped that the examples put forward will give at least some idea of the vast scale and complexity of the problem and, above all, of the urgent need to continue and intensify this type of research by drawing upon the combined skills of everyone involved.

The focus in some cases will be on the works by a number of artists operating in the same workshop and using the same forms of expression, but with the introduction of slight variations that make it possible to identify the hand of the individual author.

To conclude, despite all the difficulties and limitations, the process of attribution is not a sterile pastime, because the acquisition of new elements or a new name increases our knowledge of African art and enriches our understanding of it.

The "Master of the Slanted Eyes"

At first glance the universe of Dogon sculpture presents such marked differences that establishing authorship in a field of artistic activity that spans many centuries appears a hopeless task. But this is not so.

Two sculptures, one in the Louvre (no. 113) and the other in a private collection (no. 114), can be attributed to a great artist called the "Maître des Yeux Obliques" by Hélène Leloup, due to his figures' slanted eyes.

This particular hallmark is accompanied by a large number of recurrent features including the way the parts of the body are articulated, the positioning of the bracelets and bangles, and, above all, the shape of the head. The coiffure of small plaits following the line of the skull, the excessively shaved temples to enhance the elongation of the head, further emphasized by the vertical incisions that delimit the area of the face, the identical position and shape of the tiny ears, the marked accentuation of the arrow-shaped nose, and the small spade-shaped beard all make his works unmistakable. Nothing is known about their function in the society where they originated or how they arrived in Europe.

Curiously enough, the two figures considered here both wear the same spiral-shaped iron earrings as the woman pounding millet (no. 12), who also has steatopygia as well as similar tattoos on her cheeks and breasts. While the same shaving of the hair and similar rendering of features can also be seen in sculptures such as the celebrated couple playing the balafon (no. 13) and the horseman now in the Musée Dapper, Paris,[10] the dating for these two works is several centuries earlier than the one in the Louvre, which would suggest that some figurative conventions were maintained over a long period of time.

Two great Benin artists

The spoils of the punitive expedition that destroyed the city of Benin in 1897 (see no. 36) included, among the various artworks, about one thousand bronze plaques (many of which were damaged), similar to the decorative panels on the doors of Romanesque basilicas. Some scholars suggest that the African artists may have found the model for these plaques, and in particular their rectangular format, in illustrations brought by European sailors. Systematic examination would make it possible both to put these sculptures into thematic and perhaps also chronological order, and to distinguish the personalities of the more significant artists.

I am able to present the sculptures below thanks to the sharp eye of William Fagg, a pioneer of research in this field, who also coined the names by which their authors are known.

The "Master of the Circled Cross"

One of these artists is the "Master of the Circled Cross", who was probably active around the end of the 16th century and owes his name to the small crosses in the background of the approximately twenty-five works attributed to him.[11] He is the only author of large figures, for which he invented the device of spreading the scene over two plaques, evidently to be seen together, perhaps for technical reasons that limited the size. Unfortunately, due to the division of the spoils that followed the destruction of the city, the two halves of the work shown here are now in different museums and can only be seen together in exhibitions.

Two of the plaques feature a warrior or dignitary of the Edo court (nos. 115–115a) and the other two a Portuguese figure (nos. 116–116a). Both are distinguished by the attributes of their nationality and status: a leopard skin, a tall mitre-like hat, three spears and a decorated shield in the first case; a pleated skirt, an elegant sleeveless doublet, a very large hat perched upon a mass of hair, a staff of office and a sword in the second.

The perfectly frontal representation and the motionless, vertical pose of the slender figures (especially the Portuguese), enhanced by the deft positioning of the spears and the staff, the accompanying fishes and snake, and the use of low relief, make the creations of this master of bronze quite unique. William Fagg describes his elegant, solemn figures as endowed with "calligraphic beauty".

According to Paula Ben-Amos, the fishes and the snake on the two plaques are references to the reign of Esigie and would therefore suggest a date at the beginning of the 16th century.

Sophisticated slenderness also distinguishes the figures of the third plaque attributable to the master (no. 117), for which division into two halves was not required. In this frontal image of an Oba and two attendants, the author has chosen a more subtle register and the three figures are shown in the same dress of simple elegance, linked by their arms, slender cylinders bent at right angles in a masterly geometric pattern that isolates and focuses attention on the monarch.

A plaque formerly in the Schwarz Collection, Amsterdam, and almost certainly by the same hand shows a presumably Portuguese hunter in very similar dress with the same features, hair and spade-shaped beard. An additional and very important element is the fact that the hunter is in exactly the same position as the figure on the two plaques, with his arms bent at right angles, the right raised and holding a quiver, the left lowered and holding a large bird with a long beak.[12]

Two Portuguese figures in the same dress, apart from their headgear, appear on a work that William Fagg regards as another plaque "probably meant to be nailed to a door".[13]

Unlike the other pieces, this has rounded edges and, above all, is made lighter by the large openings, which make it an anomaly among the works of this kind. As in plaque no. 117, the two figures are linked by their arms, which are symmetrically positioned and guide the eye to a vessel held up like a trophy. The heads are shown in bold profile turned to face this object at an angle of 90 degrees to the bodies.

115. "Master of the Circled Cross"
Benin, Nigeria, 16th c.
Plaque with the upper half of a Benin dignitary or warrior
Bronze, 38 x 37 cm
Staatliche Museen zu Berlin, Ethnologisches Museum, Berlin

115a. "Master of the Circled Cross"
Benin, Nigeria, 16th c.
Plaque with the lower half of a Benin dignitary or warrior
Bronze, 40 x 37 cm
Museum für Völkerkunde, Hamburg

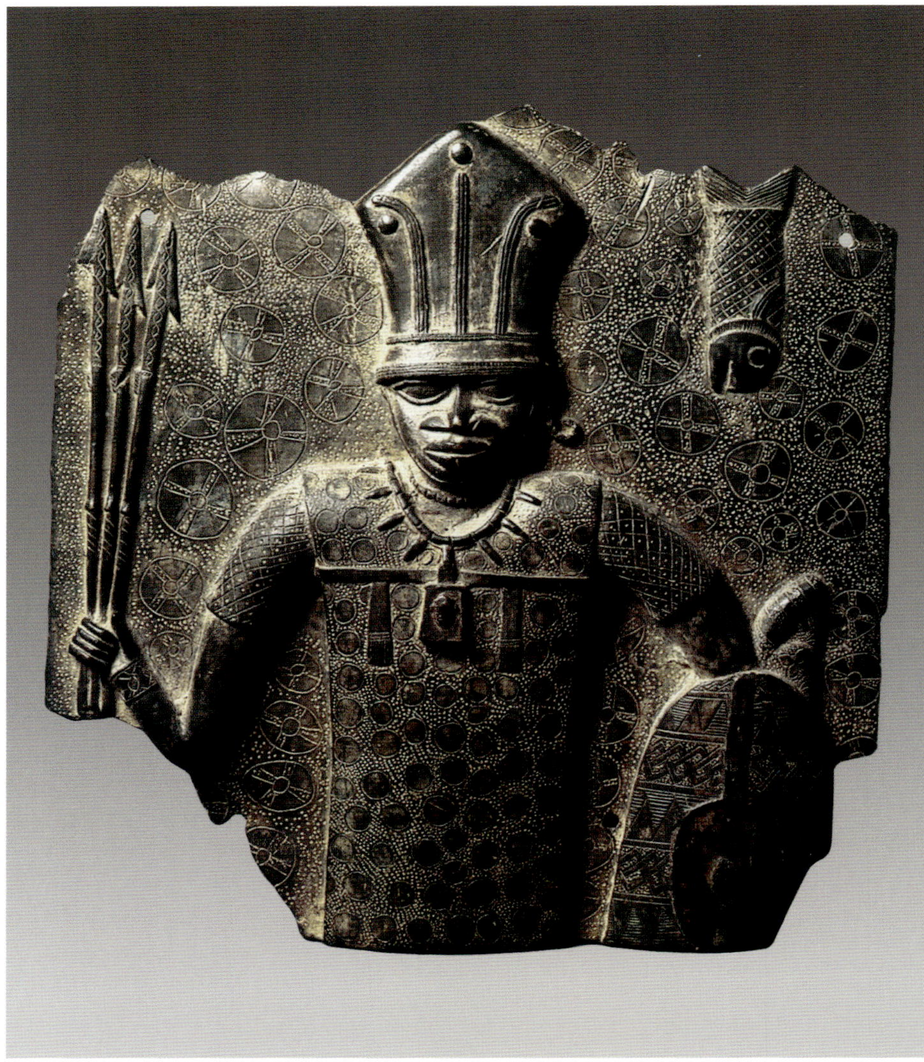

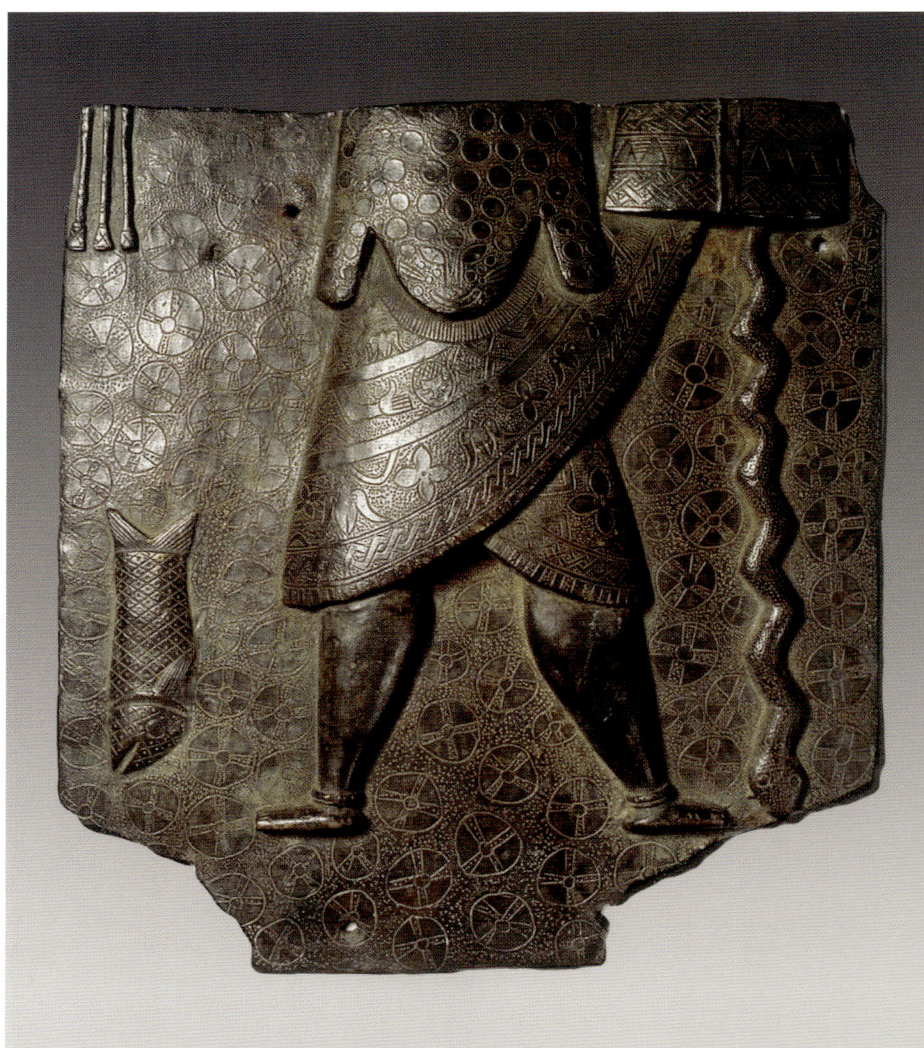

116. "Master of the Circled Cross"
Benin, Nigeria, 16th c.
Plaque with the upper half
of a Portuguese male figure
Bronze, 42.5 x 41.5 cm
The British Museum, Ethnography
Department, London

116a. "Master of the Circled Cross"
Benin, Nigeria, 16th c.
Plaque with the lower half
of a Portuguese male figure
Bronze, 40 x 38.6 cm
Museum für Völkerkunde, Vienna

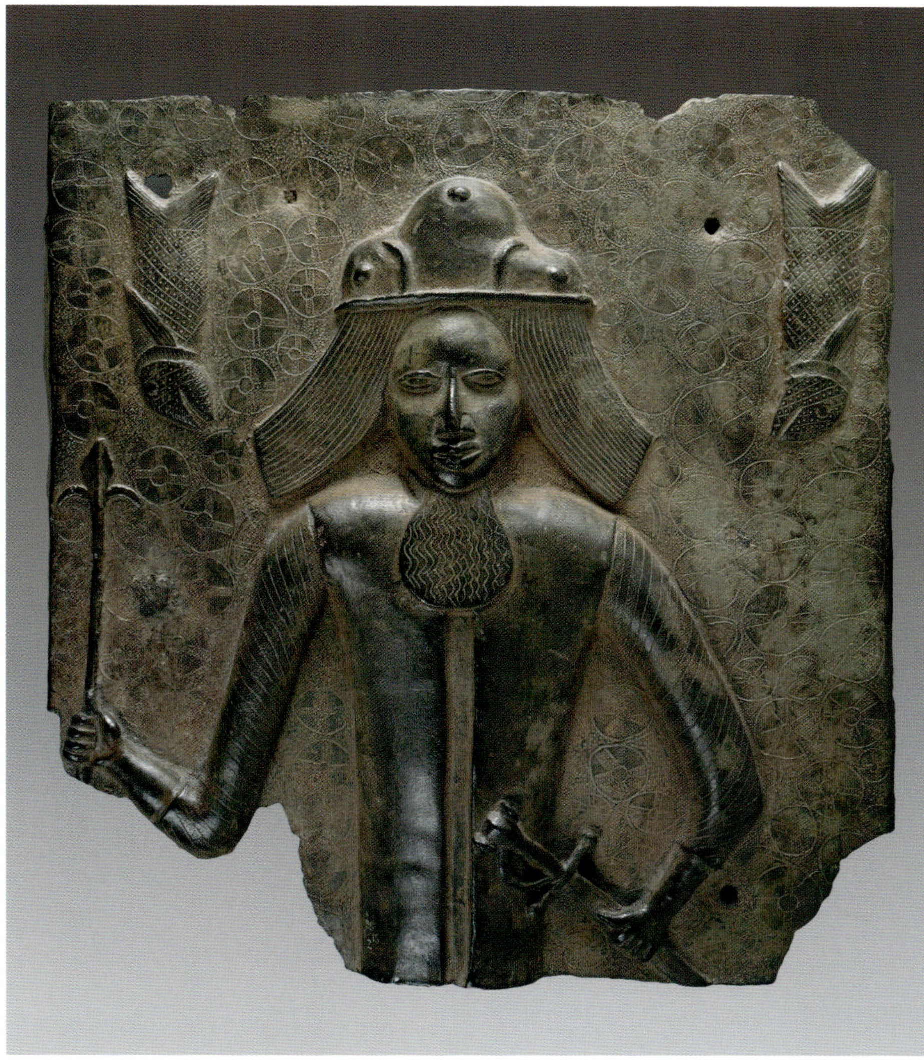

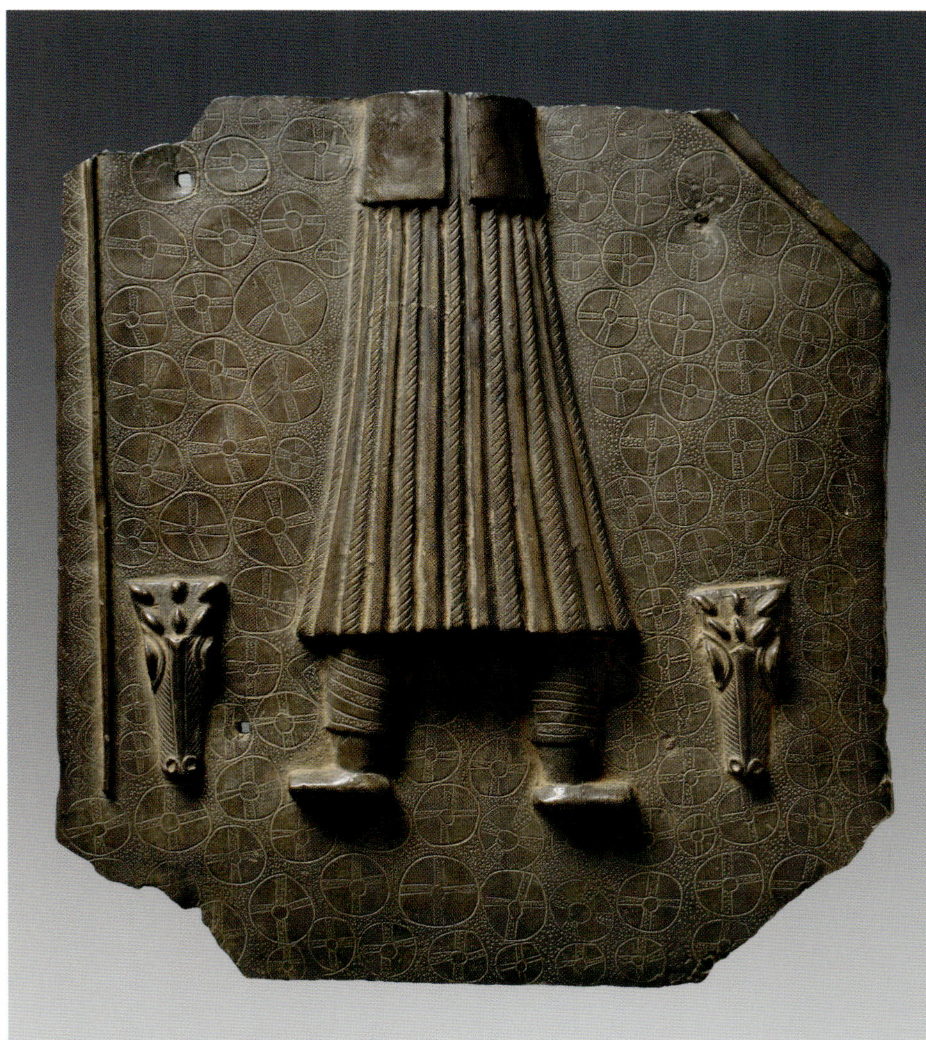

117. "Master of the Circled Cross"
Benin, Nigeria, 16th c.
Oba and two attendants
Bronze, 42 x 47 cm
The British Museum, Ethnography Department, London

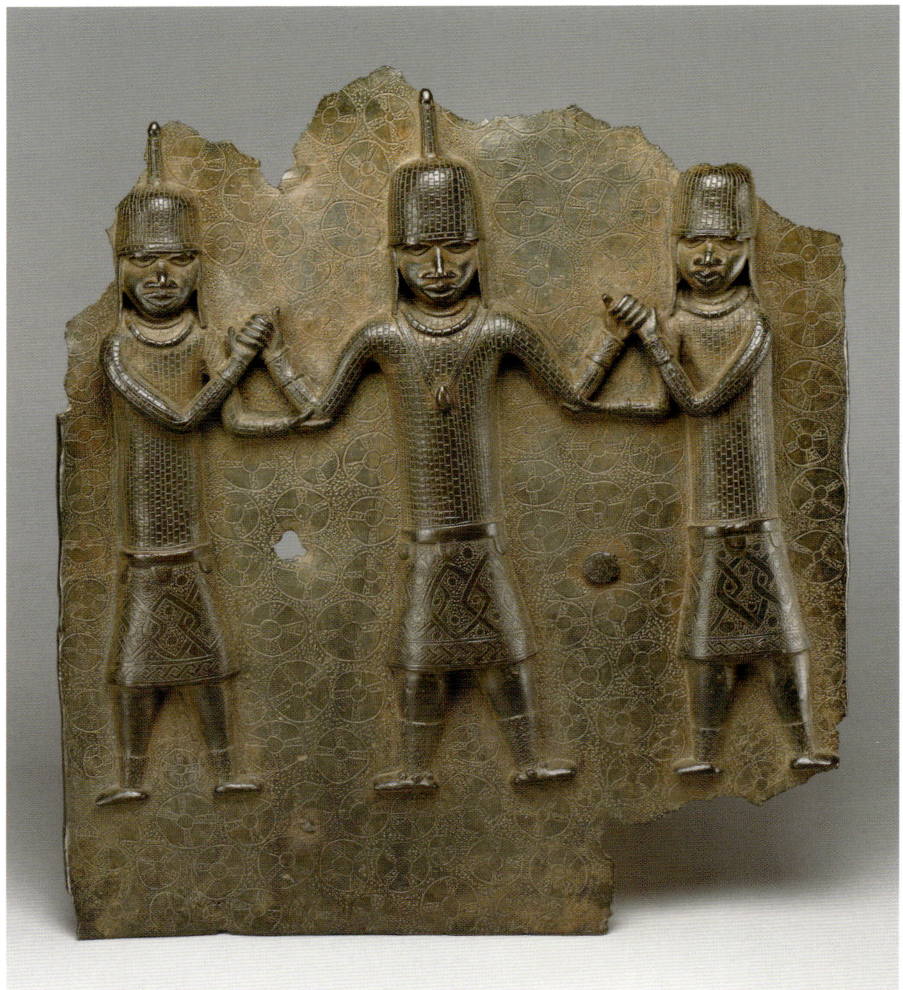

The "Master of the Leopard Hunt"

The name "Master of the Leopard Hunt" was coined for the author of seven plaques again by William Fagg, whose seminal *Nigerian Images* (1963) devotes two illustrations to the sculptor's most characteristic works, one plaque with a leopard hunt and another with a bird hunt.

The first (no. 118) shows what the British scholar calls a "synoptic vision" of five Portuguese hunters and two huge leopards, shown in profile in a kind of maze, created by the very long branch surrounding the scene like a wall and offshoots of foliage. Like the tree in the two following plaques, this is a symbolic representation of the forest in which the action takes place. The outstretched arms of the hunters and the very long tails of the animals contribute to the maze-like effect of the composition, which is balanced and rendered more attractive by the elegant four-leaf sprigs.

According to Felix von Luschan, the two animals could be lions or rather "fabulous beasts deliberately depicted by the artist in that way".[14] It is in any event certain that apart from the presumed mane and the curious tail ending in three tufts, they correspond to the leopard image that is a recurrent feature of Benin art, both plaques and sculptures in the round.[15] In fact, they have the same eyes, the same leaf-shaped ears (which appear, however, in all images of quadrupeds), and the same mouth with terrible fangs, shown as a triangular opening juxtaposed to the triangular spray of whiskers in relief.

The composition on the plaque now in the National Commission for Museums and Monuments, Nigeria (no. 119) is simplified and almost stark. It shows two members of the Amufi guild hanging from ropes secured to a tree and engaged in a ritual acrobatic dance "intended to demonstrate access to invincible mystical powers".[16]

The representation is rigorously frontal and the two dancers perform their "flight" against a bare background, closed at the top by the sturdy branches of a simplified tree, which extend horizontally as though to frame the scene

118. "Master of the Leopard Hunt"
Benin, Nigeria, 16th–17th c.
Leopard hunt
Bronze, 55 x 39 cm
Staatliche Museen zu Berlin,
Ethnologisches Museum, Berlin

119. "Master of the Leopard Hunt"
Benin, Nigeria, 16th–17th c.
Amufi acrobats
Bronze, 43.5 x 37.5 cm
The National Commission for
Museums and Monuments, Nigeria

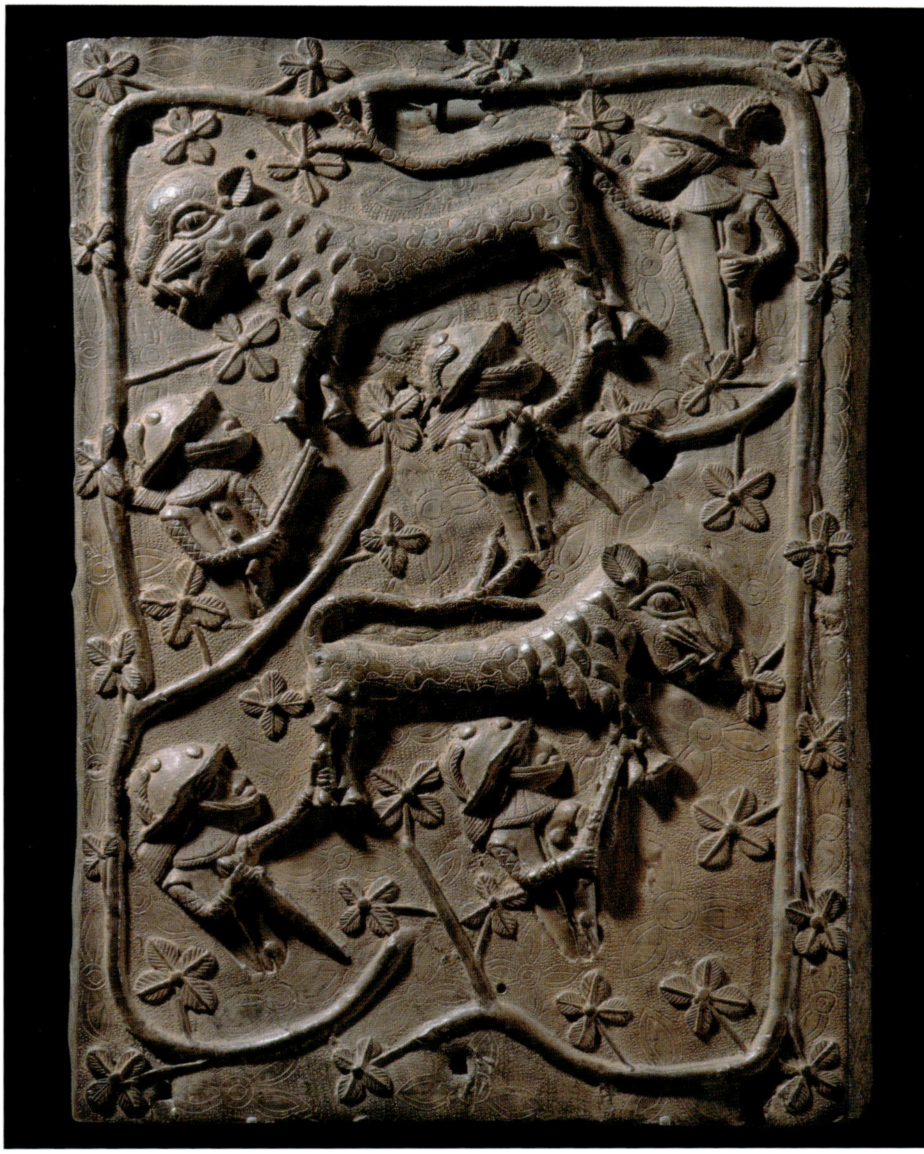

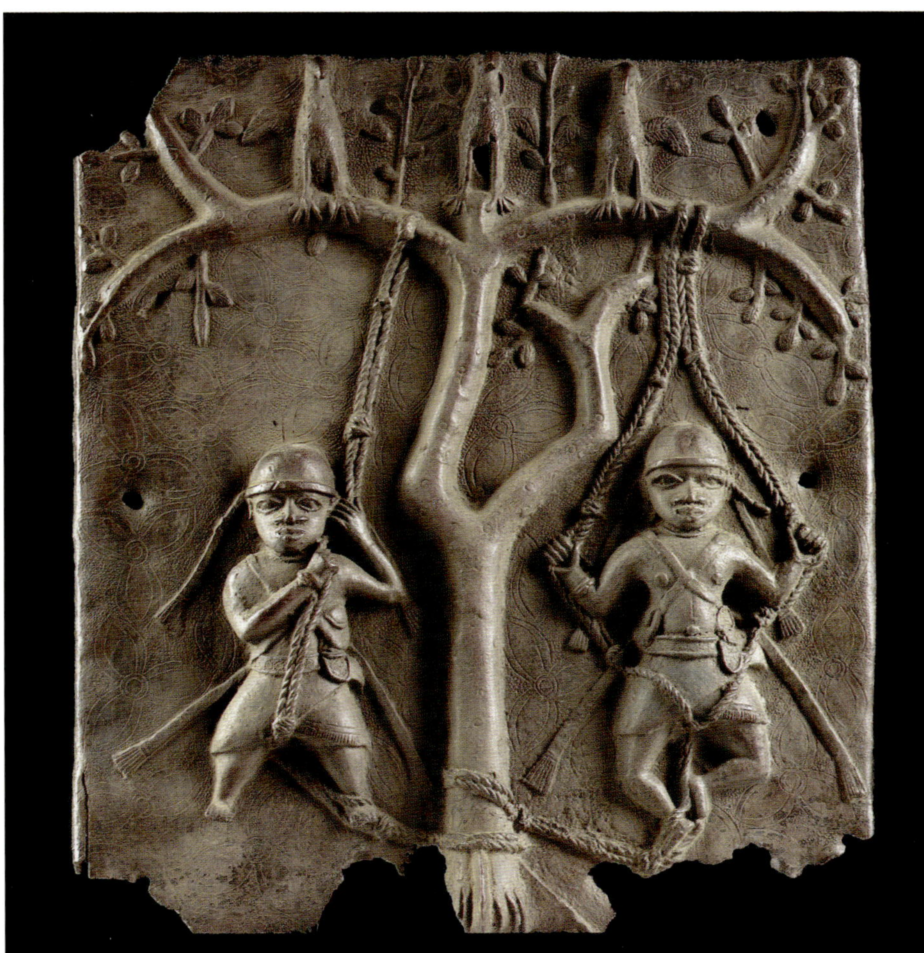

120. "Master of the Leopard Hunt"
Benin, Nigeria, 16th–17th c.
Bird hunt
Bronze, 45 x 34 cm
Staatliche Museen zu Berlin, Ethnologisches Museum, Berlin

121. "Master of the Estense Salt Cellar"
Sapi, Sierra Leone, 15th–16th c.
Salt cellar
Ivory, 29 cm
Galleria e Museo Estense, Modena

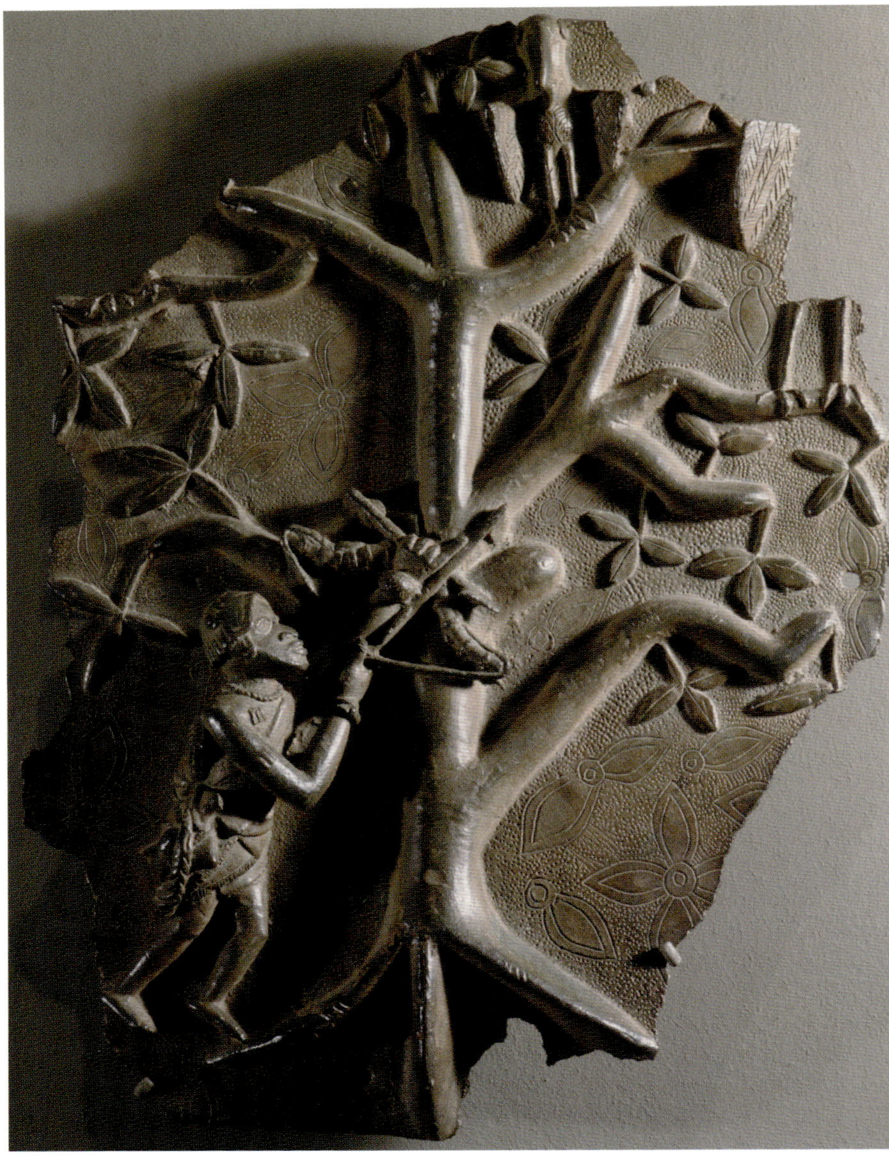

below. The three birds with open wings perched upon them are perhaps ibis or more likely white vultures symbolically associated with the sea god Olokun, dispenser of wealth and fertility. Thus they set a kind of allegorical seal on the ceremony taking place below.

The archer dominating the unfortunately damaged plaque of the bird hunt (no. 120) is, instead, set in a crowded space more similar to that of the leopard hunt. The scene here is occupied by the bird and the tree with its roots, leaves and large branches as well as the hunter carved in high relief with great realism and extraordinary precision of detail, despite the small size of the work. The man is about to shoot an arrow at another enormous bird, certainly bigger than him to judge by its long legs and the visible section of wing. The large, slanting, parallel branches of the tree in the centre of the scene seem to indicate the line of aim, in a composition that has a deftly handled perspective.

The "Master of the Galleria Estense Salt Cellar"

The hand of some individual artists can also be identified among the works in ivory produced by African artists for export to Portugal in the 16th century (the subject of the previous chapter, to which readers are referred for general information). These include the "Master of the Symbolic Execution", in the Museo Pigorini in Rome,[17] the author of two salt cellars and the monumental horn now in the Louvre,[18] and some sculptors of oliphants decorated with hunting scenes. We shall confine ourselves here to the works of a highly sophisticated artist combining fertile imagination, extraordinary sensitivity to form and superlative technical skill. He is unquestionably the author of

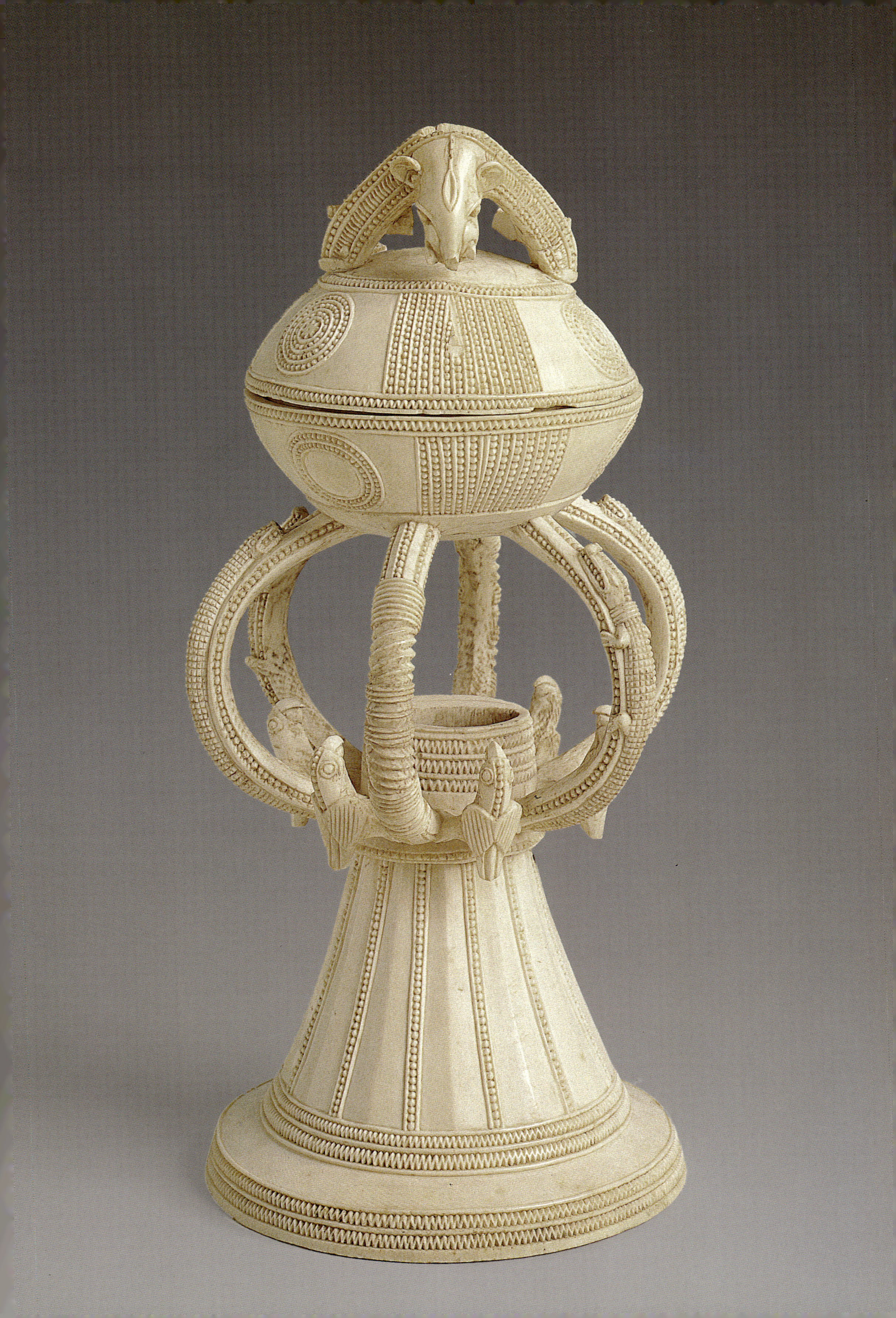

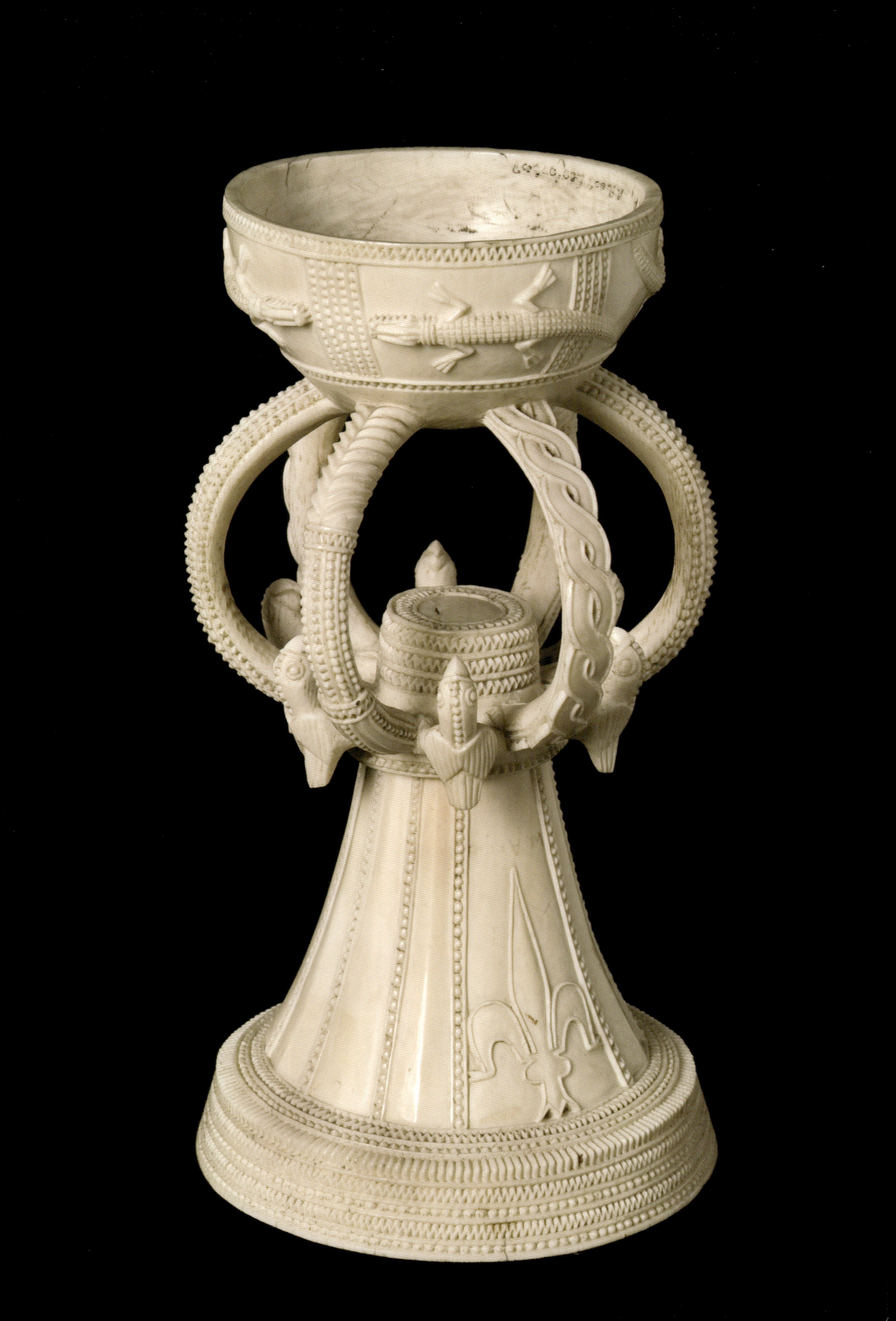

122. "Master of the Estense Salt Cellar"
Sapi, Sierra Leone, 15th–16th c.
Salt cellar (lid missing)
Ivory, 20.2 cm
Pitt Rivers Museum, Oxford University, Oxford

123. "Master of the Estense Salt Cellar"
Sapi, Sierra Leone, 15th–16th c.
Spoon
Ivory, 24 cm
The British Museum, Ethnography Department, London

124. "Master of the Estense Salt Cellar"
Sapi, Sierra Leone, 15th–16th c.
Fork
Ivory, 24.5 cm
The British Museum, Ethnography Department, London

four salt cellars (one with no lid and two bases), two spoons and perhaps a fork.

The salt cellar (no. 121) now in the Galleria e Museo Estense, Modena (inv. 2433), is the most complete piece. It was almost certainly in the collection of the Este family, who moved to Modena in 1625 after the annexation of Ferrara, the ancient capital of their dukedom, by the Papal State. The earliest and somewhat vague documentation dates from as late as 1866 and simply describes the item as an "ivory bowl with carved base and lid fashioned out of a single piece",[19] which says nothing about the exceptional quality of the small work and the inventiveness of its author.

Rising from the smooth truncated cone of the base are slender arches with parrots perched between them and snakes and crocodiles with long flat tails climbing up them. The somewhat flattened vessel itself is again anomalous with respect to the spherical compartments of most of the other salt cellars, but works extremely well within the overall economy of the work, where the airy spherical cage formed by the arches is the dominant element.

The human figure originally carved on the lid, of which only remnants of the feet now survive, must have been a chief to judge by the fine decoration on the back of the three-legged stool adorned with a boar's head on which he was seated.

The decoration of the second salt cellar (no. 122) is more sober. The arches between which the parrots are perched are decorated solely with geometric motifs, rows of granules and interwoven bands. Two pairs of juxtaposed crocodiles are, instead, carved on the wall of the vessel. A stylized fleur-de-lis can be seen on the base, which is also adorned with vertical rows of granules like the previous piece. These and the crocodiles also form part of the decoration of two fragments, one of which displays a fleur-de-lis similar to the one on the salt cellar now in Oxford.[20]

With enough certainty the same artist can be identified as the author of the spoons now in the British Museum (no. 123) and the Museo de América in Madrid. It is not only the way of representing the snakes and crocodiles that is identical, but also the artist's skill in arranging volumes and voids, so as to create elegant knots in the slender handles of the spoons with animals

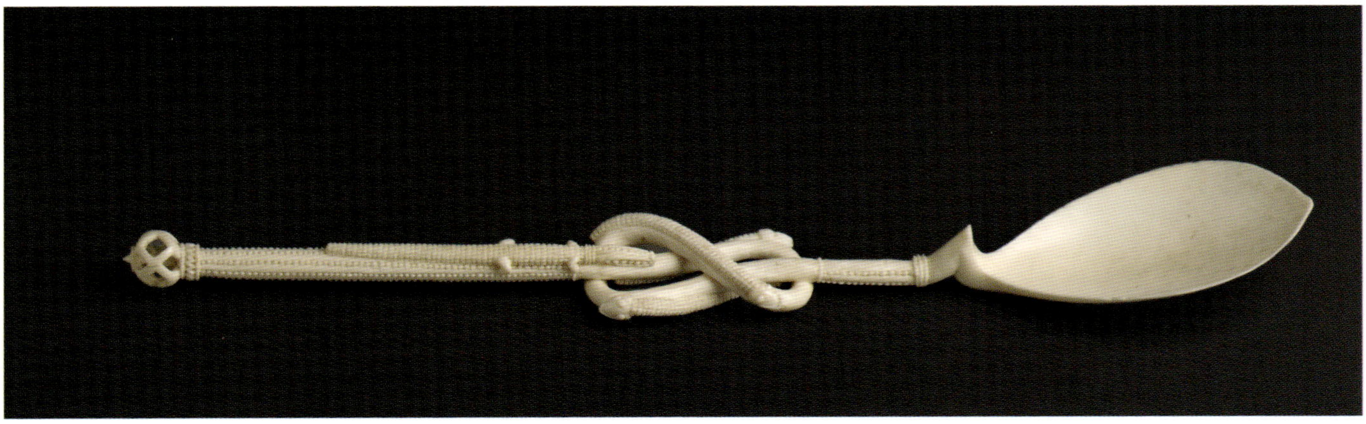

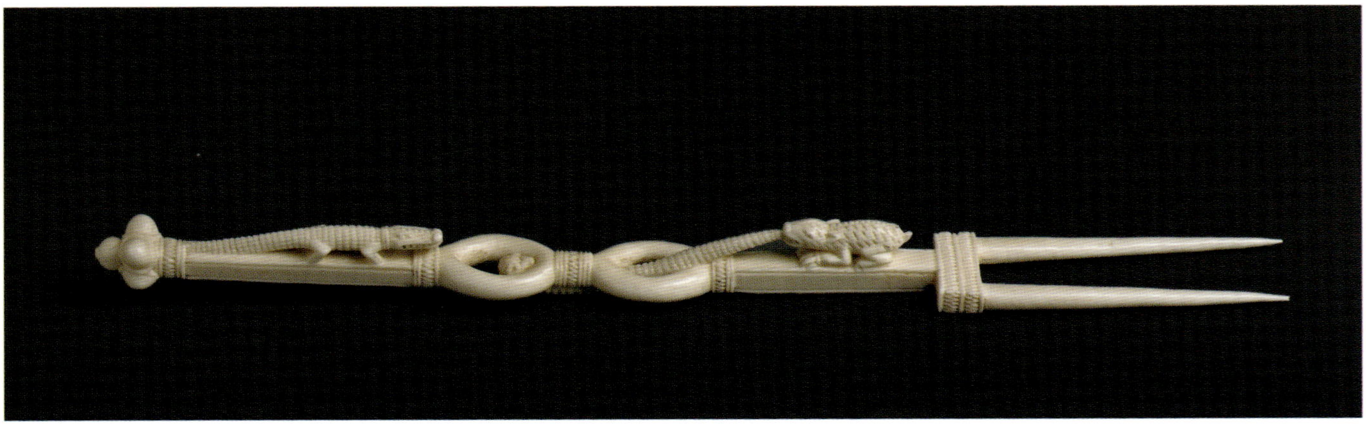

125. "Master of the Slender Figures"
Bamana, Mali (Segu region)
Standing female figure
Wood, 38 cm
University of East Anglia, Norwich
(Rosa and Lisa Sainsbury Collection)

crawling along them. The fork (no. 124), also in the British Museum, was probably carved by the same artist. The rectangular and more rigid handle has two rings through which a snake is threaded, its tail caught in the jaws of a quadruped (a dog?) near the prongs, while a crocodile approaches threateningly from the other end.

The miniature scale of this universe does not make the author of the salt cellars and the other ivories any less great than the artists who created larger works, just as Pisanello, the author of superb medallions, was in no way inferior to the great sculptors of his time.

A great workshop of Bamana sculptors

The more recent art of the Bamana people offers an opportunity to present the output of a workshop active in the Segu region, where at least three artists and some followers produced scores of works, differing in subject matter but sharing certain iconographic features, over a period of decades in the late 19th and early 20th century.

The works are male and female images, including horsemen, antelopes (male and female), masks surmounted by human figures, antelope and crocodile protomes, and puppet heads in a stark, rigorous, hieratic style. Unfortunately, for reasons of space, only a few examples can be illustrated here, in the hope that they will give at least some idea of the workshop's very varied output.

Human figures, standing or seated on stools, account for the majority of the works and can be divided into two groups, which in any event have many

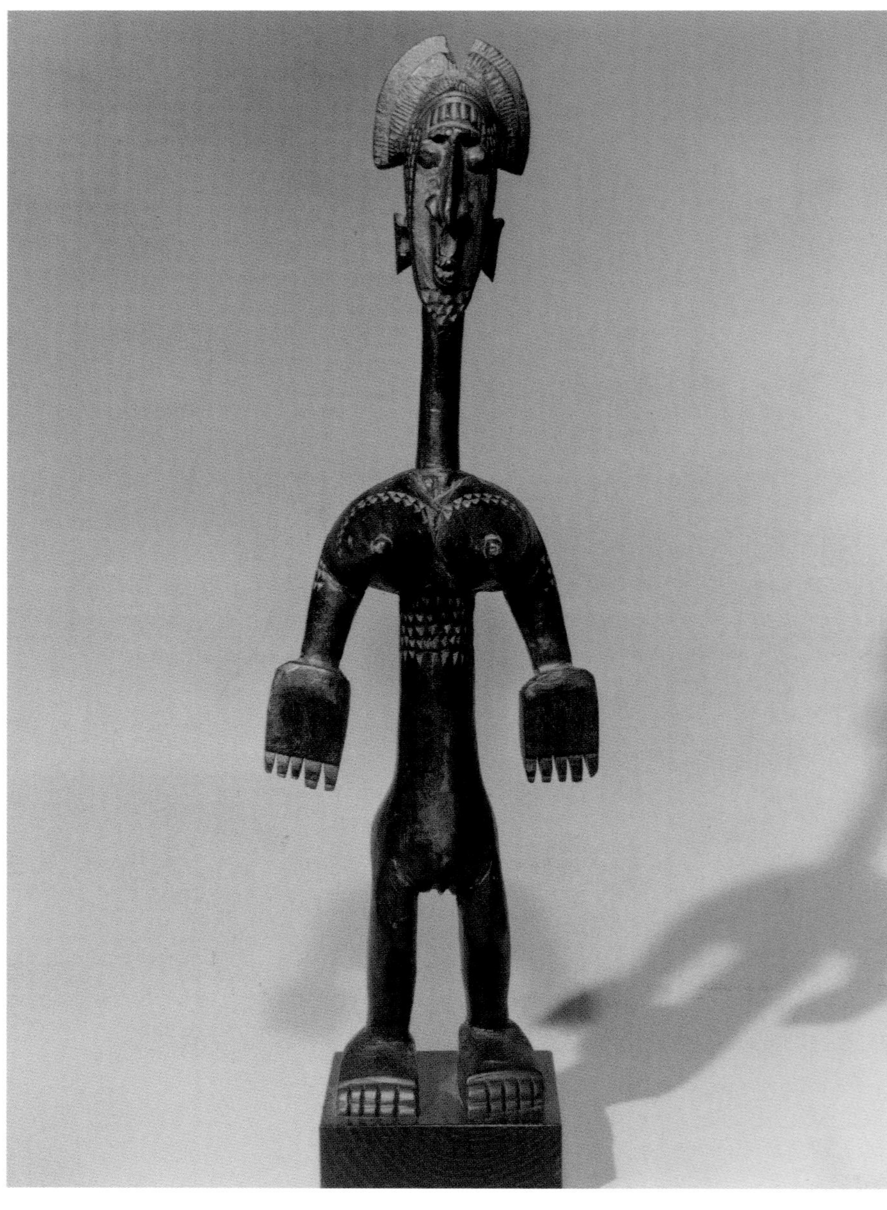

Pages 152–153
126. "Master of the Aquiline Profile"
Bamana, Mali (Segu region)
Seated female figure
Wood, 67 cm
Formerly in the Pierre Vérité Collection, Paris

127. "Master of the Slender Figures" (?)
Bamana, Mali (Segu region)
Horseman
Wood, 56 cm
Museum Rietberg, Zurich

elements in common in addition to their general form. These include the pose; absence of musculature; large and strongly projecting head; flat, narrow face; long nose with arrow-shaped nostrils; coiffure of finely carved plaits; discreet and elegant scarification; sloping shoulders with the same accentuated curve; breasts of the same shape (pointed for women and hemispherical for men); triangular buttocks; short arms with no joints; large shovel-like hands with the palms facing outwards and enormous feet. One unusual detail in the seated figures is the representation of kneecaps.

Some structural differences and details do, however, reveal the work of different hands. While the figures in one group (no. 125) are slender with very long necks and rounded ears, those in another (no. 126) are sturdier with shorter necks. Above all, the latter have more massive heads with the line of the forehead continuing into the beak-like nose, which gives them an unmistakable profile, and ears tending towards the triangular. The legs of the stools are also different: rectangular blocks in the first case and tapered at the join with the seat in the second.

The arched nose, which is also present in some representations of antelopes, as we shall see later, is reminiscent of the Baga sculpture from Guinea. As Dominique Zahan suggested to me some thirty years ago, this similarity may not be coincidental, but rather the result of contact between the Baga and the inhabitants of the Middle Niger in medieval times.

On the basis of the characteristics of their works, I suggested that the first of these two artists should be called the "Master of the Slender Figures" and the second the "Master of the Aquiline Profile".

The group of human figures also includes some horsemen, which are almost certainly the work of the "Master of the Slender Figures" or a sculptor very close to him in style. As an exemplar of them all, see the specimen in the Museum Rietberg in Zurich (no. 127), in which the mount, with its short, sturdy body, is an unexpected invention since it resembles a mythological beast rather than a horse, a cross between a quadruped and a dragon with a very long neck and a small head, whose ferocity is, however, somewhat mitigated by decoration.

The antelopes (*Ci-wara*) created in the workshop are images of male and female animals that were attached to headdresses worn by a pair of young dancers, during propitiatory ceremonies to ensure the fertility of the soil.

Like the human figures, these can be attributed to different artists whose works are recognizable within the framework of a rigorously adopted common model, due to small differences in the volumes of the various parts of the body. These carvers can be referred to as the "Master of Antelopes 1" and the "Master of Antelopes 2". The possibility remains, however, that the same sculptors were also responsible for producing the human figures and horsemen, as suggested by certain similarities in the rendering of the heads in the first case and the decoration and form of the breast harness and the neck in the second.

In accordance with the traditional iconography, the female antelope is represented with a smaller male on its back. The streamlined bodies of the two animals and the spiral horns pointing vertically upward are similar (no. 128).

The male antelopes are completely different from the females. They are a simplified and conceptualized image of the animal and can only be linked to the female antelope through the representation of the body. The upper and visually more important part is a brilliant invention in that while the simultaneously monumental and airy mane accompanies the curve of the slender arched neck, naturally joined to the pointed, bird-like head, the robust horns slope backwards at an angle to the mane in a sort of counterpoint.

The masks combine various formal and iconographic elements of the works described above, and their essential components – the human face (or rather the front part of the head) and the upper structure – offer a kind of compendium of the motifs developed in the workshop. The upper structure

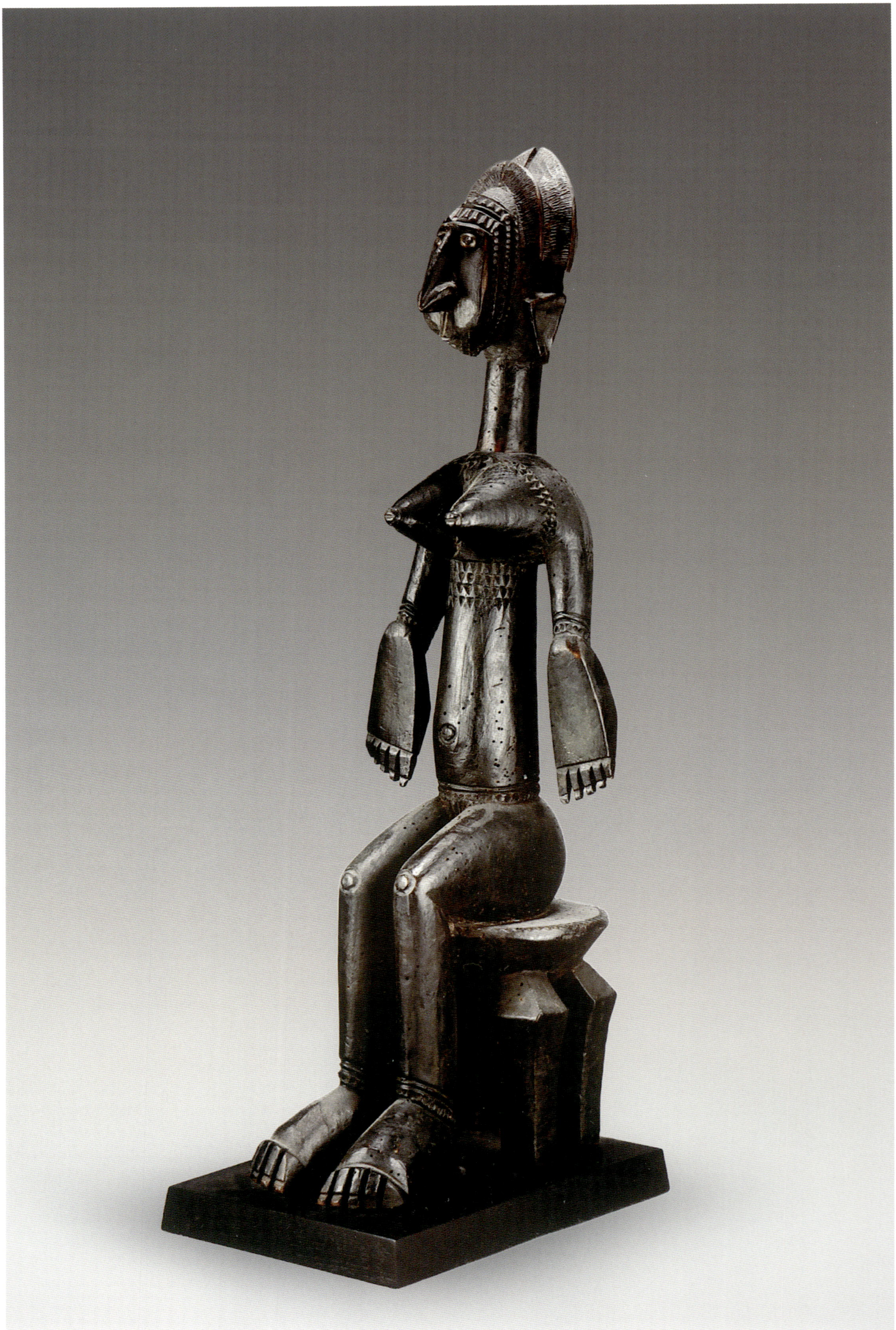

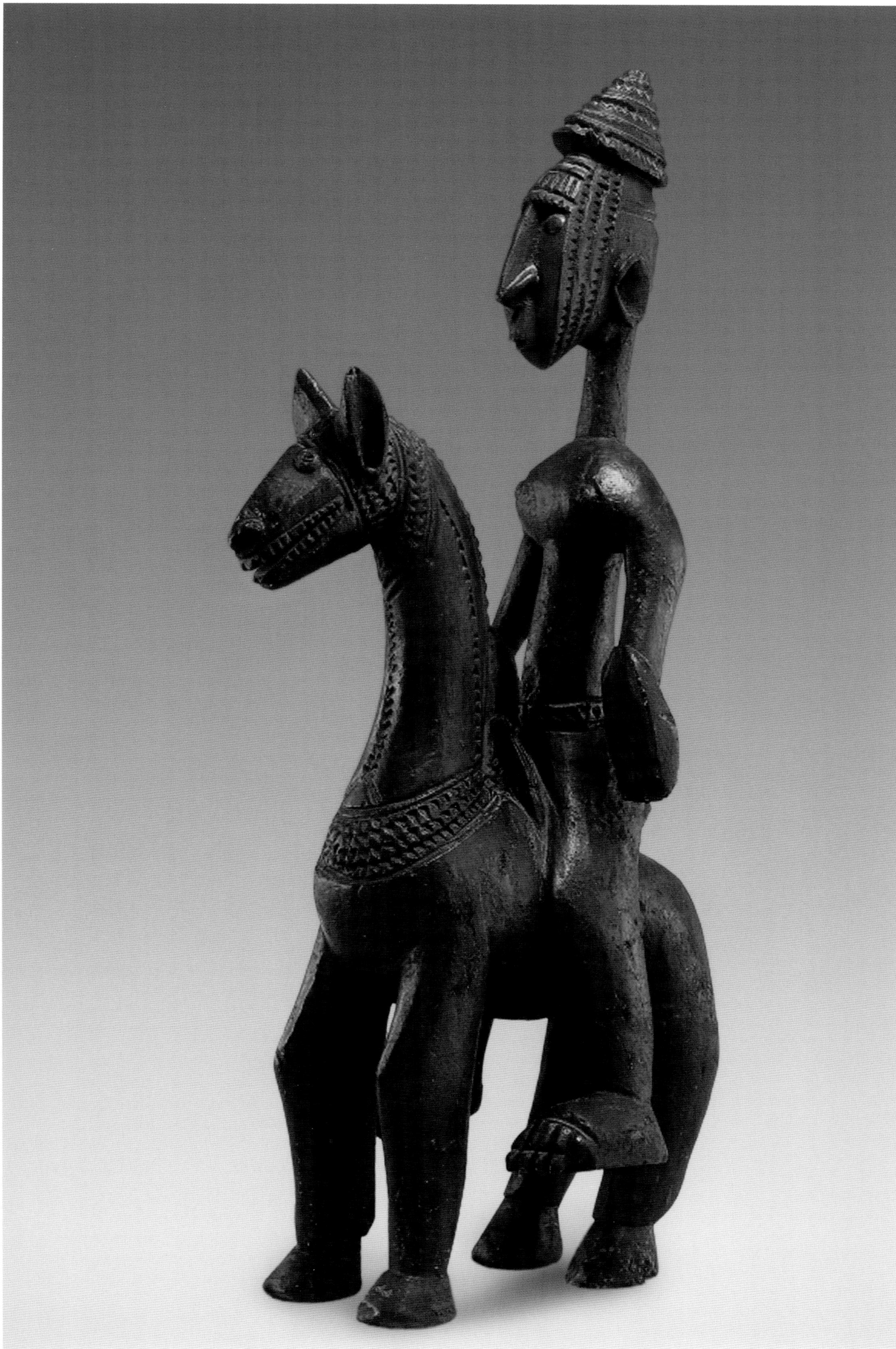

128. "Master of Antelopes 1"
Bamana, Mali (Segu region)
Female antelope
Wood, 70 cm
Musée du Quai Branly, Paris
(formerly in the Musée de l'Homme)

129. "Master of the Slender Figures" (?)
Bamana, Mali (Segu region)
Mask surmounted by human figure
Wood, 72 cm
Galerie Ratton-Hourdé, Paris
(formerly in the collection
of the painter Marcel Gromaire)

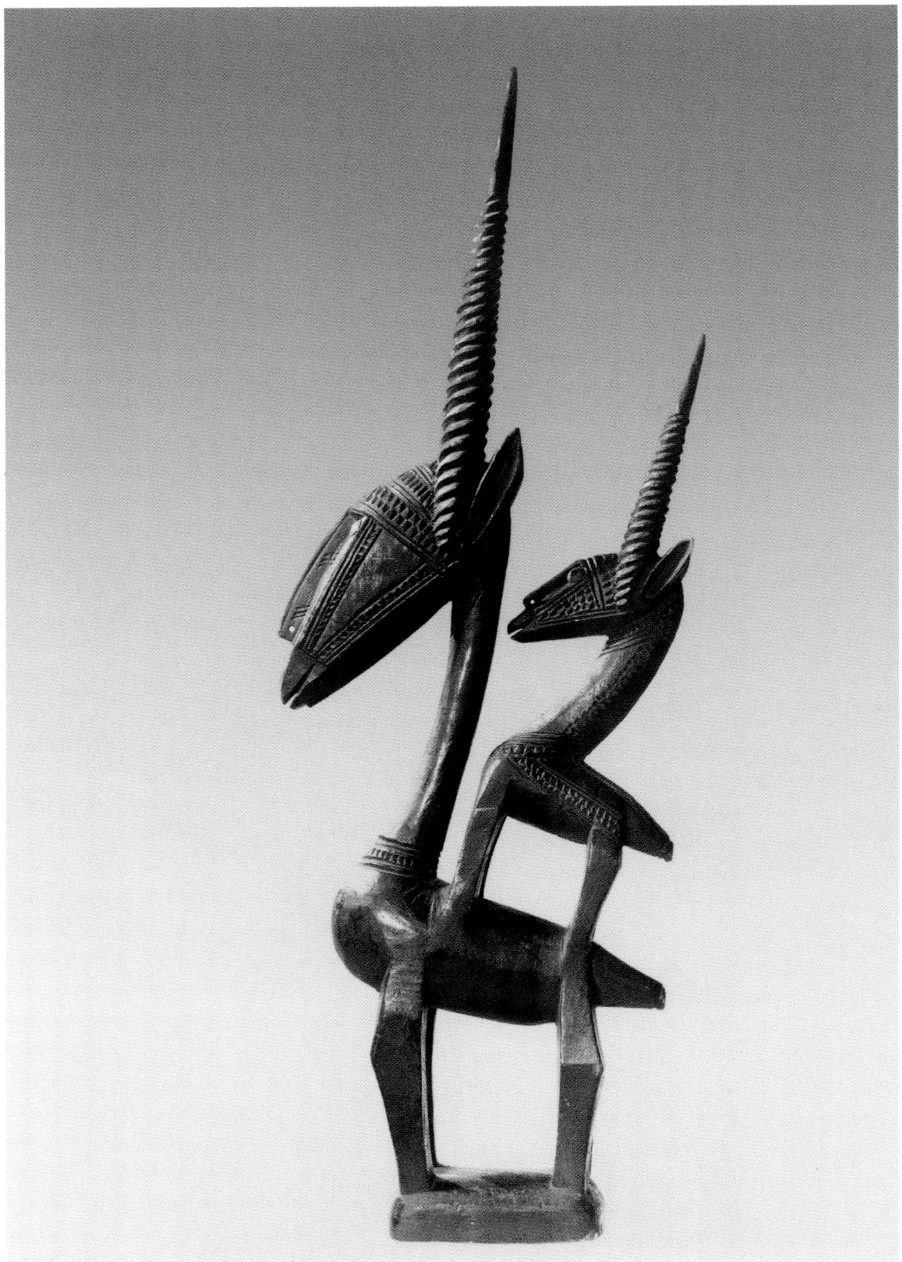

consists of four vertical horns with a human figure in the centre (no. 129) or six horns with an antelope or crocodile head in front.[21] See, for example, the mask with antelope in the British Museum, and the mask with a crocodile in a private collection in Paris, formerly in the Vérité.[22]

With its continuous curve of forehead and nose, the face proper recalls the work of the "Master of the Aquiline Profile" with the addition of a small beard beneath the bottom lip and two narrow, horizontal tattoos on the cheeks. The human figures in the upper structure are, instead, closer to those of the "Master of the Slender Figures". The antelopes and crocodiles are more difficult to attribute. The masks are, however, distinguished by the form of the ear: small and solid in one group, larger, thinner and crescent-shaped in the other.

As regards the period when the workshop was active, the only evidence is provided by the years in which the works were acquired or bought by public and private collections in the West. The earliest "official" dates are in the first decade of the 20th century. A mask with an antelope protome, now in the Museé du Quai Branly, was acquired by the members of the Desplaignes Mission in 1906.[23] A female antelope was purchased in the same year by the British Museum and another was donated to the Musée de l'Homme in Paris by Charles Monteil in 1908.[24] One seated female figure was acquired around 1912 for the collection of the present-day Museé Royal de l'Afrique Centrale in Tervuren[25] and one for the British Museum in 1919.

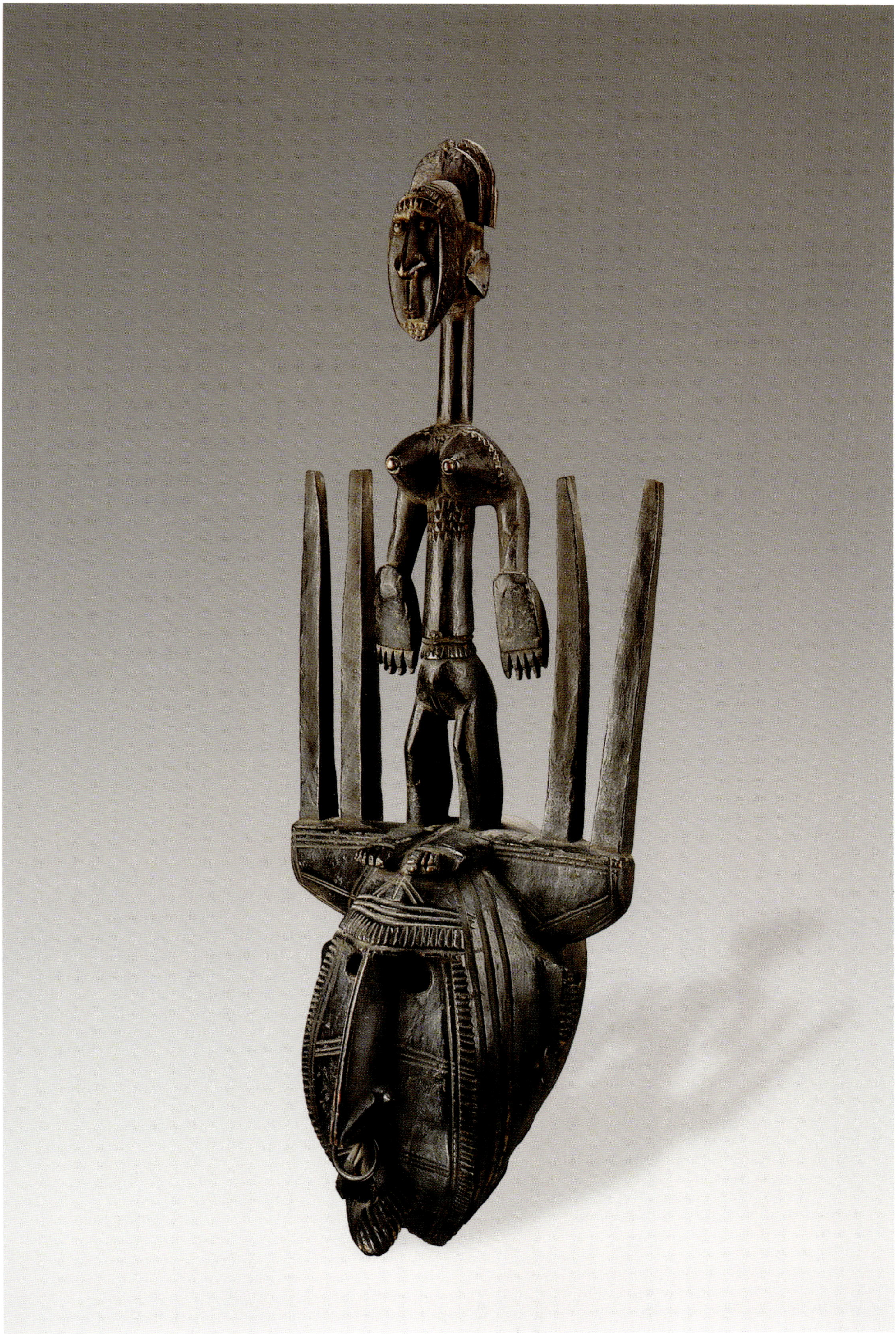

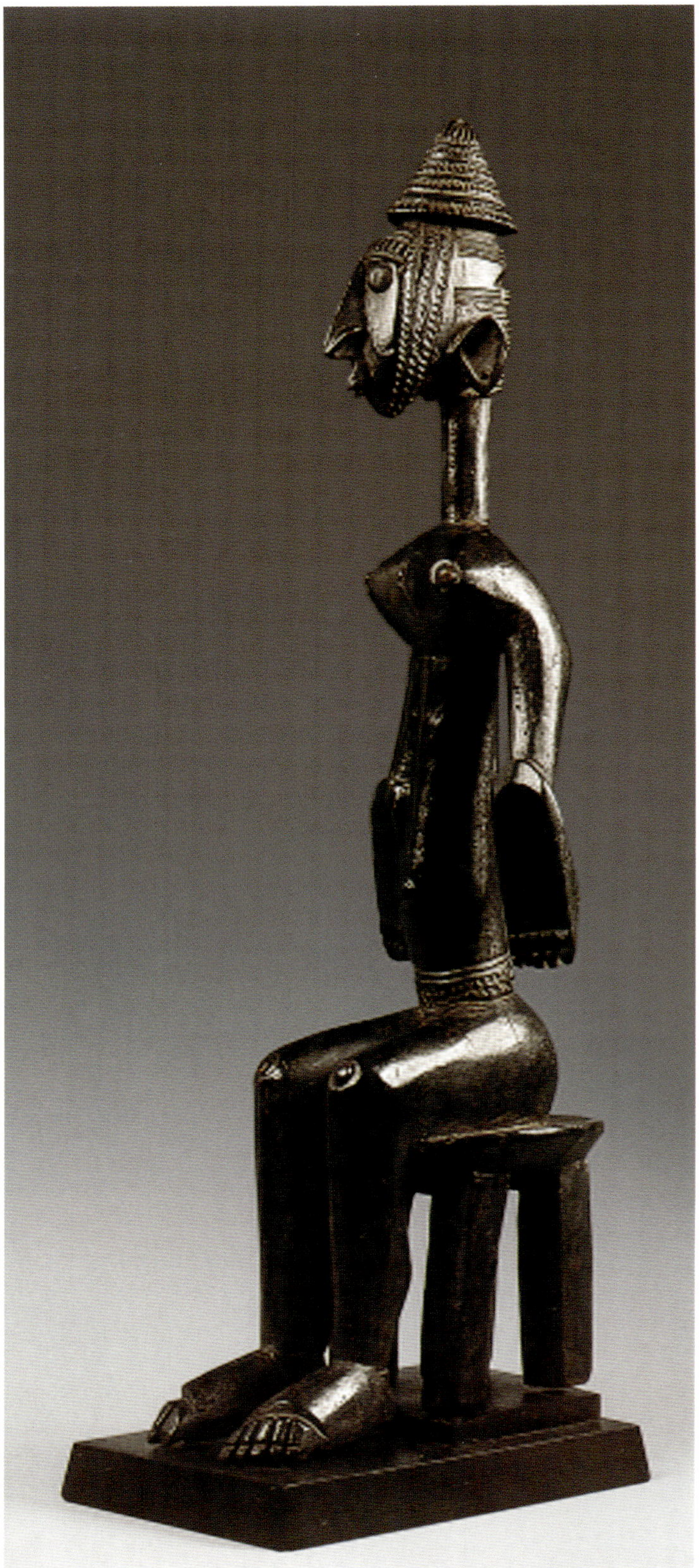

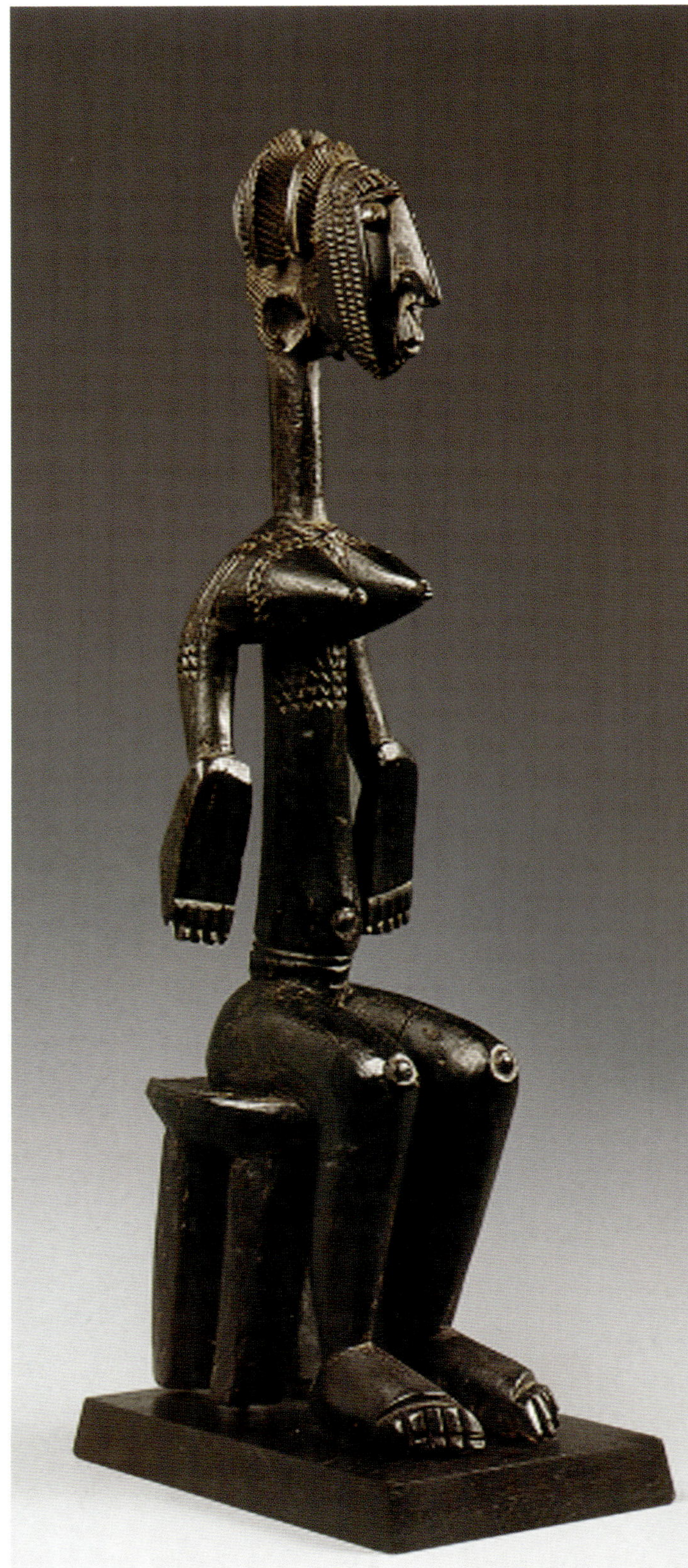

130–131. "Master of the Slender Figures"
Bamana, Mali (Segu region)
Seated male and female figures
Wood, 60 cm and 54 cm
Galerie Ratton-Hourdé, Paris

Two more dates can be added to these definitively established ones. First, a seated figure owned by the great painter Henri Matisse probably came into his possession in the period when Parisian artists developed a keen interest in African art, namely, before 1915,[26] and a standing female figure appeared in a catalogue by Marius de Zayas published that same year.[27] It was also more or less the same period that saw the arrival in Europe of the female figure and the two masks in the Pierre Vérité Collection in Paris, according to information personally received from their former owner. Many other items from this prolific workshop were acquired by Western collections in subsequent years.

While these dates would seem to suggest that the workshop was active for a number of decades starting in the late 19th century, a pair of seated figures (nos. 130–131) attributable to the "Master of the Slender Figures" that appeared a few years ago were apparently acquired in 1868 by a certain Monsieur Bal, stationed in Mali in that period,[28] which would mean that this prolific workshop came into operation at least thirty years earlier.

The Baule workshops and artists

The art of the Baule people enjoyed immediate popularity on the Western scene from its very first appearance due to its appealing qualities, and many works were soon bought up for museums and private collections in Europe and then America. Their large number made it easier first to group items with similar characteristics and second to identify them as the work of particular artists or workshops producing standard models with a greater or lesser degree of variation.

Susan Vogel, the greatest scholar of Baule art, has gathered information in situ helping both to clarify the function of the sculptural items[29] and to identify corpuses of works attributable to a dozen workshops or individual artists. At least four or five sculptors operated in one of the latter, which she calls the Nzipri Circle,[30] in the second half of the 19th century. In the catalogue of the above-mentioned exhibition 'Masterhands/Mains de Maîtres', Bernard de Grunne attributes the workshop – which he calls the "Masters of Sakassou"[31] and was active between 1840 and 1880 – with the authorship of fifteen statues and two masks,[32] one of the largest homogeneous sets identified in African art.

The common features of the human figures include verticality and slenderness that are not synonymous with weakness, but rather reflect the essential core of the form with its large feet, legs slightly bent as though in preparation for the upward thrust of the body, rounded calves and slender thighs, elongated trunk, and breasts for the female figures that are comparatively small and pointed or sometimes flattened against the chest. The rear view also confirms the adoption of a common model, with small hemispherical buttocks, clearly defined shoulder blades and the groove of the spine continuing up to the nape of the neck.

The oval heads are unmistakable, above all, because of the large slit eyes, prominent lips and small, circular ears. The differences in coiffure could be related to differences in function or to formal choices made independently by the various sculptors. The same holds for the positioning of the thin arms, which mostly hang down with the large hands on either side of the navel, but are also placed behind the back with the forearms crossed. One exemplary figure (no. 132) shows the right arm held up at an angle across the chest parallel to the downward-stretched left arm. Together with other elements, this small but by no means insignificant detail bears witness to creative independence on the part of the authors of the works, produced in order to meet the religious and social needs of the community, but given a personal interpretation, as is the case for every true work of art.

The two masks attributed to this workshop, one male and one female, are recognizable by virtue of the heart-shaped face, the hemispherical eyes and the shape of the lips. The coiffure of the female figure, half in parallel plaits and half gathered in a chignon, is surprising but not unusual, according to Susan Vogel. Above all, it does not disrupt the serene composure of the work.

132. "Master of the Sakassou Workshop"
Baule, Ivory Coast, 1840–80
Female figure
Wood, 63 cm
Private collection

133. "Master of Totokro"
Baule, Ivory Coast
Portrait mask
Wood, 32.4 cm
Formerly in the Charles Ratton Collection, Paris

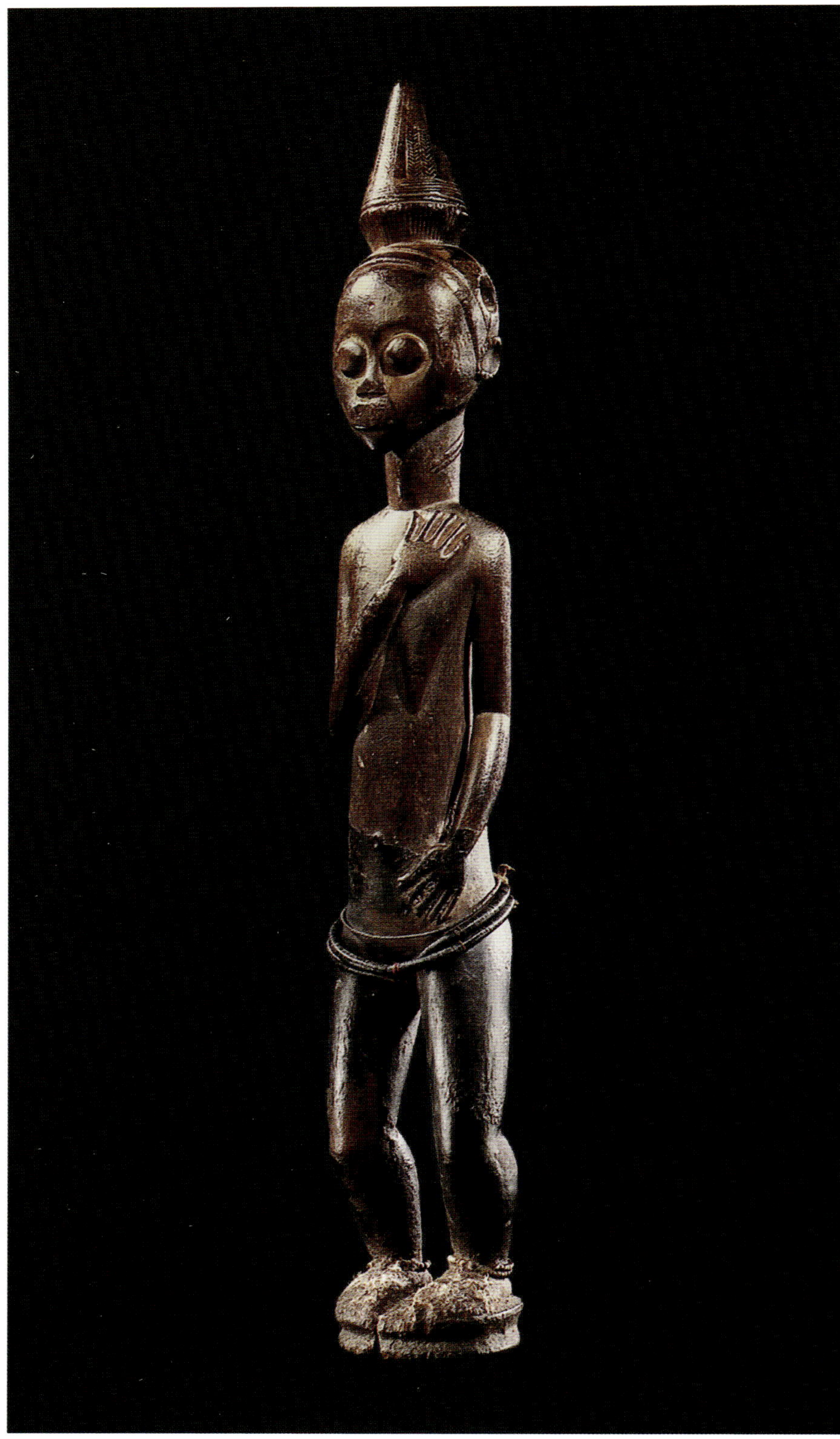

The other Baule artist presented here, again identified by Susan Vogel, is the "Master of Totokro", so named after the village near Dimbokro in the southern part of the Ivory Coast, from which one of his works came onto the market in Abidjan around 1970. In support of her attribution and reconstruction of the author's artistic personality, the American scholar has published four masks that have common figurative characteristics while also preserving their own formal identity (nos. 133–134).[33]

She associates these four works with another two masks, a pair of human figures and a monkey now in the Musée municipal d'Agen ("a donation perhaps from the 1930s"),[34] which show no sign of ageing, because they were probably acquired as soon as they were carved. Vogel has also published a beautiful female figure, recorded in 1994 in a village close to Totokro, and drawn attention to a male figure acquired by the Cleveland Museum of Art in 1931.

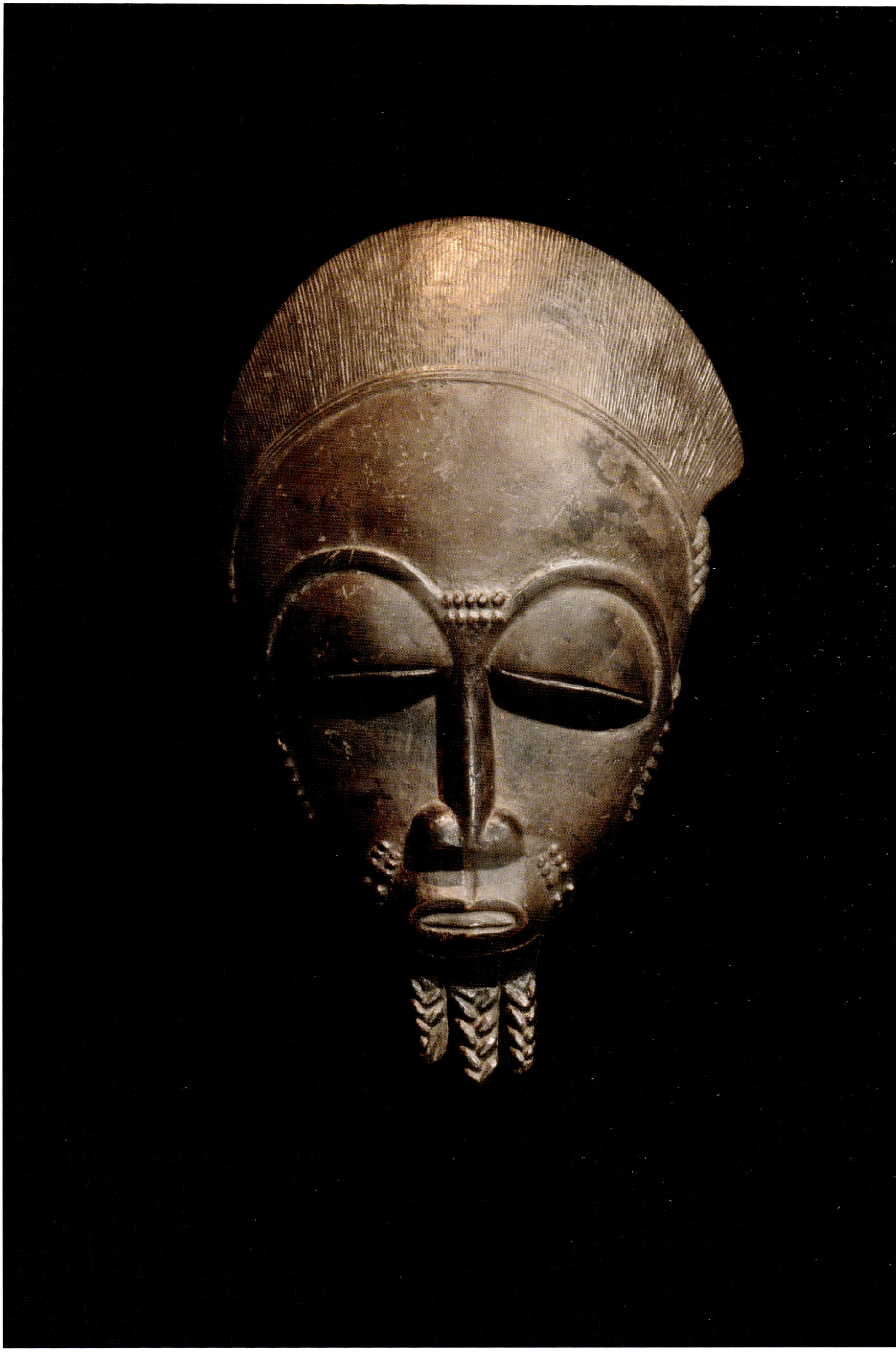

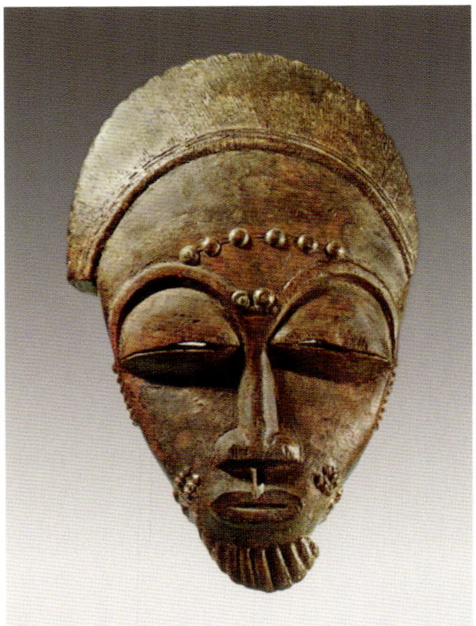

134. "Master of Totokro"
Baule, Ivory Coast
Portrait mask
Wood, 30.5 cm
Galerie Bernard de Grunne, Brussels (formerly in the Franco Monti Collection, Milan)

135. "Master of Bouaflé"
Guro, Ivory Coast
Mask
Wood, 35.8 cm
Museum Rietberg, Zurich (formerly in the Von der Heidt Collection)

The most striking quality of the masks is the thoughtful composure and serenity suggested by the unadorned volumes, the balance of the various constituent elements of the faces, and the subtle expressive distortions. The broad forehead beneath the coiffure (an elegant diadem of narrow plaits) echoes the shape of the huge, mysterious eyes hidden behind their almost completely closed lids. Slight asymmetries in the coiffure and the eyes bring the splendid faces to life.

Vogel regards the attribution of the masks to one author as unequivocally confirmed not only by formal similarities, but also by the unmistakable and unrepeatable marks left on the rough backs of the works by the blade of an axe with a small notch. Since the old method of sharpening axes on a stone did not completely eliminate the slight flaws in the blade, the American scholar's brilliant observation can be fruitfully applied, with all due caution, in the examination of other works.

As regards the period in which the sculptor was active, the mask once owned by Charles Ratton arrived in Paris before World War I, according to the information obtained from the celebrated dealer. Confirmation is provided by the presence of the fourth item (all trace of which has now been lost) in the catalogue of the 'Oriental Exhibition' at the House of Artists in Budapest, 1911.[35] The presumed date when the works, which were probably purchased immediately after they were carved, came into the possession of the Agen Museum would suggest that the "Master of Totokro" executed them between 1900 and 1939.

A Guro artist: the "Master of Bouaflé"

While Susan Vogel is in the front line with regard to the study of Baule art, the pioneers of the art of the Guro, a neighbouring people in the Ivory Coast, are Hans Himmelheber, Eberhard Fischer and Lorenz Homberger, the organizers of the major exhibition 'Die Kunst der Guro' at the Museum Rietberg, Zurich, in 1985. The event and the accompanying catalogue featured the works of many artists active in the first half of the 20th century, who were named after the localities in which some of their works were found.

If we confine ourselves to the makers of masks, the list includes the masters of Gonate, Gohitafla, Yasua, the Douno and Bouaflé, whose recognizable and very different works are now held by numerous public and private collections. Unfortunately, for reasons of space, it is necessary here to focus solely on one work by the "Master of Bouaflé", active in the early decades of the 20th century.

The works of this artist are unmistakably characterized by subtle stylization and what Eberhard Fischer describes as a "slightly sentimental" style.[36] An elegant zigzag pattern in relief (a stylized beard?) emphasizes the oval of the elongated face, surmounted by a small animal, one or two horns (no. 135) or a human figure. The author's hand is revealed most of all in the profile, where the sinuous line of a very broad forehead starts from the scalloped join of the coiffure and continues naturally along the smooth nose, before turning abruptly to pass almost seamlessly over the narrow slash of the small, sulky mouth and around the receding chin. The element that makes the work of this master unmistakable is, however, the shape of the eyes: long, narrow slits set at a sharp angle. The pointed horns, which practically constitute an extension of the coiffure, add a further thrust to the already flowing lines of the mask.

The master also carved some heddle pulleys adorned with very small human or animal heads, which are recognizable due to the unmistakable shape of the slanted slit eyes.

Olowe of Ise, a great Yoruba master

While practically all African artists are known only by pseudonyms, many Yoruba sculptors operating in Nigeria in the first half of the 20th century are associated by name with the works they created. The best-known of those active in the Ekiti region include Agbonbiofe, Areogun, Bamgboye, Bambgbose,

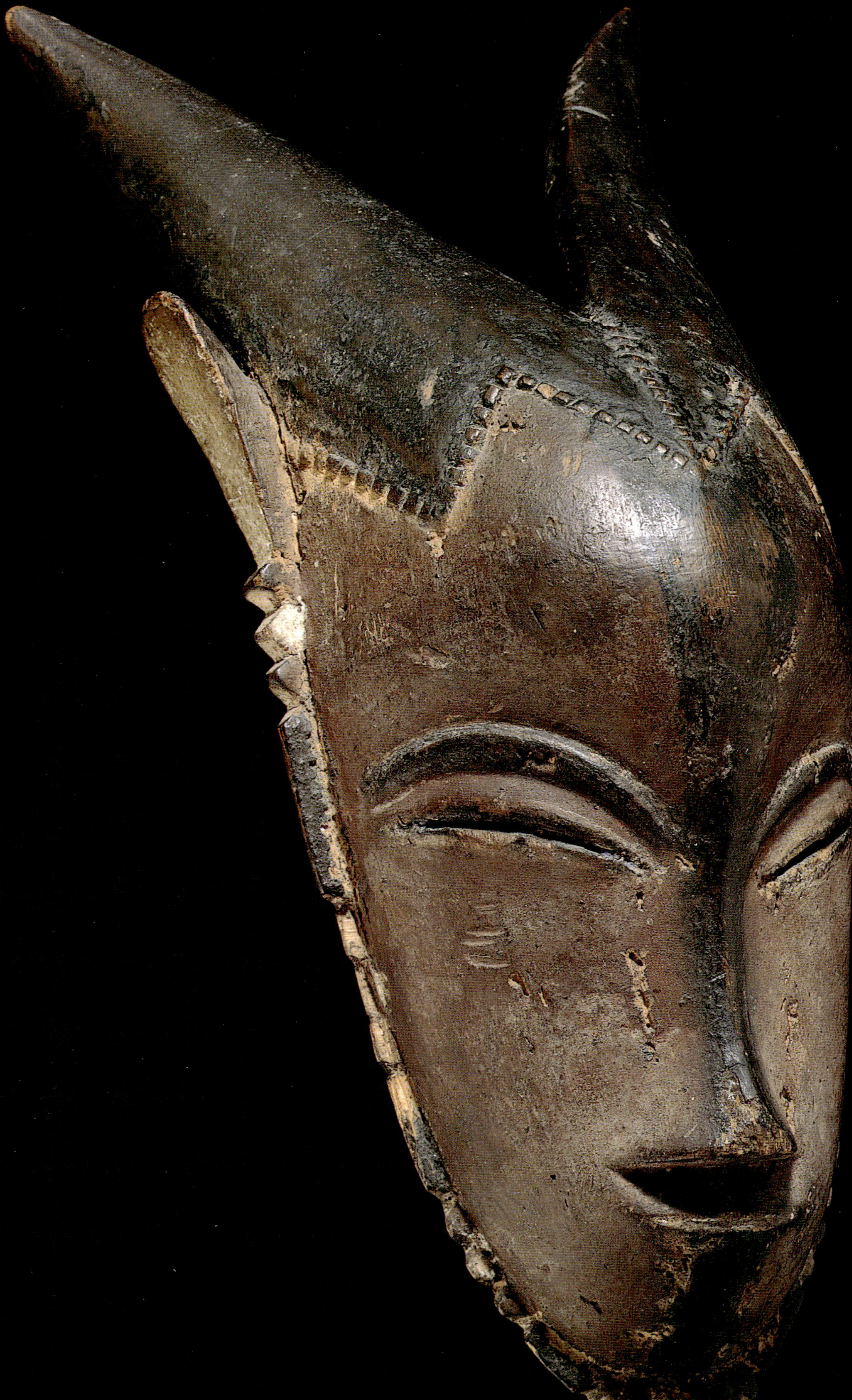

136. "Master of the Isare Warrior"
Yoruba, Nigeria, ca. 1925
Warrior carried by a healer (?)
Wood damaged by termites, 83 cm
The National Commission for Museums and Monuments, Nigeria

137. Olowe of Ise
Yoruba, Nigeria, 1910–14
Palace door
Wood and pigments, 127 cm
The British Museum, Ethnography Department, London

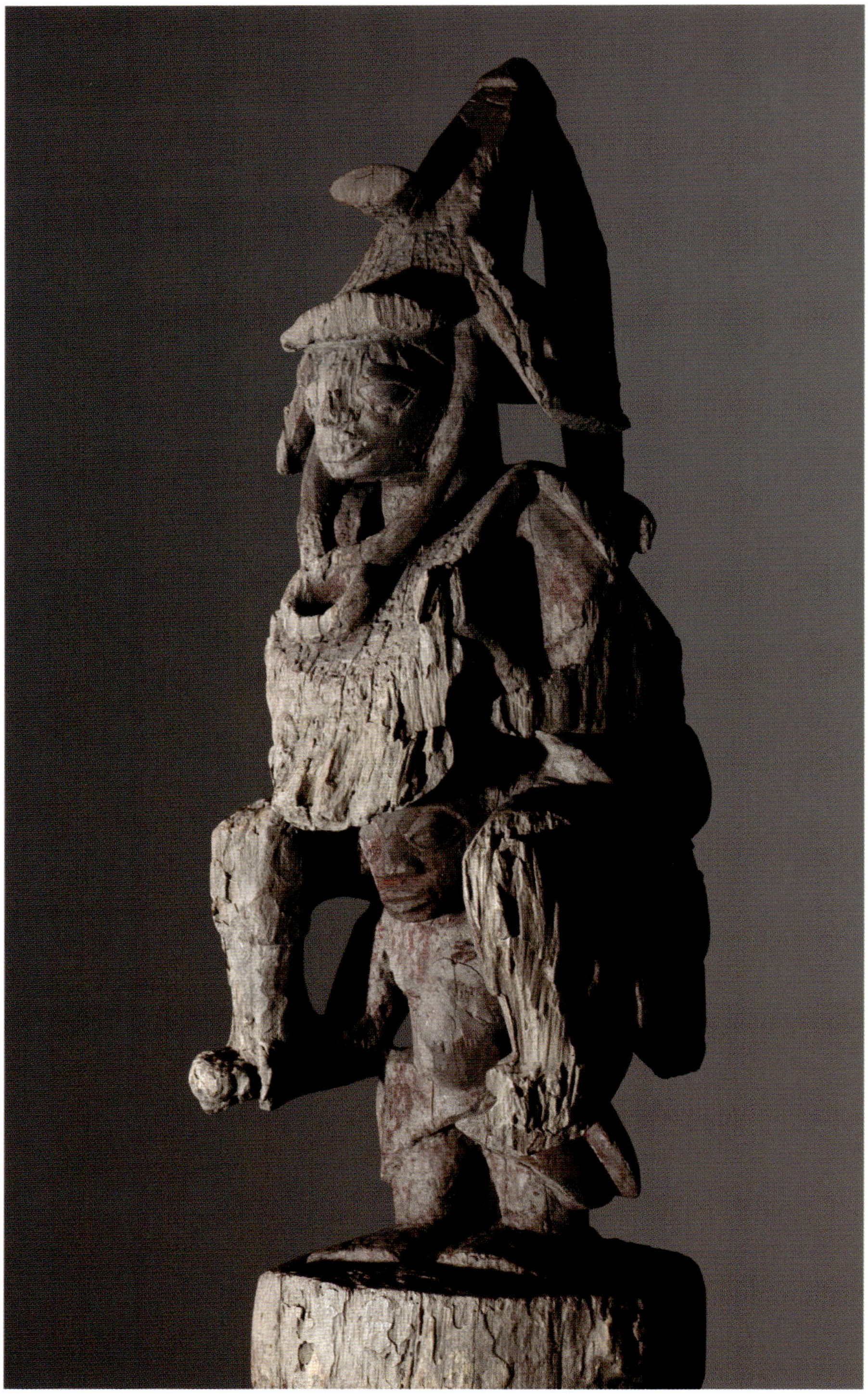

Osamuku and Olowe of Ise, who is specifically featured here. The complete list would be much longer.

A great sculptor active in the second half of the 19th century is, instead, known only as the "Master of the Isare Warrior", after the name of the locality in the Osi area where William Fagg discovered the extraordinary figure of a warrior being carried by a "retainer" (no. 136) in 1958 together with a female image. The sculpture is described by the British scholar as "one of the richest works of Yoruba sculpture in existence",[37] despite the severe damage due to termites and exposure to the elements.

Olowe of Ise (c. 1873/78–1938) was the first African artist to be featured in a solo show, organized in 1998 at the National Museum of African Art, Washington, D.C., by Roslyn Walker, its director at the time.

Highly esteemed by the local rulers and important Yoruba dignitaries who commissioned him to produce artworks, Olowe was both skilful and versatile. He carved doors and pillars for the verandas of palaces and the houses of dignitaries, vessels of all shapes and sizes, isolated figures and groups,

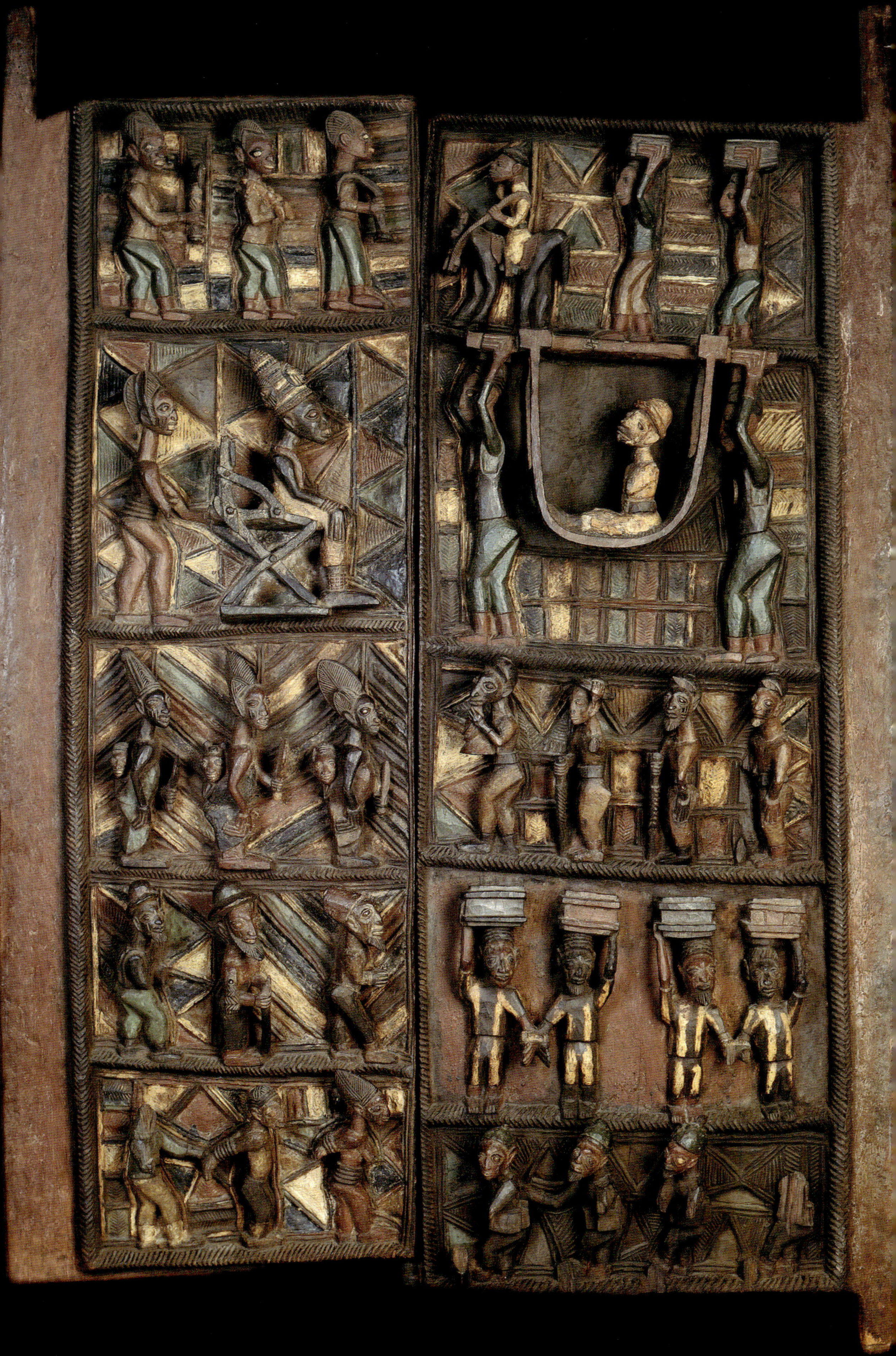

138. Olowe of Ise
Yoruba, Nigeria, before 1938
Veranda pillar
Wood and pigments, 210 cm
Staatliches Museum für Völkerkunde, Munich

139a–b. Olowe of Ise
Yoruba, Nigeria, before 1938
Veranda pillar
Wood and pigments, 212 cm
Staatliches Museum für Völkerkunde, Munich

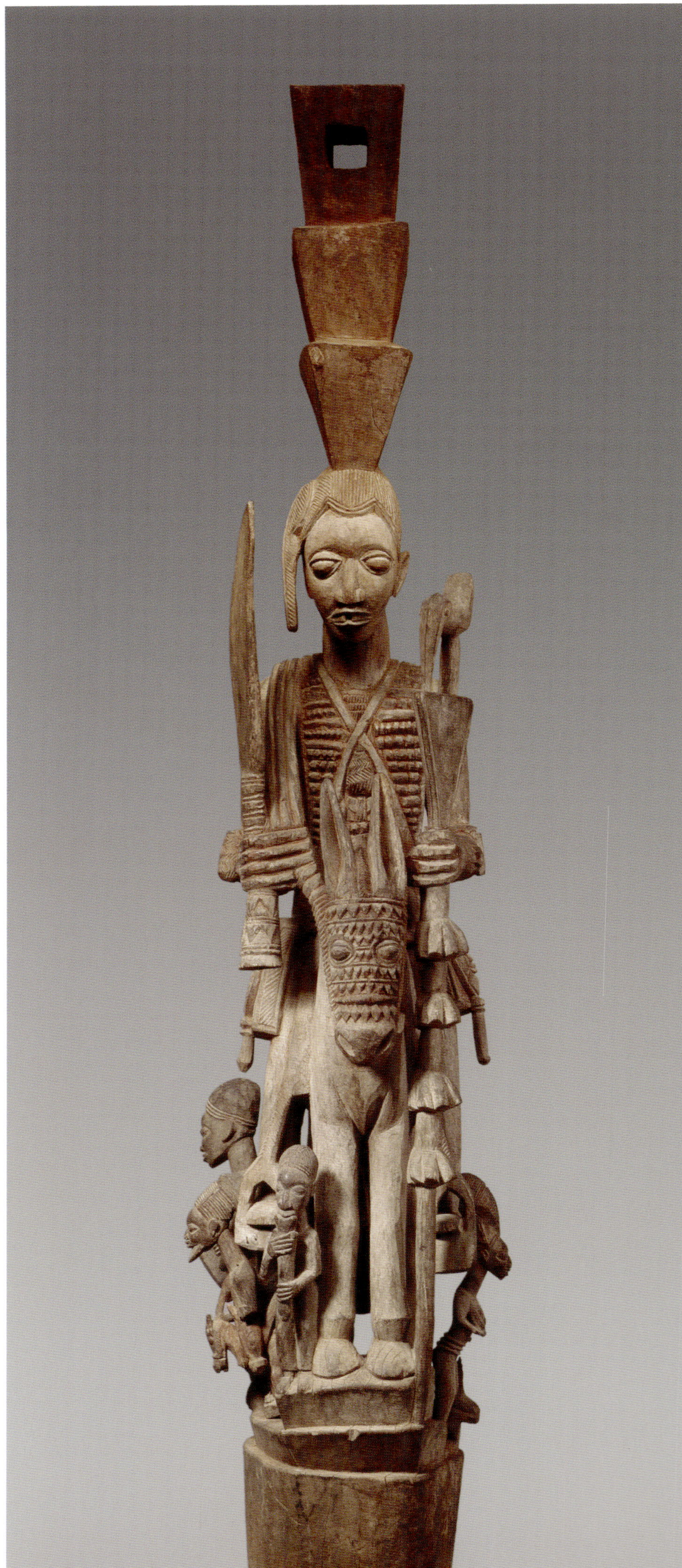

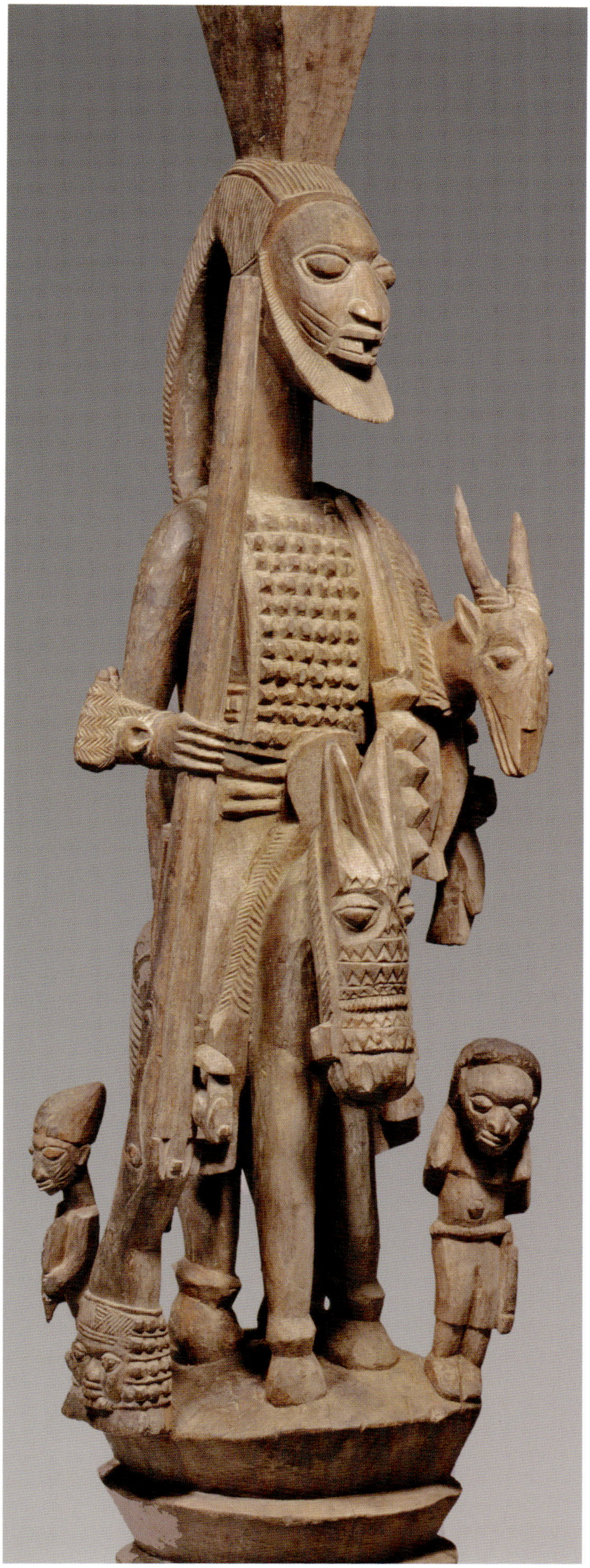

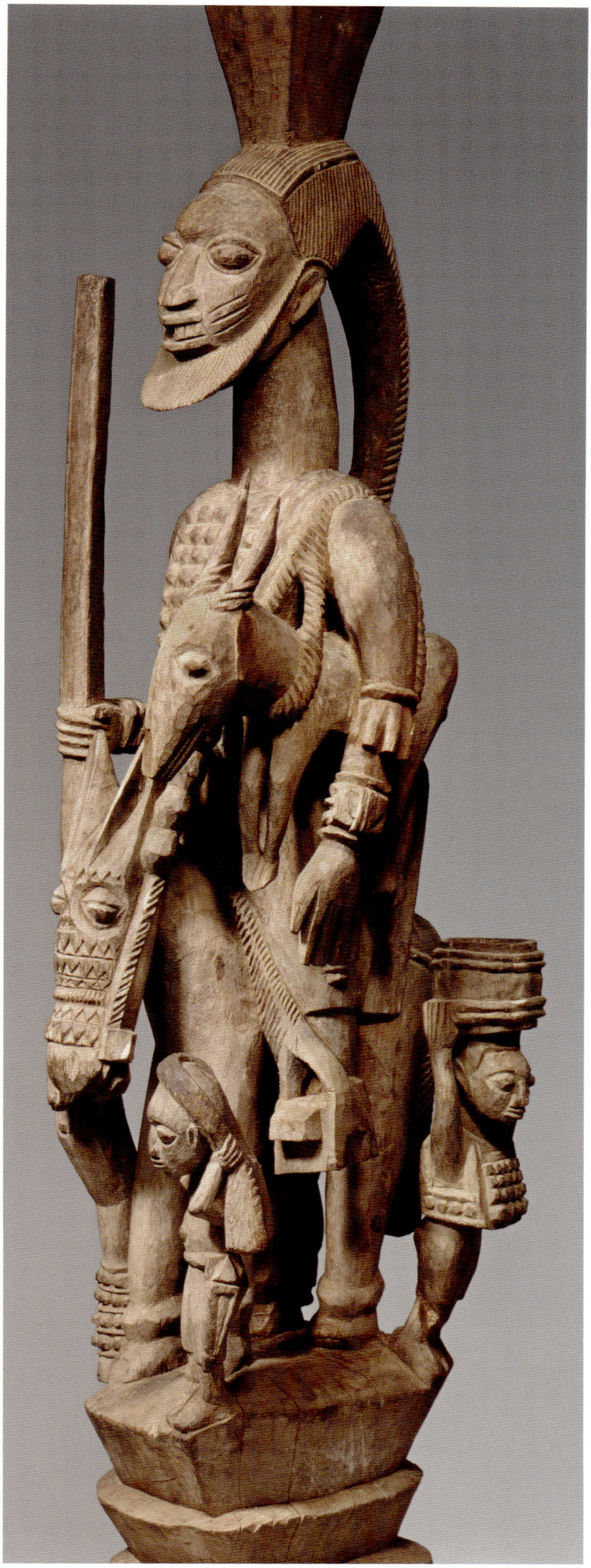

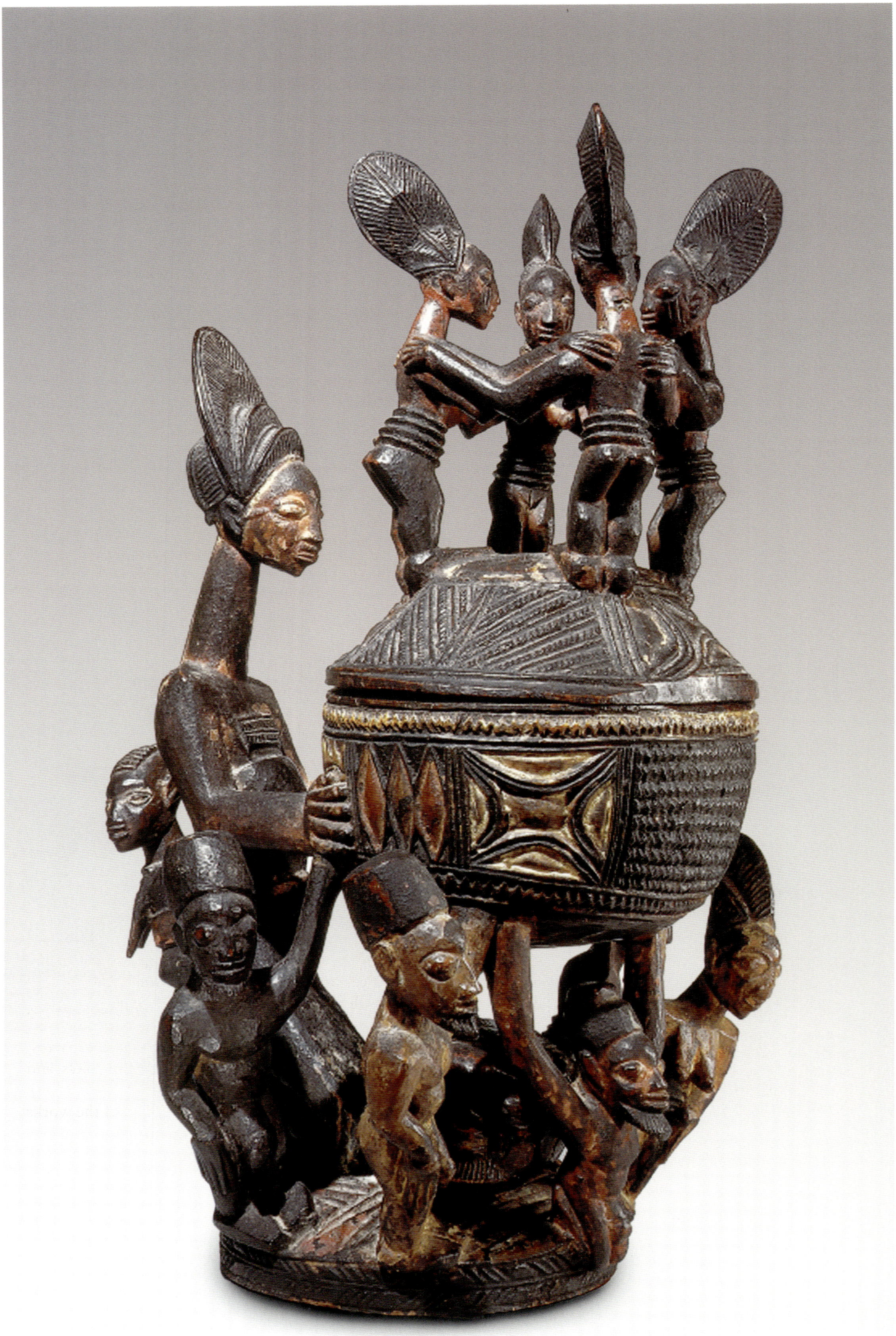

140. Olowe of Ise
Yoruba, Nigeria, ca. 1925
Vessel decorated with figures
Wood and pigments, 63.7 cm
National Museum of African Art,
Washington, D.C.

masks, drums, mortars, mirror cases and dolls, imprinting all of them, large or small, simple or complex, with the hallmark of his personality. The catalogue of the Washington exhibition, with the illustrations of the forty-five sculptures, bears witness to this versatility.

His work has been known in Europe since 1924, when the door (no. 137) he carved about ten years earlier[38] for the palace of the Ogoga (ruler) of Ikere, sent to London for the British Empire Exhibition, was requested by the British government for the British Museum, where it has been ever since.[39] The ten scenes sculpted into the surface of the each panels recount the visit to Ikere of two representatives of the British crown, Major Reeve-Tucker and Captain Ambrose.

The meeting of the latter, borne in a litter, with the enthroned monarch occupies the two largest panels. Curiously, the European visitor is represented on a much smaller scale than the African king. As William Fagg observes, "Olowe has carved Captain Ambrose himself as almost a suppliant of the king"[40] rather than a representative of the colonial power.

While the figures on the doors made by the other Yoruba artists listed above are flat and static, these are dynamic, often carved in the round and clearly protruding from the vertical plane of the panel as though projected into space.

The Nigerian artist's best-known and most monumental works are, however, pillars for the verandas of important figures in Yoruba society. Those illustrated here (nos. 138–139) are from the compound of the Onymon family in Ogbagi. Over two metres in height, they bear witness to Olowe's rich vein of invention. Two horsemen of considerable size, probably a priest in the first pillar and a hunter in the second, tower over retinues of smaller figures.

As Roslyn Walker acutely observes, the small scale of the capitals accentuates the size of the figures below, which "seem to project beyond the dimensions of the capital".[41]

Olowe is also the author of some vessels probably used to contain cola nuts. The monumental item purchased some fifteen years ago by the National Museum of African Art in Washington (no. 140) is considered one of the masterpieces of 20th-century Yoruba art.[42]

The sobriety of the geometric decoration on the spherical vessel enhances the highly animated yet disciplined throng of figures surmounting and supporting it. While four women in a circle with their hands on one another's shoulders form an elegant diadem on the lid, a kneeling figure enormous in size compared to others provides a visual link between this group and the one below.

Mention should also be made of the colours, both sober and bright, that enrich the sculptures and add vivacity to the images.

Great sculptors of the Cameroonian chiefdoms

The political requirements and culture of the great 19th-century chiefdoms of Cameroon[43] fostered the activities of masters and workshops commissioned to create the works needed to celebrate the ruling dynasty and ensure the consolidation of power and smooth functioning of society.

The emblematic works in this connection, for which the term "court art" does not seem inappropriate, are great supporting pillars of palace verandas, as in Nigeria, symbolic portraits of kings, queens, chiefs and minor chiefs, and the emblems of rulers.

The attitude of Cameroonian society towards the authors of the works was ambiguous, according to the scholars who have examined the art of the region. Among the Bangwa (a group of the Bamileke people inhabiting the central part of the western plateau of Cameroon), for example, sculptors were even regarded as the property of their patrons and their names were in any case forgotten in the space of a few decades.[44] The only artist to have escaped this oblivion is Ateu Atsa (ca. 1840–1880), court sculptor to the monarch Assunganyi and identified by Bernard de Grunne as the author of twenty-two works.[45]

141. "Master of the Rings"
Bangwa, Cameroon, ca. 1840–80
Commemorative statue
Wood, 87 cm
Private collection (formerly in the Dartevelle Collection)

142. "Master of the Rings"
Bangwa, Cameroon, ca. 1840–80
Maternity figure, commemorative statue
Wood, 82 cm
Staatliche Museen zu Berlin, Ethnologisches Museum, Berlin

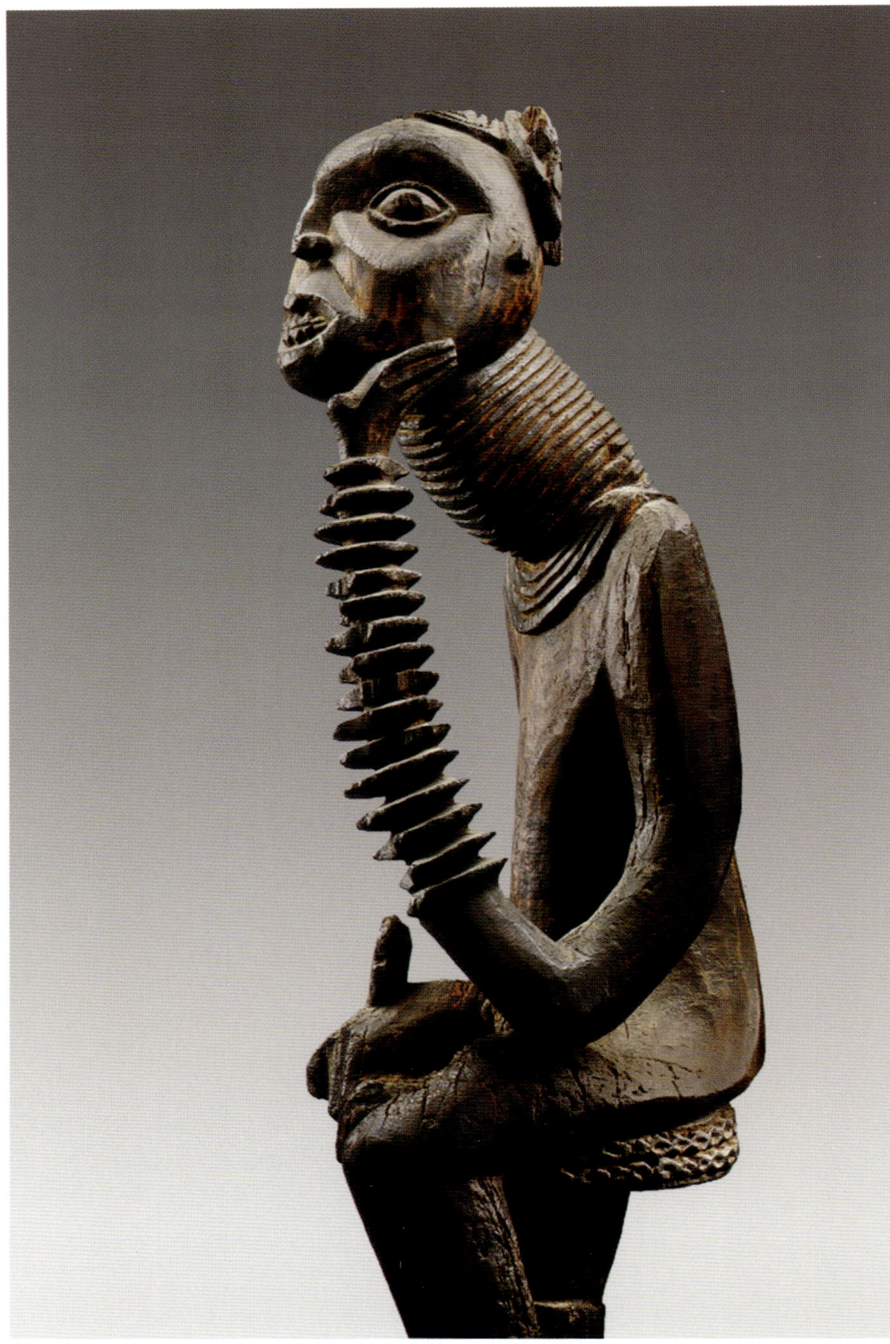

Two great Bangwa sculptors

In my opinion, however, the most extraordinary Bangwa sculptor in the second half of the 19th century is the author of the seated figure acquired by Robert Brain in 1965–67, formerly in the collection of Pierre Dartevelle, and of the maternity figure acquired by Gustav Conrau in 1899 and now in the Ethnologisches Museum, Berlin.

The first is a male figure seated on a typical stool with a single support structure (no. 141). While the right arm and leg are now lost, the chin rests on the left hand in a thoughtful attitude. The missing right hand may have held an emblem of sovereignty such as a sceptre or pipe. The large oval head, whose features display real ferocity, surmounts a body reminiscent of some monstrous insect. Note the triangular indentations of the cheeks on either side of a small nose with flaring nostrils and above all the large mouth with cruel teeth.

While the metal necklaces and ivory bangles on the figure were traditional attributes of the Bangwa chiefs, this extraordinary artist not only increased the number of the latter to sixteen but also made them equal in size and number to the rings encircling the abnormally long neck, thus making the unnatural elongation of the arm formally coherent within a structure of great ex-

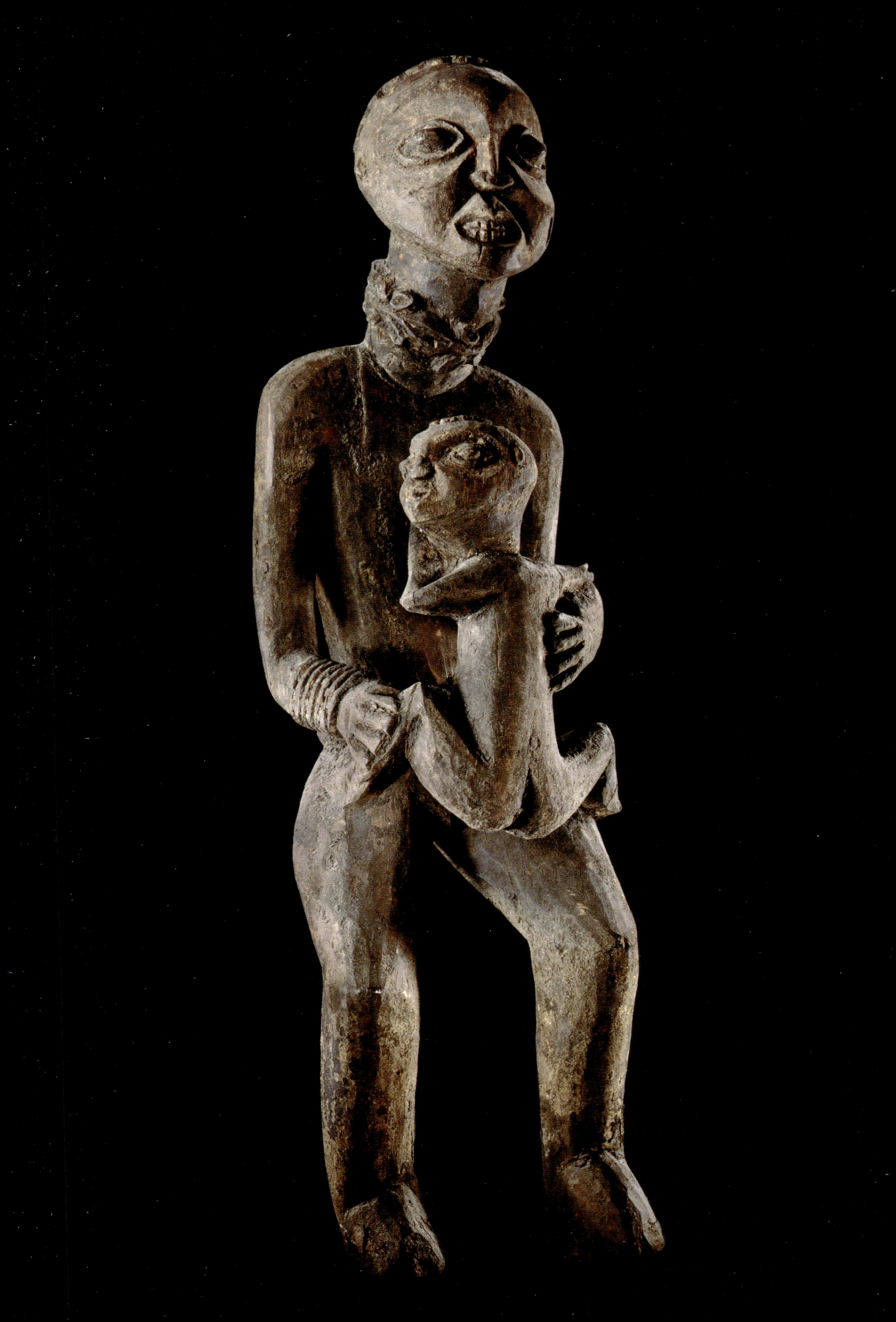

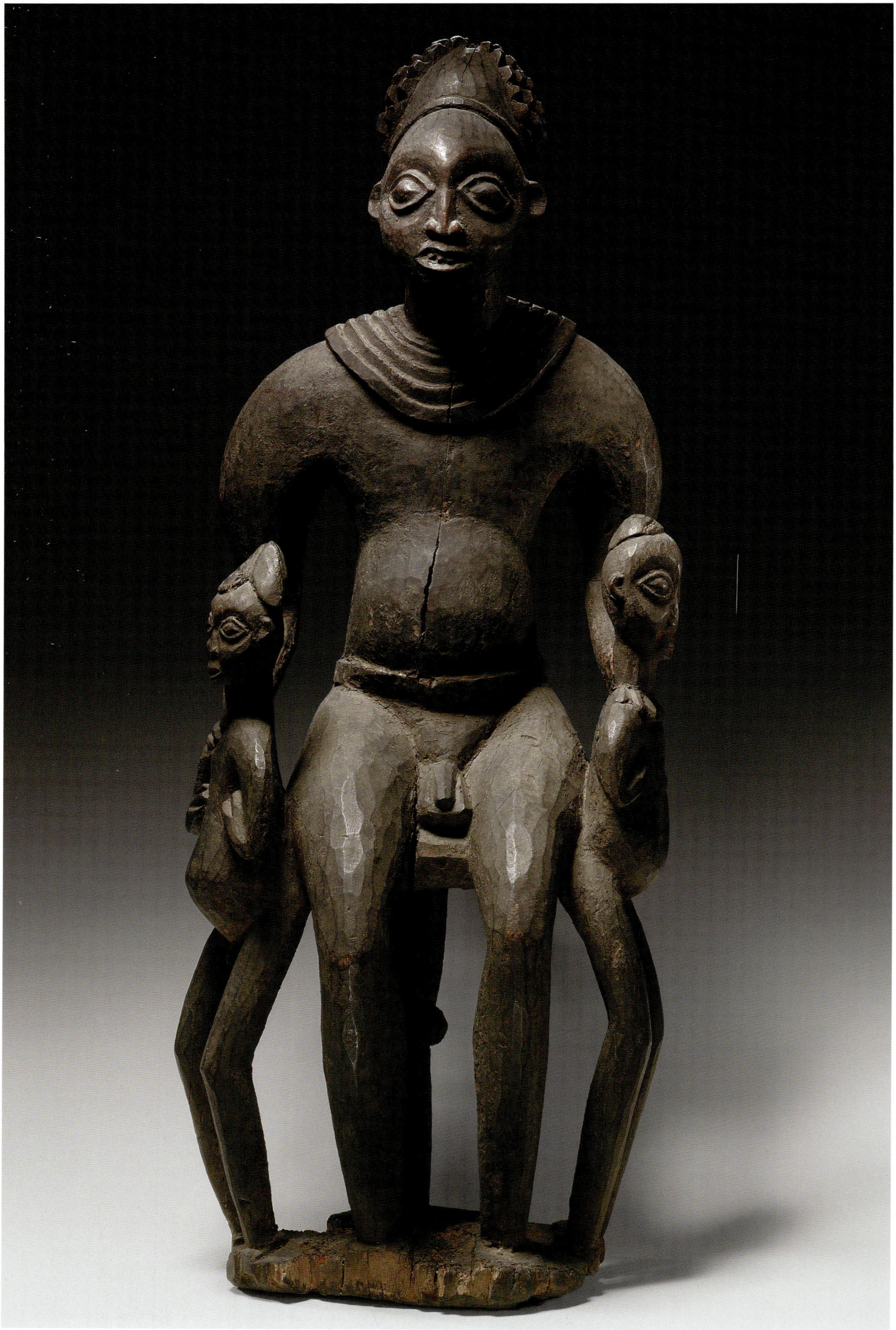

143. "Master of the Berlin Tanyi"
Bangwa, Cameroon,
second half of 19th c.
Commemorative statue
Wood, 89 cm
Staatliche Museen zu Berlin,
Ethnologisches Museum, Berlin

144. Anonymous artist
Bangwa, Cameroon,
second half of 19th c.
Commemorative statue
Wood, 79 cm
Private collection

pressive power. It was on the basis of this highly individual iconographic and volumetric solution that I coined the name "Master of the Rings" for this artist.

The second work (no. 142), whose date of acquisition in situ by Conrau (1899) delimits the period in which the master was active, is a maternity figure referred to locally as a mother of twins, despite the fact that there is only one child. The woman's high social status is indicated only by the bracelets and the elegant necklace of cowry shells.

The heads of the mother and child display the same features as the previous figure, while their naturally proportioned bodies, formed by simple volumes, are shot through with tension evident above all in the frontal view. The tilting of the woman's torso is balanced by the unlikely position of the child, who has the same adult features as the mother, but seems to be affectively detached from her (their heads are turned at right angles to one another), in accordance with a representative convention recurrent in most African maternity figures.

Susan Vogel has attributed three works to another artist active in the same chiefdom during the same period. The first (no. 143), now in the Berlin ethnological museum, is an imposing male figure flanked by two smaller ones (interpreted by the experts on Bangwa sculpture as a father of twins). The other two are commemorative figures seated on typical stools with a single support structure, one in the Musée Dapper and the other in a private collection (only one is shown here). Since the Bangwa title for the father of twins is *Tanyi*, according to Brain and Pollock,[46] and the Berlin sculpture is the best exam-

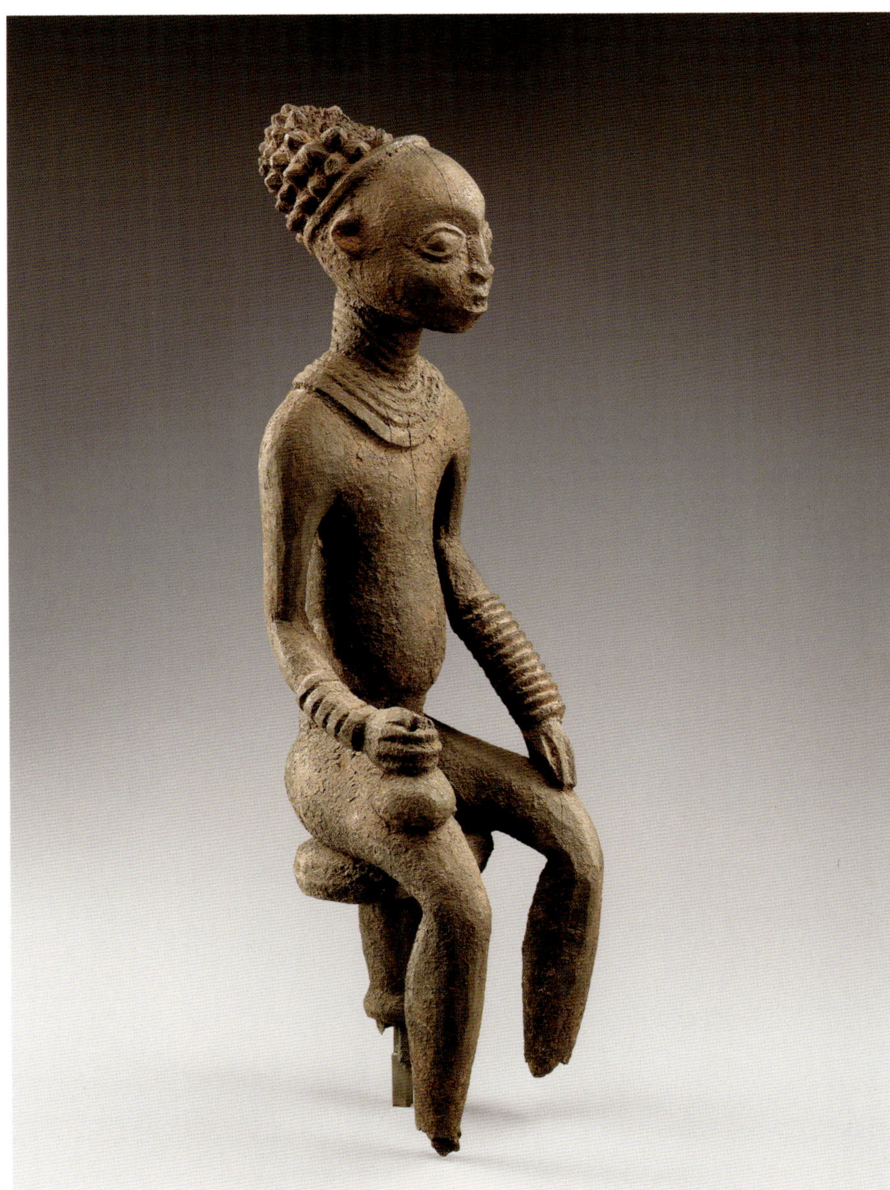

ple, Susan Vogel has suggested that the author of these three works should be known as the "Master of the Berlin Tanyi".[47]

The figures bear some similarities to those by the "Master of the Rings", but are distinguished by the softness of the delicate, sensitive facial features and an aura of spiritual serenity in harmony with the elegant rendering of the slim body in smooth volumes.

The existence of similar sculptures that are not, however, the work of these masters (no. 144) suggests that other sculptors were active alongside them and followed their methods.[48]

The "Master of Bamessi"

Authors of works from areas other than the Bangwa chiefdoms are also identifiable. An example is provided by the sculptor of a group of monumental helmet-like anthropomorphic masks from the Tikar region. Placed on top of the head, they made the wearer, whose face was hidden by a hood of fibres, look like a giant and were used by dancers in the yearly ceremonies to ensure the fertility of the soil, as well as at funerals and receptions for important personages.

The two examples shown here differ only in their coiffure. The first (no. 145), now in the Portland Art Museum in Oregon, was acquired in 1932 in the village of Bamessi by the missionary, collector and scholar Paul Gebauer, the source of our information on the use of these works. The second (no. 146) was purchased at the end of the 1960s and is now in the Civiche Raccolte Artistiche del Castello Sforzesco, Raccolte Extraeuropee in Milan.

145. "Master of Bamessi"
Tikar/Bekom, Cameroon
Mask
Wood, 46.5 cm
The Portland Art Museum, Portland

146. "Master of Bamessi"
Tikar/Bekom, Cameroon
Mask
Wood, 52 cm
Civiche Raccolte Artistiche del
Castello Sforzesco, Raccolte
Extraeuropee, Milan

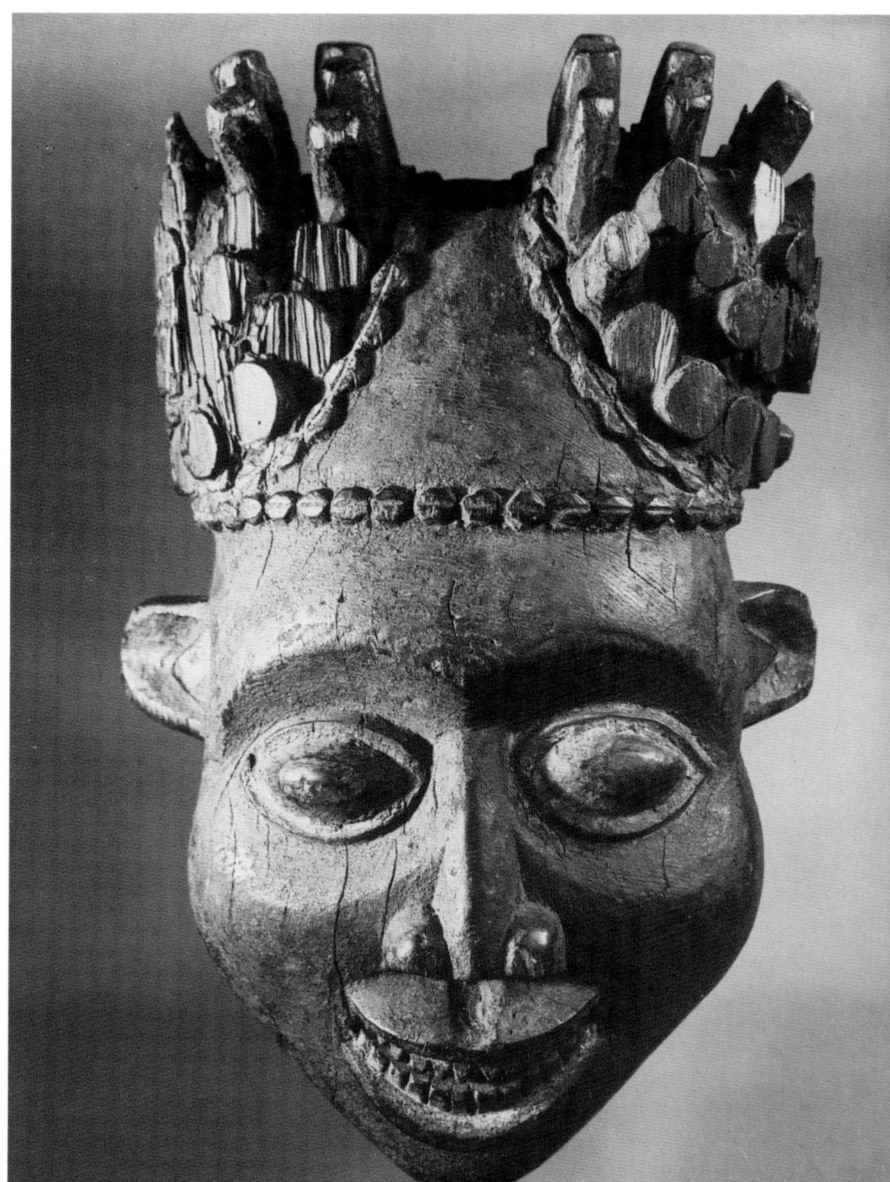

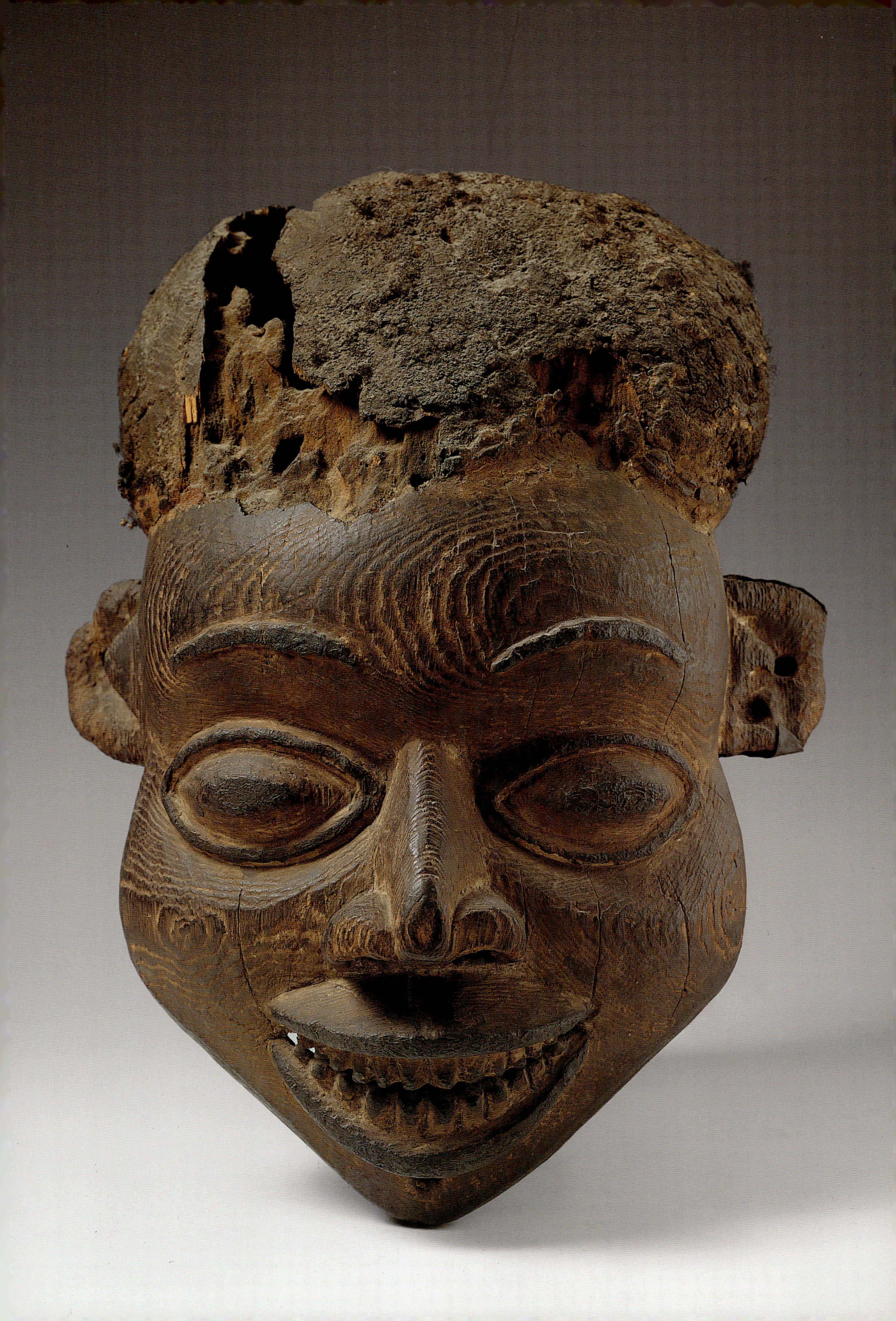

147. "Master of Ntem"
Fang, Gabon, ca. 1800–60
Reliquary figure
Wood, 50.8 cm
Dallas Museum of Art, Dallas
(Eugene and Margaret McDermott Art Fund)

147a. Rear view of the reliquary figure no. 147

Seen from the front, the masks have a very unusual shaped outline but retain a natural appearance. The features of the face are rendered in expressively emphasized full volumes, such as the perfect oval of the large eyes reiterated in the curve of the eyelids and eyebrows, carved in relief, and the splendid crescent-shaped mouth, half-open in a smile that seems to extend to the cheeks, making them fuller. The result is an impression of joyful vigour and exuberant vitality that makes the works by this artist quite unmistakable. Referred to provisionally as the "Master of Bamessi" after the name of the village where the work in the Gebauer Collection was acquired, he could equally well be called the "Master of the Winning Smile".

Ancestral protectors: the reliquary figures of the Fang and Kota peoples

The Fang of Gabon, Cameroon and Equatorial Guinea and the Kota of Gabon used to place wooden figures on cylindrical caskets of bark or woven fibre baskets containing the bones of important ancestors of the community. These relics were consulted in connection with decisions affecting the community and also performed a protective function. Propitiatory sacrifices were made to the ancestors, whose intercession was requested on every important occasion in the life of the family and the community.

The Ntem Masters

Curiously enough, Fang reliquary carvings, both complete figures and heads, are still the most sought-after and expensive African works of art, even though they are by no means the rarest traditional sculptures. They first appeared on the Western market around 1910, when incipient interest in the so-called primitive arts gave the young Paul Guillaume the idea of having Fang sculptures shipped from Gabon for sale to collectors and gallery owners.[49]

Although the Fang were spread out over a vast area, the iconography of their sculptures is comparatively homogeneous in general terms, at least at the level of the major regional subgroups. The works having recognizable personal characteristics are, however, numerous and isolated at the same time. For this reason, unlike grouping by geographical area, the attribution of works to a particular author or workshop is no easy task.

In the section of the exhibition 'Masterhands/Mains de Maîtres'[50] (2001) devoted to Fang art, Luis Perrois showed seven sculptures – three of which had passed through the hands of Paul Guillaume – and attributed five of considerable antiquity and with similar characteristics (no. 147) to artists of the Mvaï group, the authors of numerous other works. The Ntem Valley and river in northern Gabon, where the reliquaries were carved between 1750 and 1860, provided him with a name for their authors. The reliquary illustrated here, and two more in the Seattle Art Museum and the Léonce and Pierre Guerre Collection in Marseille,[51] are almost certainly by the same artist.

Seen from the front, the squatting figures have an unmistakeable shape divided into three main volumes: an imposing, prognathous head on a thick neck; the block of the massive torso with rippling pectorals, short arms and a very large navel; and the thighs and lower legs. This division is repeated in the rear view (no. 147a), where the protruding buttocks and the vertical element for attaching the figure to the reliquary casket combine with the legs to form a sort of base for the upper part that is particularly evident when viewed from the side. Some figures also have tattoos in the abdominal region.

A combination of distortion and sobriety – the broad, rounded forehead crowned by an imposing coiffure that stretches out behind to balance the volume of the buttocks, the mysterious slit eyes and the disdainful mouth – and a rigorous volumetric arrangement[52] characterize the ancestral figures carved by the Ntem masters, where power and balance are blended in works of restrained monumentality.

Abstraction and symbolic representation in the art of the Kota

Like the neighbouring Fang, the Kota people inhabiting the southeast part of

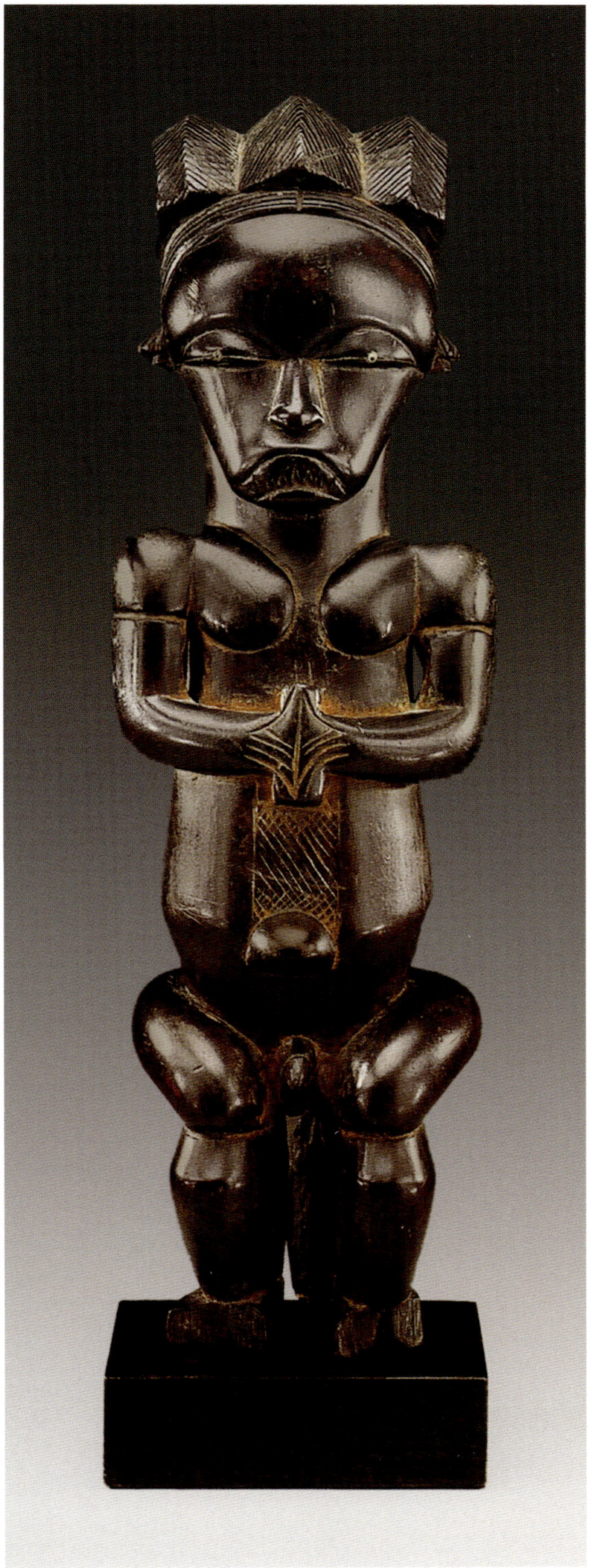
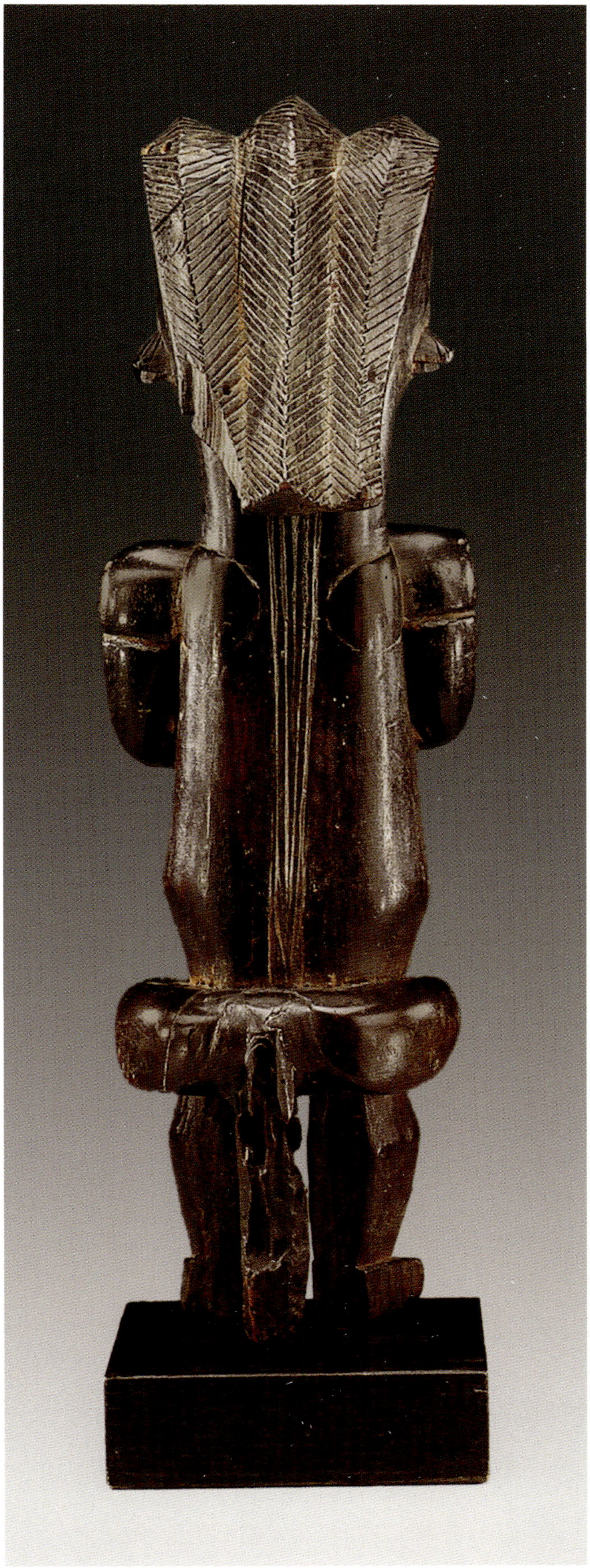

148. Kota artist
Gabon
Double-faced reliquary figure (convex face)
Wood, brass and copper, 63 cm
Staatliche Museen zu Berlin, Ethnologisches Museum, Berlin

148a. Another view of the double-faced reliquary figure no. 148 (concave face)

Gabon also used to place figures on the woven baskets containing the bones of family ancestors.

The first items of Kota sculpture arrived in France and Germany in the last quarter of the 19th century in the wake of the expeditions led by Pierre Savorgnan de Brazza and Oskar Lenz. The French items, which were exhibited at the Musée du Trocadéro, Paris, are faithfully reproduced in an illustration that appeared in *Le Tour du Monde* in 1888 (e.g. the panoply on p. 39). The reliquaries may, however, have been produced a few centuries earlier, as the local mines were able to supply the copper used for their lids before importation of this metal from Europe began in the 19th century.

While performing much the same function, the Kota reliquary figures are completely different also in conceptual terms from those of the Fang and the other peoples in the region. They are in fact symbolic representations of ancestors tending towards abstraction and very similar to bas-reliefs. Wooden shapes of moderate thickness are covered with thin sheets, plates and wires of copper and brass, which are attached to the support with nails or staples and follow the course of its raised and recessed areas, to form a sort of skin. The combination of the two metals and the interplay of concave and convex surfaces create chromatic effects of magical intensity.

The human figure is predominantly represented by an unconventional rendering of the head alone with elements whose interpretation is uncertain. According to Efraim Andersson's indigenous informants,[53] the element above the face is a moon symbol and the side pieces are the cheeks of the personage represented. If this is so, it means that the typical Cubist procedure of breaking up the subject and representing it as a whole in terms not only of what is seen but also what is known was adopted independently and much earlier by the Kota artists.

The lower part of the reliquary, consisting of a thin cylinder and a lozenge, is an extreme metaphor of the human body that confirms the Kota artists' capacity for abstraction and enhances the majesty of the head.

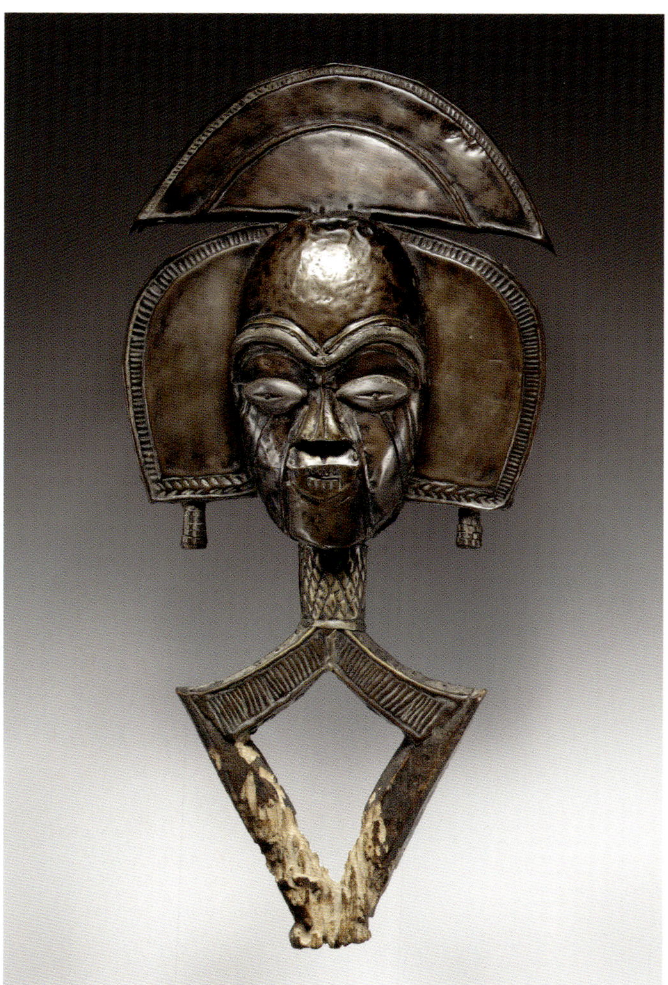

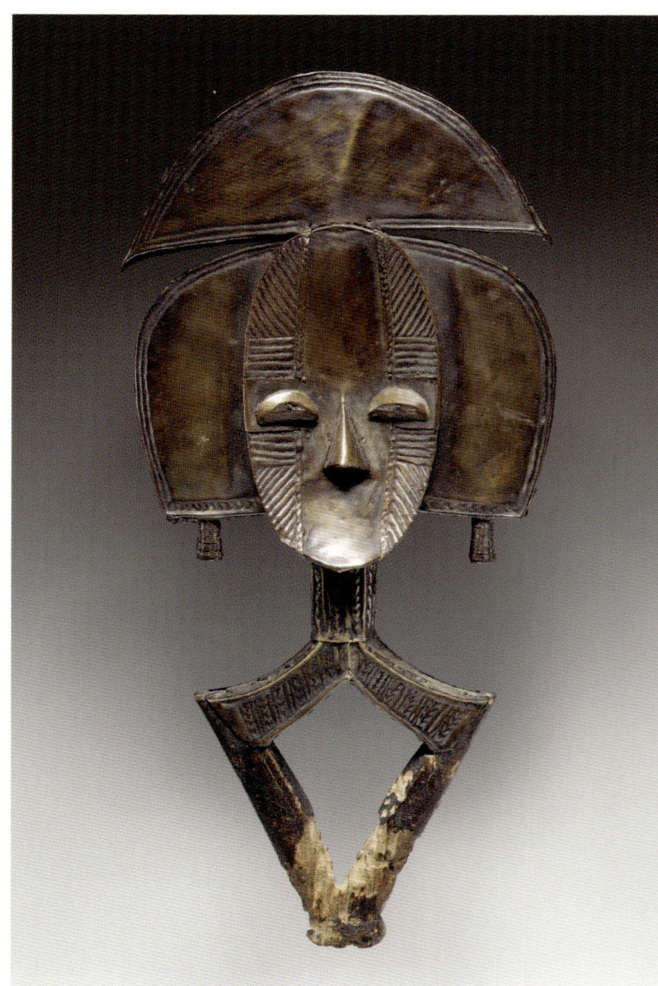

149-149a. Sébé Master
Kota, Gabon
Reliquary figure
Wood, brass and copper, 53 cm
Private collection

Within a shared overall framework of solemn, severe and indeed ascetic frontality, the regional sub-styles are highly diversified and the faces display differing degrees of abstraction. The images of 170 works published by Alain and Françoise Chaffin[54] and the illustrations of studies by other scholars who have examined the Kota[55] make it possible to assess the differences between the various types of reliquary. There are some whose convexity tends to make the stylized features less distant from reality and some of a concave character in which the representation is a sort of allusive sketch. In between are hybrid faces in which concavity and convexity predominate to different degrees. The situation is made even more complicated by the existence of Janus-like figures having concave and convex faces at the same time (nos. 148–148a), not to mention the very different ways of rendering the features, above all the eyes, and the elements surrounding the face.

It is possible, however, within the complex and manifold universe outlined above, to pick out groups of reliquaries with similar characteristics that reveal their origin in a particular workshop and in some cases the hand of a single artist. Given the large number of works exemplifying each of the types noted above, we shall confine ourselves here to just one example.

Louis Perrois selected five reliquaries (out of the many similar items held by museums and private collections) for the above-mentioned 'Mains de Maîtres' exhibition and attributed them to the Sébé Master, an artist active in Gabon in the region of the River Sébé, a tributary of the Ogoué.

While adopting the most typical form of the reliquary figures, with a crescent at the top and side pieces, he reinvented it in line with his own figurative vision (nos. 149–149a). In order to obtain the desired results, he combined a broad, rounded forehead with a small, concave, heart-shaped face dominated by large, round eyes. He also used sheets and strips of metal with the utmost skill and introduced relief elements that animate the composition, such as the contour running from the top of the head as far as the pendants of the

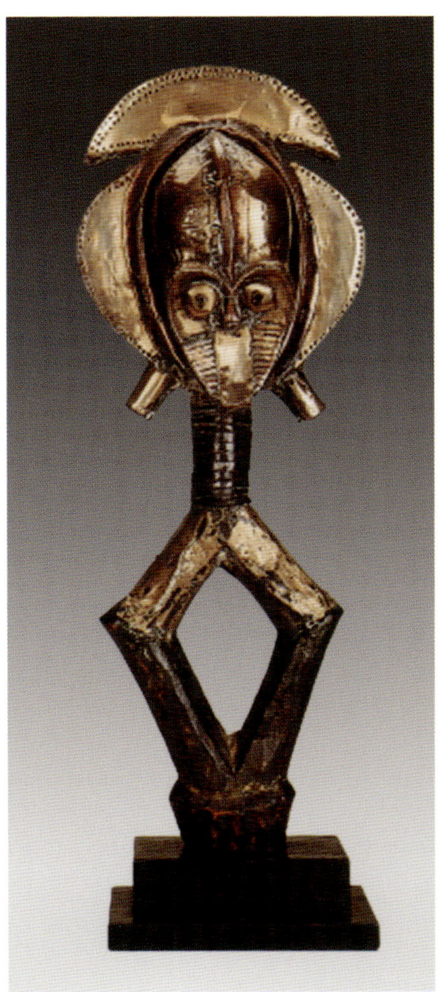

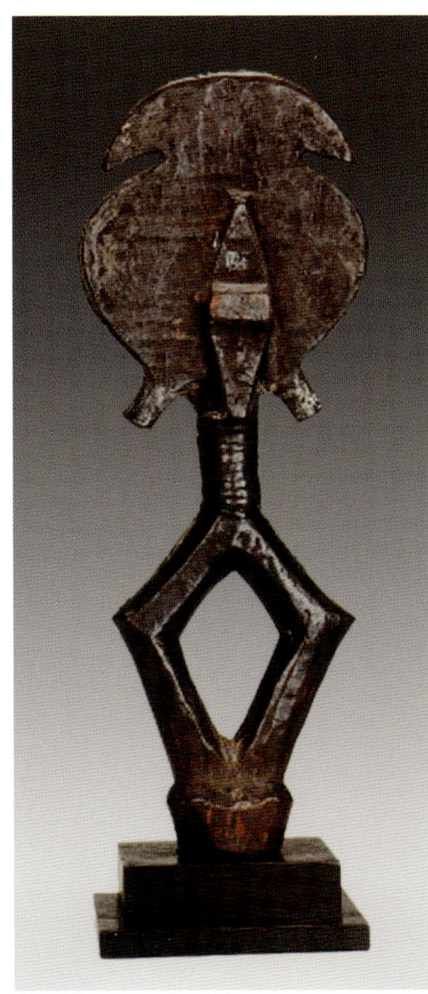

coiffure and the strip that crosses the forehead vertically and is visually linked to the lower strip of the face.

By simultaneously adopting and moving beyond the figurative conventions of his community, the artist succeeded in creating a group of original works that acquire a universal value, while respecting tradition.

Great Yombe workshops

The wealth of Kongo[56] statuary, and particularly that of the Yombe group, provides a broad range of examples of the artists' oeuvre: from the aristocratic austerity of the "Master of Kasadi" to the domestic, human quality of the "Master of Boma-Vonde" and the apparent aggressiveness of the colossal figures carved in the River Chiloango Workshop.

The "Master of Kasadi"

The universal theme of maternity frequently recurs in the statuary of the Kongo peoples and is addressed with greater or lesser degrees of originality by the different artists depending on their personalities. According to Albert Maesen, the meaning and function of the mother and child images are probably connected with the fertility cult.

The "Master of Kasadi" is identified as the author of over a dozen sculptures, the first of which, now in a private collection, was acquired in 1898. He lived in the late 19th and early 20th century, presumably in the village of Kasadi in the present-day Democratic Republic of the Congo, where two of his works were found.[57]

Six maternity figures can almost certainly be attributed to this stylistically meticulous artist on the basis of close similarities in pose, the handling of volumes, and structural and decorative elements. However, attribution is more problematic, though still very likely, for another seven items: three figures with magical-religious functions,[58] a staff surmounted by a female figure[59] and three (or perhaps four) masks.

In the mother and child images, two examples of which are illustrated here (nos. 150–151), the woman is represented in a way that emphasizes her social and cultural prestige. Every element works to create this impression, from the dignified pose and absolute frontality to the refined tattoos, the bracelets and necklaces, and the headdress usually reserved for personages of high rank. No Yombe sculpture equals the aristocratic austerity of the volumes and their crystalline formal clarity. The woman is sitting cross-legged like certain figures in ancient Egyptian art. The vertical, column-like torso and neck support a well-proportioned head with perfect features: large open eyes, dainty shell-like ears, the mouth slightly open to show the characteristic filed teeth, and an intense expression of wonder and remote detachment.

The profile of the rounded and slightly bulging shoulders is unmistakable, as is the perfect alignment of the two bracelets and the double line above the breasts delimiting the highly decorated upper part of the torso. The pattern in relief embellishing the figure's back (no. 150a) is to be found in a photograph of a woman taken by a researcher from the Musée Royal de l'Afrique Centrale, Tervuren,[60] at the beginning of the 20th century and has been in the figurative heritage of the Kongo for many centuries, as attested by a fragment of terracotta, 16th-century oliphants and other antique artefacts (see nos. 106–110).

Naturalism and stylization also combine in the figure with magical-religious functions (no. 152) and in the splendid masks now in the Tervuren museum[61] to create images of unparalleled nobility and intensity of expression (no. 153). The pierced pupils and the biconvex outline in relief suggest an inner awareness that illuminates a profoundly spiritual face, which is further enhanced by the white patina.

The "Master of Boma-Vonde"

The cross-legged seated position, the child lying in the lap, the hat of palm thread with geometric decoration, and the necklace of glass beads – all fea-

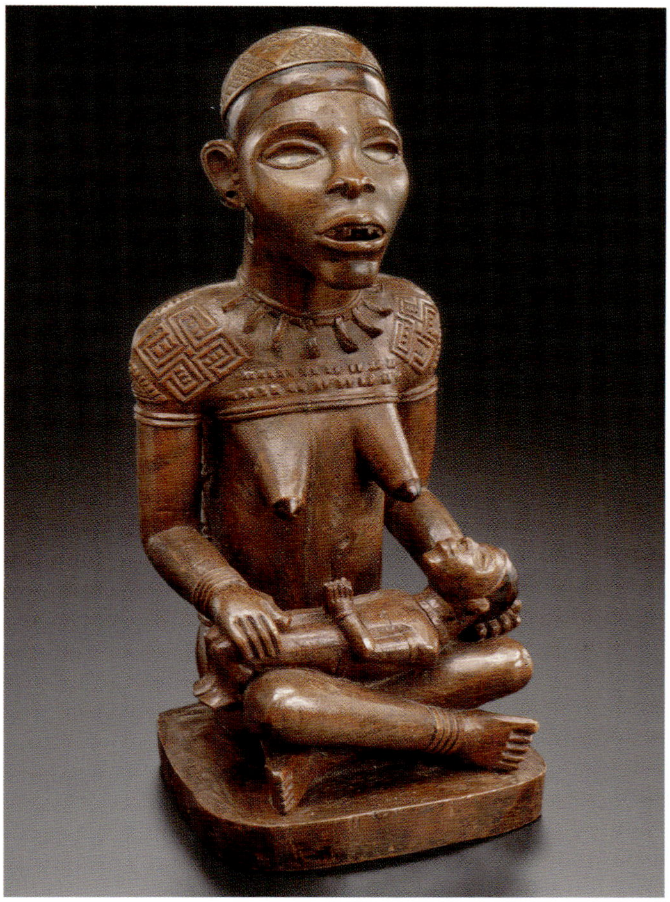

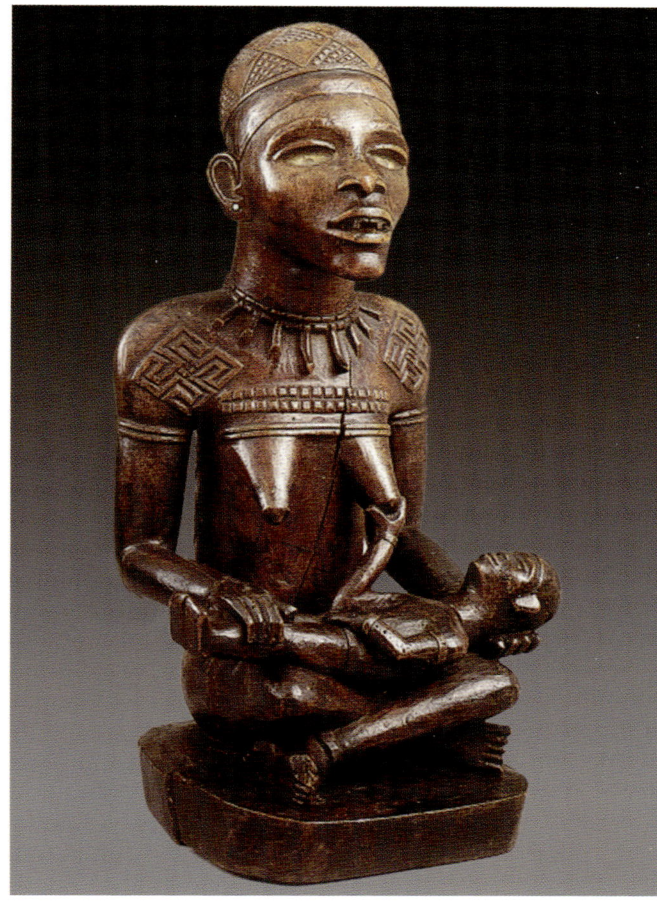

150. "Master of Kasadi"
Kongo (Yombe), Democratic Republic of the Congo
Maternity figure
Wood and traces of clay, h. 29 cm
Musée Royal de l'Afrique Centrale, Tervuren

150a. Rear view of the maternity figure no. 150

151. "Master of Kasadi"
Kongo (Yombe), Democratic Republic of the Congo
Maternity figure
Wood, h. 27.3 cm
Drs Daniel and Marian Malcolm Collection, Tenafly (USA)

152. "Master of Kasadi"
Kongo (Yombe), Democratic Republic of the Congo
Figure with magical-religious functions
Wood, h. 33 cm
Private collection

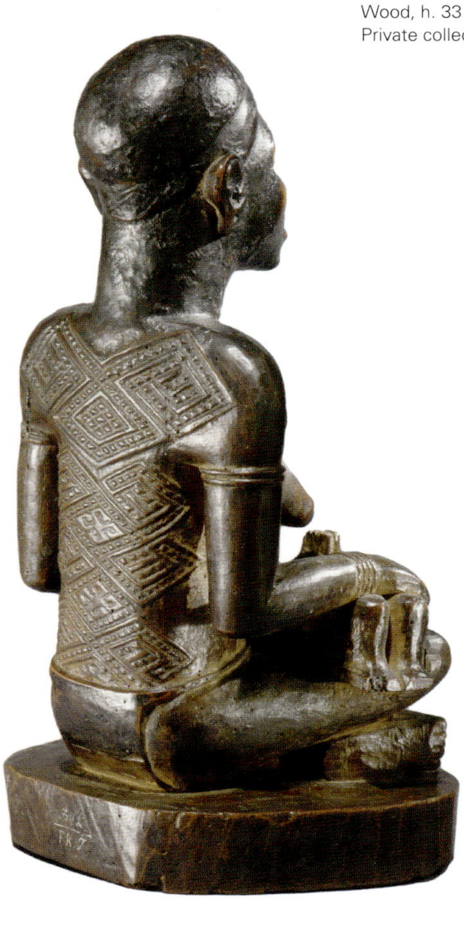

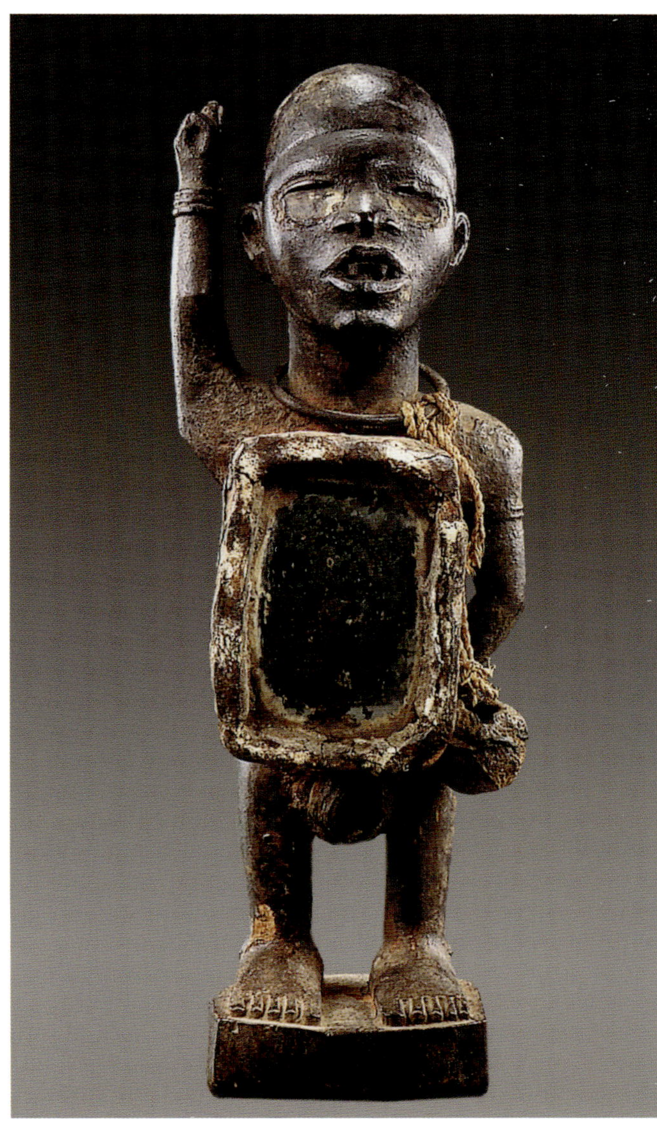

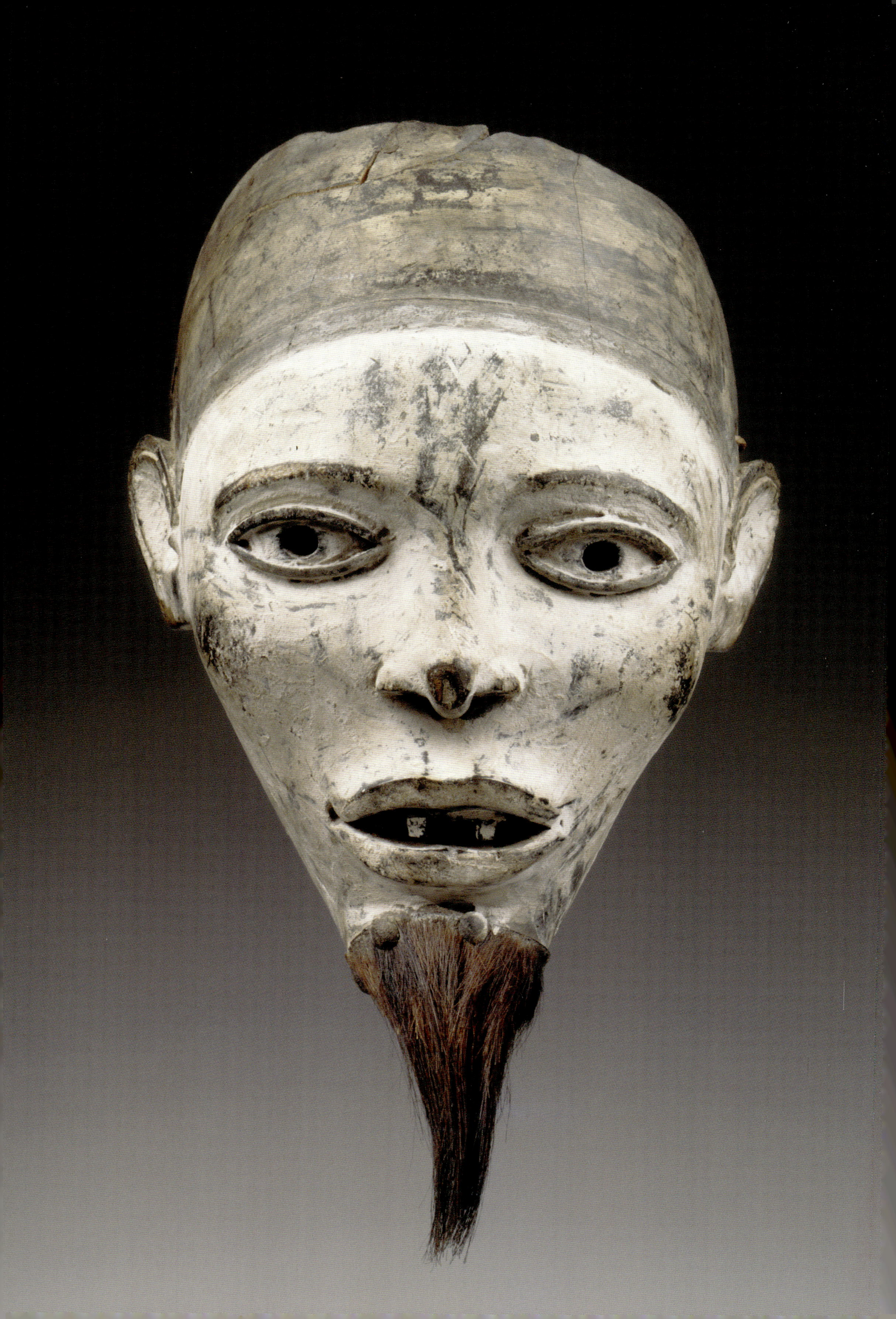

153. "Master of Kasadi"
Kongo (Yombe), Democratic Republic of the Congo
Mask
Wood, kaolin and animal hair, h. 23 cm
Musée Royal de l'Afrique Centrale, Tervuren

154. "Master of Boma-Vonde"
Kongo (Yombe), Democratic Republic of the Congo
Maternity figure
Wood, 23.7 cm
Museo Nazionale Preistorico Etnografico "L. Pigorini", Rome

155. "Master of Boma-Vonde"
Kongo (Yombe), Democratic Republic of the Congo
Ceremonial staff
Wood, h. 70 cm
Private collection (formerly in the H. Goldet Collection, Paris)

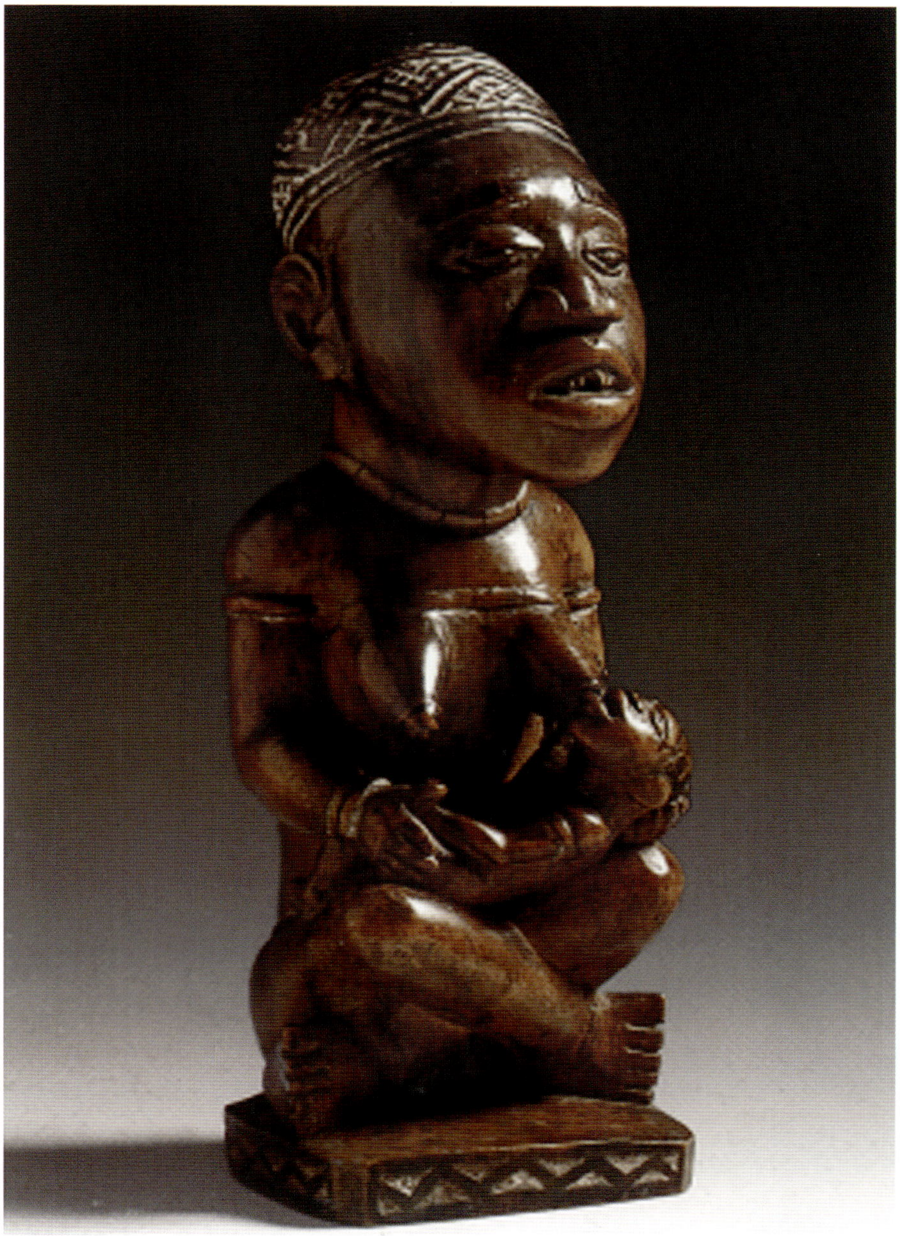

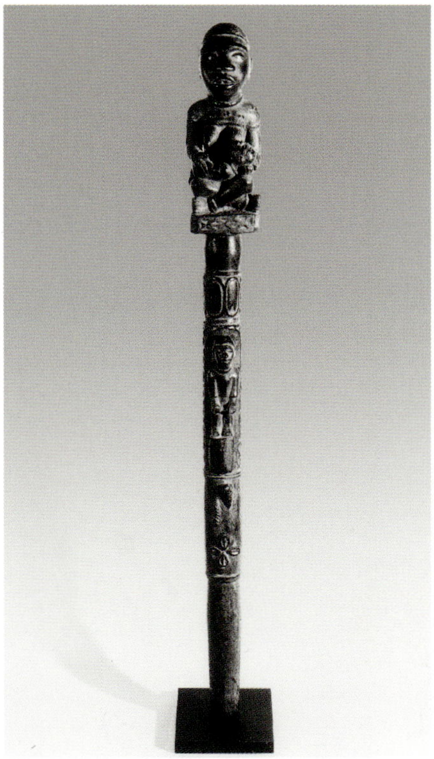

tures seen in the works of the previous group – also reappear in another four figures (no. 154)[62] and in the ornament on a staff (no. 155). The formal similarities suggest that these are the work of a single artist referred to provisionally as the "Master of Boma-Vonde" after the name of the locality where the first of his sculptures recorded in a European museum was acquired.[63]

Even though the woman is looking up and not at the child (as in the maternity figures of the previous group and most of the Africans works on this theme), this artist's sculptures strike a different note, suggesting a warm relationship between the mother and child, and creating an impression of quiet, human domesticity and fertile power. The soft rendering of the full volumes, especially the large egg-shaped head and the absence of geometric decoration, makes the images more human and earthly without detracting from their formal clarity or diminishing their expressive power.

Magical statues at the service of the community

The creativity of the Kongo artists of the past seems to have expressed itself in two very different ways. On the one hand, we have the refined delicacy of small female figures, particularly the moving mother and child images; on the other, the disturbing violence of the statues with magical-religious functions once described as nail fetishes, which were supposed to reveal, neutralize and punish individuals harmful to the society or any of its members, by means of particular rituals that involved driving nails or blades into the statues.

The final appearance of these works is the result of a genuine collective effort made by the sculptor who creates the statue, the priest, who activates it by placing magical material into the special receptacle (normally on the abdomen with a mirror or shell as a lid, as in the cases illustrated here), and the supplicants asking the spirit to intercede on their behalf, who drive nails or blades into it (or have the priest do so).

One scholar has aptly compared the magical charge of these works to the energy pent up in the core of a nuclear reactor.

The giants of the River Chiloango

A powerfully monumental and seemingly aggressive quality distinguishes a group of large figures in similar poses, which were made by Yombe artists in a workshop situated in the region of the River Chiloango in either what is now the Democratic Republic of the Congo or in neighbouring Cabinda, in the late 19th and early 20th century.

The artists' ethnic group and the place of provenance were identified by Robert Visser, who came into possession of the first sculptures, now in museums in Berlin, Detroit, Mainz and Stuttgart.

Other pieces were also acquired during more or less the same period, including the two shown here (nos. 156–157), which are now in the Museo Nazionale Preistorico Etnografico "L. Pigorini", Rome, and the Musée Royal de l'Afrique Centrale, Tervuren. It is thus possible to draw significant comparisons and identify key elements, starting with similarities such as the striking physicality of the figures.

The massive oval head and the expressive face, dominated by large eyes and a half-open mouth, are similar in both figures. The profile of the broad, arched shoulders sharply divides the smooth, rounded back from the rugged

156. "Master of the River Chiloango Workshop 1"
Kongo (Yombe), Democratic Republic of the Congo or Cabinda
Figure with magical-religious functions
Wood, metal blades and nails, fibres, fabric, shell, mirror and resin paste, 112 cm
Museo Nazionale Preistorico Etnografico "L. Pigorini", Rome

157. "Master of the River Chiloango Workshop 2"
Kongo (Yombe), Democratic Republic of the Congo or Cabinda
Figure with magical-religious functions
Wood, metal blades and nails, fibres, fabric, animal hide, shell, mirror and resin paste, 114 cm
Musée Royal de l'Afrique Centrale, Tervuren

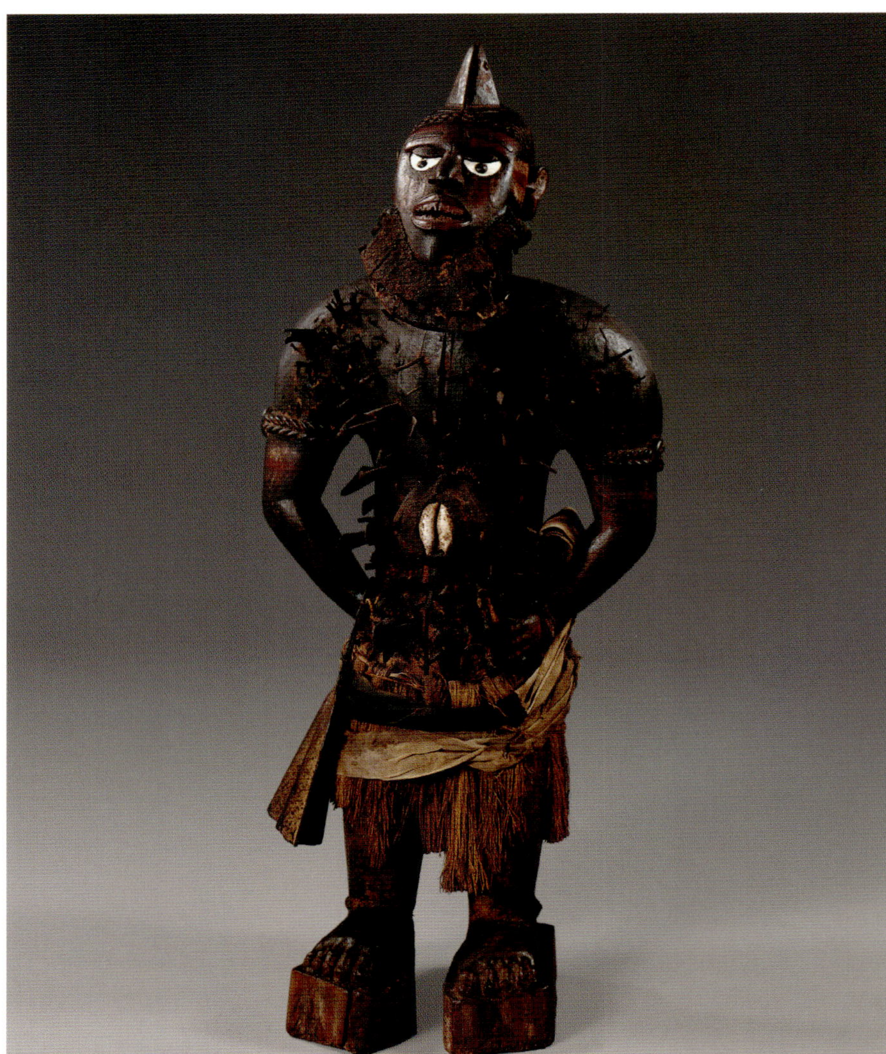

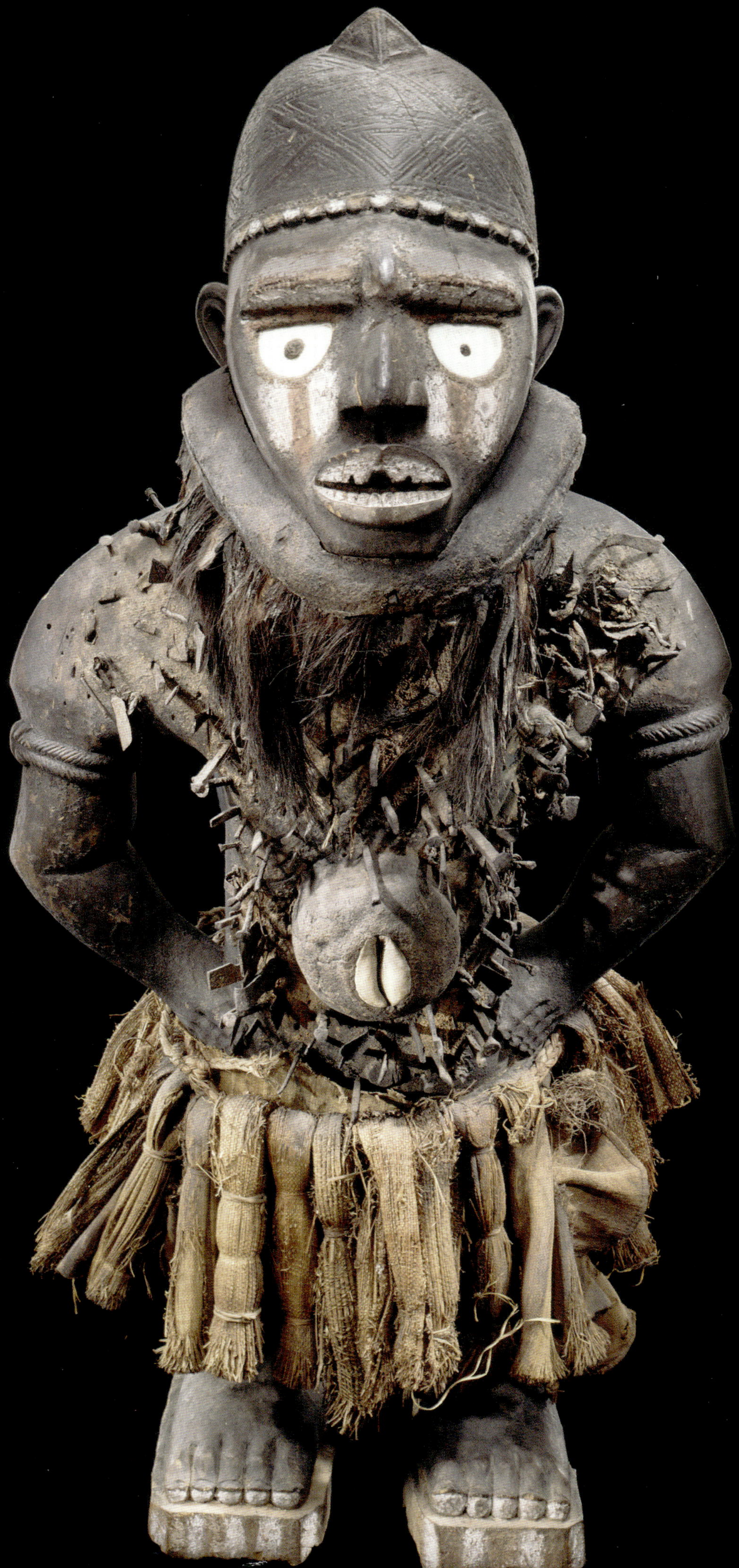

surface of the front, almost as though to emphasize its dramatic quality. Evidence of production in the same workshop and use in the same context is also provided by the similarity of the magical items: the shape and position of the receptacle, the shell serving as a lid, the nails and blades, the beard of resinous material[64] and the straw skirt.[65]

There are, however, also some differences – not always very evident though significant – between the two figures, such as the half-closed eyelids of the statue in Rome. The most important of these include the fact that the head of the latter, which is raised in challenge, has more regular proportions and appears more streamlined due to the tall point of the headdress. Moreover, while the shoulders of this figure – whose broad back is as smooth and taut as a sail – describe a harmonious curve, this is interrupted in its Belgian counterpart by the tight bangles.

Adoption of the general iconography and canons of the workshop did not, therefore, prevent the artists from expressing their own personality and creating works that are of a high formal quality, but also different and distinctive.

The aggressive and beneficent Songye figures

François Neyt has isolated a group of works that possess formal similarities from among the numerous magical Songye sculptures and attributed them to an atelier in the Belande region.[66] The common elements are best exemplified by the extraordinary androgynous "giant" now in the Mestach Collection, Brussels (no. 158).

The torso and limbs are powerfully square in shape, with the exception of the tiny, pointed breasts, whose tenderness is enhanced by contrast with the huge, flat and perfectly circular navel.

The colossal head, triangular in frontal view, is as wide as the shoulders and as long, including the headdress, as the torso. Its features are simplified and powerful, with large, wide-open eyes and a flattened nose whose flared nostrils spread in a fan shape that continues down to the disproportionately large crescent-shaped mouth, which is half-open with the teeth showing.[67] The semicircular ear carved into the head continues the line of the lower jaw that is decorated with geometric scarification marks.

A thin strip of copper running from the nose to the hemispherical forehead connects the face to a sort of sunburst crown with a large, curved horn in front, emerging from the upper section and pointing downwards. A headdress of feathers and a narrow iron collar with two hoe blades attached complete the sculpture.

The same artist is almost certainly the author of another slightly smaller figure, also in a private collection, which does not have a sunburst crown but has the same unfinished left hand and right foot, almost a kind of signature.

It is surprising to learn that these sculptures, *mankishi* in the Songye language, which are normally laden with objects that are difficult to decipher (horns, cowries, fur, glass beads and metal) and just as terrifying in appearance as those of the Kongo, "serve as protection against negative forces that beset people in the form of infertility, disease, death and bad harvests".[68]

The figures are therefore protective or therapeutic sculptures at the service of the community or individuals and not connected with the political power structure. While the larger examples, over one metre tall in some cases, served an entire village and an entire community, the smaller ones were used on a more individual basis.

Magical substances were either hung on the sculpture or placed in a cavity inside it or a horn secured to the head, and were only effective if mixed in accordance with the formulas of the specialist in magic (*nganga*), who was considered the true creator of the work in that, according to Dunja Hersak, the Songye attached importance only to the effectiveness of the sculptures (whose appearance does not reveal their function) and ignored their formal qualities.

158. Songye artist (Belande region)
Democratic Republic of the Congo
Figure with magical-religious functions
Wood, horn, metal, feathers, ritual agglomerate, 112.5 cm
Willy Mestach Collection, Brussels

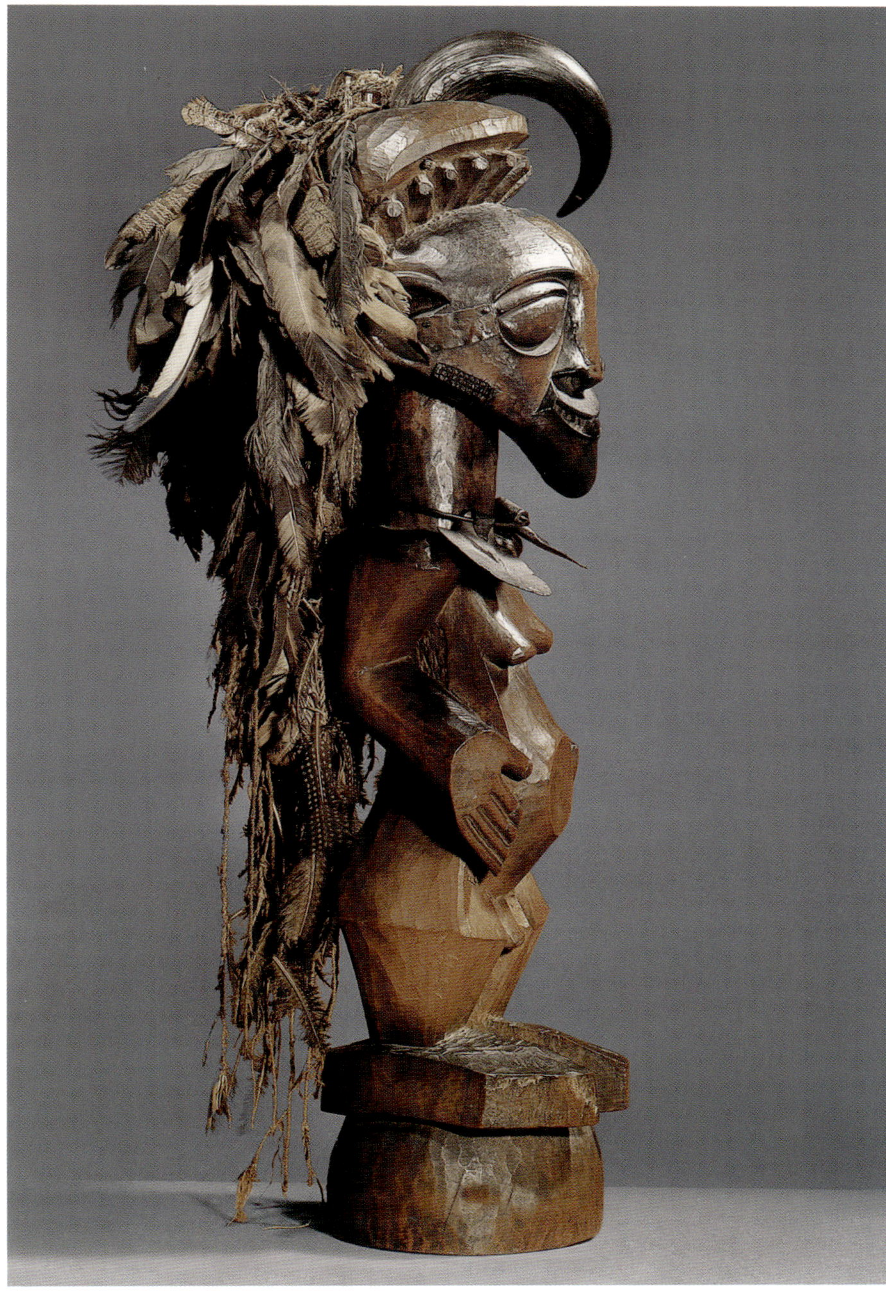

The first African sculptor to emerge from anonymity: the "Master of Buli"

The "Master of Buli", a name invented out of convenience that began to appear after World War II in studies and in many exhibition catalogues, is the first African artist to have been identified, albeit provisionally, as the author of a specifically recognized corpus of works. It was Frans Olbrechts who revolutionized studies in African art history by identifying ten sculptures at the famous exhibition held in Antwerp in 1937 as the work of the same artist. The name was coined on the basis of the only information then available, namely the fact that two of the works (the one shown here, no. 159, and a stool with a female caryatid formerly in the Révérend Père Henri Maurice Collection) come from the village of Buli.

Subsequent studies by specialists have made it possible to double the number of works that share similar stylistic features and make comparisons between them, thus pinpointing slight differences and suggesting the authorship not of a single artist, but a workshop with at least two or perhaps three carvers (see below), a hypothesis put forward by William Fagg some forty years earlier.[69]

Louis de Strycker and François Neyt identified the village of Kateba, located 130 km north of Buli in a region with a majority of Hemba inhabitants, as the place where the artist probably lived between 1810 and 1870, and renamed him the "Master of Kateba" for this reason.

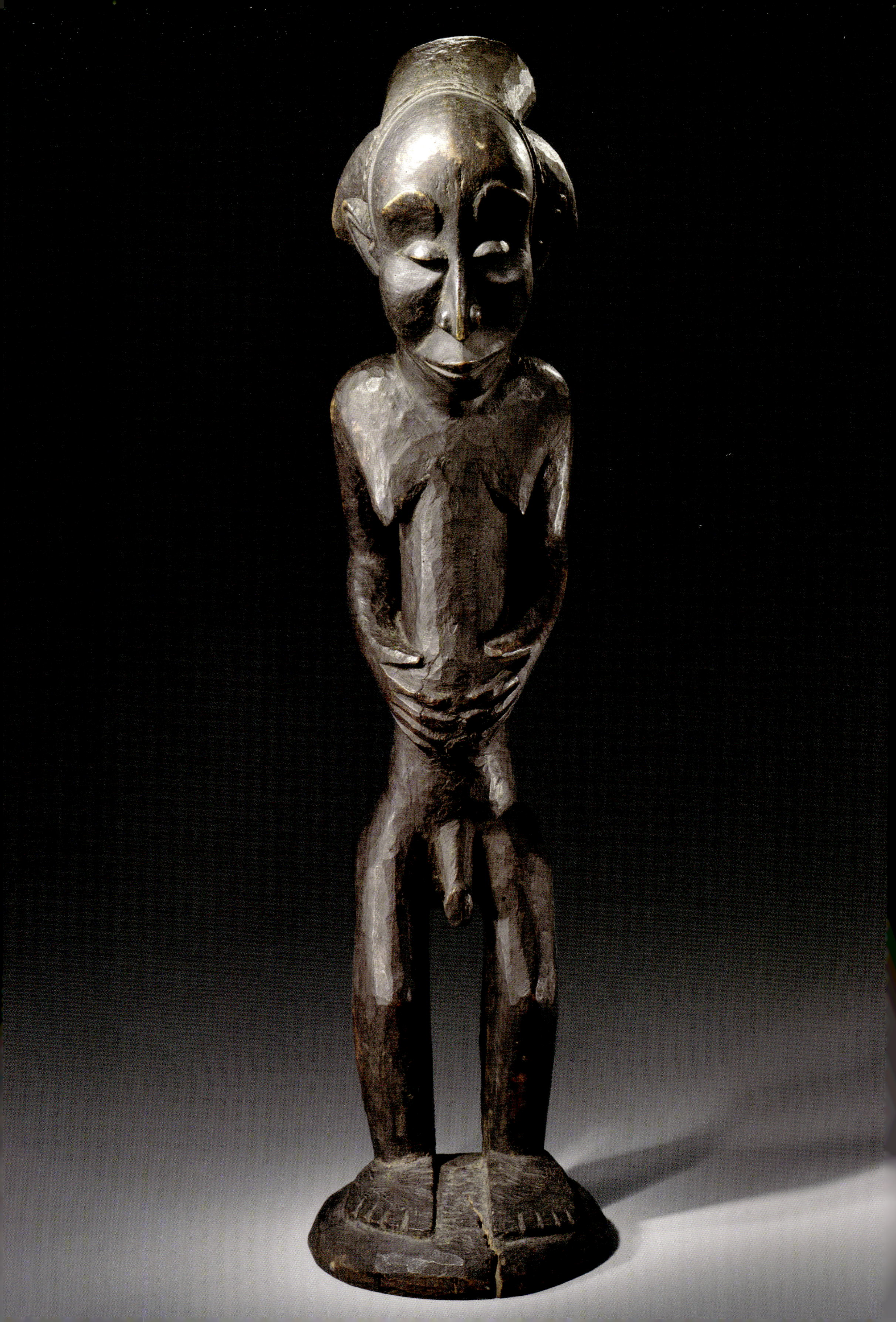

159. "Master of Kateba"
(formerly "Master of Buli")
Luba-Hemba, Democratic Republic of the Congo, 19th c.
Figure of male ancestor
Wood, 84 cm
Staatliche Museen zu Berlin, Ethnologisches Museum, Berlin (gift of F.W. Göring, 1903)

160. "Master of Kateba"
(formerly "Master of Buli")
Luba-Hemba, Democratic Republic of the Congo, 19th c.
Stool with female caryatid
Wood, 52 cm
The British Museum, Ethnography Department, London (purchased in 1905)

A section of the repeatedly cited exhibition 'Masterhands/Mains de Maîtres', made it possible to view seven sculptures produced in the workshop and reopened the debate on the authorship of the entire group of works, which had grown to more than twenty over the years. In the catalogue, de Grunne[70] attributes six of the set to the "Master of Buli", seven or eight to a second sculptor referred to as the "Master of Buli the Elder" and another seven to the "Master of Buli the Younger".[71] Claude-Henri Pirat,[72] instead, rules out the existence of any Elder or Younger Master of Buli, and attributes no fewer than fifteen works to the "Master of Kateba", and regards the remaining five, all stools, as copies. The question is therefore still open and in the absence of documentation, which is unfortunately nonexistent, first-hand comparison of all the sculptures proves indispensable.

Reasons of space make it necessary to confine the examples to only three of the works, which are all on the list drawn up by Frans Olbrechts, starting with the figure (no. 159) now in the Ethnologisches Museum, Berlin.

The upright position and the absence of scarification highlight the taut slenderness of the body, which is a hallmark of this artist's figures. In combination with the gauntness of the face, accentuated by contrast with the imposing coiffure in four chignons, this imbues the figure with an intense and poignant human quality.[73]

The position of the kneeling female caryatid supporting the stool (no. 160) now in the British Museum, London, which is unanimously attributed to this master, necessitated a less static approach that makes the woman's thinness and the length of her limbs less evident. Already monumental in size, accounting for a third of the entire volume of the work, the head is made still

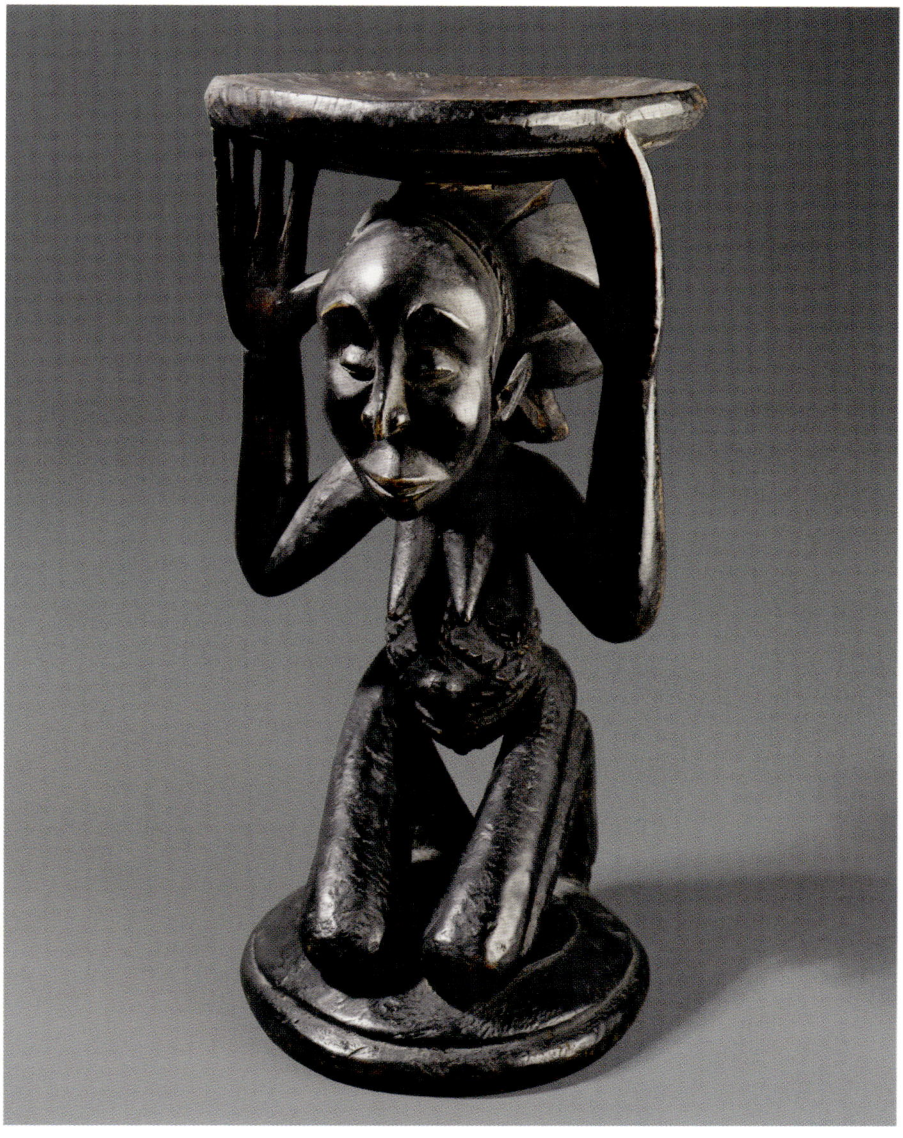

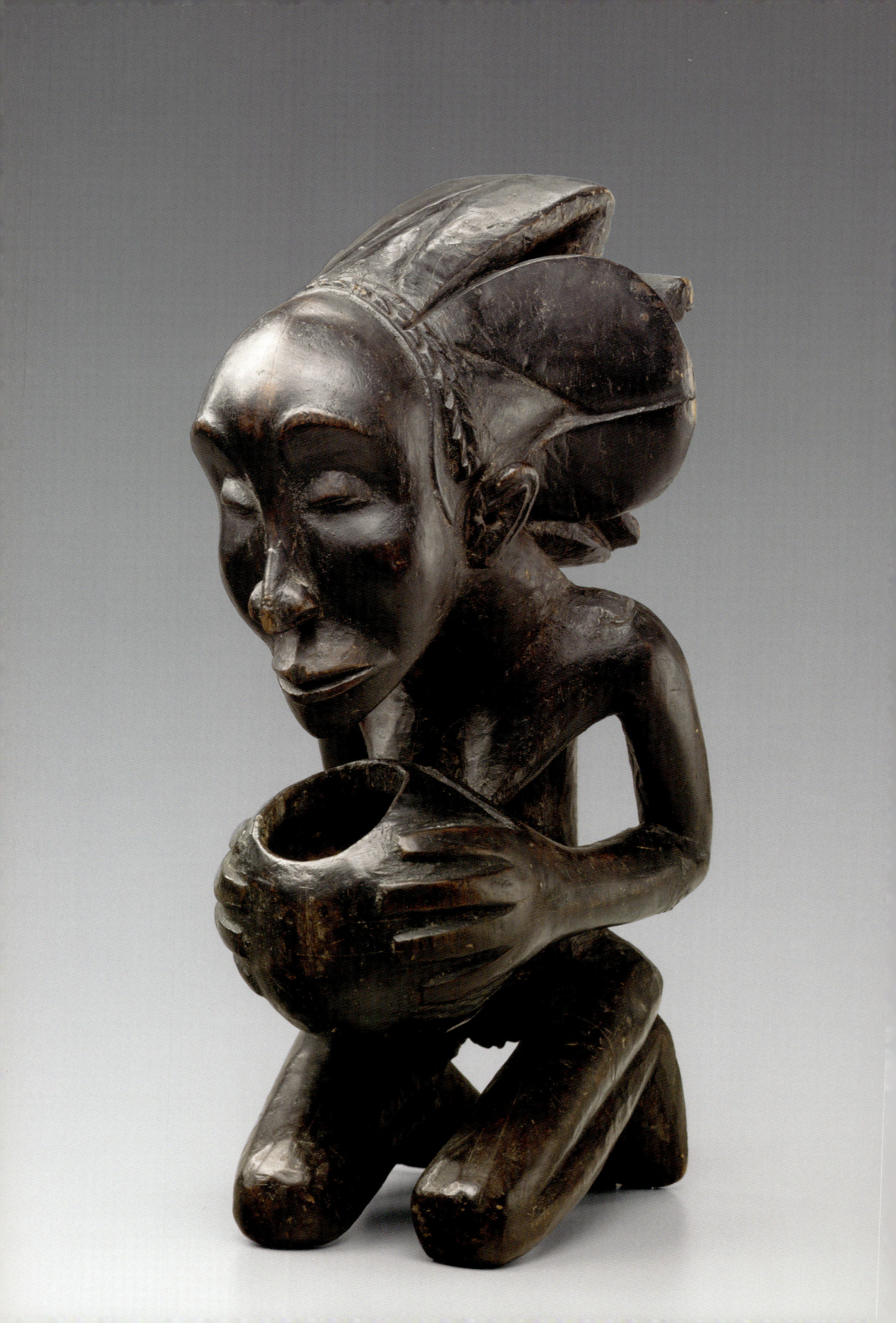

161. "Master of Kateba"
(formerly "Master of Buli")
Luba-Hemba, Democratic Republic of the Congo, 19th c.
Kneeling female bowl-bearer
Wood, 46 cm
Musée Royal de l'Afrique Centrale, Tervuren (acquired at Buli by H.-A. Bure between 1905 and 1907)

more imposing by the coiffure in four chignons. The exquisitely human features of the face, enhanced by the large open hands, are the same as those of the standing figure, but slightly softer. The abdomen, embellished with decoration in relief, is more rounded and sets off the small pointed breasts. The concentration of most of the volumes in the upper half of the work accentuates the impression of fragility conveyed by the figure.

According to François Neyt,[74] the large number of stools with caryatids is due to the practice adopted by Prince Ilunga Buki in the first half of the 19th century of giving some of his regalia to several of the local chiefs in the region he ruled over.[75]

The absence of the two disks that enclose the caryatid in the stool makes the already enormous head of the female bowl-bearer now in the Tervuren Museum (no. 161) appear still more imposing. The rear view is dominated by the monumental cross-shaped coiffure typical of the Hemba, which distinguishes the sculptures attributed to this workshop. The expressiveness of the woman's elongated face, the subtle volumetric echoes, the perfectly spherical container held between large flattened hands that almost seem to form part of it, and the interplay of the slender, cylindrical volumes of the trunk and limbs all contribute, in my opinion, to making this one of the master's most harmonious and moving works.

The "Master of the Cascade Coiffure"

The oeuvre of the "Master of the Cascade Coiffure" brings us back to the world of "miniatures", works that are very small in size but great by virtue of the lucid perfection of their volumes and the rigorous, coherent organization we have already admired in the Yombe maternity figures. The observations made here will be developed further in the chapter on artefacts whose formal quality is high, a category that unquestionably poses problems due to the difficulty in separating value judgements from functional considerations in the case of objects like the headrests examined here, items widely used in Africa that are both practical and symbolic.

In the society of the Luba Shankadi, an important group in the great Luba empire, the headrest served first and foremost to protect the monumental coiffures that usually distinguished the men and women of the ruling families during sleep. In addition to its primary aesthetic function, the coiffure also indicated social status, it was an actual symbol of power and was so obvious that the first explorers to enter the region referred to the Luba as the "hairstyle people". Fashioned in different styles using wicker frames, the coiffures could take up to fifty hours to create.

The headrests shown here were carved by two highly original artists active around the end of the 19th century in a Luba workshop located, according to François Neyt,[76] in the small kingdom of Kinkondja near Lake Kisale. (The records of the Museo Nazionale di Antropologia e Etnologia in Florence describe the item in its possession as found in the village of Kicondja in 1902.) Two of the three or four artists active there were true masters of their art, whose works (about fifteen in all) share common formal and iconographic elements.

The total absence of musculature distinguishes their figures from the full, rounded works typical of Luba sculpture. The true hallmark is, however, the extraordinary monumental coiffure in two supremely elegant, enormous wings (nos. 162–162a–163), unquestionably accentuated here for expressive purposes, which prompted William Fagg and Margaret Plass to refer to the author as the "Master of the Cascade Coiffure".[77] This name coined for the sake of convenience is provisionally adopted here.

Though the example in Florence is static, another two figures show movement and even suggest rotation,[78] while maintaining a rigorous equilibrium, based on the alignment and correspondence of the various parts. In the frontal and rear views, the flow of the diagonals of the coiffure and the outstretched upper arms in a sort of musical crescendo is interrupted by the brusque hor-

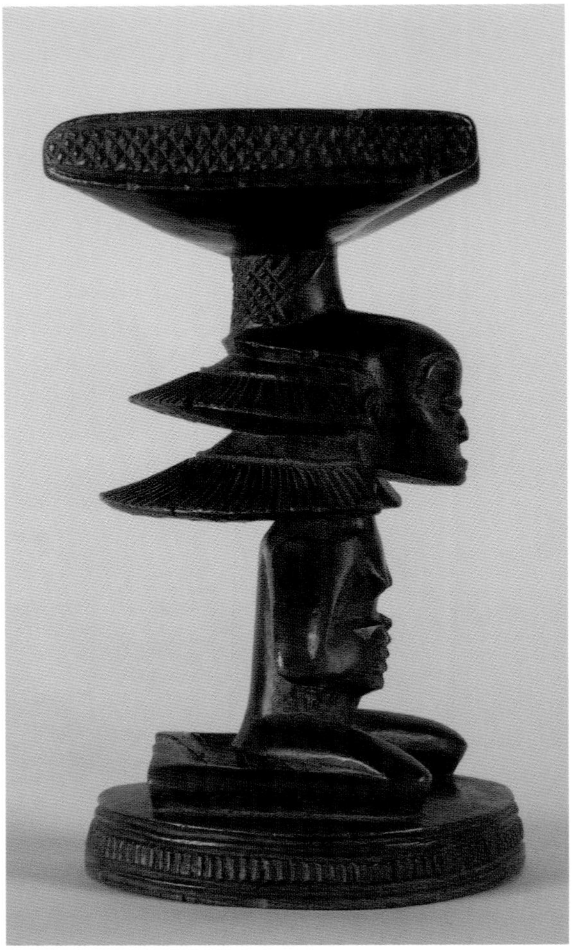
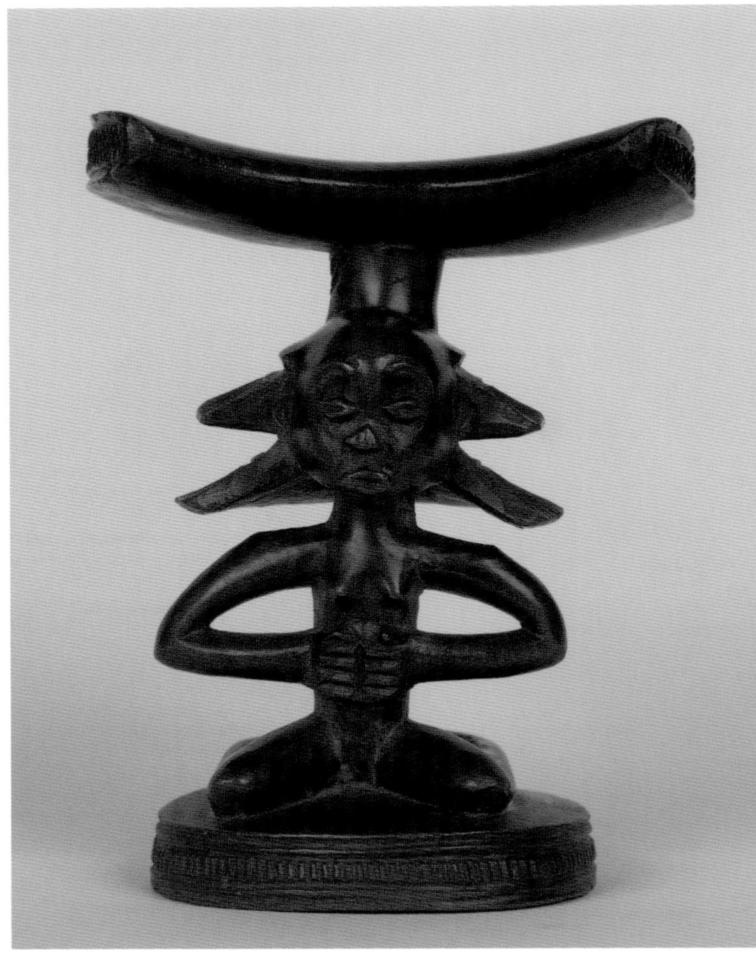
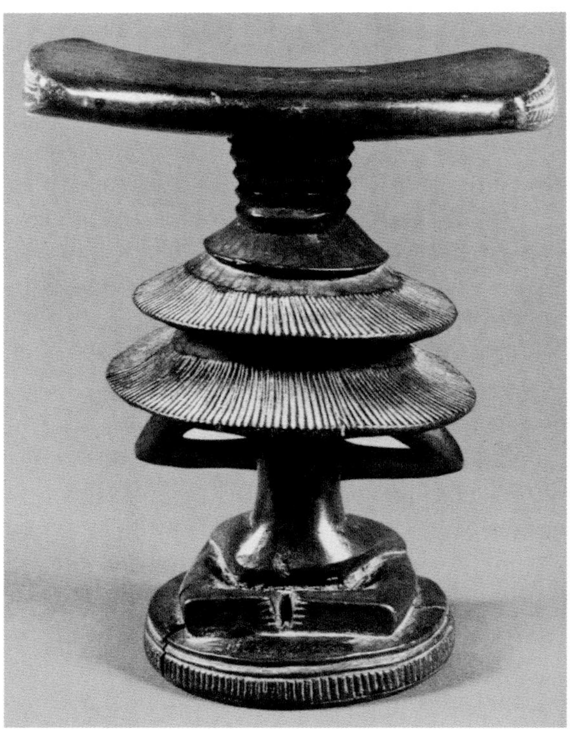
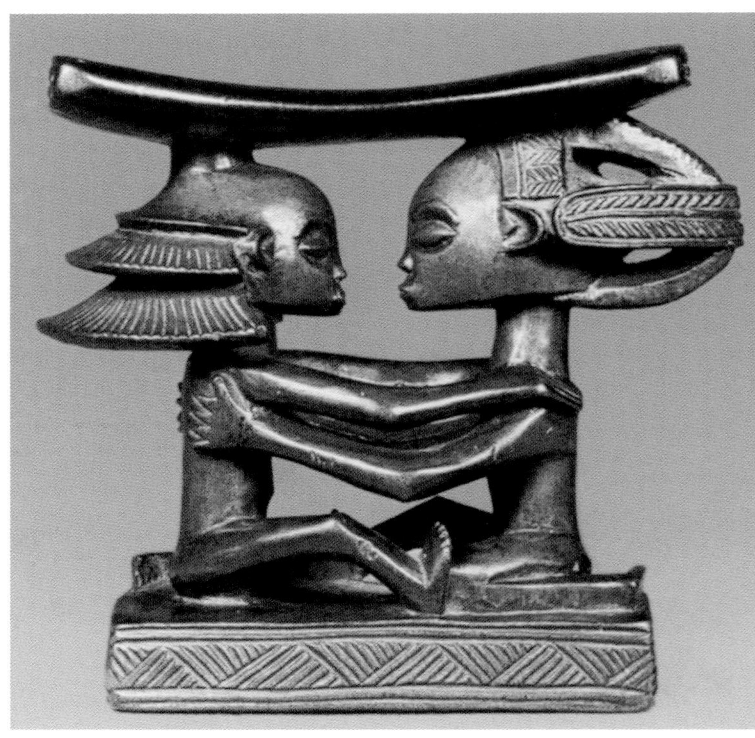

162–162a. "Master of the Cascade Coiffure 1"
Luba, Kingdom of Kinkondja, Shaba region, Democratic Republic of the Congo
Headrest
Wood, 15.5 cm
Museo Nazionale di Antropologia ed Etnologia, Florence

163. "Master of the Cascade Coiffure 1"
Luba, Kingdom of Kinkondja, Shaba region, Democratic Republic of the Congo
Headrest, rear view
Wood, 18.4 cm
Staatliche Museen zu Berlin, Ethnologisches Museum, Berlin

164. "Master of the Cascade Coiffure 2"
Luba, Kingdom of Kinkondja, Shaba region, Democratic Republic of the Congo
Headrest
Wood, 19 cm
Nationalmuseet, Copenhagen (formerly in the Carl Kjersmeier Collection)

izontal of the forearms. In profile, the protruding volume of the head balances the imposing mass of the coiffure, becoming pure form projected into space.

In the headrests with a double caryatid (there are two series by two different craftsmen), the figures are animated by a subtle tension arising from the contrast between the rigorous underlying geometry, created by the rectangle formed by the base, the top and the erect torsos of the two figures, and the fluid interplay seen in the legs and particularly the very long outstretched arms.

The only two known works of one of the two sculptors – one now in the Pavillon des Sessions, Musée du Louvre[79] and the other (no. 164) in the Nationalmuseet, Copenhagen – have the same basic form as those mentioned above, but are distinguished by greater finesse in the definition of the features of the less flattened face, by globular eyes with no incisions to simulate pupils, and in general by soft flowing contours and surfaces that attenuate the rigour of the structure. They are also and more obviously distinguished by the splendid cross-shaped coiffure of one of the two caryatids, which suggests a link with the Hemba, the Luba's neighbours to the north-east and who often intermingled with them.

The "Master of the Kunda"

Various names have been coined for the Luba-Hemba sculptor of a substantial group of works (those identified to date comprise two human figures, a double figure, three stools, four bow and arrow stands and a ceremonial staff).[80] He is called the "Master of Warua" by Leo Frobenius, who acquired the Janus-like figure for the Ethnologisches Museum[81] in Berlin in 1904, the "Master of the Sopola Court" by François Neyt,[82] and the "Master of the Kunda" by Mary Nooter Roberts, Allen E. Roberts and Bernard de Grunne.[83] The latter is the name adopted here. On the basis of the information available and the places where his works were found, we can say that this great sculptor was active in the second half of the 19th century and the first quarter of the 20th in a vast area west of Lake Tanganyika and north of Lake Moero in the present-day Democratic Republic of the Congo. The huge extent of the area might also suggest that he was an itinerant artist who travelled to the courts of his patrons.

According to Albert Maesen, the stools, the arrow racks and probably also the ceremonial staff are emblems of power and often carved by the same artist, who specialized in making prestigious insignia, as in this case, and was capable of adapting the constraints imposed by the fixed theme to his need for absolute formal rigour. The recurring female figure reflects the predominant position of women in the Luba matrilineal society. According to Mary Nooter Roberts and Allen E. Roberts, the bow and arrow stands (and hence also the other insignia) may have been crafted for a single monarch and then bestowed on his various vassal chiefs.

The double figure in Berlin and the single figure in Tervuren both bear a sort of crown with a cavity for unidentified material, possibly sacrificial in nature. The former is therefore catalogued as an *Opferschale* or libation goblet.

The stool illustrated here (no. 165) is now in the University of Pennsylvania, Philadelphia, which bought it from the Parisian dealer Charles Vignier in 1919. It was acquired between 1913 and 1916 by Joseph van den Boogaerde, a Belgian colonial official, as attested by a photograph of the sculptures in his possession taken in 1916.[84] This shows a large number of important Congolese works of art including the female bowl-bearer by the "Master of Buli" (no. 161).

As Henry Usher Hall wrote with great lucidity in his description of the stool in 1923, the author "subordinated his realism to the structural requirements of this piece of furniture, and in doing so has turned out an object really elegant in outlines and proportions."[85]

The American scholar acutely pinpointed the sculptor's extraordinary ability – evident in all of his works – to reconcile his own drive for absolute geometric rigour with the limitations imposed by a fixed theme within the constraints of a tradition. In addition to this general distinguishing feature, however, the artist's works bear precise similarities in their solution of particular compositional problems and even in many details, which, taken together, go beyond the traditional norms and become the artist's signature style.

In the three stools, the woman's arms, bent upwards at a right angle, combine with the seat to provide a rigorous square frame for the spherical volume of the enormous head, which presents even closer similarities in the large slit eyes and the very high, rounded forehead delimited by the broad regular arch of the eyebrows and the join of the hair in the form of a diadem. The extremely elegant and unmistakable coiffure is gathered behind into two groups of four plaits arranged to form cross, which pinpoints precisely the centre of the square delimited by the woman's arms and upper edge of the seat. The lower element that stretches down to cover the neck is unique and unmistakable.

The author's drive for geometric perfection is equally evident in the bow and arrow stand shown here (nos. 166–166a). While the figures adorning these items have bent arms and hands supporting elongated, pointed breasts in accordance with traditional iconography, the calibrated arrangement of the volumes – delimited above by the horizontal line of the shoulders and below by the large feet harmoniously integrated into the hemispherical base – is a wholly individual element, as is the whole formed by the short bow legs and the central support that seems to emerge from the genitals. The angle between the breasts echoes but inverts the angle between the vertical elements above designed to hold the bow and arrows.

165. "Master of the Kunda"
Luba, Democratic Republic of the Congo (southeast region)
Stool with caryatid
Wood, 41.9 cm
University of Pennsylvania, Museum of Archaeology and Anthropology, Philadelphia

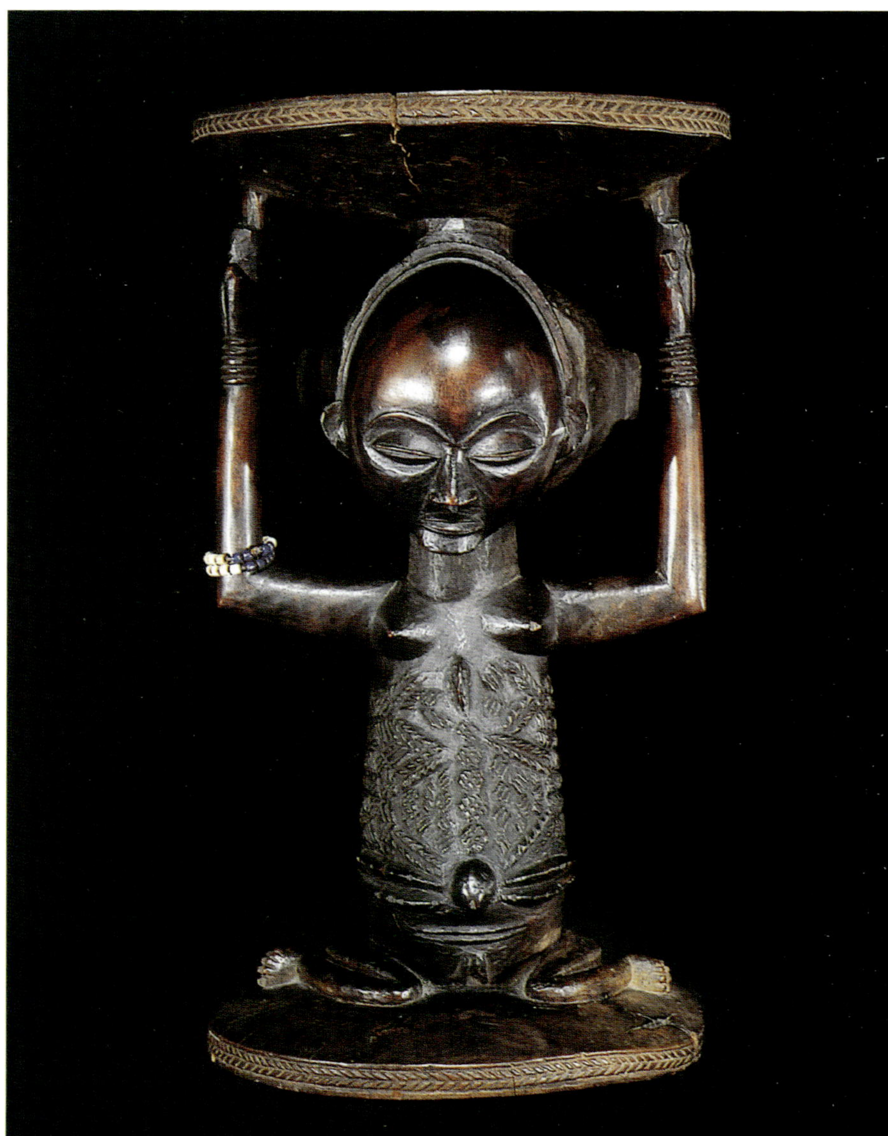

166. "Master of the Kunda"
Luba, Democratic Republic of the Congo (southeast region)
Bow and arrow stand with caryatid
Wood, 64.4 cm
Private collection (formerly in the G. de Miré Collection, Paris)

166a. Rear view of the bow and arrow stand no. 166

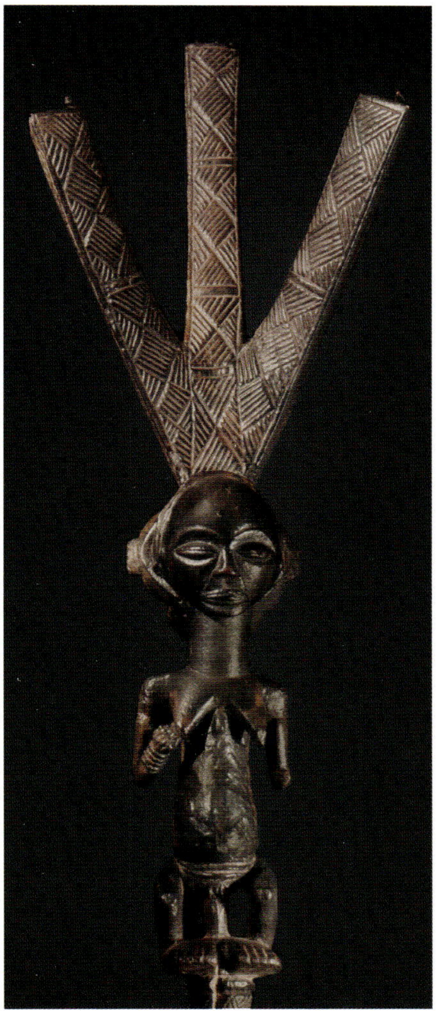

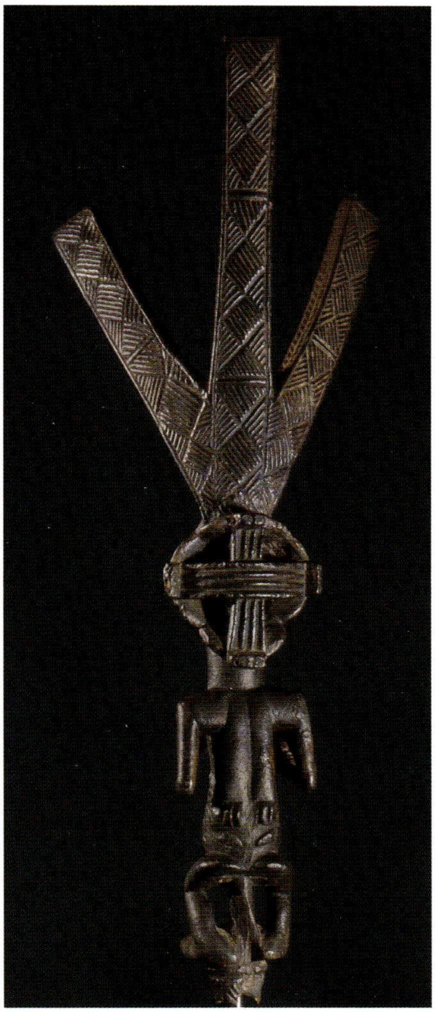

With only one exception,[86] subtle scarification marks in a rigorous geometric pattern cover the abdomen of the caryatids and the other human figures carved by this artist and animate their surfaces.

An examination of the compositional canons of the works by Maria Teresa and Valerio Zanobini confirms the great knowledge of geometry – constructive geometry of a practical rather than ideal nature[87] – possessed by this brilliant artist, who made highly expressive works with a powerful and disciplined structure.

The Moxico School

Marie-Louise Bastin's decades of research have revealed the richness of Chokwe art and the breathtaking beauty of a substantial group of sculptures, in which she identifies the style of their place of origin, the region in south-eastern Angola from which this people migrated in the second half of the 19th century to occupy lands further north until they reached the present-day Democratic Republic of the Congo.

The scholar has identified a number of the earliest works – those attributed to the Chokwe homeland – with similar formal characteristics and attributed them to various sculptors active in the regions of Muzumba and Moxico. The primary function of this court art is glorification of the chief, mostly represented standing, but sometimes seated or squatting, always naked, and often equipped for the hunt with a stick and a large rifle, proof that the statues were made after firearms were introduced into the area. The same artists also created splendid sceptres, tobacco mortars and tiny snuff boxes embellished with complete human figures or heads.

For reasons of space, we shall present only three works made by two masters from the Moxico region, in which power and refinement combine in a perfect synthesis that makes them unmistakable, and has no equal among the artworks produced later.

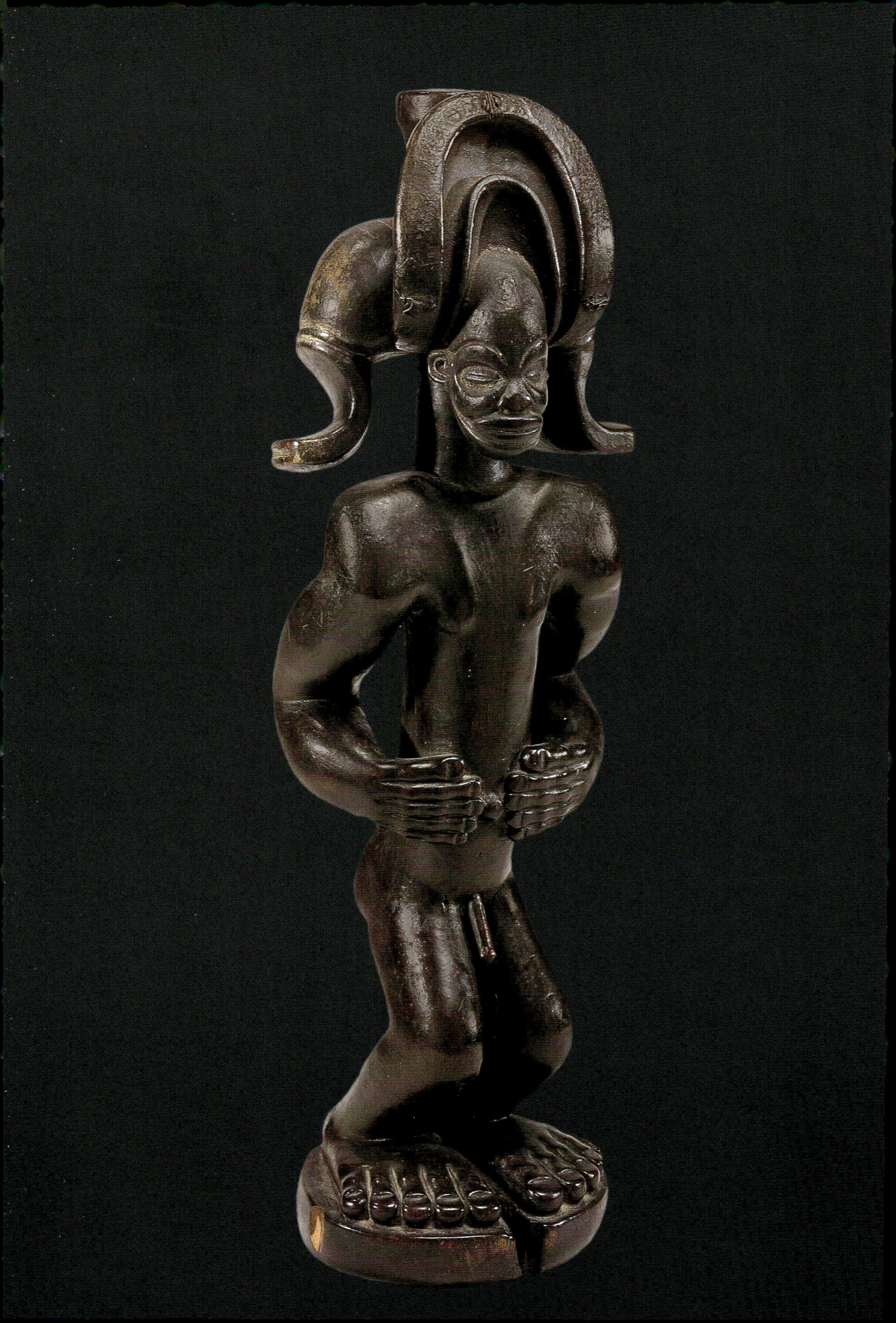

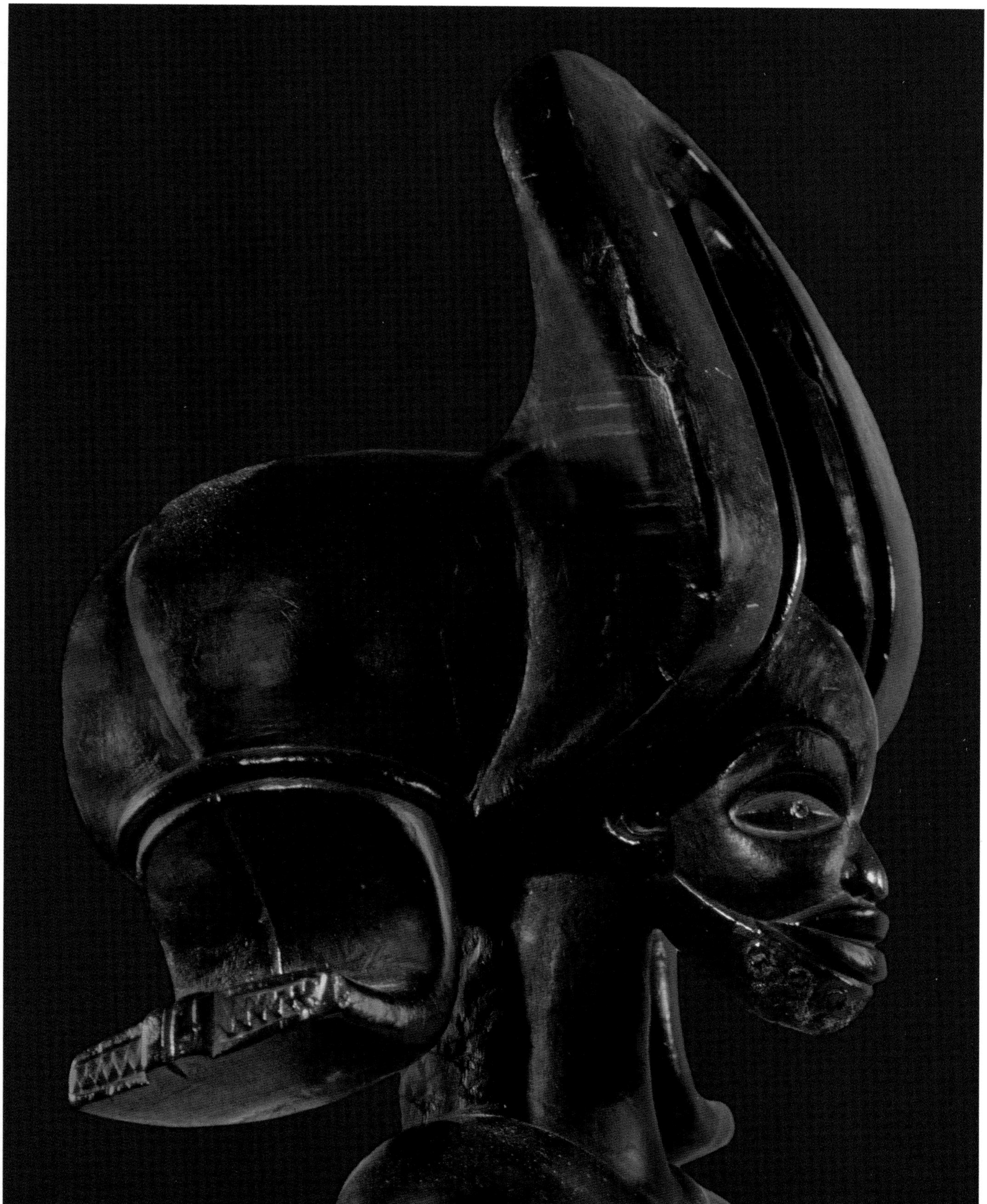

167. "Master of the Moxico School 1"
Chokwe, Angola, 19th c.
Chief figure
Wood, 35.5 cm
Museu Nacional de Etnologia, Lisbon

168. "Master of the Moxico School 1"
Chokwe, Angola, 19th c.
Chief figure (detail of head)
Wood, 37 cm
Private collection (formerly in the René Rasmussen Collection, Paris)

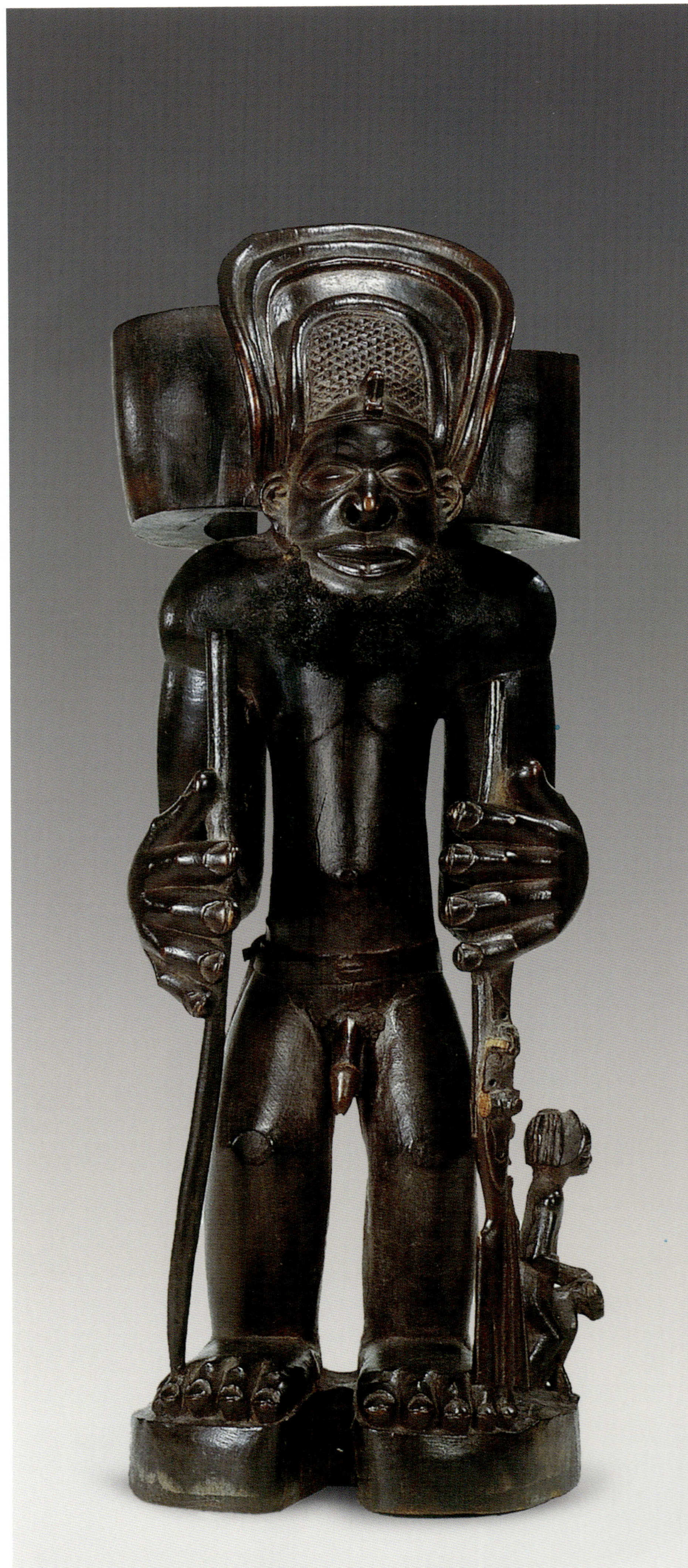

169. "Master of the Moxico School 2"
Chokwe, Angola, 19th c.
Portrait of Chibinda Ilunga
Wood and human hair, 40 cm
Museu de Antropologia
da Universidade, Porto

The sculpture (no. 167) in the Museu Nacional de Etnologia, Lisbon, is one of these absolute masterpieces by virtue of the subtle blend of Apollonian grace and emphatic expressiveness, of composure and overstated accentuation, which reveals the hand and the mind of a great artist.

The dynamic arrangement of the trunk and limbs, which could almost be described as gently powerful, is soft and rigorous at the same time. Observe the juxtaposed angles of the cylindrical arms and legs and in particular the strong hands and feet integrated into the harmonious structure of the beautiful body.

The small head with its serene and authoritative features is extended and brought into line with the overall balance of volumes by the fantastical, yet realistic, structure of the huge headdress, in which rounded shapes and Bernini-like baroque volutes combine harmoniously, as though to set their seal on the perfect synthesis of power and refinement noted above.

Referred to here as the "Master of the Moxico School 1", this artist is almost certainly also the author of a similar and oddly asexual figure (no. 168) formerly in the René Rasmussen Collection.

Marie-Louise Bastin has attributed the statue of Chibinda Ilunga, now in the Museu de Antropologia da Universidade in Porto,[88] and three sceptres surmounted by a human figure to the great artist referred to here as the "Master of the Moxico School 2". Chibinda Ilunga is the name of the legendary hunter from another people who, according to the oral tradition, took the place of a deceased Chokwe chief by marrying his daughter Lueji and founded a new dynasty.

All the hallmarks of the great sculpture of the Moxico School are again present in work no. 169: shoulders with powerful musculature echoed in the small hemispherical buttocks, strong cylindrical arms and legs, and large feet and hands holding a stick and rifle. The comparative slenderness of the torso compared to the arms and legs makes the expressive focus on the limbs even more effective. The flared nostrils and the clearly defined lips in low relief are further features that distinguish this master's works.

In keeping with his princely rank, the hunter wears a majestic headdress in the simplified shape of two huge, smooth, horizontal wings that heightens the figure's monumentality. The very small figure on the plinth with the same features is a guardian spirit.

[1] Vogel 1999, p. 42.

[2] "*nous n'avons pas affaire ici à un sous-style régional, mais bien à l'œuvre d'un même artiste, ou tout au moins à celle d'une même école ou d'un même atelier*" (Olbrechts 1959, p. 71). Due to the outbreak of World War II, this insight was not made known until 1946, when Olbrechts published his *Plastiek van Congo* in Flemish. The book was then translated into French in 1959 with the title *Les Arts Plastiques du Congo Belge*. It was in 1935 that the young ethnologist Hans Himmelheber published the results of his 1933 study on artists of the Baule and Guro peoples under the title *Negerkünstler*. See Fischer 1999, p. 68.

[3] Albert Maesen, François Neyt, Louis de Stryker, Bernard de Grunne and Claude-Henri Pirat. See Bassani 2001[a].

[4] Fagg 1951, p. 414.

[5] Fagg 1982, p. 35.

[6] Haskell 1931, pp. 89–90.

[7] It should be noted in passing that Leo Frobenius had referred to the Nigerian artist Adugbologe by name about a century earlier.

[8] It is worth remembering that the first show devoted exclusively to an artist of ancient Greece, namely Polykleitos, was only held in 1996.

[9] The catalogue lists the names of about three hundred sculptors.

[10] *Dogon* 1994, p. 135.

[11] Fagg 1991, pp. 69–70.

[12] See Dark 1973, pl. 50, ill. 103.

[13] Fagg, Plass 1964, p. 111.

[14] "*das man es also mit bewusst als solchen dargestellten Fabeltieren zu tun hat*" (Luschan [1919] 1968, p. 52).

[15] See chapter 1, no. 40.

[16] *Benin* 2007, pp. 334–335.

[17] Sapi artist, Sierra Leone, 15th–16th c. Salt cellar, ivory, 43 cm, inv. 104079.

[18] Bassani 2000, pp. 285–287; Bassani 2008, pp. 77–83.

[19] "*Scodella d'avorio con piede e coperchio intagliato e formato da un solo pezzo*" (inv. 1154).
[20] The broad-tailed crocodiles also appear on the salt cellar in Edinburgh but not the snakes and birds. See Bassani 2000, no. 728.
[21] In two masks that appear to be by different hands, the antelope protome is flanked by two female figures. See Bassani 1978[b], figs. 41–44).
[22] Bassani 1978[b], vols. 1 and 2.
[23] The mask is illustrated in the catalogue of the exhibition organized by Marius de Zayas at the Modern Gallery, New York, in 1916 (pl. 19).
[24] A mask surmounted by a crocodile was acquired by Charles Monteil in 1908 together with the female antelope donated to the Paris museum.
[25] Inv. 79.1.391. Information provided by Huguette van Geluwe.
[26] Included among the 24 works illustrated in the celebrated album published by Paul Guillaume in 1917 with a preface by Guillaume Apollinaire. The caption of pl. V reads as follows: "*Idole de la région de Bobo-Dioulasso (Sudan)*".
[27] The catalogue also includes a male antelope (no. 17) from the Musée d'Ethnographie, Palais du Trocadéro, and a standing female figure (no. 16) from a private collection.
[28] *Sculptures* 2008, p. 60.
[29] For information on the function of these works, see the studies by Susan Mullin Vogel.
[30] Vogel 1999, pp. 50–51.
[31] Grunne 2001, pp. 59–79.
[32] The masks are illustrated in Vogel 1997, pp. 142–143.
[33] One of the two masks not illustrated belongs to a private collection in London while the fourth, carved by the same hand, was shown in 1911 in the 'Keleti Kiállítás' (Oriental Exhibition) in the Müvészhában (House of the Artists) in Budapest.
[34] Vogel 1999, p. 53.
[35] *Keleti* 1911.
[36] Fischer 1999, p. 76.
[37] Fagg 1982, pp. 45–46. See also Picton 1994, fig. 1.2.
[38] Pemberton 1989, note 28.
[39] The British government offered the Ogoga a throne in exchange and the door was replaced with a new one carved by the same hand.
[40] Fagg 1969, p. 56.
[41] Walker 1998[a], p. 72.
[42] Pemberton 1989, p. 208, note 242. See also Fagg 1991, pp. 141–143.
[43] Kingdoms of different population size and density (from few to many hundreds of thousands of inhabitants) typical of the Cameroonian grasslands. Each sovereign would live in a palace embellished with works of art.
[44] Brain, Pollock 1971, p. 40.
[45] Grunne 2001, pp. 98–103 and nos. 23–27. See also Lintig 2006, pp. 120–123.
[46] Brain, Pollock 1971, p. 90.
[47] Susan Vogel (1985, p. 121) suggests that a figure with bound wrists shown in Brussels in 1977 (cat. 66) and a headdress in Lübeck (Fuhrmann 1922, pl. 92) are by the same sculptor.
[48] See also the male figure in the Ethnologisches Museum, Berlin, inv. III C 23280, and the maternity figure in the Afrika Museum, Berg en Dal, inv. XD18, both purchased in the early 20th century. These works are illustrated in Robbins, Nooter 1989, no. 800, and *Cameroon* 2008, cat. 52, 53.
[49] In 1917, now established as one of the great Parisian art dealers, Guillaume published *Sculptures nègres*, one of the first works on African art, with a foreword by the poet Apollinaire.
[50] Perrois 2001[a], pp. 120–139.
[51] Sold by the heirs at Sotheby's in Paris (catalogue Pierre Guerre, 15.4.2011, no. 7).
[52] The vertical axis is suggested by the alignment of the genitals, the navel, the joined hands, the nose and the central element of the three-part hairstyle. It continues on the back with the groove of the spine and the element for attaching the figure to the reliquary casket.
[53] Andersson 1953.
[54] Chaffin 1979. The authors took some 1100 works into consideration, half of which were examined first-hand.
[55] Especially Efraim Andersson, Louis Perrois (1979, 60 items) and Jean-Louis Paudrat (13 items).
[56] Kongo is the modern name of the people formerly referred to as Congo. See note 32 in the chapter *Commissioned Art: Afro-Portoguese Ivories*.
[57] Lehuard 1989, II, pp. 459–468.
[58] Joseph Cornet suggests that one of the items illustrated in Leloup 1998 (p. 14), should be regarded as a Sundi rather than a Yombe work on the grounds of remnants of a red patina: "*des restes de patine rouge font pencher vers les Sundi plutôt que vers le Yombe*". The similarities to the maternity figures strike me, however, as sufficient evidence to retain the attribution to an artist of the Yombe group.
[59] The Metropolitan Museum of Art, New York, wood, 121 cm. See Lehuard 1989, II, p. 468. The Tervuren Museum also has two bedposts (inv. RG35776 and RG38560) decorated with seated figures that were certainly produced by the workshop.
[60] See also Lehuard 1989, II, pp. 456–458.
[60] The masks were probably worn by the priest-healer in healing rituals. The colour white is associated with death.
[62] See Bassani 1981, nos. 3–8. Some works are illustrated frontally and in profile.
[63] The name "Master of the de Briey Maternity" (for the first group of works) and "Master of the Roselli-Lorenzini Maternity" (for the second one) were attributed early on after the names of the collectors the pieces belonged to: see Bassani 1981, pp. 66–84.
[64] The "beard" of the Pigorini statue is damaged.
[65] Two iron bells, whose function is unknown, hang from the arms.
[66] Neyt 2004, nos. 1–6.
[67] A characteristic also found in works of different provenance.
[68] Petridis 2001, cat. 38.
[69] Fagg 1965, p. 103; Fagg 1970, p. 186.
[70] Grunne 2001, pp. 187–188.
[71] The set as a whole consists of two standing male figures, three statuettes, eleven stools with one caryatid, two stools with two caryatids, two female bowl bearers and one headrest.
[72] Pirat 2001, pp. 89–90.
[73] Another similar sculpture, bought in Kankundé in 1972, is now in the Malcolm Collection. The African who sold it apparently indicated a sculptor by the name of Ngongo Ya Chintu as the author but this, according to M. Nooter Roberts (*Africa* 1999, p. 160), is "a generic honorific for sculptor, and not a specific birthname".
[74] Neyt 1993, p. 95.
[75] The prince ruled over the region on behalf of the great king Kumwimbe Ngombe (1810–40), who expanded the Luba empire considerably.

[76] Neyt 1993, pp. 184–185.
[77] Fagg, Plass 1964, p. 88.
[78] See the example formerly in the collection belonging to Charles Ratton.
[79] Formerly in the collections of Baron Lambert and Hubert Goldet.
[80] See Bassani, Zanobini 1990.
[81] Inv. IIIc 19996. The first of the master's works to arrive in Europe. This name was then adopted by Susan Vogel (1985, no. 125), and by the author of the book (Bassani, Zanobini 1990, passim).
[82] Neyt 1993, p. 84.
[83] Nooter Roberts, Roberts 1996, pp. 221–231; Grunne 2001, pp. 190–192.
[84] Grunne 2001, fig. 31.
[85] Hall 1923, p. 125.
[86] A human figure in a Belgian private collection: Bassani, Zanobini 1990, no. 9; Grunne 2001, no. 73.
[87] Bassani, Zanobini 1990, pp. 31–97, 121–164.
[88] The statue was acquired by Captain Artur da Fonseca Cardoso in 1903–04 in the Moxico region together with other works with similar stylistic characteristics. It was on the basis of this information that M.L. Bastin coined the term "Moxico School", which is adopted here. See Bastin 1994, no. 113.

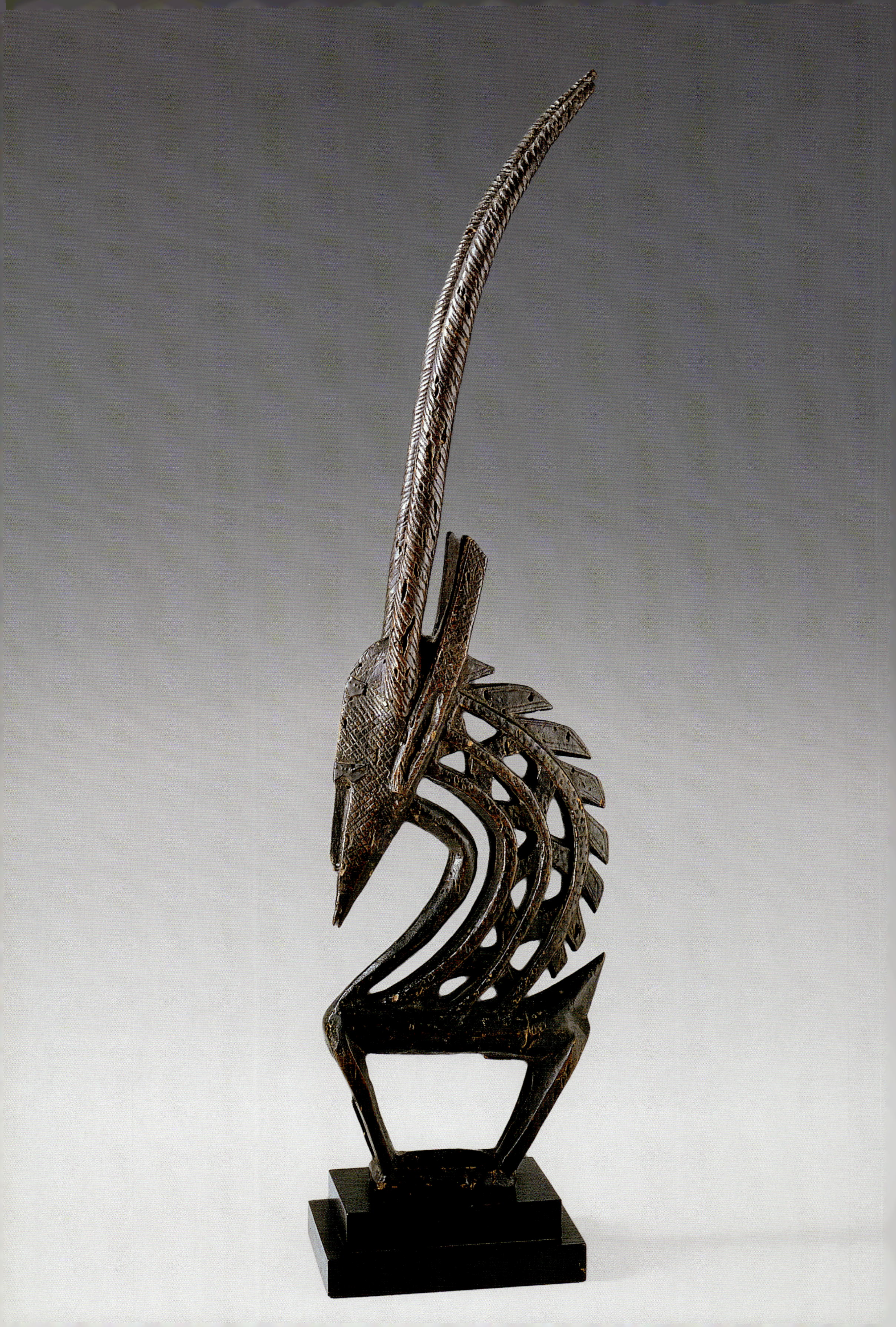

Function and Form of the Works

The fact that the functions of artworks in the religious and social practices of communities within the same people, and, in particular, of different ethnic groups, are the same, or at least similar – as far as we know – does not necessarily imply the use of common formal solutions.

The study of this aspect of the artistic creation of Africa of the past cannot, unfortunately, adopt the same instruments that are available in the study of European art.

In Europe written documentation about the author of a work, and when and where it was made, nearly always enables us to identify who introduced a new form, to reconstruct the stages of diversification, and to specify at what time and in what way the differences were produced, as well as the mechanisms and modes by which they became a legacy shared by other artists.

This documentary context does not exist for the majority of African works of art. The differences to be found in the form of works having the same function can only be hypothetically explained by an artist's invention, which occurs at a time that is usually not known to us, of a work that his community has requested from him – the archetype – and the community's acceptance of the result. The new form, which has thus become a common legacy, is reprised with varying degrees of faithfulness and skill by the artists of that society. Over time, increasingly important variations are introduced that generate sub-styles but these are often impinged upon by external influences.

Formal differences between works with the same functions (or at least similar functions) are more marked when they are between different peoples. In such cases there is even a lack of sufficient elements to allow us to establish which people created the first artwork for a particular purpose – whether for cult purposes or not – which thus prevents us from reconstructing the circumstances from which the differences derived.

We can only suppose that a particular artist responded to his society's request by inventing an object to meet a new religious need. Once the object obtained the consensus of the community, it would become the model for works by sculptors within that society, who would execute them with the individual variations inevitable in every creative act, as in the case of antelopes among the Bamana, a hypothesis that explains the differences that exist between them. The cult would subsequently be adopted by neighbouring peoples who, in turn, would commission the required objects from their own artists, and these would be created in accordance with the figurative norms prevalent in the new community.

However, the opposite situation also exists, in which very similar works have a different meaning and purpose, and which in some cases may even be diametrically opposed. Such an antithetical situation might only be revealed to us by the presence or absence of substances whose purpose is to propitiate the intervention of the supernatural entity to which the works lend physical concreteness.

This short chapter provides a few examples of above conditions.

170. Bamana artist
Mali (Segu region)
Dance headdress in the form
of a male antelope
Wood, 84 cm
Civiche Raccolte Artistiche
del Castello Sforzesco, Raccolte
Extraeuropee , Milan

171. Bamana artist
Mali (Bamako region)
Dance headdress in the form of an antelope
Wood, metal and cowries, 83 cm
Musée du Quai Branly, Paris (formerly in the Musée d'Art Moderne de la Ville de Paris)

172. Bamana artist
Mali (Sikasso region)
Dance headdress in the form of an antelope
Wood, 56 cm
Private collection

Bamana dance headdresses

The antelope-shaped dance headdress of the Ciwara society, doubtless the best known artworks by the Bamana of Mali, is an emblematic example of the first case, namely, diversification of artistic production within the same society.

The antelope is a metaphor for an indefatigable farmer and refers to a myth in which a fantastical being taught man how to cultivate the land. The sculptures, tied to a wicker headpiece, were attached to the heads of the dancers, who, dressed in fibre costumes and leaning on two sticks, mimed the animals' leaps in couples (male and female).

The ways of representing the animal vary according to the community the artist belonged to, though attribution to an artist of a particular region is often uncertain.

Strength and elegance are the distinctive features of the Segu style headdresses to which the first example belongs (no. 170). A simply sculpted body provides the base for a large pointed head on a neck decorated with a perforated mane (the serration symbolizes the animal's zigzagging run, but also the sun's path in the tropics) and long horns.

From the side, the small body is shaped like a trapezium and is wider towards the top, as though the animal were about to leap; the serrated mane between the body and the head is a perfect arabesque of solids and voids, and looks like a compressed spring ready to be released. Seen from the front, the face is as sharp as a blade and the slender spiralling horns as long as the whole body, ac-

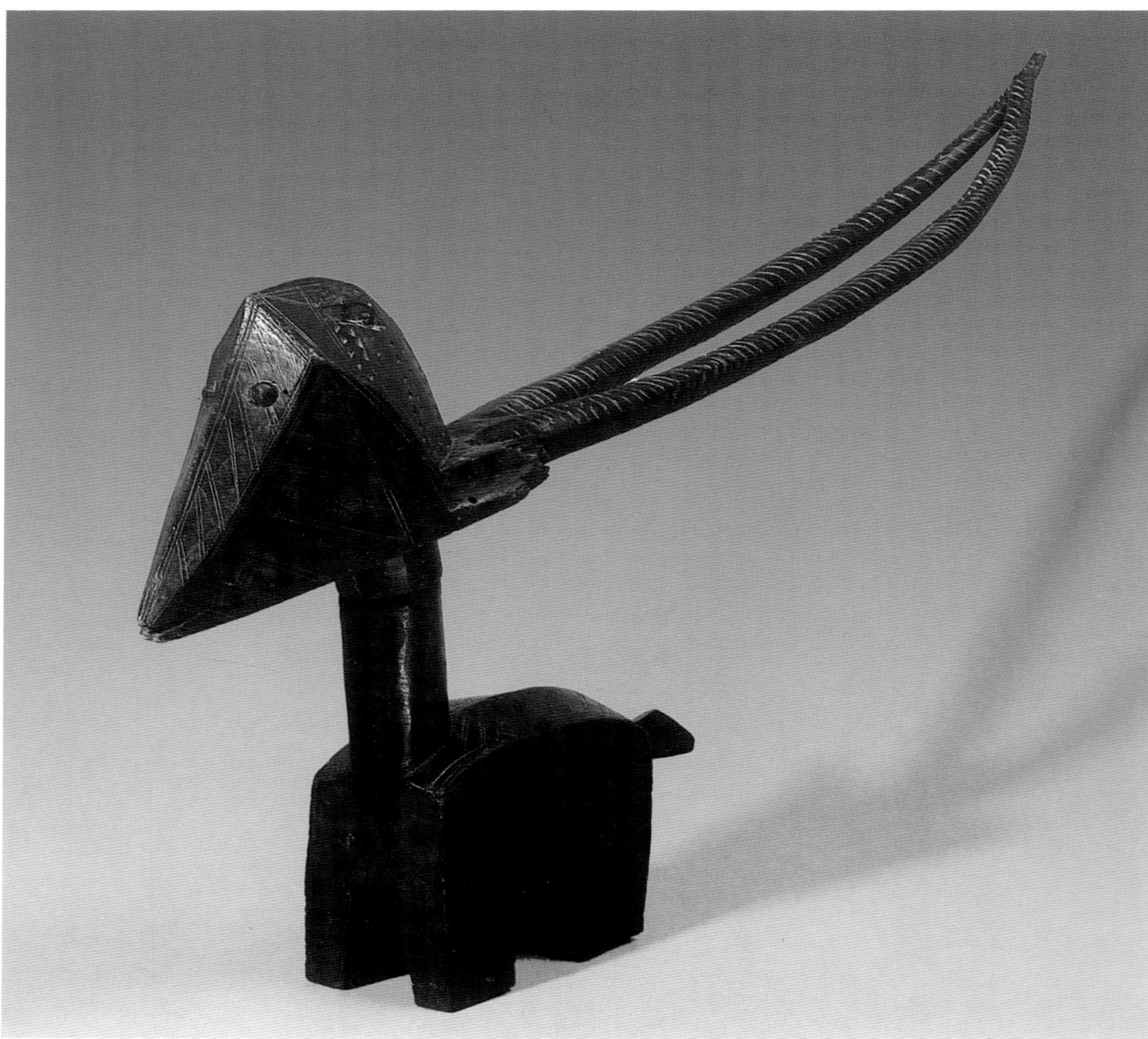

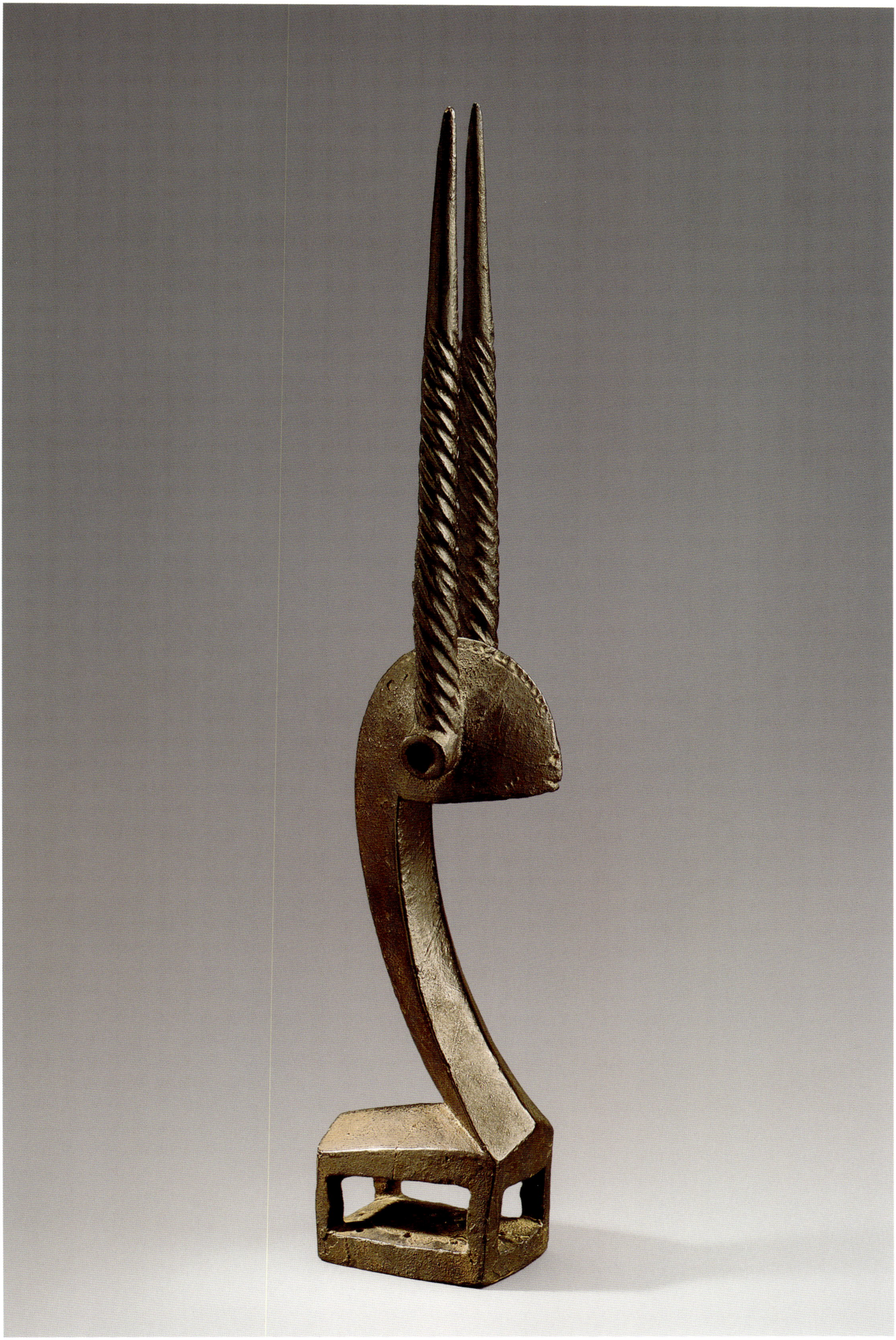

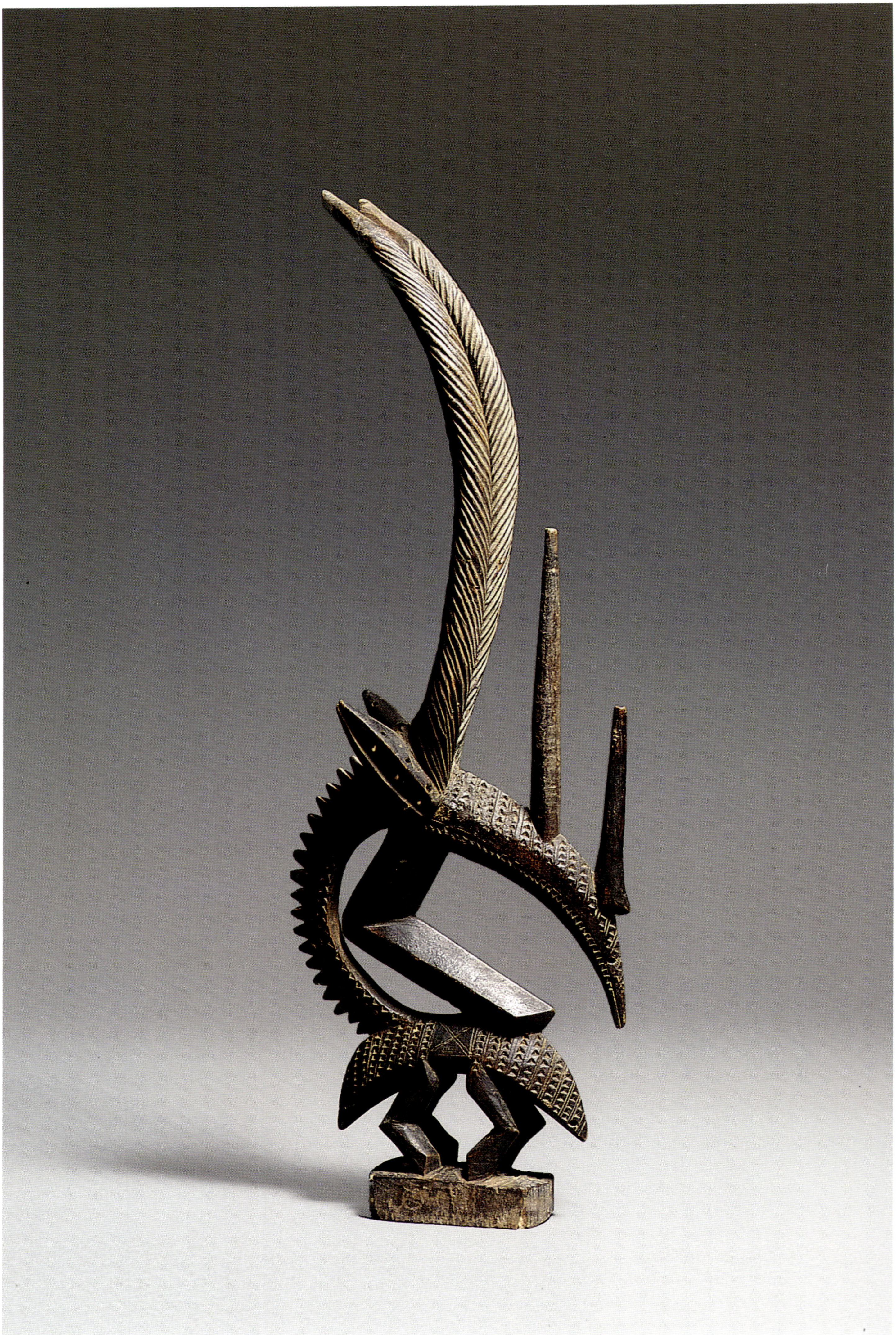

173. Bamana artist
Mali (Bouguni or Dioila region)
Dance headdress in the form
of an antelope
Wood, 51 cm
Staatliches Museum für Völkerkunde,
Munich

centuating the vertical dimension of the sculpture, which, in William Fagg's apt description, has a kind of "gothic quality".

In contrast, it is the use of primary volumes that distinguishes the beautiful antelope in the Bamako style, which, after passing through the collections of the famous Parisian dealer Louis Carré and that of Dr Maurice Girardin, entered the Musée du Quai Branly (no. 171). The compact body on square legs and the cylindrical neck that supports the large head formed by a pyramid and a hemisphere are combined in a such a spare and expressive volumetric fusion that if it were not a work by an African artist, we would attribute it to the early period of Cubism. The slender horizontal length of the horns accentuates the solid mass of the animal's body. Unlike the previous example and those that follow, this type of antelope is not carved from a single piece of wood – the head is fixed to the neck with metal clips.

The distinguishing element of the third sculpture (no. 172) is its simplification, verging on abstraction, yet the impression of an antelope quivering and about to leap emerges powerfully from its volumes. The sharp curve of the neck guides the gaze towards the simplified though not static head. The deep incisions in the spiralling horns accentuate the verticality of the work, which the small plinth that symbolizes the body does nothing to diminish.

Finally, in the headdress in the Staatliches Museum für Völkerkunde in Munich (no. 173), only the long arching horns and the serrated curve of the mane retain the idea of an antelope, because the rest is a fantastical combination of different forms in which that of the scaly anteater predominates, which can be recognized by the scales covering its body. The dynamism of the composition of curves and counter curves is accentuated by the contrast with the smooth, straight volumes of what are presumably the neck and legs, which are unnaturally, though skilfully, bent at right angles, with the corners juxtaposed.

Fang, Kota and Mahongwe ancestral figures

The works of art of the peoples of Gabon illustrate the second case, namely the diversity that exists between sculptures with the same (or at least similar) functions in different groups. The nature of these works – reliquary figures that were placed on the baskets containing the bones of important ancestors – is briefly described elsewhere in this volume.

The ancestors of the Fang are evoked in two types of sculpture: heads or full-length figures. The use of the former, which according to Günter Tessmann are rarer, was introduced earlier than the full length figures.[1] Though marked differences exist between the works, especially in terms of the volumes and proportions of the parts of the body, it is evident that they belong to a common figurative universe despite originating in different communities.

The main qualities of the small head seen here (no. 174) – which was once part of the famous collection of the English sculptor Jacob Epstein, then belonged to Carlo Monzino and is now, together with other Fang masterpieces, in the Musée Dapper, Paris – are its sublime serenity and delicate modelling.

The features of the heart-shaped face, strong chin and elaborate coiffure do not detract from the evident spherical shape of the head but accentuate its sophisticated purity. The loss of the large brass discs that presumably represented the eyes contributes to the feeling of mysterious spirituality that the work emanates.

The female figure (no. 175) in the Musée Dapper also passed through the hands of Jacob Epstein and Carlo Monzino, and had previously belonged to George de Miré and Louis Carré. It is a kind of icon of Fang art, so much so that it deserves the name *Pahouin Venus*, given to it in the catalogue of the London exhibition 'Primitive African Sculpture' held in 1933. It is an exemplary work in the second category of reliquary figures.

The round head crowns a firm young body, created by a coordinated assemblage of well-balanced, symmetrical, bulbous volumes. The width of the block comprising the shoulders and pectoral muscles corresponds to the width of that of the sturdy thighs and legs, which are best appreciated in the side view.

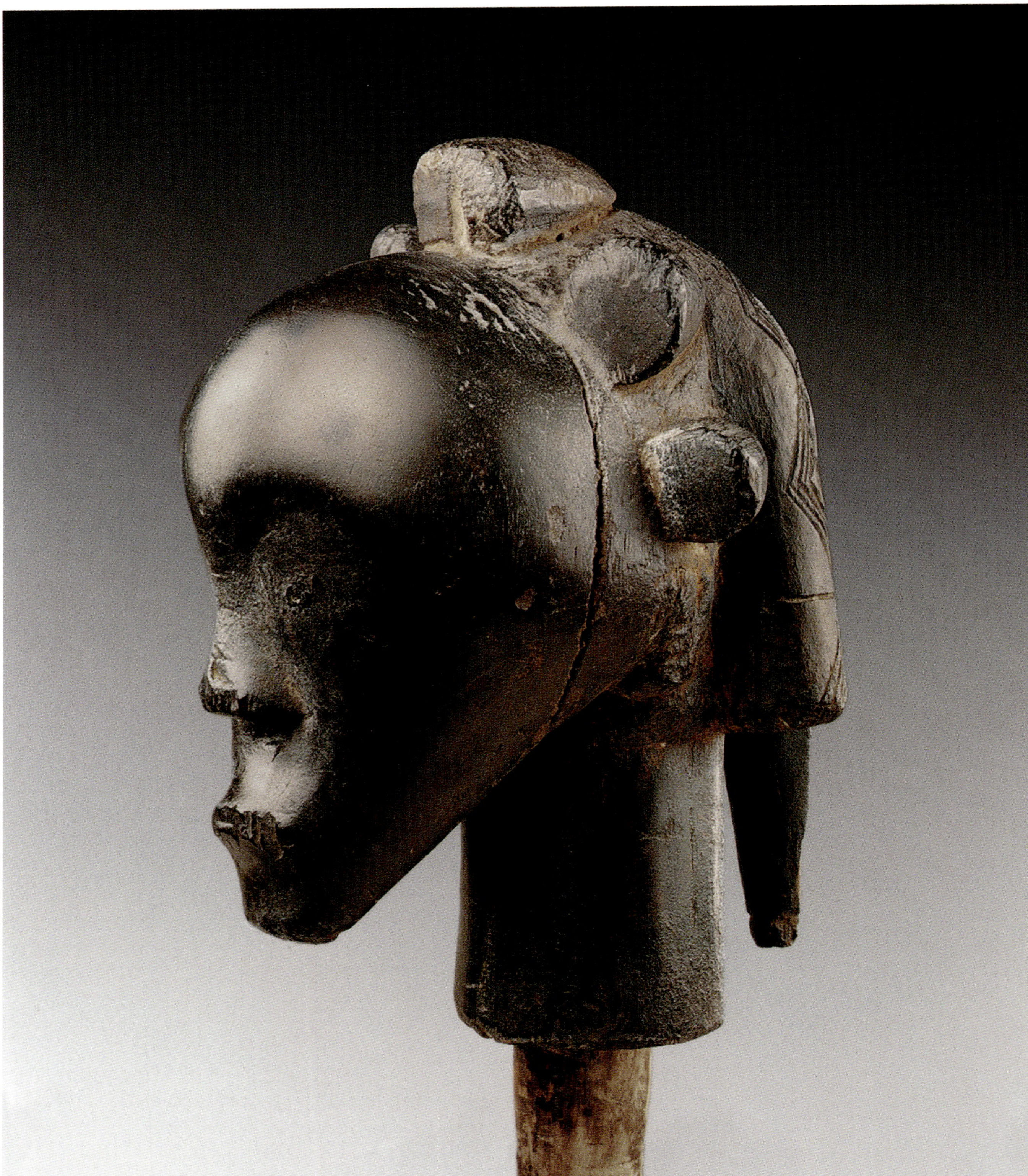

174. Fang artist
Betsi group, Gabon
Reliquary figure
Wood, 29 cm
Musée Dapper, Paris

175. Fang artist
Betsi group, Gabon
Reliquary figure
Wood, 43 cm
(56 cm with the support)
Musée Dapper, Paris

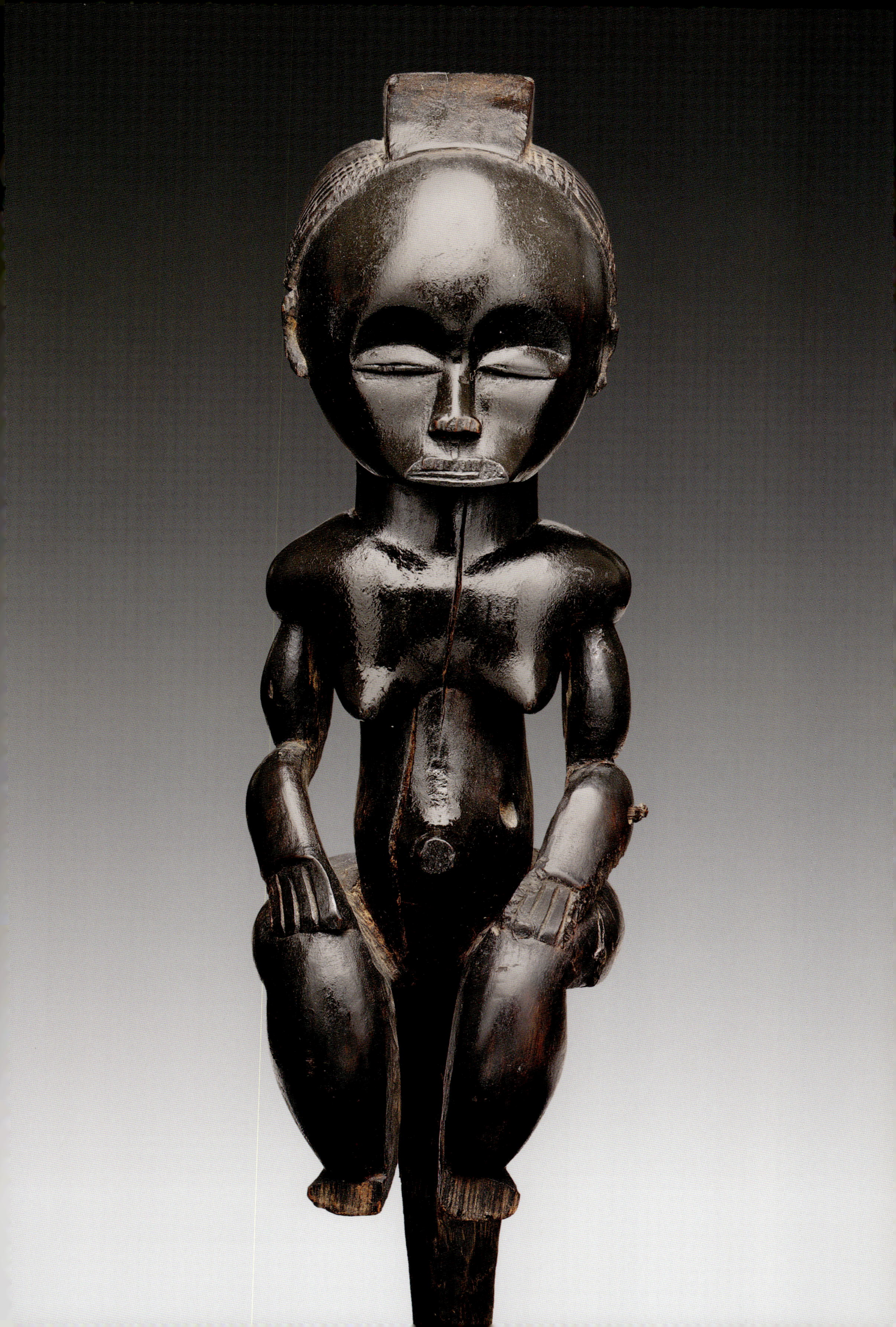

When viewed from behind, the stiff forms of the coiffure are tempered by the complementary curves of the hollows in the back and buttocks.

The severe features, especially the half-closed eyes, imbue the unnaturally large head (it is as wide as the shoulders) with a sense of great starkness, which is moderated by the gentleness of the rounded forehead and youthful breasts. The impression created by this reinvented anatomy and perfect balance of sublimated forms is one of tranquil sensuality.

Figures that are totally different from those of the Fang, both in structure and general conception, perform a similar function in the neighbouring Kota and Mahongwe groups. In their formal abstract gauntness these arbitrary images in wood covered with thin pieces or strips of copper or brass retain no link with the physical reality that they presumably symbolize, namely the body of a mythical ancestor.

Like those of the Fang, Kota reliquary figures share common structural characteristics but their forms differ slightly, as has been seen in nos. 148–149, so here we will confine ourselves to a single example (no. 176). The sharp distinction between the lower, slightly concave part of the face and the convex visor-like forehead, combined with the round penetrating eyes and the pyramidal nose on the smooth central strip that divides the metal plates of the cheeks, together create a sense of monastic austerity, but of a warrior order of monks.

The Mahongwe artists' work is reduced even more to essentials than that of the Kota. The references to reality in their figures are minimal, but this does

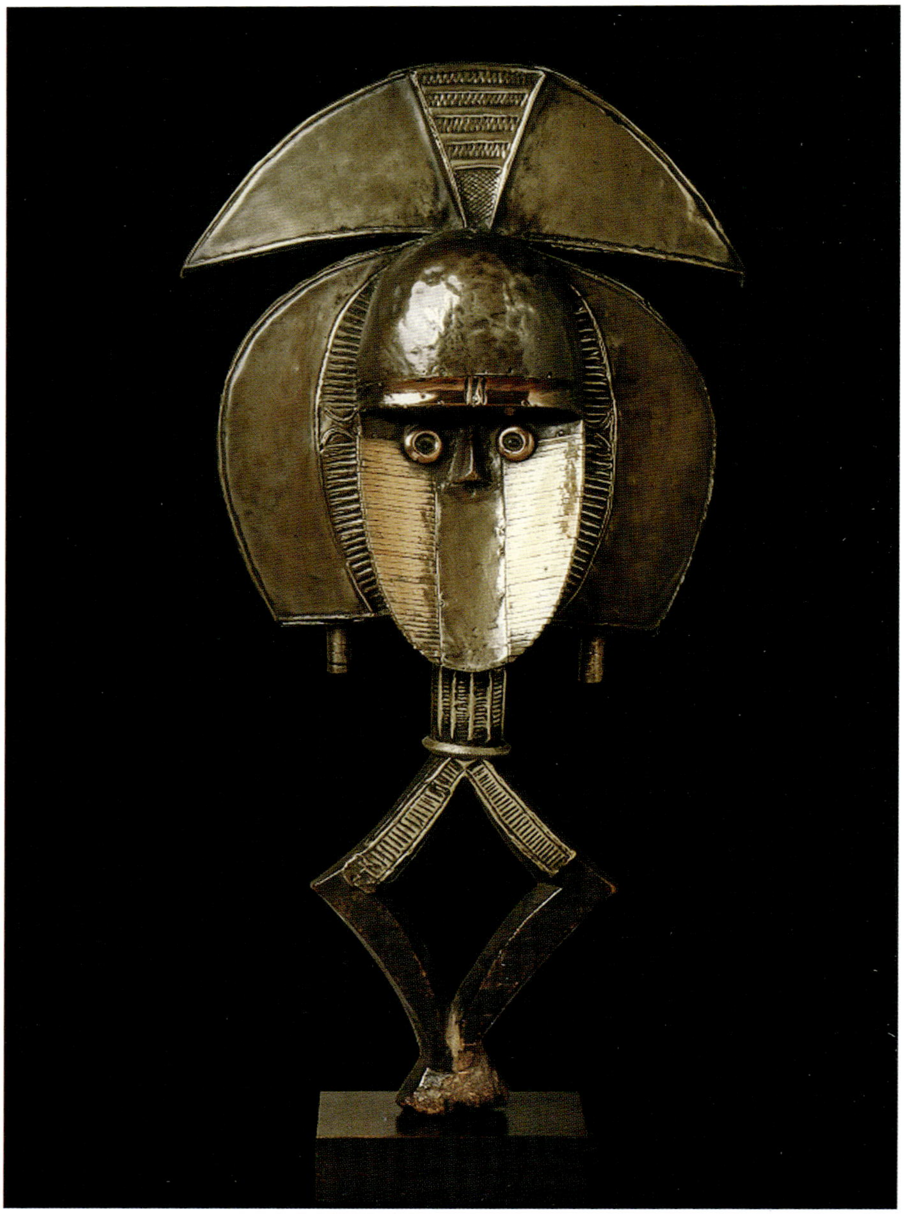

176. Kota Obamba artist
Gabon
Reliquary figure
Wood, brass and copper, 57.5 cm
Private collection

177. Mahongwe artist
Gabon
Reliquary figure
Wood, brass, copper, fibres and fur, 57 cm
Musée du Quai Branly, Paris

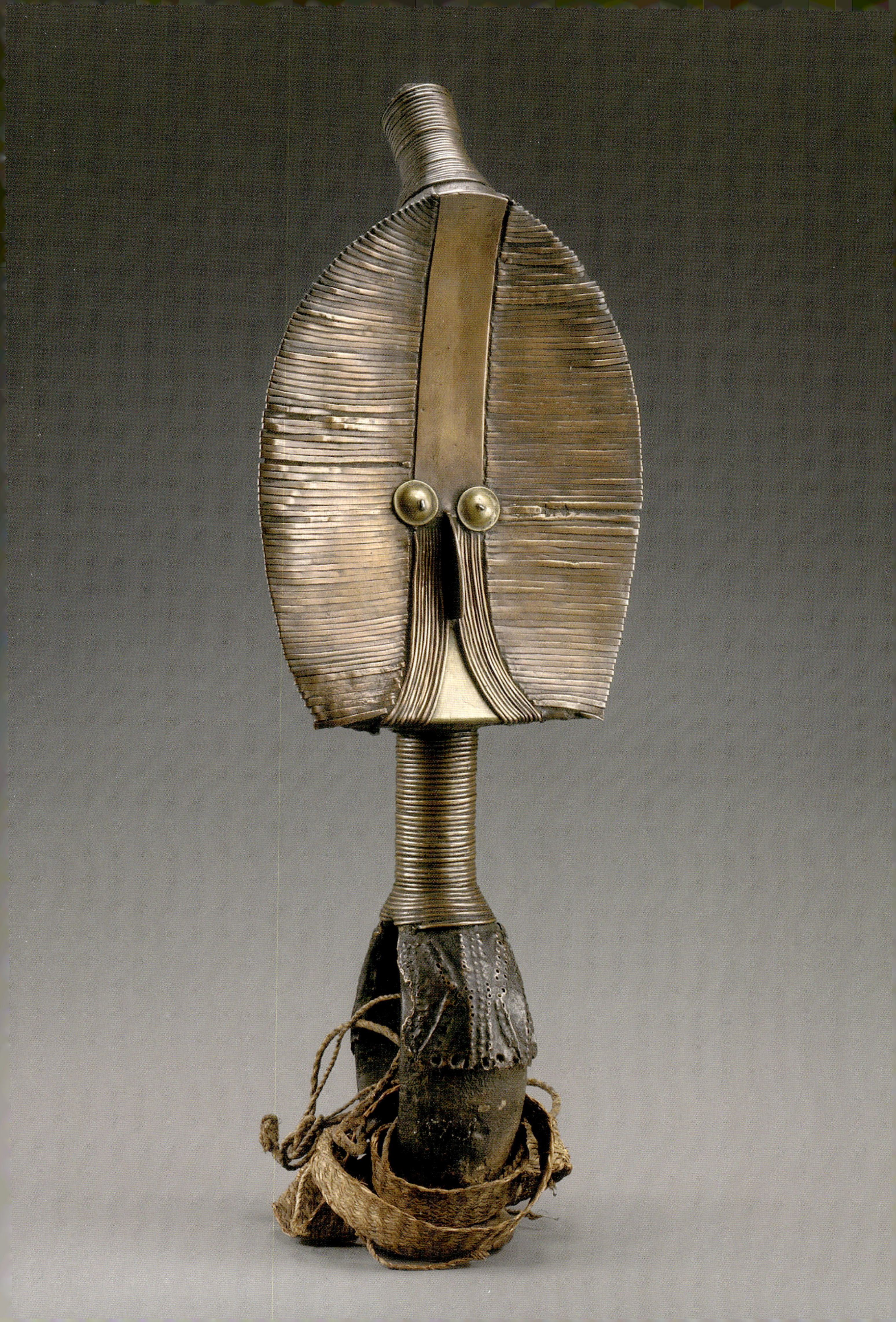

178. Baule artist
Ivory Coast
Male figure (groom in the afterlife)
Wood and fibres, 39 cm
Private collection

not diminish their communicative power: on the contrary, it is increased on the spiritual plane.

The large head of figure no. 177 is an oval, delicately concave shield, with the lower section truncated, covered with thin, horizontal strips of metal; the orthogonally placed lozenge on which it rests is, perhaps, the body. Two small hemispherical reliefs set close together and a pointed piece of metal – the eyes and nose – create a human face, divided by a smooth band (the forehead?). As the band descends beneath the eyes, it turns into two groups of wires, like the ones that circle the neck and the truncated cone on the top of the head that may represent the hairstyle. The combination of the merely apparent simplicity of the work and the ordered composition of the elements that compose it produces a sculpture of evocative and poetic power, rendered moving by its tendency towards the absolute.

The Baule figures – same form, different function

The vocabulary of the Baule from the Ivory Coast does not have a word that expresses clearly and unambiguously the qualities that bring a work of Western art to life. As has been exhaustively documented by Susan Vogel, the meanings of the symbols represented in the objects take precedence over the actual nature of the works themselves.[2] However, many works made to meet the needs of the society's spiritual life also express ideals of beauty in a way not unlike what occurred in religious art in the Western world.

The human figure is the Baule artists' favourite subject. The main function of the images is to give visible form – *présentifier* to use Lucien Stéphan's apt term[3] – to the groom (*blolo bian*) or bride (*blolo bla*) whom, according to Baule culture, every man and woman has in the other world. These entities must be propitiated with particular attentions, and a dialogue established to inculcate a benevolent attitude and prevent the psychological and sexual life of their earthly spouse being disturbed.[4]

In addition to the statues of the "groom" or "bride", other similar figures are used in the healing and divining practices of the trance diviners, important members of the society endowed with special powers. The sculptures are the "residence" of forest spirits (*asiè usu*), thought to be monstrously ugly, who must, however, be ingratiated with images of great beauty.

One example of spirit-bride is given in the chapter devoted to attributions (no. 132) like the figure reproduced here (no. 178). Its impressive head – even wider than the shoulders – weighs heavily on the slender, compact body. The thin arms that adhere to the body serve a purpose in the overall design, since they frame the relief decoration whose simplicity matches the sober nature of the figure. This has a secret life of its own that is revealed in the subtle irregularities in the alignment of the central axis.

The figures used by the trance diviners are formally no different from those of the "grooms" and "brides" of the other world and they can only be identified in certain cases by traces of substances sprinkled on them during propitiatory rituals.

This is the case of a male figure in a private collection (no. 179) that differs from the previous work in the feeling of calm power that it emanates. The compact mass of the trunk and sturdy arms becomes even broader in the strong legs. The enormous volume of the head with its serene features is made more appealing by an elegant coiffure in the form of a sunburst that crowns the hemispherical forehead. The triangular face is bounded on the upper side by the horizontal relief of the half-closed eyes and lengthened below by the plaits of the beard that seem to direct the gaze towards the hands placed near the navel.

The bowl in the right hand and the traces of sacrificial patina suggest that also the figure in the Malcolm Collection (no. 180) was a diviner's ritual object. The first quality to become apparent that distinguishes this sculpture from the previous one is the structural complexity of its soft though unaffected forms, which, taken as a whole, create a strong coherent image. The thin face is animated by the strong and tender features. The expressive hands with their long

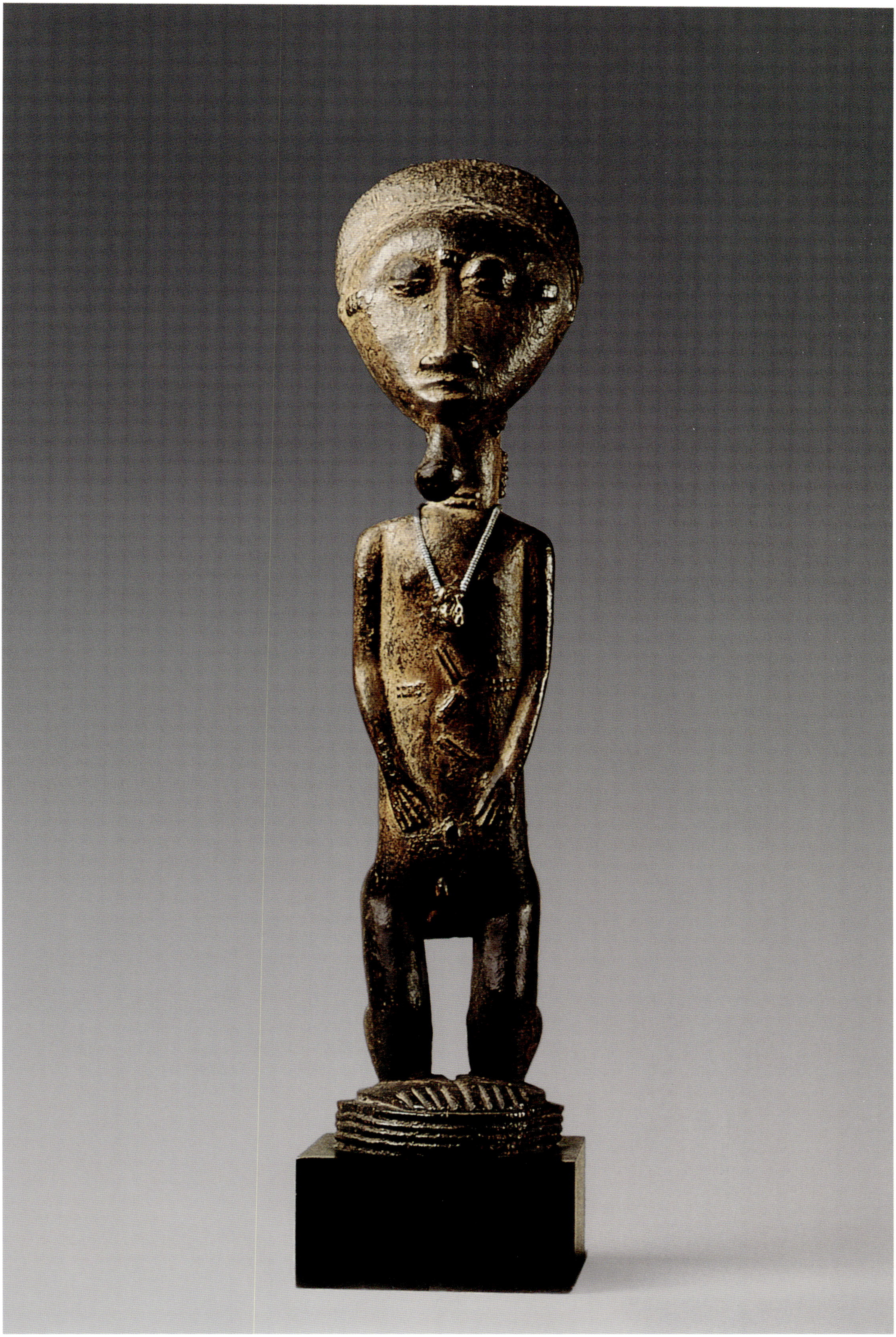

179. Baule artist
Ivory Coast
Male figure used in divination
Wood and fibres, 50 cm
Private collection

180. Baule artist
Ivory Coast
Male figure used in divination
Wood and fibres, 31.8 cm
Drs Daniel and Marian Malcolm
Collection, Tenafly (USA)

181. Baule artist
Ivory Coast
Male figure used in divination
Wood, fibres, metal and glass beads, 37 cm
Private collection

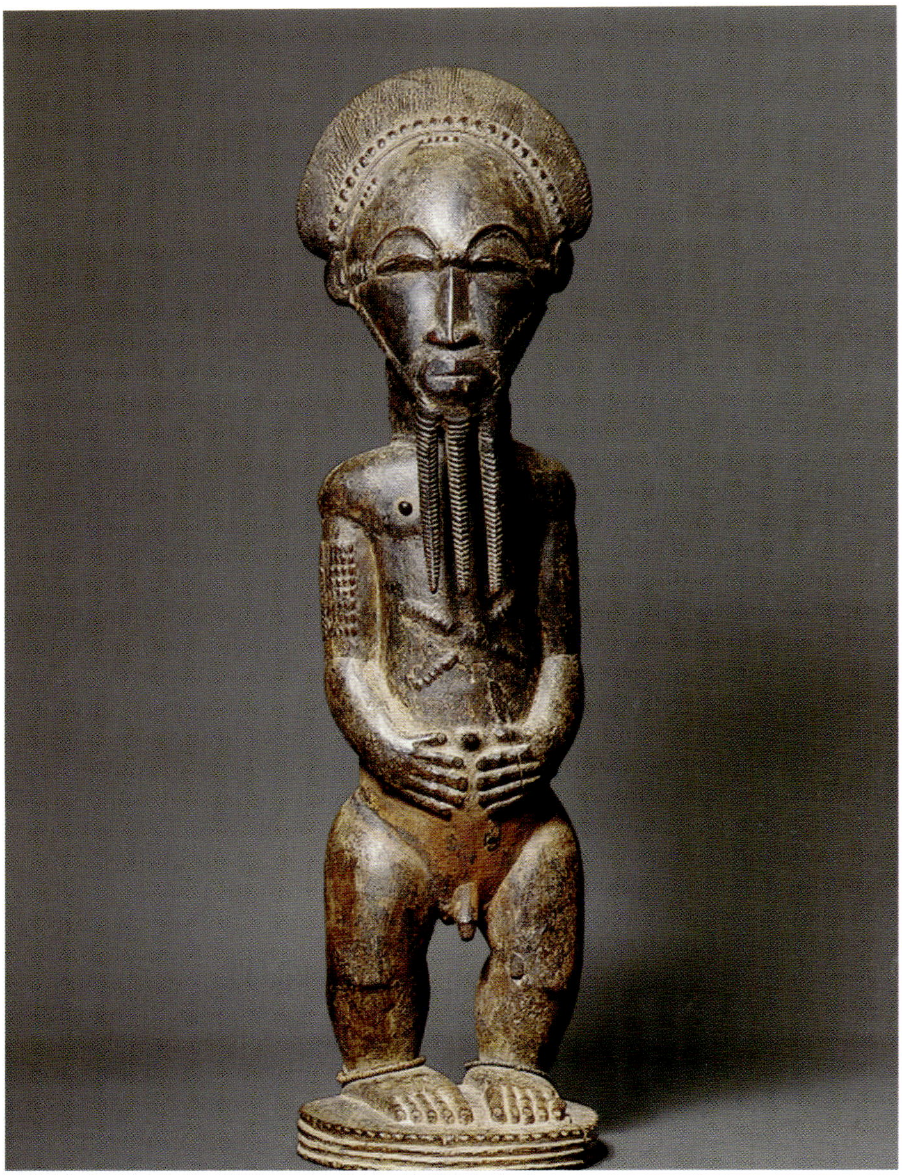

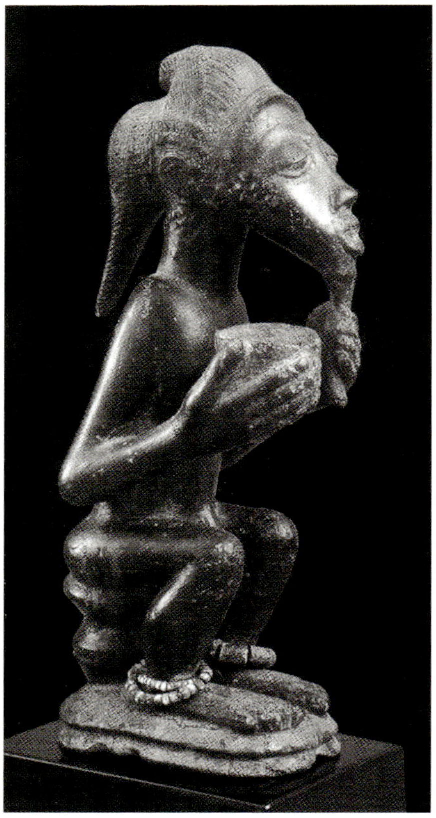

fingers – one holds the figure's beard and the other a bowl – and the very long feet do not disrupt the harmony of the figure, but are an integral part of it.

The head is more skilfully constructed and complex than those of the other figure, which was almost certainly sculpted by the same artist or a very close follower (no. 181).[5] The elegant coiffure that descends to taper below the shoulders perfectly balances the mass of the proudly raised head. The relief of two small plaits above the double curve of the ears smoothly marks the transition between the two volumes.

The few examples given here are merely an incentive to continue scholarly investigation. This is a field in which the concerted efforts of ethnologists, researchers of archival documents, art historians, physicists and chemists with the knowledge and the equipment of their professions can together produce results that exceed what have till now been all realistic expectations. Despite the inevitable approximation deriving from study of societies with no written language, they have the capability to reveal the functions of the works and the dates and places where they were produced, indispensable information for the reconstruction of the history of African art.

[1] Tessmann 1913, vol. 2, p. 117.
[2] Vogel 1997, passim; Boyer 2008, passim.
[3] Kerchache, Paudrat, Stephan 1988, p. 239.
[4] The practice of sculpting images dates from the late 19th or early 20th century.
[5] Bassani 1989, no. 51; there are two such figures but one is not illustrated here. For both, see Vogel 1997, p. 120.

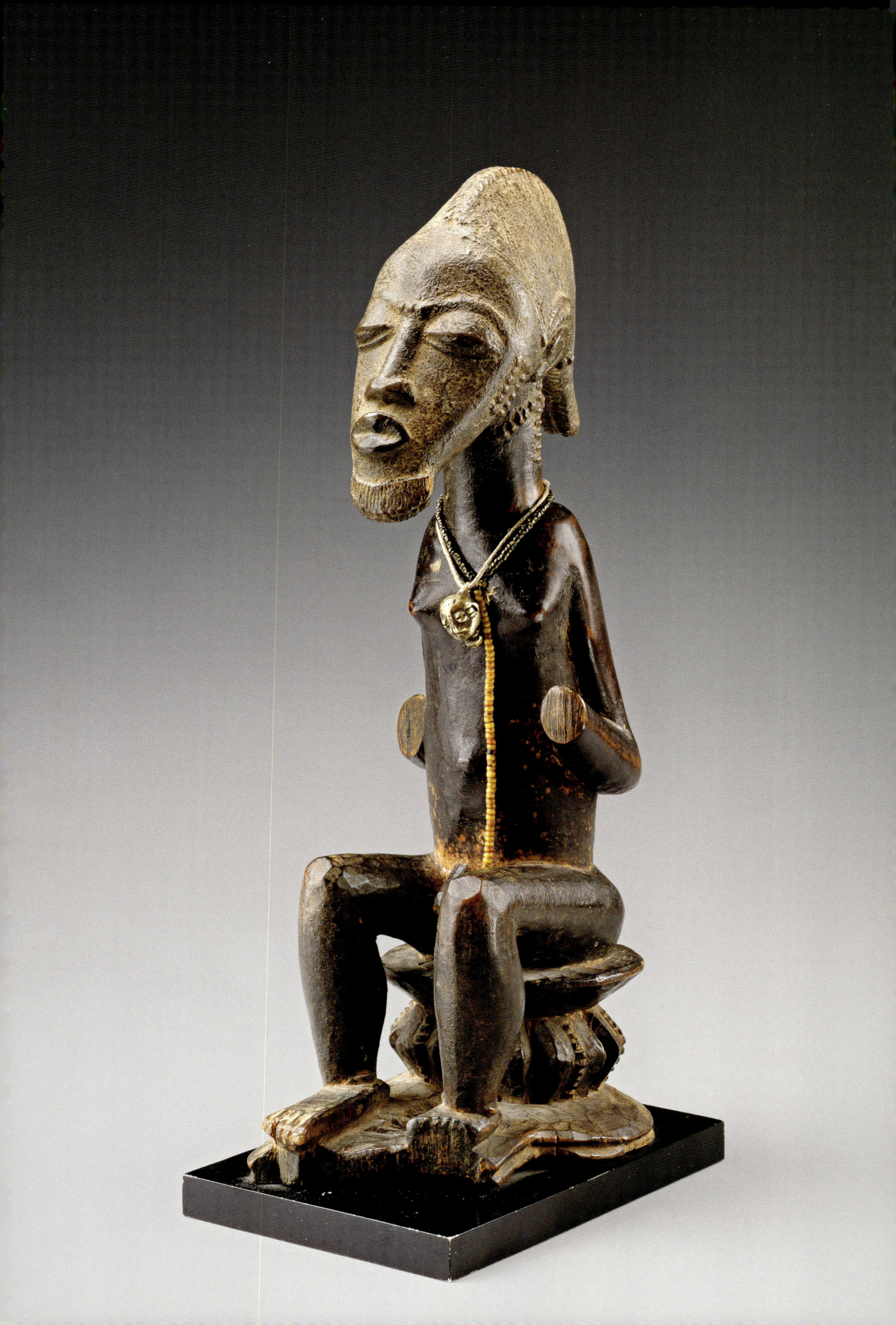

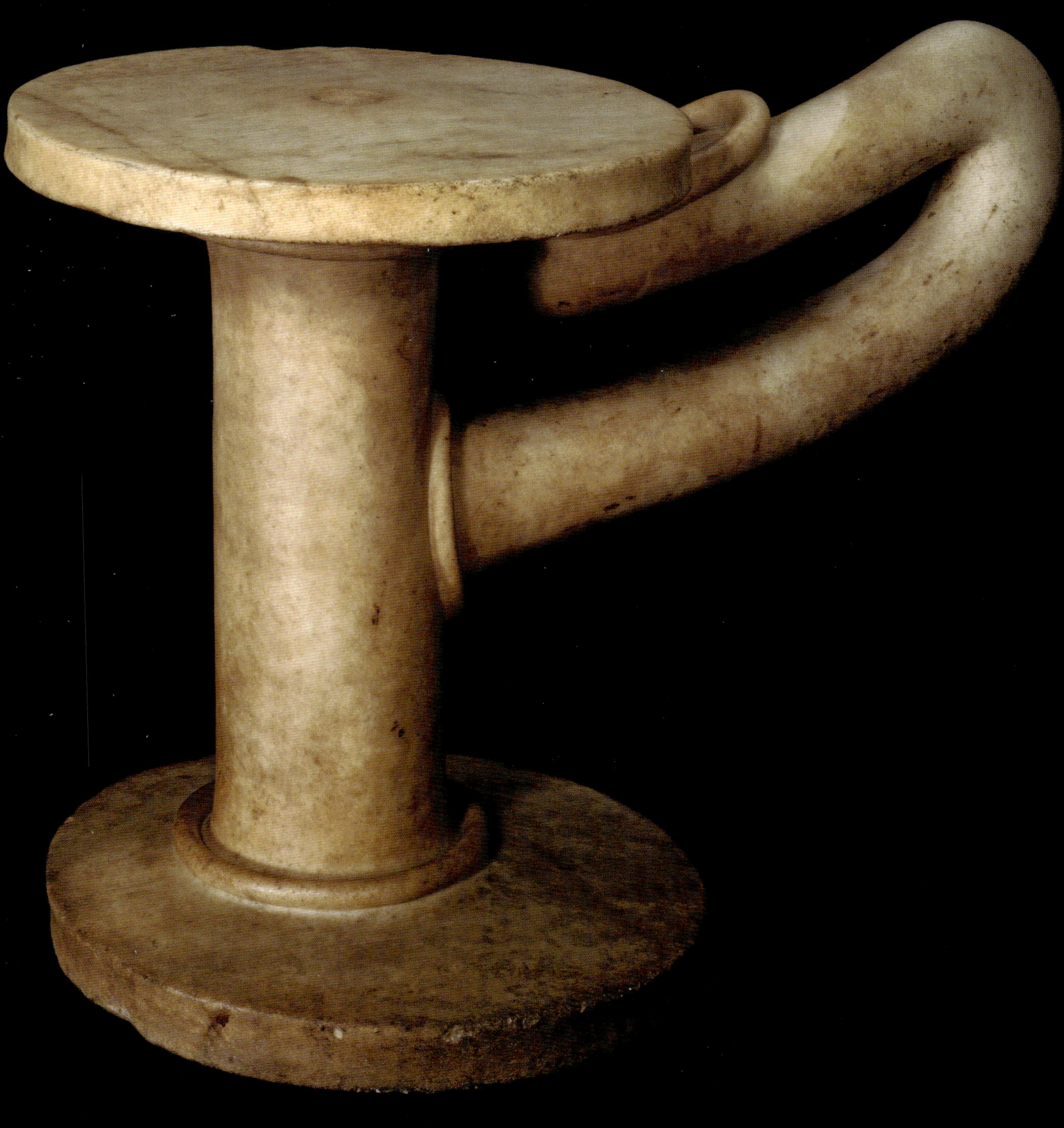

Artefacts – Works of Art

The allocation of an object to practical usage does not limit its artistic dimension but represents its creator's ability to give it a formal value. This is as true for objects made in Africa as for those produced anywhere else in the world, the West included, in which the combination of functionality, inventiveness and formal rigour produces surprising results, works whose formal perfection and ingenuity stimulate equal admiration.

The many non-African antique objects with a practical, though more often symbolic purpose in various museums throughout the world – first and foremost the famous salt cellar by Benvenuto Cellini – exemplify this. The analogy could even be extended to Western works that come under the label of "industrial design", whose form and function harmonize so well that they can be found in many museums of contemporary art, in particular the Museum of Modern Art in New York. However, there is a substantial difference between these items and African objects: the former are mass-produced and the latter are unique pieces, although this may also be true of many Western artefacts.

Apart from the above considerations, distinguishing between an artefact, a ritual object and a work of art is far from easy. Establishing the predominant characteristic – the object's functional/symbolic aspect or its formal quality – is nearly impossible in the many cases where the two are equally important and coexist, as often happens. Additionally, it is even more difficult to determine whether the functional aspect is real or symbolic.

For these reasons many works that are evidently artefacts, such as seats, headrests, boxes and spoons, are also examined in other chapters in this volume, because factors like their age, the client that commissioned them or their attribution to a particular author or workshop were thought to be more important. Moreover, here it has been preferred to deal with several versions of the same object rather than to extend the range of categories, since we believe that this solution shows to advantage the richness of the African figurative universe. It should once again be pointed out that the works described here are only a small sample and could be added to extensively with other examples that are equally representative and valid from the formal standpoint.

The works are in homogeneous groups and described in a sequence that moves from the north to the south of Africa, with the exception of antique objects. As in the chapter devoted to attributions, these are listed before the items presumably made in the 19th and 20th centuries.

Antique works

Ceremonial seats and thrones

The precious quartz seat from Ife, dated to between the 12th and 15th centuries and now in the British Museum (no. 182), is perfect in its simplicity and purity of form and admirably suited to its purpose. Its age, which laboratory analysis is unable to reveal, has been deduced from the fact that a similar seat

182. Ife artist
Nigeria, 12th–15th c.
Ceremonial seat
Quartz, 54 cm
The British Museum, Ethnography Department, London

183. Ife artist
Nigeria, 14th–15th c.
Ceremonial vessel
Brass, 12.4 cm
The National Commission for
Museums and Monuments, Nigeria

184–184a. Edo artist
Benin, Nigeria, 16th c.
Ceremonial seat
Bronze, 34 cm
The National Commission for
Museums and Monuments, Nigeria

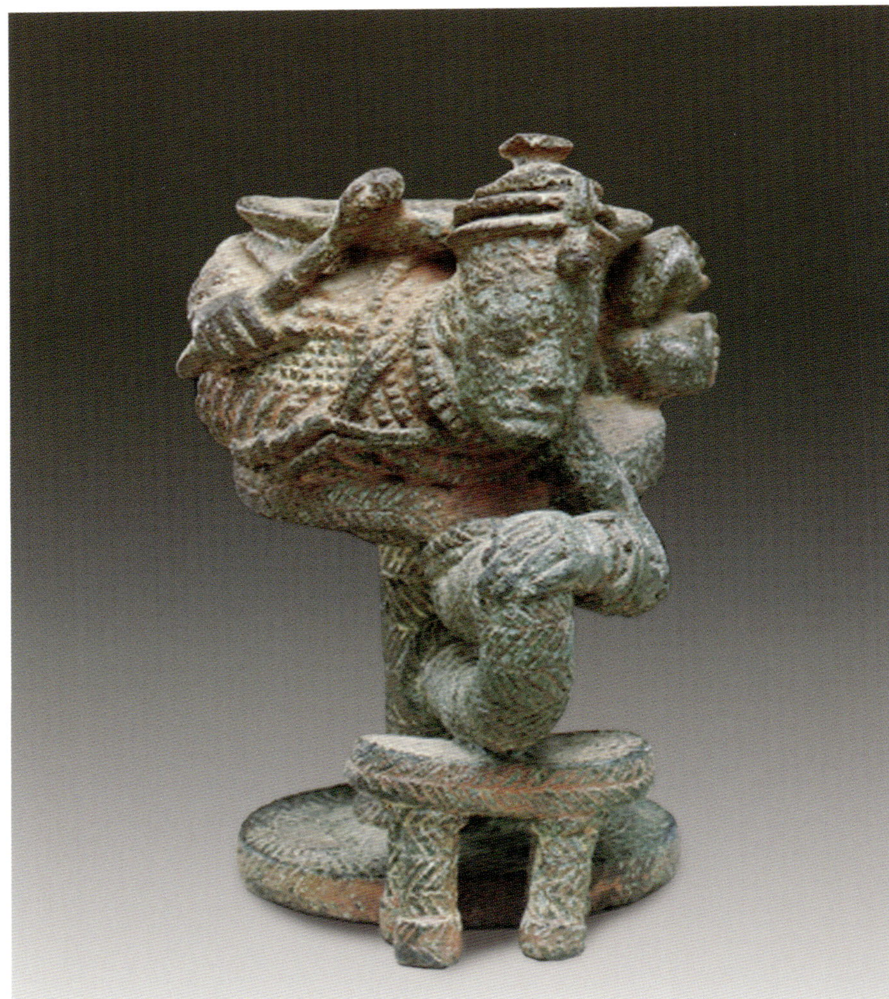

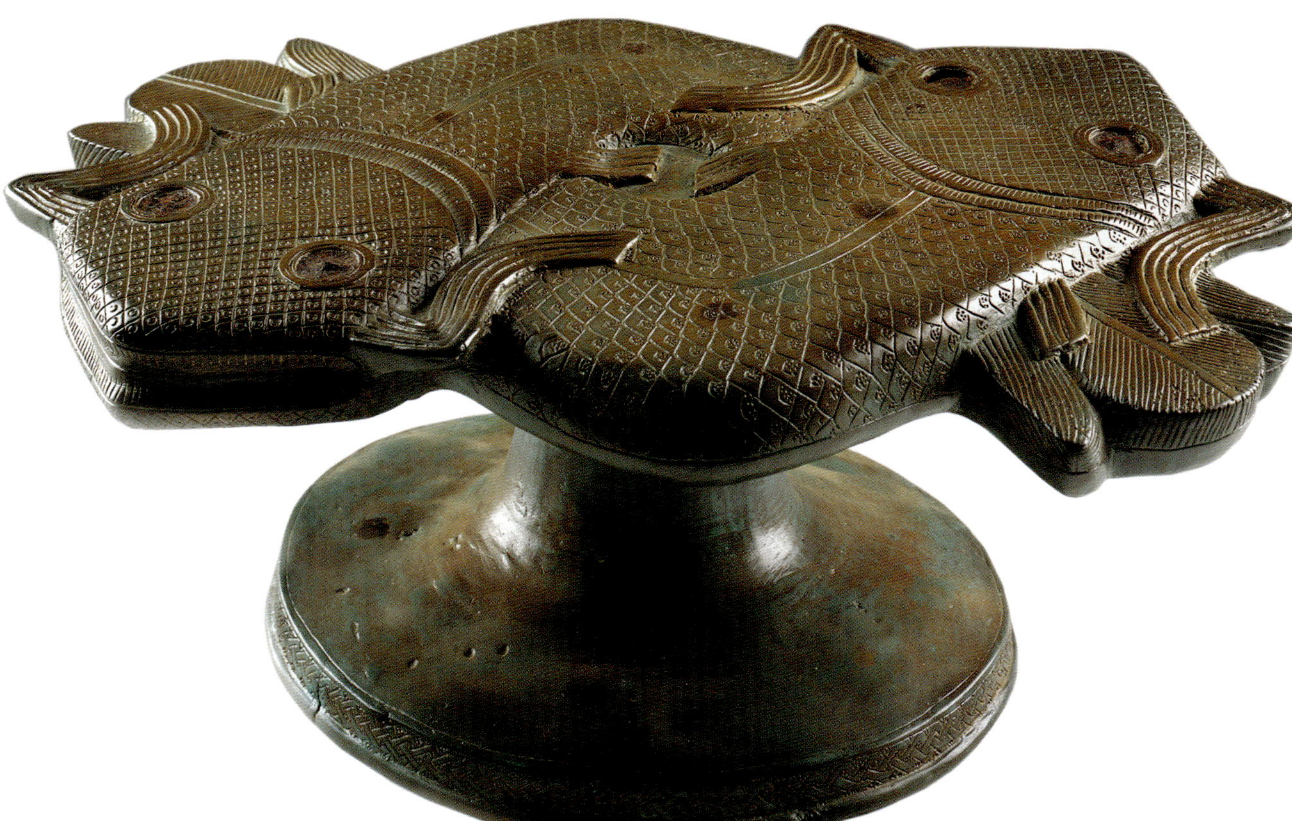

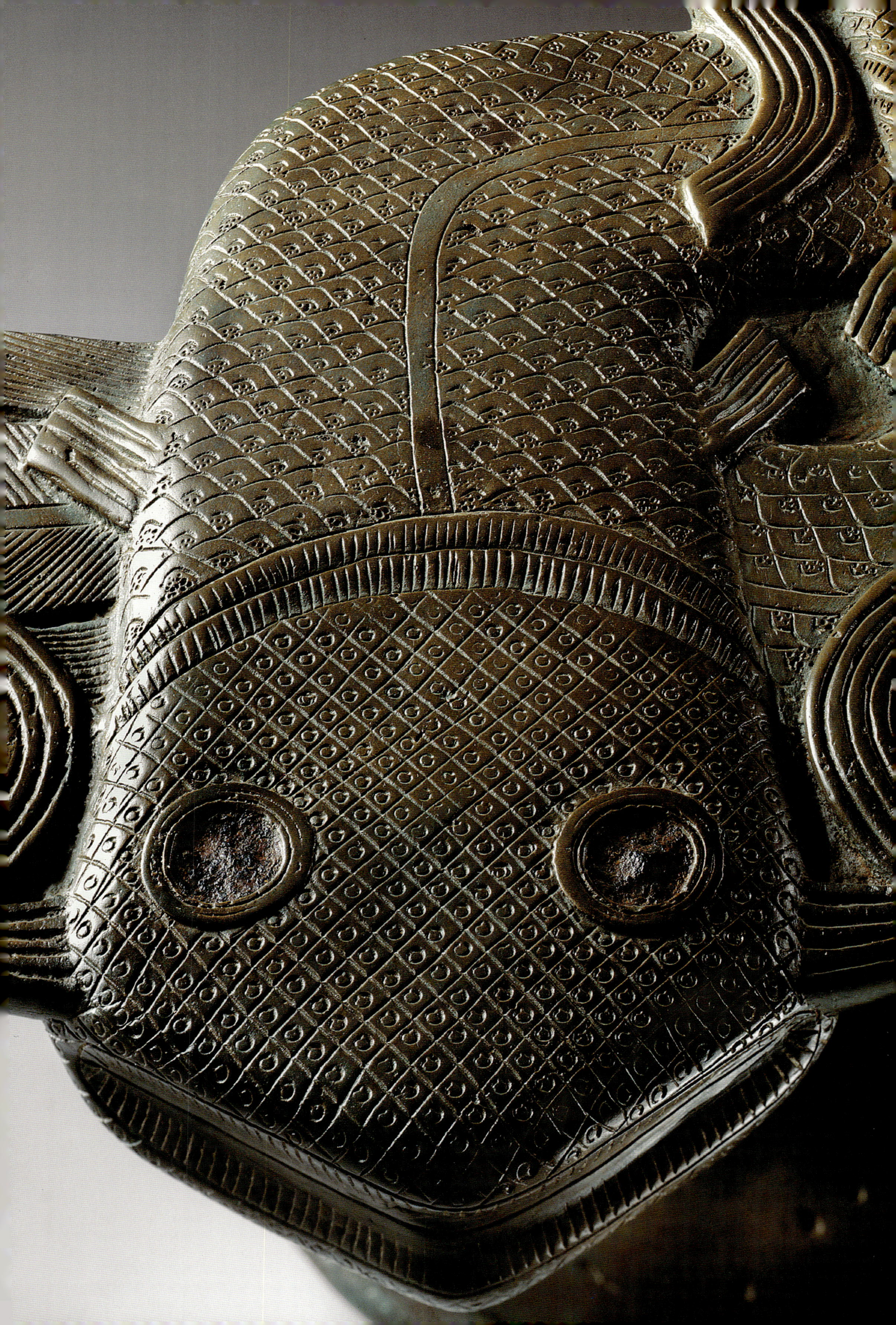

appears on a piece of terracotta,[1] and from a miniature sculpture dated to the 12th–15th century, in which an identical seat supports a vessel enveloped by a human figure (no. 183). The similarities to the quartz seat, with the exception of the surface decoration, are incontrovertible: the small circles in relief visible at the join and the base of the support and the insertion of the handle. The latter, according to Henry J. Drewall, may represent the stylized trunk of an elephant.

Unlike the seat from Ife, the 16th-century seat from Benin (no. 184), composed of two extraordinary interlocking catfish, is a triumph of imagination. The catfish is the symbol of Olokun, the deity of the waters, and of the sovereign of divine right. Their big pointed heads and the symmetrical curves of their flattened bodies and waving whiskers together express a sense of controlled movement heightened by the intricate, refined yet spare geometric decoration that simulates the scales. This is a work of vibrant formal elegance that would have been the envy of a European "Art Nouveau" artist four centuries later.

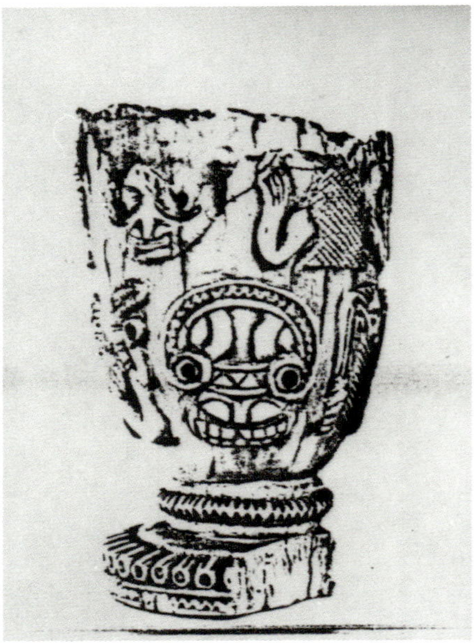

185. Owo artist
Yoruba, Nigeria, 17th c.
Goblet
Ivory, 10.6 cm
Hampshire County Museum, Winchester (UK)

Goblets and vessels

A date can only be tentatively provided at present for a large group of goblets, jugs, boxes and lidded vessels all in ivory and sharing the same decorative elements, made by artists from the city of Owo, capital of the ancient kingdom of Yoruba. It is likely that this entire group of ivory objects dates from the 17th–18th century and was produced during a relatively short period, given the thematic and formal similarities between the works.[2]

Taking into consideration only the goblets and vessels, it is thought that a badly damaged example, in the Hampshire County Museum, Winchester (UK) since 1853, was found in the ruins of Basing House, the former residence of the Marquis of Winchester, which was destroyed by Cromwell's troops in 1645 (no. 185). A second goblet donated to the Metropolitan Museum of Art, New York, by Mr and Mrs Pearls, was in the collection of the Princes of Ligne in Belgium before 1825, while three vessels with lids were donated to the Museum für Völkerkunde, Berlin, in 1831 by a certain Mr Friedländer, who is supposed to have "inherited them from Königsberg".

Due to the uncertainty of dates, only one vessel will be examined here, one of those held by the museum in Berlin (no. 186). According to information gathered last century, this object would have been used to contain small objects, usually gifts. Its compact oval form, which is monumental despite its small size, is contained within an imaginary cylinder defined by the rim of the lid and the base of equal diameter. The superb high-relief decoration, divided in two independent registers, shows a human face, monstrous creatures and fantastical animals in the lower section, and, in the upper, in addition to

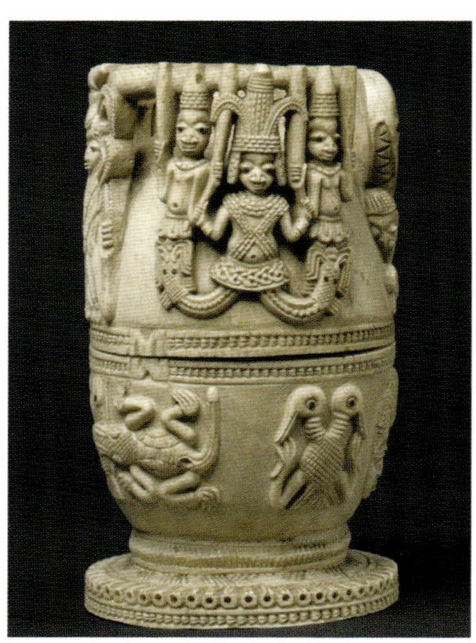

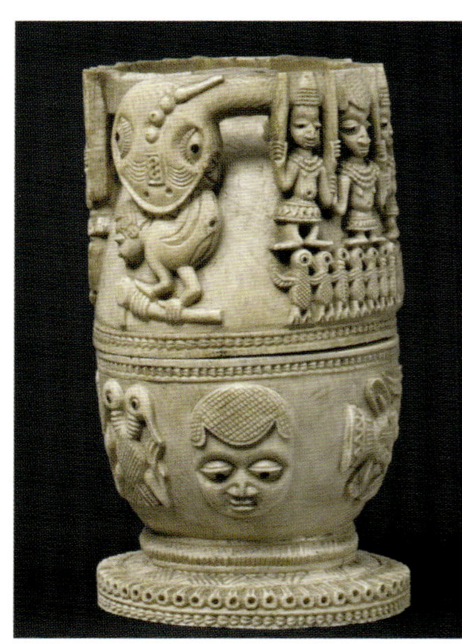

186. Owo artist
Yoruba, Nigeria, 17th–18th c.
Vessel with lid
Ivory, 23.5 cm
Staatliche Museen zu Berlin, Ethnologisches Museum, Berlin

186a. Another view of the vessel no. 186

187. Congo artist
Ancient Kingdom of Congo, Republic of the Congo, Democratic Republic of the Congo, Angola, 17th c.
Vessel with lid
Vegetable fibres, l. 29 cm
Linden-Museum, Stuttgart

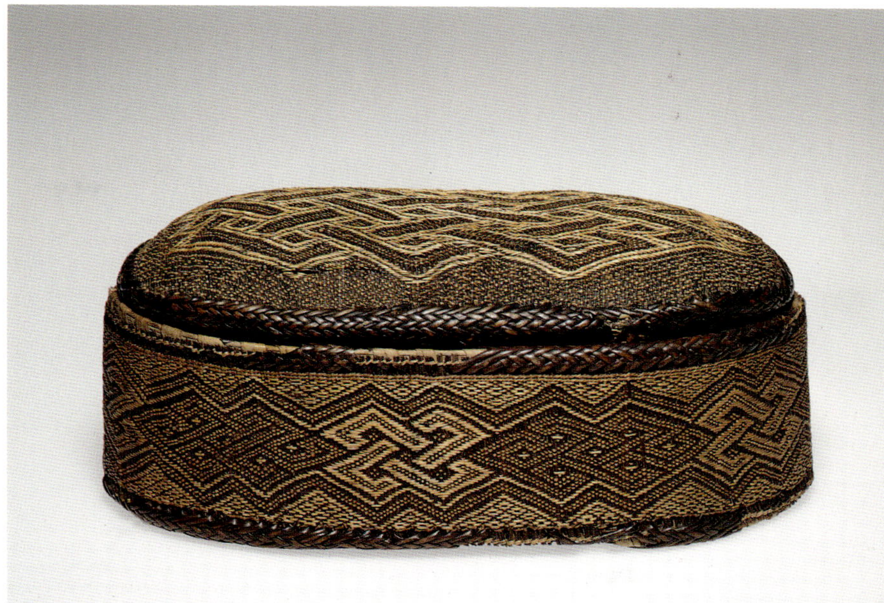

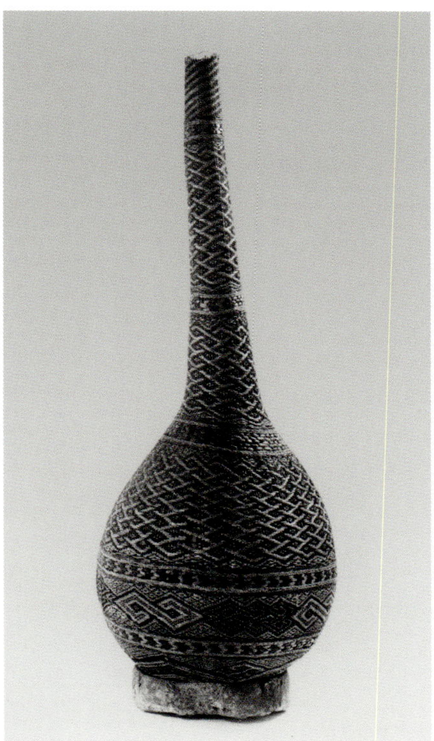

188. Congo artist
Ancient Kingdom of Congo, Republic of the Congo, Democratic Republic of the Congo, Angola, 17th c.
Flask
Gourd, vegetable fibres and wood, 52 cm
Ulmer Museum, Ulm

the gigantic head of a python sinking its fangs into a man (no. 186a), a portrait of the king wearing a crown of feathers and flanked by two dignitaries. In keeping with Yoruba mythology, his legs are carved in the form of catfish.[3]

The implications suggested by the existence of a series of small hollow cylinders in the decoration on both the base of the Owo goblets and some Benin salt cellars have been pointed out in the description of the latter.

Kongo vessels

Some vessels from the ancient kingdom of Kongo, formerly present in 17th-century European collections, can quite rightly be considered works of art, due to their perfect volumes and highly complex polychrome geometric decoration. This is adapted in each case to the size of the object and perfectly and elegantly integrated into the shape with an extraordinary sense of rhythm. The box from the Linden-Museum in Stuttgart (no. 187), which was formerly in the *wunderkammer* of the dukes of Württemberg, and the flask in the Ulmer Museum in Ulm (no. 188), acquired with the famous collection of the dealer Christoph Weickmann (1617–81), are among the most representative examples.

The characteristics of the decorative motifs in the figurative legacy of the Congo people are dealt with in the chapter devoted to the specially commissioned works (the 16th-century oliphants – see nos. 105–106 – are the earliest) in which examples are also given of fabrics decorated with the same geometric motifs.

Their presence on the containers described here is evidence of the vessels' early date and provide another example of the level of refinement attained by the society for whom these perfectly crafted objects were created.

Recent works

Thrones and ceremonial seats

In 1994 Sandro Bocola organized a fine exhibition entitled 'African Seats' at the Vitra Design Museum in Weil am Rhein, which featured 173 seats from all over Africa. Many of them could be considered works of art and in some cases actual masterpieces.

The Bidjogo throne from Guinea Bissau, the first article in the exhibition (no. 189), is a good example with which to begin. Despite their small size, the simple monumental human figures that embellish it contribute greatly to its artistic quality. However, what above all renders this a superb work of art, and would turn more than one Western designer green with envy, is the perfection and harmony of the volumes that compose the monumental yet light whole, from the circular base to the central support. This latter element starts round

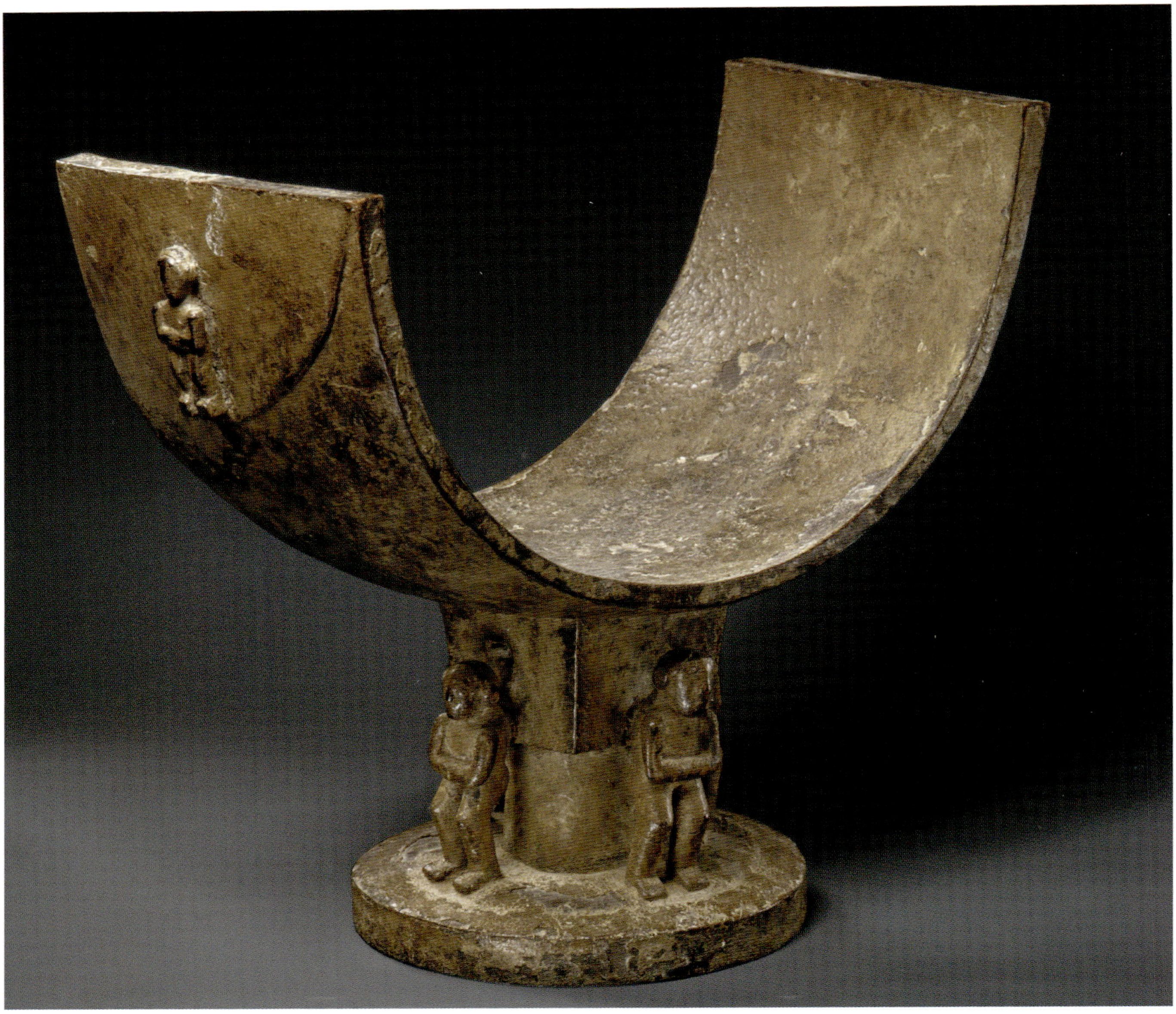

189. Bidjogo artist
Guinea Bissau
Royal seat
Wood, 39.5 cm
Staatliche Museen zu Berlin,
Ethnologisches Museum, Berlin

190. Yoruba artist
Nigeria (Igbomina region)
Ceremonial seat (?)
Wood, 47.5 cm
Jeffrey Hammer Collection,
Los Angeles (formerly in the Gaston
T. de Havenon Collection)

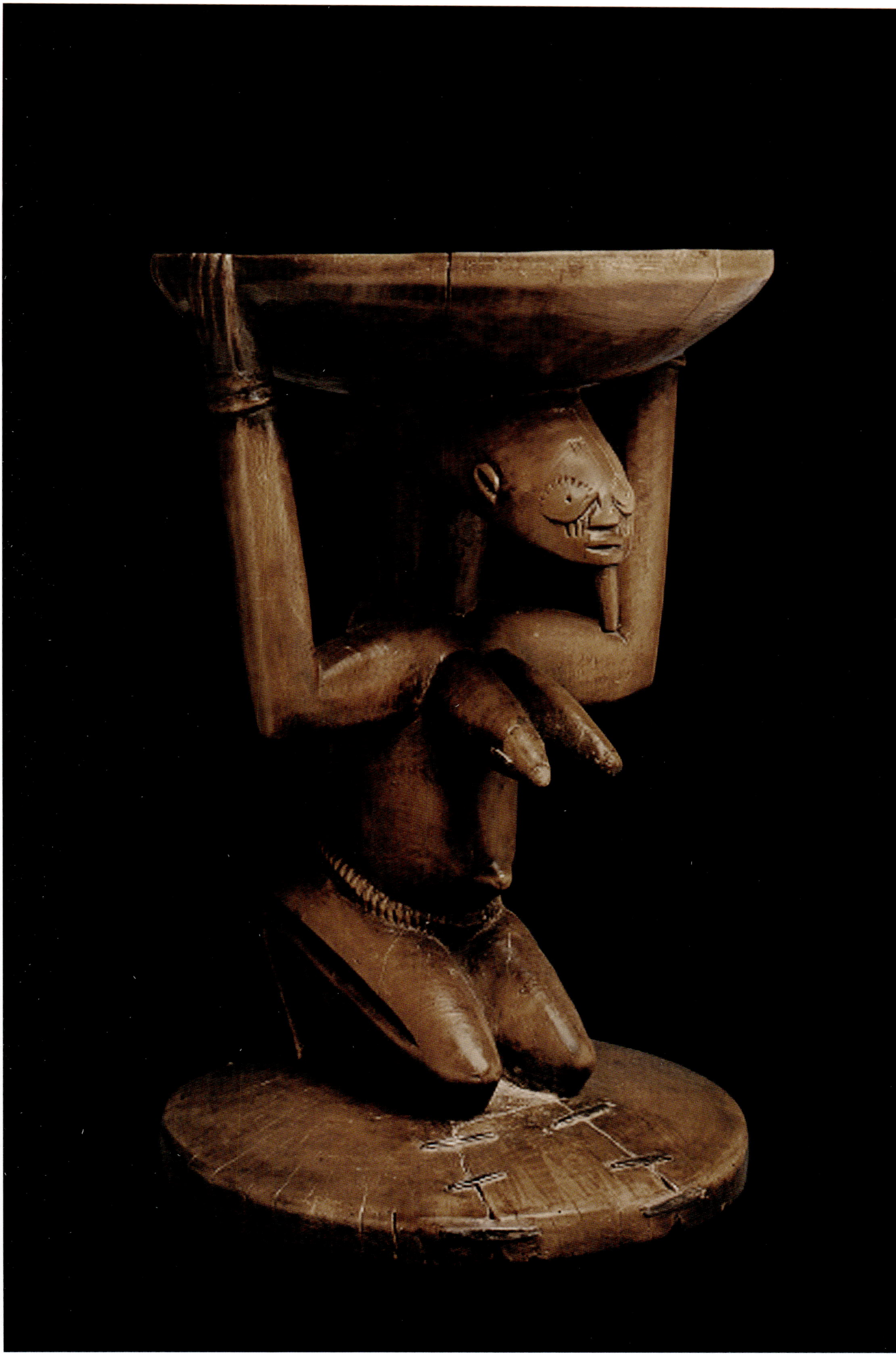

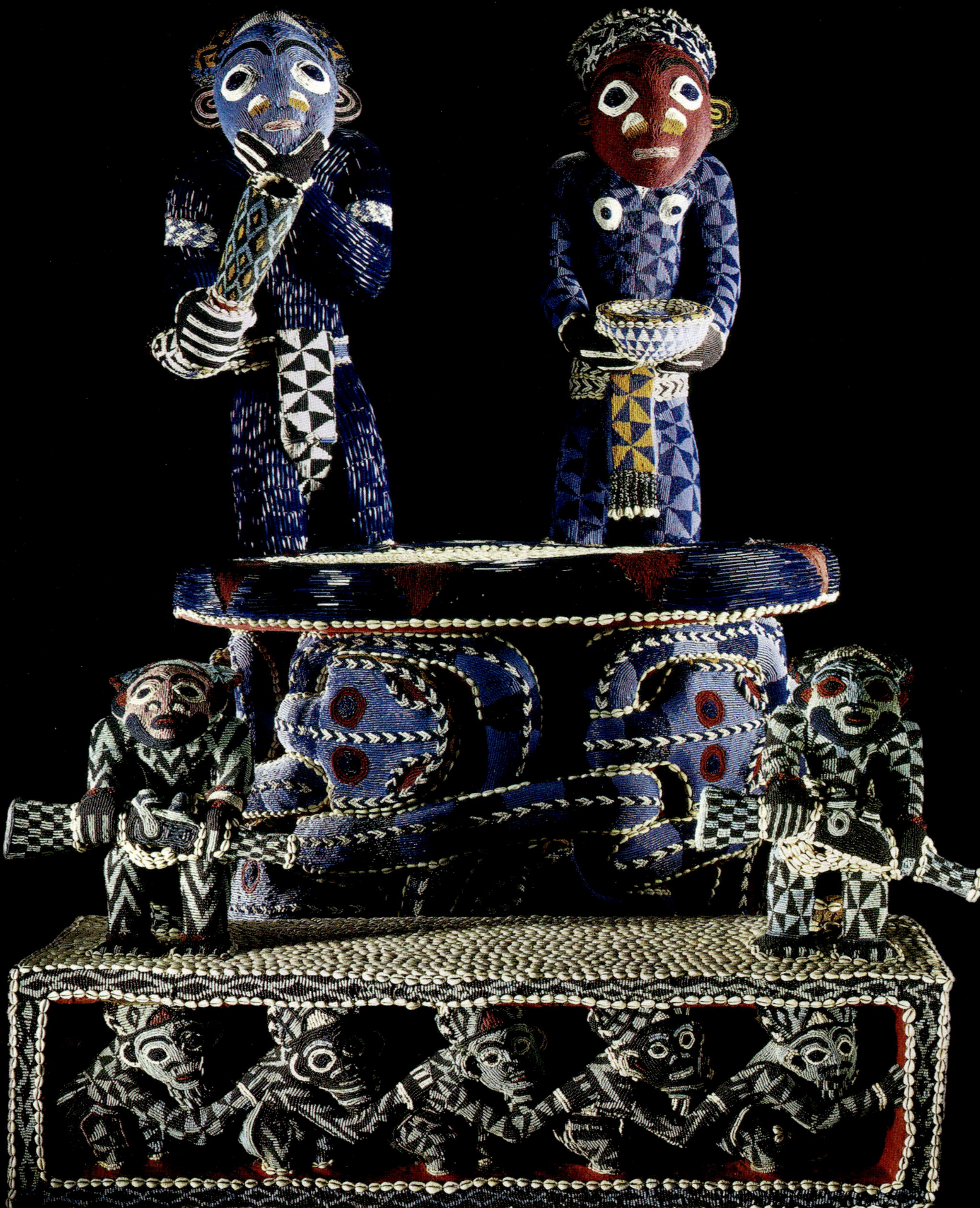

191. Bamum artist
Cameroon, 19th c.
Throne and footrest of Sultan Njoya
Wood, fabric and glass beads, 175 cm
Staatliche Museen zu Berlin, Ethnologisches Museum, Berlin (donated by Sultan Njoya to Kaiser Wilhelm II in 1908)

192. Bamum artist
Cameroon, 19th c.
Ceremonial seat
Wood, iron and bronze, 54 cm
Formerly in the Paolo Morigi Collection

but is transformed to a quadrangle so as better to show off the perfect semicircle of the actual seat through contrast.

An artist active in the 19th–20th century in the Igbomina region of Nigeria created the Yoruba seat (was it used for ceremonial purposes?) formerly in the Gaston T. de Havenon Collection (no. 190). Its function, whether practical or ritual, unfortunately remains uncertain.

The composition is dominated by a splendid kneeling female nude. Her manner is determined; the component parts of her slender yet firm figure, which joins the base to the seat, are composed in a strict rhythm. The verticality of her raised arms, long neck and the lip ornament suspended beneath her chin accentuates the parallel, oblique thrust of her large head stretched forward, the young breasts pointed like two bullets, her navel and bent legs, ordered in a clear sequence.

The most spectacular thrones and seats are those made in Cameroon, in particular for the monarchs and dignitaries of the Bamum group in the northeastern savannah area. The most famous example held by the ethnographic museum in Berlin (no. 191) was given to the German emperor in 1908 by Sultan Njoya (r. 1887–1931).[4] The emperor was supposed to receive a copy but as it was not ready in time he was presented with the original.

The throne used for official occasions had been carved for Njoya's father Nsangu (r. 1860–86/87) by a Nguot artist and covered with beads by a Menyam artist.[5] It is a spectacular work in which each element has a symbolic significance that reflects the essence of Bamum regality. The imposing snakes that coil around the base are an icon of royalty.[6] According to Hans-Joachim Koloss, the two figures that form the back represent male and female twins, who were thought to possess supernatural powers; the former is holding a libation horn (which replaced the glass bottle that existed there before the throne was donated) and the latter a bowl with kola nuts, both symbols of the ruler's wealth. Two men armed with rifles stand on the footrest whose front is decorated with a crowd of prostrate figures, probably servants. There are virtually identical

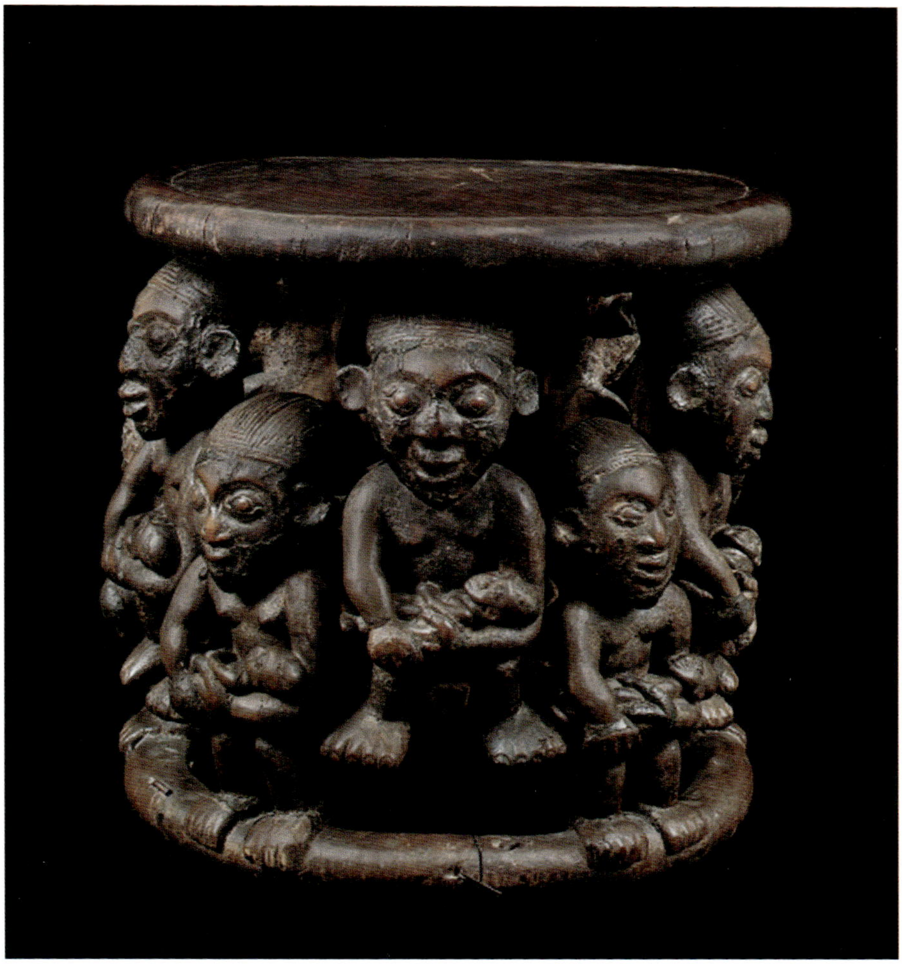

193. Luba artist
Kiambi workshop, Democratic Republic of the Congo
Seat with female caryatid
Wood and glass beads, 53 cm
Private collection

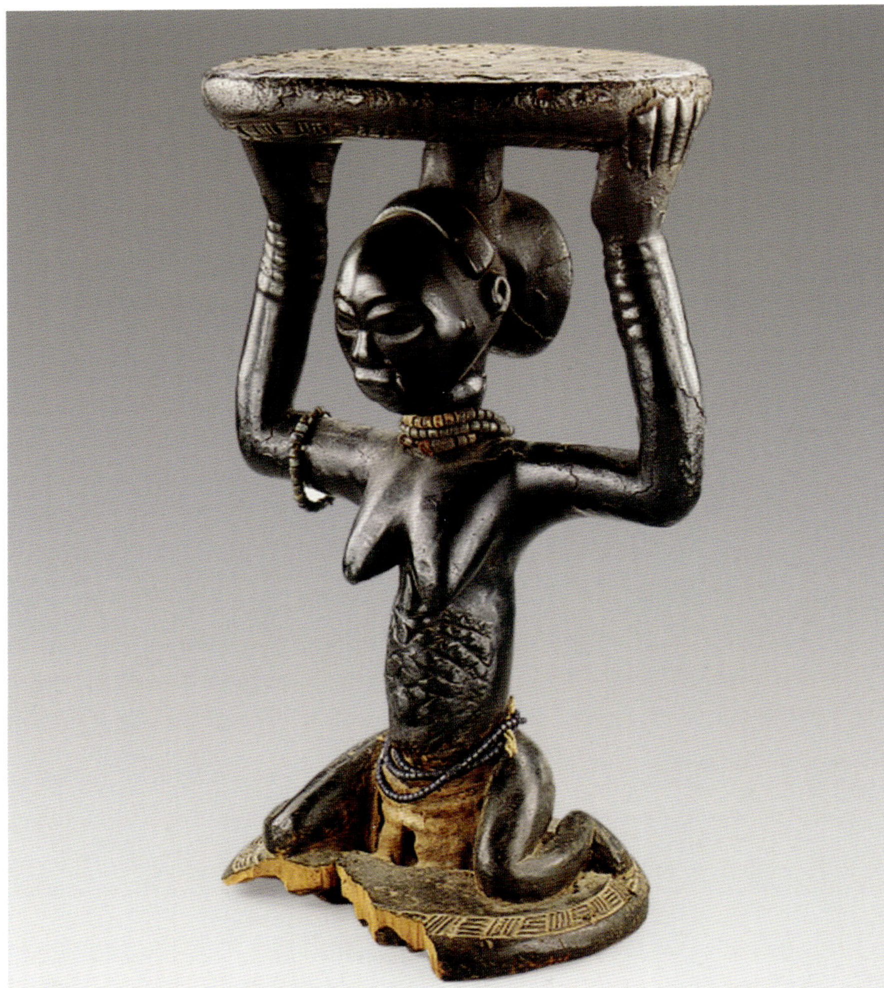

figures on a stool now in the Musée Barbier-Mueller in Geneva, which Sultan Njoya gave to the German captain Hans Glauning in 1905.

The organization of the complex volumetric-thematic construction involving vertical, horizontal and diagonal elements that skilfully alternate movement and stillness – the two large upright figures, the huge horizontal snakes, the figures leaning forward on the footrest – is one of the most fascinating aspects of this monumental work decorated with magnificent and colourful beadwork.

The attraction of Bamum works of art does not necessarily depend on their eye-catching decoration. The monochrome of the superb seat formerly in the Morigi Collection[7] (no. 192) actually heightens the perfection of its form. The artist has fully exploited the cylindrical block of wood. The crowded support for the circular seat is formed by ten fully figured and almost identical female figures, gentle and powerful at the same time, each with a baby in her lap. The rounded shapes of the figures are covered with thin copper plating that has been partially lost, which renders them soft and tender.

Although the mothers are all portrayed sitting in a circle with their babies lying in their laps, the composition is given dynamism by the fact that the figures are set on two levels, though remaining visually and physically linked. The children's bodies follow the rhythmical rise and fall of the circle in a hymn to maternity and the fullness of life, which makes this seat one of the most moving works by a Bamum artist.

Stools with caryatids have an important and symbolic political function in the complex hierarchy of Luba society in the Democratic Republic of the Congo in that they are reserved for sovereigns and important religious personages. The crouching, kneeling or standing female figure (usually there is only one, unlike the examples from Cameroon) that supports the seat alludes to women's political role in society.

In the stool shown here (no. 193; attributed by François Neyt to a workshop near the village of Kiambi in the south-east of the country) the female body

194. Yamwezi artist
Tanzania
Ceremonial seat
Wood, 107 cm
Staatliche Museen zu Berlin, Ethnologisches Museum, Berlin

194a. Rear view of the ceremonial seat no. 194

perfectly integrated into the stool's structure seems to support the seat effortlessly, in a flow of volumes that rise from the bent legs of the solid base to the circular seat at the top of the composition. The slim bust, as straight as the shaft of a column, broadens out into the elegant curve of the long, powerful raised arms. Although these are perfectly functional in the overall volumetric design, it is the full youthful breasts and large head that are the most impressive features.

The slim neck is matched by the size and shape of the cylinder that joins the seat to the woman's beautiful spherical head, rendered even more imposing by her monumental coiffure. Seen from behind, her hair has been styled in a discreet cross shape that harmonizes with the parallel reliefs of the bangles on her forearms. The subtlety of forms in the figure's expressive face, in which the beautiful oval eyes predominate, also seems to emphasize the simplicity of the smooth hair above the rounded forehead.

The surfaces of the carving, embellished by a thick patina, are given a sense of movement by the bracelets in relief and the decoration on the abdomen and around the edge of the seat.

Unlike the previous examples, the symbolism of the figure and other motifs that decorate the thrones of the Nyamwezi chiefs in Western collections is still not clear, nor is the thrones' precise function. According to Marc Felix[8] these were used by the chiefs during initiation ceremonies and meetings to resolve disputes.

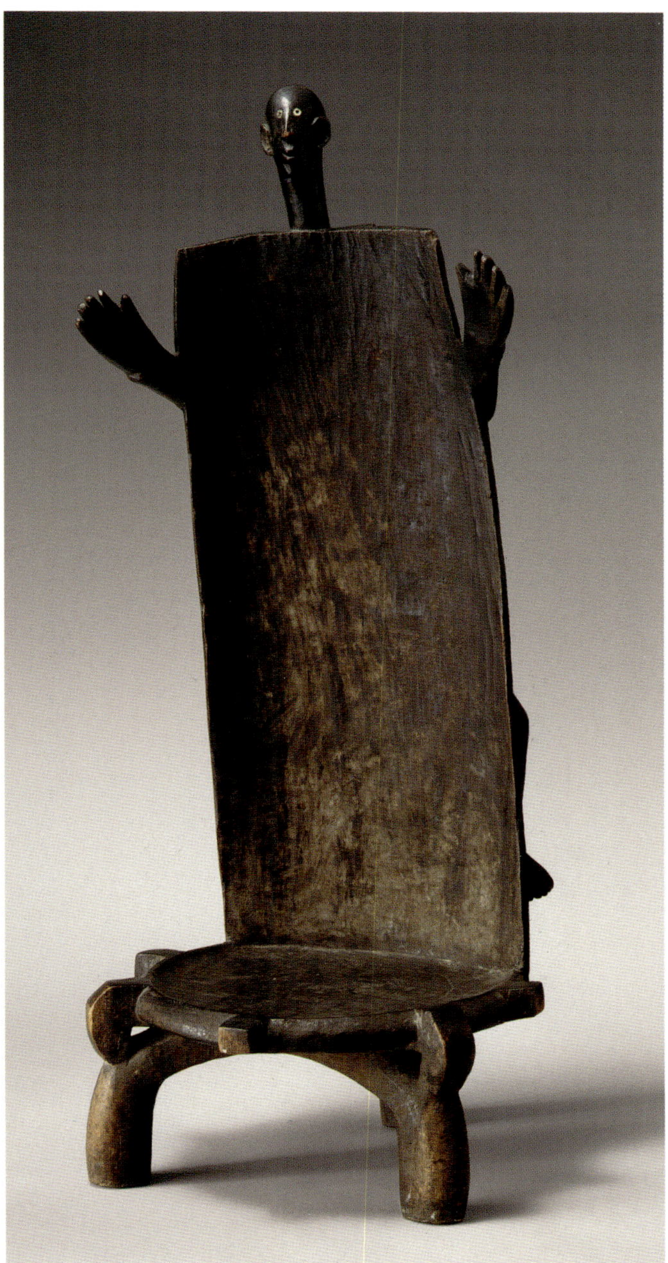

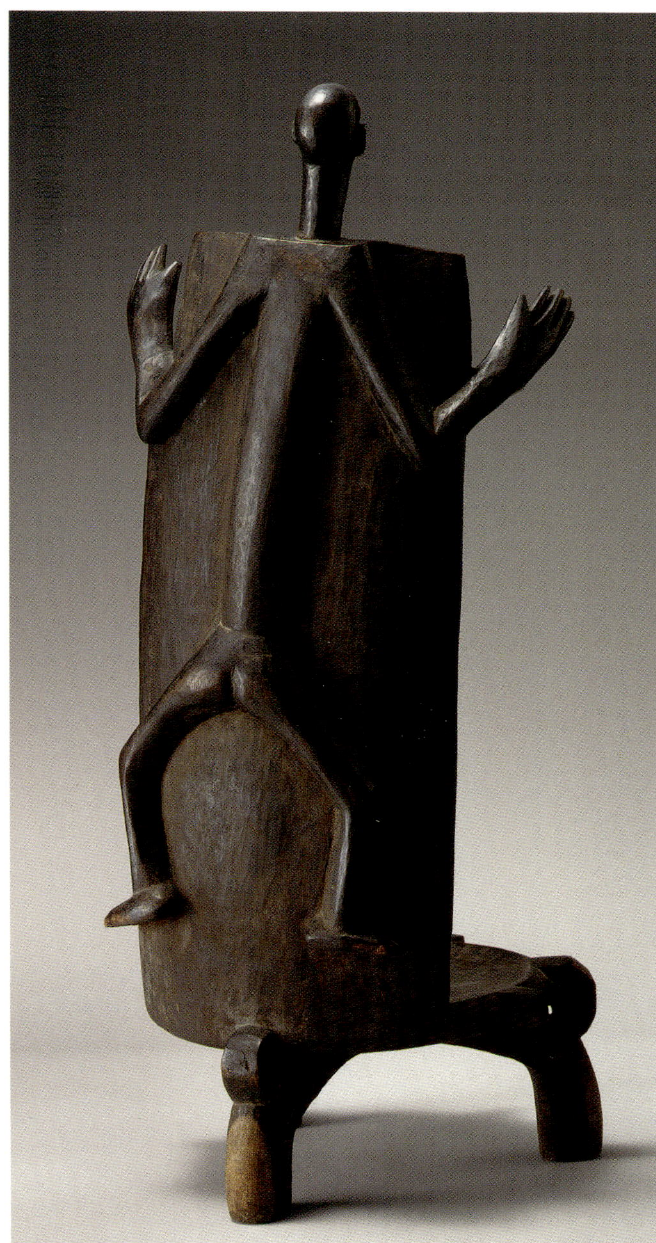

The piece in the Berlin museum (no. 194), acquired at the end of the 19th century, is certainly the most famous of these artefacts. From the formal standpoint the artist has conceived it by associating two separate, yet linked and congruent views. Seen from the front, the practical purpose of the work with its slightly curved, very tall back, on which the head and large open hands of a protective "ghost" appear like an apparition, seems obvious: it was to receive the chief and enhance his dignity.

Seen from the back (no. 194a), the "ghost" materializes in its mysterious humanity. Composed of simple, ordered reliefs, the figure occupies the whole surface of the throne's back and is virtually integrated into it. The slightly asymmetrical volumes, the movements of the flexed legs and the very long arms, bent as though embracing the throne, and the figure's trunk slightly inclined with respect to the central axis of the back of the throne to introduce a hint of movement, give the sense that the ghost has suddenly appeared, an impression reinforced by the small head and piercing eyes seen from the front.

The examples described here may suggest that all African seats have human or animal figures, but this is not the case. Most of them consist only of pure volumes. These are often so refined and their combination so ingenious that they are no inferior to objects produced in the West under the heading "industrial design". One example is the Congolese seat in the Musée du quai Branly presented by Sandro Bocola in the exhibition 'African Seats' (1994): a distillation of simplicity and boldness, a successful balance of solids and voids that could only have been conceived by a true artist with clear foresight of the formal effect that would be created by the curved elements that compose his work.

Headrests

Headrests are characterized by the same combination of functionality, symbolism and imagination. Those attributed to the "Master of the Cascade Coiffure", or rather of the two masters we spoke of in the chapter on attributions, are doubtless the most famous of these status symbols, but they are not the only ones produced by Luba sculptors.

Despite its diminutive size, the example in the British Museum, donated by Mrs Webster Plass (inv. 1956 AF 27–270), is of the same high quality as its more famous "brothers". Here two identical, noble and serene female figures, with the same youthful bodies, pert breasts and scarification on their abdomen, support the upper board with one arm, while they have their other arm around each other in a gesture of tender solidarity, as seen in the rear view. Here the animated, articulated reliefs of the shoulders, buttocks, characteristic cross-

195. Songye artist
Democratic Republic of the Congo, 19th c.
Headrest
Wood, 14 cm
Musée du Louvre, Pavillon des Sessions, Paris (formerly in the Stephen Chauvet Collection)

196. Luluwa artist
Western Kasai, Democratic Republic of the Congo, 19th c.
Headrest
Wood, 22 cm
Musée Royal de l'Afrique Centrale, Tervuren

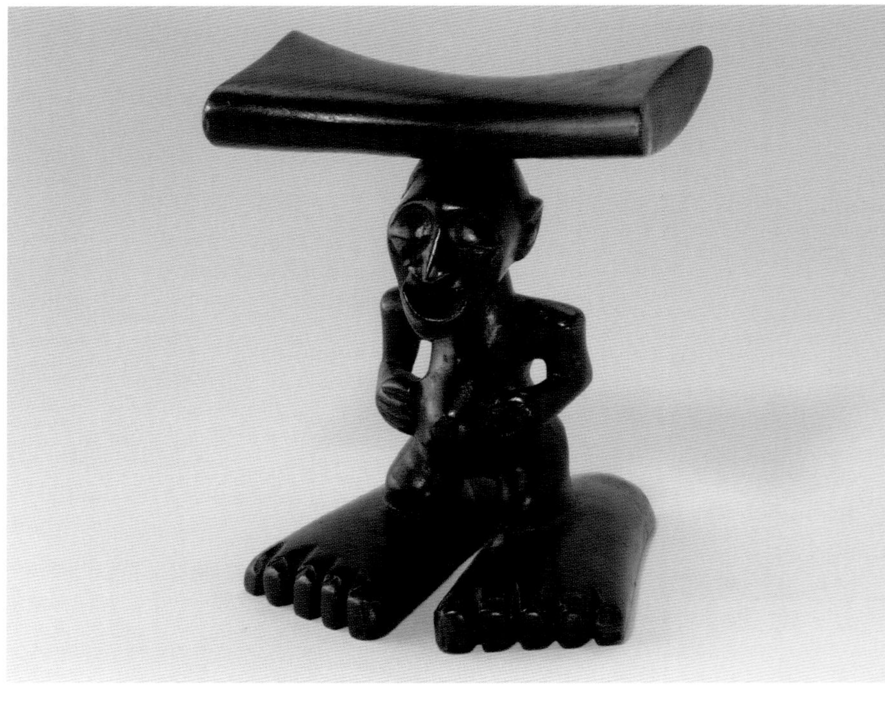

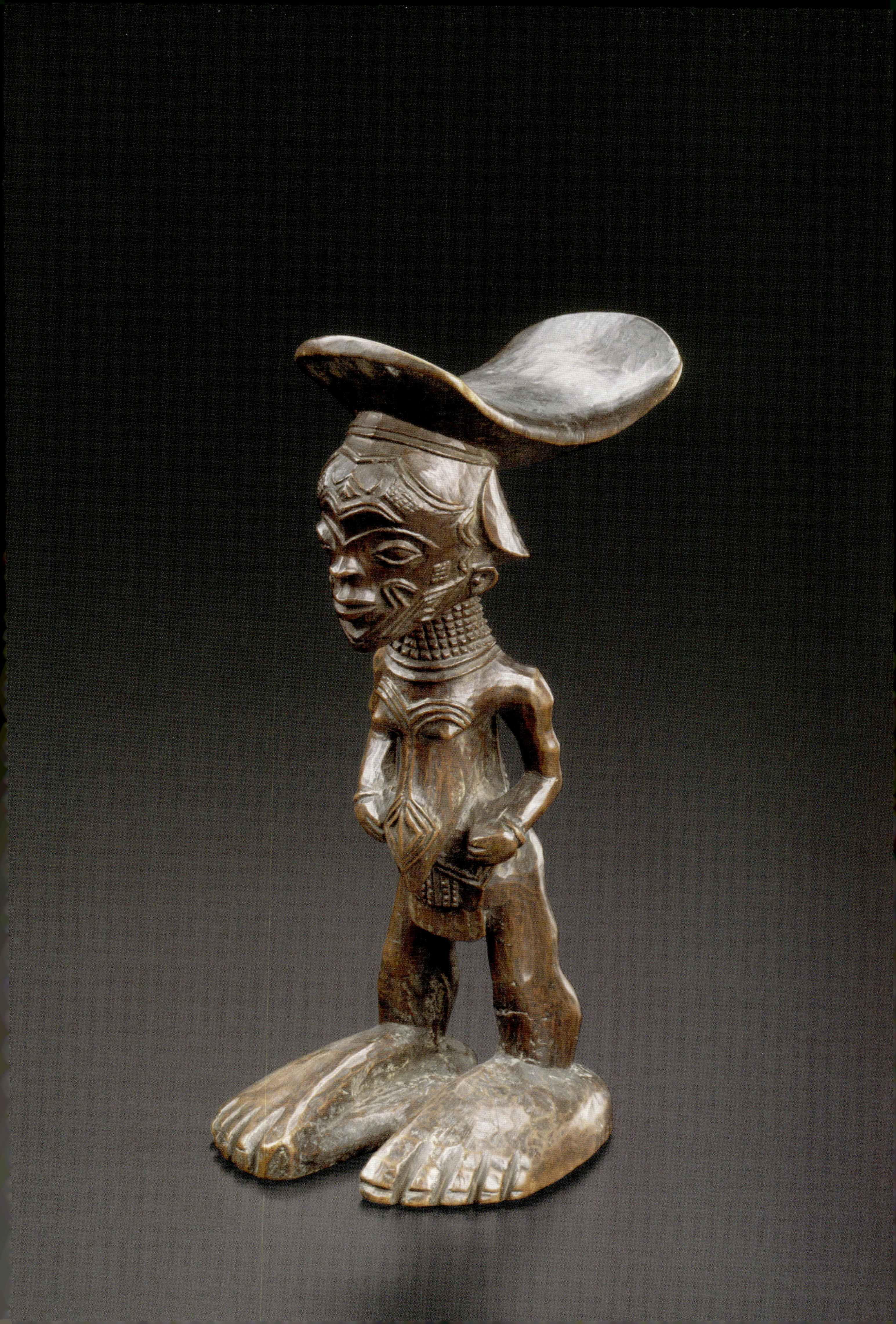

197. Zande artist
Democratic Republic of the Congo
Box-headrest
Wood and bark, 38 cm
Musée Royal de l'Afrique Centrale, Tervuren

198. Shona artist
Zimbabwe, 19th c.
Headrest
Wood, 13 cm
Private collection

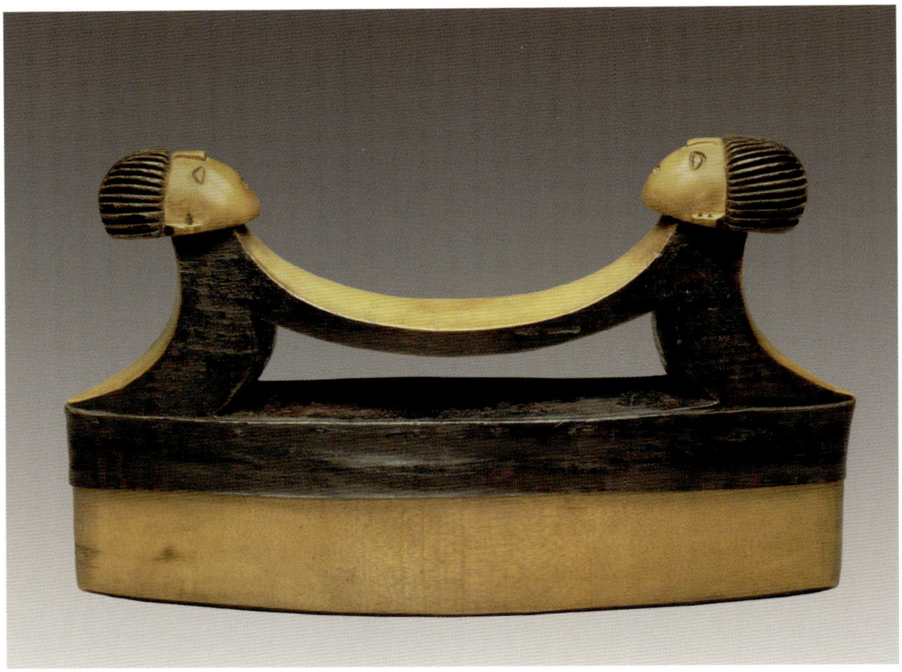

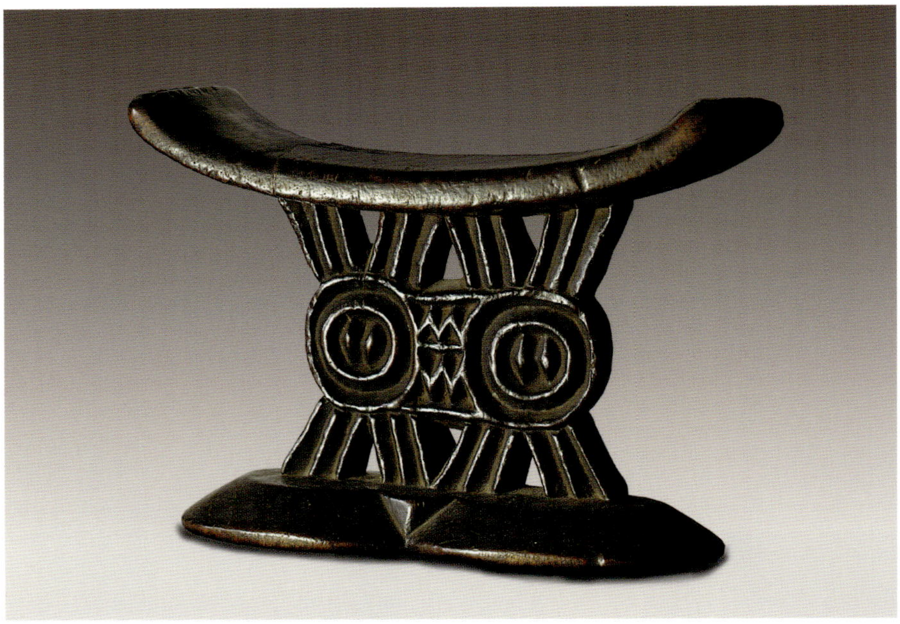

shaped hairstyles, and especially the volumes of the narrow entwined arms, counter the static quality and apparent detachment suggested in the front view by their forward-staring eyes and mainly vertical arrangement of their parallel stocky volumes. These already seem squashed by the weight that the board they support is to sustain.

What the two figures represent is not certain. A similar headrest, perhaps by the same artist, is in the National Museum of African Art in Washington, D.C.[9]

The artist who sculpted the impressive Songye headrest, on exhibit at the Pavillon des Sessions in the Louvre (no. 195), certainly had a personal idea of the man. His image is the opposite of the two serene women in the previous headrest. The features of this sexless figure are aggressive and his body becomes heavier lower down until it explodes in outsize rectangular feet set at right angles to the board. Everything is integrated in a volumetrically and figuratively coherent composition, which, in addition to providing a solid base for the upper structure, expresses a feeling of authority and power.

This headrest, sculpted by an artist who was probably active at the end of the 19th century,[10] was in the famous collection that belonged to Dr Stephen Chauvet before 1923.

The rare Luluwa headrest is governed by a different spatial concept (no. 196). Since it does not have the usual circular base, here too the static bal-

Pages 230–231
199. Kuba artist
Western Kasai, Democratic Republic of the Congo
Libation goblet in the shape of a human head
Wood and copper, 19 cm
Musée Royal de l'Afrique Centrale, Tervuren

200. Kuba artist
Western Kasai, Democratic Republic of the Congo
Anthropomorphic libation goblet
Wood, 21 cm
Musée Royal de l'Afrique Centrale, Tervuren

ance is created by the enormous feet of the forward-leaning figure that supports the cantilevered concave headboard.

The oblique body and two horizontal elements form a volumetrically daring yet visually harmonious structure whose surface is embellished by reliefs typical of the figures in this ethnic group, though here used with discretion. Constantine Petridis[11] considers it possible that this piece was created as a status symbol rather than for a practical purpose.

The human figure is also found in the curious Zande box-headrest (no. 197), though in a stylized form. This unusual combination of functions and its large size make this piece uncommon, but what makes it a true work of art is the imaginative and precise use of volumes. The long arms of two human figures create a single, smooth, ribbon-like volume that supports the sleeper's neck and connect naturally to the two lateral blocks that represent the bodies. These lean forwards (the curved backs have the same radius as the arms) to form a harmonious whole with the base. The upward-facing, delicately featured heads provide confirmation that the oval design was a deliberate choice by the artist.

In contrast, the human figure is not represented in the Shona headrest (no. 198), which is quite different from the three previous ones. It too was sculpted in the 19th century, as can be deduced from the thick patina, wear and tear and the writing on the remains of the label stuck to the underside of the base.

Its shape is dictated by its function and by the figurative tradition of the artist's community. However, he has turned these constraints into a stimulus to use the elements at his disposal to advantage and create a work that is both functional and elegant.

The harmonious functional and decorative elements – concentric circles, parallel lines and a sort of honeycomb pattern – save it from being merely useful and make it an exquisite example of applied art.

Similarities in shape and some decorative elements, particularly along the edges and in the centre of the board, suggest that at least two other pieces are by the same sculptor.[12]

Libation goblets

The goblets for libations of palm wine produced by certain peoples in the Democratic Republic of the Congo, particularly the Kuba, for the members of the wealthy ruling classes, are the most famous in the whole of Africa. They are both practical objects and symbols of the power and wealth that defined their owners' social standing.

The humble material of which they are made is wood rather than the precious metals used for antique Mediterranean goblets that had the same purpose, but this does not diminish the fascination and beauty given by the opulence and originality of their forms and their refined geometric decoration. The most spectacular goblets are those in the shape of a head or a human figure.

The serene, somewhat stylized lines of the first example (no. 199) – an ideal figure rather than a portrait – follow the usual conventions of Kuba statuary. Special attention is paid to the elements that suggest authority, such as vertical scarification from the forehead to the tip of the nose, emphasized here by the copper strip indicative of the owner's social rank, and the hair shaved at an acute angle on the temples, adapted to and enhancing the particular shape of the skull. The reliefs and hollows that delineate the facial features create a harmonious design in keeping with the elegant simplicity of the cylindrical stem.

The stem of the second goblet (no. 200) is formed by the lower section of a male body, which makes it resemble a Gothic caprice or one of those disturbing figures in the paintings of Hieronymus Bosch. In this African sculptor's work, however, the powerful pelvis, the penis and the sturdy volume of the large almost webbed feet emphasize the figure's physicality, and contribute

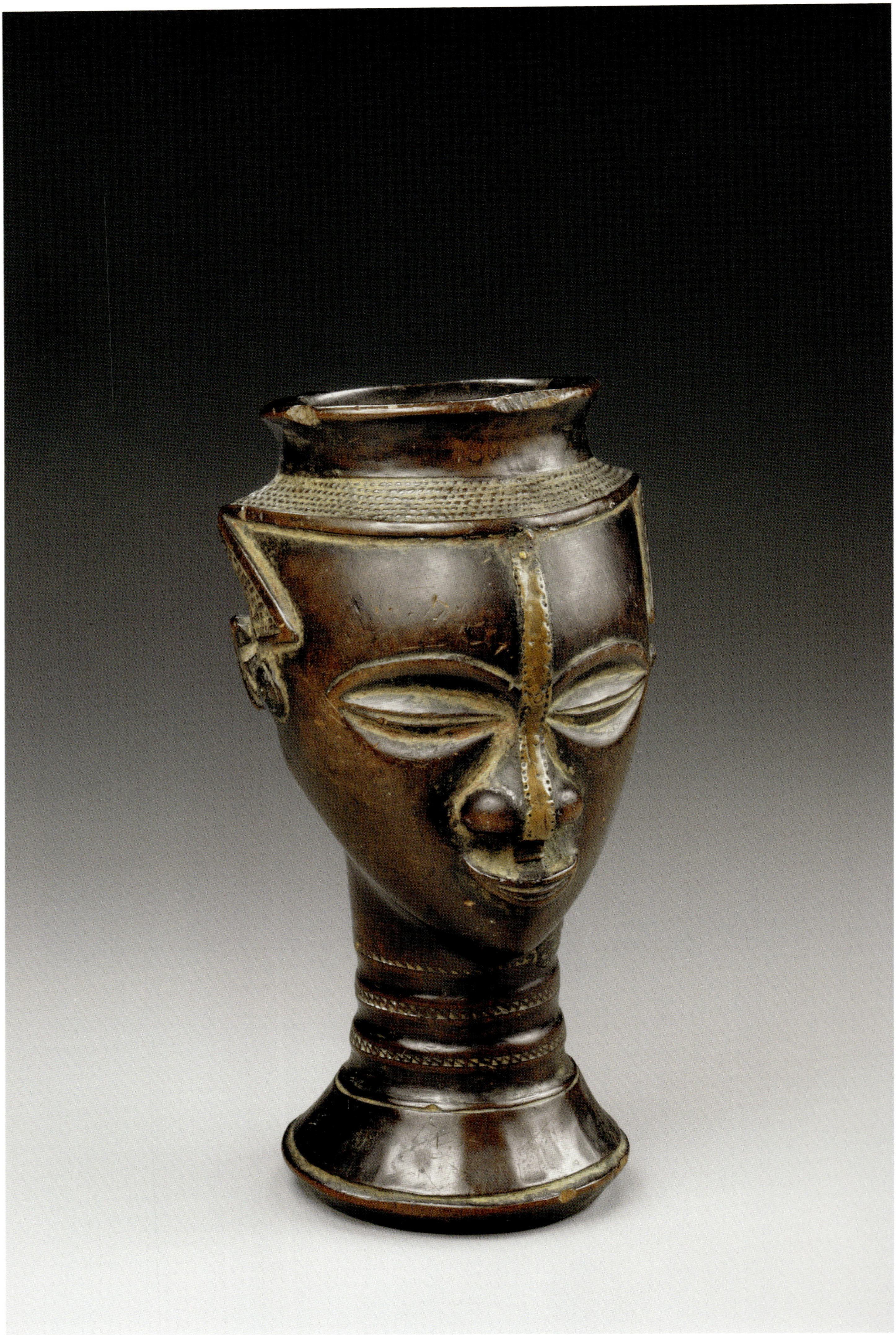

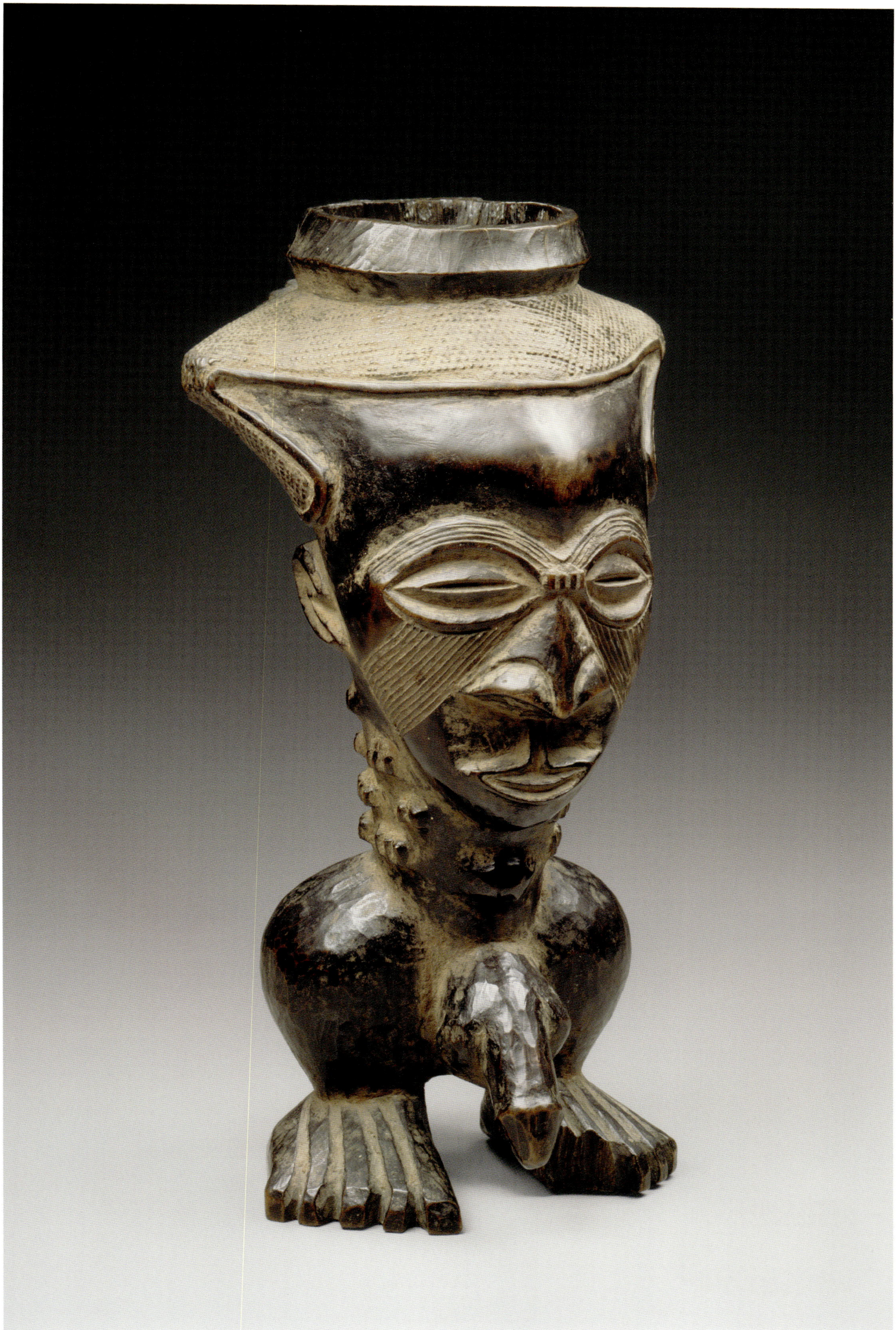

201. Luba artist
Democratic Republic of the Congo
Libation goblet in the shape of a head
Wood, l. 20 cm
Private collection

202. Kuba artist
Western Kasai, Democratic Republic of the Congo
Cosmetic box
Wood with natural patina, 21.6 cm
Staatliches Museum für Völkerkunde, Munich

Bottom
203. Chokwe artist
Angola, 19th c.
Mortar-snuffbox
Wood, h. 14 cm
Casa Museu Teixeira Lopes, Vila Nova de Gaia, Porto

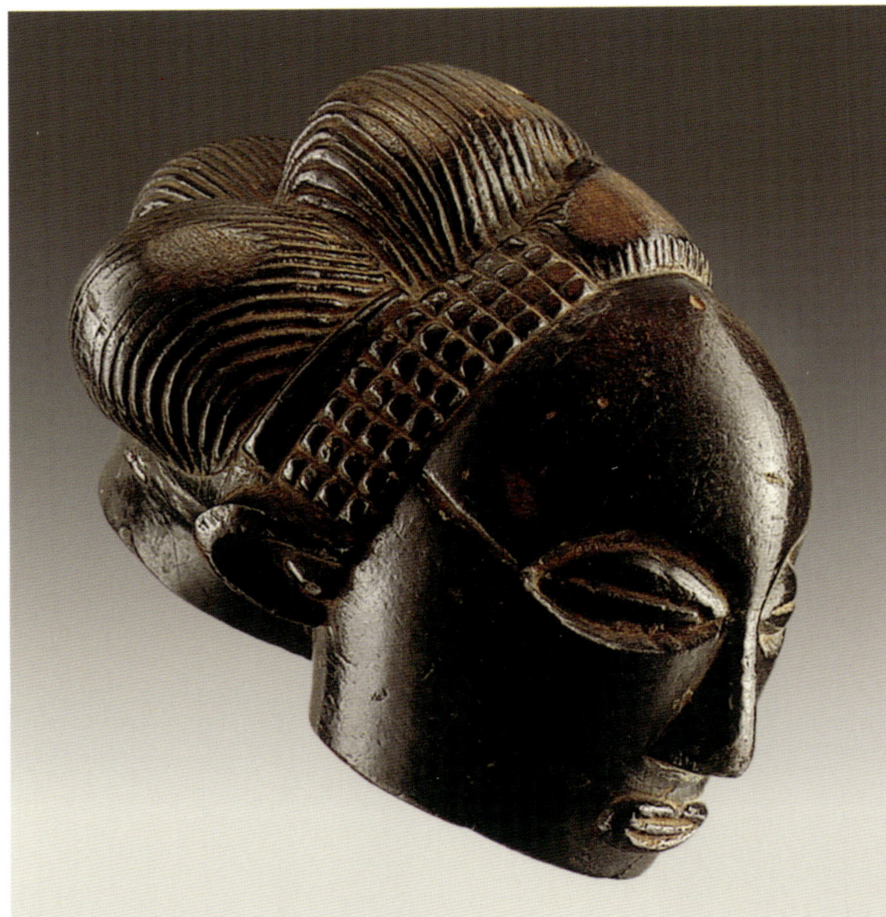

to the impression of strength conveyed by the large head with its resolute features. The entire work is faithful to the established figurative tradition, in which every element, including the scarification marks, is part of a coherent design.

The Luba goblet (no. 201) is completely different functionally and formally since it is horizontal in design in order to accommodate two vessels side by side. The function has determined the form and the beautiful voluminous coiffure, whose chignon is enhanced by parallel lines, sets off the smooth perfection of the serene face dominated by the large, half-closed eyes.

Goblets like this one, which are extremely rare and, according to Albert Maesen[13], were kept in a secret place, were used during the enthronement ceremonies of new sovereigns and on important occasions when honour was paid to the spirits of the ancestors.

The sex of this figure is uncertain, but scholars are inclined to think it is a female.

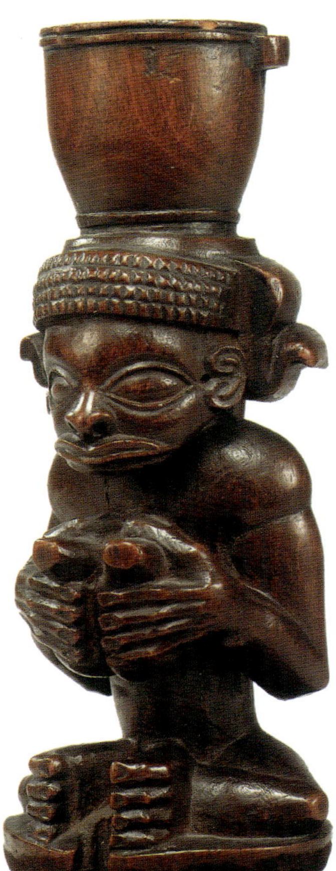

Cosmetics boxes

The same successful combination of geometric decoration and the representation of human features is found in other Kuba wooden artefacts. In the most successful cases, they are true works of art, like this beautiful wooden box (no. 202). It was probably made to contain *tukula* (red *pterocarpus* powder mixed with fat), which was used as a cosmetic.

The conventionally stylized facial features – there are similarities to the illustrated goblets – are slightly raised on the shield-shaped lid polished by handling, and blend harmoniously with the dynamic, geometric motifs artistically distributed over the whole surface.

Mortar-snuffbox

The Chokwe artists of the golden age of the Moxico School in Angola (there are three examples of their works in this volume, nos. 167–169) also carved tiny figures that convey the same feeling of controlled power as the larger

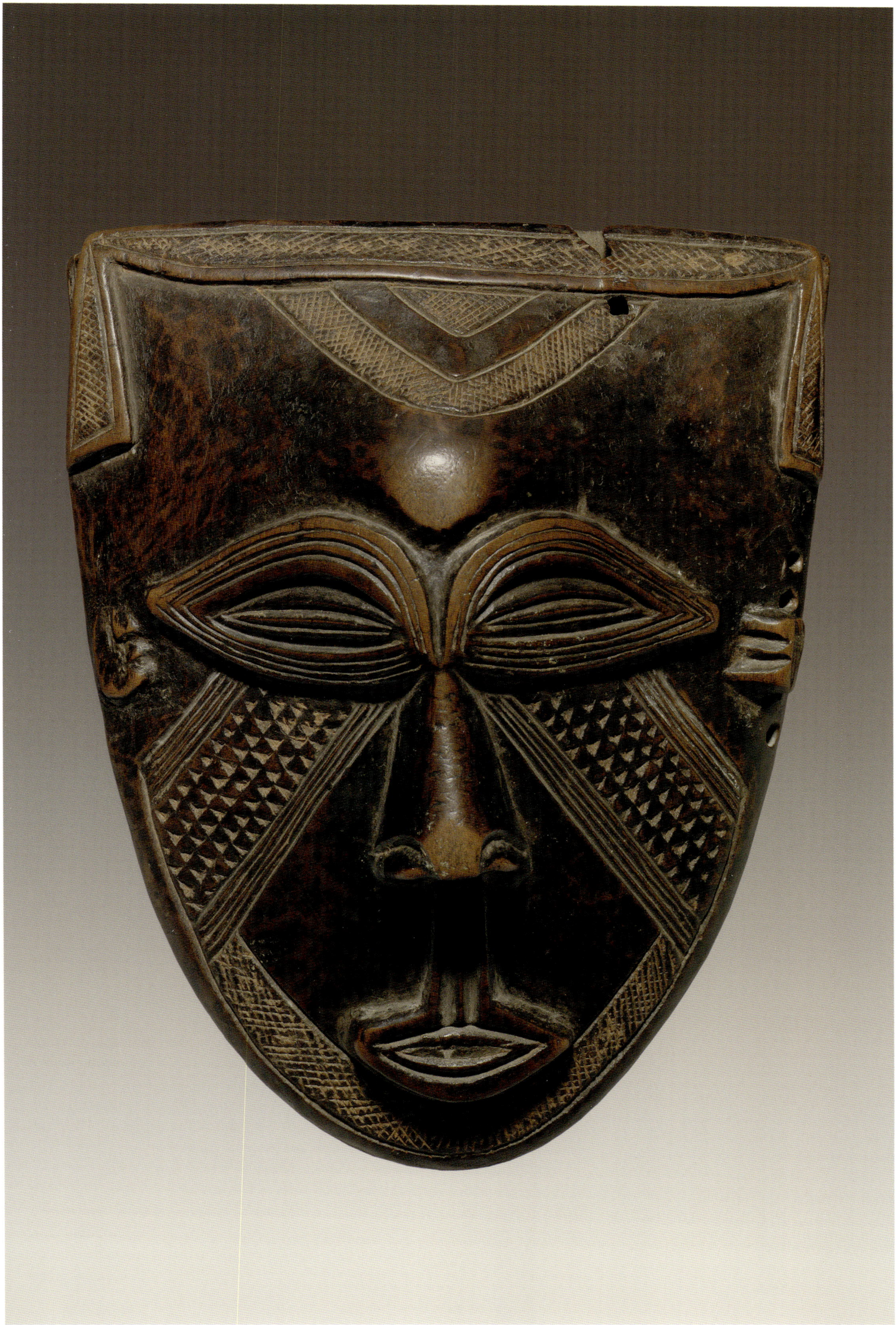

204. Zulu artist
Republic of South Africa
Spoon
Wood, 57 cm
Musée du Louvre, Pavillon des Sessions, Paris (on deposit from the Musée national d'Histoire naturelle, Paris)

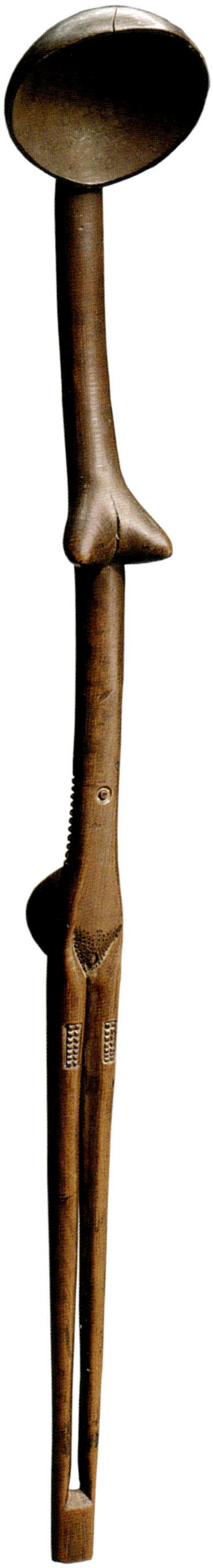

sculptures. A perfect example is given by the mortar-snuffbox (no. 203) in the form of a monumental female figure just a few centimetres in height, which could be made ten times bigger and not lose any of its refined perfection.

It possesses all the elements that distinguish classical Chokwe sculpture: powerful shoulders and forearms, large hands holding a sanza (finger piano), large feet rendered with strong horizontal volumes and a strong-willed face. The expression is achieved through the deft use of distortion and exaggeration, as in the overlarge but thin-lipped mouth, the large eyes and the unusually elegant ears.

The vessel surmounting the figure that determines its function (its lid is missing), plays the same volumetric role as the large coiffures that usually decorate works by the Moxico School, but here the upper section has been reduced for functional and compositional reasons.

Spoons

The Zulu spoon now in the Louvre (no. 204), whose purpose is unknown, is, in my opinion, the most extraordinary African spoon on account of the boldness of its design, the simplicity of its volumes and its superb craftsmanship.

The slim and slightly arched handle is a tensed but not rigid human body, its upward movement culminating in the hemispherical, hollow head-cum-bowl. The small conical breasts and diminutive buttocks – the arms have been deliberately omitted – are the only obtruding volumes and give proportion to the structure. With the subtle incisions that mark the navel, the genitals and the scarification (perhaps indicating membership of a caste), they create a fascinating figure, a dancer on her points.

If the spoon were the work of a Western artist, we would have no difficulty in labelling it generically as "surrealist". The African sculptor who made it never came into contact with the "masters" in Paris, yet in creating this artefact to meet the practical and ritual needs of his community, he obeyed the imperative of perfection that drives true artists in every society.

Bowls

The attraction of this odd-looking bowl (no. 205), whose function is not known, is its unusual shape. However, it is evident from the form and the position of its different parts that the artist intended to evoke the human body: the head, the torso with its minute breasts, the abdomen and the legs.

If this interpretation is correct, the procedure is the same as the one that Picasso and Giacometti adopted (here again we can draw an inevitable though perhaps inappropriate comparison with Western art), the former in his very famous *Guitar* of 1912 and the latter in *Spoon-Woman* of 1926–27. In the work by the African sculptor, the head and abdomen are also represented by hollows rather than volumes, with the same attention and, perhaps, with a little more human warmth.

The procedure is reversed on the back where two square reliefs represent the woman's hair and back.

Heddle pulleys for looms

Tiny pulleys for looms, artefacts that are widespread throughout Sub-Saharan Africa, are often exquisite works of art. This quality, that has no influence on function, is therefore proof of the aesthetic sense and need for beauty among the African peoples who use this artefact. The examples decorated with human and animal heads produced by the Guro and Baule sculptors from the Ivory Coast are the most conspicuous evidence of this.

A section of the exhibition 'Die Kunst der Guro Elfenbeinküste', mounted at the Museum Rietberg in Zurich in 1985, contained over one hundred pulleys, all of them different, which confirmed both the artists' inventiveness and their creative skill.

A delightful small female head is the decoration on the first pulley shown here (no. 206). The facial features, rendered with subtle physiognomic traits

205. Zulu artist
Republic of South Africa
Bowl
Wood, 31 cm
Horstmann Collection, Zug

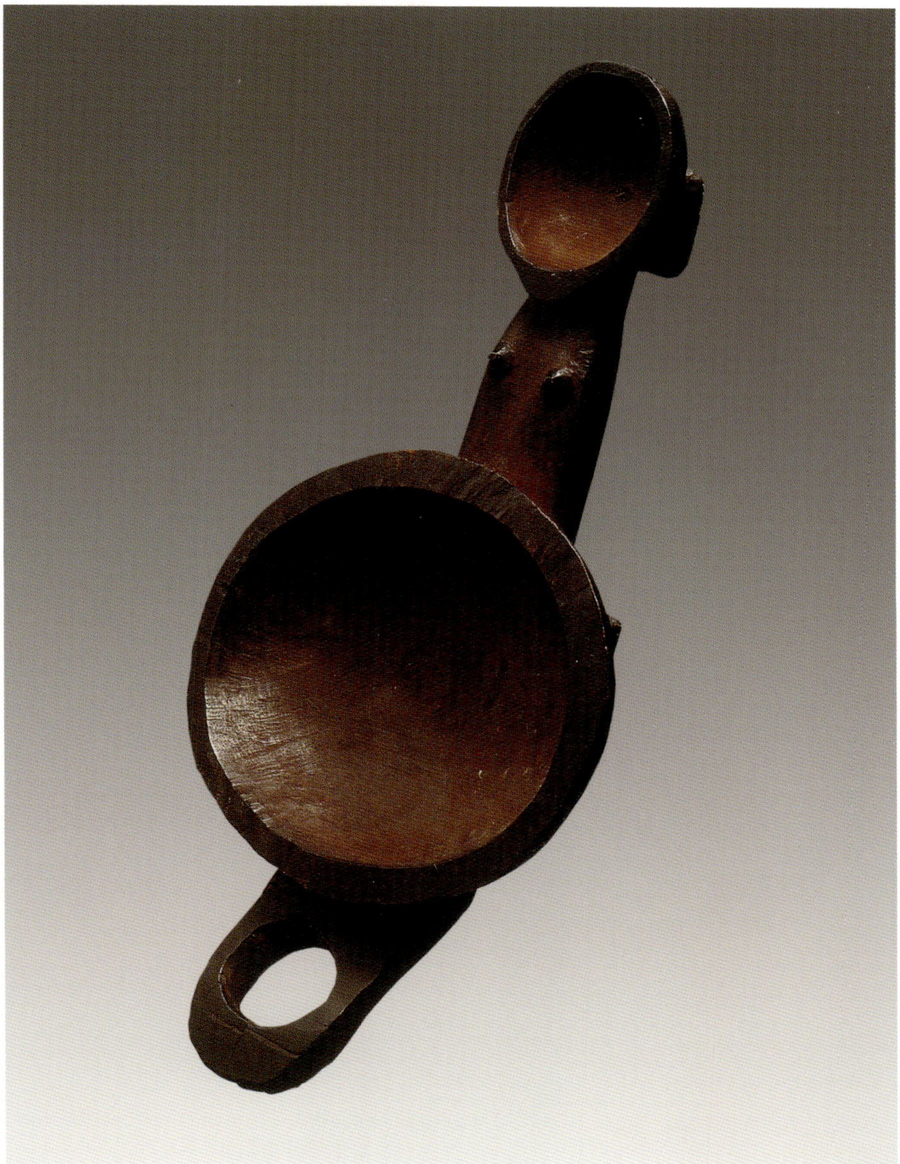

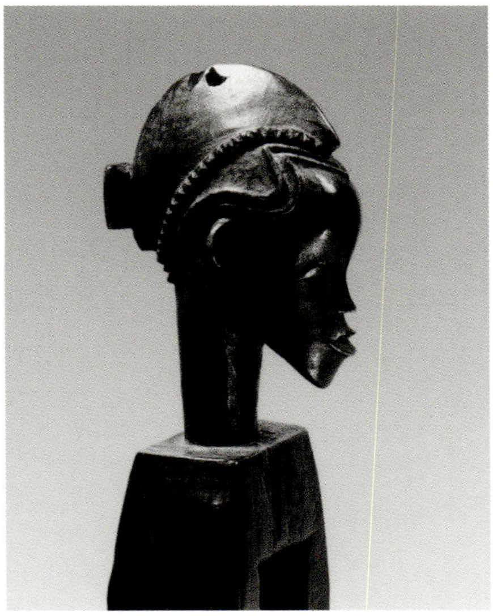

206. Guro artist
Ivory Coast
Heddle pulley with human head
Wood, 12.1 cm
Museum Rietberg, Zurich (formerly in the Han Coray Collection)

that do not detract from the elegant profile, are the same as those of large statuary. The volume of the high forehead is amplified by the relief of the wavy hair and extended by the crest that harmoniously follows the curve down to the nape of the neck, where it ends in a horizontal chignon.

The ornament on the second pulley (no. 207) is the small head of an animal that has been identified by various scholars as a bat or a fox, but, in my opinion, is a hare. The simplified volume – set horizontally on a taut neck – becomes, as if by magic, the expressive face of the lively animal thanks to the addition of pointed ears, two simple but effective triangular incisions for the eyes and the calibrated opening of the mouth, with its tiny, even and fierce-looking teeth.

The third pulley (no. 208) combines two themes. A human head wearing an animal mask is the decoration in which the human and the animal become naturally fused. This is a rare reference to Guro religious ideas. The monumental rigidity of the body of this small artefact is redeemed by the elegant decoration on the long ringed neck, surmounted by a sphere that simulates the head.

Musical instruments

Like the other artefacts illustrated above, certain musical instruments can also be considered works of art due to the originality of their conception, their refined form and decoration. In this case, too, only four examples will be given to illustrate these qualities, the first of which is the Baule gong mallet (no. 209).

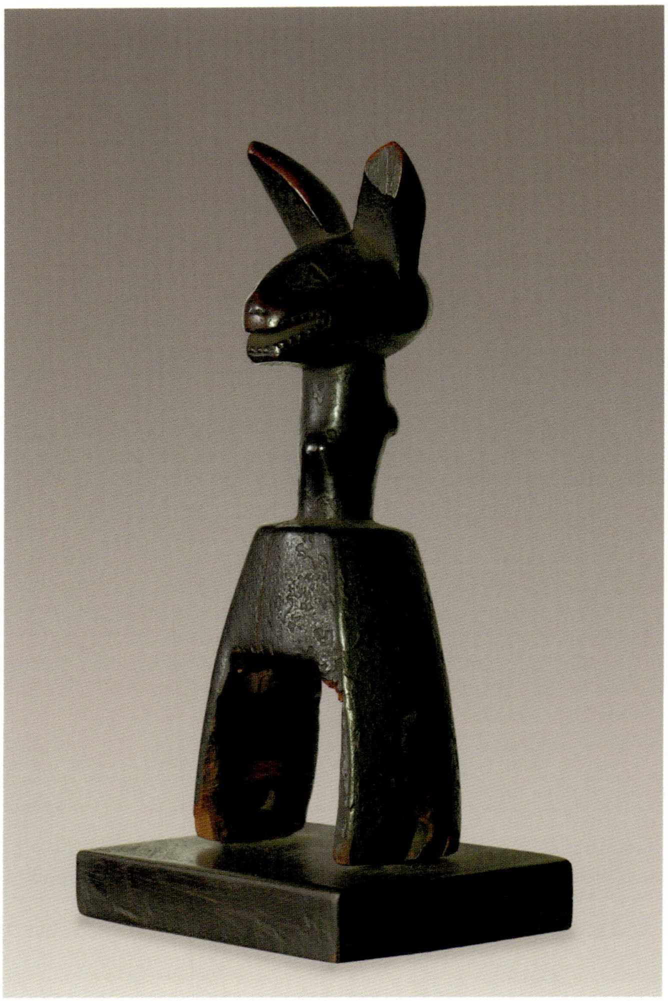

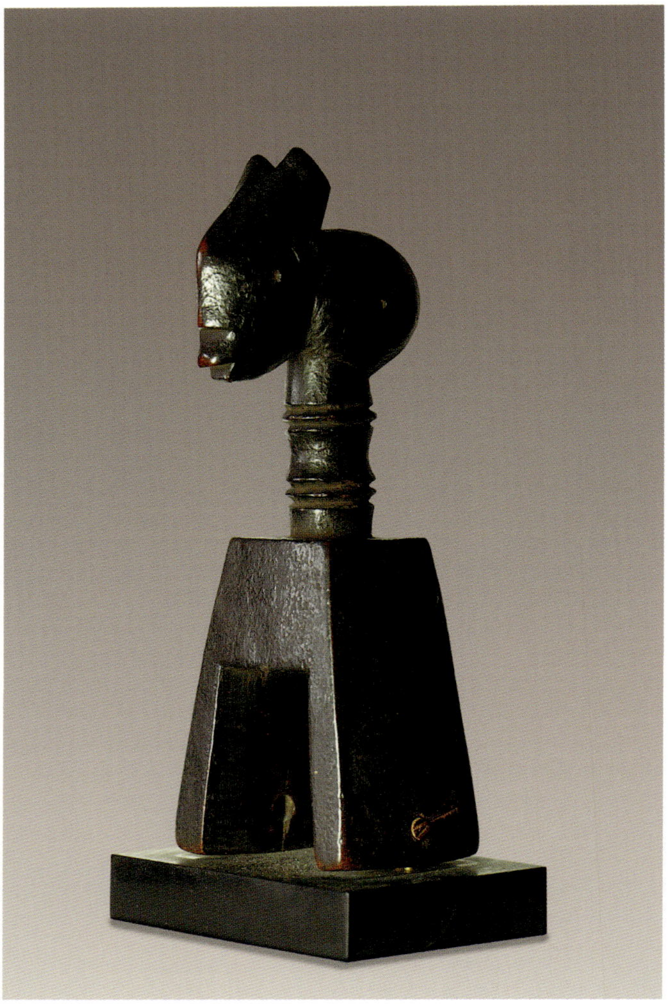

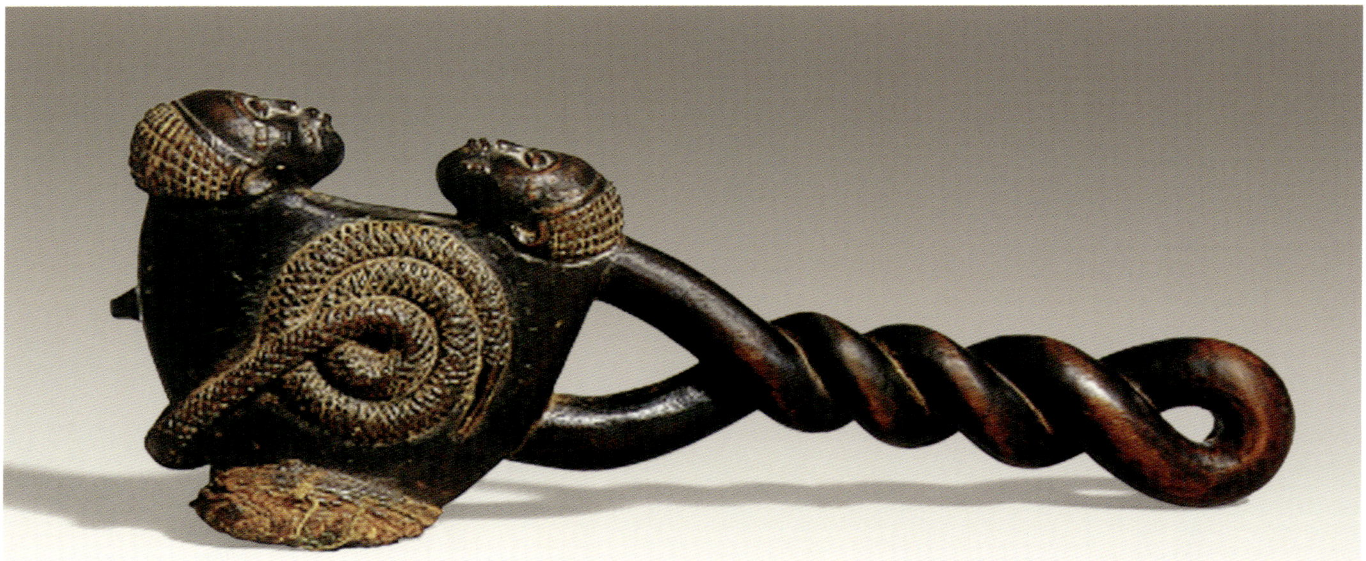

207. Guro artist
Ivory Coast
Heddle pulley with hare's head
Wood, 16.6 cm
Private collection

208. Guro artist
Ivory Coast
Heddle pulley with masked head
Wood, 15.5 cm
Private collection

209. Baule artist
Ivory Coast
Mallet for gong
Wood and fabric, 23 cm
Private collection

210. Zande artist
Democratic Republic of the Congo
Anthropomorphic sanza
Wood and bamboo, 61 cm
Musée Royal de l'Afrique Centrale,
Tervuren

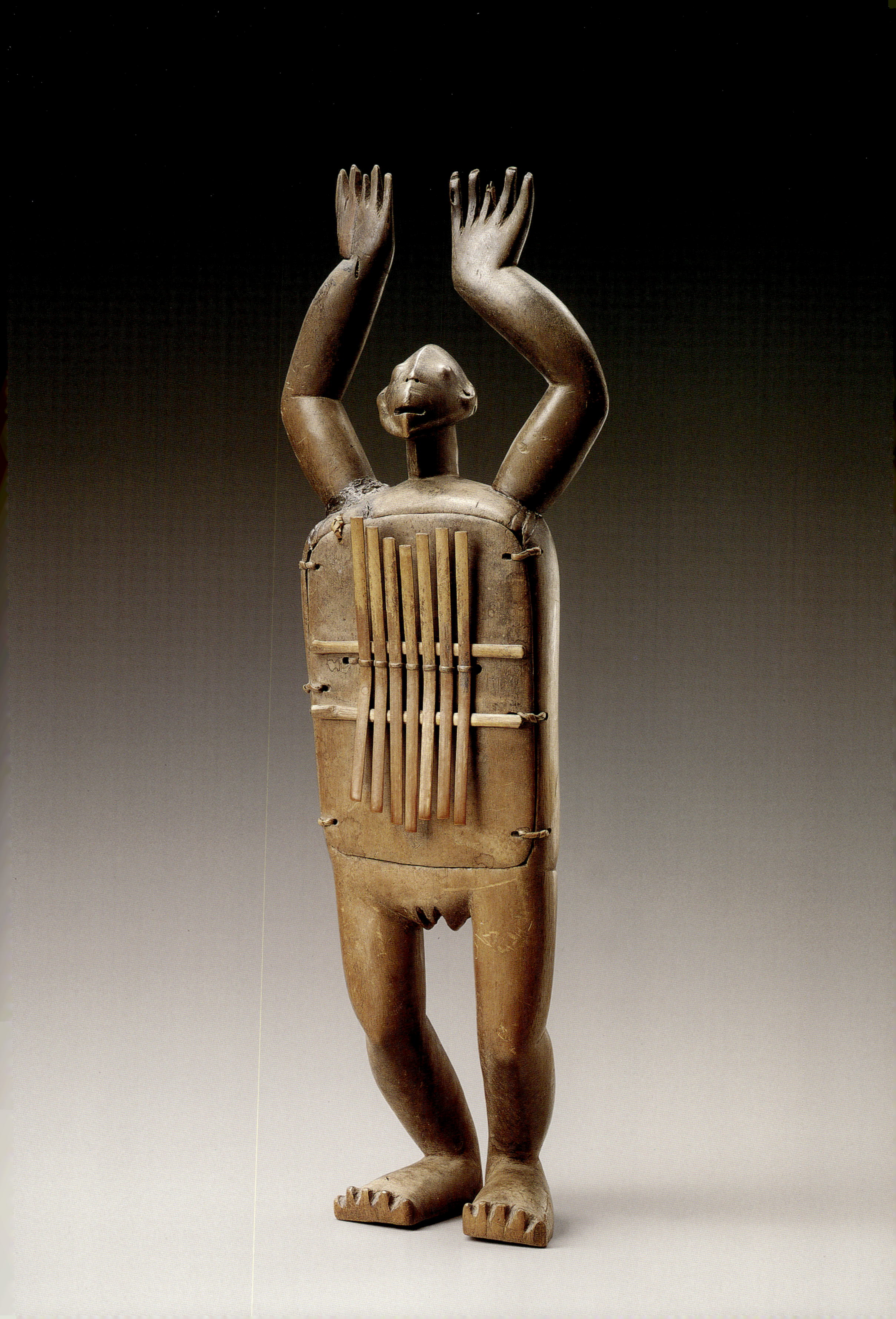

Its extremely inventive and skilful sculptor has concentrated an entire world in the small volume of the mallet head, attached to an elegant spiral handle. There are two human heads with perfectly delineated features, an enormous snake with a coiled body stretching from one side of the mallet head to the other to bite the leg of an antelope that is also being attacked by a leopard. The texture of the hair, animal's fur and reptile's coils enhances the gleam of the smooth surfaces and creates a link between the images that make up the scene.

The second musical instrument illustrated here is a sanza, which is very common in Africa. It consists of a simple sound box with lamellas attached to the top which, when plucked, emit a sound that is amplified by the sound box. The sanza in the Tervuren Museum (no. 210) is exceptional both in size and its unusual design. It has human features that do not serve a functional purpose. The form it takes perhaps corresponds to some unidentified cultural/religious symbolism but, given the result, it is undoubtedly dictated by an aesthetic need on the part of the commissioner or the artist.

The latter was certainly ingenious, since he has combined music and dance in a most convincing whole. The notion of movement is rendered by the slight flexion of the legs planted on two large feet for stability, and especially by the arms raised in a gesture extended by the open hands. These are enormous compared to the small head, rather like that of a mysterious insect, to emphasize the power and position of the limbs and accentuate their expressiveness.

By contrast, the beauty of the Mangbetu drum (no. 211) lies in the perfection of its sculptural form, which, because of the absence of any figurative decoration, can be appreciated without distraction. The perfect oval of the

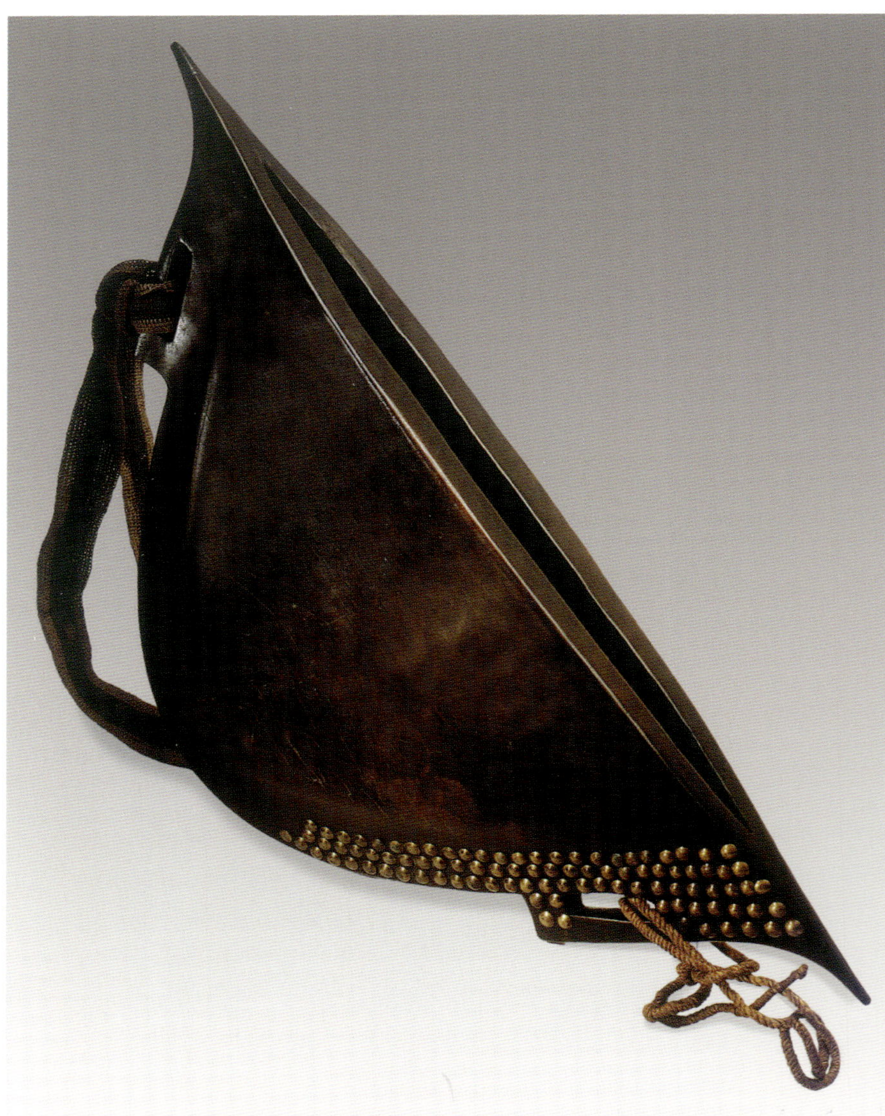

211. Mangbetu artist
Democratic Republic of the Congo
Slit drum
Wood, brass tacks and fibres, 66 cm
Formerly in the M. and D. Ginzberg Collection, New York

212. Yangere artist
Central African Republic
Slit drum
Wood, 231 cm
Musée du Louvre, Pavillon des Sessions, Paris (on deposit from the Musée du Quai Branly; gift of Pierre Savorgnan de Brazza)

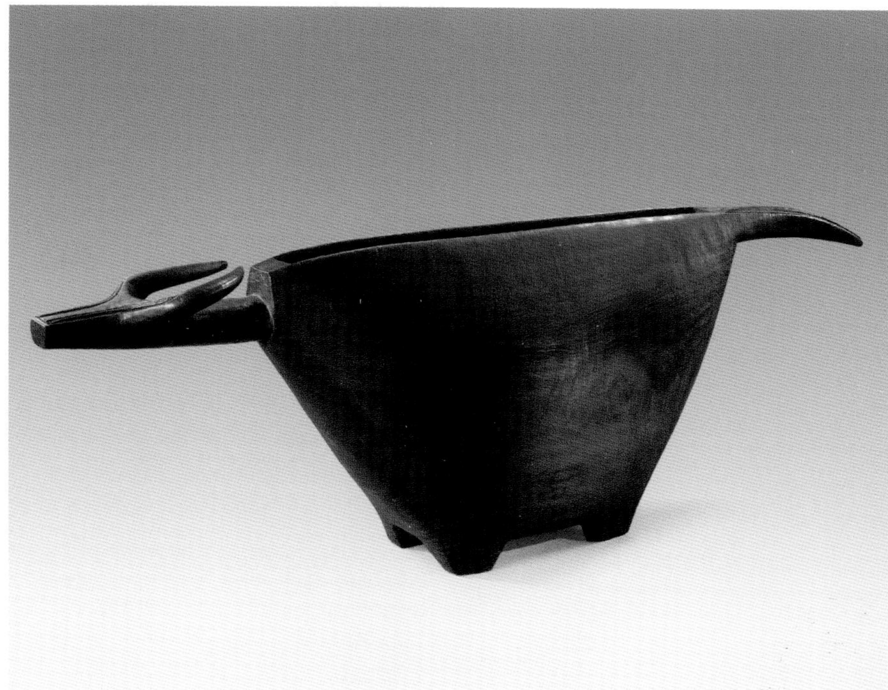

slightly rounded body of the instrument is reprised in the opposite direction in the curve of the two handles that become narrower towards the top and end in a point – a daring solution that makes the work more attractive. Drums like this were usually part of a musical group that played during festivities and special ritual ceremonies.

In addition to being symbols of power, large drums made out of a single piece of wood were used in the central regions of Africa mainly to send messages over a great distance. The example attributed probably to a Yangere artist (no. 212), which is extraordinary in size but even more so in sculptural quality, was collected by Pierre Savorgnan de Brazza (who established the French colonies in Central Africa) and donated to what was then the Musée du Trocadéro, later the Musée de l'Homme, in Paris. From here, in 2000, it was transferred with 45 other works to the Louvre to evince the excellence of African sculpture alongside masterpieces from all over the world.

This instrument is the size of a buffalo whose powerful form has been reinvented in simple volumes. The animal's body is a compact block with trapezoid, slightly rounded sides which, seen from the side, widens unnaturally towards the top as if it were about to take off. The head with its beautiful horns and the pointed tail furrowed with appropriate incisions accentuate the work's fluidity, so that it looks as though it had been modelled in a wind tunnel, the forces of which have left traces on the surface of the large drum.

[1] The National Commission for Museums and Monuments, Nigeria.
[2] Two bangles and a bracelet with a decoration similar to that on the vessels are held by the ethnographic museum in Copenhagen. In 1689 they were in the Kunstkammer of the kings of Denmark. See Bassani 2000, nos. 17, 18, 19.
[3] Drewal, Pemberton, Abiodun 1989, p. 108.
[4] After his conversion to Islam in the early 20th century, Njoya took the title of sultan. Among other things, Njoya invented a Bamum script.
[5] Artists from the peoples ruled by the Bamum: the former were wood carvers, the latter were specialized in decorating the works with multicoloured beads sewn onto a fabric that covered the sculptures.
[6] Similar pairs of snakes frequently decorate Bamum thrones. There is an example of this, without the bead decoration, in the Musée du Quai Branly, Paris, another now in the Rautenstrauch-Joest-Museum, Cologne (probably a gift from Sultan Njoya to the German governor of Cameroon, Jensko von Puttkamer) and a third in the Musée Barbier-Mueller, Geneva.
[7] Sotheby's, Paris, 6/6/2005, no. 28. Although the seat was acquired in the remote Yoko region, the outpost of the Fulbe lamidate of Tibati (Harter 1986, p. 168), it is definitely a Bamum artefact.
[8] Felix 1990, p. 370.
[9] See Nooter Roberts, Roberts 1996, p. 100.
[10] A plaster cast of the work was in the Musée du Trocadéro in 1892 (Bouloure 2000[c], p. 193).
[11] Petridis in *Tervuren Museum* 1996, no. 100.
[12] See Bassani 2007, no. 66, and Ginzberg 2000, p. 42.
[13] *Trésors* 1995, nos. 158-159.

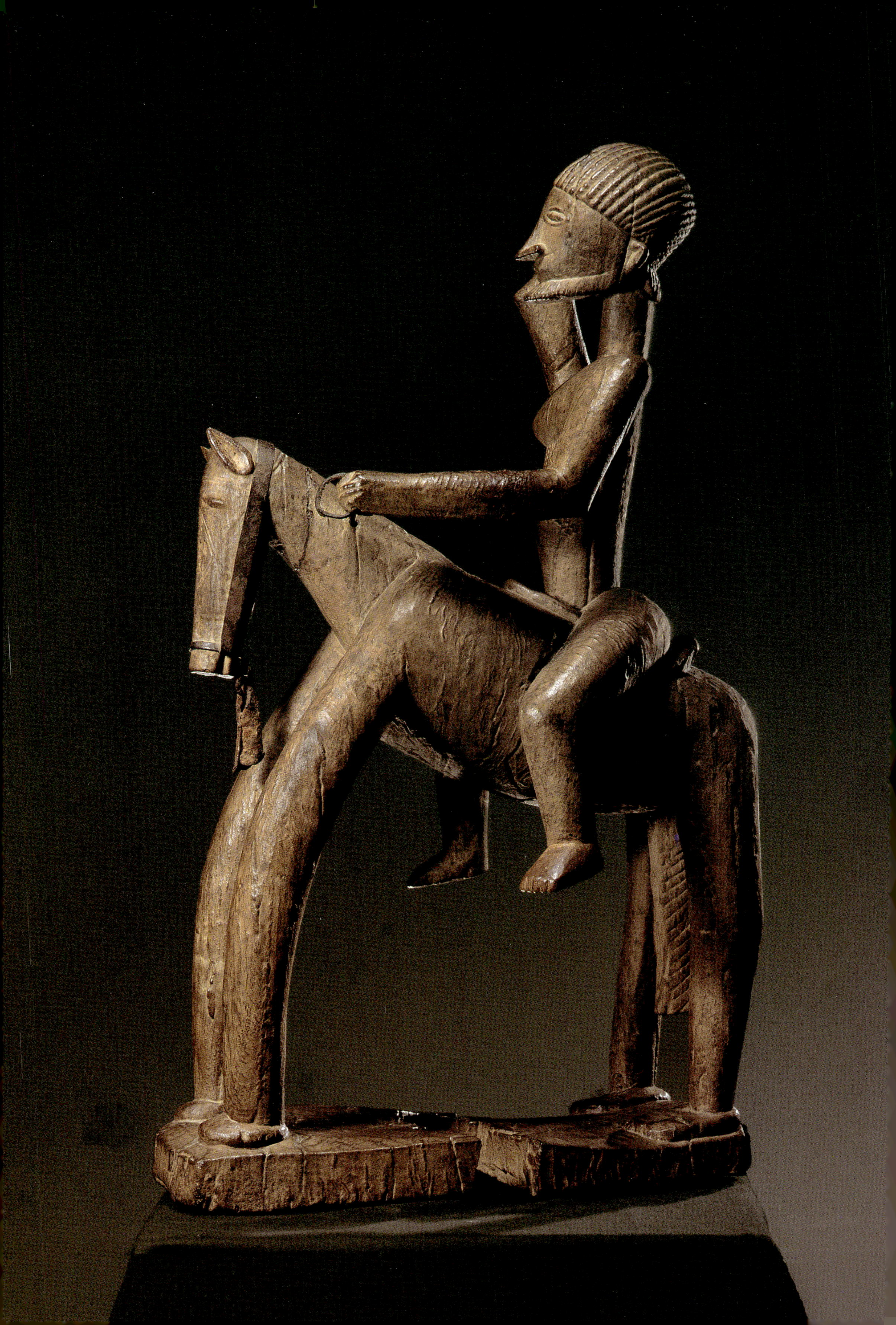

A Variety of Formal Solutions

The works in this section, which are only a sample and an incomplete one at that, give an overview of the variety of formal solutions invented by traditional African sculptors to meet their society's demand for artworks. This multiplicity has already emerged in previous chapters, in which the works themselves illustrate the diverse aspects of the artists' creativity.

The apparent dearth of subjects in African art of the past, which is almost solely devoted to the human figure, is redeemed by the extraordinary range of figurative inventions that combine tradition, imagination, faithfulness to reality, transgression and expressive choices that reveal the artists' intention of both arousing an aesthetic emotion and responding to the spiritual and societal needs of his community.

Terms such as realist, expressionist, cubist, surrealist and abstract, which are customarily adopted, with various shades of meaning, by Western art critics may be useful – though reductive – in describing African sculptures, but only when alluding to generic formal affinities with works created in the Western world. It is incorrect and misleading to suggest that they are universal categories known to traditional African artists, since the latter were unaware of their meaning, indeed their very existence. Hence, I use them here simply because I am unaware of more suitable linguistic expressions. However, when one looks for African works that exemplify these terms, one realizes just how inappropriate the terms are.

It must be added that it is not at all easy to enclose works of African art within the stylistic boundaries given above due to the variety and often combination of forms they represent. African sculptors combine creative freedom with a respect for their community's canons but in many cases they go beyond these to produce new, highly original forms that often challenge conventional models. These are then adopted over time by artists in the community to become the norm. Moreover, the so-called purity of tribal styles increasingly proves to be an arbitrary simplification by the West. The more we examine works produced by the same group, the more differences emerge, because African art, as we know it, is the fruit of a dynamic, age-old process driven by external influences, borrowing and rejection.

Stylistic regions are difficult to delimit, partly because their boundaries often differ from geographical or ethnic ones. They are also characterized by areas of transition created by the migratory movements of peoples and the mobility of individual artists. The latter have always travelled, mutually influenced each other and assimilated new ideas and new formal solutions, just as they have in Europe.

The works chosen for this section reflect my own experiences and preferences, consequently they only partially represent the dominant trends in the art of the different peoples and the continent as a whole.

213. Dogon artist
Mali, 15th–16th c. (?)
Equestrian figure
Wood and iron, 75 cm
Private collection

Realism

After examining thousands of sculptures, mostly of human figures, one realizes that the majority can be described generically as "realistic" in the sense that the

214–215. Baule artist
Ivory Coast
Male figure and female figure
Wood, kaolin, fibres and glass beads, 55.2 cm and 52.1 cm
The Metropolitan Museum of Art, New York

essential parts of the human body are always recognizable, though subjected to simplification and distortion. Of course, we are not talking about a faithful, unimaginative copy of reality and it is precisely the expressive distortions, however great or small they might be, that evince how each artist has produced an individual interpretation of the canons that are part of his community's heritage.

Where Nigerian art of the past is concerned, the reader is referred to the brief descriptions given in the first chapter; it should also be noted that the creations by Ife artists (nos. 28–35) fall perfectly into the category of "realism" if it is qualified by the adjective "idealized".

The same description also fits the earliest works of the Benin sculptors (nos. 37–38, 40–41, 43–46) to a certain degree, while in those belonging to the late period there is an increasing tendency to treat the subject in a celebratory and impersonal manner that gives it a certain stiffness. This can be seen in head no. 42 in which the residual human element in the face is dominated by celebratory attributes like the necklace and the headgear.

The common denominator of works created by the artists from the early Mali peoples (the Dogon and others who either succeeded each other or coexisted in the Bandiagara region throughout the second millennium AD) is a geometrized realism combined with a severe solemnity that transforms every image of a woman into an ancestral mother and that of every man into a priest or mythical hero. The horseman illustrated here (no. 213) is the quintessence of this style. In Edenic nudity, the man sits proudly on his powerful steed, while the ascetic aura that emanates from his beautiful, spiritual and heroic head is muted by the narrow plaits that cover his head like a soft helmet.

The accentuated slant of the horse's body is a bold invention, accompanied by remarkable formal control. The expanded space between the animal's four legs, which resemble large columns – the forelegs are immense – accentuates the verticality of the rider.

This sculpture, which has not been dated scientifically, shares several volumetric and formal solutions with that of the horseman (no. 11), assigned to the 16th–18th century, it is distinguished from the latter by the nudity and austerity of the figure.

The significance of the rare Dogon equestrian statues is not clear. Some scholars hold that they are images of *Hogon*, or religious leaders, which are in some way linked to the myth of the creation of the world, while other experts simply consider them portraits of important figures in society.

Moving closer to the present, Baule sculpture offers examples of refined realism and of the idealization of the human figure rendered through elegant volumes, subtle body decoration and serene features, the latter being qualities also found in the masks (see nos. 133–134).

The two figures by the same sculptor now in the Metropolitan Museum in New York (nos. 214–215) are another example of the above. The fact that they form a couple would suggest that they are receptacles for spirits of nature (*asie usu*) which, as mentioned in a previous chapter, are imagined as being monstrously ugly.

By contrast, these two slender figures are distinguished by soft, meticulous modelling. The fluid synthetic forms blend smoothly and gently into one another in a vertical flow, and enhanced by the subtly calculated surface details, such as the volumes of the breasts, the well-shaped, slightly flexed legs and the understated relief decoration on the woman's belly. Tiny irregularities endow the bodies with a delicate vitality that harmonizes with the composed faces to which the kaolin patina gives a gleaming luminosity. Free of excessive naturalistic details, the images exude a calm solemnity and reserved dignity like certain Gothic-Renaissance sculptures.

However, the Baule artists also produced statues of dog-faced baboons, the finest example of which is probably the one held by the Louvre (no. 216). The seemingly irreconcilable contrast with human figures is actually far less marked if one excludes the savage head in which the cold ferocity of the monster is concentrated. Beneath the remains of the propitiatory libations that have

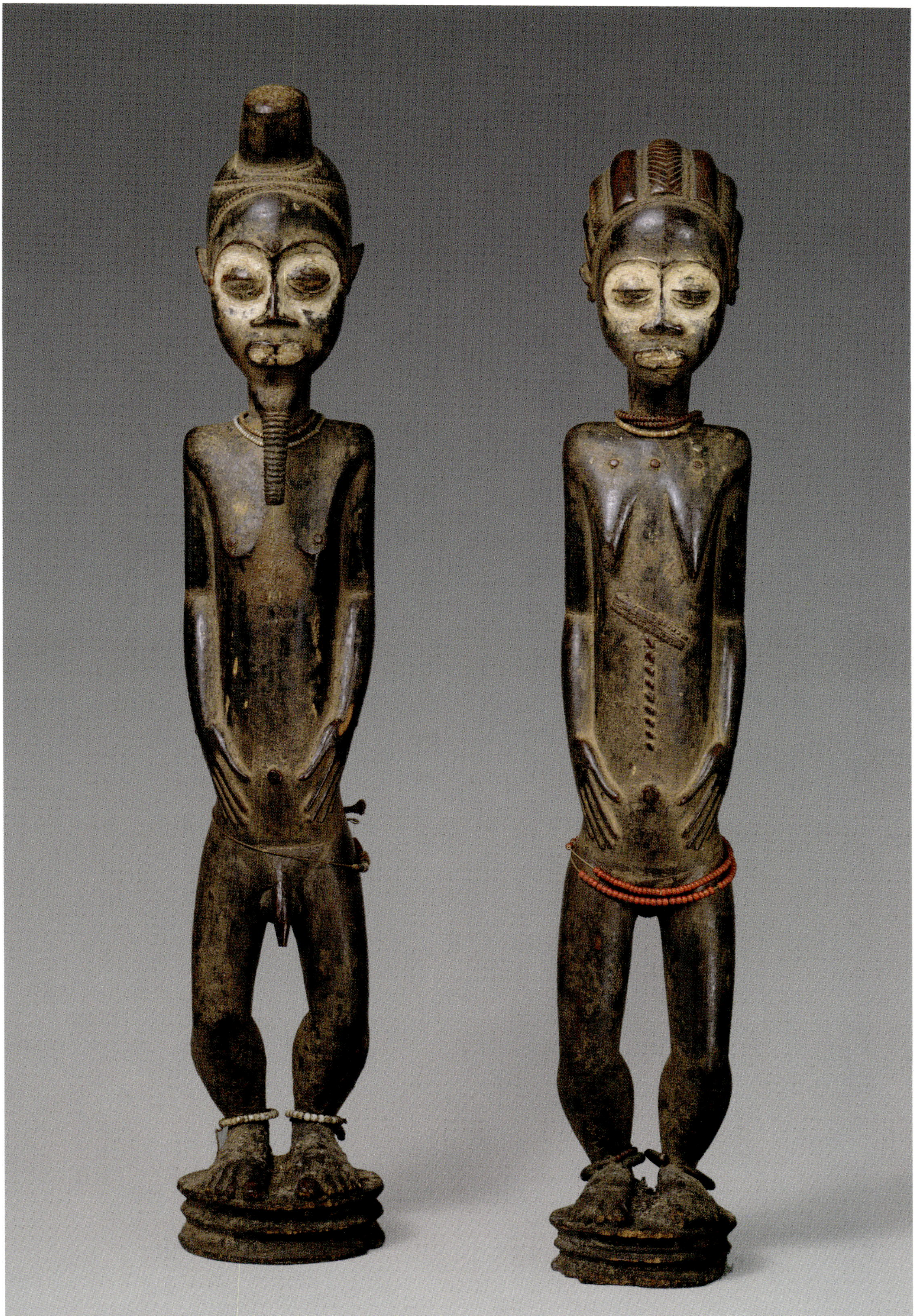

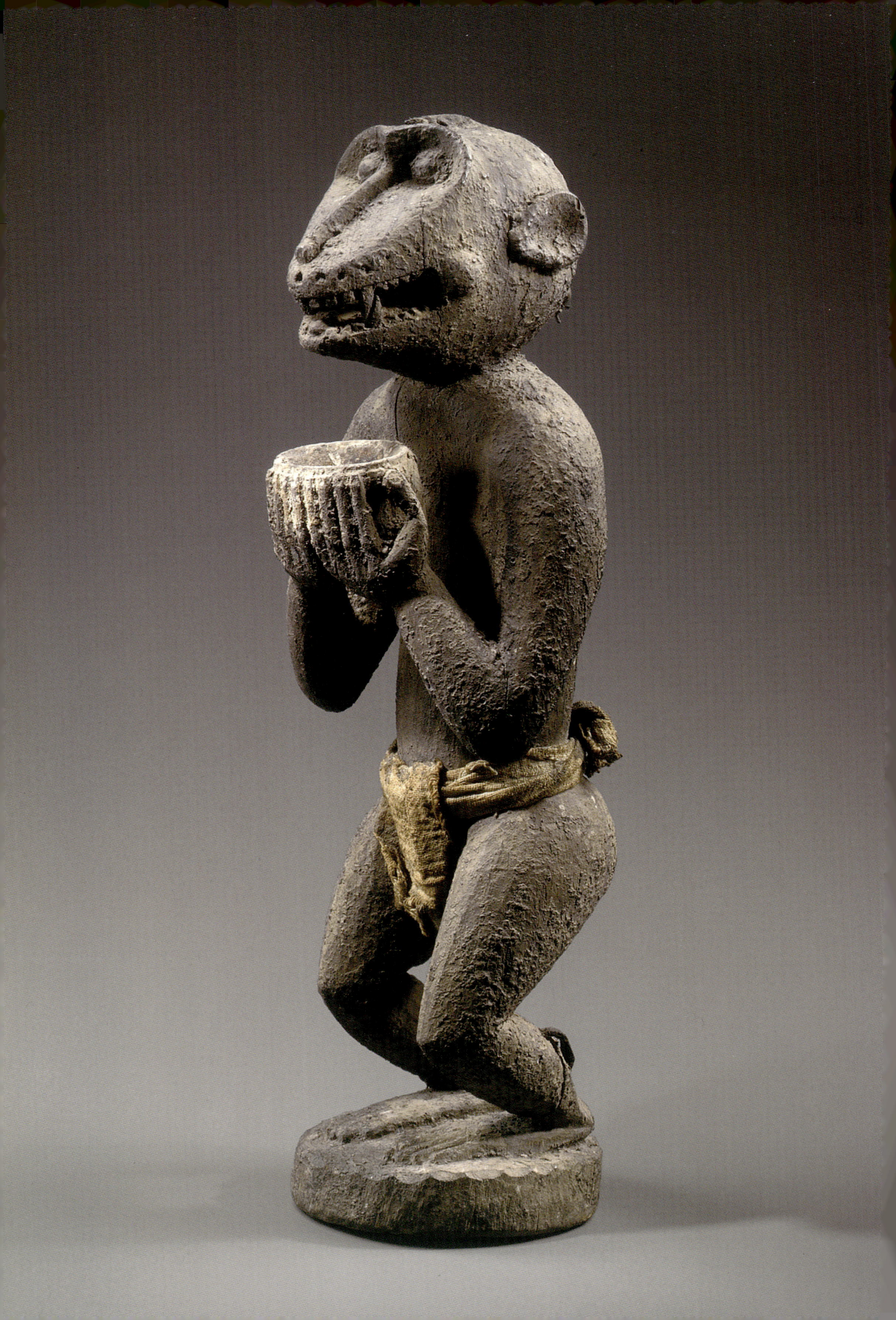

216. Baule artist
Ivory Coast
Dog-faced baboon
Wood, fabric and sacrificial material, 53.5 cm
Musée du Louvre, Pavillon des Sessions, Paris (on deposit from the Musée du Quai Branly)

217. Lobi artist
Burkina Faso
Head with religious-protective functions
Wood, 44 cm
Horstmann Collection, Zug

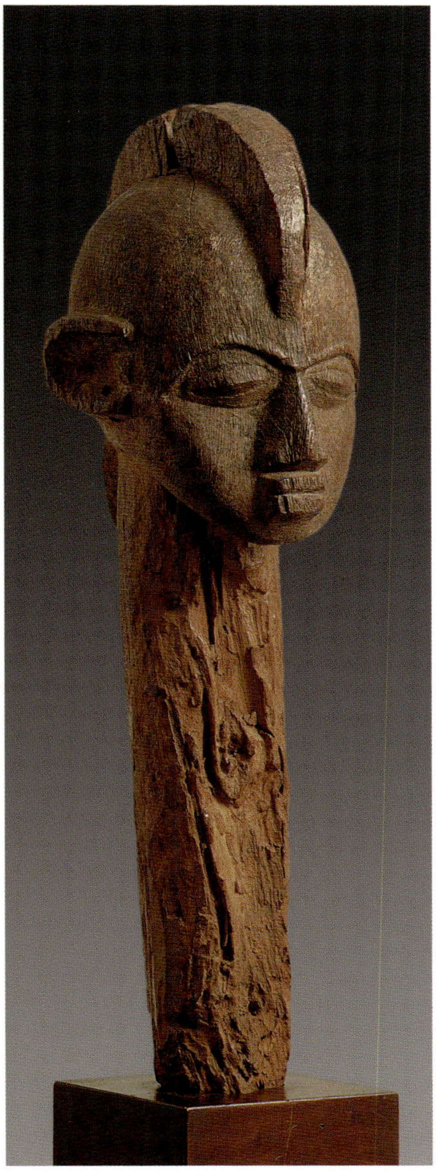

sedimented in the thick crusty patina, the forms of the body are slim, the shoulders gently rounded, the arms and legs well-shaped, the feet elongated and the hands expressive, as in the most accomplished human statuary produced by the Baule people. On the whole, however, the fusion of elegance and savageness creates a slight and disturbing feeling of uneasiness.

The statues of dog-faced baboons usually hold a goblet for sacrificial offerings and are vehicles for the spirits of the bush in which the spiritual entity becomes one with the effigy that embodies it.

The majority of wood sculpture created by the Lobi in Burkina Faso also has a realistic quality, as can be seen in the tender female image formerly in the Monti Collection[1] and in the monumental head (no. 217) whose precisely defined features are also somewhat stylized. The explicitly oval shape, accentuated by the curve of the striking crest-like coiffure, the large ears that echo the form, and the features of the delicate yet powerful face combine to create a figure of extreme composure and hieratic eloquence. The extreme austerity of the sculptures conception and the subtly rendered features combine with the ancient patina to give the work a venerable quality, a touching nobility. The eroded neck suggests that the work was planted in the ground, however, its worn surface sets off to advantage the perfect smoothness of the head enhanced by the bright patina.

Heads with a long neck and entire figures, which are held to possess supernatural powers that can be invoked to protect the owner and his tribe, are placed in special sanctuaries.

A large number of the works created by sculptors from the various Fang groups in Gabon, Cameroon and Equatorial Guinea can also be described as "realistic", as we have seen in nos. 174–175. This is further exemplified by the justly famous figure and head illustrated here. The large head, held proudly erect above the powerful, almost quivering body, is the strong point of this monumental figure (no. 218), whose complex articulation attests to the artist's plastic sensibility. The huge staring eyes light up the unadorned face whose unsurpassable majesty is revealed by the side view. This enables the viewer to see how the proud profile is softened by the perfect semicircle of the forehead and by the upper part of the coiffure, which is divided into thick, tapering, vertical plaits that harmonize with the profile of the face.

A similar though less monumental coiffure enhances the head (no. 219) reproduced by Carl Einstein in *Negerplastik* in 1915.[2] The calm, radiant spirituality suggested by the ample hemispherical brow that dominates the small, delicately shaped triangular face distinguishes this head from the previous one. This very famous work has passed through a series of collections, starting with that of the Brummer brothers at the beginning of the last century, then those of the sculptor Jacob Epstein, Carlo Monzino and, lastly, the Musée Dapper – like the previous figure and nos. 174–175.

The inclusion of the Kongo figure (no. 220) amongst the realistic sculptures is justified solely by the extraordinarily beautiful head, since it is the only human element that emerges from the mass of pelts that form the primitive cape – actually an attribute of royalty. The contrast between the cape and the face, which is sculpted with a deeply felt tenderness, accentuates the gentle expression of the latter. The features – especially the beautiful lips – are disarmingly naturalistic, which is unusual in Kongo sculpture, and give the face an adolescent charm tempered by a kind of thoughtful awareness. This is heightened by the contrast that exists between the pelts of wild animals and the pale face that gleams like ivory, that together create a successful combination of realism and expressionism.

Conversely, imposing male figures are the most representative artworks produced by the Hemba, another people from the Democratic Republic of the Congo. François Neyt devoted an exhaustive study (1977) to the sculpture of this ethnic group in which he revealed the existence of an impressive gallery of large-scale images, and defined an assortment of a dozen or so stylistic regions, each with its own approach.

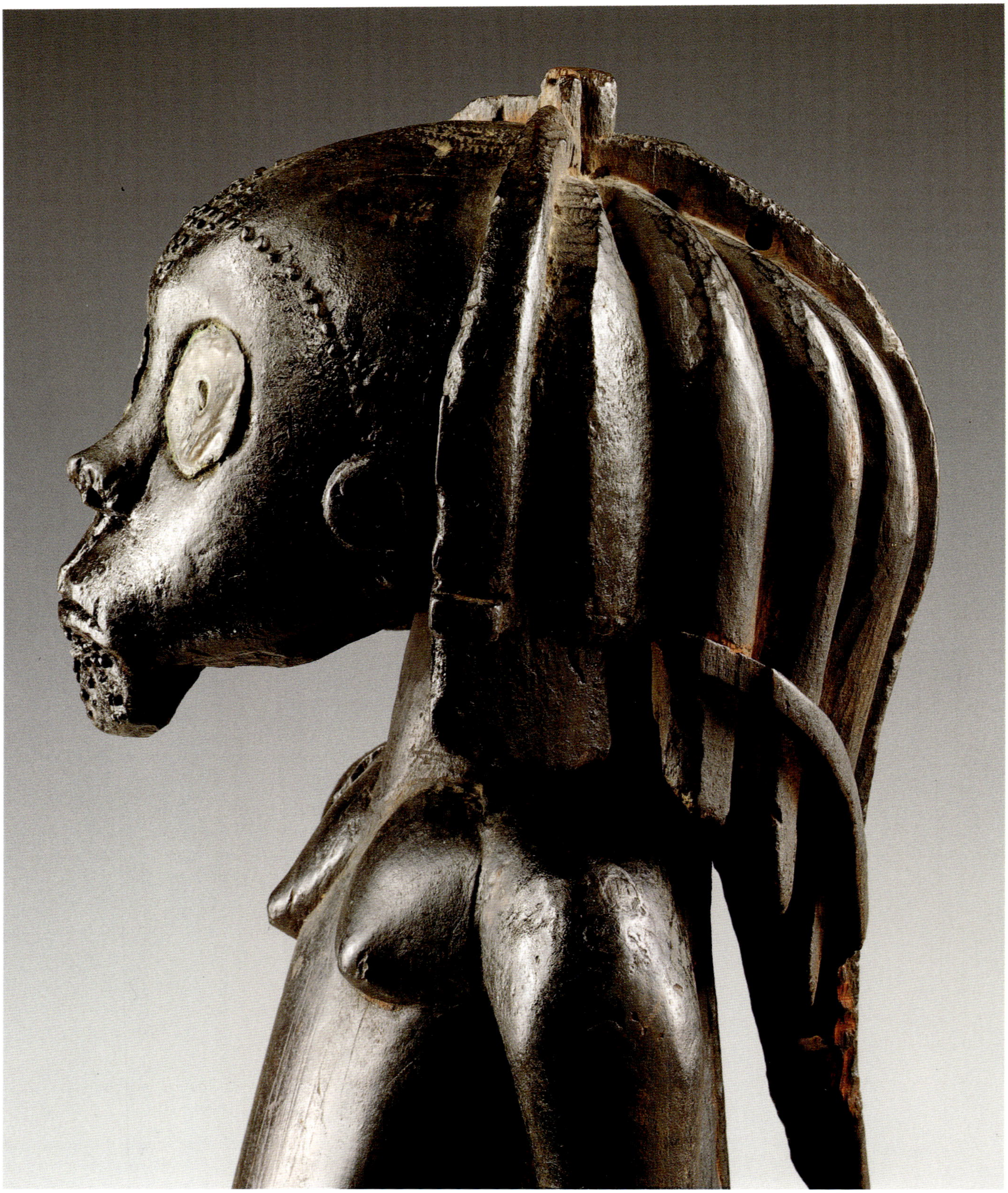

218–218a. Fang artist (Betsi)
Gabon
Reliquary male figure
Wood and brass, 70 cm
Musée Dapper, Paris (formerly in the Jacob Epstein and Carlo Monzino collections)

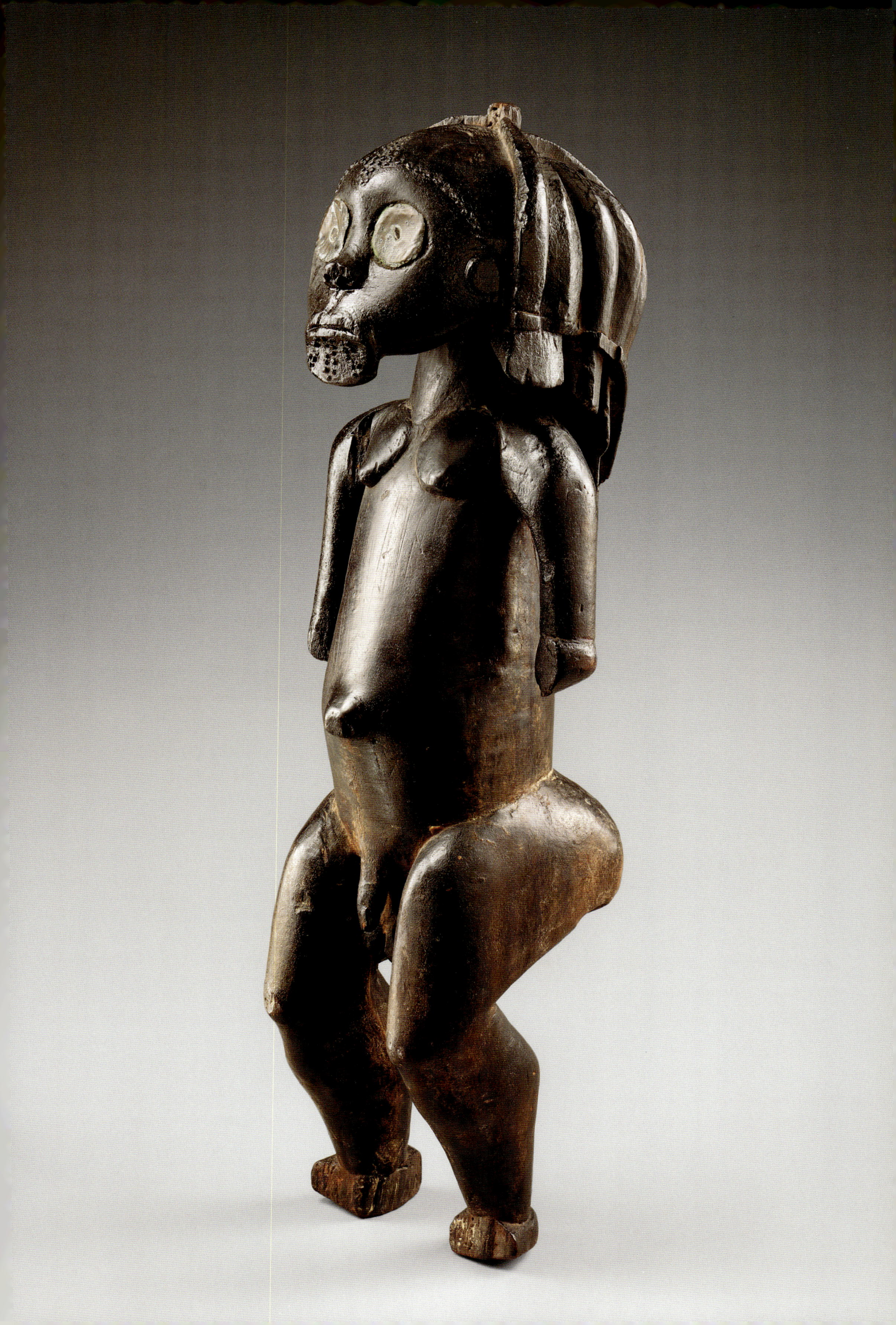

219. Fang artist (Betsi)
Gabon
Reliquary head
Wood, metal and resin, 34 cm
(63 cm including support)
Musée Dapper, Paris (formerly in the Jacob Epstein and Carlo Monzino collections)

220. Kongo artist
Democratic Republic of the Congo
Figure with magical-religious functions
Wood, glass, fabric, feathers and pelts, 34 cm (excluding feathers)
Staatliches Museum für Völkerkunde, Munich

Pages 250–251
221. Hemba artist
Democratic Republic of the Congo
(Luika region)
Ancestral figure
Wood, skin, fabric and raffia, 81 cm
Staatliche Museen zu Berlin, Ethnologisches Museum, Berlin

222. Hemba artist
Democratic Republic of the Congo
(Luika region)
Ancestral figure
Wood and woven fibres, 69 cm
Private collection

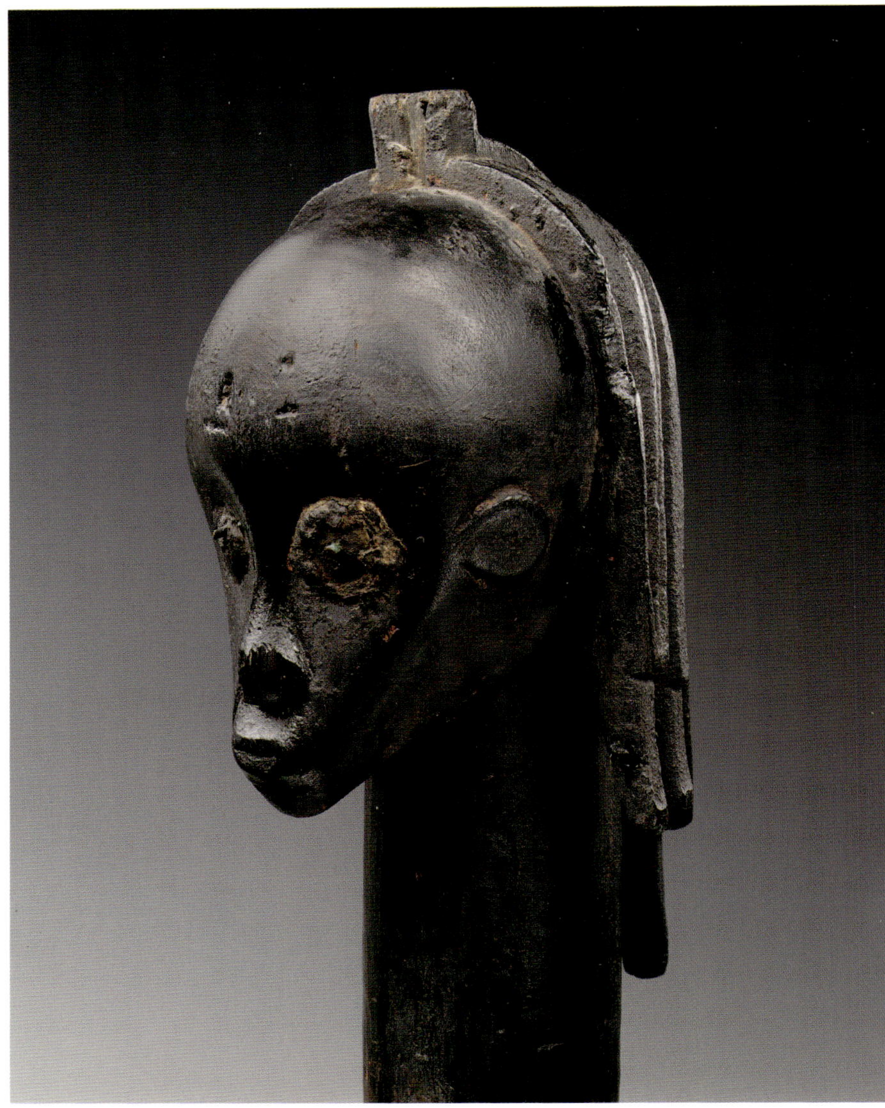

The figure held by the Ethnologisches Museum in Berlin (no. 221) was brought from Africa in 1891 and is probably the first work of its kind to have arrived in Europe. It is typical of the traditional style of the Niembo – the largest Hemba subgroup – indeed, its considerable size and formal coherence make it one of the most representative examples of this style.

The large head, given extra length by the typically cruciform coiffure, stands regally on the polished body softened by the rounded shoulders and enlivened by the slightly protruding abdomen and small, pointed breasts. The expressive features of the pensive face trimmed with an elegant beard perfectly combine reserve and superhuman authority, as befits the portrait of an ancestor in all his splendour.

The second figure (no. 222) is also in the Niembo style, but the formal differences between this and the previous sculpture are clearly evident, not so much in the various details as in the general definition of the volumes, which are particularly accentuated here. The posture is typical of an ancestor – arms hanging down and hands resting on hips – as is the structure of its various parts, but a strong impression is received of the muscles, despite not being represented anatomically, beneath the fluid, lustrous surfaces typical of Hemba statuary.

However, the main difference lies in the large head with its resolute, even aggressive, features. The powerful neck, with a protruding and pointed Adam's apple, supports the elongated mass of the head which, inclined slightly forward, is compensated volumetrically and visually by the extremely elaborate, monumental quadrilobate coiffure that opens up like a magnificent flower behind. The facial features are less generic and conventional, in other words they are more personalized, and the profile view reveals their haughty imperiousness to the full.

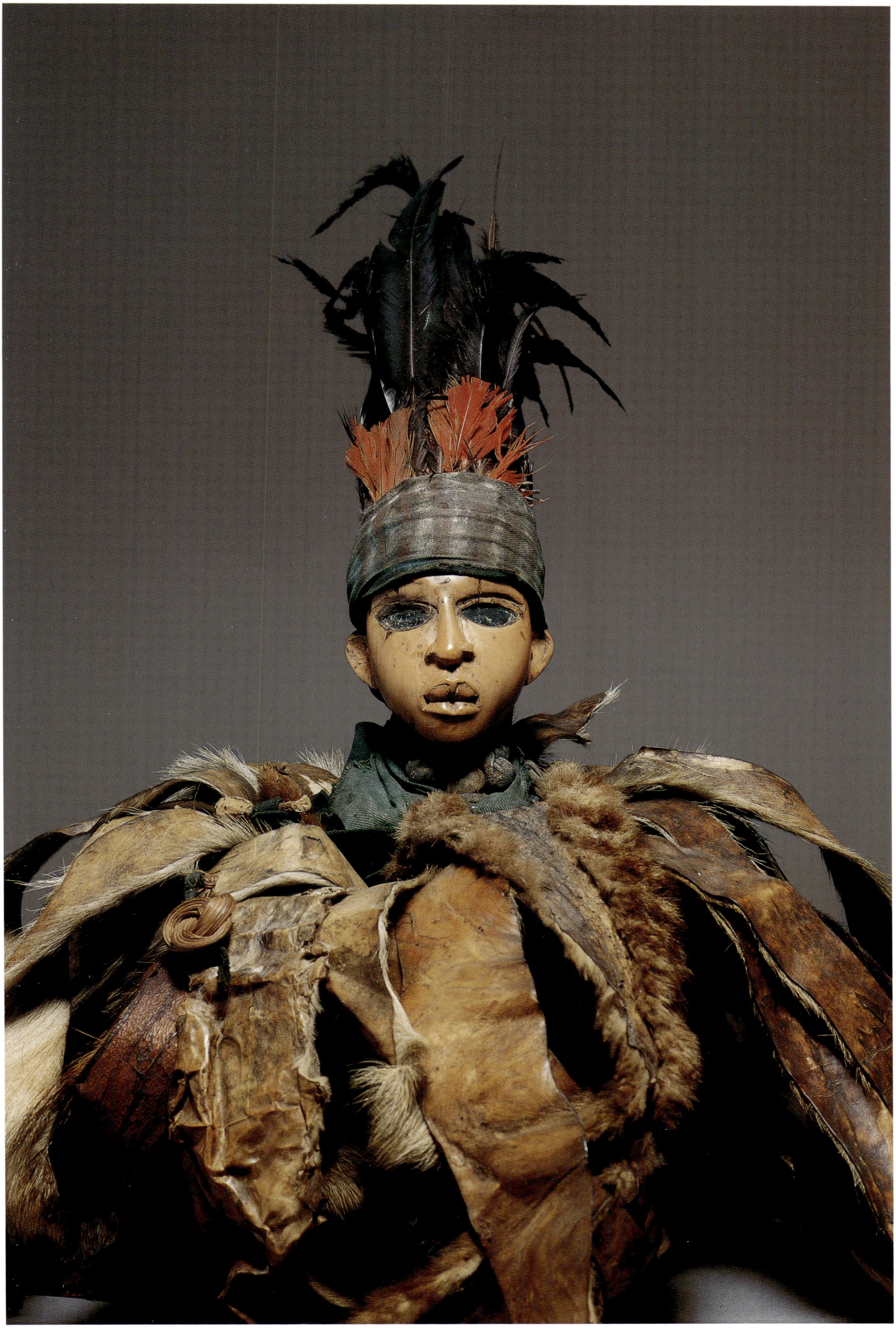

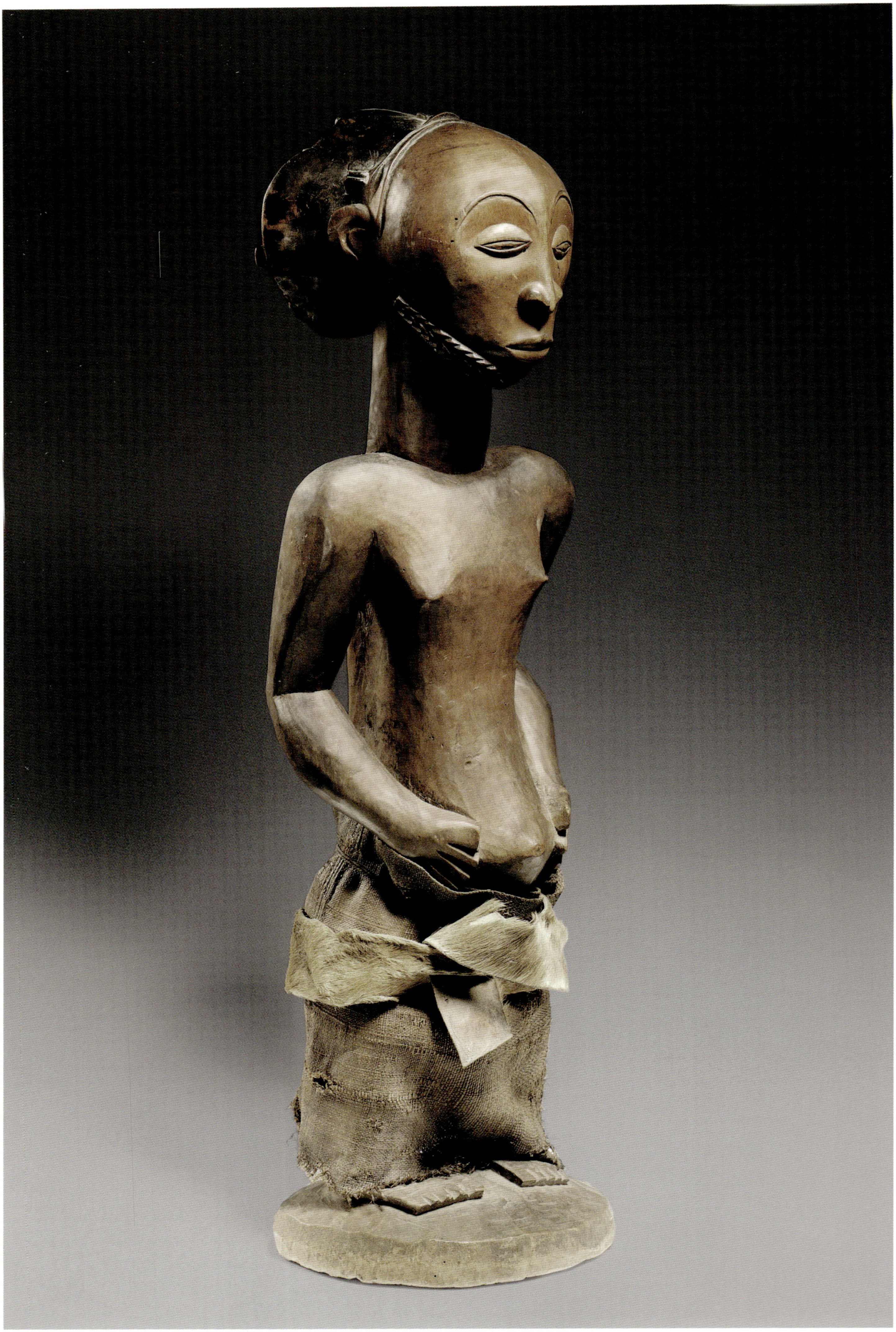

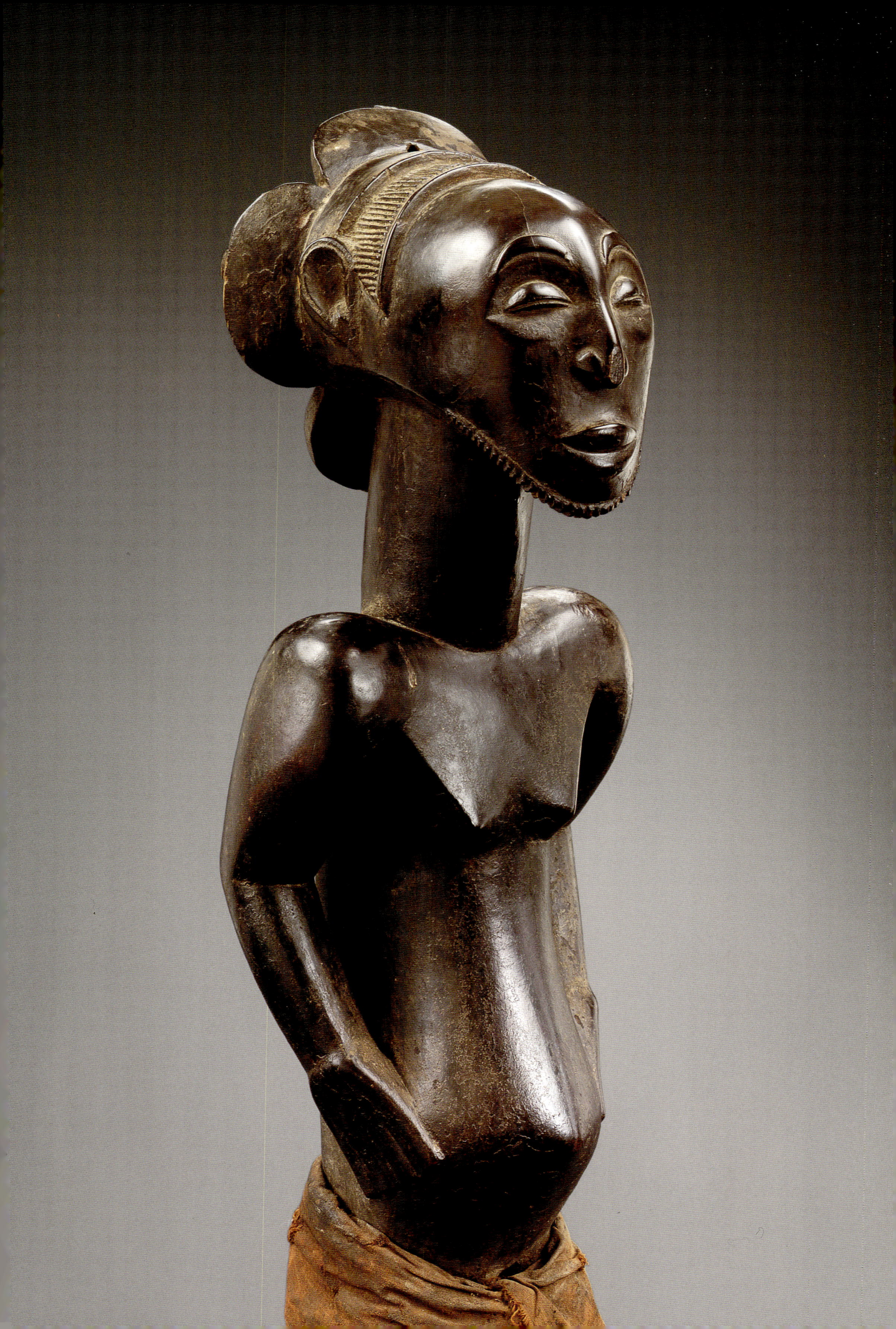

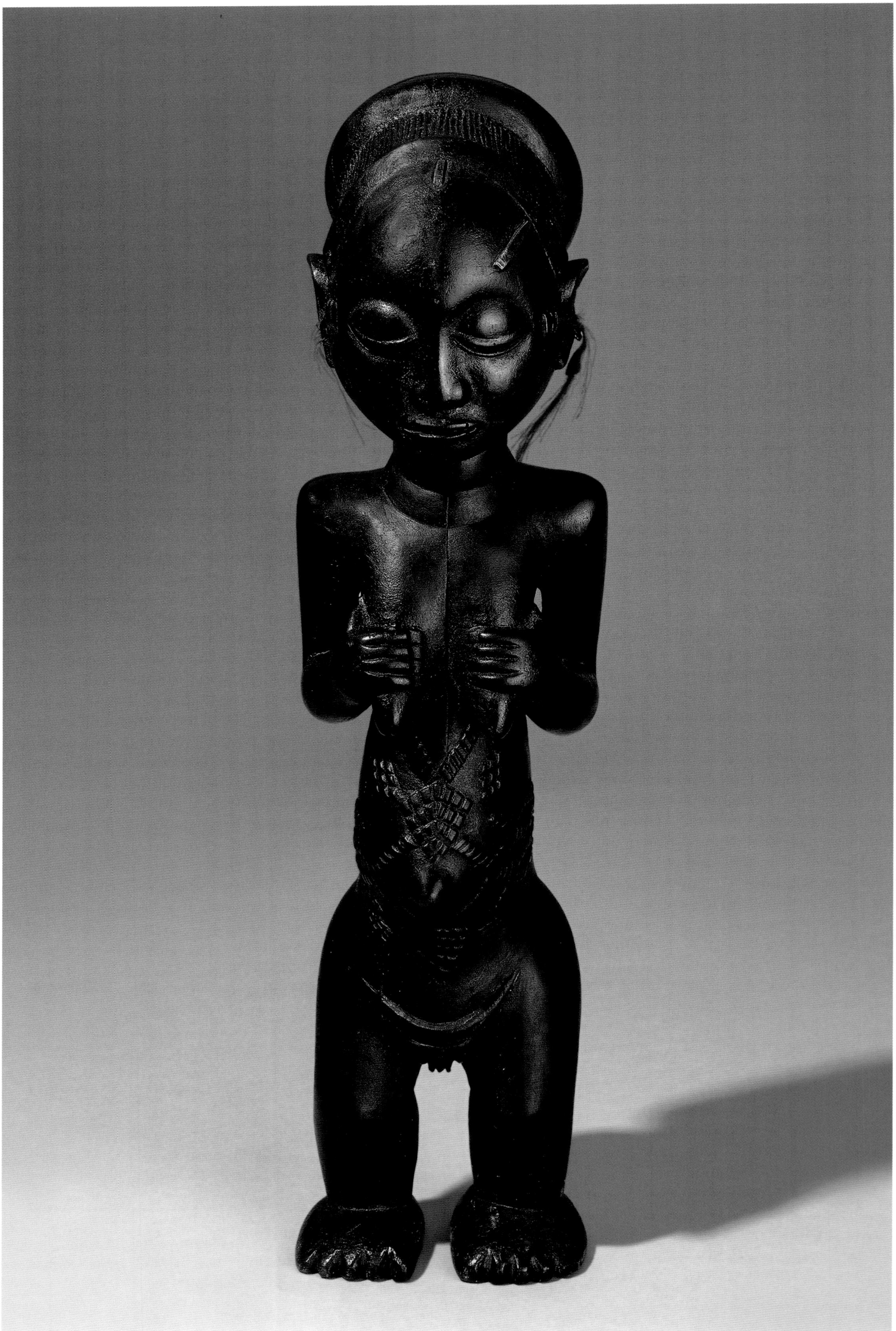

223. Luba artist
Democratic Republic of the Congo
Ancestral figure
Wood, 45.7 cm
The British Museum, Ethnography Department, London

224. Ngbaka artist
Democratic Republic of the Congo
Male figure
Wood, metal and fibres, 48.3 cm
Present location unknown (formerly in the de Miré and Charles Ratton collections, Paris, and Chaim Gross Collection, New York)

Luba art differs from that of the Hemba in that women are the principal subject, though they are rarely represented outside of decoration on ceremonial instruments or symbols of power.

The figure now held by the British Museum (no. 223) – one of the few and possibly the most perfect of its kind known to exist – possesses a sublime human quality that seems to embody both the figure's consequence and reserve. The discreet decoration, the ample forehead topped by the simple, elegant coiffure, the confident set of the mouth and, above all, the large, half-closed, perfectly shaped eyes, express both spiritual intensity and grave awareness, in keeping with the role of women in Luba society.

The size of the head, which is certainly out of proportion to the rest of the body and therefore not wholly realistic, is in keeping with the overall volumetric scheme of the figure, which is divided into four large blocks: the head and the shoulders, the arms, the abdomen, and the legs. It should be noted, however, that not all Luba figures adhere to these proportions or typology.

During the centuries prior to 1800, the Luba had created a vast empire along the upper reaches of the River Lualaba, and in their society a woman – either the mother or wife of a chief or king – always occupied a prominent position in political and religious life as well as in the family.

The Ngbaka male figure formerly in the prestigious art collection of the New York painter Chaim Gross (no. 224), is held to be "the finest from the area" by William Fagg,[3] and can also be assigned to the realist universe.

The sculpture comes from the vast region that straddles parts of the Democratic Republic of the Congo, the Central African Republic and the Sudan

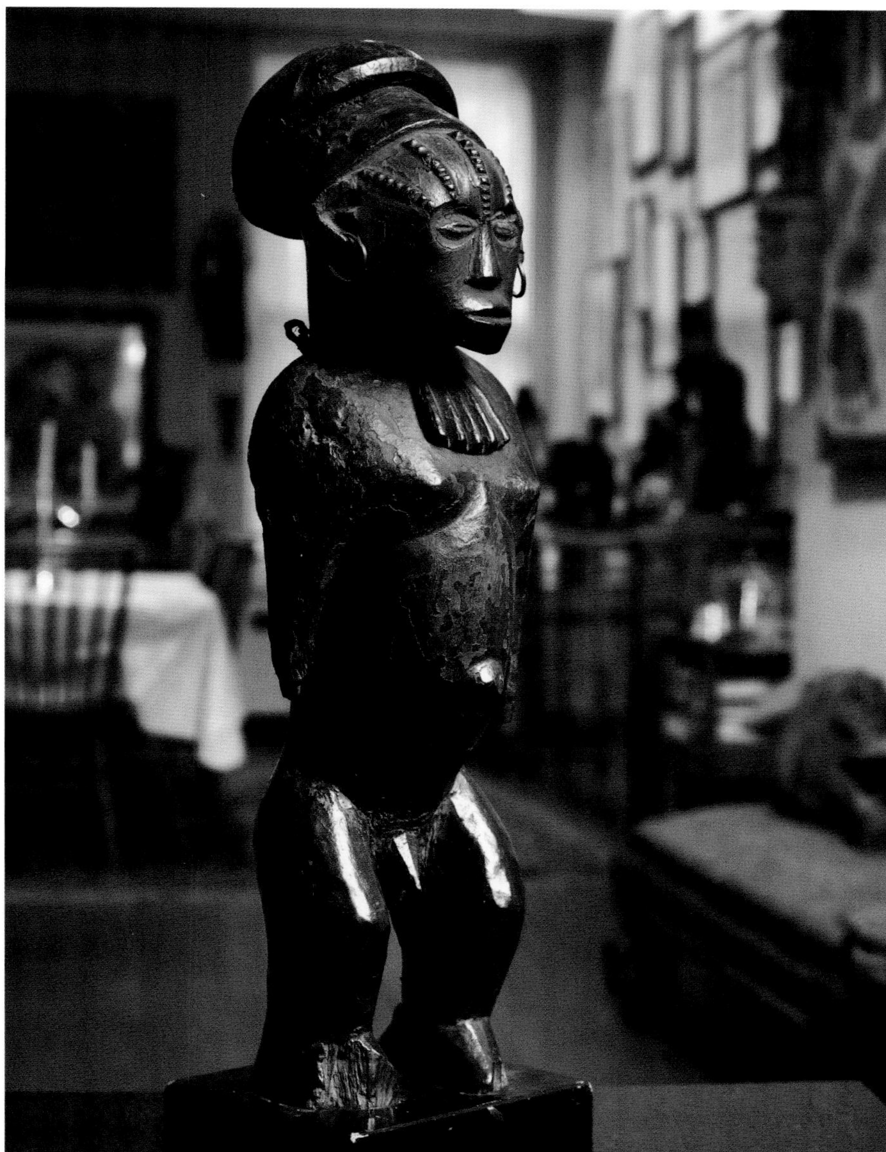

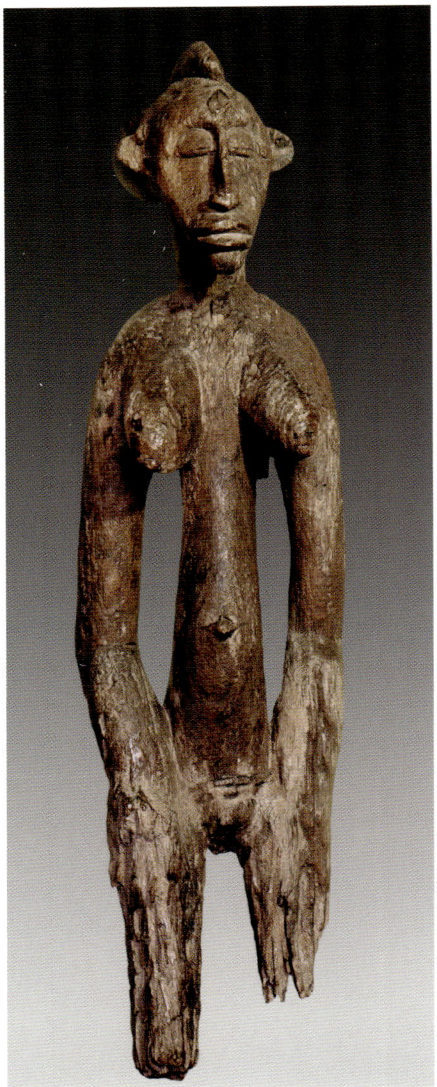

225. "Master of Lataha"
Senufo, village of Lataha, Ivory Coast
Female Poro society figure (base missing)
Wood, h. 95 cm
Museum Rietberg, Zurich

226. "Master of Lataha"
Senufo, village of Lataha, Ivory Coast
Male Poro society figure
Wood, h. 110 cm
The Metropolitan Museum of Art, New York

227. "Master of Sikasso"
Senufo, Mali
Female Poro society figure
Wood, seeds, shells and latex, 90.5 cm
Private collection

and is thought to be an idealized portrait of Sètò, the mythical ancestor of the Ngbaka.[4]

The sturdy, well-proportioned body and proud head with regular features endow the sculpture with a sense of monumentality despite its relatively small size. The superb – and unusual – vertical keloid decoration on the forehead accentuates its breadth and is echoed by the reliefs that decorate the upper chest, creating a visual link that heightens the unity of the work. The side view shows the undulating line of the body, which is emphasized by the unusual flattening of the spine from the neck to the buttocks and by the odd shape of the arms, which are short and triangular (the end of the right arm is missing), rather like a penguin's flipper.

An extremely rich multilayered patina attests to the antiquity of the work, datable to around the mid-19th century, which is an important example of the archaic style prior to the contact made with Europeans.

A Ngbaka figure similar to the one illustrated here is visible in a photograph taken in 1912–13, in which it is standing next to the famous crouching figure in stone by André Derain[5] on a mantelpiece in the Paris apartment of the modern art dealer Daniel-Henry Kahnweiler.

The further one ventures into the immense universe of African sculpture, the hazier the notion of "realism" becomes, in the sense that the main subject, namely the human body, is subjected to ever greater simplifications and distortions, as demonstrated by the large scale Senufo sculptures illustrated here.

These figures, known as *déblé*, were usually sculpted in pairs, consisting of a man and a woman, who represent the primordial ancestors. They were carried in ritual processions on special occasions in the community's life by young initiates of the Poro society, who pounded them on the ground to mark the rhythm of the dance. This function explains the fact that the feet of the statue are replaced by a massive cylindrical base.

The well-known pair of statues held respectively by the Museum Rietberg in Zurich (no. 225) and the Metropolitan Museum of Art in New York (no. 226) is the work of a master with an unmistakable style, who influenced the creators of other sculptures formerly kept in the sacred wood at Lataha in the Korhogo region, Ivory Coast. The two figures are constructed with simple volumes, consisting in long, well-shaped arms, sloping shoulders and the slightly swollen belly that virtually continues the curve of the rounded thighs and, in the female figure, anticipates the line of the full, soft breasts. The heads are masterpieces of expressiveness in their rough detachment, and the strong point of each figure: in each one, the long imperious nose divides the hollow of the face bounded above by the curved eyebrows and below by the large, half-open mouth. The half-closed eyes, heavy lids and mouth together induce a feeling of inner calm in keeping with the solemn physicality of these monumental figures, rendered vibrant by the eroded surface.

Unfortunately, the base and lower part of the legs of the Zurich sculpture are mutilated – they were probably eaten away by termites – but this has in no way diminished the figure's solemn presence.

The ritual use of the two works, and of other sculptures located in the same place, ceased around the middle of the last century, following the establishment of an iconoclastic cult in the region. This development caused the traditional religion to be abandoned and subsequently the desecration and destruction of a large number of sculptures.

A drastic narrowing of the torso and limbs distinguishes the splendid female figure now in a private collection in America (no. 227) from the two previous works and, indeed, from the majority of known pieces. The short legs, which function in relation to the overall design, link the cylindrical base to the body surmounting it. The frontal view shows the body's oval structure – created by the rounded shoulders, abnormally long arms and large hands clenched in two fists on either side of the sex – which the tense, slender trunk divides exactly in half. The simplified, slightly rigid features of the suitably proportioned head give the figure an austere mien.

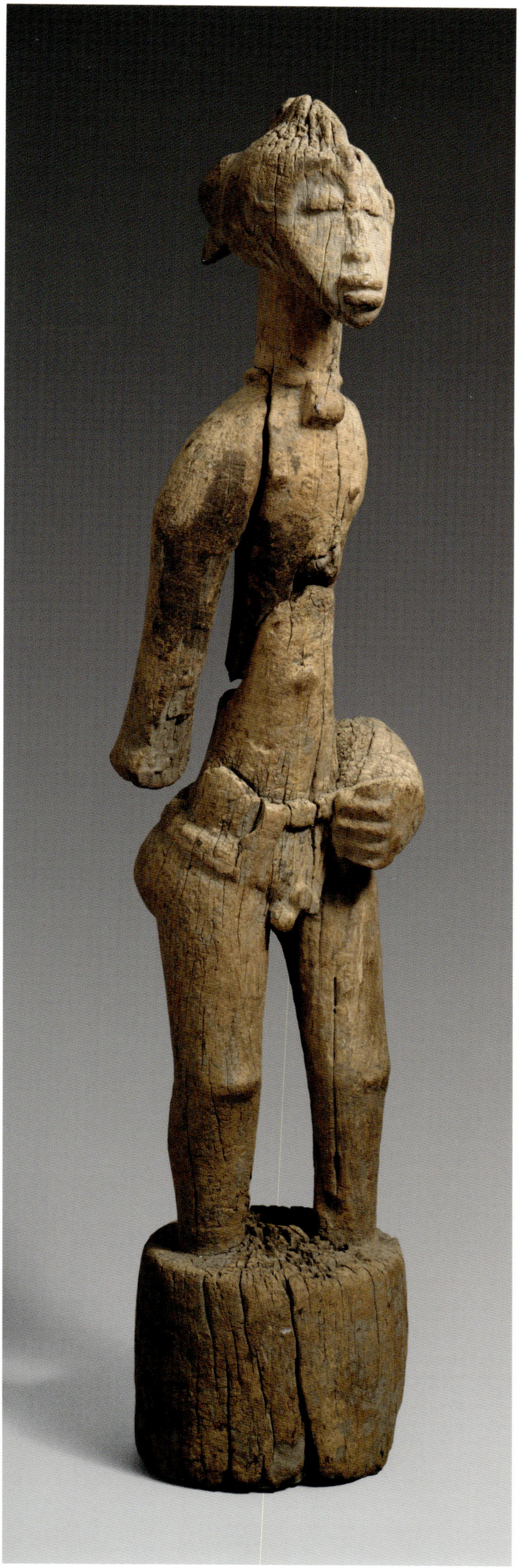
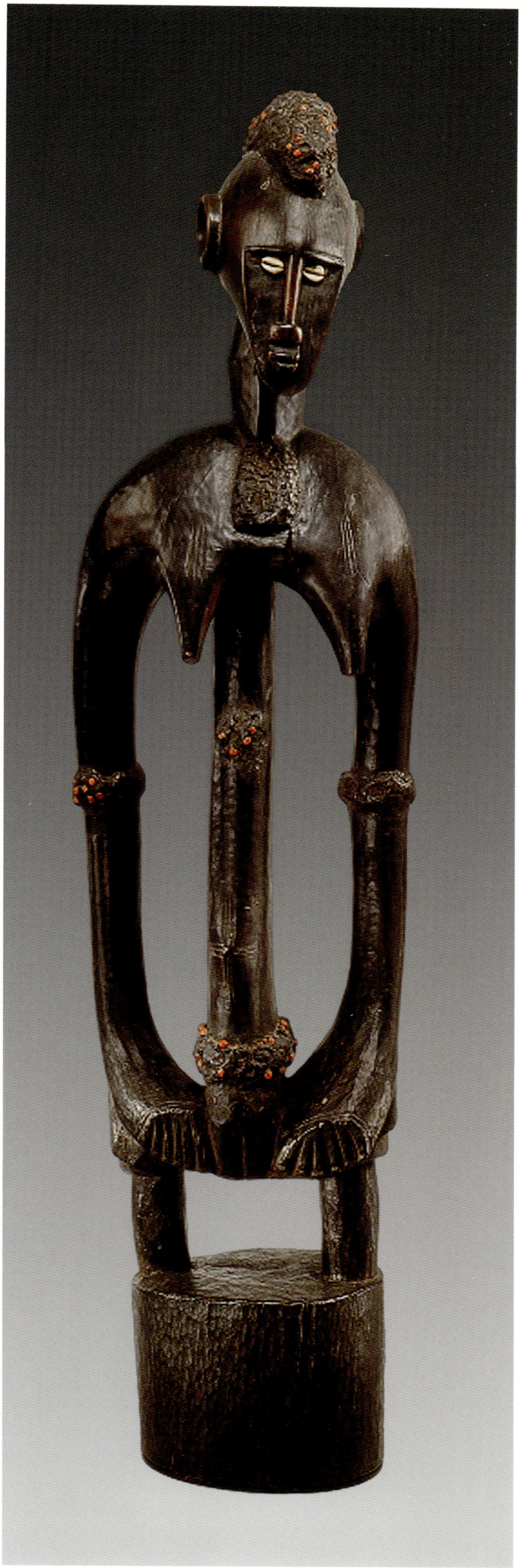

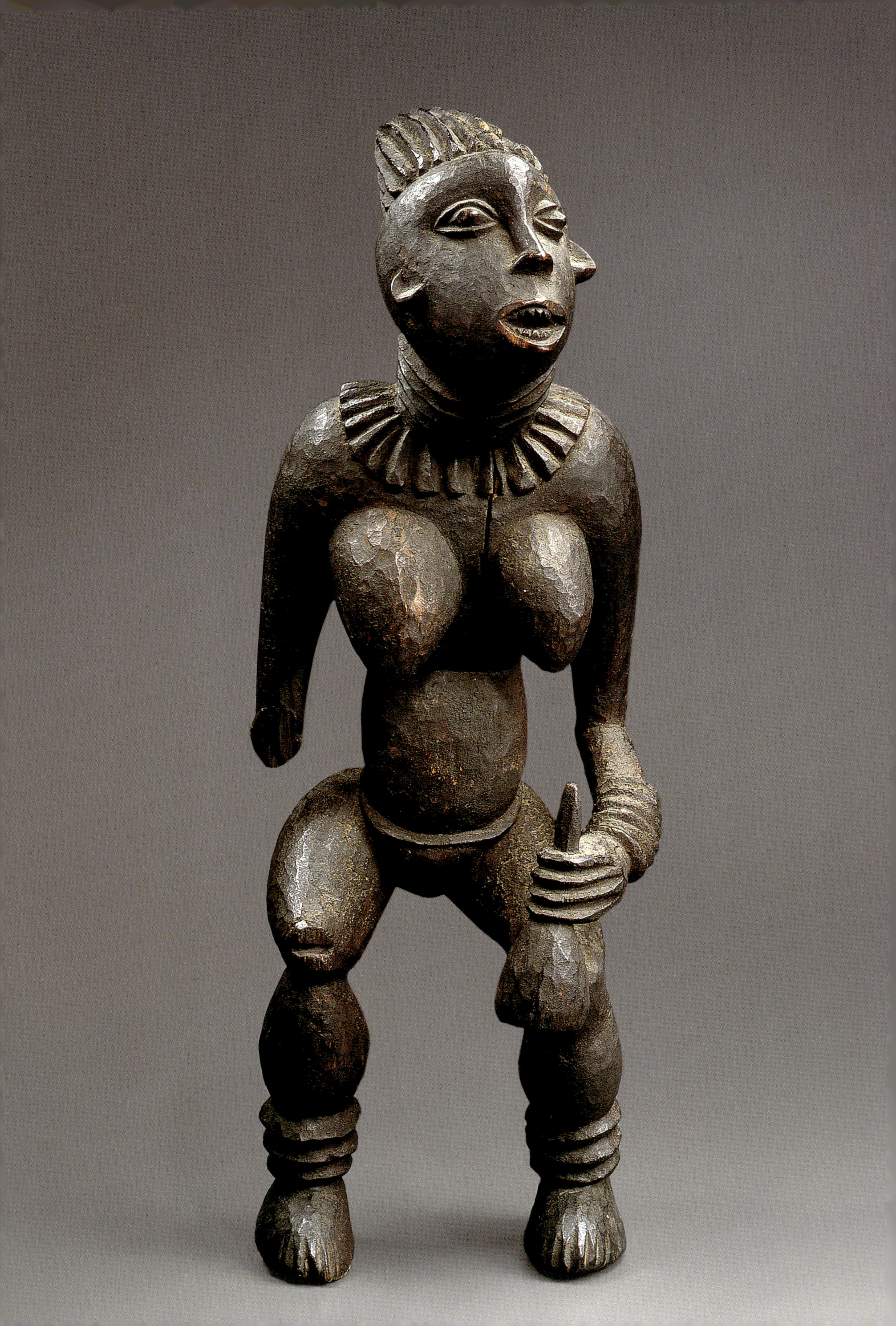

228. Bangwa artist
Cameroon
Commemorative statue of a princess
Wood and pigments, 85 cm
Musée Dapper, Paris

229. Man Ray
La Mode au Congo, 1937
Black and white contact print,
9 x 6.6 cm
Courtesy Fondazione Marconi, Milan

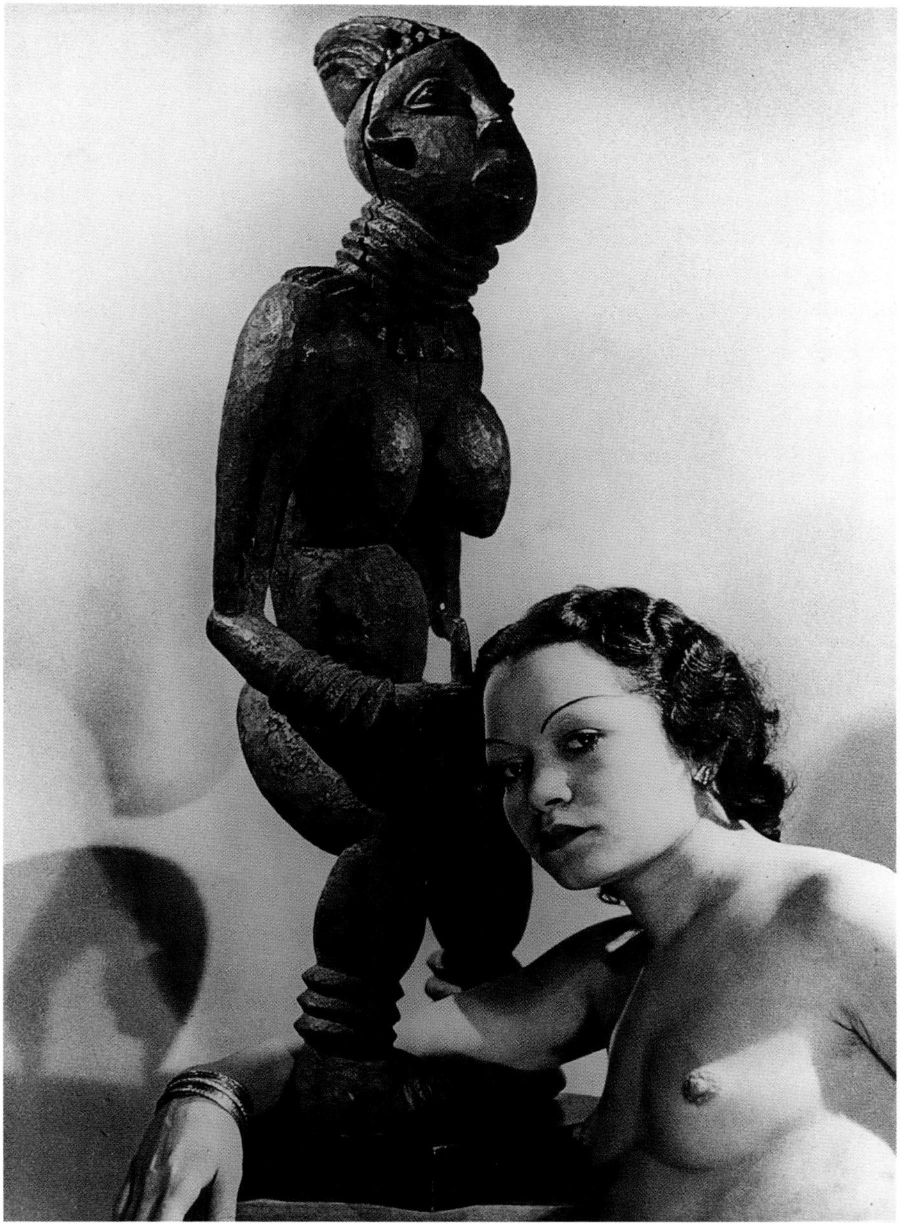

The result is an effective airy structure in which the deliberately ample voids establish a dialogue with the stylized though animated volumes. The subtle asymmetries in the structure and the hint of movement introduced by the slight deviations from the central axis are indications of hidden life about to become manifest.

This sculpture, collected by Frédéric-Henri Lem in 1935 and dated to the first half of the 19th century, has been attributed, along with two others, to the "Master of Sikasso".[6]

The large female statue brought to Europe by Gustav Conrau at the end of the 19th century is a monument to Bangwa art (no. 228). It has an additional quality to those of the other figures illustrated so far, which is both exceptional and rare in African art: the extraordinary dynamism that enlivens its opulent forms and skilfully breaks up the frontality.

An intense vitality is suggested by the unusual yet extremely controlled movement of all the body parts in tension (is it a dancing figure?) and by the deliberate choice of oval volumes: the bent legs, the torso, the breasts, and the proudly held head with striking features, all of which can be seen to advantage in the three-quarter view. The bracelets, ornate necklace and headdress indicate a high-ranking figure, possibly a wife or the mother of a king.

The work has passed through famous collections, including that of Helena Rubinstein, and was photographed next to a white female model by Man Ray in a series of well-known images (no. 229).

230. Dan artist
Liberia
Mask
Wood, 24 cm
Musée Dapper, Paris

231. Dan artist
Liberia
Mask
Wood and hair, 21.5 cm
Civiche Raccolte Artistiche del Castello Sforzesco, Raccolte Extraeuropee, Milan

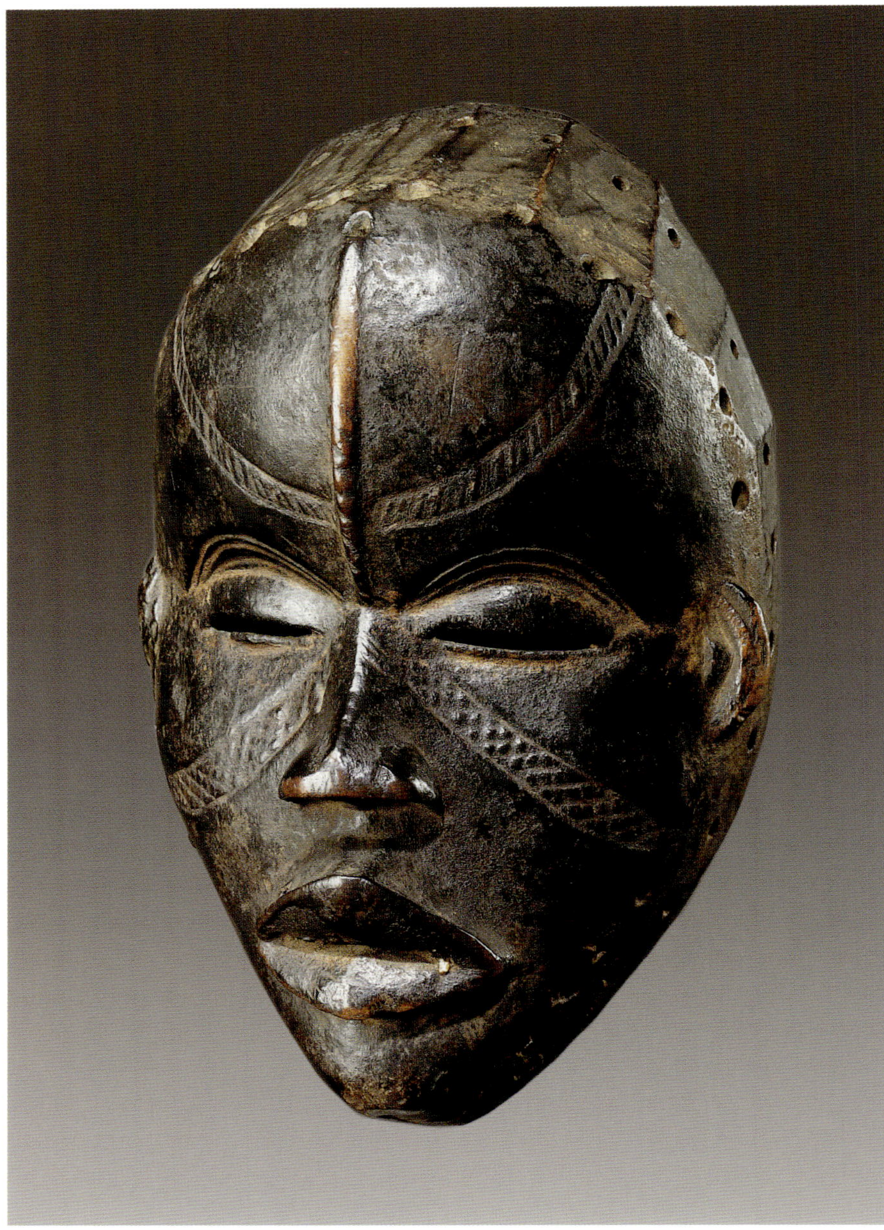

Moving on to the rich world of African masks, the Dan piece in the Musée Dapper (no. 230) is a perfect example of idealized realism. The refined yet very simple decoration subtly enlivens the surface of the oval face, enhancing the beautiful half-closed eyes, the soft and slightly protruding lips, the regular nose, the high forehead and the tiny ears. The slightly eroded surface and the thick patina with reddish lights set off the tenderly modelled features and help to create the feeling of timeless elegance of the work.

Dan masks come in countless styles, however, ranging from the somewhat simplified representation to the extreme stylization and distortion of the human face. The results are elegant serenity, as is the case here, or intense and violent expressiveness. The assignment of a particular style to a specific region is very difficult due to the stylistic assimilation and differentiation that have occurred over time.

The mask in the Milan civic collections (no. 231), which is as thin as the wall of a shell, is distinguished by the exceptionally refined and sober plastic solutions adopted by the artist. The large smooth forehead, delimited by the arched eyebrows in perfect relief and partly covered by a simple yet elegant coiffure in fibres, crowns the pointed face with its small nose, flared nostrils and pronounced lips. However, the dominant feature of the mask is the large sockets of the round eyes, above and below which the composition is divided into two equal halves, since they give the work a solemn and mysterious aura complemented by the shiny black patina.

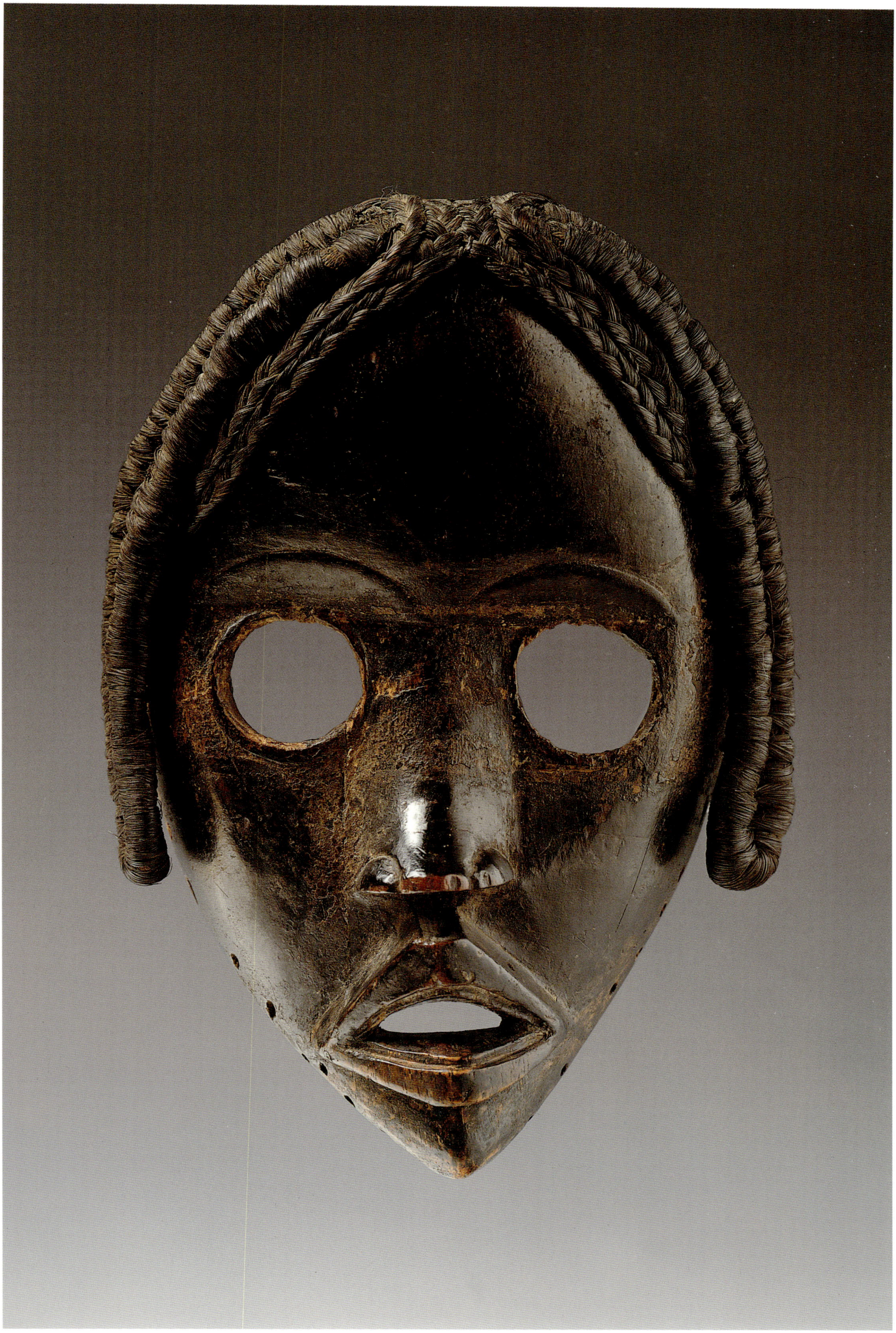

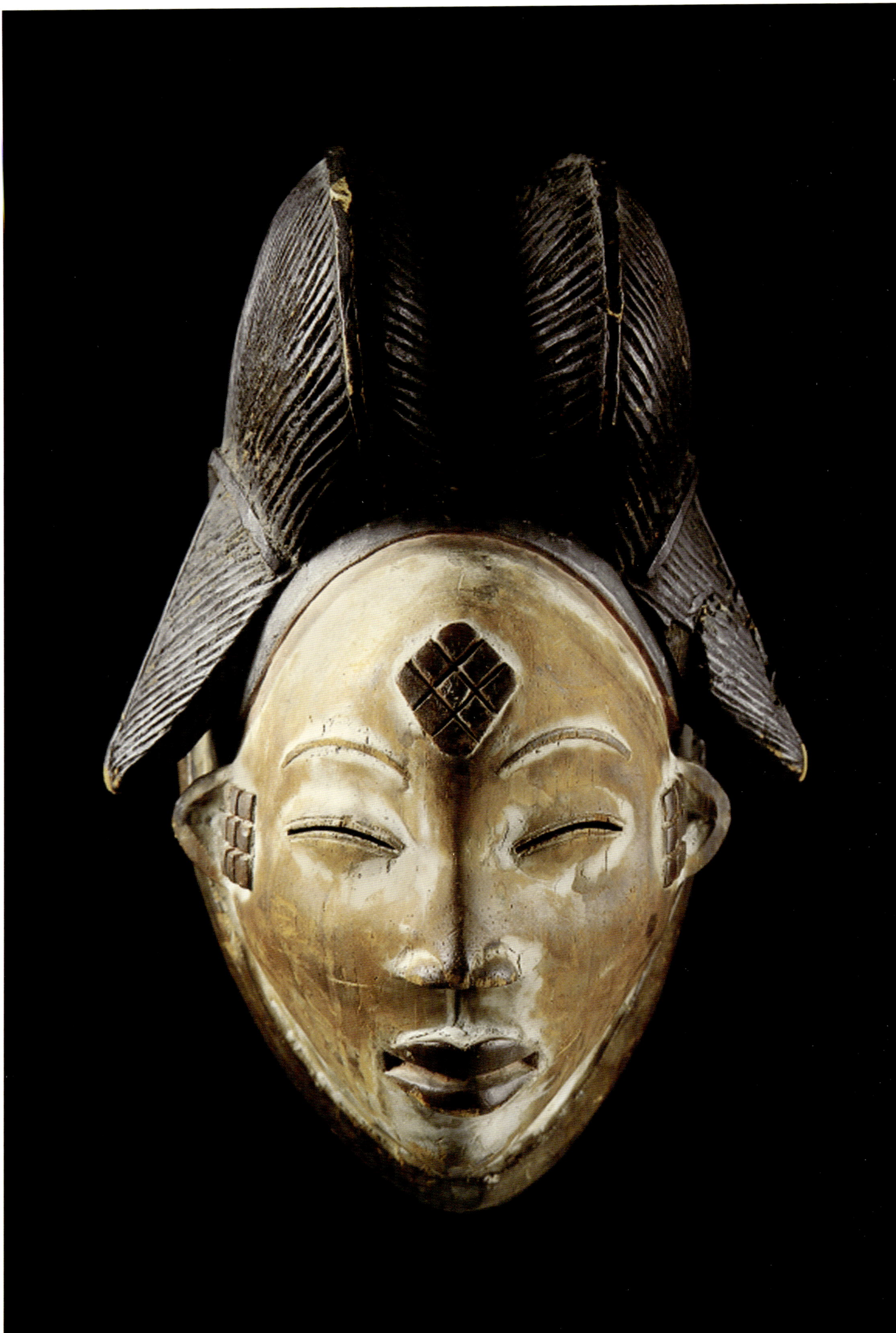

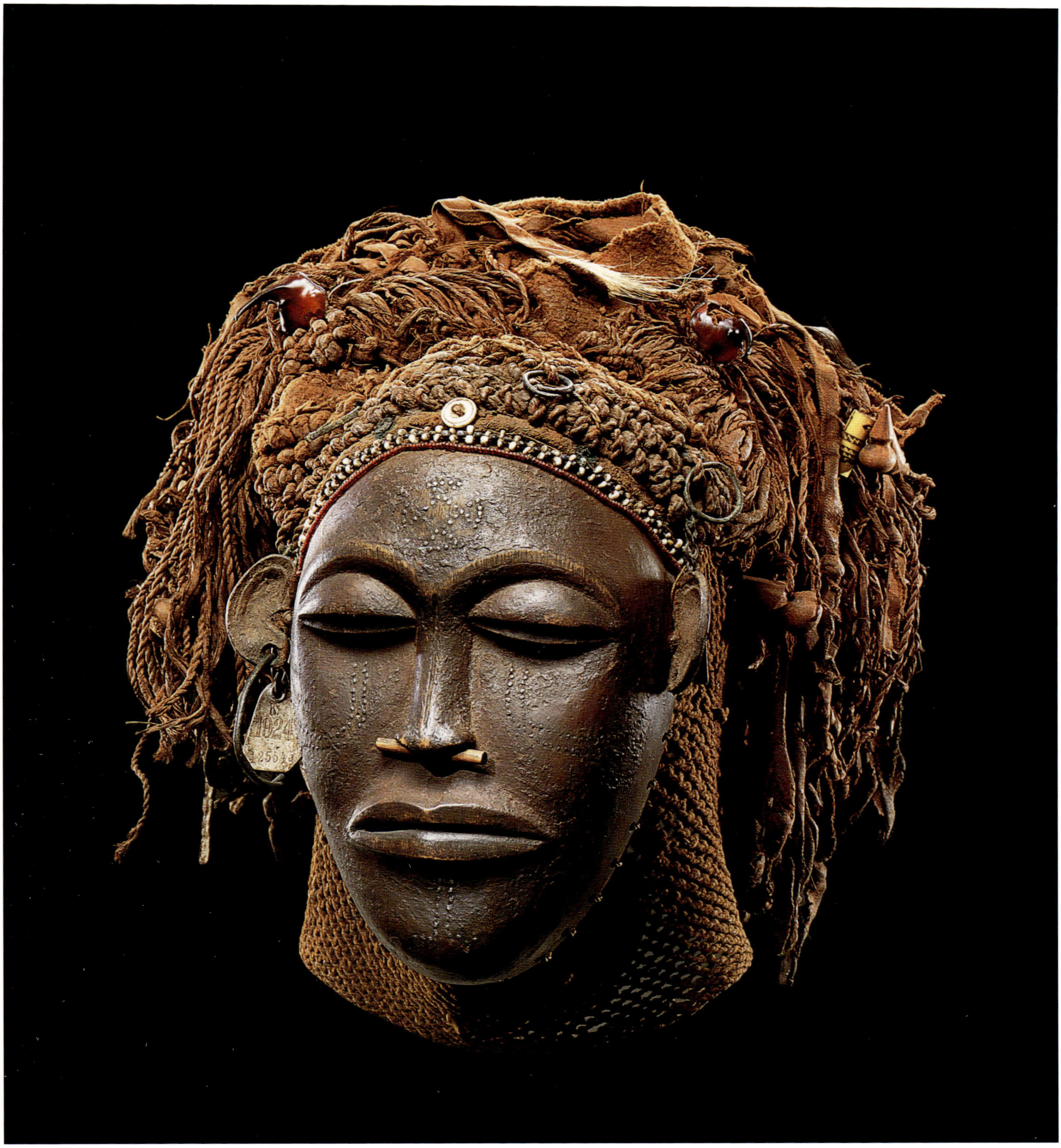

232. Punu artist
Gabon
Mask
Wood and kaolin, 26 cm
Private collection (formerly in the Hubert Goldet Collection, Paris)

233. Chokwe artist
Democratic Republic of the Congo
Mask
Wood, fibres and metal, 21 cm
Musée Royal de l'Afrique Centrale, Tervuren

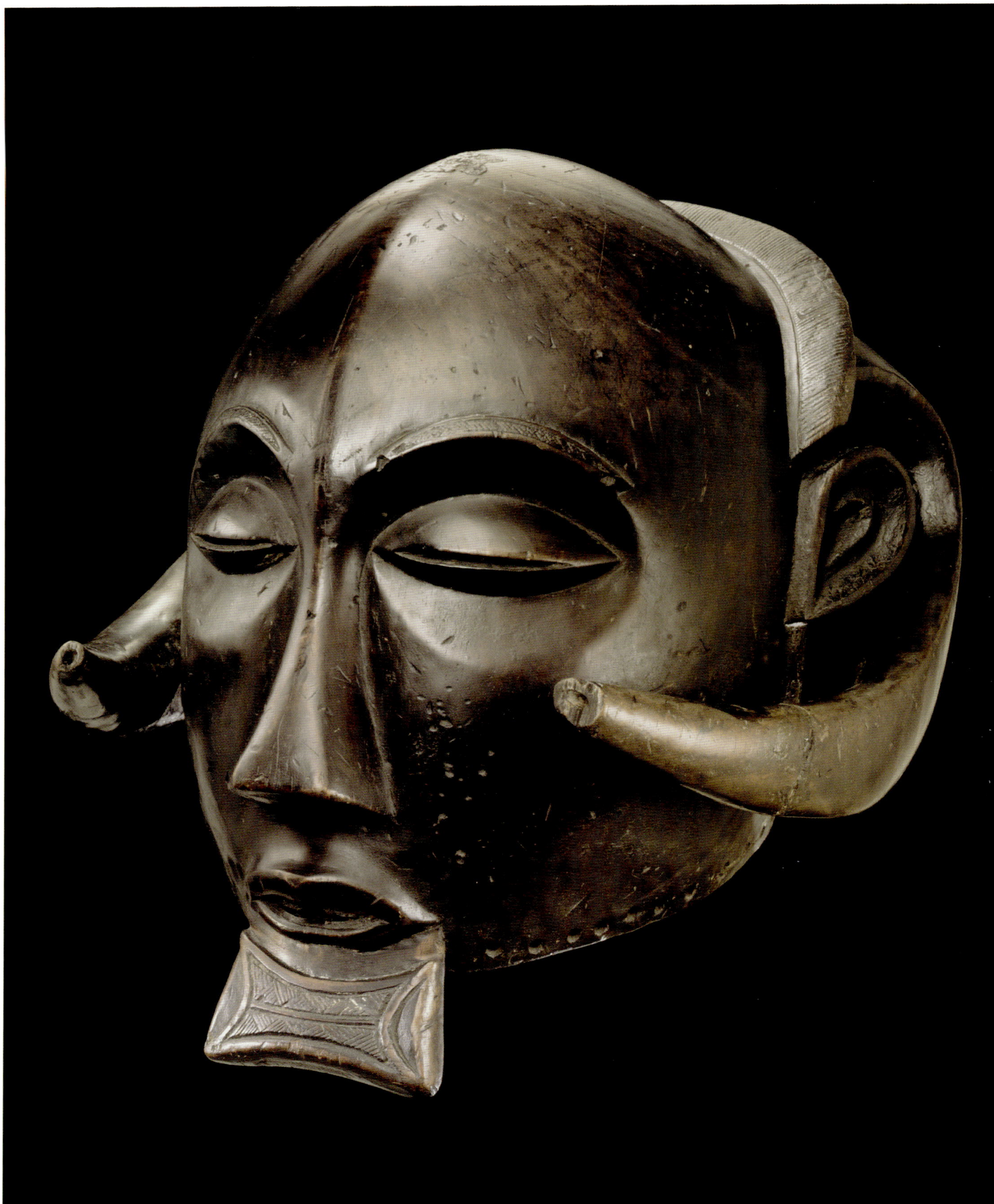

234. Luba artist
Democratic Republic of the Congo, 19th c.
Helmet-mask
Wood, 39 cm
Musée Royal de l'Afrique Centrale, Tervuren

According to Eberhard Fischer and Hans Himmelheber,[7] in the cultural universe of the Dan masks are not representations of spirits but the means through which spirits manifest themselves. In other words, they embody supernatural powers that are required to be present at every important event and when social control is exercised.

The adjective "realistic" can also be applied, though with some qualification, to masks created by other peoples, especially the Dan. See, for example, the white Punu mask from Gabon, formerly in the Goldet Collection (no. 232), in which naturalism and spirituality are harmoniously combined. Known to have been in Europe as early as the mid-19th century, it is unquestionably an antique work. The mask is made interesting by gentle, even but not mawkish features set harmoniously in the oval face enlivened by slight asymmetries. Note the almost imperceptible differences in the level of the upward slanting eyes, eyebrows, ears and scarification marks, and the lips that are fractionally out of line with the regularly shaped nose: these are all minimal variations that attest to the artist's sensibility. The abrasion of part of the kaolin that originally covered the face has revealed the warm tint of the ground that blends with the black hair, which is styled in two soft chignons that extend in stylized wings on either side of the forehead.

In the past, masks like these were used in funeral ceremonies whose function was to establish the bond between the dead and the living. The dancers who wore the masks usually stood on stilts, and their white faces – a colour associated with death by many African peoples – took on a somewhat ghostly aspect when seen from below.

Examples of realism also occur frequently in Chokwe art, as has been seen in previous works (nos. 167–169). Another instance is given in the features that animate the brilliant surface of the oval face – the idealized symbol of woman as an ancestor and source of life – in the stunning mask in the Musée Royal de l'Afrique Centrale, Tervuren (no. 233), which are rendered in a surprisingly lifelike and sober manner. The large well-defined lips harmonize with the half-closed eyes beneath the strongly arched eyebrows, suggesting a kind of spiritual intensity heightened by the wild, luxuriant coiffure.

The Belgian scholar Marie-Louise Bastin has attributed this mask to the style of the period of expansion, which began with the Chokwe emigrating towards Kasai in the second half of the 19th century.

The celebrated helmet-mask – a virtually unique work in the panorama of Luba art – in Tervuren (no. 234) can also justifiably be considered a masterpiece of realistic African art, whose parts are governed by a subtle and rigorous volumetric schema dominated by the sphere.

An immense shaved forehead framed by a horizontal plait extends above the large eye sockets, half-closed eyes, elegant eyebrows and small mouth. Two plaits, like pointed horns, accentuate the roundness of the overall volume, and their unusual forward curve encloses ears of a similar shape. Only the small square appendage – a beard or ornamental element – contrasts with the overall roundness, while enhancing its formal coherence and noble purity. The significance and function of this monumental work unfortunately remains a mystery.

The face on the Konde mask in a private collection in Belgium (no. 235) is also constructed around the sphere. The mask has both the lifelike quality of a portrait and the expressiveness of a work of art. This is created through the accentuations, reductions and simplifications introduced by the artist. Examples are seen in the strange triangular upper lip, which is perfectly integrated into the play of reliefs, and the large circular pavilions of the ears whose simplified volumes echo the shape of the head. Incidentally, the head was originally covered with real hair.

The geometric decoration is, unusually, sculpted rather than executed in applied wax and echoes the facial features, creating a perfect harmony between the volume and the surface embellished by a rich, shiny patina.

These masks (*mapiko*) created by Konde sculptors were used in the dances that marked the end of the rites of passage from boyhood to manhood.

235. Konde artist
Mozambique or Zimbabwe
Mask
Wood and hair, 27 cm
Private collection

236. Dogon artist
Mali
Ancestral couple
Wood and iron, 57.8 cm
Art Gallery of Ontario, Toronto
(formerly in the Murray Frum
Collection)

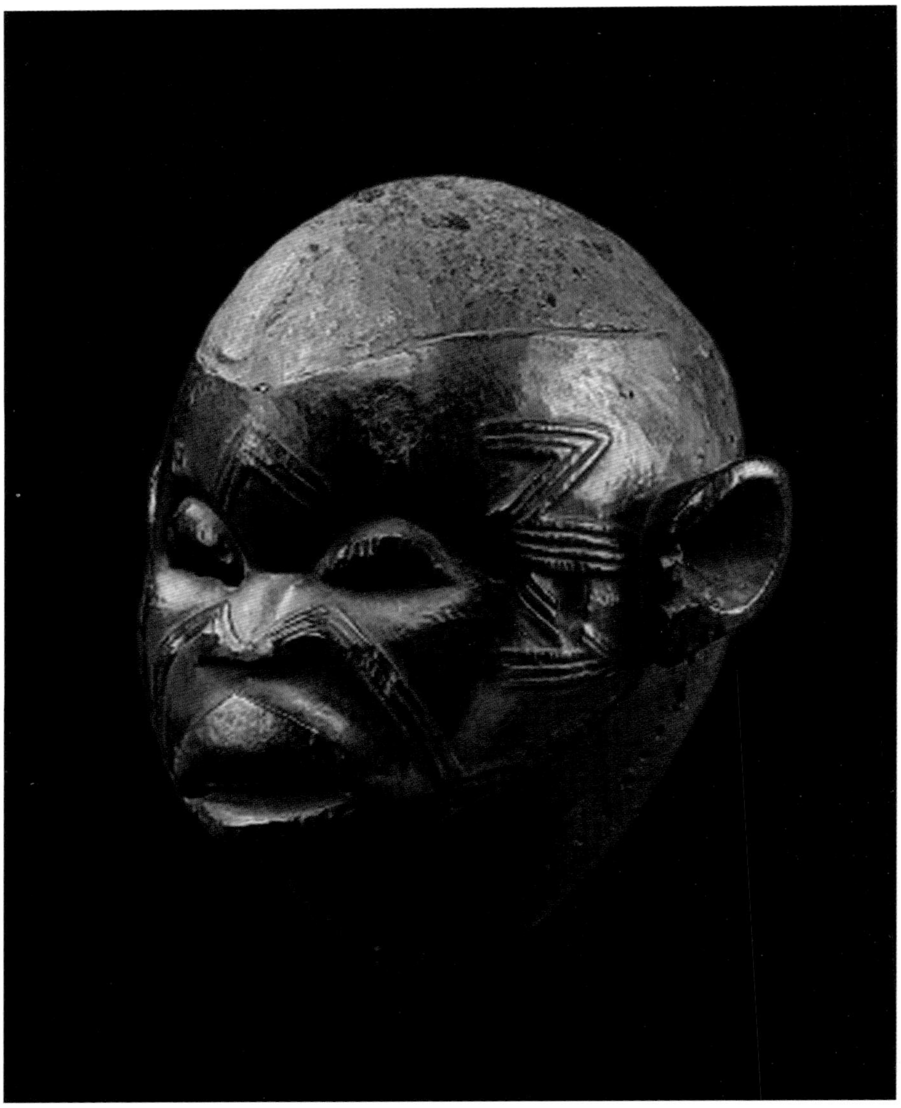

Cubism

The label "cubist", which signifies the representation of human figures and objects in geometrically recognizable forms, has been attributed more often than others to African art due to its treatment of the various parts of the human body as independent and volumetrically defined elements, and the apparently arbitrary assemblage of these elements.

The adjective would be justified if the sculptures in this chapter had been created by European artists, but it is inappropriate and simply convenient to apply it to the works by great African sculptors that we admire so much. Unfortunately, I have no better descriptive term. African artists were not familiar with Picasso or Braque and they certainly would have been surprised to hear their creations described with a reference to the theories of the celebrated Paris school. They would simply have rejected the definition, since they considered their distortions of visible reality to be of a metaphysical rather than formal nature.

Not only were African artists unaware of the definition, the reasons for the creation of African artworks are manifold and correspond to needs that are different from European ones, in that they are symbolic, religious and social. This does not mean that African artists did not abide by formal artistic language, indeed their usage of it is all too evident, to the extent that no result could be considered purely fortuitous.

The use of pure volumes can already be seen in works made between 500 BC and 500 AD by Nigerian Nok artists, who used spheres, cones and cylinders to fashion the heads and bodies of their terracotta figures, with results of surprising expressiveness (nos. 19–20).

Many of the more recent works can legitimately be placed in the "cubist" category. Indeed, a few decades ago William Fagg described an extraordinary

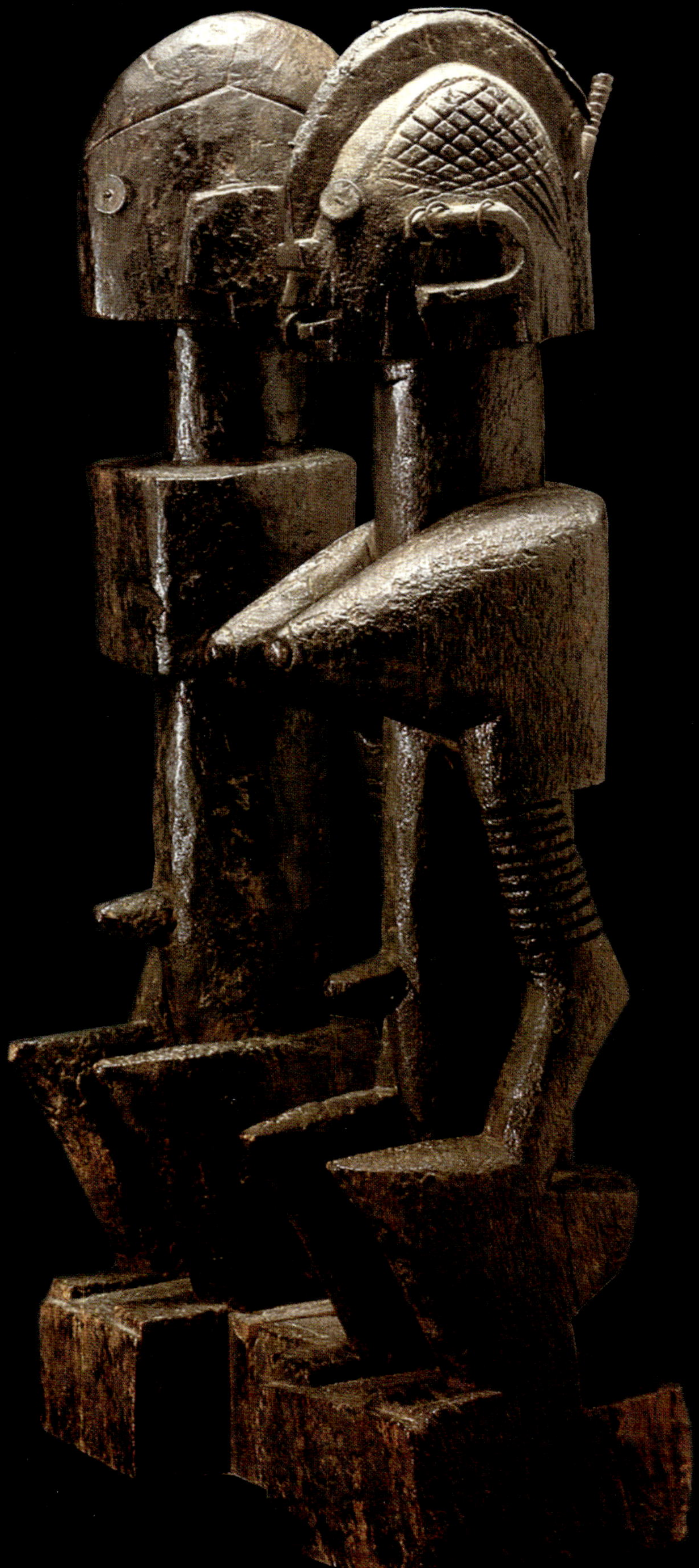

237. Bamana artist
Mali
Human figure
Wood, 59.5 cm
Horstmann Collection, Zug

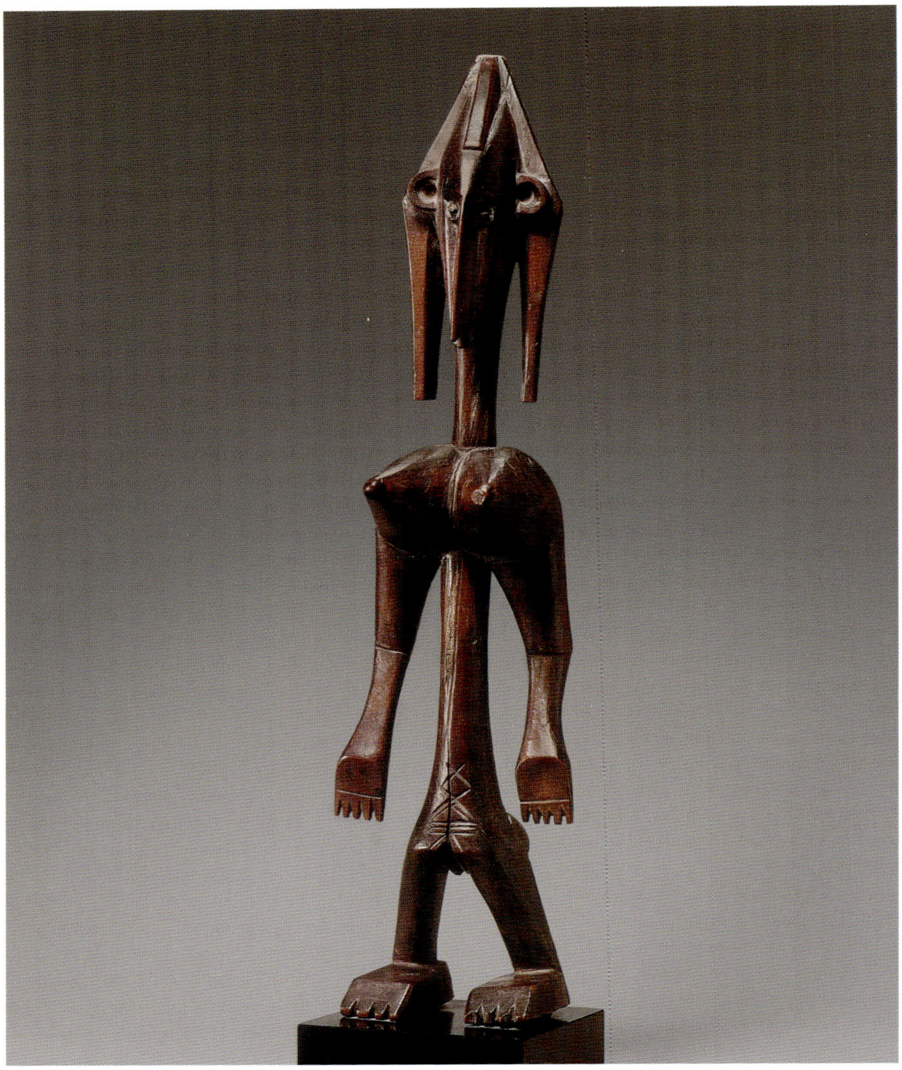

sculpture that was formerly in the Frum Collection (no. 236) as "an uncompromisingly cubistic piece".[8]

This definition is certainly justified by the successful combination of almost pure volumes, the rhythmic assemblage of the different blocks and their evident complementariness.

According to Helène Leloup, this sculpture – one of the most rigorous and compelling images of a male-female couple in African art – originated in the vicinity of the village of Dogo south of the Bandiagara Escarpment, and marks "the transition from the Dogon to the Bamana style",[9] which would perhaps explain the volumetric scheme of the work.

The artist who produced the Bamana figure in the Horstmann Collection (no. 237) went still further by visualizing and rendering his subject, the human figure, in absolutely rigorous geometric forms. He appears to have responded to Paul Cézanne's exhortation – naturally without being aware of it – to represent nature by means of pure volumes.

The reductive operation is taken to the extreme in the head, whose various parts are represented by forms that could not be more arbitrary: the cylindrical ears that interact with the round eyes, and the extremely long nose, whose powerful verticality is continued on the forehead with an element representing the hair. The harmonious volumes that lengthen the head have been assembled in a masterly fashion.

The extreme geometrization in no way interferes with the unity of the work; on the contrary, it is crucial to the creation of a coherent image of a female with a powerful visual impact.

The portrait of a queen from the Cameroonian savannah (no. 238) provides a different example of the "cubist" representation of the human figure. The work is distinguished by the bold articulation of the smooth yet powerfully defined masses: the spherical head enlivened by the pronounced, expressive facial features, the perfect cylinders of the powerful neck and limbs, the swollen belly, and the heavy conical breasts. In the three-quarter rear view the deconstruction and reduction of the body parts to pure volumes is even more evident. However, these volumes are organized according to a strict compositional scheme which, while not excluding movement, albeit almost imperceptible, endows the image with a formal coherence and monumentality without suppressing its exuberant vitality.

The sculpture portrays Queen Nana, the wife of King Metang, who ascended to the Batufam throne in 1912. The work is part of a group of statues that was first photographed by F. Christol in 1925 outside the Batufam palace. The group consists of six images of kings and queens, presumably created at different times over the course of more than a century.[10] The grouping of the pieces, which was by no means accidental, will enable us to study the development of sculpture in this small kingdom, but only after the Batufam authorship has been established and all the figures have been identified, thereby allowing their chronological sequence to be determined.

A further example of so-called "cubism" is the Songye "giant" held by the British Museum, London (no. 239), which is one of the most imposing figures used for magical-religious purposes of its kind. With the exception of the strongly protruding conical abdomen and the cylindrical neck enhanced by the bead necklaces, the volumes of the body are rigid and angular, making the figure seem more like an automaton than a human being. The geometrization is condensed in the powerful head with metal decoration that accentuates the angular features and heightens the expressiveness. It is further emphasized by the sharp aggressiveness of the forward-pointing horn – the only natural element in the whole sculpture.

Regarding the beneficent function of such figures – a surprising aspect given their hostile appearance – the reader is referred to the discussion of works nos. 156–157.

The universe of African masks, perhaps even more than that of figures, also offers examples of works that could be termed "cubist".

The Bamana Kore mask (no. 240), now in the civic collections of Milan, is one of the most carefully structured known to exist. Here the sculptor's approach is taken to extremes. An unbroken ridge delimits the concave face of the animal (a monkey?), from which emerges the volume of the perfectly triangular, imperious nose. This is seamlessly joined to the ridge at the top of the face to lend unity to the structure. The open rectangular eye sockets bring light to the deepest part of the concave surface without breaking the continuity. Executed with a remarkable economy of means, the sculpture is rendered exceptional by the rigorous, absolute volumes and essential, unmodifiable curves.

The plastic solutions invented completely independently by the artist are the same as those arrived at by the artists of the Paris school at the beginning of the 20th century. Thus, it was no accident that William Rubin noted similarities between this mask and a series of studies executed by Picasso in 1908, in the catalogue of the major exhibition '"Primitivism" in 20th Century Art'.[11]

The Kore is the last of the Bamana initiatory societies. It is characterized by eight levels and shows man the path from his animal nature to wisdom. Each level has its zoomorphic mask or its particular emblem. The monkey mask represents the eighth level and the dancers who wear it imitate the movements of the animal during the dances performed in the dry season to invoke abundant rain.

The solution adopted by some Grebo artists of sculpting eyes with cylindrical reliefs instead of holes – which we would consider revolutionary – is held by William Rubin to have influenced Picasso (who owned a Grebo mask) in the creation of his sculpture *Guitar.*

Grebo masks fall into two distinct categories that might approximately and arbitrarily be described as tending towards the realistic and the geometric. The one illustrated here (no. 241) – which is similar to the mask owned by

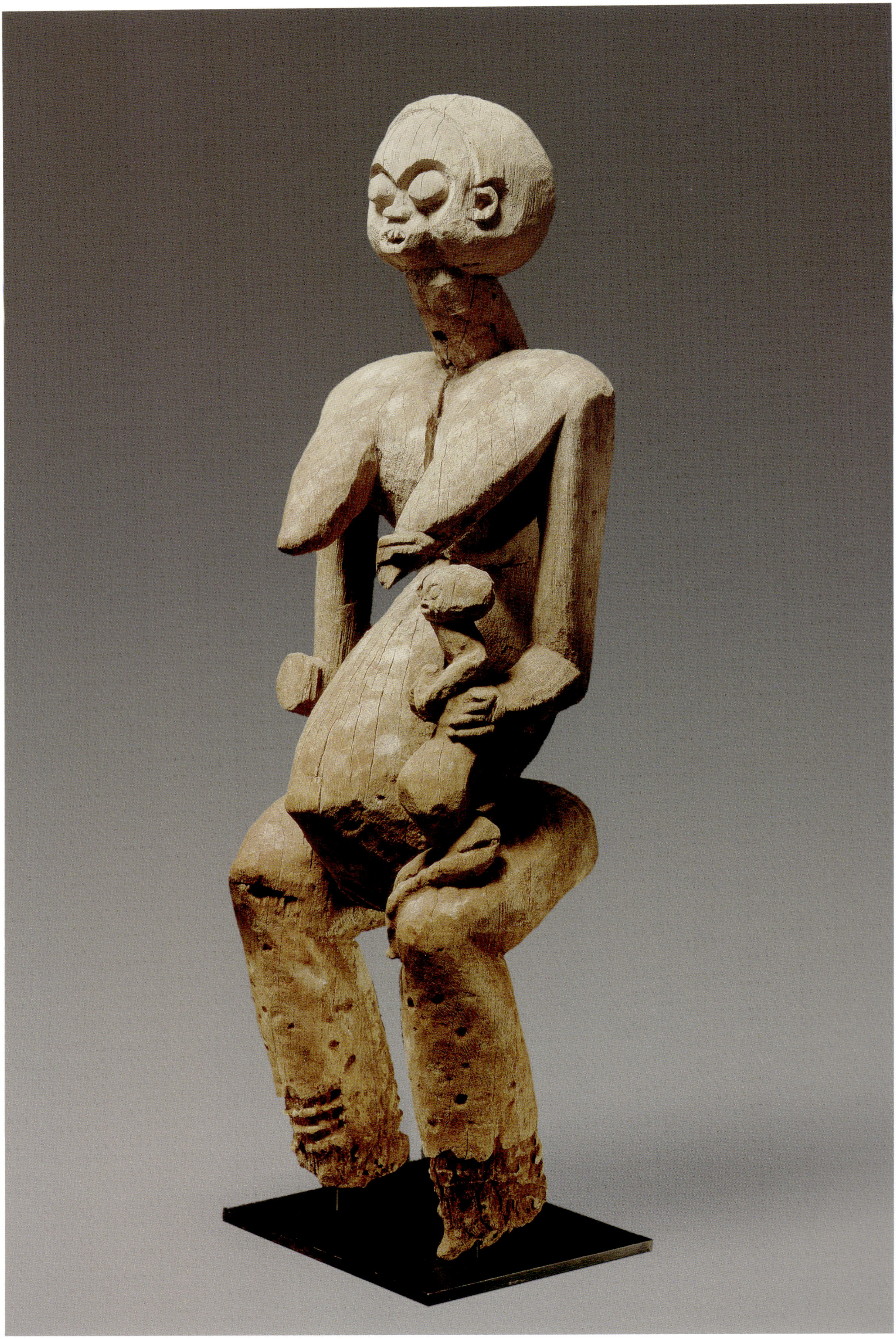

238. Bangwa artist
Cameroon
Statue of queen and child
Wood, 103 cm
Art Gallery of Ontario, Toronto
(formerly in the Murray Frum
Collection)

239. Songye artist
Democratic Republic of the Congo
Figure with magical-religious
functions
Wood, metal, glass beads, plant
fibres, horn and skin, 101.6 cm
The British Museum, Ethnography
Department, London

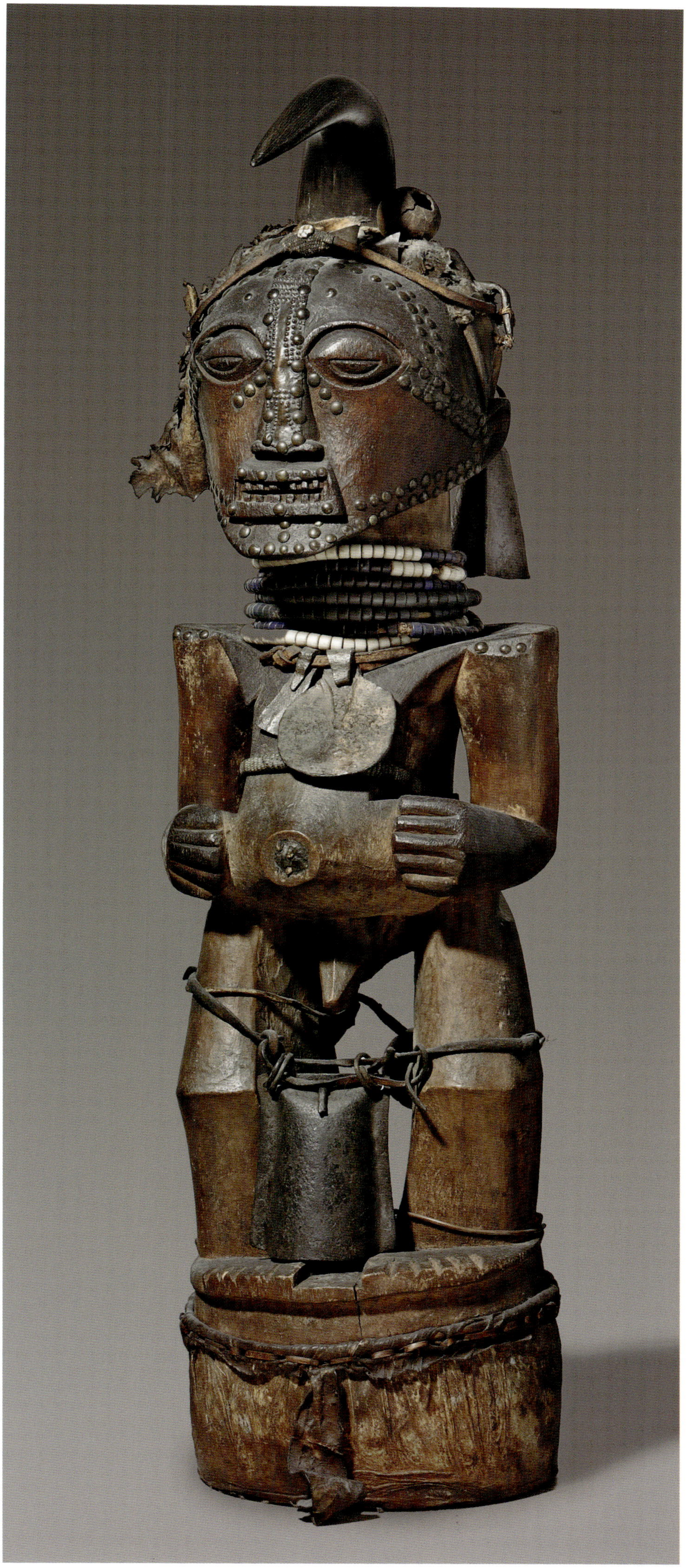

240. Bamana artist
Mali
Kore society mask
Wood, 25 cm
Civiche Raccolte Artistiche del Castello Sforzesco, Raccolte Extraeuropee, Milan

241. Grebo artist
Liberia
Mask
Wood and kaolin, 45.1 cm
Private collection (formerly in the Mario Meneghini Collection)

Pages 272–273
242. Songye artist
Kasai, Democratic Republic of the Congo
Mask
Wood, fibres and colour, 50 cm (excluding fibres)
Private collection

243. "Master of Bamendjo"
Bamileke, Cameroon
Monumental mask
Wood, 67 cm
Museum Rietberg, Zurich (formerly in the Von der Heidt Collection)

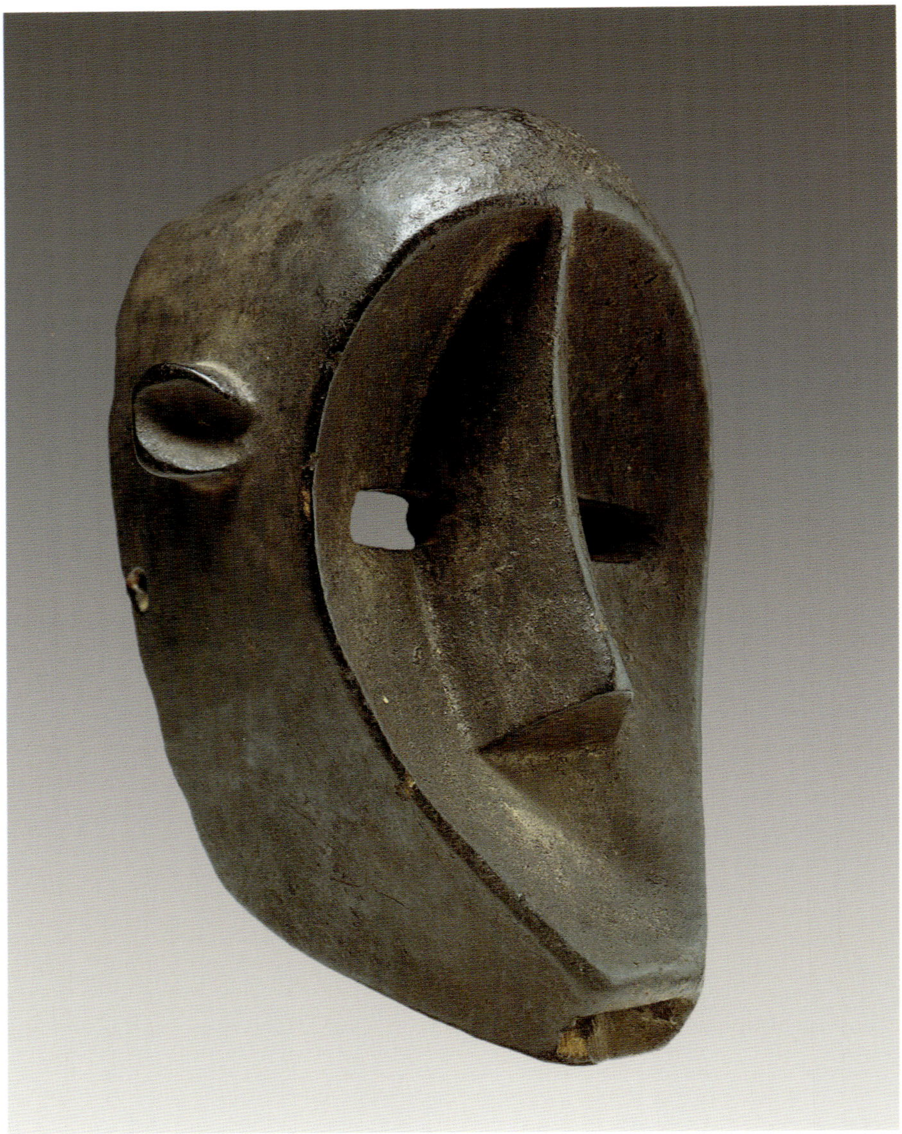

Picasso, which was probably acquired on a trip he made with Braque to Marseille in 1912 – is certainly one of the finest examples of the second category on account of its compositional rigour and powerful expressiveness.

The facial features grouped in the lower half of the mask are represented as basic volumes that project from the flat surface. The smooth, slightly curved forehead is animated by two symmetrical disks and three vertical reliefs to accentuate its height, and appears to be hinged above the eyes: a shallow horizontal groove divides the two volumes comprising the face but the break is counteracted by the central relief that rises seamlessly from the nose to unify the two halves.

According to Mario Meneghini,[12] Grebo masks embody the invisible spirits that dwell in the forest.

The magnificent Songye masks known as *Kifwebe* can quite justifiably be included among the works that could be defined as "cubist", especially the male masks, whose protruding lineaments are represented by forms that are well-defined volumetrically but completely arbitrary. So much so that one would be inclined to attribute them to a European sculptor of the beginning of the last century if one did not know that they were independent creations of proven African origin. The execution of these masks, as exemplified by the one illustrated here (no. 242), is free yet well-disciplined, as is evident from the extraordinary severity created by the sharpness of the strongly defined volumes that make no concessions to softness, and their rigorous assemblage. They are volumes that come straight out of a treatise on solid geometry: two cylindrical sections, a pyramid and a parallelepiped are positioned perfectly and protrude strongly from the surface of the mask.

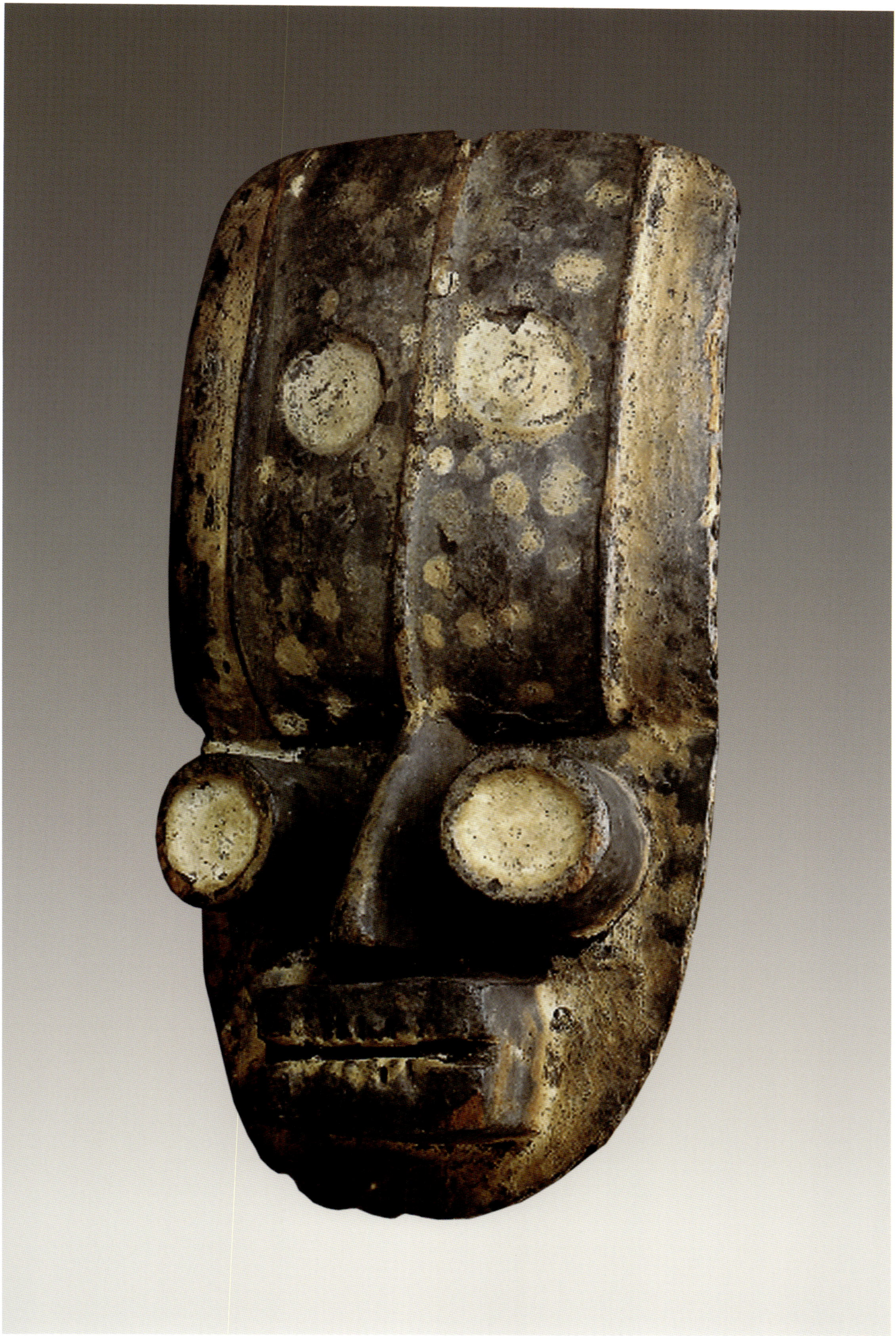

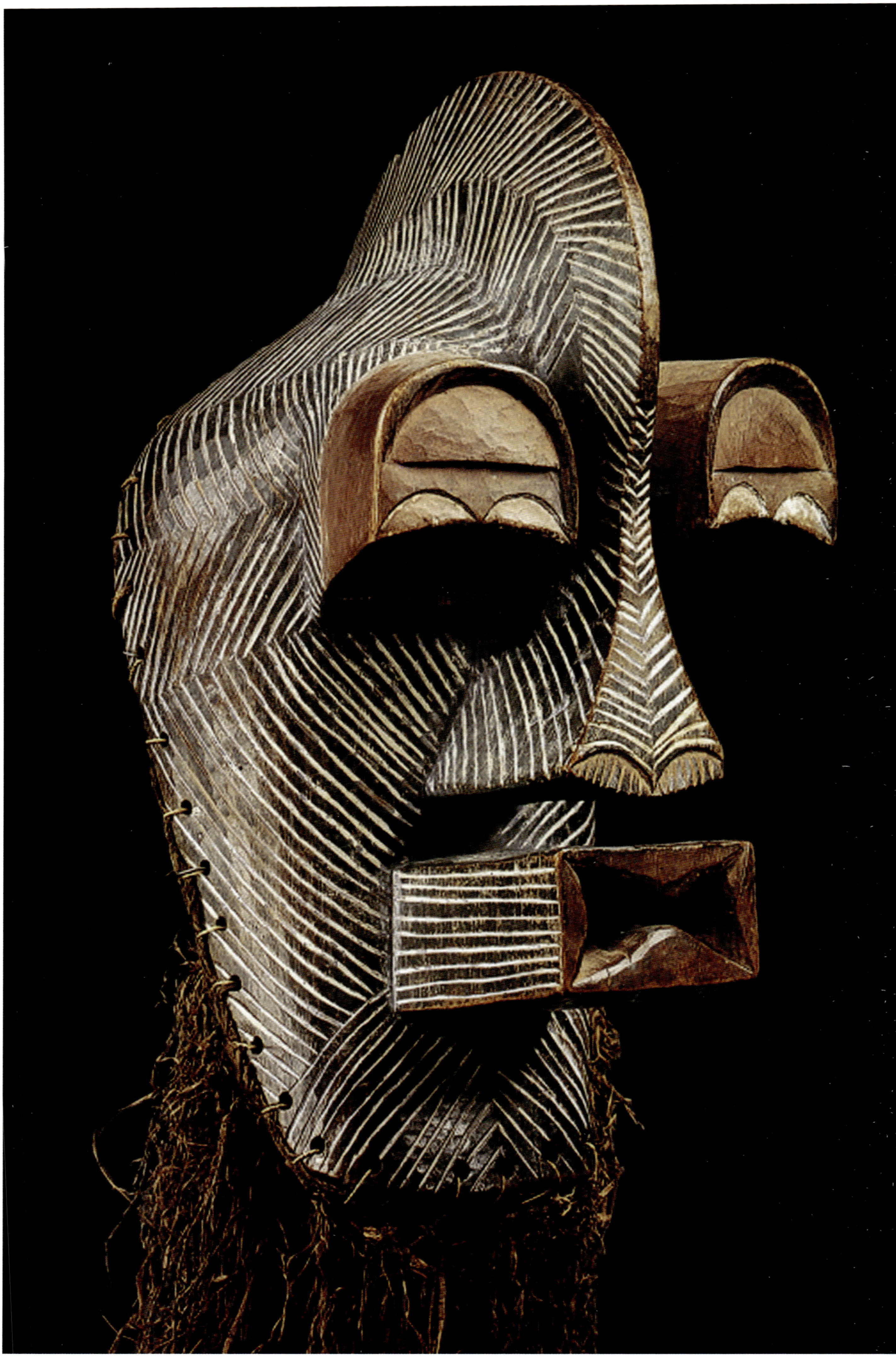

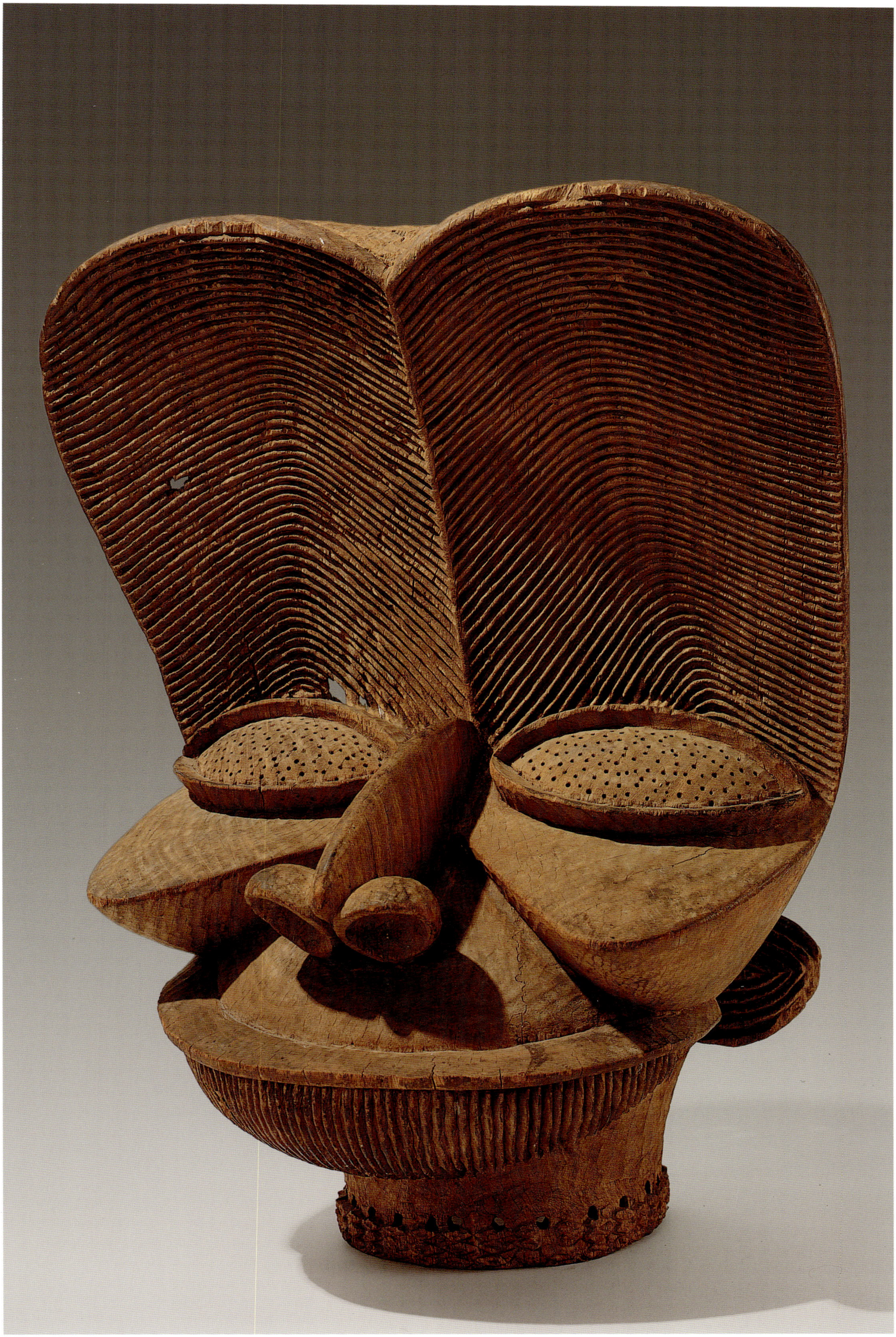

244. Chamba artist
Nigeria
Double figure
Wood, 58 cm
Horstmann Collection, Zug

The dense, skilfully rendered pattern of white kaolin incisions that covers the surface accompanies and enhances the modulations that culminate in the blade-like crest high up on the forehead of this mask: an evocation of a giant insect-man characterized by an extremely violent expressiveness that is not rendered less disturbing by the geometric precision of the features.

Male, like the one illustrated here, and female masks (the former being larger and more aggressive than the latter) were worn by members of a secret society to exercise social and political control over the community and to forcibly collect taxes that went to the heads of the society itself. The masked dancers were seen as supernatural creatures, ferocious alien beings who could not be opposed. These masks are presently used only for traditional dancing.[13]

The adjective "cubist" can also be legitimately applied to some rare Cameroonian masks, incorrectly referred to as 'Bacham'. The volumetric solutions of unequalled creative boldness that underpin them constitute a real challenge even for those of us accustomed to the audacious formal approaches of Western artists.

The diverse elements of the monumental head no. 243 are stripped of their naturalistic connotations and transformed into striking independent components within a disciplined schema in which the deconstructed and counterpoised volumes are arranged in a coherent expressive whole. The forehead dominates the strongly protruding articulated block of the cheeks, the nose with its unusual hemispherical nostrils and, above all, the enormous mouth. The subtle relief of the elegantly shaped, convex eyes links the lower part of the face to the very high forehead, which is like a taut veil enlivened by the slender central crest.

Until fairly recently, not more than about a dozen of these masks were known in the West. They came from different chiefdoms, each of which held only one example.[14] The first mask known in the West, which was formerly in the Museum für Völkerkunde, Leipzig, and is now lost, was collected in 1904. The second, illustrated here and now in Zurich (no. 243), was collected in 1914 and published (nos. 13 and 14) in *Afrikanische Plastik* by Carl Einstein in 1920. Two photos of the mask appeared. A third mask, acquired in 1925, is presently held by the Fowler Museum of Cultural History at the University of California, Los Angeles. Although the function of these monumental masks is not known, it appears to be connected with royalty in some way. Tamara Northern[15] has posited that they may have played a part in the enthronement of a king and also his funeral. And Pierre Harter[16] has suggested that they may also have been used in the designation of a king's successor.

Surrealism

A characterizing element of Surrealist European artworks is the unusual combination of incongruous components designed to create astonishing images subject neither to the laws of logic nor reason, namely, a re-evaluation of the imaginary. Many African sculptures would appear to fit this definition. The artists who produced them were not motivated by the desire to desecrate, and although the combination of elements may appear incongruous to us, it was not so for the recipients, since it was done for cultural and religious reasons of which, in many cases, we are unaware. Here we are limiting ourselves to a few examples, starting with the disconcerting Chamba sculpture (no. 244), which is also very rare and was unknown until a few decades ago.[17] However, there is no disputing the ingeniousness of the artist who, possibly with the intention of representing figures in the mythological universe of his people, invented this surreal couple whose equal is to be found only in the fantastical figures featured in European medieval codices.

The anatomy is completely unrealistic. The shoulders hunched forward, the large fan-shaped hands and the eyeless heads with large protruding ears and lipless rectangular mouths open in a kind of scream give the two figures a pathetic, stunned look. But the brilliant idea, the stroke of genius – possibly to acknowledge a myth adhered to by the people to which the artist belonged

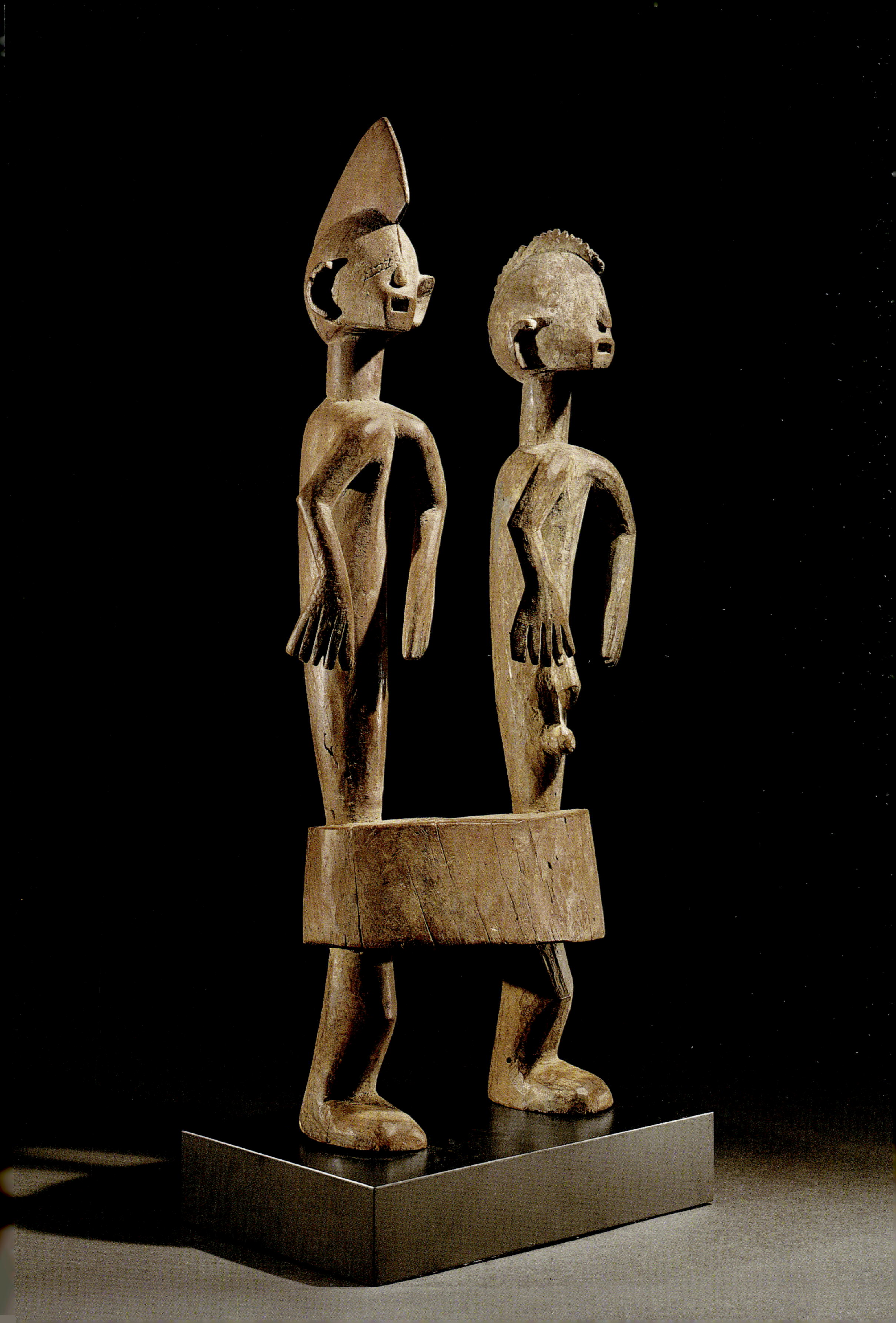

245. Kpelle artist
Guinea
Mask
Wood, fur and copper, 44 cm (including beard)
Civiche Raccolte Artistiche del Castello Sforzesco, Raccolte Extraeuropee, Milan

246. Luba artist
Democratic Republic of the Congo (Shaba region)
Mask
Wood, fur and colour, 39.2 cm
Musée Royal de l'Afrique Centrale, Tervuren

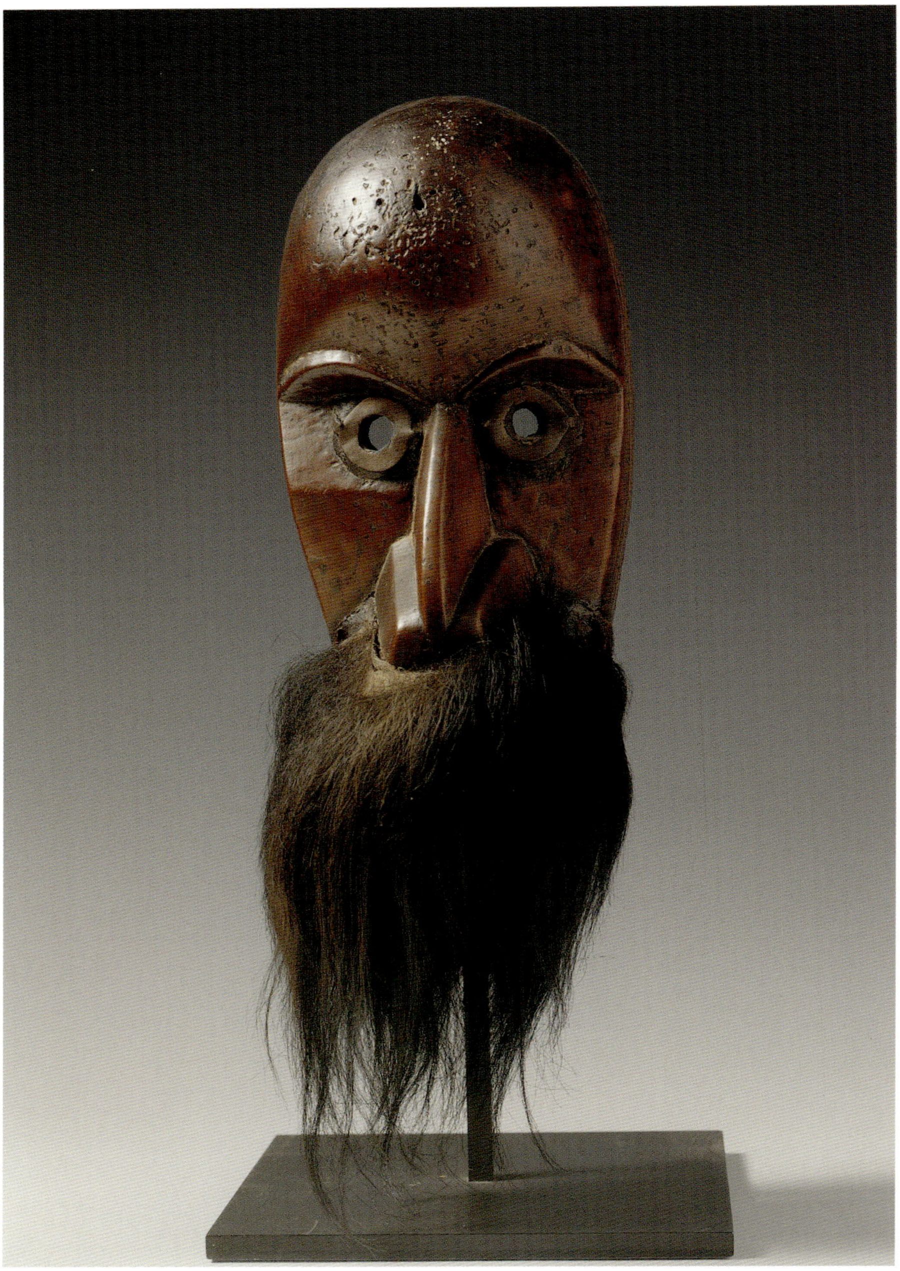

– was to insert their tapered trunks into a thick roundel from which only one pair of short, sturdy legs emerges beneath. The artist has created a disquieting monster with two bodies.

Works that could be described as "surrealist" are often to be found among masks in which human and animal elements are combined, as in this Guinean example (no. 245) with a large hemispherical forehead and enormous nose, which could also be the monstrous beak of a bird of prey. The penetrating gaze of the round eyes ringed with copper and set beneath elegantly arched eyebrows gives a dynamic expression to the face (or muzzle?) with unusually pronounced cheekbones. A long beard made of monkey hair conceals a large animal-like mouth with a mobile lower jaw. The result is the head of a hybrid creature, an image of a mysterious animal-man, which the brilliant deep-red surface and the black monkey hair endow with a subtle fascination.

A similar mask was purchased by Leo Frobenius in 1916, and is now in the Museum für Völkerkunde, Munich.

In the rare Luba mask held by the Musée Royal de l'Afrique Centrale, Tervuren (no. 246), whose meaning and use are still uncertain, the features of a human being and probably those of a lion are combined to disturbing effect. François Neyt[18] has suggested that the mask might be a symbol of royalty or, alternatively, the attribute of a member of a society of "lion-men" who clandestinely and bloodily administered justice in some parts of Central Africa.

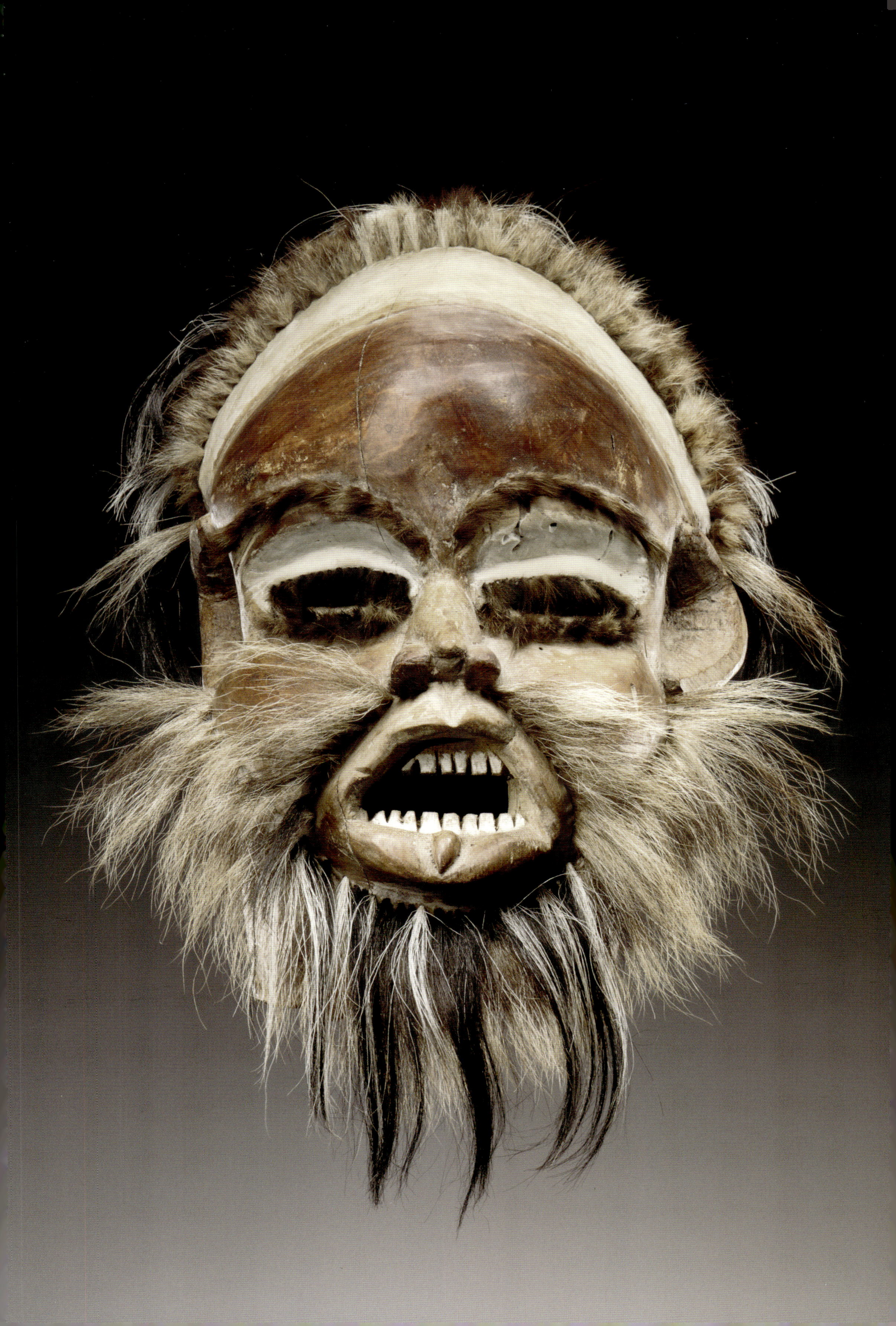

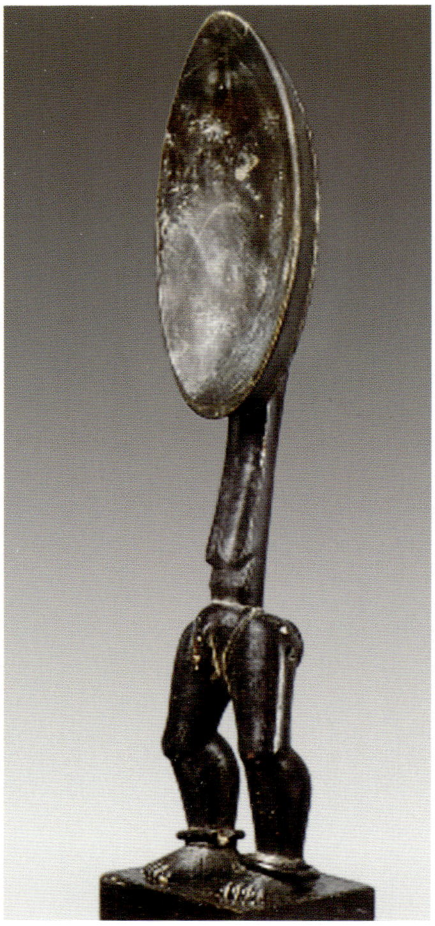

247. Dan artist
Liberia, Ivory Coast
Spoon
Wood and metal, 52 cm
Private collection

248. Kuba artist
West Kasai, Democratic Republic of the Congo
Libation goblet
Wood, 15 cm
Private collection

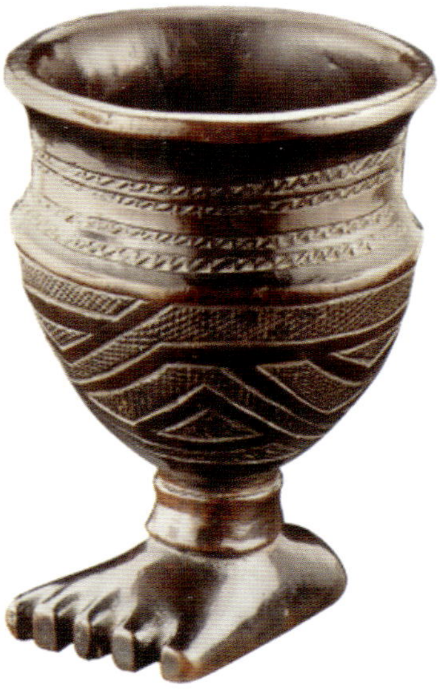

Here, the imperturbable calm of the faces – mostly female – of the shiny monochrome Luba sculptures has vanished, erased by the telling and expressive use of colour and horsehair that gives the regular features a dramatic, animated quality without radically altering them. The use of white kaolin to accentuate the curve of the forehead and the eye sockets, together with the white teeth in an abnormally large, wide-open mouth, cleverly creates another mask on top of the first. The addition of hair in suitable lengths and colours, such as the white and black tufts on the chin, completes the image and gives it a kind of feral intensity.

The large Dan spoon (no. 247),[19] whose handle is formed by two well-shaped legs, genitals that, unusually, are male, and small rounded buttocks, might also be considered a surrealistic image in the West. A stylized trunk, enlivened by an elegant relief composed of two skilfully rendered concave parts, connects the pelvis to the head/bowl in the shape of a perfect oval that is subtly echoed by the sculpted festoons on the back. The relief decoration on the trunk gives thrust to the limpid composition, confirming the anonymous sculptor's plastic sensibility.

The function and symbolic value of the spoons made by the Dan and the We peoples in Liberia and Ivory Coast, displayed during special festivities, are emblems of women enjoying particular social status.

The adjective "surrealist" would also be more than justified to describe the work of the sculptor who created the intriguing vessel no. 248, had he been a Western artist. The volume of the goblet and the large square foot out of which it appears to grow, are so perfectly integrated that they appear to represent a spontaneously developed organism. The motivation behind this work by the Kuba sculptor was naturally in keeping with the ideas of his group, but unfortunately it escapes us. We can only appreciate his ability to make an artefact that is not only flawless from a formal standpoint, but is also a testimony, along with the others illustrated here, to the high quality of the works and the African sculptors' imaginative way of conceiving them.

Abstractionism

Complete abstraction, as practised in Western art, does not exist in African sculpture. However, we frequently find works in which the link with visible reality is tenuous and nuanced. It is mainly a question of natural forms being reduced to the essential, echoed or alluded to, thus it would be more correct to describe the works as tending towards abstraction.

The reliquary figures created by the Kota and by the Mahongwe in Gabon, for example, are arbitrary images fashioned in wood covered with thin sheets or strips of copper and brass, several of which are illustrated earlier (see nos. 176–177). They attest to the skill with which these artists used geometric forms, whose abstract formal spareness no longer has any connection with the physical reality they are presumed to symbolize, namely the body of a mythical ancestor.

The few works that follow will perhaps help to clarify what has been said above. The extraordinary Kwele mask (no. 249) – if this work is really a mask – is, in my opinion, one of the finest examples of the African sculptor's skill in visual abstraction. Here the artist has consciously ignored reality, opting for the powerful evocation of form through a kind of stylization unusual in its rhythmic repetition of elements.

A boldly conceptualized representation of the iconographic theme – the human face – combined with features reduced to the essential – the subtle relief (a nose perhaps?) that divides the perfect oval – and the arbitrary multiplication of the elements – the closed or half-closed eyes in the perfectly defined sockets – give this work a crystalline formal sharpness that seems to illustrate a concept of Brancusi's, according to whom simplicity was complexity resolved.

In his introductory essay in the catalogue of the previously mentioned exhibition '"Primitivism" in 20th Century Art', William Rubin spoke of "the reiteration of root signs that articulate the faces of many Picasso figures of the twenties and thirties"[20] in relation to this mask.

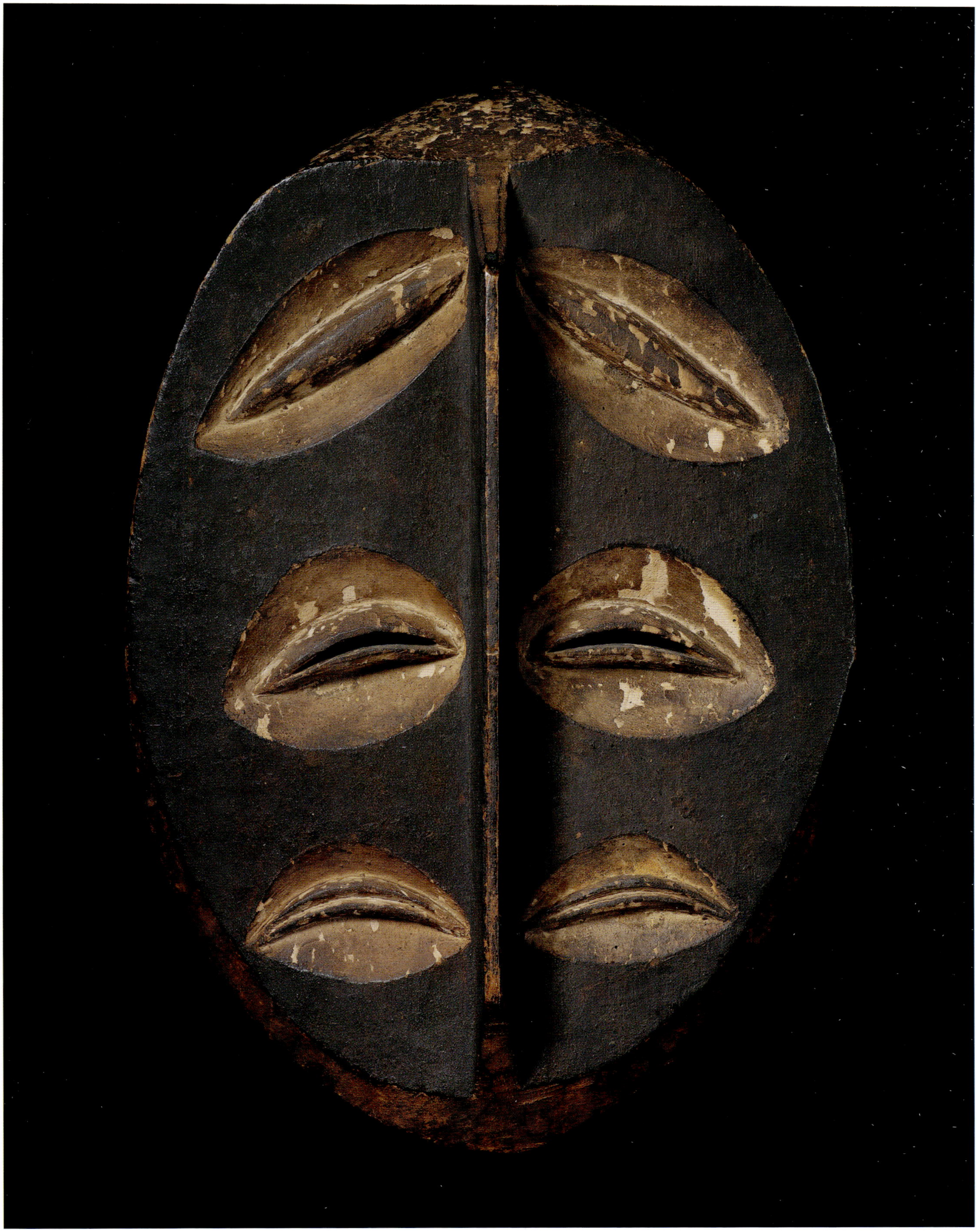

249. Kwele artist
Gabon
Mask (?)
Wood and pigments, 58 cm
Musée du Quai Branly, Paris

250. Ndengese artist
West Kasai, Democratic Republic of the Congo
Human figure
Wood and pigments, 139 cm
Musée Royal de l'Afrique Centrale, Tervuren

This can be seen, for example, in Picasso's *Head* of 1928 in which a stylized eye is repeated three times along a vertical axis.

The mask – acquired in Africa between 1930 and 1935 by Aristide Courtois, an official in the French civil service in what was then the colony of Gabon – was in several famous Paris collections, such as those of Charles Ratton, the painter Charles Lapicque and André Fourquet, before it was purchased by the Musée du Quai Branly.

Decorativism

Body decoration is currently practised in many African societies. The motifs, which are painted, tattooed or created through scarification, often cover the whole body and are also reprised in artworks, as can be seen in the Kongo maternity figure (no. 150–150a) and the Luba seat (no. 165).

The term 'decorativism', used by Western critics to signify the predominance of decorative motifs in a work of art, is also inappropriate for describing African sculptures since the decoration on them is never merely ornamental, but contains a complex message that the recipients are able to decipher according to their level of preparation. Therefore, the decoration is more like an identity card, personal data incised on the skin. Here the Western term is used, as in the case of the other formal categories, due to the lack of a more suitable definition.

The images, probably of chiefs, like the one illustrated here (no. 250), which were created in the past mainly by sculptors of the small Ndengese ethnic group in Kasai, are famous for the low-relief decoration that covers them entirely.

The austerity of the cylindrical and inordinately elongated torso and arms is accentuated by the white decoration that envelopes them in an ornate sheath. The intricate and regular geometric motifs of which it is composed constitute a kind of sign language[21] the recipients were certainly familiar with. The lower part of the body is synthesized in a semicircular block that also forms the base of the figure, which is an ingenious device.

The fluid structure, verticality, rigour of the colours – the white of the columnar body and the black of the head – combined with the grave reserve of the features create a mysterious image imbued with remote dignity.

A link with the art of the Kuba, to whom the Ndengese are related, is suggested by the shape of the head, and above all by the manner in which the hair is rendered in some figures and goblets created by the former.

Body decoration is also a characteristic feature of Luluwa sculpture, and evinces a cosmetic practice that was once widespread among the upper classes but abandoned before 1881.

However, the German explorer Hermann von Wissmann, who visited the region that year and acquired the first pieces to arrive in Europe, makes no reference to the fact. Tattoos, held to be a sign of beauty, indicated the elevated rank of a man or woman in society; moreover, the motifs depicted on the sculptures were exaggerated with respect to reality.

The ample spherical forehead and the cheeks of the maternal figure in this image of a mother and child carved by a Luluwa artist (no. 251) are covered with an elegant decoration created with artistically arranged keloids. These are echoed by the slender ringed neck and discreet motifs that adorn the slim, gleaming body. The tiny child lying trustingly in its mother's arms is placed on the diagonal, thus enlivening the composition.

Figures depicting a woman and child or a pregnant woman, which were associated with the fertility cult, were sculpted on the instructions of the priest-healers and destined for mothers who had either had an abortion or repeatedly lost their babies, in order to induce normal pregnancies.

The mask created by a Tsaye artist, which was in the collection of the Parisian painter Isaac Païles in the early decades of the last century (no. 252), is one of the few high-quality works of this kind that is certainly antique (along with the one that belonged to André Derain and is now in the Musée Barbier-

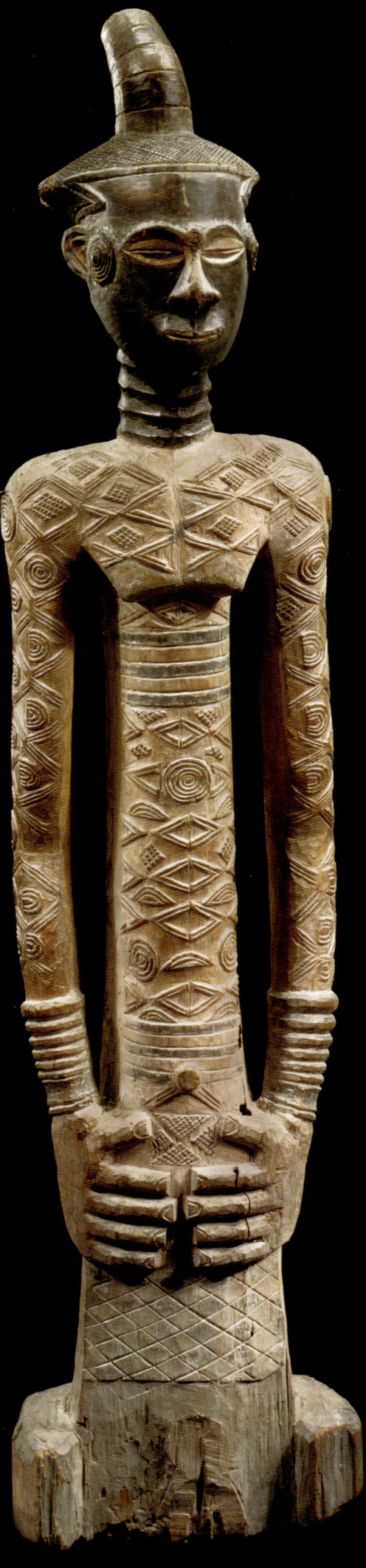

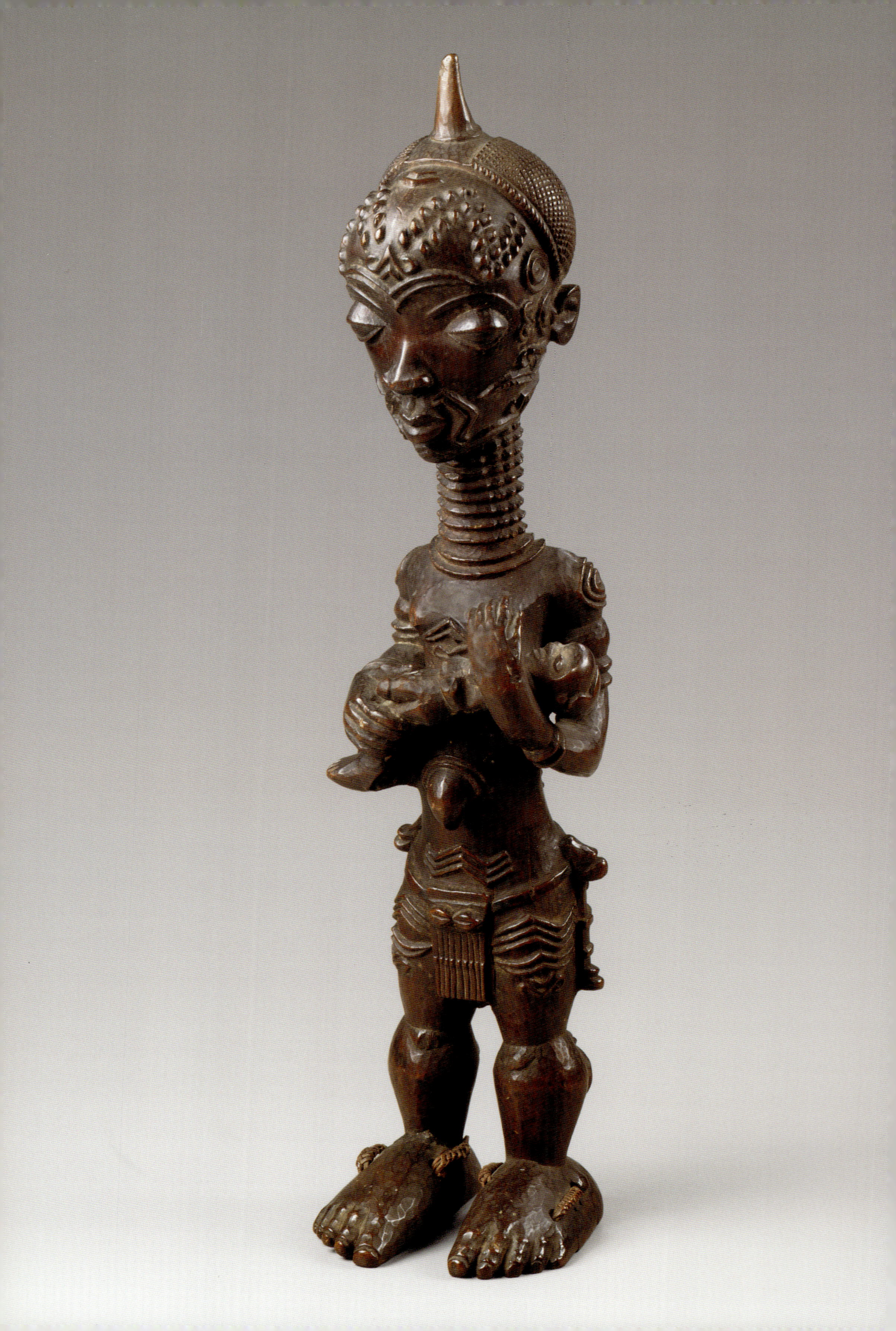

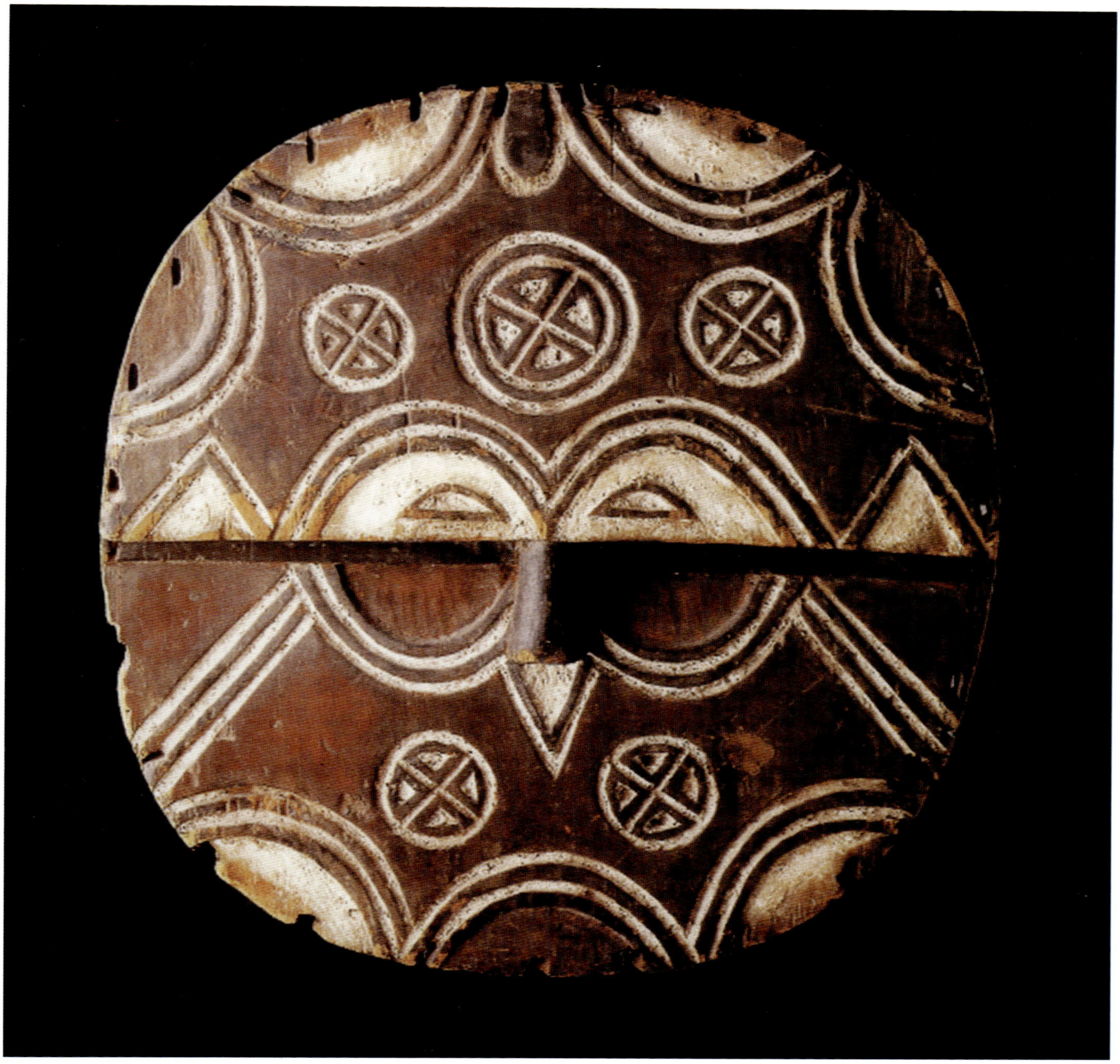

251. Luluwa artist
Democratic Republic of the Congo
Maternity figure
Wood, 41 cm
Musée Royal de l'Afrique Centrale, Tervuren (work acquired in 1886)

252. Teke artist (Tsaye)
Gabon, Republic of the Congo
Mask
Wood and pigments, 30.5 cm
Private collection (formerly in the Isaac Païles and Jean-Claude Bellier collections, Paris)

Mueller, Geneva) and illustrates what is said above concerning motifs that only appear to be decorative.

The elegant patterns that cover the surface of the mask, which at first glance may seem like an imaginative though formally sophisticated decoration, are actually a free representation of the human face. The surface of the large disk is animated by a slight and extremely subtle difference in level between the upper and lower halves. The eyes and the nose are placed respectively in these two fields and are the only human features that can be recognized due to their shape and position, though they also suggest the image of a nocturnal predator like an owl. The composition is unified by the circular eye sockets, whose surfaces are distributed equally above and below the relief line. The sobriety of the colours, namely reddish-brown and white, is almost certainly traditional and blends with and accentuates the complex decoration predominated by circles and the circular section.

The imaginative and disciplined arrangement of the motifs offers undeniable proof of the graphic skill and expertise in abstraction achieved by the artist who conceived and executed this masterly and fascinating work.

The use of these masks in the ceremonies performed by the Kidumu society, whose purpose was to strengthen the social and religious unity of the population, appears to have become obsolete at the beginning of the last century.

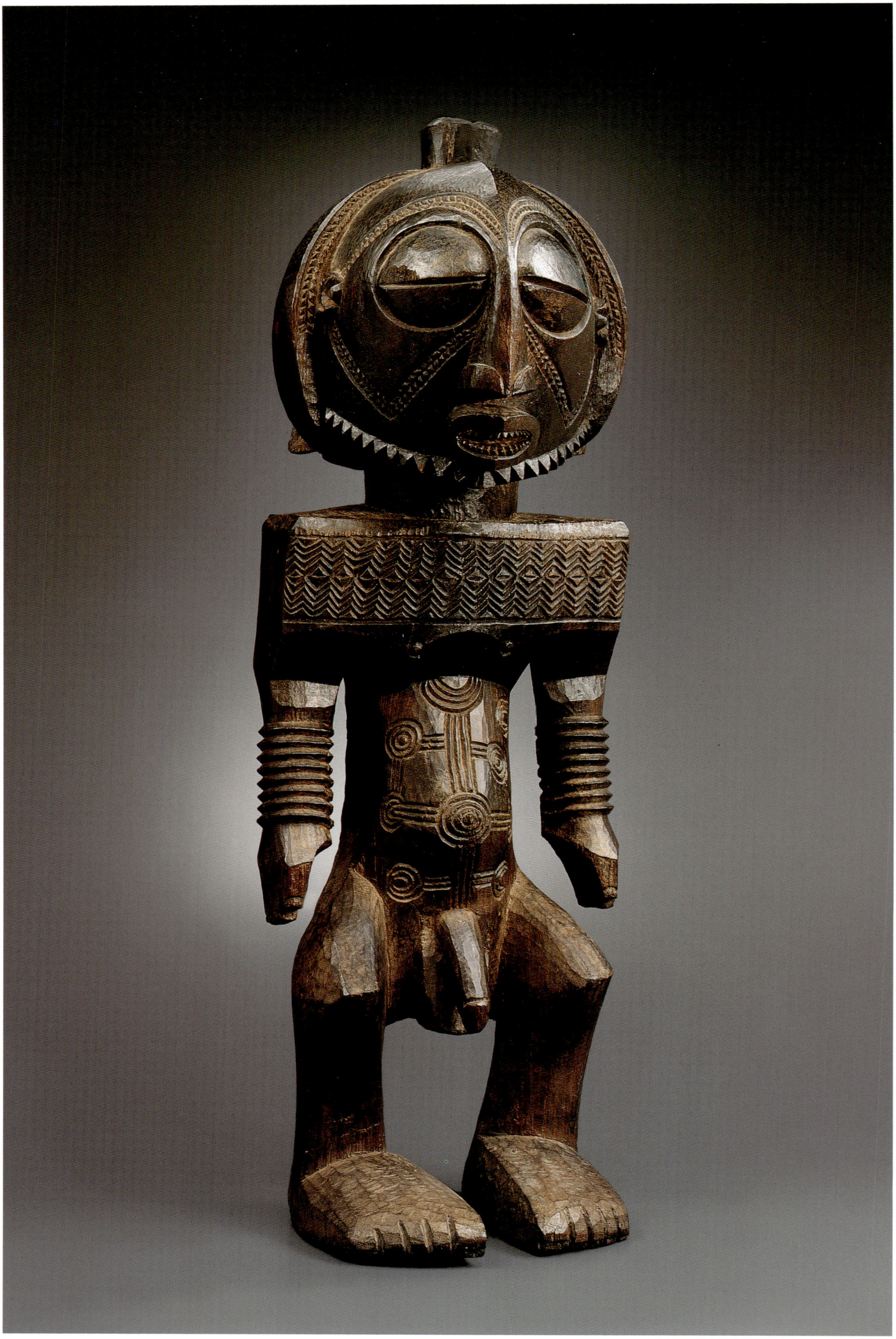

253. Boyo artist
Democratic Republic of the Congo
Royal effigy
Wood, 99.5 cm
Private collection

Pages 286–287
254. Bamileke artist
Chiefdom of Bamendou (?), Cameroon
Royal mask
Wood, 86 cm
Musée du Louvre, Pavillon des Sessions, Paris (Pierre Harter Bequest)

255. Baule artist
Ivory Coast
Mask
Wood, 22.5 cm
Horstmann Collection, Zug

The majority of examples in circulation are, in fact, recent replicas used in dances for entertainment, if not actual fakes.

Works that do not fit into formal Western categories, or are a combination of them

As I have stressed repeatedly, attaching a formal label to an artwork by an African people is always a very difficult operation and, in any case, inappropriate. The dozen or so works characterized by extremely diverse solutions that follow – which were neither created on a whim nor works that violated the accepted norms, but a combination of those norms and individual creativity – illustrate the difficulty and the inevitable arbitrariness of any classification.

The striking royal effigy created by a Boyo artist (no. 253), a kind of otherworldly figure who emanates a feeling of supernatural majesty, is the perfect example to introduce this last group. The extraordinary combination of the rigorously defined volumes and their perfectly integrated decoration proves a successful formula. The construction of the impressive head is based on the sphere, and therefore reminiscent of the round Luba masks. The eyes are the most striking feature of the large, sun-like face. They are enormous, hemispherical and set in completely circular eye sockets. A thin slit – like a horizontal hinge – separates the almost completely closed lids from the bottom of the eye: a characteristic also seen in many figures by the Bembe and Luba, neighbours of the Boyo.

The body composed of geometrized forms and covered with elegant engraved motifs is an appropriate support for the monumental head. In particular, the rectangular block of the chest and the short cylindrical arms enlivened by bracelets show the spherical mass of the head to advantage. The work was photographed in the mid-20th century by the Belgian scholar Luc Zangrie (pseudonym of Luc de Heusch) in the Kabambare region with five other statues. He described it as the image of a royal ancestor of the *Baka kunga*, one of the four Sumba royal families of the Boyo people, which, by then, had already been reduced to just a few thousand individuals.

Two similar figures (one of which was possibly by the same artist who made the work reproduced here), all trace of which was lost during World War II, were in the collections of the Museo di Antropologia e di Etnologia in Florence[22] from the beginning of the 20th century. This suggests that this superb example of the traditional art of a society at its peak was produced before the end of the 19th century.

However, it is in the creation of masks that the imagination – or what we in the West consider to be imagination – of African artists appears to know no limits when it comes to the cross-fertilization of apparently disparate forms and the accentuation or reductive stylization of elements that give the work its shape.

The monumental piece formerly in the Pierre Harter Collection and now in the Louvre (no. 254) is rendered unmistakable by the realism with which the features of the human face are rendered and also by the way in which their representation is adapted to the expressive needs of the artist through his daring and discerning formal choices. The work's powerful vitality is suggested by the oval shape of the swollen forms articulated in independent blocks of the reinvented head: the huge cheeks, the bulging forehead, the slanting upturned eyes, and the frames containing the six reptiles (giant lizards or possibly symbolic crocodiles) of what we presume to be the hair. The various parts of the mask are linked and governed by appropriate volumetric and formal relationships. The airy lightness of the openwork hairstyle further enhances the fullness and vitality of the head.

The meaning of the work as suggested by Pierre Harter[23] – human mortality suggested by the six reptiles, and fertility signified by the prominent forehead and the swollen cheeks (symbolizing a pregnant belly and breasts filled with milk) – is rich and complex, but still has to be confirmed.

Three similar masks (of inferior quality according to the author of the entry in *Les Rois Sculpteurs*) respectively in Berlin, Bremen and Chicago, were ac-

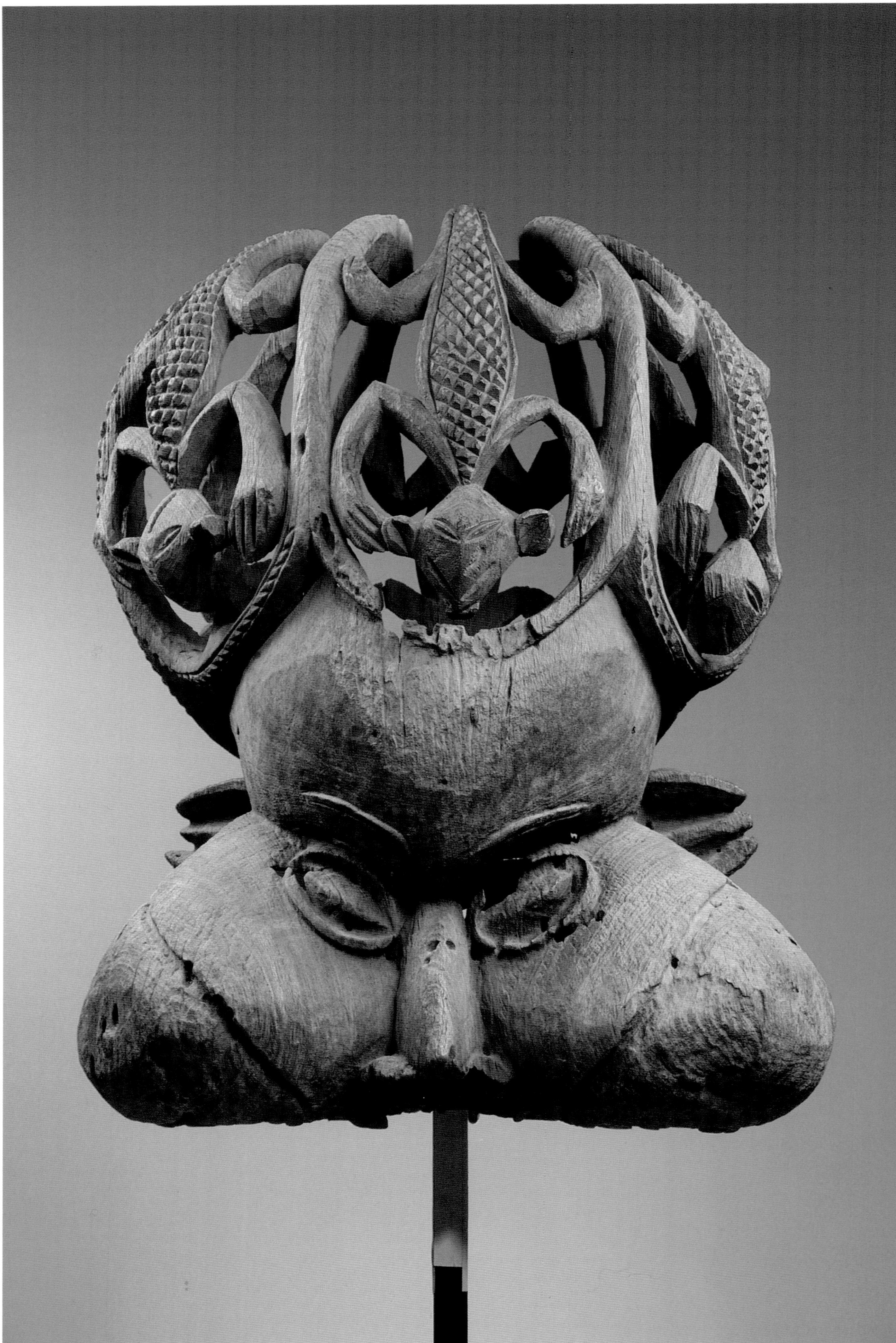

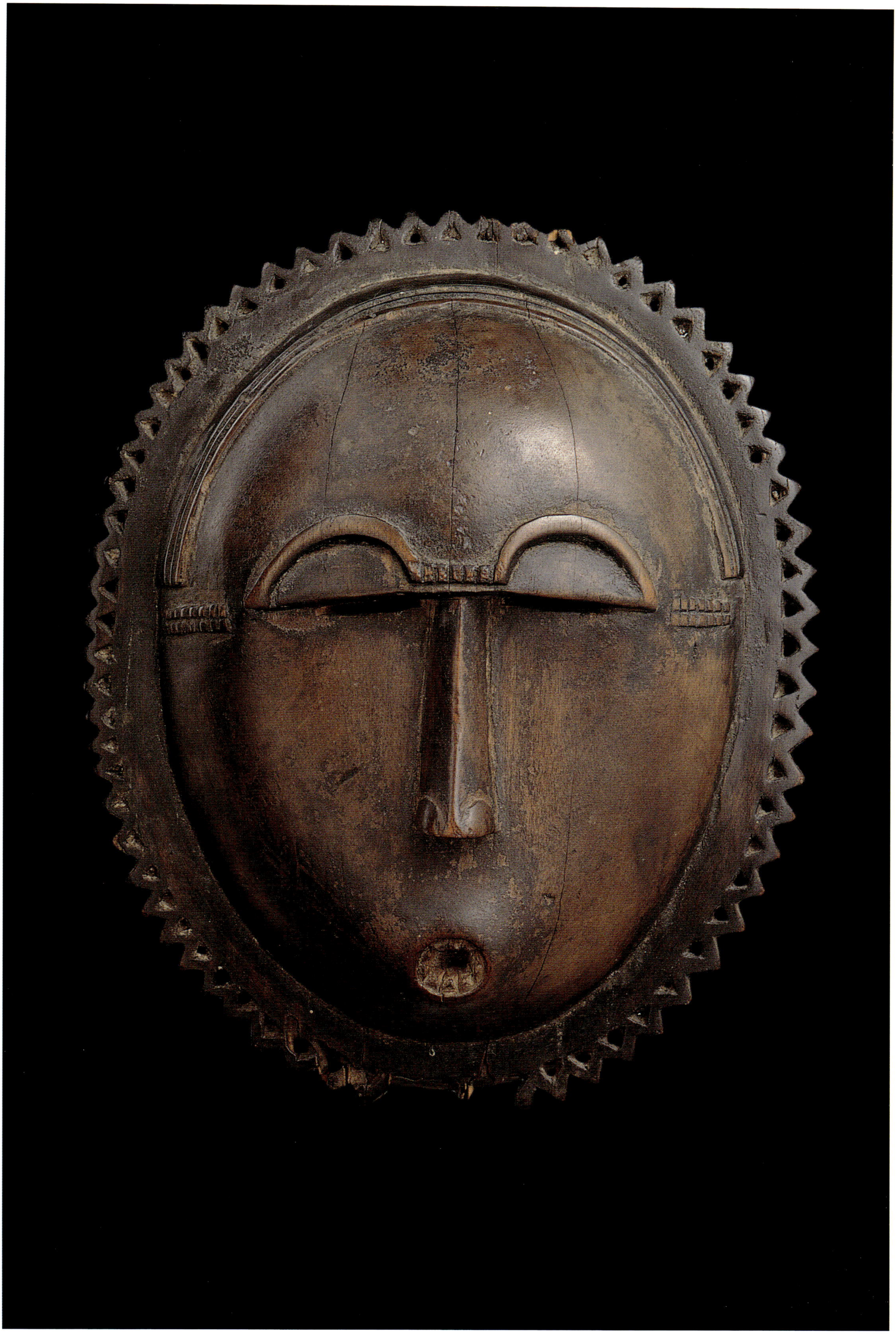

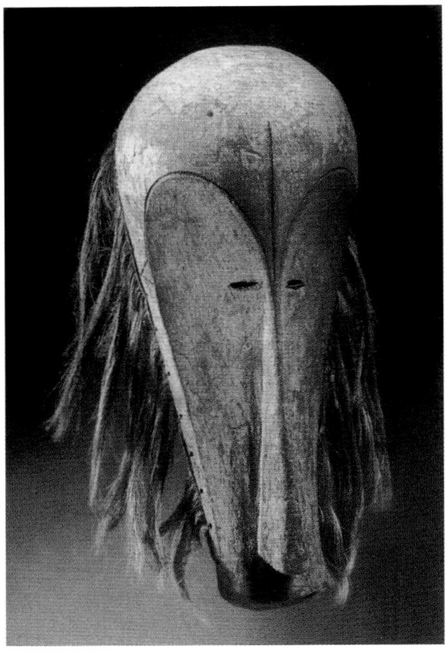

256. Fang artist
Gabon
Mask
Wood, kaolin and plant fibres, 56 cm
Denver Art Museum, Denver (work acquired by A.N. Bennett in 1890)

257. Kwele artist
Gabon
Mask
Wood and colour, 55 cm
Musée Dapper, Paris

quired at the beginning of the last century in different localities. The different provenances, together with the exaggerated volume and size of the cheeks and the motif of the hairstyle, which are not in keeping with the usual Bamileke style, make the origin of this mask uncertain, although they do not detract from its monumental beauty.

The restrained geometry of the Baule mask in the Horstmann Collection (no. 255), a celebration of female beauty, is the exact opposite of the overwhelming vitality of the Cameroonian mask. The majority of the elements typical of representations of the human face in the artworks of the Ivorian people are present here: hair in the form of a semicircle, barely indicated by a subtle relief with three engraved lines; arched eyebrows in the same shape; eyes reduced to slits; a straight, slender nose (the only vertical element in the composition); a small round mouth.

The expressive repetition of the circular form, accentuated by the serrated edge, the slight convexity, and the fine balance between geometric rigour and the allusive subtlety with which the different parts are rendered, are an added value that gives the work a purity of expression and distinct formal unity that set it apart from the other Baule pieces.

With their tendency towards abstraction contrasting the rotundity typical of the ancestral figures, the white Fang masks (see nos. 174–175) provide a good example of the formal universe of many African peoples. The white Fang mask in the Denver Art Museum, acquired in 1890 (no. 256), is one such, along with the few famous masks of this kind now in Berlin and Paris.

The extremely simplified structure pivots on the carefully balanced choice of convex and concave elements: the immense hemispherical forehead and the extremely long nose separating the two hollows of the face, which almost reach the chin. The eyes, represented by two slits, are placed close together in these hollows, at the bottom of which is the small mouth, which is almost invisible, perhaps because the wearer of the mask was not to be recognized.

The elegant motif formed by the blackened finely engraved lines that delineate the eyebrows and the middle of the forehead is the only decoration and stands out against the white ground: the colour of death.

Little is known about the meaning of this type of mask. It was used by the Ngil society, which exercised fierce police and judicial control over the people, constituting a kind of "Inquisition", according to Laburthe-Tolra.[24] Its activities were banned by the French colonial authorities in around 1910 because of the abuses committed by the society's members.

The shape of the famed Kwele mask (no. 257) now in the Musée Dapper is an oval with a point at the bottom and it is set in an oval frame. The form is enhanced by the thinness of the material and, here too, by subtle reliefs. The eyes and the nose, though simplified, are perfectly rendered and cleverly made to occupy a limited space in the heart-shaped face. The abnormal distance between the nose and the tiny mouth, which is barely hinted at on the lower edge of the oval, and the slanting eyes shaped like coffee beans accentuates the sockets beneath the large eyebrows. Their graceful curve is anticipated by the division, at top centre, into two parts of what are presumably horns; in turn, these are given dynamism by the reflections of light on the length of their faces. This eloquent structure is deceptively simple; all the elements work together to create a perfect whole and reveal the artist's clear formal-volumetric vision.

According to Leo Siroto, masks like this one were used in complex initiatory rituals in which the ruler's successor was chosen. There is a similar work in a private collection in Italy.[25]

The masterly fusion of rectilinear and curved volumes, which only appear to be incompatible, distinguishes the Bamana mask (no. 258) formerly in a French private collection. It is formed by the seamless fusion of a hemispherical cranium and an elongated parallelepiped rendered both compact and light by the carefully studied voids. The slender yet emphatic ridge that runs the whole length of the sculpture links the two volumes while at the same time accentuating the transition from one to the other.

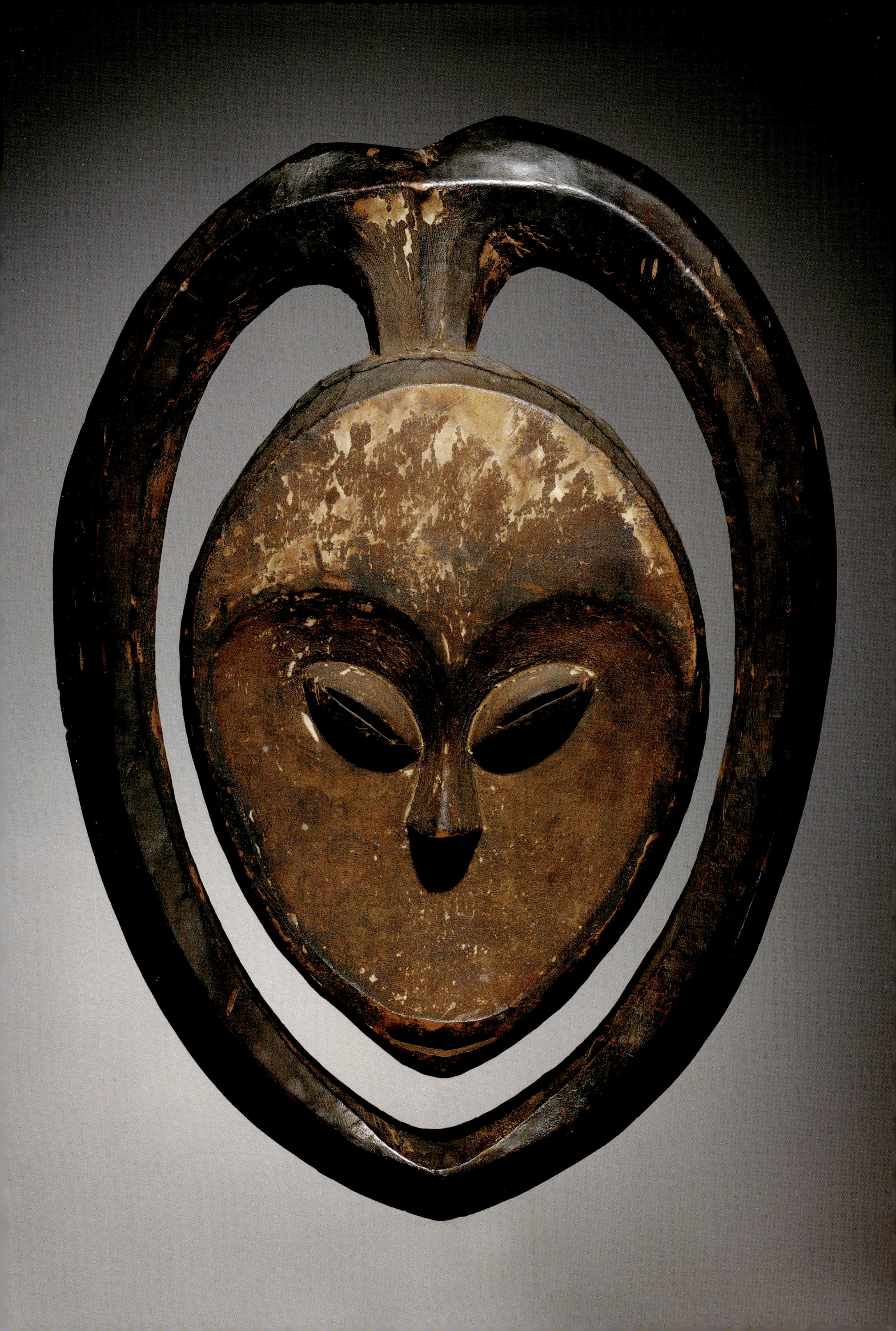

258. Bamana artist
Mali (Segu region)
Kono society mask
Wood, 50 cm
Private collection (formerly in the Gaillard Collection)

259. Boa artist
Democratic Republic of the Congo
Anthropomorphic mask
Wood and colour, 27 cm
Raccolta Congolese Capitano Emilio Piola, Parma

Pages 292–293
260. Igbo artist
Nigeria
Mask
Polychrome wood and fibres, 46 cm
Civiche Raccolte Artistiche del Castello Sforzesco, Raccolte Extraeuropee, Milan

261. Jaba artist
Nigeria
Vessel with religious function
Wood, 42 cm
Horstmann Collection, Zug

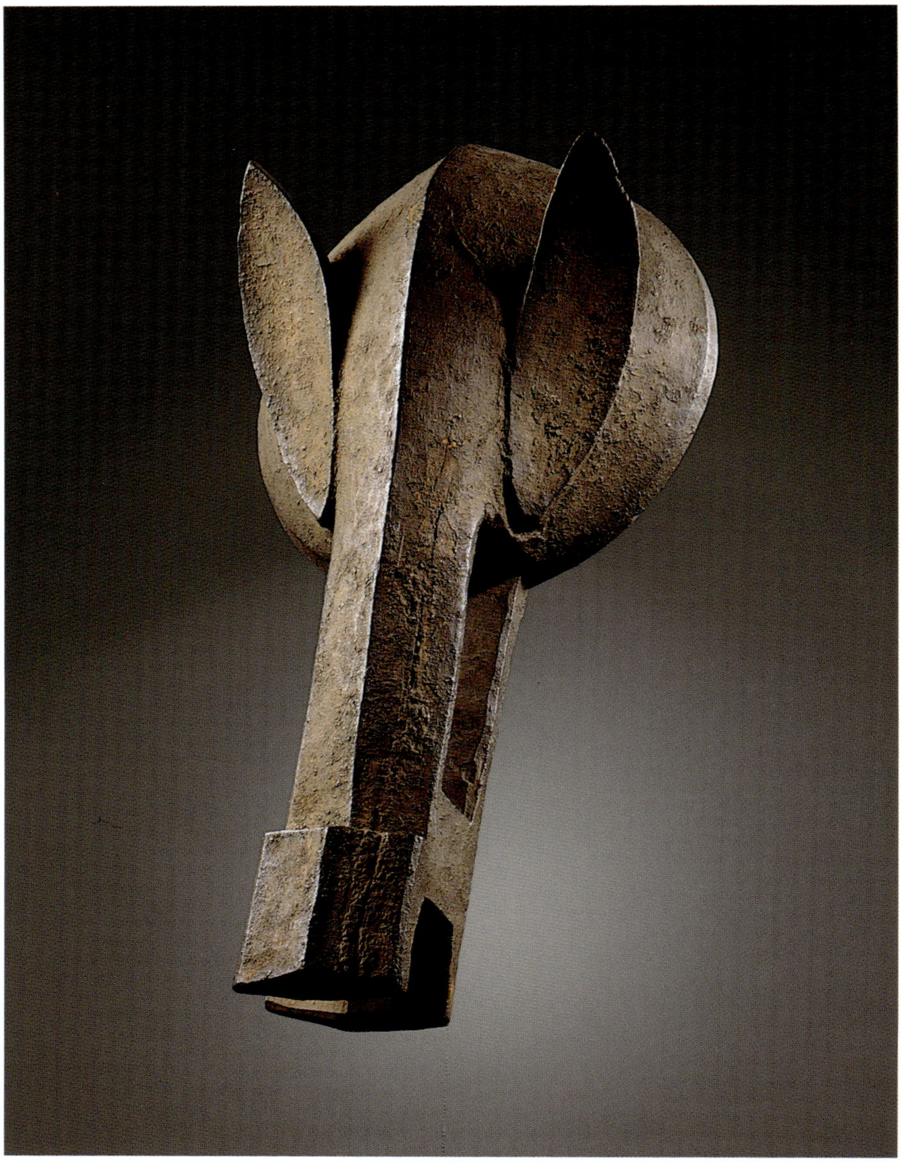

The muzzle terminates in a skilfully rendered relief that possibly represents the animal's nostrils, and the shapely ears each in the form of a leaf – unusual in this type of mask – blend with the extremely synthetic plasticity of the sculpture whose pure volumes maintain a subtle link with reality.

The dances performed by people wearing Kono society masks/headgear like this one – worn horizontally on the head of a dancer concealed beneath a feathered costume – had the function, in the Bamana world of the past, of making women and fields fertile and, above all, of frightening away creatures that devoured souls.[26] It is not certain what kind of animal is represented; according to some scholars it is an elephant, albeit highly stylized.

The extremely large ears with circular holes are the dominant feature of the fine Boa mask held by the University of Parma (no. 259), one of the few pieces to have arrived in Europe intact. Acquired at the beginning of the last century by Captain Emilio Piola, the work is not only marked by daring formal invention but also attests, though in a far less striking way, to the distortion of reality practised at an earlier time by Boa artists.[27]

The extraordinary boldness with which the artist stylizes the facial features, distributes the spaces and makes sophisticated use of black and white to create a rhythmic surface, results in a flawless work in which expressiveness melds with compositional balance. Even a cursory examination reveals the subtle interplay between the curves and the circumferences, and the coherence of the diverse elements that make up the terrified and terrifying ghostly face.

Information gathered during the last century tells us that masks like this one were used in war by the Boa, who lived in the north of the Democratic Re-

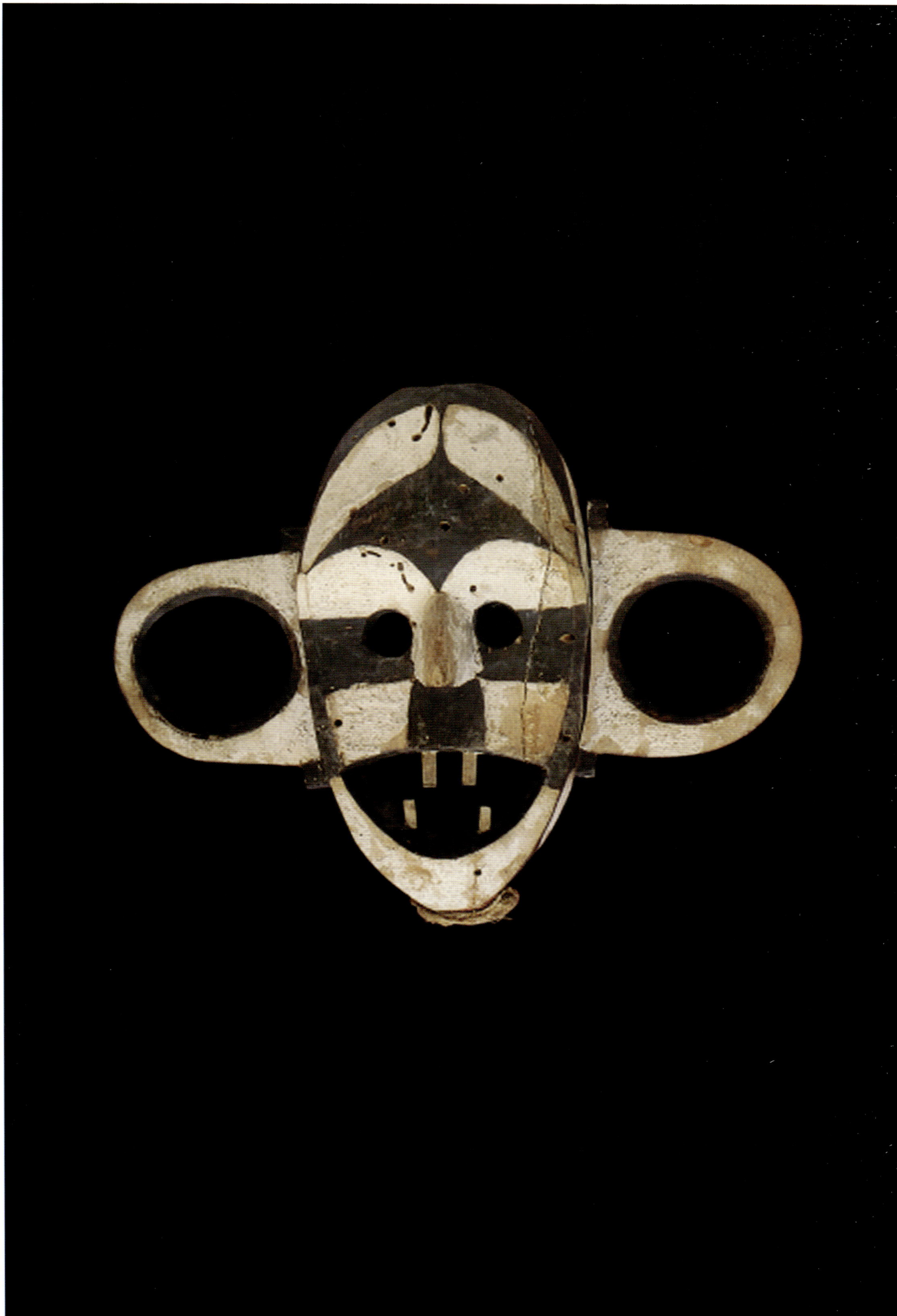

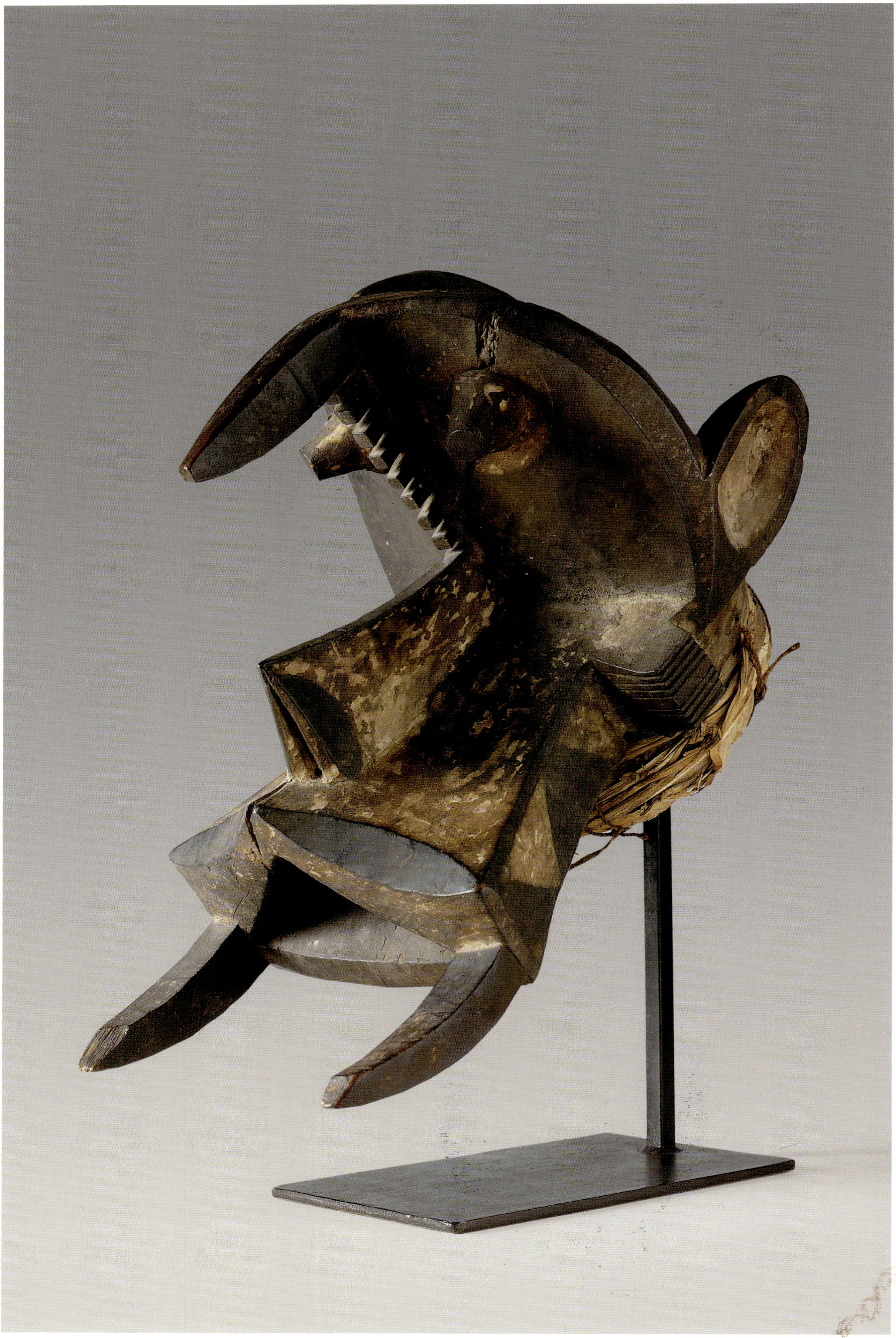

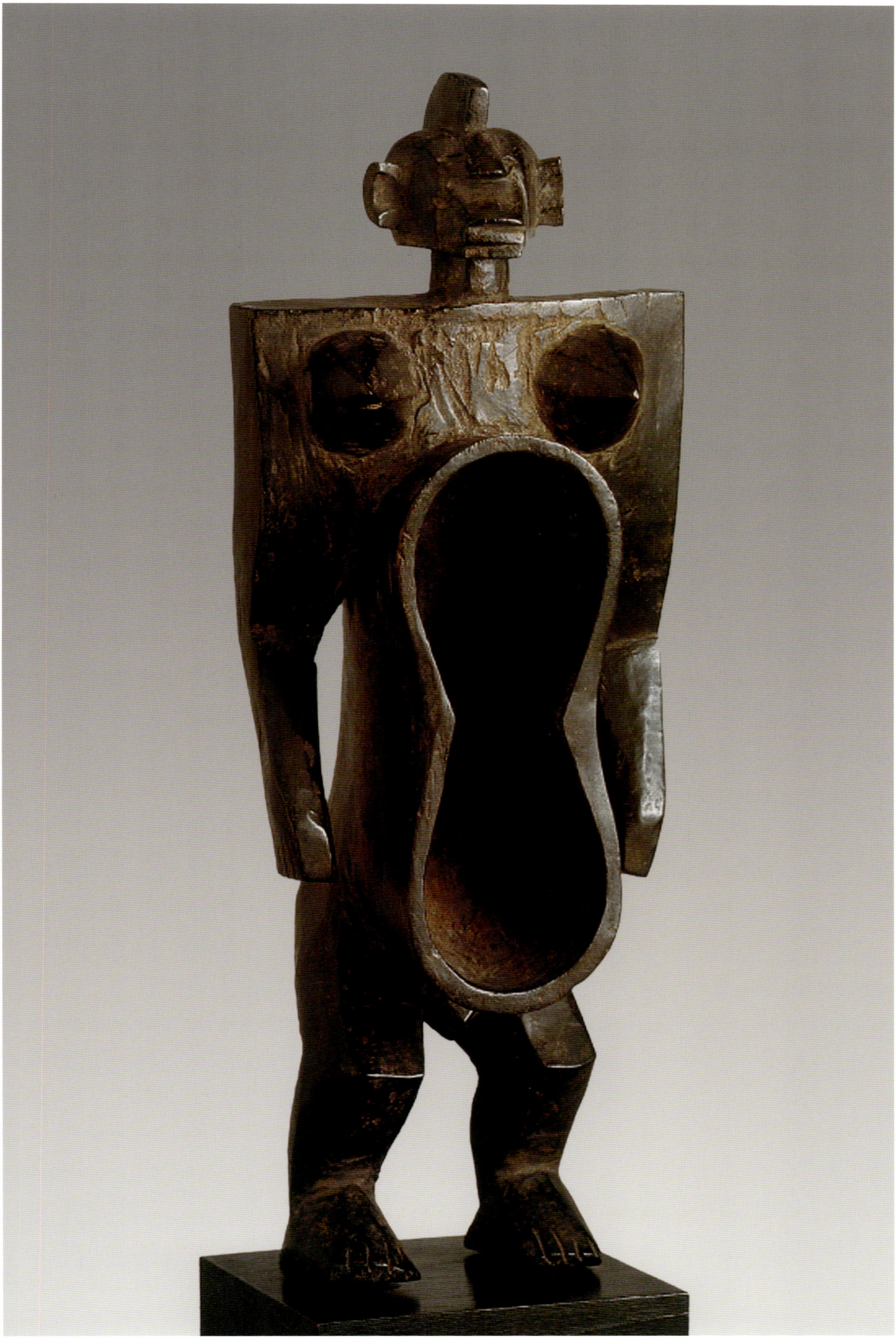

262. Ife artist
Nigeria, 12th–15th c.
Female head
Terracotta, 26 cm
The National Commission for Museums and Monuments, Nigeria

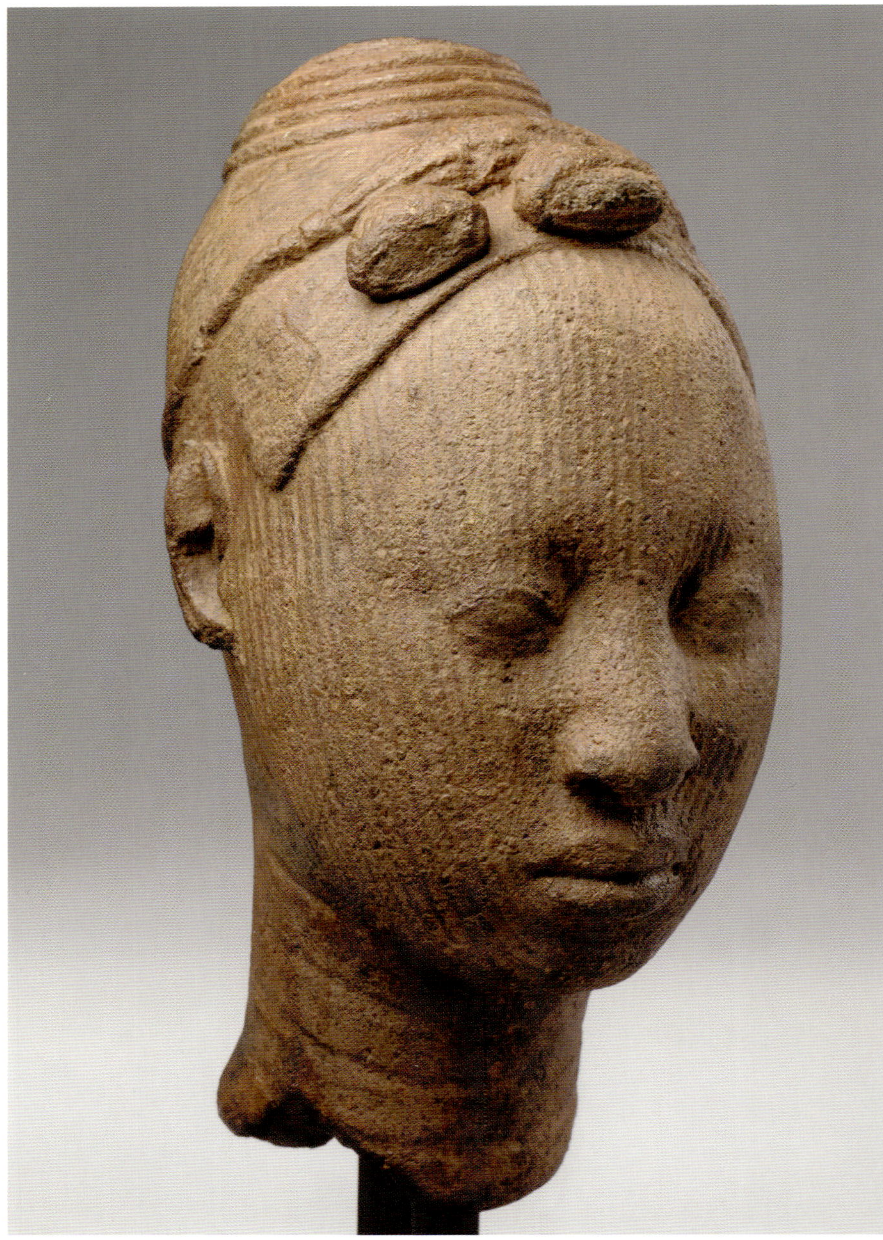

public of the Congo, and were intended to terrorize the enemy during battle.[28] The painter Alberto Magnelli owned a similar mask, which is now in a private collection in Italy.[29]

The elements that should enable identification of the species of animal (presumed to be an elephant) in mask no. 260 are radically stylized and their assemblage clearly arbitrary. The theory that the artist, an Igbo from Nigeria (from the subgroup known as the Izzi or Ezzi) intended to portray an elephant, which is supported iconographically by the two large tusks and the pointed appendage, interpreted as a trunk, that continues the line of the forehead, still has to be proved. On the other hand, the work's formal qualities are rendered outstanding by its essential volumes, by the sensitive treatment of the surfaces enlivened by subtle curves and by the kaolin-based geometric decoration, now partly worn away. A sharp vertical incision bisects the cranium that juts out at right angles to the cheeks, creating large, imposing eye sockets to dramatic effect. The aggressive reliefs, including an elegantly stylized human nose, are governed by the rhythm that brings the whole composition together. Subtle touches, like the blunted corners and certain refined details, reveal the hand of an artist who was able to produce a bold yet rigorous structure with a powerful expressiveness while respecting the figurative canons of his people's culture.

In the past, Igbo masked dances were organized by members of the different age-groups, especially on the occasion of seasonal festivals, in order to show that they were capable of working for the good of the community as agents of social control.

The section of formally composite sculptures is completed by the extraordinary vessel created by a Jaba artist from Nigeria (no. 261), which was used, according to Roy Sieber,[30] to drink palm wine during particular ceremonies linked to the cult of the dead. Considered from a formal standpoint, the work combines different solutions in a perfectly balanced way. If the sculpture had been produced by a European artist, it could be described as cubist on the strength of the geometrically rendered volume of the immense square block of the shoulders and back, of the parallelepipeds of the limbs, of the conical breasts and the cylindrical ears. At the same time, the figure's expressive violence, which is concentrated mainly in the head – itself an assemblage of pure volumes – denoted by a savage force, could be described as expressionist if it were not for the deep vessel that transforms the man into a disturbing hybrid, and thus it might quite justifiably be classed as surrealist.

I would like to end this panorama of African sculpture through the ages with an Ife terracotta head (no. 262) that combines realism and idealization, an image that reaffirms the infinite stylistic wealth that African sculptors have brought to humanity's artistic heritage, which they have undoubtedly enriched. At the same time, we must remember that the traditional African artist made his works in line with the norms of his community, though his art was only governed by them completely if, as William Fagg observed years ago, he was a "poor artist". This is not the case, at least in my opinion, with the artists who produced the works used to illustrate the subjects dealt with in this volume, even though there are no absolute or immutable canons according to which they might all be defined as masterpieces.

[1] See Bognolo 2007, no. 30.
[2] Einstein 1915, nos. 16–17. The sculpture had already been published in Warnod 1912, and in the Czech arts magazine *Umělecký měsíčník* in 1913.
[3] Fagg 1970, p. 94, cat. no. 103.
[4] *Ubangi* 2007, p. 121.
[5] Rubin 1984, p. 301.
[6] Lem 1949, no. 45; *Visual Encounters* 2009, IV, no. 2.
[7] Fischer, Himmelheber 1984, p. 8.
[8] Fagg 1981, no. 5.
[9] "*la transition entre les styles dogon et bamana*" (Leloup 1994, no. 135).
[10] Lecoq 1953, nos. 92–95.
[11] Rubin 1984, pp. 294–295.
[12] Meneghini 2006, no. XXXII.
[13] Cornet 1971, no. 132.
[14] The masks are produced for commercial reasons nowadays.
[15] Northern 1984, no. 99.
[16] Harter 1986, p. 39.
[17] The sculptor made two or three similar statues. See Kerchache, Paudrat, Stephan 1988, nos. 518–520.
[18] Neyt 1993, p. 208.
[19] The large ritual spoons produced by the Dan tribe symbolize the women who can lay claim to a high standing in society.
[20] Rubin in *"Primitivism" in 20th Century Art* 1984, p. 60.
[21] *Trésors* 1995, no. 142.
[22] Inv. 12213, 12314.
[23] *Rois Sculpteurs* 1993, pp. 121–122.
[24] Laburthe-Tolra, Falgayrettes-Leveau 1995, pp. 53, 56.
[25] *Passione d'Africa* 2009, no. 63.
[26] J.-P. Colleyn, in *Bamana* 2001, p. 188.
[27] Calonne-Beaufaict, 1909.
[28] Burssens 1995, no. 242.
[29] *Passione d'Africa* 2009, no. 3.
[30] Sieber, 1961, pp. 12–13. Two similar sculptures, formerly in the Musée Barbier-Mueller and attributed to the Koro people, are now in the Musée du Quai Branly, inv. A 89.1–2 and A.97.444.

Bibliography

Note
The bibliography on African arts is endless, as are the exhibitions. I have selected the texts that are connected directly or indirectly with the works illustrated here. Further information, however, can be obtained from the books and articles cited in the studies listed in this bibliography.

A

Abiodun, Drewal, Pemberton
Abiodun R., Drewal H.J., Pemberton J. III, *Yoruba Art and Aesthetics*, Zurich 1991.

Africa 1992
Africa. Nas vésperas do mundo moderno, Lisbon 1992.

Africa 1995
Africa: The Art of a Continent, T. Phillips (ed.), London 1995.

Africa 1999
Africa. Art and Culture. Masterpieces of African Art; Ethnological Museum Berlin, H.-J. Koloss (ed.), Munich 1994.

African Seats 1994
African Seats, S. Bocola (ed.), Munich 1994.

Allison 1968
P. Allison, *African Stone Sculpture*, London 1968.

A New York Collection 2010
A New York Collection – Arts d'Afrique, Sotheby's (auction cat.), Paris 30 June 2010, no. 14.

Andersson 1953
E. Andersson, *Contribution à l'Ethnographie de Kuta*, vol. I, *Studia ethnographica upsaliensa*, vol. VI, Uppsala 1953.

Angola figures de pouvoir 2010
Angola, figures de pouvoir, C. Falgayrettes-Leveau (ed.), Paris 2010.

Anquandah, Van Ham 1985
J. Anquandah and L. Van Ham, *Discovering the Forgotten Civilization of Komaland, Northern Ghana*, Rotterdam 1985.

Arte da Africa 2003
Arte da Africa – Obras primas do Museu etnologico de Berlin, P. Junge (ed.), Rio de Janeiro 2003.

Arts du Nigeria 1997
H. Waterfield, H. Joubert (eds.), *Arts du Nigeria: Collection du musée des Arts d'Afrique et d'Océanie*, Paris 1997.

B

Bamana 2001
Bamana: The Art of Existence in Mali, J.-P. Colleyn (ed.), New York, Zurich, Ghent 2001.

Barbot 1732
J. Barbot, *A Description of the Coasts of North and South Guinea*, in Churchill's *A Collection of Voyages and Travels*, London 1732, vol. V.

Barbot on Guinea 1992
Barbot on Guinea: The Writings of Jean Barbot on West Africa 1678–1712, P. Hair (ed.), London 1992.

Bassani 1975
E. Bassani, "Le figure da reliquiario dei Kota", in *Critica d'Arte*, Florence, no.139, 1975, pp. 21–32.

Bassani 1977[a]
E. Bassani, *Scultura africana nei musei italiani*, Bologna 1977.

Bassani 1977[b]
E. Bassani, "Kongo Nail Fetishes from the Chiloango River Area", in *African Arts*, vol. X, no. 3, April 1977, pp. 36–40.

Bassani 1978[a]
E. Bassani, "Les sculptures Vallisnieri", in *Africa-Tervuren*, XXIV, 1978–1, pp. 15–22.

Bassani 1978[b]
E. Bassani, "Una bottega di grandi artisti Bambara", 1 & 2, in *Critica d'Arte*, nos. 157–159, January–June 1978, pp. 209–228, and July–December 1978, pp. 181–200.

Bassani 1981
E. Bassani, "Due grandi artisti Yombe. Il 'M° della maternità Roselli-Lorenzini e il M° della Maternità De Briey'", in *Critica d'Arte Africana*, no. 178 di *Critica d'Arte*, July–September 1981, pp. 66–84.

Bassani 1989
E. Bassani, *La grande scultura dell'Africa Nera*, Florence 1989.

Bassani 1992
E. Bassani, "La tromba del Musée Calvet di Avignone – Testimonianza della grande arte della Sierra Leone nei secoli XV e XVI", in *Critica d'Arte*, 7th series nos. 9–10, Florence 1992, pp. 109–18.

Bassani 1994
E. Bassani, "The Oliphant in the Musée Calvet at Avignon", in *Journal of the History of Collections*, no. 6, Oxford 1994, pp. 69–78.

Bassani 1995
E. Bassani, "Raffaello ai Tropici?", in *Critica d'Arte*, 7th series, no. 4, Florence 1995, pp. 57–63 and 77–79.

Bassani 2000
E. Bassani, *African Art and Artefacts in European Collections 1400–1800*, London 2000.

Bassani 2001[a]
E. Bassani, *Arts sans artistes? Problèmes d'attribution dans les arts traditionnels de l'Afrique subsaharienne*, in Grunne 2001, pp. 13–31.

Bassani 2001[b]
E. Bassani, *Two Lost Boyo Masterpieces*, in *Faszination der culturen - für Arnold Duchateau zum 70. Geburtstag von seinen Freundeskreis*, A. Tunis (ed.), Berlin 2001, pp. 37–50.

Bassani 2003
E. Bassani, *Africa: capolavori da un continente*, Florence 2003.

Bassani 2005[a]
E. Bassani, *Arts of Africa: 7000 Years of African Art*, Milan 2005.

Bassani 2005[b]
E. Bassani, *Marfins Sapi-Portugueses*, in *Um Olhar do Porto: Uma collecção de artes decorativas*, Funchal 2005, pp. 15–22.
Bassani 2007
E. Bassani, *Maestri di arte africana. Forme e stili. 84 sculture della collezione Horstmann,* Mendrisio 2007.
Bassani 2008
E. Bassani, *Ivoires d'Afrique dans les anciennes collections françaises*, Paris 2008.
Bassani (forthcoming)
E. Bassani, *New Notes on the Afro-Portuguese Ivories and Updating of the Previous Ones.*
Bassani, Fagg 1988
E. Bassani, W. Fagg, *Africa and the Renaissance: Art in Ivory*, New York 1988.
Bassani, McLeod 1989
E. Bassani, M. McLeod, *Jacob Epstein Collector*, Milan 1989.
Bassani, Zanobini 1990
E. Bassani, M.T. and V. Zanobini, "Il Maestro del Varua", *Quaderni Poro*, 6, Milan 1990.
Bastin 1978
M.-L. Bastin, *Statuettes Tshokwe du héros civilisateur Tshibinda Ilunga*, Arnouville 1978.
Bastin 1982
M.-L. Bastin, *La Sculpture Tshokwe*, Meudon 1982.
Bastin 1994
M.-L. Bastin, *Sculpture angolaise: Mémorial de Cultures*, Lisbon 1994.
Bedaux 1972
R.M.A. Bedaux, "Tellem, reconnaissance archéologique d'une culture de l'Ouest africain au Moyen Âge: recherches architectoniques", in *Journal de la Societé des Africanistes*, 42, 1972, pp. 103–185.
Bedaux 1988
R.M.A. Bedaux, "Tellem and Dogon Material Culture", in *African Arts*, vol. XXI, 1988, pp. 31–49.
Bedaux 1992
R.M.A. Bedaux, *Des Tellem aux Dogon: recherches archéologiques dans la boucle du Niger (Mali)*, in *Dall'archeologia all'arte tradizionale africana*, proceedings of the meetings (Nov.–Dec. 1991), G. Pezzoli (ed.), Milan 1992, pp. 83–101.
Ben-Amos 1980
P. Ben-Amos, *The Art of Benin*, London 1980.
Benin 2007
Bénin: Cinq siècles d'art royal, B. Plankensteiner (ed.), Antwerp 2007 (Fr. ed.).
Benin 2007
Benin: Kings and Rituals. Court Arts from Nigeria, B. Plankensteiner (ed.), Antwerp 2007 (Eng. ed.).
Blackmun 2007
B.W. Blackmun, "Qui sont les personnages représentés dans l'art de Benin? Confrontation de l'ivoire et du bronze", in *Benin: Cinq siècles d'art royal*, Antwerp 2007, pp. 161–169.
Bognolo 2007
D. Bognolo, *Lobi*, Milan 2007.
Bonanni 1709
F. Bonanni, *A P. Philippo Bonanni Societatis Jesu, Musaeum Kircherianum sive a Padre Athanasio Kirchero in Collegio Romani Societatis Jesu pridem inceptum Nuper restitutum, auctum, descriptum et iconibus illustratutum*, Rome 1709.
Bontinck 1979
F. Bontinck, "La provenance des sculptures Vallisnieri", in *Africa-Tervuren*, XV, 1979–4, n.p.
Bosman 1705
W. Bosman, *A New and Accurate Description of the Coast of Guinea*, London 1705 (1907).
Boubé 1993
G. Boubé, *Un village des morts à Bura en République du Niger: Un site méthodiquement fouillé fournit d'irreplaçables informations*, in *Vallées du Niger*, J. Devisse, J. Polet, S. Sidibé (eds.), Paris 1993, pp. 359–377.
Boullier 2000
C. Boullier, *Sculpture Sokoto*, in *Sculptures* 2000, pp. 122–123.
Bouloré 2000[a]
V. Bouloré, *Sculpture prédogon (?)*, in *Sculptures* 2000, pp. 77–79.
Bouloré 2000[b]
V. Bouloré, *Sculpture tellem (?)*, in *Sculptures* 2000, pp. 80–83.
Bouloré 2000[c]
V. Bouloré, *Sculpture songyé*, in *Sculptures* 2000, pp. 191–193.
Boyer 2008
A.M. Boyer, *Baule*, Milan 2008.
Brain, Pollock 1971
R. Brain, A. Pollock, *Bangwa Funerary Sculpture*, London 1971.
Broggini 1992
F. and R. Broggini, "Per un'ulteriore interpretazione delle terrecotte del Komaland (Nord-Ghana)", in *Dall'archeologia all'arte tradizionale africana*, proceedings of the meetings (Nov.–Dec. 1991), G. Pezzoli (ed.), Milan 1992, pp. 51–63.
Burssens 1995
H. Burssens, *Masque pongdudu*, in *Trésors* 1995, no. 242.

C

Calonne-Beaufaict 1909
A. de Calonne-Beaufaict, *Les Ababua: observations sociologiques*, Brussels 1909.
Cameroon 2008
Cameroon: Art and Kings, L. Homberger (ed.), Zurich 2008.
Chaffin 1979
A. and F. Chaffin, *L'Art kota. Les figures de reliquaire*, Meudon 1979.
Circa 1492 1991
Circa 1492: Art in the Age of Exploration, J.A. Levenson (ed.), Washington, D.C. 1991.
Cole, Ross 1977
H. Cole, D.H. Ross, *The Arts of Ghana*, Los Angeles 1977.
Cornet 1971
J. Cornet, *Art of Africa: Treasures from the Congo*, London 1971.
Cornet 1982
J. Cornet, *Art Royal Kuba*, Milan 1982.

D

Dam-Mikkelsen, Lundbaek 1980
B. Dam-Mikkelsen, T. Lundbaek, *Etnografiske genstande i Detkongelige danske Kunstkammer 1650–1800 – Ethnographic Objects in the Royal Danish Kunstkammer 1650–1800*, Copenhagen 1980.
Dapper 1668
O. Dapper, *Naukeurige Beschrijvinge der Afrikaensche gewesten* […], Amsterdam 1668.
Dapper 1686
O. Dapper, *Description de l'Afrique* […], Amsterdam 1686.
Dark 1973
P.J.C. Dark, *An Introduction to Benin Art and Technology*, Oxford 1973.
Delange 1965
J. Delange, "Afrique Noire", in *Chefs-d'œuvre du Musée de l'Homme*, Paris 1965.
Dembow 1991
J. Dembow, *Rapport des progrès obtenus au cours du projet archéologique au Congo*, University of Texas, 1991.
Desplagnes 1907
L. Desplagnes, *Le plateau central nigérien*, Paris 1907.
Die Kunst der Dogon 1995
Die Kunst der Dogon – Museum Rietberg Zürich, L. Homberger (ed.), Zurich 1995.
Dinastía y Divinidad 2009
Dinastía y Divinidad. Arte Ife en la antigua Nigeria, Santander 2009.
Dogon 1994
Dogon, J.L. Paudrat (ed.), Paris 1994.
Drewal, Pemberton, Abiodun 1989
H.J. Drewal, J. Pemberton III, R. Abiodun, *Yoruba: Nine Centuries of African Art and Thought*, New York 1989.
Drewal, Schildkrout 2009
H.J. Drewal, E. Schildkrout, *Kingdom of Ife: Sculptures from West Africa*, London 2009.
Duchâteau 1990
A. Duchâteau, *Benin, Trésor Royal: Collection du Museum für Völkerkunde Vienne*, Paris 1990.
Duchâteau 1991
A. Duchâteau, *Tesori reali del Benin. Arte di un antico regno africano dalla collezione del Museum für Völkerkunde Vienna*, Florence 1991.
Duchâteau 1994
A. Duchâteau, *Benin: Royal Art of Africa from the Museum für Völkerkunde, Vienna*, Houston 1994.

E

Eisenhofer 2003
S. Eisenhofer, *Antica arte plastica in Africa. La città di Ife e la cultura di Nok*; and *Uno stato di bronzo e avorio. Il regno del Benin e la sua arte di corte*, in Bassani 2003, pp. 46–48, 65–69.
Eisenhofer 2007
S. Eisenhofer, *Les messagers d'Olokun: les Portugais et le Royaume de Benin*, in *Benin* 2007, pp. 54–55.
Einstein 1915
C. Einstein, *Negerplastik*, Leipzig 1915.
Einstein 1920
C. Einstein, *Afrikanische Plastik*, Berlin 1920.
Ekpo 2005
V.I. Ekpo, *Nok, Igbo-Ukwu, Ife, Tsoede, Nok, Benin, Esie, Calabar*, in E. Bassani 2005[a], pp. 48–154.
Eluyemi 2003
O. Eluyemi, *Arte nell'antica Nigeria*, in Bassani 2003, pp. 43–45 and entries 1–12.
Eluyemi 2005
O. Eluyemi, *Nigeria*, in Bassani 2005[a], pp. 42–47.
Eyo 1995
E. Eyo, *Carved Monolith (Bakor)*, in *Africa* 1995, pp. 374–375.
Eyo 2000
E. Eyo, *Sculpture Nok*, in *Sculptures* 2000, pp. 114–118.
Eyo, Willett 1980
E. Eyo, F. Willett, *Treasures of Ancient Nigeria*, New York 1980.
Eyo, Willett 1984
E. Eyo, F. Willett, *Tesori dell'antica Nigeria*, Florence 1984.
Ezra 1986
K. Ezra, *A Human Ideal in African Art: Bamana Figurative Sculpture*, Washington, D.C. 1986.
Ezra 1988
K. Ezra, *The Art of the Dogon: Selection from*

the Lester Wunderman Collection, New York 1988.
Ezra 1992
K. Ezra, *Royal Art of Benin: The Perls Collection in the Metropolitan Museum of Art*, New York 1992.

F
Fagg B. 1990
B.E.B. Fagg, *Nok Terracottas*, London 1990.
Fagg 1951
W. Fagg, "The Dilemma Which Faces African Art", in *The Listener*, 13 September 1951, pp. 413–415.
Fagg 1963
W. Fagg, *Nigerian Images: The Splendor of African Sculpture*, New York, London 1963.
Fagg 1965
W. Fagg, *Les Univers artistiques des tribus d'Afrique noire*, Paris 1965.
Fagg 1968
W. Fagg, *African Tribal Images: The Katherine White Reswick Collection,* Cleveland 1968.
Fagg 1969
W. Fagg, *The African Artist*, in *Tradition and Creativity in Tribal Art*, D.P. Biebuyck (ed.), Berkeley 1969.
Fagg 1970[a]
W. Fagg, *African Sculpture*, Washington, D.C. 1970.
Fagg 1970[b]
W. Fagg, *The Tribal Image: Wooden Figure Sculpture of the World*, London 1970.
Fagg 1981
W. Fagg, *African Majesty: From Grassland and Forest. The Barbara and Murray Frum Collection*, Toronto 1981.
Fagg 1982
W. Fagg, *The Yoruba Artist: Regional Styles*, in Fagg, Pemberton 1982, pp. 35–49.
Fagg 1991
W. Fagg, "One Hundred Notes on Nigerian Art from Christie's Catalogues 1974–1990, A Selected Anthology edited by Ezio Bassani with a biography and bibliography by Frank Willett", in *Quaderni Poro*, 7, Milan 1991.
Fagg, Pemberton 1982
W. Fagg, J. Pemberton III, *Yoruba. Sculpture of West Africa*, New York 1982.
Fagg, Plass 1964
W. Fagg, M. Plass, *African Sculpture: an Anthology*, London and New York 1964.
Felix 1990
M.L. Felix, *Mwana Hiti: Life and Art of the Matrilineal Bantu of Tanzania*, Munich 1990.
Fernandes 1951
V. Fernandes, *Description de la Côte Occidentale de l'Afrique (Sénégal au Cap du Monte Archipels)*, Th. Monod, A.Texeira da Mota, R. Mauny (eds.), Bissau 1951.
Fernandez 1966
J.W. Fernandez, "Principal of Opposition and Vitality in Fang Aesthetics", in *Journal of Aesthetics and Art Criticism*, vol. XXV, no. 1, 1966, pp. 63–64.
Fischer 1999
E. Fischer, *African Sculptures: From a 'Masterpiece' to a 'Master's Piece', German contributions to the study of Individual African Sculptors*, in Perrois, Lehuard 1999, pp. 65–81.
Fischer, Himmelberger 1984
E. Fischer, H. Himmelheber, *The Arts of the Dan in West Africa*, Zurich 1984.
Fischer, Homberger 1984
E. Fischer, L. Homberger, *Die Kunst der Guro, Elfenbeinküste*, Zurich 1985.
Formes et figures 2002
Formes et figures. L'art africain dans la collection Horstmann, Milan 2002.
Forman, Dark 1959
W. and B. Forman, P. Dark, *Benin Art*, London 1959.
Foy 1900–01
V. Foy, "Zur Frage de Herkunft einiger alter Jagdhörner: Portugal oder Benin?", in *Abhandlungen und Berichte des Konig. Zoolog. und Anthropologish- Ethnographischen Museum zu Dresden*, 9 (1900–01), pp. 20–22.
Frobenius 1911
L. Frobenius, *Auf dem Wege nach Atlantis*, Berlin 1911.
Frobenius 1912–13
L. Frobenius, *Und Afrika sprach I. Auf den Trummern des Klassischen Atlantis*, Berlin 1912–13.
Frobenius 1913
L. Frobenius, *The Voice of Africa*, London 1913.
Fuhrmann 1922
E. Fuhrmann, *Africa. Kulturen der Erde*, 6, Hagen 1922.

G
Gebauer 1979
P. Gebauer, *Art of Cameroon*, Portland 1979.
Ghana 2003
Ghana: hier et aujourd'hui – Yesterday and Today, C. Falgayrettes-Leveau (ed.), Paris 2003.
Gillon 1979
W. Gillon, *Collecting African Art*, London 1979.
Ginzberg 2000
M. Ginzberg, *Africa. Arte delle forme*, Milan 2000.
Goldwater 1960
R. Goldwater, *Bambara Sculpture from the Western Sudan*, New York 1960.
Griaule 1948
M. Griaule, *Dieu d'eau: entretien avec Ogotemmêli*, Paris 1948.
Griaule 1968
M. Griaule, *Dio d'acqua*, Milan 1968.
Grunne 1980
B. de Grunne, *Terres cuites anciennes de l'Ouest Africain (Ancient terracottas from West Africa)*, Louvain-la-Neuve 1980.
Grunne 1991
B. de Grunne, "Heroic Riders and Divine Horses: An Analysis of Ancient Soninke and Dogon Equestrian Figures from the Inland Delta Niger Region in Mali", in *The Minneapolis Institute of Arts Bulletin*, vol. LXXVI, 1991, pp. 76–96.
Grunne 1998
B. de Grunne, *Naissance de l'art en Afrique noire*, Paris 1998.
Grunne 2001
B. de Grunne, *Masterhands: Afrikaanse beeldhouwers in de kijker – Mains de maîtres: À la découverte des sculpteurs d'Afrique*, Brussels 2001.
Guerre 2011
P. Guerre, *Art d'Afrique*, Sotheby's (auction cat.), Paris 12 June 2011, no. 7.
Guillaume 1917
P. Guillaume, *Sculptures Nègres: 24 Photographies précédées d'un avertissement de Guillaume Apollinaire et d'un exposé de Paul Guillaume*, Paris 1917.
Guillaume, Munro 1929
P. Guillaume, T. Munro, *La sculpture nègre primitive*, Paris 1929.

H
Hall 1923
U.H. Hall, "Notes on some Congo and West African Woodcarvings, II. The Southern Congo Interior", in *The Museum Journal*, June 1923, vol. XIV, no. 2.
Hall 1927
H.U. Hall, "Notes on some Congo and West African Woodcarvings. II. The Southern Congo Interior", in *The Museum Journal*, Philadelphia, June 1927, vol. XIV, no. 2, pp. 175–187.
Hans Baldung Grien 1961
Hans Baldung Grien: Hexenbilder, introduction by G.F. Hartlaub, Stuttgart 1961.
Hart 1995
W.A. Hart, "Continuity and Discontinuity in the Art of Sierra Leone", in *Quaderni Poro*, 9, Milan 1995.
Hart (forthcoming)
W.A. Hart, *African Ivories and Eighteenth-Century English Antiquarians* (forthcoming).
Harter 1986
P. Harter, *Arts Anciens du Cameroun*, Arnouville 1986.
Haskell 1931
A.L. Haskell, *The Sculptor Speaks*, London 1931.
Himmelheber 1935
H. Himmelheber, *Negerkünstler. Ethnographische Studien über die Schitzkünstler bei den Stämmen Atutu und Guro im innern der Elfenbeinküste*, Stuttgart 1935.
Horae Beatae Mariae Virginis 1498
Horae Beatae Mariae Virginis [...], Philippe Pigouchet for Simon Vostre, Paris 1498.
Horae Beatae Mariae Virginis 1499
Horae Beatae Mariae Virginis [...], Thielman Kerver, Paris 1499.

I
Igbafe 2007
P.A. Igbafe, *A History of the Benin Kingdom: an Overview*, in *Benin: Kings and Rituals* 2007, pp. 41–53.
Incisa della Rocchetta 1966
G. Incisa della Rocchetta, "Il Museo di curiosità del Card. Flavio I Chigi", in *Archivio della Società Romana di Storia Patria*, 3rd series, vol. 89 (1966), pp. 141–192.
Instructions sommaires 1931
Instructions sommaires pour les collecteurs d'objets ethnographiques, Musée d'Ethnographie, Paris 1931.
Inventario semplice 1680
Inventario semplice di tutte le materie esattamente descritte che si trovano nel Museo Cospiano – Non solo le notate nel libro già stampato e composto dal sig. Dottore Lorenzo Legati, ma ancora le aggiuntevi in copia dopo la Fabrica, Bologna 1680.

K
Kamer 1974
H. Kamer, *Ancêtres M'bembé*, Paris 1974.
Keleti 1911
Keleti Kiállítás a Müvészhában IV: A Müvésház Keleti Kiállításabol, Budapest 1911.
Kerchache, Paudrat, Stephan 1988
J. Kerchache, J.L. Paudrat, L. Stephan, *L'Art africain*, Paris 1988.
Krieger 1965
K. Krieger, *Westafrikanische Plastik I*, Berlin 1965.
Krieger 1969
K. Krieger, *Westafrikanische Plastik II*, Berlin 1969.

L
Laburthe-Tolra, Falgayrettes-Leveau 1995
Ph. Laburthe-Tolra, Ch. Falgayrettes-Leveau, *Fang*, Paris 1995.

LaGamma 1988[a]
A. LaGamma, "Authorship in African Art", in *African Arts*, XXXI/4, 1988, pp. 18–22.
LaGamma 1988[b]
A. LaGamma, "Beyond Master Hands: The Lives of the Artists", in *African Arts*, XXXI/4, 1988, pp. 24–37.
LaGamma 1997
A. LaGamma, *Master Hand: Individuality and Creativity among Yoruba Sculptors*, New York 1997.
Langlois 1954
P. Langlois, *Art Soudanais: Tribu Dogon*, Brussels and Lille 1954.
Laude 1968
J. Laude, *La Peinture française (1905-1914) et l'Art nègre*, 2 vols., Paris 1968.
Lecoq 1953
R. Lecoq, *Une civilisation africaine: Les Bamiléké*, Paris 1953.
Lehuard 1989
R. Lehuard, *Art Bakongo: les centres de style*, 2 vols., Arnouville 1989.
Leiris, Damase 1959
M. Leiris, J. Damase, *Sculpture of the Tellem and the Dogon*, London 1959.
Leloup 1994
H. Leloup, *Statuaire Dogon*, Strasbourg 1994.
Leloup 1998
H. and Ph. Leloup, *Kongo, Objets de bois, objets d'ivoire*, Paris 1998.
Leloup 2000
H. and Ph. Leloup, *Bambara*, Paris 1998.
Leloup 2009
H. Leloup, *Statue anthropomorphe*, in *Musée du Quai Branly* 2009, pp. 28–33.
Leloup 2011
H. Leloup (ed.), *Dogon*, Paris 2011.
Lem 1949
F.H. Lem, *Sudanese Sculpture*, Paris 1949.
Lenz 1876
O. Lenz, "Expédition dans l'Ogouée", in *Revue Maritime et Coloniale*, vol. 54, 1876, pp. 529–534.
Lintig 2001
B. von Lintig, "Ateu Atsa, les sculpteurs, les prêtres-rois et la mémoire iconographique des Bangwa du Cameroun", in Grunne 2001, pp. 95–119.
Lintig 2006
B. von Lintig, *Cameroun*, Paris 2006.
Luschan (1919) 1968
F. von Luschan, *Die Altertüme von Benin* (3 vols, Berlin and Leipzig 1919), New York 1968 (1 vol.).

M
Maesen 1960
A. Maesen, *Umbangu: Art du Congo au Musée royal du Congo belge*, Brussels 1960.
Marees (1602) 1905
P. de Marees, *A Description and Historical Declaration of the Golden Kingdom of Guinea* (1602), in *S. Purchas, His Pilgrims* (1625), Glasgow 1905.
Mark 2007
P. Mark, *Portugal in West Africa: The Afro-Portuguese Ivories*, in *Encompassing the Globe: Portugal and the World in the 16th and 17th Centuries – Essays*, Washington, D.C. 2007, pp. 77–85.
Massing 2007[a]
J.M. Massing, *Stone Carving and Sixteenth-Century Ivory Sculpture in Sierra Leone*, in *Studies in Imagery*, London 2007, pp. 199–241.
Massing 2007[b]
J.M. Massing, *Stone Carving and Ivory Sculpture in Sierra Leone*, in *Encompassing the Globe: Portugal and the World in the 16th and 17th Centuries*, Washington, D.C. 2007, pp. 65–76.
McIntosh 1980
S.K. and R.J. McIntosh, *Prehistoric Investigations in the Region of Jenne, Mali*, Oxford 1980 (*Cambridge Monographs in African Archaeology*, 2, BAR international series 89).
McLeod 1980
M. McLeod, *Treasures of African Art*, New York 1980.
Meneghini 2006
M. Meneghini, *Collecting African Art in Liberia and Neighbouring Countries 1963-1989*, Varese 2006.
Monbrison 1993
A. de Monbrison, *Collection Kerbouc'h*, Paris 1993.
Monti 1966
F. Monti, *Le maschere africane*, Milan 1966.
Morigi 1980
P. Morigi, *Raccolta di un amatore di arte primitiva*, Berne 1980.
Musée du Quai Branly 2009
Musée du Quai Branly – La collection, Y. Le Fur (ed.), Paris 2009.

N
N'Diaye 1995
F. N'Diaye, *L'art du pays Dogon dans les collections du Musée de l'Homme*, Zurich 1995.
Neyt 1977
F. Neyt, *La grande statuaire Hemba du Zaïre*, Louvain 1977.
Neyt 1993
F. Neyt, *Luba: Aux sources du Zaïre*, Paris 1993.
Neyt 2004
F. Neyt, *Songye: La redoutable statuaire Songye d'Afrique centrale*, Antwerp 2004.
Nooter Roberts, Roberts 1996
M. Nooter Roberts, A. Roberts, *Luba Art and the Making of History*, New York and Munich 1996.
Northern 1973
T. Northern, *Royal Art of Cameroon: The Art of Bamenda/Tikar*, Hanover 1973.
Northern 1984
T. Northern, *The Art of Cameroon*, Washington, D.C. 1984.
Nyendael 1705
D. van Nyendael, *A Description of Rio Formosa, or the River of Benin*, in *A New and Accurate Description of the Coast of Guinea* […], W. Bosman (ed.), London 1705.

O
Olbrechts 1941
F.M. Olbrechts, "Bijdrage tot de kennis van de chronologie der afrikaansche plastiek", in *Inst. Royal Colonial Belge, Sect. des sciences morales et politiques, Mémoires* (Brussels) t. X f. 2, 1941, pp. 3–35.
Olbrechts 1943
F.M. Olbrechts, "Contribution to the Study of the Chronology of African Plastic Art", in *Africa*, vol. XIV, no. 4, October 1943, pp. 183–193.
Olbrechts 1946
F.M. Olbrechts, *Plastiek van Kongo*, Antwerp 1946.
Olbrechts 1959
F.M. Olbrechts, *Les Arts plastiques du Congo belge*, Brussels 1959.
Olfert Dapper's (1668) 1998
Olfert Dapper's Description of Benin (1668), A. Jones (ed.), Madison 1998.

P
Passione d'Africa 2009
Passione d'Africa. L'arte africana nelle collezioni italiane, C. Dandrieu, F. Giovagnoni (eds.), Milan 2009.
Paudrat 1984
J.L. Paudrat, *From Africa*, in *'Primitivism' in 20th Century Art*, 1984, I, pp. 125–175.
Paudrat 1986
J.L. Paudrat, *Introduction,* in *La voie des ancêtres*, Ch. Falgayrettes (ed.), Paris 1986, pp. 4–8.
Paudrat 1994
J.L. Paudrat, *Résonances mythiques dans la statuaire du Paus Dogon*, in *Dogon* 1994, pp. 55–81.
Pemberton 1989
J. Pemberton III, *The Carvers of the Northeast*, in Drewal, Pemberton, Abiodun 1989.
Perrois 1972
L. Perrois, *La statuaire Fan Gabon*, Paris 1972.
Perrois 2001[a]
L. Perrois, *Les Maîtres du Ntem: les sculpteurs fang mvaï du Nord Gabon*, in Grunne 2001, pp. 121–139.
Perrois 2001[b]
L. Perrois, *Le Maître de la Sébé: Les figures de reliquaire kota 'à tête de mort' de l'est du Gabon*, in Grunne 2001, pp. 140–159.
Perrois 2006
L. Perrois, *Fang*, Milan 2006.
Perrois, Grand-Dufay 2008
L. Perrois, C. Grand-Dufay, *Punu*, Milan 2008.
Perrois, Lehuard 1999
L. Perrois, R. Lehuard, *Ni anonyme ni impersonnel*, conference proceedings, Arnouville 1999.
Petridis 2001
C. Petridis (ed.), *Frans M. Olbrechts 1899–1958: In Search of Art in Africa*, Antwerp 2001.
Picton 1994
J. Picton, *Art, Identity and Identification: A Commentary on Yoruba Art Historical Studies*, in *Yoruba Artist* 1994.
Picton, Willett 1967
J. Picton, F. Willett, "On the Identification of Individual Carvers: A Study of Ancestor Shrine Carvings from Owo, Nigeria", in *Man*, vol. II, no. 1, 1967, pp. 62–70.
Pirat 1996
C.-L. Pirat, "Le Maître de Buli: Maître isolé ou 'atelier'? Essai de catalogue raisonné", in *Tribal Arts*, III/10, 1996, pp. 54–77.
Pirat 2001
C.-L. Pirat, "Le Maître de Buli: Réouverture du dossier", in *Tribal Arts*, VII-1, no. 26, 2001, pp. 82–95.
Pitt Rivers, Lane 1900
A. Pitt Rivers, F.H. Lane, *Antique Works of Art from Benin, Collected by Lieutenant-General Pitt Rivers*, London 1900.
Power of Form 2002
The Power of Form: African Art from the Horstmann Collection, texts by E. Bassani, M. Bockmühl, P. McNaughton, Milan 2002.
'Primitivism' in 20th Century Art 1984
'Primitivism' in 20th Century Art: Affinity of the Tribal and the Modern, W. Rubin (ed.), 2 vols., New York 1984.
'Primitivisme' dans l'art du 20e siècle 1991
'Primitivisme' dans l'art du 20e siècle: Les artistes modernes devant l'art tribal, W. Rubin (ed.) (J.L. Paudrat for French ed.), 2 vols., Paris 1991.
'Primitivismo' nell'arte del XX secolo 1985
'Primitivismo' nell'arte del XX secolo: Affinità tra il tribale e il moderno, W. Rubin (ed.) (E. Bassani for Italian ed.), 2 vols., Milan 1985.
Praetorius 1619
M. Praetorius, *Theatrum Instrumentorum*, Wolfenbüttel 1619.

Purchas 1584
S. Purchas, *Hackluytus Posthumous or Purchas, His Pilgrims*, London 1584.
Purchas 1625
S. Purchas, *Hackluyts Posthumous or Purchas his Pilgrims, 1584*, London 1625.

Q
Quando Dio Abitava a Ife 2005
Quando Dio abitava a Ife, C. Beltramo-Ceppi Zevi (ed.), Florence 2005.
Quarcoopome 2003
N.I. Quarcoopome, *Les portraits funéraires akan*, in *Ghana* 2003, pp. 93–132.

R
Read, Dalton 1898
C.H. Read, O.M. Dalton, "Works of Art from Benin City", in *Journal of the Royal Anthropological Institute of Great Britain and Ireland*, 27, 1898, pp. 362–383.
Rivière 1929 [ed. 1991]
G.H. Rivière, *Le Musée d'Ethnographie du Trocadero*, Documents, 1, 1929 (1991).
Robbins, Nooter 1989
W.M. Robbins, N.I. Nooter, *African Art in American Collections*, Washington, D.C., and London 1989.
Rois sculpteurs 1993
Rois sculpteurs (Les). Legs Pierre Harter. Art et pouvoir dans le Grassland Camerounais, L. Perrois (ed.), Paris 1993.
Rubin 1984
W. Rubin, *Picasso*, in *'Primitivism' in 20th Century Art* 1984, vol. I, pp. 241–341.

S
Sallée 1985
P. Sallée, "L'arc et la Harpe. Contribution à l'histoire de la musique du Gabon" (unpublished Ph.D. thesis, University of Paris X, Nanterre), Paris 1985.
Sculptor's Eye 2008
Sculptor's Eye (The): African and Oceanic Art from the Renée and Chaim Gross Foundation (Sotheby's auction catalogue), New York 15.5.2008.
Sculptures 2000
Sculptures – Afrique, Asie, Océanie, Amériques, (Musée du Louvre – Pavillon des Sessions), J. Kerchache (ed.), Paris 2000.
Sculptures 2008
Sculptures de l'ancien Soudan, Galerie Ratton-Hourdé (sales catalogue), Paris 2008.
Shaw 1970
T. Shaw, *Igbo Ukwu*, 2 vols., London 1970.
Sieber 1961
R. Sieber, *Sculpture of Northern Nigeria*, New York 1961.
Sieber, Walker 1987
R. Sieber, R.A. Walker, *African Art in the Cycle of Life*, Washington, D.C. 1987.
Sièges Africains 1994
Sièges Africains, S. Bocola (ed.), Munich 1994.
Strycker, Neyt 1975
L. de Strycker, F. Neyt, *Approche des arts hemba*, Villiers-le Bel 1975.
Sudan 2004
Sudan: Ancient Treasures. An Exhibition of Recent Discoveries from the Sudan National Museum, D.A. Welsby, J.R. Anderson (eds.), London 2004.

T
Tagliaferri 1974
A. Tagliaferri, *Fabulous Ancestors. Stone Carvings from Sierra Leone & Guinea*, Milan 1974.
Tagliaferri 1989
A. Tagliaferri, *Stili del potere. Antiche sculture in pietra dalla Sierra Leone e dalla Guinea*, Milan 1989.
Tessmann 1913
G. Tessmann, *Die Pangwe*, Berlin 1913.
Tervuren Museum 1996
Tervuren Museum (The): Masterpieces from Central Africa, G. Verswijver, E. De Palmenaer, V. Baeke, A.-M. Bouttiaux-N'Diaye (eds.), Munich and New York 1996.
Townshend 1827
G. Townshend Fox, *Synopsis of the Newcastle Museum, late the Allan, formerly the Tunstall, or Wycliffe Museum [...]*, Newcastle 1827.
Trésors 1995
Trésors d'Afrique – Musée de Tervuren, G. Verswijver, E. De Palmenaer, V. Baeke, A.-M. Bouttiaux-N'Diaye (eds.), Tervuren 1995.

U
Ubangi 2007
Ubangi, J.L. Grootaers (ed.), Brussels 2007.
Umělecký měsíčník 1913
Umělecký měsíčník, no. 8, April–May 1913 (frontal view); no. 9, June 1913 (profile view).

V
Vallées du Niger 1993
Vallées du Niger, J. Devisse, J. Polet, S. Sidibé (eds.), Paris 1993.
Visual Encounters 2009
Visual Encounters: Africa, Oceania, and Modern Art, O. Wick, A. Denner (eds.), Fondation Beyeler, Basel 2009.
Vogel 1985
S. Mullin Vogel, *African Aesthetics. The Carlo Monzino Collection*, Milan 1985.
Vogel 1997
S. Mullin Vogel, *Baule: African Art Western Eyes*, New Haven and London 1997.
Vogel 1999
S. Mullin Vogel, "Known Artists but Anonymous Works. Fieldwork and Art History", in *African Arts*, vol. XXXII, no. 1, Spring 1999, pp. 40–55.
Vogel, N'Diaye 1985
S. Mullin Vogel, F. N'Diaye, *African Masterpieces from the Musée de l'Homme*, New York 1985.

W
Walker 1998[a]
A.R. Walker, *Olówè of Isè: A Yoruba Sculptor to Kings*, Washington, D.C. 1998.
Walker 1998[b]
A.R. Walker, "Olówè of Isè: 'Anonymous' Has a Name", in *African Arts*, vol. XXXI, no. 4, Autumn 1998, pp. 38–47.
Wardwell 1966
A. Wardwell, "Some Notes on a Substyle of the Bambara", in *Museum Studies*, Chicago 1966, pp. 112–128.
Warnod 1912
A. Warnod, "L'Art négre", in *Comœdia*, 2 January 1912.
Welsh 1904
J. Welsh, *A Voyage to Benin Beyond the Country of Guinea Made by Master James Welsh. Who Set Forth in the Year 1588*, in *The Principal Navigations, Voyages, and Discoveries of the English Nation*, R. Hackluyt (ed.), London 1904.
Willett 1967
F. Willett, *Ife in the History of West African Sculpture*, London 1967.
Willett 1992
F. Willett, *Archaeology and the History of Nigerian Sculpture*, in *Dall'archeologia all'arte tradizionale africana*, proceedings of the meetings (Nov.–Dec. 1991), G. Pezzoli (ed.), Milan 1992, pp. 37–50.
Willett 1999
F. Willett, *Benin*, in *Afrika: Kunst und Kultur, Meisterwerke afrikanischer Kunst, Museum für Völkerkunde Berlin*, H.J. Koloss (ed.), Munich 1999, pp. 41–46.
Willett 2003
F. Willett, *The Art of Ife: A Descriptive Catalogue*, with a chapter by B. Blackmun, *The Art of Ife*, Glasgow 2003.

Y
Yoruba 1991
Yoruba: Art and Aesthetics, L. Homberger (ed.), Zurich 1991.
Yoruba Artist 1994
Yoruba Artist (The): New Theoretical Perspectives on African Artists, R. Abiodun, H.J. Drewal, J. Pemberton III (eds.), Washington, D.C., and London 1994.

Z
Zayas 1916
M. de Zayas, *African Negro Art: Its Influence on Modern Art*, New York 1916.

Photo Credits

© 2012. Foto Scala, Firenze: nos. 19, 23a–b, 31, 34, 35, 40, 43, 44, 184, 184a, 262

© 2012. Foto Scala, Firenze / BPK, Bildagentur für Kunst, Kultur und Geschichte, Berlin: nos. 48, 98, 102, 115, 118, 120, 142, 143, 148, 148a, 159, 186, 186a, 189, 191, 194, 194a, 221

© 2012. Foto Werner Forman Archive / Scala, Firenze: nos. 91, 91a, 119, 133, 136, 150a, 166, 166a, 168

© 2012. Image copyright The Metropolitan Museum of Art / Art Resource / Scala, Firenze: nos. 9, 15, 74, 214, 215, 226

© 2012. Andrea Jemolo / Foto Scala, Firenze: nos. 24, 29a-b, 32a-b, 33a-b

© 2012. Musée du quai Branly, photo Arnaud Baumann / Scala, Firenze: no. 22

© 2012. Musée du quai Branly, photos Hughes Dubois / Scala, Firenze: nos. 8, 21, 69, 69a, 113, 204, 212, 216, 254

© 2012. Musée du quai Branly, photo Patrick Gries / Valérie Torre / Scala, Firenze: no. 2

© Archives Musée Dapper, photos Hughes Dubois: nos. 1, 6, 64, 66, 144, 174, 175, 218, 218a, 219, 228, 230, 257

© ARSI – Archivum Romanum Societatis Iesu, Roma: no. 85

© Lessing/ Contrasto, Milano: no. 56

© Linden-Museum, Stuttgart, photo A. Dreyer: no. 187.

© Musée du quai Branly, photo Patrick Gries / Scala, Firenze: no. 249

© Museum Kunst, Vienna: nos. 37, 38, 41, 42, 50, 82, 104, 116a

© Museum of Art, Dallas: nos. 147, 147a

© Photograph by Franco Khoury, National Museum of African Art, Smithsonian Institute Washington, D.C.: no. 140

© Réunion des Musée Nationaux / Musée du Louvre / Michéle Bellot, distr. Archivi Alinari Firenze: no. 4

© Réunion des Musée Nationaux / Musée du Louvre / Jean-Gilles Berizzi / Thierry Le Mage, distr. Archivi Alinari Firenze: no. 195

© S-MNPE "Museo Luigi Pigorini", Roma Eur - su concessione del Ministero per i Beni e le Attività Culturali: nos. 67, 68, 71, 107, 154, 156

© Trustees of The British Museum, London: nos. 36, 45, 49, 55, 62, 75, 75a, 84, 97, 116, 117, 123, 124, 137, 160, 182, 223, 239

Armeria Reale, Torino: nos. 88, 88a

Art Gallery of Ontario, Toronto: nos. 236, 238

Civiche Raccolte Artistiche del Castello Sforzesco, Raccolte Extraeuropee, Milano: nos. 170, 231, 240, 245, 260

Collection RMCA Tervuren, photos R. Asselberghs, RMCA Tervuren ©: nos. 150, 153, 157, 161, 196, 197, 199, 200, 210, 233, 234, 246, 250, 251

Hughes Dubois, Bruxelles / Paris: nos. 10, 12, 13, 14, 58, 59, 63, 172, 222 (and cover), 258

Horstmann Collection, Zug: nos. 65, 205, 217, 237, 244, 255, 261

Andrea Jemolo, Roma: no. 54

Courtesy Fondazione Marconi, Milano: no. 229

Denver Art Museum, Denver: no. 256

Image © Sotheby's: no. 224

Institut de Recherches en Sciences Humaines, Niamey: no. 18

Paolo Manusardi, Milano: nos. 231, 240, 245, 260

Andrea Melzi, Milano: nos. 198, 207, 208

Musée Calvet, Avignon: nos. 61, 61a

Musée National du Mali, Bamako: no. 16

Musei Civici d'Arte Antica, Bologna: nos. 72, 72a

Museo Civico di Palazzo Madama, Torino: no. 96

Museo degli Argenti, Firenze. Soprintendenza Speciale per il Patrimonio Storico, Artistico ed Etnoantropologico e per il Polo Museale della Città di Firenze - su concessione del Ministero per i Beni e le Attività Culturali: nos. 105, 106, 162, 162a

Museu de Antropologia de Universidade, Porto: no. 169

Museu Etnográfico da Sociedade de Geografia, Lisboa, photo Carlos Ladeira: no. 167

Museum Rietberg, Zürich: nos. 127, 135, 206, 225, 243

Nicolò Orsi Battaglini, Firenze: nos. 105, 106, 162, 162a

Pitt Rivers Museum Archive, University of Oxford, Oxford: nos. 47, 122

Staatliches Museum, Monaco: nos. 81, 138, 139, 139a, 173, 202, 220

The National Commission for Museums and Monuments, Nigeria: nos. 20, 25, 26, 28, 30, 51, 52, 99, 183

Ulmer Museum, Ulm: no. 188